John Curry

An Historical and Critical Review of the Civil Wars in Ireland

From the reign of Queen Elizabeth to the settlement under King William

John Curry

An Historical and Critical Review of the Civil Wars in Ireland
From the reign of Queen Elizabeth to the settlement under King William

ISBN/EAN: 9783337324797

Printed in Europe, USA, Canada, Australia, Japan

Cover: Foto ©ninafisch / pixelio.de

More available books at **www.hansebooks.com**

AN

HISTORICAL AND CRITICAL

REVIEW

OF THE

CIVIL WARS IN IRELAND,

FROM THE

Reign of QUEEN ELIZABETH,

TO THE

Settlement under KING WILLIAM.

EXTRACTED

From PARLIAMENTARY RECORDS, STATE ACTS, and other authentic Materials.

By J. C. M. D.
John Curry
Author of the HISTORICAL MEMOIRS of the IRISH REBELLION in 1641.

Audi alteram Partem.

DUBLIN:

Printed, and sold by J. HOEY, and T. T. FAULKNER, Parliament-street;
G. BURNET, Abbey-street; and J. MORRIS, Fishamble-street, N°. 9.
MDCCLXXV.

ADVERTISEMENT.

ALTHOUGH this REVIEW is in the Nature of an Appeal to the enlightened Part of the Public, yet it has been the Author's earnest Wish that, in exhibiting every interesting Truth, he should give no Cause of Offence to any Party among us. His Design is to conciliate, not to irritate; and, in the Execution of such a Design, it was incumbent on him, to remove the false Grounds of a Torrent of Invectives, which have of late borne down repeatedly on our good Sense; and which, if not stopped in its Course, may sweep away before it some practicable Schemes for Public Prosperity. If some of the pre-occupied, as is but too common, reject several Facts hereafter related, because they were taught to reject them early in Life: yet they will take the less Offence at our Author, as his Materials are almost entirely taken from those very Authorities, on which the Invectives we have mentioned, are said to be founded; and, consequently, can admit of no Dispute concerning their Credibility.

ATTENTIVE solely to the Choice and Importance of his Matter, the Author has delivered himself all along in a plain unadorned Narration; little solicitous about Elegance of Periods, Strength of Colouring, or other Arts of Composition, which are but too often employed to give a wrong Direction to the Reader's Judgment, especially, when the Writer has any wrong Bias on his own.

ERRATA.

Introduction: p. x. l. 11. for *laws*, read *lures*.
              p. xiii. l. 28. for *render*, read *renders*.
              p. xiv. l. 25. for *of our conduct*, read *on our conduct*.

Passim, in the Notes, instead of *Relig.* read *Reliquiæ*.
        p. 75. l. 19. after *clear*, read *and*.
        p. 108. l. 6. for *taking*, read *take*.
        p. 220. l. 2. for *was*, read *were*.
        p. 238 l. 19. for *return*, read *returned*.
        p. 206. l. 3. after *affronted*, leave out *the*.
        p. 185. l. 25. for *instruction*, read *instructions*.
        p. 187. l. 14. for *than*, read *that*.
        p. 188. l. 23. after *parliament*, insert *and*.
        p. 196. l 9. for *sequal*, read *sequel*.
          ib. note, l. 3. for *time*, read *year*.
        p. 341. l. 3. for *came*, read *come*.
        p. 147. l. 11. for, *which Clanrickard imputes*, read, *which lord Clanrickard seems to impute*.
        p. 148. l. 7. after *complaint*, add, *to them*.
          ib. l. 8. after *month*, add, *of June*.
        p. 243. note (5), for *vol. iii.* read *vol. ii. fol.* 52.
        p. 268. l. 28. for *serous*, read *serious*.
        p. 385. l. 5. after *wars*, dele *parenthesis*, and add, *to your majesty was high*.
        p. 354. l. 5. after *forfeitures*, insert *and*.
        p. 313. l. 26. for *rish*, read *Irish*.

INTRODUCTION.

HAD the learned Author of the following Review, proposed to himself no other end, than to detect the misrepresentations of contemporary writers, who derived an interest from the circulation of false history, his service to the public would not be deemed inconsiderable. His merit would be still greater, had he sat down professedly, to expose the mistakes of other less interested, but more dangerous writers, who have gained reputation from genius, and authority from rank, to give a currency to false facts, and to pronounce false judgments on the true. His merit in both these cases, is indeed clear; but it is secondary to a nobler object.

" On a review of our history from the invasion of Henry the Second, King of England, to the revolution in sixteen hundred and eighty-eight, he discovered the calamities of this nation, flowing invariably from public misrule, private interests, barbarous manners, and the rage of parties. He beheld the fires of faction and discontent, unabated thro' every age; and found these calamities filling their measure in the sixteenth century, thro' a fresh supply of combustibles, from ecclesiastical contentions, which have set all Europe in a flame for near a hundred and fifty years, and have hardly ceased preying on the good sense and morals of our own people to the present day, to the disgrace of the human understanding." He saw popular phrensy, unsettled principles, and the lust of dominion, mingling early with our spiritual contests, and that the christian doctrine, which fatally, had so little influence before those contests began, had so much less after their commencement, that Protestants and Papists, Churchmen and Puritans,

INTRODUCTION.

Puritans, fcrupled not occafionally, to load their adverfaries with feveral crimes, which were not committed, and with odious principles which were not profeffed. The iniquity was common and great; and it became the more horrible, by making religion fubfervient to it. Party power was the object, and to obtain it the morality of the gofpel and of nature, was, for the time fufpended, as binding only in the intercourfes of private life, not in public concerns; where any means, for fecuring the end, were deemed admiffable. All this, I fay, our Author has difcovered in his review of thefe times, and with fome furprife he faw alfo, (what our theory of mankind could perhaps never reach) that there was one principle common to both parties, which with equal guilt and abfurdity, each party juftified, and reprobated alternately, as each were fufferers or gainers by it. This was the principle of perfecution which operated with all its terrors, as every dominant party could, by fraud or violence, obtain the dangerous power of giving the law and the gofpel of the times. In the progrefs of his refearches, our Author beheld alfo, that the new parliamentary eftablifhment in matters concerning religion, on the commencement of Queen Elizabeth's reign, was excepted to, not only by the men averfe from any peculiar national fyftem, but by zealous reformers alfo, who claimed the liberty of expounding the divine fcriptures in their own way; and who exclaimed highly againft the civil reftraints they were laid under, on the fcore of their right of explaining for themfelves, inftead of admitting others to explain for them. On reforming principles they were certainly in the right, and candour muft oblige us to confefs, that ftate intereft, not confiftency in the new religious eftablifhment, was chiefly confidered by thofe who framed it. An eftablifhment however was made: it required penal fanctions. The Puritan fuffered, and the Papift was undone.

These general and inconteftible truths involved a feries of tragical events. To develope them fairly; to fhew by the ufe made of party power, how long we have been the dupes of fhameful prejudices, for the fole gain of thofe who impofed and propagated them; to root up diftinctions which have ever operated to general mifchief, and to reftore that harmony, which

INTRODUCTION. iii

which former incidents have obstructed, was the principal design of the Author who presents us with the following HISTORICAL REVIEW. The writers he opposes had evidently another, a shameful intention to spread hates, perpetuate rancour, and oppress the living by an abuse of the dead: happily no man of the present age has any interest in such misrepresentations.

Our Author has confined himself to a period of history which to us of the present age, is of all others the most important; but as prior causes led to the events he takes into consideration, it may not be amiss to give a short retrospect of anterior times.

The conquest of Ireland (as it is improperly enough called) was effected in days, when barbarism and ignorance prevailed in most parts of Europe. This nation, long wasted by its own aristocratical confusion, and little mended by the weak monarchy erected on its ruins, by *(a)* three powerful Princes, yielded at last to a foreign government. This great revolution having from domestic divisions, many concurrent causes to forward it, was planned by the ambition of a foreign mighty monarch, and casually favoured by the iniquity of a domestic Prince, expelled the kingdom by the reigning Irish King. Several of our Irish Princes submitted to Henry the Second on the conviction that such a conduct, shameful as it was, would prove the best remedy for the national distempers. They found themselves mistaken when it was too late. Henry, who knew but little of the principles, and still less of the true spirit of legislation, was unfit for the task of reforming a perverse nation. His stay in Ireland was short, and his embarrassments on the Continent disabled him from executing the good he intended, and was capable of. Our people changed their condition from bad to worse: instead of protection they experienced the exercise of wanton and lawless power: instead of clement governors, purchased at the expence of exorbitant

(a) In 1136, the provincial King of Conaught, (called Turlogh the Great) having mastered the other provinces of Ireland, got himself acknowledged King of Ireland. In 1157, he was succeeded in that authority by Murkertach O'Loghlin, Prince of Tyrone, and head (at the time) of the old Royal Hy-Niall line. On the latter's fall in the battle of Literluin, 1166, Roderic, son of Turlogh the Great, was proclaimed King of Ireland in an assembly of the states at Dublin. He closed the line of Irish monarchs.

orbitant poffeffions, a fet of freebooters, who denied the natives the benefit of Englifh laws, and of all law. Thus have the old natives been treated, and we are not to wonder if they endeavoured to relieve themfelves by infurrections. As far as the miferable ftate of anarchy eftablifhed among them permitted, they fought and found fome redrefs in refiftance. For four hundred years they could find it by no other means; at leaft, by no means adequate to the ends of a fecure eftablifhment.

WE fhould not forget that in courfe of time, when the great adventurers from the neighbouring ifle found themfelves firmly rooted in this, they began, in turn, to hate one another, and in confequence allied with their enemies, the Irifh chieftains, for the reduction of their rivals. This coalition cemented by no cordiality, but calculated for prefent convenience, produced no good effect. They were united indeed on one common principle, that of fhaking off all dependence on England; and they did, in fact, confine the Englifh government to a pale of no confiderable extent. The policy of the latter, confifted in dividing its enemies, by treating one party as rebels, to be received into mercy, the other as aliens to be cut off, without any. Infurrections were the confequence of this fpecies of policy, and undoubtedly, the little happinefs the people enjoyed, they owed to the fad expedient of infurrection alone.

IT may be worth the while to confider, that this ftate of things was not owing to the hatred of one ecclefiaftical party to another, but to the inhumanity of Papifts againft men of the fame perfuafion with themfelves. It fhews how little the formal identity of religion can fecure human race, againft human violence, and that we often and fatally miftake, when we afcribe to difference of worfhip, diforders which take their full operation without any. Of religious conformity it can only be faid, that it includes a ftronger tendency to civil quiet, than religious difcord can; tho' examples may be produced now on the continent, of happinefs under the latter fituation of things, as we can produce many inftances of mifery under the other. But political philofophy (fo to fpeak) has enlightened feveral countries

INTRODUCTION.   v

tries on the Continent, and the people feel no civil miseries, because they do not adopt the religion pointed out to them by their masters. To them, and to these masters, an active civil obedience is sufficient.

In the case of various religions (particularly in their first establishments) jealousies are natural, and will prevail. Zeal, backed by credulity, and stimulated by hatred, will not hesitate on tracing to any odious form of religion, the political crimes of its votaries. But zeal and credulity, however they may be casually in the right, are very unfair arbiters, and will be generally found in the wrong; in both cases, and in our own country, we will find sad examples of human malevolence, suitable to the opportunities of gratification. When the oppressors of Ireland were unable to draw any justification of their measures from a diversity of religion, they were obliged to charge on the peculiar perverseness of the nation, what they dared not charge to their spiritual doctrines: but arguments supported by appeals to national dispositions to virtue or vice, cannot impose long. Those drawn from difference in religion exhibit a fairer outside; because it is possible enough that religion, ill understood, may have terrible consequences on civil society, which ought therefore to be guarded against. But such consequences, bad as they may be, must surely cease, or operate less to public danger, whenever knowledge and legislative wisdom co-operate, to bring their causes under a closer examination, than they have hitherto undergone. If the causes should be found no other than mere fugitive opinions, which distress may graft on a fair stock, judgment will interpose, and separate an evil which is temporary, from a sound principle which is permanent. Religion, good or bad, (according to the president Montesquieu,) is the surest test we have for the probity of men; and should the votaries of the best, in some circumstances, torture the sacred text to defend ill-taken measures, particularly when they have very strong temptations to do so; it will not be difficult to reduce such men from civil error, to civil obedience, because they can demonstrably be reclaimed to such obedience, even under the lashes of penal laws; as the case stands in Ireland, at present, with the Papists, who are loyal to their King, and from a sense of religious duty, would be so,

even

INTRODUCTION.

even without experiencing the royal mercy, to which alone, not to the laws of their country, they owe their present quiet existance in these Islands.

We do not think we have any disaffected Papists at this day in Ireland. The number, at least must be very inconsiderable; but the smallest is an object of attention. Relatively to these, the detection of them will be easy, (for they have a scrupulous regard to oaths,) from their refusal of a test of loyalty, and of an abjuration of every connection and principle inconsistent with it. By such a trial, legislators may be enabled to separate (so to speak) the elect of government from the reprobate; but legislators must conquer their own pre-occupations first, before such a separation can be made, or even attempted.

In former time, in the heat of contentions for power and property, pre-occupations had a foundation: they were lucrative as well as natural; at this day they are neither lucrative nor natural. At this day surely, the transient effects of transient policy should cease, and if an union, on the tenets of religion cannot be obtained, yet an union on civil principles, and civil conduct may. Good governors and wise men will not object to such an union, tho' they may be tender of proposing it, till a majority is prepared for believing what it really is, an useful measure.

Our morals as men, our interests as subjects, require the reformation here hinted at; religion, consistent with civil order, should cease to be a civil crime, and punishment should not reach those who are guilty of no other. Until people, whose principles (superstitious or orthodox) are reconcileable to our civil establishment, are trusted with constitutional immunities, Ireland cannot be happy. Nay, the great Landlords of the kingdom must be reduced to a state of real, and hereafter, undoubtedly to a state of feeling deficiency in their incomes, as the labouring and industrious (more than half the people) are rendered useless, and indeed, hurtful to the aggregate whole, by too many restraints. Laziness, dissatisfaction, and

despondency,

INTRODUCTION. vii

despondency, the offspring of insecurity, will generally prevail; nay, the very industry of the people, thus punished, will be turned against the state. A flux monied property may be acquired, by a traffic in large herds of cattle, or in imports and exports of commodities, and the wealth acquired will find its way into remote lands, when no security can be found for it at home. This, it must be granted, is but a partial evil: The British empire will lose nothing; it will in fact gain by it, as an emigration from hence to cultivate unoccupied lands in North America, must contribute to the strength of government, and increase of revenue, in those parts especially, where the British legislature have given security of property, to Protestants and Papists indiscriminately.

At the period from whence the Author of the following Memoirs sets forward, it will be found, that spiritual hatred mixed itself with our former national seeds of dissention. The perverseness so long imputed to the Irish, as a people, was no longer charged on their nature, but on their religion. Almost every moral, and civil duty, was then confined within the pale of an ecclesiastical party: every species of treachery was placed beyond it. Real crimes were disowned by one faction, imaginary crimes were imputed to another; and this state of things occasioned guilt on both sides, which in a different state, would undoubtedly be avoided. High as most of these crimes were, yet most were exaggerated, and the innocent suffered with the guilty. To complete the misery of the times, the gospel of peace was tortured to defend the measures, and sanctify the drunkenness of every governing, as well as every resisting set of men; and thus it fared in Ireland, in some time after the accession of Queen Elizabeth to the Throne.

Queen Elizabeth, whose reign began in the height of ecclesiastical rage, had admirable talents for government. To plant civil order in the place of that misrule which disgraced the three preceding reigns, was difficult. Her interest led her, and the success of her father and brother encouraged her, to change the religion then established in England. This she effected;

but

but truth must oblige us to confess, that the new church was reared on the foundations of persecution, and that the violence so justly censured in Queen Mary's reign was adopted as a justifiable measure in the present. The change was made by a quick act of legiflative power, but without that moderation, which found policy should direct in establishments of this nature. By the change, one party in the nation was ruined, another was provoked. Papists were occasionally punished without discrimination, and in the idea of party justice, this procedure appeared equitable. But the Puritan Protestant was punished also, and the clamour ran high among Dissenters, that the old beast returned, with a change only of the rider, and of the habiliments. The party for a comprehensive reformation, grew popular and encreased every day in strength and numbers, as it increased in faction and enthusiasm. The new church, even in the act of extirpating the old, created to itself, enemies on all sides, and thus it happened that the system wove by civil policy, was in a great degree unravelled by the ecclesiastical.

In Ireland where statute laws prevailed, but within a narrow circle, the new spiritual ordinances made no progress; the minds of the Irish were even prepared against any spiritual change, and they were provoked by the violence of the pale-governors in 1540, when after great excesses in Dublin and Trim, they extended their rage to the town of Monaghan, plundering not only the monastery of the observants, but putting the guardian and friars to death. In the first years of Elizabeth's reign, such bloody measures were wisely avoided: on its commencement, the Earl of Sussex appointed chief governor of Ireland, proceeded on a plan of moderation without the pale, and for some time within, where a majority still shewed themselves extremely averse to the new spiritual doctrines, established by parliament in England. The ruinous effects of a Brehon government were long felt, and owned by the old inhabitants. A change to a better civil establishment was practicable and solicited for by them: but they were strenuous for the retention of their religion; and tho' unanimous on no other principle of defence, they declared themselves unanimous in the

defence

defiance of this. In treating therefore with the provincial Irish, Lord Suffex confined himself to the reformation of civil government, chiefly without preffing any other upon them. This found policy was of short continuance, and the people without the pale were exafperated, by the fudden meafures taken againft their brethren within. Contemporary writers are unanimous in affirming, and the nature of the thing verifies the fact, that the penal laws againft the exercife of their religion, were the ftrongeft incentives to every infurrection of the Irifh fince the reformation. Thefe laws were originally framed in England, where the majority were prepared for their reception; but they were rejected in the Irifh, or properly fpeaking, the pale parliament.

THE natives of Ireland, ready at all times to recognize the temporal fupremacy of their fovereign, and reject any foreign claimant (lay or ecclefiaftical) of fuch fupremacy, merited being received into the fociety of conftitutional fubjects; and that they fhould be fo received, had been the labour of Sir Henry Sydney, one of the ableft, wifeft, and beft governors ever fent into that kingdom. But in vain! The reformation, it is true, made no progrefs for a long time without the pale, and extraordinary efforts to enforce it by arms would certainly be dangerous, as it might put an end to inteftine divifions among the people, which hitherto proved fo ufeful towards their reduction. To favour thofe divifions was previoufly the more politic alternative, and the Queen received the fubmiffions of many Irifh chieftains at her court very gracioufly, difmiffed them with honours and prefents, and left them free as to the concerns of their fpiritual confcience.

IT was otherwife within the pale, and its environs. Here even the feneschals of counties exercifed plain tyranny over the poor people, and fuch particular feverities were then inflicted, even in the opinion of the Lord Deputy himfelf, "as were fufficient to drive the beft and quieteft ftates into fudden confufion *(a)*."

(a) Lord Mountjoy's Letter. Pacat. Hibern. fub finem.

INTRODUCTION.

The evils of persecution were sorely felt in England particularly, and in several districts of Ireland, during the greater part of Queen Elizabeth's reign. One party was punished without discrimination, and the other (and indeed both) without sound policy. These evils encreased in the two succeeding reigns, when these three kingdoms, for the first time have been united under one sovereign. James the first whom the trumpeters of faction, charged with favouring Popery, was a great and determined enemy to his popish subjects. His administration in Ireland, with little exception, is a full proof of this. His trimming conduct towards the Papists of England, antecedently to his accession, is no proof to the contrary, for they gained nothing (and he intended they should gain nothing) by the laws he held out to them. Learned without knowledge, cunning without wisdom, one of his first gracious proclamations imported a general jail delivery to all his subjects, excepting murderers and Papists, and this coupling of the latter with such criminals produced a resentment, which degenerating into mad revenge, contributed in a considerable degree, to the detestable Powder Plot, entered into soon after, by a few desperate men, to get rid of their persecutors.

Charles the successor of James trod (and trod ruinously) in his father's steps. He wanted to impose the English religion on his Scotish subjects. The covenanters would not bear the introduction of, what they deemed a superstitious liturgy, among them. They defended themselves against it by insurrection, and the parliament sitting at Westminster approved of their conduct. The Northern Irish finding affairs embroiled in Great Britain, and dreading fatal consequences from the resolutions denounced against Papists in the English House of Commons, entertained the thought of availing themselves of the present opportunity, of frustrating the intentions of their enemies, and of shaking off the bondage they groaned under, from the time of the late Queen's demise. But they meant to compass this end by means equally justifiable, with those employed by the Scotch covenanters, and still without an impeachment of their loyalty.

The

INTRODUCTION.

The memory of paſt grievances, the dread of preſent deſtruction made theſe men deſperate. For forty years before the period we mention, the whole body of Iriſh Papiſts bore miniſterial invaſions of the moſt diſtreſſing nature to the human mind. The lands poſſeſſed by their families for ſeveral ages, were in the Court-Caſuiſtry of that age pronounced invalid and reſumable tenures, tho' no charge of treaſon or rebellion could be made to the heirs in actual poſſeſſion. Upon this pretence of defective titles ſome have been ruined, others threatened with ruin: and this was not all. The court harpies grown impatient at the paſſive conduct of the proprietors, attempted to provoke them to open rebellion, by exerciſing the moſt galling tyranny over their conſciences, by fining, impriſoning, and puniſhing in various ſhapes, ſuch Papiſts, as refuſed to join in the eſtabliſhed form of worſhip. Here then we ſee how the natives have been alarmed, in regard to property, and ſpiritual liberty, and how they were tortured by ſtate inquiſitors for not ſubmitting to religious doctrines, which ſpiritual directors may preach, but which no civil power on earth has a right to impoſe!— They ſurely who vindicate the rights of the Scots to inſurrection in 1640, can with no good grace condemn that of the Iriſh in 1641.— We do not defend either, but we may ſafely aſſert, that he who ſhould at this time of day advance, with my Lord Clarendon, that the Iriſh had no civil or religious grievances to complain of during the forty years antecedent to the Ultonian rebellion in 1641, has but a wretched alternative in option between wilful ignorance, and barefaced diſhoneſty.

We have advanced that the Iriſh in general wanted, in theſe confuſed times of King Charles I. to redreſs grievances by legal and conſtitutional means, and truth will warrant our ſaying ſo. They were firmly attached to our monarchical form of government; they were cordially loyal to the reigning Prince, and ready to make a diſtinction between the ſeverity of the law, and the diſpoſition of the monarch, notwithſtanding the unworthinefs of his deputies, who betrayed him and them. By their reprefentatives in parliament they made the higheft profeffions of their affection, and were fincere. What then provoked to the fudden and defperate meafures which followed? The anfwer is eafy and ready. This devoted people found the King's upright intentions fruftrated by an adjournment of the feffion of parliament in 1641, fo contrary to the King's order, as well as intereft. In that proceeding they difcovered how the Lords Juftices had been leagued fecretly with the Puritans at Weftminfter; how the King had been betrayed, and the hands of his enemies ftrengthened; how the claim to their own patrimonies (the hereditary poffeffions of feveral ages) had been kept up, and the intention of granting them to undertakers from England referved. What idea could this difobedience to the King, this infecurity to the fubject, fuggeft? It did not produce jealoufy and miftruft alone: it confirmed them in a certainty, that a majority of the more antient and wealthy proprietors were to be ruined, for the advantage of needy ftrangers, as was intended by Lord Strafford's plan. All grew impatient, the Northern men, already ruined, grew defperate. The latter rofe up in arms in the fatal month of October 1641. And feveral counties have all at once been expofed to the barbarities of an exafperated multitude; an evil which would not remain to be a ftain on the face of our annals, had the feffion been continued as the King intended, and had the bills prepared for the fecurity of the antient proprietors of the kingdom been paffed into laws. Had this, I fay, been the cafe, the defperadoes of Ulfter would be kept down by their Southern fellow fubjects, who had no concern in the peculiar complaints of that party. But the Lords Juftices and their agents took care to remove this line of feparation, and render the men in poffeffion as infecure, as the men ejected. This fact is one of the moft important in the hiftory of this ifland, and fhould be well underftood. I fay no more of it here, that I may not anticipate on the following Hiftorical Review, wherein the details are given with equal candor and judicioufnefs.

The

INTRODUCTION.

The Earl of Clarendon has left us an account of those times in the stile rather of a pleader, than of an historian. He was doubtless a nobleman of great abilities, but very unjust to the Irish nation. In representations anticipated by spiritual hatred and national prejudices, this man of strength, resigns all his vigour. No longer master of his subject, he yields himself up a willing captive, to such informations as were correspondent to his prior ideas of the people he undertakes to describe. He appears to have been incapable of receiving second impressions, and we can hardly on this account, charge him with delivering us a conscious untruth. History in such hands is neither better nor worse, than what the writer is enabled to make it, according to the degree of his partiality or aversion; and he must have little knowledge of men, who knows not, that this species of human infirmity, is but too often an ingredient in some of the best, as it always is in the worst characters, with whom the infirmity ends in vice. In the best, it resembles a cancerous excrescence on a beautiful face, and grows but too often out of our fairest principle, that of religion, from which it should, if possible, be rooted. Were religious indifference useful in any instance, it would be in this before us, where the more a man is lukewarm in religious party-zeal, the nearer he approaches to the character of a true patriot and good citizen. But there is a strength of mind superior to religious indifference itself, which gives all the qualifications necessary to constitute a good man, and judicious historian. This strength the Earl of Clarendon and other great men (Protestants and Papists) wanted, and still want. As painters of former times, they may give a good likeness: as contemporaries they are intolerable; of all men the most likely to be deceived, and the most laborious to deceive. The mischief they circulate is in proportion to their abilities, and that rank in life, which render those abilities conspicuous.

It is, indeed, to be lamented, that Mr. Hume, one of the ablest writers of the present age, should as an historian suffer himself to be so far led astray by such contemporaries as we have hinted at, as to transfer all or moſt of the miſchiefs of the year 1641 in Ireland, from the original authors, to the unfortunate Iriſh alone. Parties leſs aggrieved in Scotland were up before them, and drew the ſword not only with impunity but with advantage. The Iriſh in Ulſter who wanted to regain the lands they loſt, followed the example. We do not juſtify the act in either kingdom. We only advance in alleviation of the Iriſh crime, that the majority of the nation have, in the two reigns of James and Charles, ſuffered a cruel bondage of thirty eight years with little intermiſſion, and had now the moſt alarming proſpect of extirpation before them. They did not mean to withdraw their allegiance from the King; even the weak leaders of the Northern rabble had no ſuch intention. The latter began, and acted ſingly. Their outrages on their firſt ſetting out were kept within ſome bounds; moſt of the innocent Proteſtants in the neighbouring diſtricts had time to eſcape into places of ſecurity, before many murders were committed. The Papiſts in the other provinces had no ſhare in their guilt; they immediately publiſhed their deteſtation of it.

In general, they were ſteady to their duty as chriſtians, and to their loyalty as ſubjects. They in their own defence took up arms, not againſt the King, but againſt the King's enemies, who announced their exciſion in public reſolutions, and parliamentary votes. This is the truth of the fact. Mr. Hume paſſes it over as of no importance to the ſubject of his hiſtory.

He appears to have ſat down with an intention to cure us of our unhappy-party prejudices, by pointing out their terrible conſequences, in the laſt age, of our conduct as legiſlators, and our feelings as men. In general his obſervations are admirable, and ſtand in the place of excellent inſtructions, enforced by ſtriking examples. His miſtakes at the ſame time are hurtful, and a wound from ſuch a hand muſt be painful. But happily it cannot be mortal, in the caſe before us, as abundant materials of true information are ſtill preſerved entire. The documents in the following

Review

INTRODUCTION.   xv

Review will shew that Mr. Hume's representation of Irish affairs in 1641, is not true history, but fine and pathetic writing. Pity it is, to find such a man adopting the untruths of Sir John Temple, and spreading them on a new canvas heightened with all the colourings of his art. The piece has certainly cost him some labour; for horror and pity are wrought up here in high tragical strains. But the Irish certainly have not sat for the picture; and Mr. Hume in this part of his history must admit the justness of a charge, that he has given a wrong direction to the passions, he has taken so much pains to excite.

Mr. Hume is still alive to review and correct some mistakes in his history; and should he decline doing justice in the case before us (what must not be supposed) he, and not truth, will be affected.

The changes of religion in these kingdoms produced a most memorable æra in our history; and however the reformation hath operated, in spreading the base of civil liberty, yet it divided us into parties, and for a time produced terrible struggles for power and property in both kingdoms; in Ireland especially these things had a period. When all power was set on one side, and that contention ceased, yet the hatred which commenced with the original disputes remained, and exerted itself with remakable violence, in the framing of penal laws, which doubtless should be but few, in countries which exist by industry, unless the object of such laws, be too formidable not to require its removal at any expence to the public. In this light hath Popery been held, from the very commencement of Queen Elizabeth's reign, and is seen in no other to this day. No experience of Papists being known and acknowledged good subjects in other Protestant countries; no experience of their good conduct in our own, could hitherto remove the idea of their being enemies by principle to our Protestant establishment. Sir William Blackstone, who has enlightened these nations by his admirable commentaries on our laws, pronounces on this subject, like those who are content with the first impressions they receive, and think but little on a subject, in which they are but little concerned.

" While

"While Papists," he says, "acknowledge a foreign power, superior to the "sovereignty of the kingdom, they cannot complain, if the laws of that "kingdom will not treat them on the footing of good subjects." With great deference to so great an authority, this judgment includes a charge, which it is impossible to support, unless it can be proved that English and Irish Papists are men of different principles from their brethren in Hanover and Canada. But this is not the case; the majority of English Papists even in the days of Queen Elizabeth (who stripped them of power and liberty) acknowledged no authority superior to her sovereignty, and renounced to the authority of Pius the Fifth, who wanted to withdraw them from the allegiance they owed her. This they have done, without any breach with the Roman see in matters purely spiritual; in things, I mean, which regard the next life, not the present. The Papists of Ireland have, in a Formulary lately drawn up by themselves, renounced any authority, civil or temporal, claimed or unclaimed, by any foreign Prince or Prelate whatsoever, recognizing at the same time his Majesty's title, and professing their allegiance to be due to him solely. Thus it is at present, even in Spain and Portugal, where no subject would dare own or recognize any foreign power superior to the sovereignty of those kingdoms; and nearer home in France, the sovereignty of that kingdom is so jealously guarded, against all foreign pretenders and pretensions, that a professor who should bring this matter even into doubt, would be degraded from his office, if he did not meet with a severer punishment. Pity it is, that a point of knowledge, so much within his reach, should escape Judge Blackstone; pity it is indeed, that so great an authority, should be employed to give weight, and perhaps perpetuity to a popular error, so injurious to a million of his Majesty's good subjects; for so I venture to denominate them, notwithstanding the hurt they do the public through a legal incapacity to serve it.

We are sorry to find any necessity for saying so much on this subject, and yet a little more must be added, before we dismiss it.

INTRODUCTION.

The supremacy of Popes in matters merely spiritual, and directed as it ought to be, for the preservation of harmony and unity in the church, cannot be formidable to princes;——thus restricted, it had for many ages been useful to them. The abuse of this supremacy, and every ill-grounded claim foreign to it, may be removed, and (let me add) has been removed. In the present age, Popes have no more the power of deposing Kings, or of absolving subjects from their allegiance, than they had in the days of Constantine, who permitted a legal establishment of their religion in Rome, the capital of his empire. The claim to this deposing power began and operated only in times of bigotry and ignorance, and has been often opposed even in the darkest; in the dawn of knowledge it could not do much mischief; it could not operate in the light; and if any among us should be still found blind; should any spiritual doctor among us attempt to justify such a claim, he may be easily detected by putting him to the test of his civil orthodoxy. Such a man, if a christian, will not abjure to the public, what he teaches in private. It is against such a man that the keen edge of penal laws should be employed; legislative wisdom should here draw a line of partition, instead of confounding the well principled, indiscriminately, with their opposers.

The Historical Review now presented to the public, was intended intirely for exposing, in a proper light, things over which the fatal prejudices of the times have thrown much obscurity. We would draw useful instructions from our former calamities, and reconcile, by truth, men too long divided by mistakes. We have freely condemned, in this preliminary discourse, the conduct of the Roman Catholics before the reformation: We have had no call upon us to justify it since that time in any blameable case, and, through the rebellion which succeeded the year 1641 in particular, the author of the following work has been free enough to expose and censure the violence and ambition of some among the clergy as well as laity, that the more justice might be done to the virtue and patriotism of others of the

c   same

same party. It was an age of infatuation and drunkenness, among all parties (Protestants and Papists) throughout the three kingdoms, and an historian who from prejudice cannot distinguish, or who from bye-ends will not distinguish, between the mad and the sober, will acquit himself but ill. He will not instruct, but he certainly will mislead.

The Catholics of the present age, have one great interest in common with their fellow subjects, and it consists in the peace of their country, under a monarch, who makes the happiness of all his people the principal object of his government. With this interest in quiet they never will part. Since their submission at Limerick, in 1691, they have been faithful to the government, which God has set over them; and we take great pleasure, in finding that the penal laws of the late Queen, which they did not provoke, have taken their best effects, in crowning those virtues, which, in fact, are the production of painful sufferings, not of power or wealth. Whatever their religion be, a complex system of superstition, or a summary of christian duties, it enforces obedience to the established government; their perseverance in such a religion is not a civil crime, though an hypocritical adoption of a different one, or a reward offered for obtaining the adoption, would be odious to God and man. Indeed if any danger can arise from their religion, it must be from their not professing it sincerely, and from omitting the duties it imposes on them. Every man who has a retrospect to the grievances exposed in the following work, will think himself happy, that he found his existence in this present century. In the present reign we must feel a comfort like that which succeeds to the terrors of a mighty tempest; our state bark is moored, and however many may suffer by restraints on industry and insecurity to property, yet every subject has a full permission to exercise the religion of his conscience. Can this be said of the Tudor and Stuart reigns, when men were fined, tortured, and imprisoned, to exercise a religion against their conscience? Were insurrections in those days any mighty wonders among a fierce and turbulent people? Or will not their infrequency be the chief wonder with impartial posterity?

THE

INTRODUCTION.

The intention of the author in the following Historical Review of times (most important to be well described) is, we trust, sufficiently explained. He labours to instruct, not to misrepresent; he endeavours to conciliate, not to inflame. No honest man of the present age, (Protestant or Papist) is concerned in the conduct of Protestants or Papists of any former age, otherwise than by contrasting the causes and effects in the one with those in the other, and instructing us thereby to put a proper estimate on our present happiness, and to remove any ill impression the public may still retain, in regard to times so very different from our own. This is placing a mirror before the reader, wherein beauties and deformities are fairly reflected; and whereby deductions may be made, for improving our minds and manners, by the justness of the representation.

The instruction to be drawn from the perusal of the following Historical Review has been pointed out; and if the Author has occasionally put censures on some of our Roman Catholic predecessors, relatively to some false judgments and opinions, he has not done it impertinently, to guard the present generation of Roman Catholics against such exploded notions. He knows them too well to need being so guarded. The opinions he refers to (and they were no more than opinions) may be compared to chronic distempers, which for a time make depredations on a sound constitution, and which such a constitution will in time shake off. The birth and parentage of those opinions can be easily traced, if men will be at the small pains of doing it. They were the offspring of local interests, nursed by the passions, and adopted by the politics of the age. They are now no more, and the shades which formerly enveloped the ignorant and unwary are dispersed. No Roman Catholic is now interested in errors which were but local, and have indeed been opposed by Roman Catholics in the most clouded days. In the light which time hath spread about us, Papists have got a full sight of their civil duty; and they profess and practice it. To them we need not apply.. Our present suit is to Protestants who still are jealous, and who may perhaps be loth to part with mistakes, they have been long in the habit of indulging. Some among them (and it is a good omen) have already shaken off their captivity under those mistakes; and we wish, and hope also, that others may make a philosophic effort, and reflect that the opinions we have censured were no other than what we have represented them to be, mere temporary and transient evils, from which no party (Protestant or Papist) was exempt in the times we speak of. At present no party should be punished for opinions or principles which they are ready to abjure. The Papists it is true, avow doctrines, which they are bound by conscience to retain, and which their adversaries will always condemn. It is not in this case as in the other. The opinion is fugitive, the doctrine permanent. Relatively to tenets of faith, a charge made on one side, is admitted to be just on the other. There can therefore be no mistake in a case where all parties are agreed, and no good reason can be assigned for charging men with doctrines they reject, when so many are avowed, as would justify the charge of error, if error it could be proved. Human society exposed by nature to sundry evils, requires no adventitious supply from causes wherein nature revolts, instead of bearing a part. If the terms of christian communion professed by Roman Catholics in every country, be deemed crimes punishable in any; they must stand to this in every punishing country. They must, in this case, oppose the penalties of conscience to those of law, and resignedly yield to the lesser punishment.

ENOUGH is said to shew, that an union on civil principles and practices, under the present establishment, is sufficient for all the purposes of civil security; and we need not go about to prove, that in our own Northern soil, and under our variable climate, the prosperity admitted by both, cannot be obtained, without the co-operation and mutual confidence of all our people. They must be hands of mischief indeed, that require to be tied up from this co-operation, and heads devoid of all honest principle, who should be an obstacle to such confidence. The Roman Catholics are by law excluded from permanent property. Even insecurity is annexed to a flux-monied property acquired by their industry. But the penal laws they are exposed to, have long since received a constitutional ratification,

INTRODUCTION. xxi

fication, and while such laws exist, their religion commands obedience, not resistance. They have as little the inclination, as they have the right, to seek any alleviation of their sufferings, but what they may obtain, from a Prince who has approved himself the best of Kings, at the head of a wise parliament.

BEFORE we conclude, it is but fit that the author should express his gratitude to gentlemen who have forwarded the present work by their encouragement. He does so unfeignedly; and he has a particular call upon him to confess his obligations to Mr. JAMES REYNOLDS of *Ash-Street*, whose correspondence with the great towns of the kingdom is extensive, and who omits no occasion, and indeed improves every opportunity, to approve himself a loyal subject, and good citizen.

June 12th, 1775.

AUTHORITIES quoted in the enfuing Work.

Reliquiæ Sacræ Carolinæ, or the Works of King Charles I. Octavo.
Scrinia Sacra, or Myfteries of State and Government. Octavo, Lond. Ed.
Morrifton's Hiftory of Ireland. Lond. Ed. Folio.
Pacata Hibernia. Lond. Ed. Folio.
State Letters of the Earl of Strafford. Lond. Ed. Folio.
State Letters of the Earl of Orrery. Dub. Ed. Octavo.
State Letters of Lord Arlington, by Brown. Lond. Ed. Octavo.
Borlace's Hiftory of the Irifh Rebellion. Dub. Ed. Folio.
Temple's Hiftory of the Irifh Rebellion. Quarto.
Sir John Davis's Hiftorical Relations. Dub. Ed. Octavo.
Journals of the Irifh Houfe of Commons. Folio.
Supplement to thefe Journals. Dub. Ed. Folio.
Walfh's Hiftory of the Irifh Remonftrance. Folio.
Carte's Life of the Duke of Ormond. Lond. Ed. Folio.
Carte's Collection of Original Letters. Dub. Ed. Octavo.
Earl of Caftlehaven's Memoirs. Lond. Ed. Duodecimo.
Earl of Anglefey's Letter to the Earl of Caftlehaven. Lond. Ed. Duodecimo.
Doctor Leland's Hiftory of Ireland. Dub. Ed. Quarto.
Warner's Hiftory of the Irifh Rebellion. Lond. Ed. Quarto.
Archbifhop King's State of the Proteftants of Ireland under King James. Quarto.
Mr. Lefley's Anfwer to Archbifhop King. Quarto.
The Earl of Clarendon's Life and Memoirs, by himfelf. Dub. Ed. Octavo.
Henry Earl of Clarendon's State Letters. Octavo.
Lord Effex's State Letters.
Mr. Belling's Manufcript Hiftory of the Wars of Ireland.
Sir John Dalrymple's Memoirs. Dub. Ed. Octavo.
Spencer's State of Ireland. Dub. Ed. Duodecimo.

AN HISTORICAL AND CRITICAL REVIEW OF THE CIVIL WARS IN IRELAND.

BOOK I.

CHAP. I.

Of the State of the Irish from the Time of the Invasion of Henry II.

IN order to form a right judgment of the principles, and conduct of the natives of Ireland, since the reformation (from which period only, I purpose to consider their civil dissensions) it is necessary to look back to the times preceding that event; and to take a cursory view of the manner, in which the first British adventurers, and their successors, for several ages, treated these, as they affected to call them, conquered People (1). Now it is evident from all our records, that after these adventurers got footing in that kingdom, the British colonies only, and some (*a*) few septs of the Irish, that were enfranchised by special charter, were admitted to the Benefit and Protection of the laws of England; and that the Irish, as such, were generally reputed aliens,

or

---

(1) Sir John Davis's Historical Relations, D. Ed. p. 45.

(*a*) These were the O'Neals of Ulster, O'Melaghlins of Meath, the O'Conors of Connaught, the O'Briens of Thomond, and the Mac Mouroghs of Leinster. Sir John Davis's Hist. Rel.

or rather enemies; in so much, that it was adjudged no felony to kill a mere (*b*) Irishman, in time of peace.

It is also evident, that (2) the Irish, on their parts, "did, at several times, desire to be admitted to the benefit of the law; as in their petitions to Richard II. and Lord Thomas of Lancaster, before the war of the two Houses; and afterwards, to Lord Leonard Gray, and Sir Arthur St. Leger, when Henry the VIII. began to reform that kingdom. And it was certainly a great defect in the civil policy of Ireland, that for the space of three hundred and fifty years at least after the conquest first attempted, the English laws were not communicated to its people, nor the benefit or protection thereof allowed them; for as long as they were out of the protection of the laws, so as every Englishman might oppress, spoil, and kill them without controul (3), how was it possible they should be other than outlaws, and enemies to the Crown of England? If the king would not admit them to the condition of subjects, how could they learn to acknowledge, and obey him, as their Sovereign? When they might not converse, or commerce, with civilized men, nor enter into any town or city without peril of ther lives: whither should they fly, but into woods and mountains, and there live in a wild, and barbarous manner? In a word, if the English would neither in peace govern them by the law, nor could in war root them out by the sword, must they not needs be pricks in their eyes, and thorns in their sides, to the world's end?"

On the other hand, that these people merited far different treatment from the crown of England, is manifest from hence, that when they were at last admitted to the condition of subjects, under James I. they gave many signal proofs of their dutifulness, and obedience; and as the same knowing, and impartial witness whom I have hitherto quoted, then vouched for them (4), " would gladly continue in that condition, as long as they might be protected, and justly governed, without oppression on the one hand, or impunity on the other; there being, in his opinion, no nation under the sun that did love equal, and indifferent (*c*), Justice, better than the Irish, or that would rest better satisfied

(2) Sir John Davis's Historical Relations, D. Ed. p. 16.
(3) Id. ib. p. 52.   (4) Id. ib. p. 123.

(*b*) So ridiculously, as well as tyrannously, was this distinction kept up, "That no man was to be taken for " an Englishman, who had not his upper lip shaven:" (which, it seems, the Irish had not.) " And, if any " man should be found among the English, contrary " thereunto, it was lawful to seize him, and his goods, " as an Irish enemy."   Sir John Davis, Ib. p. 92.

(*c*) " I dare affirm," says Sir John Davis, Attorney General in Ireland, in the reign of James I. " that " for the space of five years last past, there have not " been found so many malefactors, worthy of death, " in all the six circuits of this realm, which is now " divided into thirty-six shires at large, as in one cir- " cuit of six shires, namely, the Western circuit of " England. For the truth is, that in time of peace, " the Irish are more fearful to offend the law, than " the English, or any other nation whatsoever." Hist. Relat. p. 116.

tisfied with the execution thereof, altho' it were against themselves; so as they might have the protection, and benefit of the law, when upon a just cause they did desire it."

CHAP. II.

The State of the Irish, at the Beginning of the Reformation of Religion.

IN this condition of absolute slavery, the Irish remained during the reigns of Henry VIII. Edward VI. and Q. Elizabeth; when the new reformed religion was first introduced among them; a circumstance not at all likely to induce them to embrace it, even tho' they had been willing to part with their old religion, which was far from being the case. This obstacle to their reformation, was accompanied with others still greater; their new pastors were totally ignorant of the Irish language, as their flocks, for the most part, were of the English (*a*); besides, the inferior clergy, in those days, who had the immediate cure of souls, were men of no parts, or erudition; and, what was much worse, they were full as immoral, as they were illiterate (1). "The " clergy in Ireland," says Mr. Spencer (*b*), writing of this period, " excepting " the grave fathers, who are in high places about the state, and some few " others, who are lately planted in the new college, are generally bad, licen- " tious, and most disordered."

Such were the men, whose new religious doctrine, and discipline, these people were required to embrace, against the conviction of their consciences, and at the peril of their liberties, fortunes, and lives.

At the same time that the ignorance, and immorality of the reforming missionaries caused the Irish to hate, and despise their doctrine, these people held the

(1) Spencer's State of Ireland, Dub. Ed.

(*a*) " Even within the English pale," (viz. the counties of Dublin, Meath, Lowth, and Kildare,) " the Irish language was become so predominant, that " laws were repeatedly enacted to restrain it, but in " vain.—In those tracts of Irish territory, which in- " terfected the English settlements, no other language " was at all known; so that here the wretched flock " was totally inaccessible to those strangers, who were " become their pastors." Leland's Hist. of Ireland, Dub. Ed. 4to. Vol. ii. p. 194.

(*b*) He was Secretary to Lord Leonard Gray, Deputy of Ireland, in the reign of Elizabeth. " What- " ever disorders," adds he, on this occasion, " are " in the church of England, may be seen in that of " Ireland, and much more; namely, gross simony, " greedy covetousness, fleshly incontinency, careless " sloth, and generally all disordered life in the com- " mon clergymen. And besides these, they have " particular enormities; they neither read the scrip- " tures, nor preach to the people, only they take the " tythes and offerings, and gather what fruit they can " off their livings, which they convert as badly." State of Ireland, p. 131.

the persons of their own clergy, in the highest esteem and veneration (c). Of this, I shall mention one remarkable instance, out of many others, that occur in their history (2). " Towards the end of Queen Elizabeth's reign, her Ma-
" jesty's forces besieging the castle of Cloghan, and understanding that in the
" same there was a Romish priest," (to which order of men they never gave quarter,) " having also in their hands, the brother of the Constable, who had
" the charge of the castle, the commanding officer sent him word, that if he
" did not presently surrender the Castle to him, he would hang his brother in
" their sight. But to save the priest, whose life they tendered, they persever-
" ed obstinately not to yield: whereupon the officer, in their sight, hanged
" the Constable's brother. Nevertheless, within four days afterwards, the
" priest being shifted away in safety, the Constable sued for a protection, and
" rendered the castle. I do relate this accident," adds my author, " to the
" end the reader may the more clearly see, in what reverence, and estimation,
" these ignorant superstitious Irish do hold a Popish priest; in regard of whose
" safety, the Constable was content to suffer his brother to perish."

C H A P. III.

The Conduct of the English Chief Governors of Ireland, towards the Natives.

MR. OSBURNE informs us (1), that in England, during Q. Elizabeth's reign, to be a Catholic was thought to signify nothing else, but an enemy to God, and the Prince. The like prejudice prevailed also, at the same time, in Ireland; and the name of Irishman, or Papist, was deemed a sufficient justification of any act of cruelty, or injustice, committed on the person who bore it I say not this, merely on the testimony of Irishmen, and Papists; but on that also, of Englishmen, and Protestants; some of whom were eye-witnesses of the facts they relate, and had the virtue to publish their detestation of them.

In

(2) Pacata Hibernia, fol. 358.   (1) Osburne's Works.

(c) " It's a great wonder," says the same Mr. Spencer, " to see the odds, which is between the " zeal of the popish priests and the ministers of the Gos- " pel. For they spare not to come out of Spain, from " Rome, and from Rheims, by long toil and dange- " rous travelling hither; where they know peril of " death awaiteth them, and no reward, or riches to " be found, only to draw the people to the church of

" Rome. Whereas, some of our idle ministers, hav- " ing a way for credit and estimation thereby opened, " and having livings of the country offered to them, " without pains, and without peril, will neither for " the same, nor for any love of God, or zeal of " religion, be drawn forth from their warm nests, to " look out into God's harvest." Ib. p. 114.

IN a (2) Memorial presented to her Majesty and Council, by an *(a)* officer, who had served several years in her army in Ireland; some of those unconscionable courses are set forth, particularly those frequent breaches of publick faith, and the insecurity of any pardon granted to these people, on their submitting to the government; who, says the Memorialist, "without being guilty of any new crime, and even without a legal trial, were afterwards condemned, and executed, to the great dishonour of her Majesty, and discredit of her Laws."

IT would be equally shocking, and tedious, to recite all those well-attested acts of cruelty and perfidy, which were perpetrated on these people, by the order, or connivance, of her Majesty's principal Ministers in that kingdom. Two, or three instances only, which include hundreds of sufferers, will suffice for the present.

WHEN, in the year 1583 (3), the garrison of Smerwick, in Kerry, surrendered, upon mercy, to Lord Deputy Gray *(b)*, he ordered upwards of seven hundred of them to be put to the sword (c), or hanged (4). "Wingfield was commissioned to disarm them; and when this service was performed, an English company was sent into the fort, and the garrison was butchered in cold blood, nor is it without pain that we find a service so horrid, and detestable, committed to Sir Walter Raleigh. The usual, and obvious excuses for this severity, could not efface the odiousness of it; on the Continent it was received with horror."

ABOUT the same time (5), "Walter Earl of Essex, on the conclusion of a peace, invited Bryan O'Neal of Claneboy, with a great number of his relations, to an entertainment, where they lived together in great harmony, making good

---

(2) Manuscript in Trinity College, Dublin. See Append. No. 1.
(3) Borlase's Reduction of Ireland, p. 136.
(4) Leland's Hist. of Ireland, Vol. ii. p. 283.
(5) MSS. Irish Chronicle in Trinity College, Dub.

(*a*) The author, in the body of his Memorial, offers the following trial and proof of his veracity. "I desire not that your Majesty should either simply credit me, in this my plain dealing, in detecting them," (her Ministers in Ireland,) "nor them in excusing themselves. But, if it please your Highness to appoint Commissioners in that realm for the trial; if I prove not directly all that ever I have declared, let me lose your gracious favour for ever."

(*b*) "Repeated complaints were made of the inhuman rigor practiced by this Deputy, and his officers. The Queen was assured, that he tyrannised with such barbarity, that little was left in Ireland for her Majesty to reign over, but ashes, and dead carcasses." Lel. Hist. of Ireland, Vol. ii. p. 287.

(*c*) "The Italian General, and some officers, were made prisoners of war, but the garrison was butchered in cold blood." Leland's Hist. of Ireland, Vol ii. p. 283.

good cheer for three days and nights; when, on a sudden, O'Neal was surprised with an arrest, together with his brother and wife, by the Earl's order (d). His friends were put to the sword before his face; nor were the women and children spared: he was himself, with his brother and wife, sent to Dublin, where they were cut in quarters. This encreased the disaffection, and produced the detestation of all the Irish; for this Chieftain of Claneboy, was the senior of his family, and as he had been universally esteemed, he was now as universally regretted."

We don't find, however, that any remarkable commotion was excited on this account; or that any immediate provocation on the part of the Irish, was so much as pretended, for so barbarous an act of perfidy. " After the 19th year of Queen Elizabeth, viz. anno, 1577, the Lords of Conaght, and O'Rorke," says (6) Morrisson, " made a composition for their Lands, with Sir Nicholas Malby, governor of that province; wherein they were content to yield the Queen so large a rent, and such services, both of labourers to work upon occasion of fortifying, and of horse and foot, to serve upon occasion of war, that their minds seemed not yet to be alienated from their wonted awe, and reverence for the crown of England." Yet, in that same year, an horrible massacre was committed by the English, at Mulloghmaston, on some hundreds of the most peaceable of the Irish gentry, invited thither on the public faith, and under the protection of government.

The fact is thus literally (e) translated from (7) the Irish annals of Queen Elizabeth's reign. " The calends of January, on Tuesday, 1577. In this year the English of Leinster and Meath, committed horrid murders on such of the O'Mores and O'Conors, and others of the King's and Queen's county as kept the peace, sued for protection, and held no correspondence with those of their kindred, who still stood out in arms against the English government."

" The English published a proclamation, inviting all the well-affected Irish to an interview on the Rathmore, at Mulloghmaston; engaging, at the same time, for their security, and that no evil was intended. In consequence of this engagement, the well-affected came to the Rathmore aforesaid, and soon after

(6) History of Ireland, fol. Ed. p. 3.   (7) MSS. Trin. Col. Dub.

(d) " Such relations," as Doctor Leland justly observes on this occasion. " would be more suspicious, if these annals in general expressed great virulence against the English, and their government. But they do not appear to differ essentially from the printed histories, except in the minuteness with which they record the local transactions, and adventures of the Irish. And sometimes they expressly condemn their countrymen, for their rebellions against their Prince." Hist. of Ireland, Vol. ii. p. 258.

(e) By my learned, and very worthy friend, Charles O'Conor, of Balanegare, Esq; as likewise the former.

after they were assembled, they found themselves surrounded by three or four lines of English and Irish horse and foot, completely accoutred, by whom they were ungenerously attacked, and cut to pieces; and not a single man escaped."

To this massacre, the Memorialist beforementioned, probably alluded, when he complained (8), " that her Majesty's servants, who were placed in authority, to protect men for her service, had drawn unto them, by such protection, three or four hundred of the Irish, under colour to serve her Majesty; and brought them to a place of meeting, where her garrison-soldiers were appointed to be; who there, most dishonourably, put them all to the sword. This, adds he, was done by the consent, and practice, of the Lord Deputy for the time being."

CHAP. IV.

Motives for the general Discontent in Ulster.

IN the year 1589 (1), " When Sir William Fitzwilliams entered upon the government, Ireland was in the best estate that it had been in for a long time, not only peaceable and quiet, but so as any, the greatest Lord, called by letter, or messenger, readily came to the State; and none of them were known to be any way discontent. But, within three months after his taking the sword, having been informed, that the Spaniards lately (a) wrecked upon the coasts of Conaught, and Ulster, had left with the inhabitants great store of treasure, and other riches, he greedily sought to get it into his hands, pretending the Queen's service, as appeared by a commission, by which he first essayed to seize the same; but that not taking effect, he made a journey himself, into these parts, where, altogether failing of his purpose, he brought thence with him, as prisoners, two of the best affected gentlemen to the State, that were in those parts, whom he deemed to possess the greatest part of the treasure, namely, Sir Owen Mac Tooly, father-in-law to the Earl of Tyrone, who had long enjoyed a pension of two hundred pounds a year from the Queen, and Sir John O'Dogherty. The former refusing to pay for his enlargement, continued prisoner till the beginning of Sir William Russell's government,

---

(8) Lee's Memorial, MSS. Trin. Col. Dub.

(1) Morif. Hift. of Ireland, fol. 4.

(a) " Those (Spaniards) who were shipwrecked in Ireland, and cast ashore, were all put to the sword, or perished by the hands of the Executioner; the Lord Deputy, by whose orders it was done, fearing they would side with the Rebels; at least this was the pretence made use of, to excuse this barbarity."—— 'Tis said, that on the coast of Ireland, seventeen ships, and five thousand three hundred and ninety four men were then destroyed. Rapin's Hift. of Eng. Vol. ix. p. 122. Note.

vernment, who in pity difcharged him; but the old gentleman's heart was firft broken, fo as fhortly after he died. The latter was releafed, after two years reftraint; but not without paying for his liberty. At this hard ufuage of thefe two Ulfter gentlemen, all the great men of the Irifh, efpecially in thofe Northern parts, did much repine. " The loyal Irifh," fays Doctor Leland, " on this occafion, trembled for their own fafety, and the difaffected were confirmed in their inveteracy."

"ABOUT the year 1590 (2), died M'Mahon, Chieftain of Monaghan, who, in his life-time had furrendered his country into her Majefty's hands, and received a re-grant thereof, under the broad feal of England, to him and his heirs male; and in default of fuch, to his brother Hugh Roe M'Mahon, with other remainders. And this man dying without iffue-male, his faid brother came up to the State, that he might be fettled in his inheritance, hoping to be countenanced and cherifhed, as her Majefty's Patentee. But he found, as the *(b)* Irifh fay, he could not be admitted, until he promifed fix hundred cows, for fuch, and no other, were the Irifh bribes. He was afterwards imprifoned for failing in part of his payment; and in a few days enlarged, with promife that the Lord Deputy himfelf, would go and fettle him in his country of Monaghan; whither his Lordfhip took his journey fhortly after, with M'Mahon in his company. At their firft arrival, the gentleman was clapt into bolts; and in two days after, he was indicted, arraigned, and executed at his own door; all done, as the Irifh faid, by fuch officers, as the Lord Deputy carried with him, for that purpofe, from Dublin. The treafon for which he was condemned, was, becaufe, two years before, he pretending a rent due unto him, out of Ferney, levied forces, and made a diftrefs for the fame; which, by the Englifh law, adds my Author, may, perhaps, be treafon; but in that country, never before fubject to law, it was thought no rare thing, nor great

(2) Id. ib. fol. 10.

(*b*) On occafion of this manner of expreffing himfelf, which Morriffon often makes ufe of, the reader is defired to take notice of the following paffage. " This, fays he, I write of hearfay; but, as in the general relation following, I purpofe to write nothing which is not warranted, either by relations prefented to the Queen by the principal Counccllors of Ireland, or by letters interchanged between the ftates of England and Ireland, or like authentical writings; fo for the particular of the above named Lord Deputy, if, perhaps, fome may think any thing obferved by me to derogate from him, I proteft, that whatfoever I write, is, in like fort, warranted, and may not be omitted without the fcandal of hiftorical integrity, being objections frequently made by the rebels, for excufe of their difloyalty, as well in all their petitions, as treaties of peace." Morif. Hift. of Ireland, f. 8. He afterwards, indeed, mentions, in its due place, what he calls an honourable anfwer of the Deputy, to part of this charge, in which anfwer it is affirmed, " that the country feemed glad of M'Mahon's execution." But this, Morriffon himfelf, in the fame page, flatly contradicts. Ib. f. 11. And he further protefts, " that he would moft willingly have inferted his full juftification, if any fuch memorial had come to his hands."

Ibid. fol. 8.

great offence. The Marshal, Sir Henry Bagnall, had part of the country; Captain Hensflower was made Seneschall of it, and had M'Mahon's chief house, and part of the land; and to divers others, smaller portions of land were assigned; and the Irish spared not to say, that these men were all the contrivers of his death; and that every one was paid something for his share. "Certain it is," says the same (3) Historian, " that, upon M'Mahon's execution, heartburnings, and loathings of the English government, began to grow in the Northern Lords; and they shunned, as much as they could, to admit any Sheriffs, or any English among them *(c)*."

C H A P. V.

The first Causes of Tyrone's *Insurrection.*

UPON (1) the execution of M'Mahon, and the jealousy thence conceived against the English, Maguire, a Northern Lord, about the year 1593, began to declare himself discontent, and to stand upon his defence. He alleged, that he had given three hundred Cows, to free his country from a Sheriff, during the Lord Deputy's government; and that, notwithstanding, one Captain Willis *(a)* was made Sheriff of Fermanagh, having, for his guard, one hundred men; and leading about some hundreds of women and boys, all living upon the spoil of the country: upon which, says my Author, Maguire, who was Chieftain of Fermanagh, taking his advantage, set upon them and drove them into a church, where he would have put them all to the sword, if the Earl of Tyrone had not interposed his authority, and made composition for their lives, upon condition that they should all leave the country. Upon this

---

(3) Ib.   (1) Morif. ib. fol. 12.

(c) " The unhappy M'Mahon, for an offence committed, before the Law, which declared it capital, had been established in his country, was tried, condemned by a jury, said to be formed of private soldiers, and executed in two days, to the utter consternation of his countrymen. His estate was distributed to Sir Henry Bagnall, and other adventurers, together with four of the old Irish sept. The condemnation of this Chieftain, confirmed the Irish in their aversion to the English polity; which they considered as a system of hateful cruelty and tyranny." Lel. Hist. of Ireland, Vol. ii. p. 317.

(a) " A great part of that unquietness of O'Donnel's country, came by Sir William Fitzwilliam's placing one Willis there to be Sheriff, who had with him three hundred of the very rascals, and scum of that kingdom, which did rob and spoil that people, ravish their wives and daughters, and made havock of all; which bred such a discontent, as that the whole country was up in arms against them, so as if the Earl of Tyrone had not rescued and delivered him, and them, out of the country, they had been all put to the sword." Lee's Letter to Queen Elizabeth, MSS. in Trinity College.

this occasion, the Lord Deputy Fitzwilliams sent the Queen's *(b)* forces into Fermanagh, won Maguire's castle of Enniskillen, and proclaimed him a traitor. The Irish avow, that his Lordship let fall some speeches against the Earl of Tyrone himself, calling him a traitor also, (notwithstanding his late service,) which speeches coming to that Earl's hearing, he ever after said, were the first causes that moved him to misdoubt his safety, and to stand upon his defence; now first combining himself with O'Donnell, and the other Lords of the North, to defend, adds Mr. Morrisson, their honours, estates, and liberties.

This combination, however, was for some time kept secret; for (2) Tyrone still served, with the Queen's forces, against Maguire, and once valiantly fighting, was wounded in the thigh (3). " But he ceased not to complain daily of the Lord Deputy's, and Marshall's, envy against him; and of wrongs done him by the *(c)* garrison soldiers: and these wrongs not being redressed, together, with the ill government of the church, the extortions of Sheriffs, and the army's oppressing the subject, and by that means, driving many daily into rebellion, made him at last resolve to temporize *(d)* no longer." But what it was, that first provoked him to break out into open acts of hostility against the government, I shall now briefly relate.

In the year 1594, Sir William Fitzwilliams being recalled into England, Sir William Russell succeeded him in the government of Ireland. To this new Deputy, the Queen had been prevailed upon to give private orders (4), to seize upon Tyrone, and make him a prisoner, if ever he should get him in his

---

(2) Id. ib. fol. 13.   (3) Id. ib.   (4) Cambden's Eliz. p. 634.

(b) The Earl of Tyrone had, at that time, in conjunction with the English Marshall of Newry, the command of all the Queen's forces sent against Maguire. Irish Annals.

(c) The Queen had long before this, frequently, but in vain, ordered this grievance to be removed. " For that our subjects of that realm," says she, in her instructions to Sir John Perrot, anno 1583, " have been very grievously oppressed by the outrages, and insolences committed by certain ill-affected of our garrisons serving there, which hath been partly a cause of the alienation of the good-will, which they before bare unto us, we cannot (as a principal matter, wherein we look to have redress) but give you an especial charge, to see that our garrisons serving there, be kept in better discipline than heretofore they have been.—And that such abuses as have been hitherto committed by such Captains, as have had heretofore more regard to their particular profit, than to the discharge of their duties, may be met withal, and the party offending, severely punished." Desiderata Curiosa Hibern. Vol. i. p. 36.

(d) " Where it was your Majesty's pleasure," says Lee, in his Memorial to the Queen, " He (Tyrone) should have great encouragement given him, by thanks for his last great service against Maguire, it was held from him; and instead of that, they devised all means and policies to aggravate matters against him to your Majesty; which is credibly made known unto him: and more, that upon what security soever, he should come in, your Majesty's pleasure is to have him detained." Desid. Curios. Hib. Vol. i. p. 110.

his power. Tyrone had often refused to come to Dublin, on the invitation of the late Lord Deputy, from a distrust of his Lordship's honour, and on account of his known enmity to him; but Sir William Russell having sent him (5) a protection, which was an assurance of safety on public faith; he soon appeared before him at the castle, and declared, that the reason of his not having obeyed the like orders from the late Deputy, was because he knew, " that he had laid snares for his life, which it was but natural for him to avoid." He added, " that the accusations against him, were false and malicious; that he desired nothing more, than a fair and impartial trial, by which, he was confident, his innocence would fully appear; and, for that purpose, he declared, (as if, says Cambden, he thought himself sufficiently secured by the testimony of a good conscience,) that he would renounce all claim to his letters of protection, in case the aforesaid accusations of his enemies could be proved against him."

This (6) matter being seriously debated in the Council, some of that board were of opinion, that O'Neal should be then made a prisoner, notwithstanding his protection, in order to answer a charge of High Treason, which his known, and inveterate enemy, (e) Sir Henry Bagnall, had newly prepared against him. But the majority of the council, either, says my (7) Author, out of a (f) vain scruple of violating the public faith, or thro' some secret affection for Tyrone, declared, that he ought, in justice and honour, to be then dismissed; and that his trial should be deferred to another time. Of the subject of this debate, Tyrone was privately informed by the (g) Earl of Ormond, and thereupon, immediately

---

(5) Id. ib.   (6) Id. ib.   (7) Cambden, ib.

(e) This same Bagnall, had formerly urged some articles of treason against him, " which, says Morrison, were believed in England, till Tyrone offered, by his letters, to stand to his trial either in England or Ireland. Accordingly, adds my Author, he answered to the said articles, before the Lord Deputy and Council, at Dundalk, in such sort, as they who had written into England against him, now to the contrary, wrote that he had sufficiently answered them. Whereupon, the Lords of England wrote to the Earl of Tyrone, that they approved his answers, and that, in their opinion, he had wrong to be so charged.—At the same time, their Lordship's wrote to the Deputy, taxing him and the Marshal (Bagnall) that they had used the Earl of Tyrone against law and equity." Hist. of Ireland, fol. 12.

(f) Some English officers having assured certain Irish Chiefs, that upon surrendering themselves to the government, they would obtain their pardon. " These Chiefs embraced the council, submitted, and consented to attend the Lord Deputy St. Leger into England: but here, the only favour granted was, that they were not brought to immediate execution. They were committed to prison, their lands declared forfeit, and granted to those, by whose council they had surrendered." Lel. Hist. of Ireland, Vol. ii. p. 189.

(g) This Earl had some time before, received the like private orders, with respect to some Irish gentlemen to whom he had granted protection; but he was so far from obeying them, that he wrote a letter to Lord Treasurer Burleigh, in which he told him, that these orders appeared very strange to him; that the Irish

mediately fled from Dublin; and although he was quickly followed by the Deputy's order to stop him, which was sent to all the towns through which it was thought he was to pass, yet by the assistance of his friends, and the swiftness of his horses, he escaped in safety to Ulster.

O'Donnell's first cause of disaffection to the government, happened very early (8). While he was yet a lad, of the age of twelve, or fifteen years, a ship freighted with several curiosities, was, by the then Lord Deputy's order, sent to the bay of Tyrconnell; where the Master having found O'Donnell, and some of his companions, seduced them, with a display of his curiosities, to come on board his vessel; and after entertaining them there for some time, with much seeming affection, and respect, he privately ordered his mariners to sail back for Dublin, having got the prey they came for. As soon as they arrived there, O'Donnell, and his companions, were closely confined in the castle of that city, where they remained prisoners, under many wants and cruel *(b)* restraints, for more than seven years; and at last, made a desperate attempt to escape, which by the assistance of their friends, and their own resolution succeeded; though not without the loss of the life of one of O'Donnell's companions, and the extreme danger of his own. It was immediately upon his arrival in Ulster, after this escape, that he entered into the before mentioned combination with Tyrone, being then not more than twenty years old.

The (9) Queen was much displeased that her commands, with respect to Tyrone, were not executed; and the (10) Lords of the English council sharply rebuked the Deputy for having so easily suffered him to escape out of his hands. And although Sir William Russell afterwards, frequently invited him, in the most soothing manner, to come to Dublin, he could never be again prevailed upon, by any promise of safety, to put himself in his power; but immediately betook himself to open acts of hostility: the first of which, was, (after having defeated a great body of the Queen's forces) his assaulting, and demolishing,

(8) Lombard. Irish Annals.   (9) Camden's Eliz. p 635.   (10) Morrison's Hist.

Irish gentlemen in question had, according to her Majesty's instructions, delivered pledges to do good service, and put in assurances of their loyalty; and then he declares his resolution in these words: "My Lord, I will never use treachery to any man, for it will both touch her Highness's honour, and my own credit too much; and whosoever gave the Queen advice thus to write, is fitter to execute such base service than I am. Saving my duty to her Majesty, I would I were to have revenge by my sword, of any man that thus persuadeth the Queen to write to me." Carte's Orm. Vol. i. fol. lvi.

(b) "His manner of usage, says Lee, was most dishonourable and discommendable, and neither allowable before God or man.—For he (O'Donnell) being young, and being taken by this stratagem, having never offended, was imprisoned with great severity, many irons laid upon him, as if he had been a notable traitor and malefactor, and kept still amongst those, who were ever notorious traitors to your Majesty." Memorial to the Queen, Desid. Hib. Vol. i. p. 96.

lishing, in the year 1595, the fort of Black Water, which was built upon the passage into Tyrone. "In this victory, says Burlace (11), the *(i)* like of which, the Irish never gained, since the English first set foot in Ireland, Tyrone's implacable enemy, Marshal Bagnall, with others, was slain *(k) (l).*"

The several submissions, which he afterwards made, with apparent sincerity, were but of short duration; because the conditions promised him on these occasions, were never fulfilled; of which breach of articles, he frequently complained; but was only answered (12), "That the benefit of his pardon was so great, that it should have counterpoised his wrongs, and still kept him in his duty *(m).*"

(11) Reduct. of Ireland, p. 178.   (12) Morrif. Hist.

(i) The Earl of Tyrone ordered, that the dead of the enemy should be interred. 2500 were left, with their General, on the field of battle: among whom were 18 captains, and many other gentlemen, whose names were unknown. Irish Ann.

(k) About this time, one hundred and forty-four barrels of gun powder, sent from the Queen to Dublin, were stored in Winetavern-street, and took fire by accident, on the 13th of March. Numbers were lost, and that part of the town greatly damaged by the explosion. Irish Annals.

(l) In this action, one of the Queen's soldiers, by accident, set fire to a barrel of gun powder, and that set fire to a number of others ranged along the line. The explosion was terrible, and destroyed a great number of the Queen's men; and the remains of the defeated army marched back to Ardmagh in disorder. Ibid.

(m) The report which Lee, in his memorial to Q. Elizabeth makes of Tyrone's loyalty, power, and services, is very remarkable. For mentioning the designs of his enemies, "Let," says he, "those devices take effect, or otherwise have him cut off, your Majesty's whole kingdom there would moan it most pitifully; for there was never man bred in those parts, who hath done your Majesty greater service than he, with often loss of his blood, upon notable enemies of your Majesty. Yea, more often than all the other nobles of Ireland. And what quietness your Majesty has had these many years past, in the Northern parts of that kingdom, its neither your forces there placed (which have been but small,) nor their great service who commanded them, but only the honest disposition, and carriage of the Earl, hath made them obedient in these parts to your Majesty.—If he were so bad as they would fain enforce, as many as know him, and the strength of his country, will witness thus much with me, that he might very easily cut off many of your Majesty's forces, which are laid in garrison in small troops, in divers parts bordering upon his country; yea, and over run all your English pale, to the utter ruin thereof; yea, and camp, as long as should please him, under the walls of Dublin, for any strength your Majesty hath yet in that kingdom to remove him." Lee's Letter, MSS. See Append. No. 1.

"The Rebel's forces, says Borlace, when Tyrone was proclaimed a traitor, amounted to 1000 horse, and 6280 foot, in Ulster, and 2300 in Conaught; all at Tyrone's beck: whereas before, 800 foot, and 300 horse, were esteemed, on the government's side, an invincible army." Reduct. of Ireland, p. 175.6.

CHAP.

CHAP. VI.

Defmond's *Infurrection*.

THE Earl of Defmond's vaft eftate in the province of Munfter, had been an irrefiftible temptation to former Chief Governors, in this reign, to make, or to proclaim him, a rebel, their prey being enfured to them, in either cafe, by his forfeiture. And, indeed, it does not appear, that this Earl, before he was proclaimed, had committed any over-act of treafon; unlefs his private family-quarrels with the Earl of Ormond, about their refpective powers, and limits, can be deemed fuch. About a month before he was proclaimed, his Countefs had delivered up their only fon, together with Patrick O'Haly, Bifhop of Mayo, and Con. O'Rorke, a Francifcan Friar, both nobly defcended, and who had fled to her for protection, to Sir William Drury, Lord Juftice at Limerick, as hoftages, and pledges of the Earl's loyalty; nor can I find, that any thing but *(a)* meer fufpicion was then alleged againft him, and that only becaufe he refufed, or delayed, to draw out his forces againft his brother John of Defmond, who was in arms againft the Queen (1). "Whilft he held off," fays the Bifhop of Chicefter, " with delays, and delufions, he was declared a traitor, in the beginning of December, 1579, after which proclamation, the Chief Juftice Drury appointed the war to be profecuted againft him, by the Earl of Ormond." But certainly, fuch fufpicion ought, in all equitable judgment, to have been removed, by his confenting to have his only fon delivered up as a pledge of his future loyalty; who, though but an infant, was carried to London, and detained a prifoner in the tower there, for many years after. It is no fmall confirmation of his being previoufly innocent of any over-act of treafon,

(1) Thankful Remembrance, p. 43.

(a) "When the Earl of Defmond attended Drury's fummons to Kilmalock, with a well appointed company of horfe and foot, he was committed to cuftody on bare fufpicion; but, upon making the moft folemn promifes of loyalty, and fidelity, he obtained his liberty, retired from the camp, but refufed to attend the Deputy; and, therefore, was ftill confidered as a favourer of foreign invaders, and their caufe. Upon this bare fufpicion, Malby attacked his town of Rathkeal. This the Earl confidered as an unprovoked, and unwarrantable attempt, which he was juftified in repelling. Malby prepares to reduce his caftles, but Drury's death prevents him. Defmond was now fummoned by Sir William Pelham (Drury's fucceffor) he refufed to comply, but ftill profeffed his loyalty. He was then ordered to deliver up one of his caftles, as a pledge of his fidelity, (his fon was delivered up as fuch, before,) his anfwer confifted of complaints of injuries. He was therefore, by proclamation, declared a traitor, if within twenty days he fhould not fubmit. In the mean time, his territories were, purpofely, made the feat of war, and expofed to all the ravages of a neceffitous army. Defmond, in revenge, appeared before the town of Youghall, took it, cut off a detachment fent to its relief; and, then firft declared for the Catholic caufe." See Lel. Hift. of Ireland, Vol. ii. from p. 259 to 277.

treason, that, when it was resolved in council, to proclaim him a traitor (2); the Lords Gormanstown and Delvin, refused to sign the proclamation, with the other counsellors, for which they incurred her Majesty's displeasure.

But what ever excesses Desmond committed after he was proclaimed, it is certain, that he sorely *(b)* regretted them; as appears by the following letter, written by him to the Earl of Ormond; who, though his near relation, had long been his rival and enemy, and was now appointed his judge *(c)*.

My Lord, (3)

GREAT is my grief, when I think how heavily her Majesty is bent to disfavour me; and, howbeit I carry the name of an undutiful subject, yet God knoweth, that my heart, and mind, are always most loyally inclined to serve my most loving Prince, so it may please her Highness to remove her displeasure from me. As I may not condemn myself of disloyalty to her Majesty, so I cannot excuse my faults, but must confess I have incurred her Majesty's indignation; yet when the cause, and means, which were found, and devised to make me commit folly, shall be known to her Highness, I rest in an assured hope, that her most gracious Majesty will think of me as my heart deserveth; as also of those, who wrung me into undutifulness. From my heart, I am sorry that folly, bad councils, flights, or any other things, have made me to forget my duty; and therefore, I am most desirous to get conference with your Lordship, to the end I may open, and declare to you how tirannously I was

(2) Abbe Geoghegan's Hist. of Ireland, Vol. iii. p. 434.   (3) Scrinia Sacra.

(b) Desmond now saw his whole extent of territory ravaged, and depopulated without mercy; and, like an abject outlaw, was compelled to take shelter in his woods. His miserable vassals were abandoned to daily slaughter, or to the still more horrid calamity of famine. When, at the time that their lives were spared, they were frequently bereft of all means of support, Hook assures us, that they were seen following the army, with their wives and children; and begging that all might be rescued from their miseries by the sword, rather than thus condemned to waste in famine."—In this dismal situation of the once great Earl of Desmond, "His Countess fell upon her knees before the Lord Deputy, and, with tears, petitioned, but in vain, that her husband should be received to mercy. His force, as a rebel, was now too inconsiderable, and his possessions to be forfeited were of too princely an extent, for the Queen's ministers to admit of pardon, or submission." Lel. Hist. of Ireland, Vol. ii. p. 278-9.

(c) Spencer's description of the calamities brought on the people of Munster, by this war is really shocking. "Notwithstanding," says he, "that the same was a most rich, and plentiful country, full of corn, and cattle.—Yet, ere one year and an half, they were brought to such wretchedness, as that any stony heart would have rued the same. Out of every corner of the woods and glynns, they came creeping forth upon their hands, for their legs could not bear them; they looked like anatomies of death; they spake like ghosts crying out of their graves, they did eat the dead carrions, happy were they could find them, yea, and one another soon after; insomuch, as the very carcasses they spared not to scrape out of their graves, and, if they found a plot of watercresses or shamrocks, there they flocked as to a feast for the time, yet not able to continue there withal; that in short space, there was none almost left, and a most populous and plentiful country suddenly left void of man, and beast." State of Ireland, p. 158.

was used; humbly craving, that you will vouchsafe to appoint some time, and place, where and when I may attend your honour; and then I doubt not to make it appear, how dutiful a mind I carry; how faithfully I have, at my own charge, served her Majesty, before I was proclaimed; how sorrowful I am for my offences, and how faithfully I am affected ever hereafter to serve her Majesty; and so I commit your Lordship to God.

(Subscribed,) GIRALD DESMOND.

WHETHER the conference so earnestly desired in this letter was obtained, or not, does not appear. We only know (4), " that Kelly of Morierta, (of whom the Earl of Ormond had taken assurance of his fighting against the rebels) with twenty five of his kearn, did in the night-time assault the Earl of Desmond in his cabbin, then deserted by all his friends. Kelly entering the hut found that all were fled, but one man of venerable aspect, stretched languidly before a fire. The leader assailed, and wounded him. He exclaimed, " Spare me, for I am the Earl of Desmond." Kelly smote off his head, and brought it to the Earl of Ormond; by whom it was conveyed to the Queen, and impaled on London bridge (d) (e)."

UPON

---

(4) Carte's Ormond, Vol. i. Leland's Hist. of Ireland, Vol. ii. p. 288.

(d) The Irish analists, and other Roman Catholic writers, do not scruple to say, " That the vengeance of God was signal in this event," on account of this Earl's having committed great cruelties on his taking of Youghall, " which he gave up to plunder, not sparing even the churches, and whatsoever was sacred, which his soldiers polluted and defiled, bringing every thing to utter confusion and desolation, and making havock, as well of sacred vestments and chalices, as of any other chattle. Certain Spaniards, adds my author, who were with them, at that wicked exploit, perceiving by the furniture and ornaments of the churches, that the town's-men were all Catholics, and containing their hands from plunder, were reproved by some of that wicked company, for that they took not part of the spoil, as others did; but they answered, that they ought not to rob or spoil better christians than themselves; and one of the said Spaniards cut his cloak, as St. Martin did, in five parts, and distributed the same upon five children, that were stripped of their cloaths, and left naked by some of the Kearns." Theatre of Catholic and Protestant religion, p. 436.

(e) Mr. Spencer relates the first cause of disaffection, in the Desmond family, to the crown of England, as follows; " In the reign of King Edward the IVth, Thomas Earl of Desmond, being through false subornation (as they say) of the Queen, for some offence by her against him conceived, brought to his death at Tredagh (Drogheda) most unjustly, notwithstanding that he was a very good and sound subject to the King; thereupon all his kinsmen of the Geraldines, which then was a mighty family in Munster, in revenge of that huge wrong, rose in arms against the King, and utterly renounced, and forsook all obedience to the crown of England; to whom the M'Swiney's, M'Shee's, and M'Mahon's, being then servants, and followers, did the like, and have ever sithence so continued. And with them, (they say) all the people of Munster went out, and many other of them, which were mere English, thenceforth joined with the Irish against the King, and termed themselves very Irish, taking on them Irish habits and customs, which never since could be clean wiped away, but the contagion hath remained still among their posterity."
State of Ireland, p. 102.

Upon the attainder of this Earl, and his confederates (5), not less than 574,628 acres of land, English meafure, fell to the crown, and were difpofed of by Queen Elizabeth, to Englifh undertakers.

That Queen having long determined to fend James, the only fon and heir of this Earl of Defmond, (who, as we have obferved (6), from his infancy had been kept a prifoner in the tower, as a pledge of his father's loyalty) to Ireland, in hopes that his prefence there would draw off his father's followers from James Fitzthomas, who had ufurped the title of Defmond, and gave her Majefty's forces much oppofition, did in the year 1600, put that defign in execution. The young Earl landed at Youghall, October 14th, and was conducted from thence, by Captain Price, to the Prefident of Munfter at Moyallo; the Captain prefented him to his Lordfhip, together with her Majefty's letter, and letters patent under the great feal of England, for his reftitution in blood and honour.

" The Lord Prefident of Munfter, in order to make trial of the affections of the Earl's Kindred, and followers, confented, at his own requeft, that he fhould make a journey from Moyallo into the county of Limerick; the Earl came to Killmalock of a Saturday in the evening; and by the way, and at his entrance into the town, there was a mighty concourfe of people, infomuch, that all the ftreets, doors, and windows, yea, the very gutters, and tops of houfes were filled with them; and they welcomed him with all expreffions, and figns of joy; every one throwing upon him wheat and falt, according to an ancient ceremony ufed in that province. That night, the Earl was invited to fup with Sir George Thornton, and although he had a guard of foldiers, who made a lane from his lodgings to Sir George's houfe, yet the confluence of people was fo great, that he could not, in half an hour, make his paffage thro' the crowd. After fupper, he had the fame encounters in his return to his lodgings. The next day being Sunday, the Earl went to church to hear divine fervice; and all the way his countrymen ufed loud, and rude, dehortations to keep him from church; unto which he lent a deaf ear; but after fervice and the fermon, were ended, the Earl coming forth of the church, was railed at, and fpit upon, by thofe, that before his going to church, were fo defirous to fee, and falute him; infomuch, as after that public profeffion of his religion, the town was cleared of the multitude of ftrangers; and the Earl, from thence forwards, might walk as quietly, and freely, and as little in effect followed,

D   or

(5) Morrif. Hift. fol. 4.   (6) Pacata Hibernia, fol. 90.

or regarded, as any other private gentleman; nor did any of his father's followers, except some of the meanest sort of freeholders, after that, resort unto him."

As nothing can excuse the barbarous incivility of these Irish to the young Earl of Desmond on that occasion, so this passage furnishes no ill proof of the mistaken policy of the then government of Ireland, which consisted in proselyting by force, or seduction, to the established religion, the heirs of the principal Irish families, with a view of drawing their followers, and dependents after them. " For the truth is," as my (7) Author well observes in the same place, " the young Earl's religion, being a Protestant, was the only cause that bred this coyness in them all; for, if he had been a Romish Catholic, the hearts, and knees, of all degrees in the province, would have bowed unto him."

C H A P. VII.

Lord Deputy Mountjoy's, *and Lord* Verulam's *opinions of the Government of Ireland in* 1602.

AND, indeed, all thinking men saw, and regretted, that the policy of the government of Ireland, at this juncture, was as weak, as it was wicked. Lord (1) Deputy Mountjoy (2), in a letter to the Lords of the Council in England, seems to impute to its fraud, and severity, the continuance of the war even to that time. " All the Irish," says he, " that are now obstinate, are so only out of their diffidence to be *(a)* safe in any forgiveness; and though they are weary of the war, they are unwilling to have it ended, for fear left, upon a peace, there would ensue a severe reformation of religion. They have the antient swelling, and desire of liberty, in their countrymen, to work upon; their fear to be rooted out, and to have their old faults punished upon particular discontents; and, generally, all over the kingdom *(b)*, their fear

(7) Ib.   (1) In 1600.   (2) Pacat. Hibern. in fine.

(a) " When some one, who hath been a bad member, pardoned by your Majesty, hath heard himself exclaimed upon to be a notable thief after his pardon; and hath simply come in, without any bonds, or any enforcement, to an open sessions, to take his trial by your Majesty's laws, if any could accuse him; notwithstanding his coming in after this manner, there hath been order given, without any trial at all, for the execution of him. And so he has lost his life to the great dishonour of your Majesty, and discredit of your laws.—And this dishonest practice has been by consent of your Deputies." Lee's Memorial to Q. Elizabeth, MSS. College Library.

(b) " All the Irish Chieftains concurred in the same general demand of a free exercise of religion." Lel. Hist of Ireland, Vol. ii. p. 335.

fear of a persecution for religion. The least of which, alone, have been many times sufficient to drive the best, and most quiet, states into sudden confusion." Nay he even seemed to apprehend, that these fears, and their diffidence to be safe in any forgiveness *(c)*, " would keep all spirits from settling, breed new combinations, and even stir the towns themselves, to solicit foreign aid, with promise to cast themselves into their protection." In order to prevent which, he submits, to their Lordships consideration, the following particulars.

" As all pain, and anguish, impatient of the present, doth use change for a remedy, so (says his Lordship) will it be impossible for us to settle the minds of those people into a peace, or reduce them unto order, while they feel the smart of these sensible griefs, and apparent fears, which I have remembered to your Lordships, without some hopes of redress, and security." After which, he tells them, " that they should be advised, how they punished in their bodies, and goods, such, merely for religion, as did profess to be faithful subjects; and against whom the contrary could not be proved; that it would as much avail the speedy settlement of Ireland, as any thing, if it would please her Majesty, to deal liberally with the Irish Lords of the country, or such as were of good reputation among them, in the distribution of such lands, as they formerly possessed, or such as the state could make little use of for her Majesty. If they continue (adds his Lordship) as they ought to do, and yield the Queen as much commodity, as she may otherwise expect, she hath made a good purchase of such subjects for such lands." Lord Verulam (3), in a letter to Secretary Cecil, about the same time, earnestly recommended the like lenity, and forbearance, with respect to these people. " I think," says he, " that much letting of blood in the decline of the disease, is against all method of cure; that it will but exasperate necessity, and despair; and, perchance, discover the hollowness of that which is done already; which none blazeth to the best

(3) Scrinia Sacra.

(c) " When there have been notable traitors in arms against your Majesty," says the before-mentioned Memorialist, " and sums of money offered for their heads, yet could by no means be compassed, they have in the end, of their own accord, made means for their pardon, and have put in sureties for their good behaviour, offering to do great service, which they have accordingly performed, to the contentment of the State, and thereupon received pardon, and have put in sureties for their good behaviour, and to be answerable at all times at assizes, and sessions, when they should be called. Yet, notwithstanding, there have been secret commissions given for the murthering of those men. They have been often set upon by the sheriffs of shires, to whom the commissions were directed, in sundry of which shires, some of them have been killed, and others have hardly escaped. And, after all this, they have simply come, without pardon, or protection, to submit themselves to your Majesty's laws, where they have been put to their trial upon several endictments, of all which they have been acquitted, and set at liberty." Lee's Memorial to the Queen. Desid. Curios. Hib. Vol. i. p. 92.

beſt ſhew. But of all other points, to my underſtanding, the moſt effectual is the well expreſſing, or impreſſing, of the deſign of England on that miſerable, and deſolate nation; that the Queen ſeeketh not an extirpation of the people, but a reduction; and now that ſhe hath chaſtiſed them by royal power, and arms, according to the neceſſity of the occaſion, that her Majeſty taketh no pleaſure in the effuſion of blood, and the diſplanting of antient generation."

And then, as to the matter of religion, " All divines," proceeds his Lordſhip, " do agree that, if conſcience be to be enforced (wherein they differ) yet two things muſt precede its enforcement; the one, means of information, the other, time of operation; neither of which they (the Iriſh) have yet had. And there is no doubt, but to wreſtle with them is directly oppoſite to their reclaim, and cannot but continue their alienation from the government; and, therefore, a toleration of religion, for a time not definite, ſeems to me to be a matter warrantable by religion, and in policy of abſolute neceſſity: and the heſitation of this, I think, hath been a great caſting back of affairs in Ireland."

C H A P. VIII.

Proclamation of Pardon in the Province of Munſter.

THE Iriſh, during the whole time of this war, ſeem to have acted chiefly on the defenſive, notwithſtanding the vaſt deſtruction by fire, ſword, and famine, which the Chief Governors of Ireland ſtill carried through every part of their country. Of this deſtruction, the Queen herſelf expreſſed a very ſenſible feeling, when ſhe declared on that occaſion (1), " That ſhe feared the ſame reproach might be made to her, which was formerly made by Bato to Tiberius, viz. It is you! you! that are to blame for theſe things, who have committed your flocks, not to ſhepherds, but to wolves."

This private declaration of pity, her Majeſty, ſoon after, ſeconded, by a public act of truly royal beneficence, in facilitating, and inviting, ſome of theſe miſguided people's ſpeedy return to their duty. But her gracious intentions, and commands, in that reſpect, were in a great Meaſure, neglected, or diſobeyed, by her principal Miniſters in that kingdom.

(1) Cambd. Eliz. circa Initium.

"IN (2) December 1600, the Queen difpatched an order to Lord Deputy Mountjoy, to grant a general pardon to all, and every, the inhabitants of Munfter, of what condition, or ftate foever; thereby to remove from them all fufpicion of impeachment for their former offences;" "whereunto," adds her Majefty, "the greateft part of them have been violently carried, rather by the power of the arch-traitors (whom fhe, therefore, excepts from pardon,) than by any wilful defection in their loyalty." And to the end the people, wafted with the mifery of thefe wars, might not be burthened with the expences in the obtaining their pardons, or putting in fecurity for the peace, even when needful, her pleafure was, that the fees of the feal, fhould be either wholly remitted, or fo moderated by the Lord Deputy and council, that her fubjects might have caufe the more dutifully, and gladly, to embrace her princely clemency, and bounty, in that her gracious and free pardon."

IN lefs than two months after the publication of this order, upwards (3) of four thoufand of the inhabitants of that province fubmitted, for protection, to the Lord Prefident. All thefe, however, contrary to her Majefty's exprefs commands, " his (4) Lordfhip obliged to put in fuch pledges, as no governor in former times ever had done the like." How little he obferved her Majefty's commands of forgivenefs, in other refpects, appears from an hiftory, which he himfelf has left us, of the two laft years of this war. Whence we may very probably conclude, that he who was not afhamed to publifh fuch inhuman actions of his own, as are there recorded, did not fcruple to order, or commit, others, if poffible, more inhuman, which he took care to fupprefs.

CHAP. IX.

The Spaniards invade Ireland.

ON the 23d of September, 1601, the Spaniards, under (1) Don Juan D'Aguila, landed at Kinfale, full of confidence, that they would be immediately joined, in their hoftile attempts on the kingdom, by all the difcontented Irifh. But, herein, they were greatly difappointed; (2) for " no Irifh of account," fays Morriffon, " repaired to them, except fome dependents of Florence M'Carty, who was then in prifon, and had invited them over." And, although Don Juan, immediately after his landing (3), publifhed a manifefto, wherein he folemnly declared, that his defign in this expedition, was to refcue them

(2) Pacat. Hibern. fol. 116.   (3) Id. ib. fol. 121.   (4) Id. ib.
(1) Id. ib. fol. 136.   (2) Id. ib.   (3) Id. ib. fol. 200.

them from that oppreſſion and ſlavery, which they had ſo long groaned under, on account of their religion, (which alſo, he promiſed to re-eſtabliſh in a free and flouriſhing ſtate,) yet he found the generality of theſe people, and even many of their *(a)* clergy, ſo unwilling to aſſiſt him, even for theſe deſirable purpoſes (4), " that he conceived a juſt diſdain and ſpleen, againſt the nation." This is confirmed by Lord Deputy Mountjoy himſelf, who informed the Engliſh council (5), " that Don Juan, and his Spaniards, conceived malice againſt the Iriſh, in whoſe aid they too late diſcovered no confidence could be placed." It is ſcarcely credible, and yet we have the ſame Lord Deputy's teſtimony for it, that this Spaniſh general offered (6) ſix ſhillings a day to every horſeman among the Iriſh, that would join his ſtandard. " So that," adds his Lordſhip, " it is a wonder unto us, that from preſent ſtaggering, they fall not to flat defection." And, what increaſes the wonder ſtill more, is, that notwithſtanding all this, much the (7) greater part of the Queen's army, which then beſieged him in Kinſale, conſiſted of the Iriſh. But ſo very few of theſe people were ſeduced to that defection, by theſe tempting offers and declarations; and ſo ridiculouſly incenſed were the Spaniards againſt them, on that account, and thought them ſo little worthy to be ſaved in any ſenſe, that one of their officers publickly declared (8), " That he believed, Chriſt did not die for them."

As for thoſe few Iriſh, who joined the Spaniards on their firſt arrival, Sir George Carew himſelf, ſeems to have made their apology (9), by ſaying " that little wonder was to be made thereat, conſidering what power religion and gold have in the hearts of men, both which the Spaniards brought with them into Ireland."

IMMEDIATELY before the ſurrender of Kinſale, which was occaſioned *(b)* by the entire defeat of the Northern Iriſh under Tyrone, who came to relieve it, her Majeſty's army, being in purſuit of the routed enemy (10), " continued the

---

(4) Id. ib. fol 224.   (5) Morriſ. Hiſt. fol. 192.   (6) Id. ib. fol. 144.   (7) Pacat. Hibern. fol. 213.
(8) Pacat. Hibern.   (9) Id. ib. fol. 224.   (10) Id. ib. fol. 144.

(a) " Candour obliges us to acknowledge, that the Romiſh clergy, at this time, did not uniformly concur in exciting the Iriſh to inſurrections. Sullivan himſelf, confeſſes (although it was his buſineſs to repreſent the religious zeal of his countrymen in the moſt advantageous point of view) that a conſiderable party among the clergy, recommended a dutiful ſubmiſſion to the government, and oppoſed the practices of their more intemperate brethren." Leland's Hiſt. of Ireland, Vol. ii. p. 306.

(b) Morriſſon affirms, " that the reaſon moving Don Juan to make the ſurrender of Kinſale, was the malice, he and the Spaniards had againſt the Iriſh; in whoſe aid, they too late diſcovered, no confidence could judicially be placed." Hiſt. of Ireland, f. 192.

execution a mile and an half, and left it there only because they were tired of killing:" "And had it not been," says (11) Morrifion, who was then on the fpot. "for fome impediments from the wearinefs of the men, and the ill condition of the horfes for want of feeding, we had cut the throats of all the rebels there affembled." "The Earl of Clanrickard killed (12), with his own hand, above twenty Irifh; and cried out to fpare no rebels: for which the Deputy knighted him in the field, among the dead bodies. There were fome of the Irifh taken prifoners, who offered great ranfoms, but upon their bringing to the camp, they were all hanged."

MORRISSON informs us of one particular, concerning the defeat of the Irifh at the battle of Kinfale; which, for its oddity at leaft, deferves fome notice (13). "On the fame day," fays he, "an old written book was fhewn to the Lord Deputy, wherein was a prophecy, naming the ford and hill, where this battle was given; and foretelling a great overthrow to befall the Irifh in that place." Sir George Carew has given a more circumftantial account of this prophecy (14). "He had often heard the Earl of Thomond fay, that in an old book of Irifh prophecies, which himfelf had feen, it was reported, that towards the latter days, a battle fhould be fought between the Englifh and the Irifh, in a place which the book named, near unto Kinfale; and the Earl coming out of England, and landing at Kinfale, in the time of the fiege, Sir George, and divers others, heard him report the prophecy, and name the place, where, according to it, the battle fhould be fought. The day on which the victory was obtained, he and the Earl rode out to fee the dead bodies of the vanquifhed, and afked fome that were there prefent, by what name that ground was called; they not knowing to what end the queftion was afked, told the true name thereof; which was the fame, that the Earl had before reported to him. "I befeech the reader," continues the Prefident, "to believe me, for I deliver nothing but truth; but as one fwallow makes no fummer, fo fhall not this one true prophecy increafe my credulity in old predictions of that kind."

(11) Hift. of Ireland, fol. 178.   (12) Pacat. Hibern.   (13) Ubi fupra fol. 175.
(14) Pacat. Hibern. fol. 235.

CHAP.

CHAP. X.

The Cruelty of the English Army in Munster.

IN December 1600, about nine months before the arrival of the Spaniards (1), "There was not, as has already been observed, in the whole province of Munster *(a)*, one castle that held out against the Queen; nor was it known that there were five rebels in a company there." And afterwards, at the battle of Kinsale (2), almost all the insurgents of the other provinces, who were there assembled under Tyrone, were totally *(b)* dispersed. Yet the unceasing cruelty of the victors, which increased in proportion to the weakness of the vanquished, provoked these latter to have recourse, once more, to arms for their natural defence. After that battle, the English seemed determined to destroy, indiscriminately, all the remaining Irish, that came in their way; which they had sometimes done with such circumstances of barbarity, that the Irish, in despair, were often tempted to prevent them, by destroying themselves. Thus, at the taking of the castle of Dunboy, " the (3) Lord President, supposing that the besieged in their extremity would leap into the sea, which was near, posted some of the officers there with boats, who had the killing of about thirty of them, that attempted it." That garrison had sent out a messenger offering to surrender the castle, if they might have assurance of their lives; but the Lord-President, instead of granting that assurance, turned the messenger over to the Marshal, by whose direction he was (4) executed."

NOTHING

(1) Pacat. Hibern.   (2) Id. ib.   (3) Ib. fol. 570.   (4) Ib.

(a) " And now (December, 1600) there was not a castle in Munster held for the rebels, nor any company of ten rebels together, though there wanted not loose vagabonds dispersed in all corners." Morris. Hist. of Ireland, fol. 94.

(b) We are told by a contemporary Roman Catholic writer, that Tyrone's defeat at the battle of Kinsale, was a judgment from God, on account " of his soldiers, in their march thither to relieve the Spaniards, having robbed and spoiled the monasteries of Timnalage, and Kilcrea; and prophaned other churches. For, says that writer, the Queen's army consisted, for the most part, of Irish Catholic Soldiers; the English being altogether, saving a very few, consumed by cold and famine, being unable to endure the toil and labour of so unseasonable a winter campaign. Yet Tyrone's army exceeding the other in multitude of people, and ever before that time, terrible to the English, by reason of so many great overthrows given unto them, were broken, and put to flight by a few horse-men, that issued out of the English camp; being thereunto solicited, and procured by the Earl of Clanrickard, an Irish (Roman Catholic) Earl, then in the English camp. Wherefore," adds my author, " the said Earl of Tyrone, returning from that overthrow, said, that it was the vengeance of the Mighty Hand of God, and his most just judgment, which ought to be executed upon such wicked, and sacrilegious soldiers, that perpetrated such outrages upon sacred places." Theatre of religion, p. 423.

NOTHING can better shew the implacable fury of these English commanders, and the despair to which that fury drove the Irish, than some particulars of this siege, which are thus related by the Lord President himself (5). " M'Geoghegan, chief commander of the castle, being mortally wounded with divers shots in his body, the garrison made choice of one Thomas Taylor to be their chief; who, having nine barrels of powder, threw himself and it into the vault, and there sate down by it, with a lighted match in his hand; vowing, and protesting to set it on fire, and blow up the castle, himself, and all the rest, except they might have promise of life, which was by the Lord President refused. His Lordship intending to bury them in the ruins, and entering amongst them into the castle, the rest of the garrison constrained Taylor to surrender simply; who, with eight and forty more, being ready to come forth, and the Lord President's officers having entered to receive them, they found the above-mentioned M'Geoghegan lying there mortally wounded; but perceiving Taylor, and the rest, ready to surrender themselves, he (M'Geoghegan) raising himself up from the ground, and snatching a lighted candle, staggered therewith to a barrel of powder, which, for that purpose, was unheaded; offering to cast it into the same; but Captain Power took him, and held him in his arms, until he was by our men instantly killed. The whole number of the ward," continues my author, " consisted of one hundred and forty three selected men; being the best choice of all their forces, of the which no one man escaped, but were either slain, executed, or buried in the ruins; and so obstinate a defence hath not been seen within this kingdom."

IF any of the Irish that were in arms, intruded into the dwellings of their peaceable countrymen; or compelled them to pay them contribution (which they durst not refuse) these latter were always considered as harbourers, and abbettors, of rebels, and forfeited their lives, and properties, for having yielded to a force, which they could not resist. Thus we find, that the Lord President " having (6) heard, that the Munster fugitives were harboured in certain parts of that province, diverted his forces thither, burnt all the houses and corn, taking great preys, and harassing the country, *killed all man-kind that were found therein.* From thence, he went to other parts, where he did the like; not leaving behind him man or beast, corn or cattle, except such as had been conveyed into castles."

" THE

(5) Ib. fol. 318.   (6) Pacat. Hibern. fol. 106.

"The (7) ward of Castle-Lisloel, eighteen in number, when besieged by Sir Charles Wilmot, came forth upon their knees, and begged for mercy. The women and children (says my author) Sir Charles suffered to depart; but of the weaponed men, he hanged nine; the residue he detained till he had acquainted the Lord President with what he had done, who gave present orders for the execution of the rest."

The same Sir Charles Wilmott, having at another time gone to seek the enemy in their camp, " entered (8)," says the same historian, " without any resistance; for there he found nothing but hurt, and sick men; whose lives, and pains, by the soldiers, were both determined."

One would immagine, from the virulence of the expressions, and the barbarity of the actions, mentioned in this history, that it was written rather by an enemy, than a chief commander of her Majesty's forces; or that the Irish had, at this time, given some new, and extraordinary, provocation for such inhuman actions, and expressions. But it is manifest, even from this history, that, during the last two years of this war, these Irish were in no sort aggressors, or assailants; for the author himself assures us, from his own knowledge (9), " That, ever since the siege of Kinsale, they were so much afraid of the Queen's forces, that they lived in their fastnesses, supporting themselves with their own victuals, and the wines that had been sent them out of Spain."

CHAP. XI.

A dreadful Famine in Ireland.

THUS did her Majesty's Ministers in Ireland execute her orders of clemency, and forgiveness, towards these misguided people. Nor were even these incessant acts of cruelty sufficient to appease their enmity. That destruction, which their swords had left unfinished, they now industriously compleated by a general famine. Mr. Morrisson mentions this method of ending the war, with a seeming complacency, at least, without dislike. But the effects of it were too horrible to be unfeelingly related, even by an enemy. " Because (1)," says he, " I have often made mention formerly, of our destroying the rebels corn, and using all means to famish them, let me now, by

two

Id. ib.   (8) Ib.   (9) Ib. fol. 377.

(1) History of Ireland, fol. 272.

two or three examples, shew the miserable estate to which they were thereby reduced." He then, after telling us, that Sir Arthur Chichester, Sir Richard Morrisson, and other commanders, saw a most horrid spectacle of three children, whereof the eldest was not above ten years old, feeding on the flesh of their dead mother, with circumstances too shocking to be repeated; and that the common sort of rebels were driven to unspeakable extremities, beyond the records of any Histories, that he had ever read in that kind; he mentions an horrid stratagem of some of these wretched people, to allay the rage of hunger, in the following manner. " Some old women (2)," says he, " about the Newry, used to make a fire in the fields, and divers little children driving out the cattle in the cold mornings, and coming thither to warm themselves, were by these women surprised, killed, and eaten; which was at last discovered by a great girl, breaking from them by the strength of her body; and Captain Trevor sending out soldiers to know the truth, they found the childrens sculls and bones, and apprehended the old women, who were executed for the fact. No spectacle," adds Morrisson, " was more frequent in the ditches of towns, and especially in wasted countries, than to see multitudes of these poor people dead, with their mouths all coloured green by eating nettles, docks, and all things they could rend up above ground."

THE Lord Deputy and Council (3), in a letter to the Lords in England concerning their receiving the submissions of some Irish chiefs, acquainted them, " That they had received these submissions, partly for the good of the service, and partly out of human commiseration; having with our own eyes (say they) daily seen the lamentable state of the country, wherein we found every where men dead of famine." They add, " that they had been credibly informed, that in the space of a few months, there were above three thousand starved in Tyrone."

(2) Morris. ib. fol. 272.   (3) Ib. fol. 237.

CHAP. XII.

The greater, and better Part of the Irish in this War, fought for the Queen against their Countrymen.—The hard Terms of their being received to Mercy.

IN the Irish parliament of 1614, the Catholic members, in order to obtain a suspension of some penal statutes, then put in strict execution against those of their religion, alleged their ancestors signal services, exhibited in the royal army, during the wars of the former reign (1). " Chronicles of blood," said a member of that house of commons, " shew the glory of our progenitors, as the Queen's army was full of natives." Nay it was openly affirmed, in the same parliament, and might have been then easily contradicted if untrue (2), " That the gentlemen of Ireland had spent as much in that war, as the Queen herself; and that one gentleman, of only three hundred pounds a year, expended ten thousand pounds on that occasion." Most certain it is, that the principal nobility, and gentry of the kingdom, and all the cities and corporate towns, persisted in their allegiance to her Majesty, notwithstanding the many tempting offers made them by the Spaniards, in order to withdraw them from it. It is also certain (3), that more than one half of that gallant army under Lord Mountjoy, which so successfully attacked, and at last entirely defeated Tyrone, was Irish; nor did their having (4) less pay than the English, or their being exposed to endure the brunt in every action, " lessen their zeal, or activity, in the service." Yet the terms on which the submitting Irish were received to mercy, seem to have been calculated, not so much to reclaim them, as to make them still continue desperately in action. For, besides the usual pledges of their wives and children, with other cautions, which, contrary to her Majesty's merciful order of December, 1600, (before recited) were exacted from them; as a further proof of their sincere submission, and previous to their pardon, it was also required, that they should perform what was called, some signal service on their own people; which, in reality, was nothing less, than that they should basely betray, or perfidiously murder, some of their nearest kindred, or former friends. Mr. Morrison acquaints us (5), " that Lord Mountjoy never received any to mercy, but such as had so drawn blood on their fellow-rebels. Thus," says (6) he, " M'Mahon,

(1) Commons Journal, Vol. i. (2) Ib. (3) Morrif. Hist. fol. 120. (4) Id. ib. fol. 208.
(5) Ib. fol. 43. (6) Ib. fol. 77.

"M'Mahon, and M'Artmoyle, offered to submit; but neither could be received, without the other's head." But barbarous as these terms of acceptance were, they were sometimes reluctantly complied with. "I (7) have made," says Lord Mountjoy himself, "some of the subjects, already reclaimed, and in these times suspected, put themselves in blood already; for even now I hear, that Lord Mountgarret's sons have killed some of Cloncare's, and some of Tyrrill's followers, since I contested with their father about somewhat I heard suspicious of them." I shall mention one notable instance of this kind of service, contrived, and related, by the Lord President of Munster himself.

"About (8) this time," says he, "Nugent came to make his submission to the President; by whom he was told, that as his crimes and offences were extraordinary, he could not hope for pardon, unless he would deserve it by some extraordinary service; which, said the President, if you shall perform, you may deserve not only pardon for your faults, committed heretofore, but also some store of crowns to relieve your wants hereafter. Nugent, who was valiant and daring, and in whom the rebels reposed great confidence, presently promised not to be wanting in any thing that one man could accomplish; and, in private, made offer to the President, that, if he might be well recompensed, he would ruin, within a short time, James Fitzthomas, the then reputed Earl of Desmond, or his brother John. But the President, having before contrived a plot for James, gave him in charge to undertake his brother John. Accordingly, some few days after this, Nugent riding in company with John Fitzthomas, and one Mr. Copinger, permitted this great captain to ride a little before him, minding, his back being turned, to shoot him through with his pistol, which, for the purpose, was well charged with two balls. The opportunity offered, the pistol bent, both heart and hand ready to do the deed, when Copinger, at the instant, snatched the pistol from him, crying Treason! wherewith John Fitzthomas turning himself about, perceived his intent. Nugent thinking to escape by the goodness of his horse, spurred hard, the horse stumbled, and he was taken; and the next day, after examination, and confession of his intent, hanged. In his examination, he freely confessed the whole intent, which was to have dispatched John Fitzthomas, and immediately after, to have posted to his brother James, to carry the first news thereof; intending to call him aside in secret manner, to relate the particulars of his brother's murder, and then to execute as much upon him also; adding, that although they should take away his life, which he would not intreat them to spare, yet was their own safety never the more assured; for
that

(7) Id. ib. fol. 132.   (8) Pacat. Hibern. fol. 37-8.

that there were many others, whom himself perfectly knew to have sworn unto the President, to effect as much as he intended: this confession, being sealed with his death, did strike fearful terror into the two brethren; and although the plot attained not fully the desired success, yet it proved to be of great consequence."

Yet these submitting Irish, who upon very light suspicion, were obliged to comply with such cruel injunctions, were eminently serviceable to Lord Mountjoy, in the prosecution of this war. His Lordship acknowledges, in several letters to the English Council, the great assistance they had given him; and, in one of them expressly says, " That (9), if these submittees had not furnished his army with beeves, it would have been in great distress." " Yet the commanders of that army often took their cattle (10), without payment in ready money; which," says Morrisson, " grieved them;" or, if they meant to shew them particular favour, " they paid them in the new base coin, then made current by proclamation, in a shilling of which, there was not more (11) than two pence value in silver."

CHAP. XIII.

Tyrone *sues for Pardon, and obtains it.*

LORD Mountjoy was highly ambitious of putting an end to this war; an honour, which his predecessors in the government had in vain endeavoured to attain. For this purpose, he had received the submissions of many of the well-disposed Irish chiefs; and by fire, famine, and the sword, had weakened, or ruined, most of those, who still continued obstinate. He had reduced Tyrone himself to great extremity; having taken, or destroyed, most of his fortresses; and (what perhaps was more mortifying to him) having broken in pieces (1) the chair of stone, wherein, for many centuries, the O'Neals of his family had been invested with more than kingly authority. His Lordship had narrowly enquired into the conduct of former chief governors; and finding that the principal causes of their ill success, in the reduction of this people, were their incessant cruelties, and frequent breaches of the public faith, he abstained, in some measure, from *(a)* the former; and, with respect

---

(9) Morris. Hist. fol. 115. (10) Id. ib. (11) Id. ib. fol. 23. (1) Id. ib. fol. 236.

(a) The friendly, and honourable manner of his receiving, and entertaining some of the submitting chieftains of the Irish, may be seen in the following passage related by his Secretary Morrisson. " The 23d of April, his Lordship," says he, " kept St. George's feast at Dublin, with solemn pomp, the captains

respect to the latter, altho' he was not very punctual to his word in his private dealings, yet he found it absolutely necessary, for obtaining his great end, to observe it strictly in his promises of pardon, and in all public matters, wherein the honour of the state was concerned (2). " He kept his word inviolably in public affairs," says his Secretary Morrisson, " without which he never could have been intrusted by the Irish; but, otherwise, in his promises he was dilatory, and doubtful; so as, in all events, he was not without his evasion."

By these means, the tranquillity of Ulster was so far restored, in August 1602, that the Deputy told Cecil, in a letter of that date (3), " That, except things fell out much contrary to what he had good reason to expect, he presumed, if the Queen kept the Irish garrisons strong, and well provided for all the ensuing winter, she might, before the next spring, send into Ireland proper persons, with her pleasure how much, and in what manner, every man should hold his land; and what laws she would have current there; and he was confident, they would be obeyed. And after this winter," adds his Lordship, " I think she may withdraw her garrisons, only leaving wards in their places; and if I be not much deceived, you shall find, that these men will be the last of all Ireland that will forsake the Queen's party; and, I presume, after this winter, they will do the Queen good service against the Spaniards, if they come."

On (4) the 30th of March following, Tyrone came to Mellifont, where being admitted to the Lord Deputy's chamber, he kneeled at the door humbly, for a long space, making his penitent submission to her Majesty. And the next day he made a most humble submission in writing, signed with his own hand; wherein, after absolutely casting himself on her Majesty's mercy, without presuming to justify his disloyal proceedings, he among other things, most sorrowfully, and earnestly desired, that it might please her Majesty, rather in some measure to mitigate her just indignation against him, in that he did religiously vow, that the first motives of his rebellion were neither practice, malice, nor ambition; but that he was induced first by fear of his life, which, he conceived, was sought by his enemies practice, to stand upon his guard." This submission

---

(2) Morrisson, ib. fol. 236.   (3) Id. ib.   (4) Id. ib.

tains bringing up his meat, and some of the colonels attending on his person at the table, to which feast, the rebels were invited, whom his Lordship had lately received to mercy, under her Majesty's protection, till their pardons might be signed; namely, Turlogh M'Henry, captain of the Fews, Ever M'Cooley, chief of the Fearney, O'Hanlon, a Lord of Ulster, Phelim M'Feagh, chief of the O'Byrnes, and Donell Spaniagh, chief of the Cavanaghs in Leinster. These," adds my author, " were entertained with plenty of wine, and all kindness; his Lordship assuring them, that as he had been a scourge to them in rebellion, so he would now be a mediator for them to her Majesty, in their state of subjects, they standing firm and constant to their obedience." Hist. of Ireland, p. 59.

submission in writing (adds Mr. Morrisson) was presented by the Earl of Tyrone, kneeling before the Lord Deputy and Council, and in the presence of a great assembly, whereupon the Lord Deputy, in the Queen's name, promised to the Earl, for himself, and his followers, her Majesty's gracious pardon. And to himself the restoring of his dignity of the Earldom of Tyrone, and of his blood; and likewise new letters patent for all his lands, which, in his former letters patent, had been granted to him, before his rebellion (5). "Thus had the Queen's army under Lord Mountjoy, broken, and absolutely subdued, all the Lords and chieftains of the Irishry. Whereupon, the multitude being brayed, as it were, in a mortar, with sword, famine, and pestilence together, submitted themselves to the English government, received the laws, and Magistrates, and most gladly embraced the *King's pardon, and peace, in all parts of the realm, with demonstrations of joy, and comfort."

(5) Sir John Davis's Hist. Relations. * James I.

BOOK·

AN HISTORICAL AND CRITICAL REVIEW OF THE CIVIL WARS IN IRELAND.

BOOK II.

CHAP. I.

The State of the Irish under King James I.

"SOME few years before Queen Elizabeth's death, King James was at (1) the utmost pains to gain the friendship of Roman Catholic Princes, as a necessary precaution to facilitate his accession to the English Throne. Lord Home, who was himself a Roman Catholic, was entrusted with a secret commission to the Pope; the Archbishop of Glasgow, another Roman Catholic, was very active with those of his own religion. Sir James Lindsay made great progress in gaining the English Papists." And as it seems to have been part of that King's policy, in order to pave the way to his succession (2), " to waste the vigour of the state of England, by some insensible, yet powerful, means," he had his agents in Ireland, fomenting Tyrone's war, (" The Scots daily carrying munition to the rebels in Ulster.") So that the Queen was driven to an almost incredible *(a)* expence in carrying it on, and her enemies still encouraged by James's secret assistance, and promises.

"It

---

(1) Robertson's Hist. of Scotland, &c. (2) Secret Correspondence between King James and Sir Robert Cecil, p. 75.

(a) " The Queen's charge for Ireland," says Morrison, " from the 1st of April 1600, to the 29th of March 1602, was two hundred and eighty-three thousand, six hundred and seventy-three pounds, nineteen shillings and four-pence halfpenny." Hist. of Ireland, fol. 197.

"It (3) is certain," says Mr. Osburne, "that the promise, King James made to Roman Catholics, was registered, and amounted so high at least, as a toleration of their religion."

"Of (4) these intrigues, Queen Elizabeth received obscure hints from several quarters (5)." Her Majesty in a letter to the King himself in 1599, gave him to understand, ". that there were many letters from Rome, and elsewhere, which told the names of men, authorised by him (tho' she hoped falsely) to assure his conformity as time might serve, to establish the dangerous party, and fail his own."

The Roman Catholics, in the different provinces of Ireland, were, on James's accession, so much elated with the hopes of the above-mentioned toleration, and had taken up such an opinion, that the King himself was a Catholic, that they ran into some excesses, which have been since, unfairly represented by Historians, as so many overt acts of treason, and rebellion. For, on that mistaken notion, they exercised their religion publickly, and even seized on some churches for their own use. The Mayors of Cork, and Waterford, are said to have refused to proclaim the King, because they did not proclaim him precisely at the time appointed by his excellency; and the citizens of Cork would not, it seems, suffer the King's munition, and artillery, which was entrusted to their keeping, to be conveyed to a new fort, built within their franchises, but against their consent. But we can easily make it appear, that these passages admit of a much more favourable interpretation, than what has been given them. For it is not surely probable, that men, who had preserved their allegiance under a severe persecution of their religion, during all the time of Queen Elizabeth's reign, would, without any new cause, all at once, become rebels to a Prince, from whom they hourly expected a toleration of it; and whom they generally believed to be privately of their own way of thinking in that respect. They excused their delay in proclaiming the King, by assuring his Excellency, that it was occasioned (6), "Only by their desire of doing it with the greater solemnity;" which excuse appears to have been accepted; for when they had, soon after, proclaimed his Majesty, in the solemn manner they intended, Lord Mountjoy told them (7), "That in regard of their joyful, and solemn way of doing it, he was willing to interpret their actions to the best, and took their good performance for an excuse." And, as to the hindering the munition, and artillery to be carried to the fort, they
alleged

(3) Osburne's Works. (4) Robertson ubi supra. (5) Saunderson King James. (6) Morrison's History. (7) Id. ib.

alleged (8), "That the fort was commanded by a perfon, who had, on feveral occafions, fhewn great contempt, and enmity to their city; and that the foldiers there had offered them many abufes, fhooting at their fifhermen, and at the boats fent out for provifion; and ufing them at their pleafure." And they made it their reqeuft to his Excellency, that, as the fort was built within their franchifes, they might have the keeping of it for his Majefty, which they would do to their utmoft peril. They had, befides, another excufe, which was not altogether difapproved of by his Lordfhip; they knew, that the Deputy's power had determined with the Queen's life; but they did not know, that it was renewed by her fucceffor (9), "It may be," fays his Excellency, in his letter to them on this occafion, "that you have rafhly, and unadvifedly done this, upon fome opinion of the ceafing of authority in the public government, upon the death of our late fovereign, which is fomewhat more, though no way in true, and fevere judgment, excufable; and, I think otherwife, you never would have been fo foolifh." And it was then only that he firft undeceived them as to that matter, by telling them (10), "That his authority, as Lord Deputy, was renewed, and confirmed by his then Majefty's royal letters patent, under his feal; requiring them, upon their allegiance, to pay obedience to it;" and adding, "that if he fhould find they did fo, he would be glad to have occafion to interpret all things paft in the better part, and take as little notice, as he could thereof."

But his Lorfhip feems not to have waited for the effects of this letter, which is dated April the 27th; for on the firft of the following month, he marched out with an army towards Munfter, and on the 4th entered at a place called Gracedieu, near the city of Waterford; the citizens of which refufed, at firft, to receive his army into the town, being authorifed thereto by their charter; but they offered to give free and prompt admittance to his Lordfhip, and his retinue, the Chief of them having, for that purpofe, come forth, and attended him in his camp.

What Lord Mountjoy feemed principally to refent in thefe people, to fuch a degree as thus fuddenly to draw down the army upon them, was the boldnefs of feveral of the towns, and corporations (11), "in fetting up, of their own heads, the public exercife of the Popifh worfhip." For, in all his letters to the magiftrates of that province, he takes particular notice of that boldnefs; frequently affuring them (12), "That his Majefty was a good Proteftant; and even threatening one of thefe towns (13), "that if they did not defift from the public breach of his Majefty's laws, in the celebration of the Mafs, he would

(8) Id. ib.   (9) Id. ib. fol. 288.   (10) Ib.   (11) Id. ib.   (12) Id. ib.   (13) Id. ib.

would think them fit to be profecuted with the revenging fword of his Majefty's forces."

AND in truth, his Excellency, in this expedition to Waterford, appears, at firft fight, to have acted the part, rather of a meek and zealous Proteftant miffioner, than that of an incenfed leader of an hoftile army. For, upon the citizens coming forth to pay their refpects to him in his camp (14), he immediately required them to bring unto him one Doctor White, a famous Jefuit of that city, "With whom," fays Morriffon (15), "he difputed againft fome erroneous pofitions of popery; all which," adds my Author, "his Lordfhip did (as no layman, I think, could better do) moft learnedly confute." It is but juftice to obferve, that his Lordfhip, at the fame time, did as learnedly confute an erroneous pofition in the citizens charter, granted by King John; by which they fuppofed themfelves privileged to deny his foldiers entrance into their city. But his Lordfhip told them roundly, without entering into the merits of the matter (16), "That if they did not prefently open their ports to him, and his army, he would cut King John's charter in pieces with King James's fword; and that, if he entered the town by force, he would ruin it, and ftrew falt upon the ruins *(b)*."

CHAP. II.

A general Act of Oblivion.

KING James fucceeded to the Englifh throne without oppofition; and his Catholic fubjects, throughout the three kingdoms, made fignal rejoicings on that account. Upon this occafion, he not only confirmed Tyrone's pardon, but alfo received him in England, (whither he was conducted by Lord Deputy Mountjoy) with fingular marks (1) of favour; and foon after, fent him back with *(a)* honour, to take poffeffion of his eftates in Ireland; having

(14) Id. ib.   (15) Id. ib.   (16) Id. ib.   (1) Morrif. ubi fupra.

(b) "But this ftorm," fays an adverfe writer, "as foon as the Lord Deputy prefented himfelf with an army before their walls, was appeafed; and not long after, larger liberties and immunities were granted unto them, than formerly they had." Defid. Curiof. Hibern. Vol. i. p. 416. Such privileges were afterwards granted them, "That the Juftices of affize having no authority to hold their affizes there, the laws of religion (againft recufants) could not be executed." Ib. Vol. i. p. 359.

(a) Tyrone's reception by the people of Beaumorris, where he landed, was very different. "For no refpect to the Lord Deputy," fays Morriffon, "in whofe company he rode up to London, could contain many women in thefe parts, who had loft hufbands, and children in the Irifh war, from flinging dirt at him, with bitter words. And when he was to return, he durft not pafs by thefe parts, without directions to the Sheriffs to convey him, with troops of horfe, from place to place, till he was fafely embarked." Morrif. Hift. of Ireland, fol. 296.

having set forth a proclamation, forbidding all persons to reproach him, at any time after, with the rebellion formerly raised by him, and then happily suppressed.

But (2) although, by the suppression of this rebellion, the minds of the people were broken, and prepared to obedience, yet the state, upon good reason, did conceive, that the public peace could not be settled, till the hearts of the people were also quieted, by securing them from the danger of the law, which most of them had incurred, one way or other, in that great and general confusion; therefore, by a general act of state, called the Act of Oblivion, published by proclamation, under the great seal, all offences against the crown, and all particular trespasses between subject and subject, were to all such as would come into the justices of assize, by a certain day, and claim the benefit of this act, pardoned, remitted, and utterly extinguished *(b)*, never to be revived, or called in question. And by the same proclamation, all the Irishry, who for the most part, had no defence, or justice, from the crown, were received into his Majesty's immediate protection. "This," continues my Author, "bred such comfort, and security in the hearts of all men, as thereupon ensued the calmest, and most universal peace, that ever was seen in Ireland."

Yet, in the midst of this most calm, and universal peace, his Majesty, quite unmindful of all his former promises of favour to his Roman Catholic subjects, ordered a proclamation to be published, strictly forbidding the exercise of their religion to those of Ireland, banishing their clergy, and inflicting severe penalties on all such, as should be found to harbour, or entertain them; enjoining, also, the immediate execution of the act of uniformity of the second of Elizabeth; which act, tho' pretended to have been passed in the Irish parliament forty years before, was then first solemnly published.

By this act, all Roman Catholics are obliged to assist at the Protestant church-service, every Sunday and Holyday, on the penalty of twelve pence, and of what, indeed, was infinitely more grievous, the censures of the Ecclesiastical courts, for each default. A method of proceeding very inconsistent with the fundamental principles of that religion, which this act was intended to introduce, viz. freedom of conscience, and the right of private judgment.
Heylin

(2) Sir John Davis's Historical Relations.

(b) Happy, indeed, had it been for the proprietors of six entire counties in Ulster, had this solemn promise of oblivion been faithfully observed; or rather not so scandalously broken, in a few years after, as we shall presently see it was.

Heylin has juſtly obſerved another abſurdity in this ſtatute. "The (3) Iriſh," ſays he, "were obliged, under ſeveral penalties, to be preſent at the reading of the Engliſh Liturgy, which they underſtood no more than they did the Maſs; by which means, they were not only kept in continual ignorance, as to the doctrines, and devotions, of the church of England, but alſo were furniſhed with an excellent argument againſt ourſelves, for having the Divine Service celebrated in ſuch a language, as the people did not underſtand (c)."

CHAP. III.

Some Conſiderations on the two Statutes of Supremacy and Uniformity.

THE execution of the penal act laſt mentioned, and of the preceding ſtatute of ſupremacy, was the more grievous, and unjuſtifiable, as they were both well known to have been impoſed upon the nation by force, or fraud, though under the plauſible appearance of parliamentary ſanction.

As for the ſtatute of ſupremacy, there is no queſtion but the Iriſh chieftains were previouſly awed, and broken, by a military force, in order to (a) gain their conſent to it (1). "Lord Leonard Gray, to prepare the minds of the people to obey this ſtatute, began firſt, (ſays Sir John Davis,) with a martial courſe, by making a victorious circuit round the kingdom, whereby the principal ſepts of the Iriſhry were all terrified, and moſt of them broken; and then, after this preparation thus made, he firſt propounded, and paſſed thoſe laws, which made the great alteration in the ſtate eccleſiaſtical."

OF

---

(3) Eliz. (1) Sir John Davis's Hiſtorical Relat.

(c) To remedy this inconvenience, "In the reign of James I. it was ordered, that the Bible and Common-prayer ſhould be tranſlated into the Iriſh language; which was done: and every pariſh church was obliged to pay ten ſhillings for an Iriſh bible, when not one amongſt an hundred could read, or underſtand it. And therefore," adds my Author, "an Iriſh Proteſtant Biſhop did laugh at this ſtrange kind of alteration, and ſaid to ſome of his friends, "In Q. Elizabeth's time, we had Engliſh Bibles, and Iriſh Miniſters; but now we have Miniſters come out of England unto us, and Iriſh Bibles with them."—Moſt of the benefices and church-livings in Ireland, were beſtowed upon Engliſh and Scottiſh Miniſters, not one of them having three words of the Iriſh tongue." Theatre of Cath. and Proteſt. Religion, p. 245.

(a) Yet even when it came to be propoſed in parliament, "Lords and Commons joined in expreſſing their abhorrence of the ſpiritual authority aſſumed by the King." Lel. Hiſt. of Ireland, Vol. ii. p. 165. "But fear," ſays the ſame writer, "ſerved to allay the violence of thoſe, who could not be perſuaded." However, "in deſpite of legiſlative authority, they ſtill oppoſed that law with indefatigable zeal. Several incumbents of the dioceſs of Dublin, choſe to reſign their benefices, rather than acknowledge the King's ſupremacy." And ſo formidable, at leaſt ſo conſiderable was this party, "that the Archbiſhop (Brown) would not venture to fill up their benefices until he had conſulted his patron Lord Cromwell." Id. ib p. 167. Theſe incumbents objected to the legality of that ſtatute, becauſe, "two Proctors from each Dioceſs, had been uſually ſummoned and claimed to be a member of the legiſlative body, and to have a full right of ſuffrage in every queſtion; and becauſe, in this caſe, their claim was rejected." Ib. p. 165-6.

Ch. III.   CIVIL WARS in IRELAND.   59

Of the statute of uniformity, of the 2d of Elizabeth, all the Irish writers at, or near, that period, unanimously affirm, that it was surreptitiously or forcibly obtained. Mr. Lynch in his Cambrensis Eversus, informs us (2), "That it was passed by the artifice of one Mr. Stanyhurst of Corduff, then Speaker of the Irish Commons, who being in the reforming Interest, privately got together, on a day when the house was not to sit *(b)*, a few such members as he knew to be favourers of that interest, and consequently, in the absence of all those, who, he believed, would have opposed it. But that these absent members, having understood what had passed in this secret convention, did, soon after, in a full and regular meeting of parliament, enter their protests against it; upon which the Lord Lieutenant assured many of them, in particular, with protestations, and oaths, that the penalties of that statute should never be inflicted; which they too easily believing, suffered it to remain as it was. This, adds my author, I have often heard for certain truth, from many antient people, who lived at that time; and I am the more inclined to believe it, because the Lord Lieutenant's promise was so far kept, that this law was never generally executed, during the remainder of Queen Elizabeth's reign;" which was more than forty years; that is, until all, or most of those members were, probably, dead, to whom such promise had been given.

" In (3) the very beginning of that parliament, January 12th, 1559, most of the nobility, and gentry, were so divided in opinion about ecclesiastical government," says Sir James Ware, " that the Earl of Sussex, then Lord Lieutenant, thought proper to dissolve it, in the beginning of the following month." We find also (4), that his excellency, upon dissolving the Parliament, went to England, to consult her Majesty on the affairs of the kingdom; that, in a few months after, having returned to Ireland, he received orders to call an assembly of the clergy, for the establishment of the Protestant religion; and that, after this assembly had dispersed themselves, William Walsh, Bishop of Meath, not content with what offers her Majesty had proposed, was, for preaching against the book of Common-prayer, first imprisoned, and afterwards deposed, by order of her Majesty."

Now,

(2) P.   (3) Annals.   (4) Id. ib.

(b) " In this House of Commons, we find the representatives summoned for ten counties only; the rest, which made up the number of seventy-six, were citizens and burgesses of these towns, in which the Royal authority was predominant. It is therefore, little wonder, that in despite of clamour, and opposition, in a session of a few weeks, the whole ecclesiastical system of Queen Mary was entirely reversed." Leland's Hist. of Ireland, Vol. ii. p. 224.

Now, as under the words, " Ecclesiastical Government," the whole purport, and tendency of this act of uniformity are plainly comprehended, may we not reasonably conclude, from Lord Suffex's dissolving the parliament, on account of the jarring opinions of the members concerning that statute.; and from the order, which he soon after received, to call an assembly of the clergy, " for the establishment of the Protestant religion," (which order, had that act being duly and legally passed, would have been needless, if not absurd) that the statute in question was not openly, and regularly carried; but that it was forcibly, or clandestinely imposed, in the manner before-mentioned *(c)*?

CHAP. IV.

Sir Arthur Chichester's *Government.*

IN the year 1605, Lord Deputy Chichester, (" who (1) had been a pupil of the famous Arch-puritan *(a)* Cartwright, and was himself a great patron, and encourager of that sect,") " having (2) ordered the Roman Catholic Aldermen, and some of the principal citizens of Dublin, to be called before the council, exemplified under the great seal, and published, the above-mentioned act of uniformity; in regard," says my Author, " there was found to be a material difference between the original record, and printed copies; that none might pretend ignorance of the original record; and added thereto the King's injunction for the observance of it."

Mr.

(1) Presbyterian Loyalty.   (2) Harris's Hist. of Dublin.

(c) We are told by a contemporary historian, that a similar artifice was successfully made use of, the year before, to get the like act of uniformity passed in England; which, probably, was considered as a good precedent for passing the Irish act in the same manner. " The bill," says my Author, " met many rubs and lets among the members of the Commons; whereupon, by watching an opportunity to summon the favourers of it together, at one unexpected hour, when the opposers were likely to be absent, viz. Early in the morning, before the ordinary hour of resort of Knights, Citizens, and Burgesses, to the parliament-house, and upon a day unlooked for, the statists procured the said bill to be suddenly, and most unjustly (tho' not without some difficulty) passed by the greater number of voices: the rather because of the absence, and subtle circumvention of the rest of their fellow-members." Hist. of the reformation, Vol. i.

(a) This Cartwright was so staunch a non-conformist, even as to ceremonials, that in his reply to Archbishop Whitgift, he makes use of these words: " Certain of the things we stand upon, are such, that if every hair of our heads were a life, we ought to afford them, for the defence of them." Sir George Paul, in his life of Archbishop Whitgift, tells us,

" that in his prayer before his sermons," he used to say, " because they (meaning the Bishops) which ought to be pillars of the church, do band themselves against Christ, and his Truth, therefore, O Lord, give us grace, and power, as one man, to set ourselves against them." p. 47.

Ch. IV.   CIVIL WARS IN IRELAND.   41

Mr. (3) Carte has difcovered no lefs ignorance, than partiality, in his manner of juftifying the execution of this penal ftatute, at that juncture. "The Irifh Catholics," fays he, "became accidentally fubject to the fmall pecuniary penalties of it, forty years after it was made, upon their feparation from the public worfhip of the (eftablifhed) church of Ireland; and it was reafonable to imagine, that fuch a fudden defection fhould have irritated the government, and put them upon fome *(b)* wholefome feverities, to ftop it in the beginning." Here is a caufe affigned for inflicting this penalty, which never exifted but in the Hiftorian's brain. For their feparation, and sudden defection, from the public worfhip of the church of Ireland, neceffarily fuppofes their former agreement, and conformity to it; but this he could not fuppofe of the Irifh in general, without a barefaced contradiction to known facts. For fo ftedfaftly did thefe people adhere to their antient religion in that, and the former reign, notwithftanding the many alluring offers, and terrifying punifhments, made ufe of to withdraw them from it, that Chichefter himfelf, who had often employed both means of feduction, was heard to exclaim, in the rage of difappointment (4), "That he believed the very air, and foil of Ireland, were infected with popery." The barbarous incivility, already mentioned, which the young Earl of Defmond met with from his countrymen, and followers, after they were convinced of his conformity to the public worfhip of the church of Ireland, is a fufficient refutation of this miftake.

The King about this time (5), fent inftructions to the ftate, for miniftring the oath of fupremacy to the Catholic Lawyers and Juftices of Peace; and for putting the laws againft recufants in ftrict execution. Accordingly (6), "of fixteen Aldermen, and citizens of Dublin, fummoned before the Privy Council, nine were cenfured in the caftle chamber; and fix of the Aldermen were fined, each in one hundred pounds; and the other three, in fifty pounds a-piece; and they were all committed prifoners to the caftle, during the pleafure of the court. It was, at the fame time, ordered, that none of the citizens fhould bear offices, until they had conformed *(c)*."

G   Hard

---

(3) Life of Ormond, Vol. i.   (4) Analecta Sacra.   (5) Carte ubi fupra. Vol. i. fol. 21.
(6) Harris ubi fupra.

(b) Yet, in another place, he owns, "That the penalties of this act were raifed for the private gain of minifters; and had always occafioned a clamour abroad, of a terrible perfecution; and if rigoroufly executed (adds he) it would be a force upon the confciences of the poor ignorant Irifh, as they ftood informed." Carr. O. m. Vol. i. fol. 523.

(c) On this occafion, "all the old Englifh families of the pale, took the alarm, and boldly remonftrated againft the feverity of thefe proceedings. They denied the legality of the fentence by which thefe feverities were inflicted, and urged, that by the ftatute of 2d of Elizabeth, the crime of recufancy had its punifhment

HARD as this treatment of the Catholic laity was, (amidſt "the calmeſt, and moſt univerſal peace that was ever known in Ireland,") that of their clergy was ſtill more rigorous. To omit many other inſtances, the caſe of Robert Lawler deſerves particular notice. When this poor man was thrown into priſon, for exerciſing the function of a Roman Catholic prieſt, he (7), in order to remove all ſuſpicion of his maintaining, or teaching any ſeditious doctrines, made the following confeſſion, before the Lord Deputy and Council; and afterwards confirmed it on oath, viz. " That he did acknowledge his ſovereign, King James, to be his lawful chief, and ſupreme governor, in cauſes as well eccleſiaſtical, as civil; that he was bound in conſcience to obey him, in all ſaid cauſes; and that neither the Pope, nor any other foreign Prelate, or Potentate, had power to controul the King, in any cauſes eccleſiaſtical, or civil, within that kingdom, or in any other of his Majeſty's dominions." Yet this extreme condeſcenſion could not, it ſeems, prevent his condemnation. The only pretence for this ſeverity was, his having denied, privately, to ſome of his friends, who viſited him in priſon, that he had ever made ſuch confeſſion, as was derogatory to the ſpiritual authority of the Roman Pontiff; for, he told them, " that he had not acknowledged, that the King was ſupreme governor in ſpiritual cauſes, but in eccleſiaſtical." Whether this diſtinction, calculated for the private ſatisfaction of his friends, was well or ill founded, I ſhall not take upon me to determine; but certain it is, that it cancelled all the merit of his public confeſſion.

(7) Sir John Davis's Reports in fine.

puniſhment aſcertained, and that any extenſion of the penalty was illegal, and unconſtitutional.—Their remonſtrance was preſented to the Council by an unuſual concourſe of people, but the chief petitioners were confined to the caſtle of Dublin; and Sir Patrick Barnwell, their great agent, was, by the King's command, ſent in cuſtody into England." Lel. Hiſt. of Ireland, Vol. ii. p. 421-2.

The King, on this ſubject, wrote to Chicheſter, " That he thought, both the order he had taken for reformation, and the puniſhment he had inflicted upon ſome of the Aldermen of Dublin, and certain others whom his letters mention, for their contempt, to be not only juſt, but neceſſary.—And that he conceived hope, that many, by ſuch means, will be brought to conformity (in religion) who perhaps hereafter will find cauſe to give thanks to God, and him, for being drawn by ſo gentle a conſtraint, to their own good." Deſid. Curioſ. Hib. Vol. i. p. 465.

CHAP.

CHAP. V.

The Conspiracy, and Flight of the Earls.

THESE severities not having produced the desired effect, which, probably, was a new insurrection, and consequently new forfeitures, another expedient was made use of, which had been *(a)* sometimes successful, viz. private information of an intended conspiracy of the Irish, by means of an anonymous letter. But that there was in fact no such conspiracy, and that this letter was meerly a state-trick, to ensnare the innocent, by forged accusations, we have as good proof, as can possibly be had of a negative, in the manifest absurdity, and contradiction, of the different accounts, which have been left us of it.

THE first of these accounts, which is taken from Doctor Henry Jones, Bishop of Meath, and formerly Scout-master General to Cromwell's army, runs thus (1), " Anno 1607, there was a providential discovery of another rebellion in Ireland; the Lord Chichester being Deputy; the discoverer not being willing to appear, a letter from him, not being subscribed, was superscribed to Sir William Usher, clerk of the Council, and dropt in the council-chamber, then held in the castle of Dublin; in which was mentioned a design for seizing that castle and murthering the Deputy, with a general revolt, and dependance on Spanish forces; and this also for religion; for particulars whereof, adds the Bishop, I refer to that letter, dated March the 19th, 1607." Hence it appears, that the first discovery of this conspiracy arose from the anonymous letter above-mentioned.

DOCTOR Carlton, Bishop of Chichester, a cotemporary writer, has left us a prolix account of the discovery of this conspiracy, in which, however, there is no mention made of this anonymous letter. The substance of his account is what follows.

" MONTGOMERY,

(1) Preface to Borlase's History of the Irish Rebellion.

(a) This was then thought to have been a contrivance of Secretary Cecil, whom Osburne calls " an adept in state tricks," and who two years before, found the like expedient to have succeeded in the affair of the Gun powder Treason. (See an Essay towards a new history of that treason.) " Cecil," says Mr. Dod, " was an adept in framing fictitious plots, and has left instructions behind him to succeeding ministers, when, and how to make use of them against Catholics. The original of these instructions, in Cecil's own hand-writing, was formerly in the keeping of the infamous Judge Bradshaw, by whom it was shewn to Sir William Percival, who communicated it to a gentleman of great worth, who died anno 1697, and left it among other papers of remarks upon the times." Ecclesiast. Hist. Vol. iii. fol. 196.

" MONTGOMERY (2), Bishop of Derry," says he, " suspected, or was told, that Tyrone had gotten into his hands the greatest part of the lands of his Bishoprick; which he intended, in a lawful course, to recover; and finding there was no man could give him better light, or knowledge of these things, than O'Cahane (who was great with Tyrone) made use of such means, that he (O'Cahane) came to him of his own accord, and told him, he could help him to the knowledge of what he sought; but that he was afraid of Tyrone; yet he engaged, to reveal all that he knew of that matter, provided the Bishop would promise to save him from Tyrone's violence, and not deliver him into England, which the Bishop having promised, he brought O'Cahane to the Council in Dublin, to take his confession there. Upon this, processes were sent to Tyrone, to warn him to come up to Dublin, at an appointed time, to answer the suit of the Lord Bishop of Derry. There was no other intention but, in a peaceable way, to bring the suit to a trial; for the Council then knew nothing of the plot. But Tyrone having entered into a new conspiracy, of which O'Cahane was, began to suspect, when he was served with a process to answer the suit, that this was but a plot to draw him in, and that surely the treason was revealed by O'Cahane. Upon this bare suspicion, Tyrone with his confederates, fled out of Ireland, and lost all those lands in the North." Doctor Carlton adds, " that he had this account of the discovery of the conspiracy from the Bishop of Derry himself. The reader will please to recollect, that, according to the Bishop of Meath's story, the first discovery of this plot was made to the Council by an anonymous letter dropt in the council-chamber; but, by the Bishop of Derry's account, the actual flight of the Earls, and their confederates, out of the kingdom, was what alone excited in them the first suspicion of the conspiracy.

BUT let us reflect a moment on the obvious incredibility of this latter Bishop's tale. O'Cahane, a prime Catholic gentleman, possessed of a very large estate, enters into a conspiracy with Tyrone, against the Protestant religion, and government of Ireland; and yet, at the same time, he comes, " of his own accord," to a Protestant Bishop, to put him in a way to deprive the person, who was to be his chief leader in that conspiracy, of a great part of his estate, the loss of which must have proportionably lessened that leader's power to carry it on; and this he does for no other recompence, but a promise from the Bishop, that he will save him from Tyrone's violence; that is to say, from the violence of a man, with whom he was not only great, but also joined in a plot against the government. Now supposing that O'Cahane only knew that Tyrone was engaged in such a conspiracy, without being himself an accomplice

(2) Thankful remembrance, &c. p. 168.

Ch. V.   CIVIL WARS in IRELAND.   45

plice in it, would he not have thought such knowledge of his guilt a much better security, and defence, against Tyrone's violence, (as it put him absolutely in his power,) than any promise of protection from the Bishop could be? But as it is supposed, that he was actually concerned with Tyrone in that conspiracy, what can be more absurd, than to imagine, that he would, of his own accord, and without any suitable recompence, have thus provoked his leader, to seek revenge, and his own pardon by revealing his (O'Cahane's) guilt? For it is not even pretended, that O'Cahane had any thoughts, all this while, of discovering the plot; and how he could have expected to carry it on, in concert with Tyrone, after having thus provoked and injured him, is, indeed, a a mystery not easily unravelled *(b)*.

Sir John Temple's account (3) of this conspiracy is much shorter than that of either of these Bishops, but equally incoherent and absurd. " In this state," says he, " the kingdom continued under some indifferent terms of peace and tranquillity, until the *(c)* Earl of Tyrone took up new thoughts of rising into arms. And into this rebellious design he drew the whole province of Ulster, then entirely at his devotion. But his plot failed; and finding himself not able to get together, any considerable forces, he, with the principal of his adherents, quitting the kingdom, fled into Spain."

The contradiction of Tyrone's having drawn the whole province of Ulster into his rebellious designs, and at the same time, his not being able to get together any considerable forces, is too glaring, to need any further animadversion.

These are the only written accounts I have yet met with, after a very diligent search, of this conspiracy of the Earls, from which, I presume, the candid reader will conclude, that there never was any such conspiracy; and that these

(3) See his History of the Irish Rebellion.

(b) Incredible as these things are, yet in order to carry on the farce thoroughly, and to garble up O'Cahane's great estate, among the rest, O'Cahane himself was afterwards seized, as one of the conspirators, and forfeited, like the other gentlemen of Ulster. The King and Council, however, discovered some tenderness, with respect to him, before his actual seisure. For they desired the Deputy " to bring him to conformity, by shaking the rod over him; but if that would not do, his Majesty was pleased, that he should use his discretion in drawing down some force upon him." This letter is dated January 25th, 1607. And in another letter of the 20th of November following, they say, " but for O'Cahane, whom it seemeth, you have imprisoned, we like well of the course you have taken with him.—And we allow also, very well of your placing his son in the college." Desiderata Curiosa Hibern. p. 508-13.

(c) Tyrone was, at this time, so closely looked after, " that he was heard to complain, that he had so many eyes watching over him, as that he could not drink a full carouse of sack, but the state was advertised thereof, within a few hours." Sir John Davis's Hist. Relat. p. 117.

these accounts were then framed, however injudiciously, to give some colour of right to public acts of slander, oppression, and rapine.

Doctor Leland has justly observed on this occasion (4), " That it seems extraordinary, that the Northerns, who were still smarting with the chastisement they had received, in the late rebellion; whose consequence, and influence, were considerably diminished; and who were very lately reconciled to government, and invested with their honours and estates, should precipitately involve themselves in a new rebellion *(d)*." Such an event indeed, in these circumstances, not only seems extraordinary, but actually is, at least in a moral sense, utterly incredible.

CHAP. VI.

Puritan Bishops in Ireland.

DURING Sir Arthur Chichester's government, several of the established clergy were puritanically affected, if not puritans professed. Of this number, was the famous Doctor, afterwards Primate, Usher; for when in the year 1605, he was Provost of the College of Dublin, " the whole doctrine (1) of Calvin

(4) Hist. of Ireland, Vol. ii.   (1) Carte's Ormond.

(d) But the same writer endeavours to refute the only traditional account which has been hitherto handed down to us of it, (viz. that the flight of the Earls was occasioned by the treachery of one of the family of St. Laurence;) by meerly supposing, " that, if any art, or treachery had been used to render the Earls obnoxious to the law, they would themselves have explained the deep scheme, and have left some memorials, in vindication of their conduct, either in Spain or Rome, where they were entertained, and protected. But, as no such memorials (says he) have appeared, they seem to have acquiesced in the charge of conspiracy against the English government." But to this it may be answered, on a much more probable supposition, that these noblemen were not, perhaps expert at drawing up memorials; or rather, that they were in too desponding, and necessitous a condition, to do more than relate their misfortunes, and the manner in which they were brought on them, verbally, in order to obtain a subsistence from those courts, to which they fled for refuge; and that this traditional account was originally derived, and uniformly handed down to us, from such verbal relation. But let us try the force of this negative reasoning on the opposite side of the question. The King seems to have been so apprehensive, that this affair of the Earls " might blemish" (as he expresses it) " the reputation of that friendship which ought to be mutually observed between him and other Princes, that he thought it not amiss, to publish some such matter, by way of proclamation, as might better clear mens judgments concerning the same." At the same time, solemnly promising, " that it should appear to the world as clear as the sun, by evident proof, that the only ground, and motive of these Earls departure was the private knowledge and inward terror of their own guiltiness." Ib. p. 425. But neither in that, nor in any other authentic instrument, nor in any manner whatever, did his Majesty deign, ever after, to enlighten the world, even with the least glimpse of evident proof, that such was the motive of these Earls departure. And I shall leave it to the decision of every candid reader, whether this non-performance of his Majesty's solemn promise, be not a better negative proof of the nullity, and fiction of this conspiracy of the Earls, than the barenon-appearance of a memorial in their vindication, can be deemed of its reality?

Calvin, was, by his management, received as the public belief of the Irish church, and ratified by Chichester in the King's name (2). It was, in short, he that drew up those Calvinistical articles, then agreed to in convocation, which were afterwards condemned, and abolished by Lord Deputy Wentworth, containing arrant Brownism, and confirming not only the Lambeth-articles, suppressed by Queen Elizabeth, and afterwards rejected by King James; but also several particular fancies and notions of his own."

" AFTER (3) the repeal of the Irish act against the bringing in of the Scots, retaining them, and marrying with them, the Scottish Presbyters came over to Ireland in great Numbers. These the Irish Bishops condescended to ordain, not as performing the function of Bishops, for they would not receive ordination from them as such, but as meer Presbyters, assisting with some of their own Ministers, in order to qualify them to enjoy benefices in the church. And these Bishops were so exceedingly complaisant, on such occasions, that they left out all those expressions in the established form of ordination, which these Ministers excepted against; inserting and using such others, as they consented to, and approved of. After this method, Mr. Blair was publickly ordained by Doctor Ecclin, Bishop of Down, in the church of Bangor; and all those of the Presbyterian persuasion, who were ordained in Ireland, between the years 1622, and 1642, were ordained after the same method; and all of them so ordained, enjoyed the churches and tythes, though they remained Presbyterians still, and used not the Liturgy. And there was, adds my Author, a civil comprehension between them, and a sort of an ecclesiastical comprehension too; for they frequently met, and consulted with the Bishops, about the affairs of common concernment to the interest of religion; and some of them were members of the convocation in 1634." The same author informs us, " that these Presbyters employed themselves in their ministerial work, to the approbation of all the moderate, and sober Episcopalians; and particularly, of the great Primate Usher, from whom they had great applause."

CHAP. VII.

Warm Contests in the Irish House of Commons.

IN the year 1613, a parliament was called, wherein the attainder, and outlawry, of the noblemen and gentlemen of Ulster, together with several other acts, injurious to the religion, and property, of the natives, were intended to be passed. " The Irish," says Mr. (1) Carte, " on this occasion, were
apprehensive

(2) Id. ib. Vol. i. fol. 73.   (3) Presbyterian Loyalty.   (1) Life of Ormond, Vol. i.

apprehensive that some further penal laws, particularly against harbouring *(a)* Jesuits, and seminary priests, and for obliging not only Magistrates in corporations, but also professors of the law, and others to take the oath of supremacy, would be enacted." And that apprehension was but too well founded. Knox, a Scotch Puritan, and Bishop of Raphoe, had informed the Deputy, that the only sure means of extirpating Popery out of Ireland, was by the death, or banishment of the persons, and the confiscation of the properties, of Papists. And, although neither of these humane alternatives was fully adopted by his Excellency, yet, from that malignant insinuation, he certainly meditated some new, and severe parliamentary restrictions upon them at that juncture. For this purpose, several new boroughs were hastily *(b)* created in Munster, and Conaught; some, and those not a few, even after the writs had been issued. And from the antient boroughs and towns, many undue returns of aliens, and other unqualified persons, were openly procured.

UNDER these circumstances, when, on the first day of the session (2), Sir John Davis was proposed for Speaker, Sir James Geogh observed, " That he saw *(c)* many persons in the house, who had had no right to sit as members; and

(2) Reeves in Analect. Part ii. p. 14.

(a) There was actually a bill of that kind sent over by the Deputy, concerning which, the King tells him and the Council, in returning the other bills, " We think it a fit time to dispatch from hence, Sir John Davis, our Attorney General of that kingdom, with those bills which were first transmitted thither, under the great seal of England, and were lately sent for hither again, by our special direction, to the End that the bill against the Jesuits, &c. might be taken away from the rest, to be further considered by us; which we ourselves have done with our own Hands." Desid. Curiof. Hib. Vol. i. p. 325.

(b) " The Deputy" says Doctor Leland, " continued to increase the new boroughs to the number of forty; of which several were not incorporated, until the writs for summoning a parliament had already issued.—This awakened the fears of the numerous party of recusants; some additional severities against those who refused to abandon the Romish communion; some additional penal statutes, or at least the revival of those already made, were naturally dreaded." Hist of Ireland, Vol. ii. p. 445. The same author had before informed us, " That these new boroughs being most of them inconsiderable, and many too poor to afford wages to their representatives, must have been entirely influenced by government, and returned its creatures, and immediate dependents; and that they were represented by Attorneys clerks, and the servants of the Lord Deputy." Ib. p. 443.

(c) The Lords of the pale, in their humble remonstrance to his Majesty on this occasion, observe, among other things, " That the managing elections for that parliament, had generally bred so grievous an apprehension, as is not in their power to express, arising from a fearful suspicion, that the project of erecting so many corporations in places that scarcely pass the rank of the poor villages of the poorest country in Christendom, do tend to nought else, but that by the voices of a few, selected for that purpose under the name of Burgesses, extreme penal laws should be imposed on his Majesty's subjects.—That his Majesty's subjects of Ireland, in general, did very much distaste and exclaim against the deposing of so many Magistrates in the cities, and boroughs of that kingdom, for not sparing the oath of supremacy, in spiritual and ecclesiastical causes, they protesting a firm profession of loyalty, and of all kingly jurisdiction in his Highness." Desid. Curiof. Hiber. Vol. i. p. 160.

Ch. VII.   CIVIL WARS IN IRELAND.   49

and therefore moved, that their votes might be a while suspended, until a Speaker was chosen; after which the legality of their elections should be duly enquired into. But this motion being soon rejected, and Sir James urged, by the opposite party, to proceed directly in the chusing of a Speaker, he named *(d)* Sir John Everard, and was seconded by Sir Christopher Nugent, Mr. William Talbot, and several other respectable members. But Sir Oliver St. John, and Sir Thomas Ridgeway insisting tumultuously, that Sir John Davis was chosen Speaker, by a majority of voices; and the other party calling out, as loudly, to place Sir John Everard in the chair, great confusion arose among them; so that the number of votes, on either side, could not be determined, until Sir John Davis's friends having followed him to another room, those who remained within, agreed to put Sir John Everard in the chair, supposing him to be duly elected, as in truth he was by a real majority of legal voices, notwithstanding the greater number of nominal votes on the other side. But the court-members, on their return, finding him there, and conscious of their greater numbers (3) dragged him violently thence, and fixed *(e)* Sir John Davis in his place. They were emboldened to commit this outrage, by the presence of a band of soldiers completely armed, with lighted matches in their hands, who were placed, for that purpose, at the entrance into parliament. Alarmed at these proceedings, the Catholic members quitted the house, having first openly protested against the authors of such unheard-of violence, as invaders of the liberties of their country, and of the rights and privileges of parliament.

H   Not

(3) Analecta Sacra. Reeves ubi supra.

(d) "A Recusant of respectable character, who had been a Justice of the King's bench, and, on resigning his station rather than take the oaths, was indulged with a pension." Leland's Hist. of Ireland, Vol. ii. 447.

(e) A cotemporary writer, in a tract addressed to Sir Arthur Chichester himself, relates this contest in the following manner. "There were," says he, "two elections, viz. those of the recusant sect had chosen Sir John Everard, Knight, for the Speaker; and therefore in no wise would accept of Sir John Davis; and in this division, grew an uncertainty, who had most voices; whereupon, Sir John Davis with all those of the Protestancy, went out to be numbered, and before they came in again, those of the recusancy had shut the door, and had set Sir John Everard in the chair of the Speaker; but when the Protestants saw that, they quietly pulled Sir John Everard out of the chair, and held Sir John Davis therein; and thus, with great contention, the second and third days (of the parliament) were spent; but the recusants prevailed not therein, for Sir John Davis was maintained in the place.—Then did the recusants of both houses of parliament withdraw themselves, and resorted not thither any more, notwithstanding that they were often sent for by the Lord Deputy." Desid. Curios. Hibern. Vol. i. p. 168.

Not content with this protestation, these seceding members *(f)* sent four of the most considerable of their own body into England, with their complaints to the King. These were accompanied from the House of Lords, by David Roche, Viscount Fermoy; James Plunkett, Baron of Killeen, afterwards Earl of Fingall; and by the Lord Baron of Delvin, afterwards Earl of Westmeath; together with Sir Patrick Barnwell, and four lawyers.

But these noblemen and gentlemen, instead of obtaining redress of the injury complained of, were, in the end, sent *(g)* back and insulted, with this quaint and evasive answer (4), " That as Papists, they were but half subjects, and therefore, should have but half privileges;" which, by the way, was an indirect confession of the wrong done them. Nay, it appears by a public speech, which his Majesty made on this occasion, that he would not allow them to be even half subjects; which by a new quirk of Royal logic, he endeavoured to prove thus: " As men, ye consist of bodies and souls; now your souls, which are the nobler parts, ye devote to the Pope; to me ye submit nothing but your bodies, nor yet your bodies entire; for those ye divide between me and the King of Spain; him ye serve with your bodies armed, leaving to me only your naked, useless, and unarmed bodies *(h).*"

With this curious answer, he remanded them back to Ireland, ordering them at their peril, to attend the business of parliament, which was chiefly that of raising large supplies for his Majesty. And, indeed, in that respect, these half-subjects always shewed themselves abundantly more useful, than those he called his whole-subjects; as, on account of their far greater number, and opulence, they contributed more than seven-eights, in all the loans, and subsidies, that were required by him, during his whole reign. And for their chearful concurrence in granting this last supply, we shall presently find his Majesty

(4) Cox's Hist. Irel. Vol. ii. p. 25.

(f) After having obtained leave from his Majesty, in consequence of an humble address signed by the Lords Buttevant, Gormanston, Fermoy, Mountgarret, Killine, Delvin, Slane, Trimbleston, Donboyne, Lowth, Cahyr." See that Address, Append.

(g) " Two of their agents, Talbot and Lutterel, were committed prisoners, one to the Tower, and the other to the Fleet." Lel. Hist. Irel. Vol. ii. p. 451.

(h) The manner in which he justified to these agents, his having granted a commission for creating these new boroughs is still more extraordinary. " It was never before heard," said he, " that any good subjects did dispute the King's power in this point. What is it to you, whether I make many or few boroughs? My Council may consider the fitness, if I require it; but, what if I had created forty noblemen, and four hundred boroughs? The more the merrier, the fewer the better cheer." Desid. Curios. Hibern. Vol. i. p. 220.

Majesty thanking them, with the rest of the Irish Commons, in a seemingly gracious and grateful manner.

The Catholics, however, on their return to parliament, still insisted on questioning the aforesaid elections, before any other business was proceeded upon; and they prevailed so far, that an order was then passed, and repeated in the following session (5), " That the exceptions taken to these elections should be duly examined, at a more convenient opportunity." But we don't find, that such opportunity was ever after afforded them *(i)*. In this parliament, so composed, and managed, the act of attainder, and outlawry, against the noblemen and gentlemen of the six intire counties in Ulster, for the before-mentioned pretended conspiracy, was suffered to be passed.

It is well worthy of notice, that this act of the attainder of the Earls does not specify any particulars of the conspiracy lately imputed to them; not even their flight, which was the only proof, and that meerly presumptive, that was alleged for it. It barely recites, in general, as the grounds of it (6), " These noblemens having committed, and perpetrated, acts of treason against his Majesty (which, as we have already seen, they were only suspected, or accused, of having intended to commit,) and their own and ancestors former rebellion against Queen Elizabeth," (for which, as we have also already seen, they had all received his Majesty's free, and absolute *(k)*, pardon, at his accession.) It is therefore, no wonder, that while this act was under debate, a committee of the Commons was appointed to wait on the Lord Deputy (7), " to acquaint him with a scruple, that was moved, whether that attainder did look back to treasons committed before the King's time, or only since." But no other answer appears, on the part of the Deputy, but the passing of the bill.

(5) Commons Journal. Vol. i.   (6) See Irish Statutes.   (7) Com Jour. Vol. i. fol. 45, 47.

(i) His Majesty, however, soon after sent instructions to the Deputy, " That the Burgesses returned upon the new charters, from Tallagh, Lifmore, Caterlogh, Clonkiltie, Fetherd, Augher, Belfast, and Charlemount ; as also those from Kildare and Cavan, being falsely returned, should forbear to sit in that house, unless they should be again duly elected."—— And also, " that the Burgesses returned from the towns of Clogher, Athlone, and Gouran, should, forbear to sit in the house of parliament." Desid. Curios. Hib. Vol. i. p. 324-5.

(k) In one of his Majesty's letters of instructions to Sir Arthur Chichester, when first appointed Deputy, we find these words. " We think it not amiss, as well for making known, that we are careful of that state (Ireland) ; as also to root out jealousies, which have been formerly conceived, that daily advantage should be searched for by the Ministers of that realm, to molest, and oppress them for old offences, only to serve private ends ; a matter so odious to our nature, to whom generally that people have carried themselves as becometh natural and loving subjects, that we would have it one of the first works you should do, to secure them from ever being called in question for any offence done, either before, or in the precedent rebellion." Desid. Curios. Hiber. Vol. i. p. 448.

CHAP. VIII.

The King thanks the Irish for their Supply, but orders the Penal Laws to be put in Force against them.

AFTER the before-mentioned supplies had been granted by parliament, his Majesty wrote to the Deputy, (and ordered his letter to be publickly read in the house) that (1), " understanding, that the bills of subsidies were, upon the first propounding, received, and passed, with such universal consent and chearfulness, that there seemed to arise an affectionate emulation between them, who should express most love, and forwardness therein unto him; he took that evident demonstration of their dutiful zeal and affection, in such good part, that he commanded him to give them thanks in his name, and to let them know, that he was much better pleased with the free manner of that present of their affections unto him, than if they had given him ten times the value of the money, with unwilling hearts." Upon this occasion, Sir John Everard observed to the house (2), " that, as neither in Queen Elizabeth's time, nor in his then Majesty's, any subsidies had been so regularly granted, there being no denial, he did, on the knees of his heart, humbly pray in behalf of his country, that the statute of the 2d of Queen Elizabeth might be something moderated for a time; which being granted," added he, " if the King were willing to demand two, three, or four subsidies, he doubted not of any denial hereafter." And, in the same session, the whole house, among other grievances which they had laid before the Deputy, again mentioned that statute; and humbly prayed (3), " That, in the execution thereof, the clerks of the crown and peace, might not be permitted to take such excessive fees, as they did; but that these fees might be altogether forbidden to be taken, or else that the same might be drawn down, and moderated, and that, by an act of state to be observed throughout the kingdom." They further prayed (4), " That, whereas the recusant lawyers were debarred from *(a)* their practice,

(1) Ib. (2) Ib. (3) Ib. (4) Ib.

(a) " In 1614, all the Councellors of law that were in Ireland, who would not take the oath of supremacy, were put from pleading of causes in any of the four courts, or elsewhere, to speak for clients. Likewise, such as were pensioners, that would not take the said oath, were discharged of their pensions." Desid. Curios. Hiber. Vol. i, p. 320.

" The statute made the 2d of Eliz. laying a penalty of 12d. every Sunday and Holyday, for not going to church, is put strictly in execution in many places: but the said money, being a great matter of value over the whole kingdom, is not employed upon the poor according to the statute, but brought into the hands of the clerks of these courts, but how they dispose of it, the parishioners, or church-wardens know not." Petition of the Lords and Commons Agents, 1613. Desid. Curios. Vol. i. p. 249.

" Lord

practice, by special directions from his Majesty: and, forasmuch as the Commons did find by experience, that the subjects of the realm did suffer no small prejudice in their causes, for want of learned Counsel, especially at the assizes, that his Lordship would be a means to his Majesty, that such, and so many of the said lawyers might be restored to their practice, as his Lordship in his judgment should think fit, for the dispatch of said causes." To which his Lordship answered, " That the Lords of the Council in England had signified his Majesty's pleasure for silencing them, until they had taken the oath (of supremacy) but that he would acquaint their Lordships with what the Commons had signified, and with their desire." But that no redress followed, appears from hence, that in the ensuing session of May 16th, 1615, the same Commons humbly addressed the Lord Deputy to know, " Whether his Lordship had received any answer touching the practice of the Irish lawyers; and prayed, that they might be, by his Lordship's recomendation, again restored unto practice." To which we find no answer returned.

IMPRISONMENTS, on account of recusancy, were then so frequent, and grievous, that the Commons in this same session, annexed to their long list of grievances (5), a prayer, " That his Lordship would be pleased to release all those, that lay in, upon excommunications;" and at the same time acquainted him, " that a great number of the house desired, that he would recommend to his Majesty, that some suspension might be had of the statute of the 2d of Elizabeth."

THE Catholics of Ireland, on account of their number, and opulence, had contributed more liberally to the above-mentioned, and all other supplies, than all the rest of his Majesty's subjects of that kingdom; and yet the King, instead of redressing their present grievances, did, in a few months after the date of his letter of thanks before-mentioned, not only continue, but increase them; by giving particular instructions to Sir Oliver St. John, then going over Lord Deputy, to put this statute of the 2d of Elizabeth, and all other penal statutes, in strict execution; instructions, which (6) Sir Oliver seemed very well inclined to

---

(5) Commons Jour. Vol. i.   (6) Carte's Orm. Vol i. fol. 37.

" Lord Deputy Chichester confesses, " that the Justices of assize (1613) for the space of two or three years past, had bound over divers juries to the starchamber, for their refusing to present recusants upon the testimony of the witnesses, that they come not to church, according to the law.—All which jurors have been punished in the star-chamber, by fine and imprisonment." See Chichest. Ans. Def. Cur. ib. p. 262.

The reason Chichester gives for not distributing the money collected from Catholics, for not going to church on Sundays and Holydays, to the poor, as the statute 2d of Eliz. directs, is, " because the poor of the parishes are not fit to receive the same, being recusants, (Catholics,) and therefore ought to pay the like penalty." Ib. p. 275.

to *(b)* pursue: for, at his entering on the government, he did indeed proceed with vigour, in the execution of that statute; and caused presentments to be made of such as neglected coming to church, in different parts of the kingdom. The effects of this vigour were very dismal, and extensive; the treasures of the rich were thereby soon exhausted; and the poor, every where, not being able to pay this tax on their consciences, fled into dens, and caverns, from the cruel collectors of it, whither they were sometimes pursued by furious blood-hounds, set on, and followed by a Sheriff, and his posse of disbanded soldiers, equally furious and unrelenting (7). Mr. Rooth, a cotemporary writer, informs us, that in the poor county of Cavan alone, not less than *(c)* eight thousand pounds were levied, in one year, by means of this tax; ecclesiastical censures, on the same account, were severely executed, in every part of the kingdom. Those who lay under them, when found abroad, were constantly thrown into jails; and great numbers of merchants and artificers, being thus confined at home, and hindered to transact business publickly, and in the way of open commerce, were suddenly reduced to poverty and distress. Even their dead bodies did not escape the cruelty of these censures; for if they happened to die, while they yet lay under them, they were denied Christian burial, and their corpses thrown into holes, dug in the highways, with every mark of ignominy, that could be devised, and inflicted, by their cruel and bigoted judges.

C H A P. IX.

Some Account of the Ecclesiastical Courts at that juncture in Ireland.

BISHOP Burnet, in his life of Doctor Bedel, Bishop of Kilmore, hath left us a very shocking description of these ecclesiastical courts in Ireland. " They were," says his Lordship, " often managed by a Chancellor, that bought his place, and so thought he had a right to all the profits he could make out of it. And their whole business seemed to be nothing but oppression, and extortion;

(7) Analecta Sacra.

(b) " Sir Oliver St. John seemed to be actuated with peculiar zeal against Popery." Lel. Hist. Irel. Vol. i. p. 561. " A commission was issued by him to seize the liberties and revenues of Waterford, because the magistrates refused the oath of supremacy." Id. ib. p. 462.

(c) This will not seem strange, when we consider what Lord Deputy Mountjoy says in a letter to Secretary Cecil, viz. " That in the time of Tyrone's war, that Earl did raise upon Ulster, ill-inhabited as it was, with no industry, and for the most part wasted, above four score thousand pounds by the year." Morris. ubi supra. fol. 234.

extortion; the solemnest, and sacredest, of all church-censures, which was excommunication, went about in so sordid, and base a manner, that all regard to it, as it was spiritual censure, was lost; and the effects it had in law, made it be cried out upon, as a most intolerable piece of tyranny. The officers of the court thought they had a sort of right to oppress the natives; and that all was well got, that was wrung from them. Primate Usher himself, seemed so sensible of these abuses, that he told Archbishop Laud (1), " such was then the venality of all things sacred in Ireland, that he was afraid to mention any thing about them;" and that, upon some of the adverse party's having asked him, " where he had heard, or read before, that religion and mens souls were set to sale, after that manner?" His Grace was obliged to have recourse to a pitiful witticism for an answer, viz. " That there was another place, where both Heaven and God himself, were set to sale." Which whether true or false, (and false it most certainly is) was a tacit confession of the justice of the charge of public corruption against these courts. But we shall presently see, that Primate Usher's own court was not a whit less corrupt, in the opinion of the good Bishop Bedel, than those of the other Irish Bishops.

THESE corruptions were so flagrant, and long continued, that even in 1640, the dissenters in Ulster, on whom the episcopal clergy had, as we have seen, conferred many signal favours, made severe animadversions upon them. In their remonstrance to the English parliament of that year, they observed, among other abuses of these courts (2), " That the commutation of penance (which Burnet calls the worst of simony) which either should not at all be exacted, or if exacted, should be set apart for the poor, and other pious uses, came either to the Prelate's kitchen, or the Commissary's purse, or to both; and that, though the officers of these courts pretended themselves to be the advancers of virtue, and punishers of vice, yet they usually, without further satisfaction, absolved the most scandalous persons for a sum of money, and often questioned not at all such, from whom they privately beforehand had received such sum."

(1) Burnet ubi supra.   (2) Pryn's Antipathy to Bishops, Part ii. p. 374.

CHAP.

CHAP. X.

The Patience, and Submission, of the Natives.

WHILE the nobility and gentry of Ulster were, by the late act of attainder, stript of their possessions, for crimes that were either never committed, or were formerly pardoned, another design was set on foot, to seize on the estates of the natives in the other provinces, under the pretence of a judicial enquiry into defective titles. This enquiry caused a *(a)* general alarm thro' every part of the kingdom; inasmuch as (1), " no title of lineal descent, or long possession, though for several hundred years, nor even letters patent, could secure the proprietors against the predatory effects of it." But as this business was prosecuted with greatest violence in the ensuing reign, under Lord Wentworth's government, I shall defer the consideration of it till I come to speak of that period.

ONE would imagine, that some cause had been given by the Irish, or at least pretended by their enemies, for such continued severity; but nothing of that kind appears to have been the case; for all historians agree, that, except O'Dogherty's short-lived tumult, and the forged plot of the Earls, there was not the least commotion in Ireland, during that whole reign; although, had the Irish been disposed to rise, it is certain, that no people could have a more tempting opportunity, or a more plausible *(b)* pretence, than they then had (2),
" for

---

(1) Remonstrance from Trim.   (2) Carte's Orm. Vol. i. fol. 45.

(a) It was rigorously prosecuted by Sir Arthur Chichester, tho' the King in his instructions to him, upon his first appointment to the Lieutenancy of Ireland, told him, " That he had directed a commission to compound with his subjects of that kingdom for defective and imperfect titles; and that he had resolved, from thenceforth, to grant no more warrants of lands, coming within any title of concealment; because he hoped that, thereby, both his people would receive contentment, and his coffers some augmentation, by the composition with the tenants of such lands." Desid. Curios. Hib. Vol. i. p. 455-6.

(b) The Commissioners sent about this time from England, by the King, to enquire into the numerous grievances complained of by the Irish agents, set forth in their report to his Majesty, " That out of the particular instances (being many) of oppression, and extortions of the soldiers, provost-marshals, and others, they had selected three score. That in counties, where the composition, in lieu of the cess was paid, the soldiers did extort on his Majesty's subjects, by neither paying money, nor giving tickets, for what they took up. That, besides meat and drink, they extorted money from the poorer people, where they were cessed; three shillings for every night's lodging for an horse-man, and two for a foot-man, sometimes more. As also certain petty sums for their boys, and attendants, besides victuals; and these soldiers took money, not only for themselves, but likewise for other soldiers absent, which the country called black men, because they were not seen. That, in all these cases, when the people had not money, they took forcibly
some

"for King James never kept up a greater force in that kingdom, than one thousand seven hundred and thirty five foot, and two hundred and twelve horse; and these in a miserable condition, sometimes three years unpaid; and not a penny of money in the hands of either of the Treasurers, or any to be borrowed from private persons. Yet he was, all this time, settling the plantations in different parts of the kingdom; changing the (c) properties of lands, transplanting the old inhabitants, and settling colonies of strangers; while the old Irish captains, and petty Lords, were discontented at the loss of their antient power; and while there were, in remote parts of the kingdom, numbers of idle young, and active fellows, who being unprovided for a livelihood, and not daring to earn it by the sweat of their brow, were full of complaints, and eager for alterations. In Conaught alone there were seven thousand of these idle fellows booked down by officers, and given in a list to the Lord Deputy, that were fit for nothing but arms; and who then living on their friends, and relations, must have been forced to seek, and push their fortunes."

some of their cattle or household-stuff, for pawns, in lieu thereof; that the officers of the army did the same; that Sheriffs did suffer their men, and bailiffs, and followers, to take both money, and victuals from the country. And that the reason the people did not complain to the Deputy of all these oppressions and extortions, was for fear of being worse used by the soldiers at other times; and because the charges of the complaint would far exceed the damages." See that Report, in Desid. Curios. Hiber. Vol. ii. p. 365-4-2.

(c) We are told on this occasion, "That there are not wanting proofs of the most iniquitous practices, of hardened cruelty, of vile perjury, and scandalous subornation, employed to despoil the fair, and unoffending proprietor of his inheritance." Lel. hist. of Irel. Vol. ii. p. 470.

AN
HISTORICAL AND CRITICAL
REVIEW
OF THE
CIVIL WARS IN IRELAND.

BOOK III.

CHAP. I.

The State of the Irish under Charles I.

DURING the first two years of King Charles's reign, the Catholics of Ireland enjoyed some little tranquillity, for which they were indebted, not to the lenity of the Irish government, but to his Majesty's goodness alone (1), " Which had limited, from time to time, the Lord Deputy, and Council of that kingdom, by several instructions, directions, and letters, concerning them." Their gratitude, for this forbearance, was, indeed, extraordinary; and the generosity of their offer to his Majesty, on that account, could scarce be exceeded by any thing, but by that folly and fanaticism, which induced the government to reject it.

In the year 1626 (2), " The condition of the King's affairs was much perplexed in England; he was at war with the two most powerful Kings in Europe, and his subjects in the English parliament would afford him little or no assistance, but upon hard, and dishonourable terms, though they had engaged him in the first war; and seemed glad of the last, it being in defence of religion."

In

---

(1) Scrinia Sacra.   (2) Sir Edward Walker's Historic. Discourses, fol. 337.

In this perplexity of his Majesty's affairs (3), " The Roman Catholics of Ireland offered constantly to pay an army of five thousand foot, and five hundred horse, for his Majesty's service, provided they might be tolerated in the exercise of their religion (4). The toleration they desired was no more, than some respite from the oppressions, and extortions, of the ecclesiastical courts; and to have all proceedings against them in these courts, for religion, suspended; to be released from those exorbitant sums, which they were obliged to pay for their christenings and marriages; and particularly, to have the extravagant surplice-fees of the clergy, and the extraordinary warrants for levying them, abolished."

But the clergy were too much interested in these matters, not to oppose, with all their powers, the acceptance of such an offer. Upon the first tender of it (5), a protestation was drawn up against it, by Primate Usher, and subscribed by twelve Bishops; which Doctor Downham, Bishop of Derry, pronounced in Christ-church, Dublin, before the state; upon whom it had so powerful an effect, that the Catholics offer was scornfully rejected, and their religion scurrilously abused *(a)*.

These Bishops set forth in their protestation (6), " That to grant a toleration, in respect of money to be given, or a contribution to be made, by the Catholics, was to set religion to sale, with the souls of the people." And Doctor Downham had no sooner pronounced these words, but all the people in the church cried out aloud, " Amen, Amen."

But how shamefully these Bishops themselves had exposed their religion to both sale, and contempt, in their ecclesiastical courts, (from whose tyranny the Catholics were willing to purchase their redemption at so dear a rate) was then notoriously manifest. " In these courts," says (7) Bishop Burnet, " bribes went about almost barefaced; and the exchange they made of pennance for money, was the worst sort of simony." The good Bishop Bedel told Primate Usher himself, the author and principal promoter of this protestation, that (8), " Whereas he was wont to except one of these courts (meaning the Primate's) from the general corruption, yet he heard it was said, among great personages, that his Grace's court was as corrupt as others; some said, it was worse; and that

---

(3) Id. ib. (4) Carte's Orm. Vol. i. fol. 50. (5) Harris's Fiction Unmasked. Usher's Life. (6) Foxes and Fire-brands, Part ii. p. 80. (7) Life of Bishop Bedel. (8) Burnet ib.

(a) " All the Protestant clergy," says Doctor Leland on this occasion, " were seriously averse to Popery; many to a degree of rancour, imbibed among the English, and Scottish Puritans." Hist. Irel. Vol. ii. p. 481.

that of his Grace's late visitation, they saw no profit, but the taking of the money."

NAY it appears, by the journals of the Irish Commons, even in 1640, that the judges of these courts were guilty of (9) " barbarous, and unjust exactions; and that too, for such rites and customs, as had been formerly in use with the Popish natives, but were now condemned, and renounced, by Protestants, viz. money for Holy-water-clerk, for annointing, Mortuary-muttons, Mary-gallons, St. Patrick's ridges, Soul-money, and the like."

THUS, while these Bishops were simonaically extorting large sums of money from the Catholics, for their own private use (for to that alone they were applied) they expected to be considered as taking only their lawful dues: but for the King to accept of the same, or less, from these people, to enable him to carry on the most necessary *(b)* public service (on condition only of freeing them from such barbarous, and unjust extortions) was, in their Lordships opinion, nothing less than " setting religion to sale, with the souls of the people."

C H A P. II.

A free Gift raised for the King, chiefly by the Natives, for which they were rewarded by a new Persecution of their Religion.

IN this pressing exigency of his Majesty's affairs, a free gift or contribution, of one hundred and twenty thousand pounds, was set on foot in Ireland, " of which, says (1) Mr. Carte, the Catholics paid near *(a)* two thirds." And indeed, on that account, they seem to have been well entitled to that respite from legal penalties, which they are said to have then obtained. But this respite,

(9) Commons Journal, Vol. i.   (1) Life of Orm. Vol. i.

(b) " We are told in the life of Primate Usher, that this protestation (of the Bishops) had a considerable effect in retarding a project, the success of which was absolutely necessary to the King's affairs." Lel. ubi supra, Vol. ii. p. 482, note.

(a) The Catholic nobility and gentry afterwards solemnly declared, in their remonstrance of grievances, delivered to his Majesty's Commissioners at Trim, in March 1612. " That they had readily, and without reluctance or repining, contributed to all the subsidies, loans, and other extraordinary grants made to his Majesty since the beginning of his reign; and were, in parliament, and otherwise, most forward in granting said sums; and did bear nine parts in ten, in the payment thereof." App. The truth of this appears from hence, that these subsidies, loans, &c. were rated to each person, in proportion to the value of his real property; and we are well informed, " That before the year 1641, the Irish were the proprietors of ten acres of Land, to one that the English had in Ireland." Col. Laurence Inter. of Ireland, part. ii. p. 47.

respite, if any they had, must have been very inconsiderable; for in the year 1629, a severe persecution was raised against them, which was as unlooked for, as unmerited. The Council of Ireland, in their letter to the King, April 28th of that year, confess (2), " That, except what they call the insolence and excresence of the Popish clergy; (which shall be just now explained) the kingdom, as to the civil part of it, was in far better order at that juncture, than ever it was in the memory of man, as well in the general and current execution of justice, according to the laws, in the freedom of mens persons and estates, and in the universal outward submission of all sorts of settled inhabitants to the crown and laws of England; as also in the advancement of the crown-revenues, and in the competent number of Bishops, and other able and learned Ministers of the church of England." But these Bishops, it seems, and other able and learned Ministers of the church of England, were not then thought sufficient, without the help of a military force, to reclaim the Catholics from the heinous sin of serving God in the way most agreeable to their own consciences.

The cause, and manner of this persecution, are thus related by Hammon l'Estrange, who was then, or shortly after, in Ireland (3). " In this year," says he, " the Roman clergy began to rant it, and to exercise their fancies called Religion, so publickly as if they had gained a toleration." The reader, I imagine, will be surprised to find, that this ranting of the Roman clergy was nothing more, than their reading *(b)* prayers quietly to their people in one of their own chapels: " For (proceeds l'Estrange) whilst the Lords Justices were at Christ-church, in Dublin, on St. Stephen's Day, they were celebrating Mass in Cook-street; which their Lordships taking notice of, they sent the Archbishop of Dublin, the Mayor, Sheriffs, and Recorder of the city, with a file of musketeers, to apprehend them; which they did, taking away the crucifixes and paraments of the altar; the soldiers hewing down the image of St. Francis, the Priests and Friars were delivered into the hands of the pursuivants, at whom the people threw stones, and rescued them; the Lords Justices being informed of this, sent a guard and delivered them, and clapped eight Popish Aldermen by the heels for not assisting their Mayor. On this account, fifteen houses, by direction of the Lords of the Council in England, were seized to the King's use,

(2) Scrinia Sacra.   (3) See Harris's Fiction Unmasked.

(b) It hath been observed on this occasion, that " the Protestant party were zealous in their detestation of Popish idolatry, (i. e. ceremonies) that the inferiors of their clergy were poor, and sometimes scandalously profligate.—And that many of the Prelates, as well as officers of state, of English birth, were puritanically affected." See Leland's Hist. of Ireland, Vol. iii. p. 4.

use, and the Priests and Friars were so *(c)* persecuted, that two of them (adds my author) hanged themselves in their own defence."

Few I believe, will wonder, that the populace endeavoured to rescue their Priests, in such an exigency; and fewer yet, that the Popish Aldermen of Dublin did not assist their Mayor in this Priest-catching business. But it is not easy to conceive what else, but a truly puritanical excess of zeal could have excited an Archbishop of Dublin to quit his proper province, the public service of the church, on a solemn festival, to head a file of musketeers, and lead them on thus furiously to demolish a chapel, apprehend a few Priests, and terrify a number of harmless people in the midst of their devotions; and that too, " in the midst of far better order, in civil matters, and more universal subjection to the crown and laws of England, than was ever before known in the memory of man." One can hardly help thinking, that the furious puritan Venner did, some years after, copy the example of this Archbishop of Dublin, when issuing from his conventicle in Coleman-street, London, with about fifty of his disciples armed, he fancied himself commissioned from Heaven, to fall upon and kill all those whom he met within the streets, of a different persuasion from his own.

After what has been hitherto related, who can help wondering at the partiality, or ignorance of those historians, who confidently tell us (4); " That, during all this, and the former reign, the Catholics of Ireland enjoyed an undisturbed exercise of their religion; and that even in Dublin, where the seat of the King's Chief Governor was, they went as publickly, and uninterruptedly to their devotions, as he went to his."

(4) Clarendon, &c.

(c) This persecution was afterwards extended all over the kingdom. The English Council acquainted the Justices of Ireland, on that occasion, " That his Majesty in person, was pleased openly, and in most gracious manner, to approve and commend their ability and good service; whereby they might be sufficiently encouraged to go on, with the like resolution and moderation, till the work was fully done, as well in the city as in other places of the kingdom, leaving to their discretion, when, and where to carry a soft or harder hand." Scrinia Sacra.

CHAP.

CHAP. III.

The free Gift, or Contribution continued for the Service of the Government..

THE free gift before-mentioned, having been continued longer, and grown more burdensome than was expected, the people (1) " began to entertain frightful apprehensions, least it might, in fine, turn to an hereditary charge on their estates." The Protestants especially, complained loudly of it; those of Cavan in particular, who signed a petition to the Lords Justices against it, setting forth (2), " That it was plotted, and collected, without the consent of the Protestants in that country, and partly by force, praying their Lordships favourably to forbear any further imposition of any such burden upon them, until they represented their humble remonstrance to his Majesty."

RICHARD Earl of Cork, then one of the Lords Justices (3), " privately set the Protestants against this contribution; and several of the Bishops joined him in opposing it." His Grace of Canterbury told *(a)* Bishop Bedel, on that occasion (4), " That his, and the other Bishops behaviour, was not well taken by his Majesty." A scheme was, however, formed by them, for levying the whole contribution on the Catholics, by putting the statute of the 2d of Elizabeth in strict execution. Accordingly, the Lords Justices and Council, informed his Majesty (5), " That it was impossible to improve that part of the revenue *(b)*, save only by imposing the twelve-pence a Sunday on the recusants." This proposal was readily agreed to by the King (6) : " We approve well," says he, in his answer; " that this business, as you desire, may be presently put into such a state, as that the money, which shall, by that means, grow due unto us, may be ready to be levied by Michaelmas next. And as the best and surest way to bring it to effect, We do hereby authorise, and require you, forthwith to assemble our Council there, and with their privity to cause presentments

---

(1) Lord Strafford's State Letters, Vol. i. fol. 184.   (2) Id. ib. fol. 150.   (3) Id. ib. fol. 76.
(4) Id. ib. fol. 134.   (5) Id. ib. Vol. ii. fol. 91.   (6) Id. ib.

(a) " Bedel had united with the inhabitants of his diocefs, in a petition to the late Lords Juſtices, reprefenting the new contribution, as irregularly obtained, and oppreſſively levied." Lel. Hiſt. of Ire. Vol. iii. p. 26.

(b) " The prefent Lords Juſtices adviſed, that the recuſants ſhould be ſtrictly preſented ; and the weekly fines impoſed for their abſence from the eſtabliſhed worſhip, as a means of providing for the army." Lel. ib. Vol. iii. p. 8.

sentments to be duly made through the whole kingdom, according as the law you mention doth appoint." These presentments were accordingly made, and fines were imposed on such juries as refused to find them.

Lord Wentworth, then appointed Deputy, did not, it seems, like this method of raising a supply for the maintenance of the army (7). " Not," says he, " but that every good Englishman ought, as well in reason of state, as conscience, to desire the kingdom were well reduced to a conformity in religion; but because it is a great business, that has many roots lying deep, and far within the ground, which should be first thoroughly opened before we judge what height it may shoot up to, when it shall feel itself once struck at, to be loosened and pulled up." He was, therefore, for continuing the contribution, as it then stood (8), " because he thought it more safe, considering the inequality of numbers, and the ill provision of the army, to take the contribution against the will of the Protestants, than to raise the twelve-pence a Sunday, against the liking of the recusants." But his principal reason for not depending on the execution of this statute, for raising the supply, was the uncertainty of its success, or sufficiency; for as he pleasantly observed (9), " If it took that good effect, for which it was intended, which was to bring the Irish to a conformity in religion, it would come to nothing; and so would prove a covering narrower than a man could wrap himself in."

His Lordship soon brought the King over to his opinion in this particular, but was obliged to make use of Laud's assistance, to convince the Irish Bishops of the impropriety of executing the statute of the 2d of Elizabeth, at that juncture (10), " As for the laying aside," says his Grace, in his letter to Bishop Bedel, " the twelve-pence a Sunday, and not exacting it for the present, his Majesty conceives he did it upon all the considerable reasons, that could be, and those very well weighed; and therefore, I do heartily pray both you, and your brethren, to lay aside all jealousies, and to advance his Majesty's service by all the good means you can."

(7) Id. ib. fol. 75.   (8) Ib. fol. 76.   (9) Id. ib. fol. 47.   (10) Id. ib. Vol. ii. fol. 91.

CHAP. IV.

Lord Wentworth *continues the Contribution.*

THE eſtabliſhed clergy of Ireland, who made religion a pretence for preſſing the execution of the before-mentioned ſtatute (1), "were themſelves generally ignorant and unlearned; and looſe, and irregular, in their lives *(a)* and converſations." Of this particular obſtacle to the reformation of the Iriſh, Lord Wentworth was fully ſenſible, and mentioned it in ſeveral of his letters to the Miniſtry in England (2). " An unlearned clergy," ſays he in one of them, " who have not ſo much as the outward form of churchmen to cover themſelves withal; nor their perſons any way reverenced, or protected; the churches unbuilt, the Parſonage and Vicarage-houſes utterly ruined; the people untaught through the non-reſidence of the clergy, occaſioned by unlimited ſhameful numbers of ſpiritual promotions, with cure of ſouls, which they hold by commendams; the rites and ceremonies of the church run over, without decency of habit, order, or gravity, in the courſe of their ſervice; the Biſhops alienating their very principal houſes and demeſnes, to their children, to ſtrangers; and farming out their juriſdictions to mean and unworthy perſons;" ſo that, with reſpect to their project of propagating religion by enforcing this ſtatute, his Lordſhip juſtly obſerved (3), " That ſuch brainſick zeal would work a goodly reformation ſurely, to force conformity to a religion, when there was hardly to be found a church to receive, or an able Miniſter to teach the people."

THE method Lord Wentworth propoſed, for improving this part of the revenue, in preference to the tax on the conſciences of the natives, was firſt, to continue the contribution for another year; and ſecondly, to ſummon a parliament; in order to ſettle a conſtant and regular ſupply for the army. But, in order to make trial of the temper of the Catholics, (who had firſt propoſed, and actually paid more than two thirds of the former contribution,) with regard to the continuance of it for a longer term (4), " he ſent a private meſſenger of his own to Ireland, who was himſelf a Catholic, with inſtructions to invite them

---

(1) Carte's Orm. Vol. i. fol. 68.   (2) State Letters, Vol. i. fol. 187.   (3) Id. fol. 172.
(4) Id. ib. fol. 74.

(a) " Ignorance, negligence, and corruption of manners in the eſtabliſhed clergy were the conſequences of their poverty." Lel. Hiſt. Irel. ubi ſupra, p. 26.

them to make an offer to his Majesty of half a' subsidy, to be paid the next year; upon condition, that all further prosecution upon the statute of the 2d of Elizabeth might be respited, till his coming over. " The instrument I employed," says he, " knows no other, but that the resolution of the state here is set upon that course, and that I do this privately, in favour and well-wishing to divert the present storm, which else would fall heavy upon them all; being framed, and executed by the Earl of Cork; which makes the man labour in good earnest, taking it to be a cause pro aris, et focis."

The answer, which this artful message produced was (5), " That the Catholics were all very willing to continue the contribution to his Majesty, as it then was, until his Lordship's coming over; and, in order to testify their forwardness to comply, they sent his Lordship a letter to that effect, from the Earl of Antrim and others."

CHAP. V.

Lord Deputy Wentworth *arrives in Ireland.*

IN July 1633, Lord Wentworth landed in Dublin (1); " his Lordship began his administration in a manner," says Mr. Carte, " that was ungracious, and could be hardly expected from a man of his wisdom, and experience, who knew the consequence of the first steps that a Governor takes, and the impressions which they leave in the minds of the people. For, four days after his arrival, he summoned the Council by a pursuivant, according to the usual manner in that point; but summoned only a particular number, as if he intended to consult with a committee, rather than the whole body of it. This disobliged all that were omitted in the summons; and even the few he had called together were offended by a neglect, which they thought unbecoming his Lordship to offer, or themselves to bear; they assembled at two o'clock, according to their summons, but the Lord Deputy, whether out of an affectation of state, or not attending to the hour thro' a more agreeable cause (for he had, a day or two before, declared his marriage to Mistress Elizabeth Rhodes, a young lady of extraordinary merit, whom after a long absence he had met at Dublin) made them wait two hours and more, before he came to them; and then the business, under pretence of which they were summoned, was not handled, as they expected." It was, perhaps, for this, among other reasons, that at their next meeting in Council, his Lordship's proposal for continuing the contribution

(5) Id ib.   (1) Carte's Orm. Vol. i. fol. 57.

contribution for another year was far from being agreeably received; so far indeed, that he said (2), "He was put to his last refuge on that occasion, which was to tell them plainly, that there was no necessity, which induced him to take them to Council in that business; for that, rather than fail in so necessary a duty *(a)* to his master, he would undertake, upon the peril of his head, to make the King's army able to subsist, and provide for themselves amongst them, without their help (3)." The army, at this time, took up victuals in its marches, and paid nothing; as if it had been in an enemy's country; and therefore was held in abomination by the inhabitants. Having by this commination, somewhat softened their opposition, he further advised (4), "That the proposition of the next year's contribution might come from the Protestants, as it had done that year, from the Papists; and so those, no more in shew, than substance, to go before these, in their chearfulness, and readiness to serve his Majesty."

His Lordship's second proposal, of calling a parliament, to settle a constant and regular supply for the maintenance of the army, was so very differently received, that upon the bare mention of it, they readily came into his first proposal (5). "They were so horribly afraid," says he, "that the contribution-money would be set, as an annual charge, upon their inheritances, as they would redeem it at any rate; so as, upon the name of a parliament, it was something strange to see, how instantly they gave consent to this proposition, with all the chearfulness possible, and agreed to have a letter drawn up, making an offer of the next year's contribution, under their hands."

(2) Ib fol. 98.   (3) Id. ib.   (4) Ib.   (5) Id. ib.

(a) There was not among all the English Commons, a more violent opoſer of the extention of the King's prerogative, or a more ſtrenuous aſſertor of the peoples liberties, than he was while he remained plain Sir Thomas Wentworth. But being brought over to the court in 1629, he was ſworn a Privy Councellor, and made Baron; and ſoon after, a Viſcount. "The Duke of Buckingham himſelf," ſays Mr. Howel, flew not ſo high in ſo ſhort a revolution of time. He was made Viſcount with a great deal of high ceremony, upon a Sunday in the afternoon, at Whitehall. Lord Powis, who affected him not much, being told that the heralds had fetched his pedegree from the blood royal, viz. from John of Gaunt, ſwore that if ever he came to be King of England, he would turn rebel." Letters, p. 211.

CHAP.

CHAP. VI.

Lord Wentworth's *manner of modelling the Irish Parliament.*

LORD Wentworth was not, in the least degree, scrupulous as to the legal qualifications of such persons, as he intended should constitute this new House of Commons; nor indeed, did he willingly suffer any to be returned, whom he did not believe to be, some way or other, subservient to his predatory designs. " I (1.) shall labour," says he, " to make as many captains; and officers burgesses, in this parliament, as I possibly can; who, having immediate dependence on the crown, may almost sway the business, between the two parties, which way they please." One particular instance of his Lordship's management in these elections, I shall relate in his own words, because, indeed, it is in itself so extraordinary, that it would hardly gain belief, were it to be related in the words of any other person.

His Lordship had resolved to make Mr. Cateline, who was Recorder of Dublin, one of the representatives of that city; but it appears that Cateline's competitor, being either a Roman Catholic, or strenuously supported by that interest, was likely to carry the election from him. For the Catholics were generally *(a)* apprehensive, that some severe laws against the exercise of their religion were intended to be passed in that session, and therefore, were probably very active in this business of elections, in the different parts of the kingdom. This activity of theirs, was foundation enough for Lord Wentworth to pretend, in excuse of his own violent interposition in this election for Dublin (2), " That the Sheriff of that city had carried himself mutinously;" but in what respect, he does not mention, otherwise, than by a bare suspicion of his own, " that he was set on by Priests and Friars to suffer no Protestant to be returned to parliament." On this suspicion, however, he brought him (3) into the *(b)* castle-chamber, upon an Ore tenus; where, upon what he had set down under his hand, he fined him in two hundred pounds; and

five

(1) Ib.   (2) Ib. Vol i. fol. 270.   (3) Ib.

(a) This appears from Wentworth's speech to this parliament; wherein, in order to remove all such apprehensions, he tells them, " That meeting was meerly civil, religion not at all concerned one way or other. In this," adds he, " I have endeavoured to give you satisfaction, both privately and publickly. And now I assure you again, there is nothing of religion to be stirred in this parliament." State Letters, Vol. i. fol. 289.

(b) A tirannical court then held by the Deputy of Ireland, similar to that of the star-chamber in England.

five hundred pounds more, for his contempt in refusing to set his hand to another part of his examination; disabling him from ever bearing that office in the city. " Which," adds his Lordship, " wrought so good an effect, as giving order presently for chosing a new sheriff, and going on, the next day, with the election again, the voices were all orderly taken; and the conformable proving the greatest number, Catelinc, and Alderman Barry, a Protestant, were chosen."

THE Deputy had also resolved, to make this Catelinc Speaker of the House of Commons (4). " And, as I understood," says he, " there was a muttering among them of rejecting him, and chosing some other for themselves, I called the Lord Chancellor to me, and directed him to require them forthwith to assemble themselves in their House, and to chose their Speaker, who was to be presented to me by nine o'clock to-morrow morning; telling them it was not worth their contention; and that it would be taken as an ill presage of some waywardness, or forwardness of mind, if they should go about to deny such for their Speaker, as should be recommended by his Majesty's Privycouncil; or to struggle in a business, wherein the conclusion must be according to his Majesty's good will and pleasure, whether they will or no. So they departed, (adds he) and before dinner, without any noise or opposition at all, they chose the Recorder for their Speaker."

His Lordship, however, understanding, what (5) dangerous broils and tumults had happened in the House of Commons in 1614, under Sir Arthur Chichester's government, upon the like occasion of forcing a Speaker upon them, did, after Sir Arthur's example, issue a proclamation, " That neither the Peers nor Commoners should come into parliament with swords." Concerning this proclamation, I shall relate a passage of a young nobleman, of whom I shall hereafter have occasion to make frequent mention. " Pursuant to orders, the Usher of the Black Rod was planted at the door of the House of Lords, to take the swords of the Peers; and as the Earl of Ormond was coming in, he demanded his, but was refused. That officer, hereupon, shewed the proclamation, and repeated his demand in a rough manner. The Earl told him, that if he must have his sword, he should have it in his guts; and so marched on to his seat, and was the only Peer who sat that day with a sword in the House. Upon the Earl's being sent for by the Deputy that very night, to appear before the Council, and answer for his disobedience to the proclamation, he owned he had seen it, and added, " That he disobeyed both that and his Lordship's order, out of deference to an higher authority;" and then

(4) Ib. fol. 277.   (5) Carte's Orm. Vol. i. fol. 64.

then produced the Kings writ, which summoned him to come to parliament, cum Gladio Cinctus. This altercation was the beginning and cause of that great friendship, which subsisted between these two noblemen during Lord Wentworth's life."

CHAP. VII.

Some Transactions of this Parliament.

ON the 16th of July 1634, this parliament met in the castle of Dublin (1). "Undoubtedly," says Wentworth, "with the greatest civility and splendor, Ireland ever saw; there having appeared a very gallant nobility and gentry, far above that I expected; and all this accompanied with singular chearfulness towards his Majesty's affairs."

His Lordship in his speech, acquainted them (2), "That his Majesty expected an hundred thousand pounds debt to be discharged; and twenty thousand pounds a year, constant and standing revenue, to be set apart for payment of the army." He likewise told them, "That his Majesty intended to have two sessions of that parliament, the one for himself, the other for them; so as if they, without conditions, supplied the King in this, they might be sure his Majesty would go along with them in the next meeting, thro' all the expressions of a gracious and good King."

LORD Wentworth knew, that in the year 1628, the King had given the Irish his solemn promise, for a *(a)* valuable consideration, that he would, in their next parliament, (which was that now assembled) remove several grievances, that had been humbly remonstrated to him; particularly, the enquiry into defective titles; but he was sensible, at the same time, that this solemn promise would not be kept; nay, he had himself actually persuaded the King not to keep it. It was, therefore, with reason apprehended, by both his Majesty, and his Lordship, that the Commons would insist on the performance of that promise, before they granted the supplies in question; on which account, it was thought most adviseable to make two sessions of that parliament, and to give them the King's promise for both. At all events, it seems
to

---

(1) Strafford's State Letters, Vol. i. fol. 274.   (2) Ib.

(a) "A free gift of one hundred and twenty thousand pounds; of which they had paid, in 1631, one hundred and six thousand, two hundred and four score pounds, sixteen shillings and two-pence farthing. This money had been given to his Majesty, on account of the above-mentioned promise." See Straff. State Let. Vol. i. fol. 68.

to have been resolved upon, in case the commons insisted on the previous performance of the King's promise, to dissolve the parliament, and raise the supplies in an arbitrary way. Under this apprehension, his Majesty told the Deputy (3), "That it would not be worse for him, though that parliament's obstinacy should make him break with them; "for I fear," adds he, "they have some ground to demand more than it is fit for me to give."

The Deputy, however, took uncommon pains to persuade them, that in case of their free and unconditional grant of the supplies, the King would certainly confirm the promised graces; and in order to banish from their minds all diffidence in that respect (4), "surely," said he, "so great a meanness cannot enter your hearts, as once to suspect his Majesty's gracious regards of you, and performance with you, where you affix yourselves upon his grace." And yet his Lordship had not only advised his Majesty, as I have already observed, to break his solemn promise to these people; but also, in order more effectually to persuade him to do so, had even engaged to take upon himself all the danger and infamy that was likely to arise from it. For which wonderful piece of service, his Majesty, soon after, thanked him, in a letter written with his own hand *(b)*.

But left these artful insinuations should should not prevail with the Commons, he thought proper to enforce his demands by some high expressions, tending to frighten them into a speedy compliance (5). "Let me not," said he, "prove a Cassandra amongst you, to speak truth, and not to be believed. However, speak truth I will, were I to become your enemy for it; remember therefore, that I tell you, you may either mar, or make this parliament. If you proceed with respect, without laying clogs, or conditions on the King, as wise men and good subjects ought to do, you shall infallibly set up this parliament eminent to posterity, as the very basis, and foundation of the greatest happiness and prosperity that ever befel this nation. But, if you meet a great King with narrow circumscribed hearts, if you will needs be wise and cautious, above the moon, remember again, that I tell you, you shall never be able to cast your mists before the eyes of so discerning a King; you shall be found out, your sons shall wish they had been the children of more believing parents; and in a time when you look not for it, when it will be too late for you

(3) Id. ib. (4) Id. ib. (5) Ib.

(b) Wentworth,
Before I answer any of your particular letters to me, I must tell you, that your last public dispatch has given me a great deal of contentment; and especially for the keeping off the envy of a necessary negative from me of those unreasonable graces that people expected from me." Straff. State Let. Vol. i. fol. 331.

you to help, the sad repentance of an unadvised breach shall be yours; lasting honour shall be my Master's."

CHAP. VIII.

The Legality of several Elections questioned, but the Motion over-ruled.

THE very next day after Lord Wentworth had delivered his speech to parliament (which, it seems, he did with so much haughty *(a)* vehemence (1), " That he was faint at the present, and the worse for it, two or three days after,") the recusants began to call for (2) " The purging of the House;" an operation, which we may well presume, it then stood in great need of. But that motion was, with some difficulty, over-ruled. This interruption his Lordship had not foreseen; and therefore ordered, that on the following day, the supplies should be instantly moved for (3), " Not to be diverted," says he, " by any other proposition; not even by moving, that it should rest till the House had taken this purging physic, which they so hotly called for."

The supplies were accordingly moved for, on the following day, and six entire subsidies were unanimously voted to his Majesty, payable in four years.

THESE supplies were very *(b)* considerable; and far exceeded his Lordship's expectation (4). " The proportion he was guided by, was to rate every thousand pounds per annum, with forty pounds payment to the King, each subsidy; so that," says he, " the subsidies raised this first, were more than I proposed to be had in both sessions, and were given freely and without any contradiction."

HIS Lordship's observation on the Catholics calling so hotly for " the purging of the House," is worthy of some notice (5). " This warm motion for purging

(1) Id. ib. fol. 273. (2) ib. (3) Id. ib. Vol. i. fol. 278. (4) Id. ib. (5) Ib.

(a) " For this way," says he, " I was assured, they should have founds at least; and the success was answerable. For had it been low, and modestly delivered, I might, perchance, have gotten from them: It was pretty well; whereas, this way, filling one of their senses with noise, and amusing the rest with earnestness and vehemence: It was the best spoken, they ever heard in their lives." State Let. Vol i. ib.

(b) Each of these subsidies amounted to fifty thousand pounds; " And he never propounded more to the King than thirty thousand." Straff. State Let. Vol. i. fol. 273.

purging the House," says he, " doubtless with an aim of putting out a great company of Protestants, upon the point of non-residency, came not, as I was well assured, from any backwardness to supply the King; but out of an hope, by this means putting out many of the other party, to become the greater number, and so endear themselves the more with his Majesty, to make that work (granting the subsidies) wholly their own, and themselves more considerable; which would turn a greater obligation on the King, than I conceive his Majesty would be willing they should put upon him, or indeed was fit, the present condition of affairs considered." By this condition of affairs, is plainly to be understood, his Majesty's and the Viceroy's, preconcerted design, to carry on the enquiry into defective titles, notwithstanding the Royal promise to the contrary; for which iniquitous purpose, these unqualified members were still retained and protected, to the great prejudice of the real representatives of the people, and at the expence of his Majesty's justice, and honour.

C H A P. IX.

The Remonstrance of the Irish Commons to the Deputy, concerning the promised Graces.

THE Commons relying on the merit of these unconditional supplies, chearfully and unanimously granted, appointed a committee to draw up a remonstrance to the Lord Deputy, concerning his Majesty's promise; particularly, in relation to the enquiry into defective titles. In that remonstrance (a), they set forth (1), " That sensibly apprehending the manifold inconveniences that had befallen the kingdom, through the uncertainty of estates, occasioned by the embezzling, burning, and defacing of records, in times loose, and uncertain, troubled with continual war, until the beginning of his late Majesty's happy reign; and increased by the negligence, or ignorance of sundry persons, heretofore employed in passing of patents and estates from the crown; whereby many errors in law crept into these grants, whereof divers indigent persons, with eagle-eyes piercing thereinto, commonly took advantage, to the utter overthrow of many noble and deserving persons, who, for valuable considerations of service to the crown, or for money, or for both, honourably and fairly acquired their estates. That, therefore, finding in

L. themselves

(1) Strafford's State Letters, Vol. i.

(a) " The Peers also complained loudly of public grievances; pressed for the confirmation of the Royal graces; were particularly urgent for establishing the article, which confined the King's claim on their lands to a retrospect of sixty years; and frequently mentioned the Royal promise, in a manner highly offensive to an administration resolved that it should not be fulfilled." Lel. Hist. Irel. Vol. iii. p. 20.

themselves a sensible feeling of these and other grievances, they had received unspeakable pleasure from his Majesty's princely care, and tender affection towards them, expressed in the graces transmitted over by their last agents, and on his Royal word, the best of assurances, and his princely signature, which he had been graciously pleased to pass unto them, to cause the said graces to be enacted in the next ensuing parliament; that they could not sufficiently discharge their duty to his Majesty, or the trust reposed in them by their country, unless they were careful in these great affairs, to conserve the honour of his Majesty's word, in that respect, passed unto them his people, who had heretofore, by their said agents, presented a free gift of one hundred and twenty thousand pounds to his Majesty, and one hundred and fifty thousand pounds loan-money, or contribution, by them forgiven; and forty thousand pounds in these two last years, contributed by the country, amounting in the total, to three hundred and ten thousand pounds, exceeding in proportion, their abilities, and the precedents of past ages, &c. Wherefore, they most humbly prayed, that his Lordship would place the statute 21st Jacobi, entitled an act for the general quiet of the subject against concealments, in the first transmission of laws into England; the said grace being particularly promised by his Majesty, approved by both the Councils of estate in England and Ireland, and published in all the counties of Ireland, at the general assizes; and most expected of all the other graces. And that he would please to certify their universal consent, and much longing desire, to have the said statute of 21st Jacobi, and the rest of the said graces, perpetuated by acts to be passed in that parliament." This remonstrance was presented to his Lordship by Sir George Ratcliffe, Knight, Master of the Rolls, Sir James Ware, Knight, Mr. Serjeant Barry, and eight other respectable members.

" THE (2) improvement of the King's revenue, was the colour made use of by certain projectors, to obtain commissions of enquiry into defective titles; the great benefit of which, was generally to accrue to these projectors, or discoverers, whilst the King was content with an *(b)* inconsiderable proportion of land, or a small advance of the reserved rent *(c)*." One case of this kind (3), Mr.

(2) Carte's Orm. Vol. i. fol. 27.   (3) Ib.

(b) " The yearly rent reserved to the King, (in the plantation of Wexford) was five pounds for every thousand acres granted the English; and six pounds six shillings and eight-pence, for every thousand acres granted to the natives." Desid. Curios. Hibern. Vol. ii. p. 390-1.

(c) " The commissioners appointed to distribute these lands, scandalously abused their trusts; and by fraud, or violence, deprived the natives of those possessions, which the King had reserved for them." Ld. Hist. of Irel. Vol. ii. p. 467.

Mr. Carte has selected out of many others, which contains in it such a scene of iniquity and cruelty, that considering it in all its circumstances, it is scarce to be paralleled in the history of any age, or country. The case I mean, is that of the Byrne's, in the county of Wicklow, who were robbed of large estates, by Sir William Parsons and his fellow-commissioners, on pretence of this enquiry into defective titles. These State-harpies made use of every means of force and fraud, to accomplish their designs; having even tortured some witnesses, to make them swear for their purposes; and by promises of pardon, and other corrupt methods, procured thieves, traytors, and other convict criminals, to give false testimony for the same end; all which, these wretches afterwards, publickly confessed at their deaths (4).

CHAP. X.

The Commons require an Answer to their Remonstrance.

ON the 4th of November, 1634, commenced the second session of this parliament (1); and on the 12th an order was passed, "that Mr. Speaker and the whole house should attend the Lord Deputy, humbly to desire his Lordship's answer to the petition of remonstrance, formerly presented to his Lordship, either in writing, or otherwise, as his Lordship should think fit."

The return made by the Deputy, on that occasion, was by no means suitable to so respectful an application. He had already resolved (2) to "give them an answer, round and clear, as such as would stifle all replications." He, therefore, called some of them before him, and told them plainly (3), " That he would not transmit to England the statute 21st Jacobi; that such refusal was his own, their request never having been so much as sent over by him; that passing this act was not good, and expedient for the kingdom at that time; and so they were to rest satisfied, without stirring any more. As to that particular, as a thing which could not, nor would not be departed from." For the clearing of the King's honour, so essentially concerned in this contest, his Lordship had, with some difficulty, brought over the Council to represent to his Majesty (4), " That he was not bound, either in conscience, justice, or honour,

(4) See Carte's Orm. Vol. i.

(1) Strafford's State Letters, ib.   (2) Ib. fol. 338.   (3) Ib.   (4) Ib.   (5) Ib.

honour, to perform the folemn promife he had made to thefe people, for the valuable confideration before-mentioned."

When, on the 27th of November, his Lordſhip's anſwer to their remonſtrance was reported to the Commons, the Catholic members, who were principally, if not ſolely, aggrieved by the enquiry into defective titles, " were ſo ill to pleaſe (5)," ſays Wentworth himſelf, " that they loſt all temper, and broke forth into ſuch forward ſullenneſs, as was ſtrange; rejecting, hand over head, every other bill that was offered them, from his Majeſty and the ſtate."

The bills here alluded, were the two ſtatutes of Uſes and Wills (6), " By which, ſays Mr. Carte, " the Roman Catholics imagined, and not *(a)* without reaſon, that their religion would in time be affected, and by the due execution thereof, be at laſt utterly extinguiſhed, by their putting it in his Majeſty's power, to have the minors of the chief families of the kingdom, educated in the communion of the church of England. Theſe bills were, however, at length paſſed in that ſeſſion (7); and the Catholics ever afterwards conſidered them as heavy grievances, and had an eye to them, in all the complaints which they exhibited, upon occaſion, againſt the court of wards."

CHAP. XI.

A Convocation of the Clergy of Ireland.

BUT the Roman Catholics of Ireland were not the only objects of the Deputy's deſpotiſm and controul. The Proteſtant Archbiſhops, Biſhops, and other clergy, then aſſembled in convocation, with the famous Primate Uſher at their head, crouched and groaned under his more than Papal dominion. Lord Wentworth had diſcovered, that the generality of that clergy were

(5) Ib.   (6) Carte's Orm. Vol. i.   (7) Ib.

(a) " Theſe laws could not be agreeable to the recuſants, becauſe they empowered the King to have minors educated from their early years in the communion of the eſtabliſhed church." Lel. Hiſt. Irel. Vol. iii. p. 24. And becauſe Strafford had promiſed, in his ſpeech to that parliament, " that religion ſhould not be touched upon." State Let, Vol. i. p. 305.

were ſtrongly *(a)* inclined to (1) puritaniſm; and therefore he reſolved, in concert with Archbiſhop Laud (2), to compel them " to receive, implicitly, without examination, or debate," the canons, as well as the articles, of the church of England; a kind of condeſcenſion, which for the manner, as well as matter, they were exceedingly loath to yield to. It may not, perhaps, be unentertaining to the reader, to find ſome account here of this extraordinary tranſaction, from his Lordſhip's own letter to the Archbiſhop, on that occaſion.

" I FOUND (3)," ſays he, " the Lower Houſe of convocation had appointed a ſelect committee, to conſider the canons of the church of England; and that they did proceed in the examination, without conferring at all with the Biſhops; that they had gone through the book of canons, and noted in the margin, ſuch as they allowed with an A; and on the others, they had put a D, which ſtood for Deliberandum; that into the fifth article they had brought the articles of Ireland, to be allowed and received, under pain of excommunication; and that they had drawn up their canons into a body.

" I INSTANTLY ſent for Dean *(b)* Andrews, that reverend Clerk, who ſate, forſooth, in the chair of this committee; requiring him to bring along with him the aforeſaid book of canons, ſo noted in the margin, together with the draught he was to preſent, that afternoon, to the Houſe.

" BUT

---

(1) Strafford's State Letters.   (2) Id. ib. Vol. iii. fol. 381.   (3) Id. ib. Vol. i. fol. 342.

(a) " They not only ſung the pſalms after the Geneva-tune, but expounded the text to the Geneva-ſenſe." Strafford's State Let. Vol. i.

(b) Dean of Limerick. Lord Wentworth was very angry with this clergyman; and the puniſhment he intended for him, was ſomewhat ſingular. " If," ſays he, in a letter to Laud on this occaſion, " your Lordſhip thinks Doctor Andrews is to blame, and that you would chaſtiſe him for it, make him Biſhop of Ferns and Laughlin, to have it without any other commendam, than as the laſt Biſhop had it; and then I aſſure you, he ſhall leave better behind him." For that Biſhoprick, it ſeems, was then " ſo ſaddled and ſpur-gauled, (they are Wentworth's own words) that, if the devil himſelf were the rider, he could not make well worſe of it, than it was already." State Let. The Dean, however, accepted this preferment, with great thankfulneſs. " His Lordſhip elect," ſays the Deputy of him ſometime after, " gave us a farewell ſermon this Lent, that had failed ſurely, for a lean one it was; only he commended the times, and ſaid, How long! How long! have we heretofore expected preferment, and miſſed of it. But now, God be praiſed, we have it. By my troth," adds Wentworth, " they were his very words; and I had much ado to forbear laughing outright, that underſtood, how he miſtook even theſe times in this point, which did not intend this Biſhoprick to him for a preferment, but rather as a diſcipline. Yet he is a good child, and kiſſeth the rod; ſo you ſee it was not a correction ill beſtowed upon him." State Let. Vol. i.

"But (4) when I had opened the book, and ran over the deliberandums in the margin, I confefs, I was not fo much moved fince I came into Ireland. I told him, certainly, not a Dean of Limerick, but an Ananias, had been there in fpirit, if not in body, with all the fraternities, and conventicles of Amfterdam; and that I was afhamed, and fcandalized, at it beyond meafure. I therefore faid, he fhould leave the book and draught with me; and then I did command him, upon his allegiance, to report nothing to the Houfe from that committee, till he heard from me again; being thus nettled, I gave prefent directions for a meeting, and warned the Primate, the Bifhops of Meath, Kilmore, Raphoe, and Derry, together with Dean Lefly, the Prolocutor, and all thofe, who had been of the committee, to be with me the next morning.

"Then I publickly told them, how unlike clergymen, that owed canonical obedience to their fuperiors, they had proceeded in their committee; how unheard of a part it was, for a few petty Clerks to make articles of faith, without the privity, or confent of the ftate, or the Bifhops; and what a fpirit of Brownifm, and contradiction, I obferved in their deliberandums; but thefe heady and arrogant courfes, they muft know, I was not to endure, nor, if they were difpofed to be frantic, in this dead and cold feafon of the year, would fuffer them either to be mad in their convocations, or pulpits."

After this, his Lordfhip declared to them all, "That no other queftion fhould be propofed at their meeting, but that for allowing, and receiving, the articles of England, without admitting any other difcourfe at all; for that he would not endure that the articles of the church of England fhould be difputed. And finally," proceeds his Lordfhip, " becaufe there fhould be no queftion in the canon that fhould be voted, I defired the Lord Primate would be pleafed to frame it, and fend it to me, for my perufal; after which, I would fend the Prolocutor a draught of the canon, to be propounded in a letter of his own.

"This meeting thus broke, there were fome hot fpirits, fons of thunder, amongft them, who moved, they fhould petition for a free fynod, but in fine, they could not agree among themfelves, who fhould put the bell about the Cat's neck; fo this likewife vanifhed."

(4) Id. ib. fol. 342.

As for Primate Usher's part in this transaction (5), "It is very true," says his Lordship (c), "for all his silence, it was not possible, but he knew how near they were to have brought in those articles of Ireland, to the infinite disturbance and scandal of the church, as I conceive. And certainly, he could be content, I had been surprised; but he is so learned a Prelate, and so good a man, as, I beseech your Grace, it may never be imputed to him."

But to proceed with his Lordship's narrative. "The Primate accordingly framed the canon, which I," says he, "not so well approving, drew up one myself, more after the words of the canon in England, and then sent it to him. His Grace came instantly to me, and told me, he feared the canon would not pass in that form, as I had made it, but he was hopeful, as he had drawn it up, it might. He besought me therefore, to think a little better of it; but I confess, having taken a little jealousy, that his proceedings were not open and free to those ends I had my eye upon, it was too late, either to persuade, or affright me; I told his Lordship I was resolved to put it to them, in these very words: Only, for order's sake, I desired his Lordship would vote this canon first, in the Upper House of convocation, without any delay: then I wrote a letter to Dean Leslie, with the canon inclosed; which accordingly, that afternoon was unanimously voted; first with the Bishops, and then with the rest of the clergy, excepting one man, who singly did deliberate upon receiving the articles of England."

This was, perhaps, the highest exertion of lay-ecclesiastical (6) authority, that was ever known in these kingdoms. For, as by this canon, excommunication is expressly denounced against all those, who should affirm, that, "The articles of the church of England were such, as they might not, with

---

(5) Id. ib.   (6) Canons agreed upon in the synod begun, and holden in St. Patrick's church, Dublin. Anno 1634, p. 1.

(c) "The Primate is hugely against it. The truth is, I conceive, there are some puritan correspondants of his, that infuse these notions into his head." Strafford to Laud, ib. "Usher was head of the puritanic party of the clergy, and supported by the judgments and affections of almost all the Irish clergy." Lel. Hist. of Irel. Vol. iii. p. 28. He was afterwards one of the witnesses against Strafford at his trial; and had a pension from Cromwell, when he was made Protector. Ludlow tells us, "That he was desired by the fanatics, to deal faithfully with the King in the controversy that was between his Majesty and the parliament about episcopacy, according to his own judgment, which," says he, "they knew to be against it; but he answered, that if he should do as they proposed, he should ruin himself, and family, having a child, and many debts." Memoirs, Vol. i.

with a good conscience, subscribe unto;" and as the members of this convocation seem, upon the whole, to have thought them to be really such, (for otherwise, they would have more readily acquiesced in them). It appears, that these Bishops and clergy, were then obliged to subscribe to a canon, denouncing excommunication against themselves, in case they should ever after venture to publish their real opinion of these articles.

AN

AN HISTORICAL AND CRITICAL REVIEW OF THE CIVIL WARS IN IRELAND.

BOOK IV.

CHAP. I.

Lord Wentworth's *Proceedings upon the Enquiry into Defective Titles.*

WENTWORTH was well informed, what ample rewards two of his predecessors in the government of Ireland had obtained, by their activity and success, in carrying on the enquiry into defective titles (1); " One of them having had Lands bestowed upon him, which in the year 1633, were of no less than ten thousand pounds yearly value; and the other (2), ten thousand pounds in one gift." Hoping therefore, for the like, or greater, retribution, his Lordship exerted himself in that business, with uncommon resolution and vigour; " having procured inquisitions, upon feigned titles to estates, against many hundred years possession, whilst jurors refusing to find such offices, as being against their consciences, and the evidence, were censured to public infamy *(a)*, and the ruin of their estates."

(1) Sir Arthur Chichester. Straff. State Let. (2) Lord Faulkland. ib. Vol. ii. 294.

(a) " Needy projectors, and rapacious courtiers, still continued the scandalous traffic of pleading the King's title against the possessors of estates, of seizing their lands, or forcing them to grievous compositions." Lel. Hist. Irel. Vol. iii. p. 13.

The Deputy had chosen Conaught, and Ormond, to make his first essay upon, in this enquiry. His Lordship owns (3), " That he had often laboured to find a title in the crown to these countries, but was always foiled in the attempt." And, in several of his letters into England, he laments, that he could gather no light from thence into these matters. An accident, however, removed, soon after, his perplexity with regard to Ormond; but the nobility, and gentry, in some parts of Conaught, gave him great opposition. Wherefore (4), " Old records of state, and the memorials of antient monasteries, were ransacked, to ascertain the King's original title to that province; and the ingenuity of Court-lawyers was employed, to invalidate all patents granted to the possessors of lands there, from the reign of Queen Elizabeth." The Deputy even seemed to entertain thoughts of calling to his assistance the authority of his packed parliament, on that occasion (5). " This house," says he, in a letter to the Secretary, " is very well composed, so as the Protestants are the majority; and this may be of great use to confirm, and settle his Majesty's title to the plantations of Conaught and Ormond; for this you may be sure of, all the Protestants are for plantations, all the other against them; so as, these being the greater number, you can want no help they can give you therein. Nay, in case there be no title to be made good to these countries in the crown, yet should not I despair, forth of reasons of state, and for the strength and security of the kingdom, to have them passed to the King, by an immediate act of parliament."

CHAP. II.

The Earl of Ormond surrenders his Country to the King.

WE have already seen that, by the Earl of Ormond's spirited behaviour, in the beginning of this parliament, Wentworth conceived a particular friendship for him; which was so far mutual on the Earl's part, that he made a voluntary surrender of his country to the King, in whom otherwise (a) no title could be found to it. For this condescension, his Lordship was, by the Deputy's mediation, made a Privy-counsellor, in the room of Sir Pierce Crosby, lately sequestered from that board for no other cause, but his having voted in parliament against a bill, which Lord Wentworth had approved, and signed

(3) Id. ib. Vol. i. fol. 339. (4) Lel. ubi supra, p. 31. (5) Straff. State Let.

(a) " Seeing," says Wentworth on this occasion, " we have sped so well, where our title was borrowed, or at least supported by my Lord of Ormond, and, indeed, could not have stood alone upon the King's evidence, I am most confident, we shall have like success for Clare." State Let. Vol. ii. fol. 93.

signed in the Privy-council (1). " There were twenty-eight Counsellors present, when he was sequestered, and not one dissenting voice, but all for the sequestration."

The surrender of Ormond was soon followed by that of Limerick, and Clare; but the people of Conaught were not all so complaisant; altho' they too had some leading examples of that kind in their own province.

About this time Lord Wentworth acquainted his Majesty (2), " That he should be able to find for him, a just and honourable title to Conaught, against all opposition; and that the acquisition to his Majesty, in that province alone, would amount to no less than an hundred and twenty thousand acres *(b)*." It is but natural to enquire, by what means a just and honourable title could be so suddenly found, which, but a few months before, seemed to be altogether despaired of. Lord Wentworth himself shall satisfy the reader's curiosity, in that respect.

Before his Lordship left Dublin, to hold this court of inquisition in Conaught, he had given orders to his managers there, that gentlemen of the best estates and understandings, in the different counties, should be returned on the juries, which were to be held in the first trials of defective titles. This he did, not as one might imagine, on a supposition of their greater knowledge, integrity, or honour; but because, as he says himself (3), " This being a leading case for the whole province, it would set a great value, in their estimation, upon the goodness of the King's title, if found by those persons of quality." And on the other hand, if the King's title should not be found, or, as he expresses it (4), " If the jury should prevaricate," he would be sure then to have " persons of such means, as might answer to the King in a round fine in the castle-chamber; and because the fear of that fine would be apter to produce the desired effect in such persons, than in others, who had little or nothing to lose."

(1) Id. ib. Vol. i. fol. 350.   (2) Id. ib.   (3) ib. Vol. i. fol. 442.   (4) ib.

(b) " Wentworth's Project was nothing less," says Leland, " than to subvert the title to every estate, in every part of Conaught; and to establish a new plantation through that whole province. A project, which when first proposed in the late reign, was received with horror, and amazement." Hist. of Irel. Vol. iii. p. 30.

CHAP. III.

The Deputy holds his Court of Inquisition.

HIS Lordship having thus prepared matters, went himself to the Abbey of Boyle, in the County of Roscommon (1); " Where," says he, " finding that divers affrights had been put into the people's minds, concerning his Majesty's intention in this work, I sent for half a dozen of the principal gentlemen amongst them; and in the presence of the commissioners, desired that they would acquaint the rest of the country, that the end of my coming was, the next day, to execute his Majesty's commission for finding a clear and undoubted title in the crown, to the province of Conaught, proposing to begin first with the county of Roscommon; wherein, nevertheless, to manifest his Majesty's justice and honour, I thought fit to let them know, that it was his Majesty's gracious pleasure, that any man's counsel should be fully and willingly heard, in defence of their respective rights; being a favour never before afforded to any, upon taking these kind of inquisitions; as also, if there was any thing else they desired, that I was ready to hear them, and would return them a fair and equal answer thereunto; as by his Majesty I had been strictly enjoined; and to afford his good people all respect and freedom, in the setting forth, and defence of their several rights and claims (2). With this," continues he, " I left them marvelously well satisfied, for a few good words please them more than can be imagined.

" The next morning, however," adds his Lordship, " the gentlemen of the country petitioned, that the inquisition might be deferred to a longer time, they being unprovided; which I refused, as I had caused notice of it, by a Scire Facias, to be issued from the Chancery, twenty days before; which was more also than had formerly been accustomed, in cases of that nature. So presently," proceeds he, " we went to the place appointed, read the commission, called and swore the jury, and so on with our work."

Sir Lucas Dillon was foreman of this jury, and seems to have behaved, on that occasion, entirely to the Deputy's *(a)* liking. Nevertheless, after the lawyers

(1) ib.   (2) ib. fol. 442.

(a) " In truth," says he of this gentleman, " he deserves to be extraordinarily well dealt withal; and so he shall be, if it pleases his Majesty to leave him to me." State Let. Vol. ii. fol. 444.

lawyers on both fides, had done speaking, Lord Wentworth made a speech to the jury, which did not at all encourage them to use that freedom which he had promised to allow them, in returning an impartial verdict; but on the contrary, rather convinced them, that his Lordship had already pre-judged the cause against their countrymen. For, among other things, he told them, " That his Majesty was indifferent, whether they found for him, or no; that he had directed him to press nothing upon them, where the path to his right lay so open, and plain before him; but yet, that of himself, and as one that must ever wish prosperity to their nation, he desired them first to descend into their own consciences, to take them to counsel, and there they should find the evidence for the crown clear, and conclusive. Next to beware, how they appeared resolved, or obstinate against so manifest a truth; or how they let slip out of their hands, the means to weave themselves into the Royal thoughts, and care of his Majesty, thro' a chearful, and ready acknowledgment of his right, and a due and full submission thereunto. That if they would be inclined to truth, and do best for themselves, they were undoubtedly to find the title for the King. But, if they were passionately resolved, to go over all bounds to their own will; and, without respect at all to their own good, to do that which were simply best for his Majesty, then he should advise them roughly and pertinaciously, to deny to find any title at all; and there," says he, " I left them to chant together, as they called it, over their evidence; and the next day, they found the King's title, without scruple or hesitation."

CHAP. IV.

The Deputy's Severity towards the Jury of the County of Galway.

THE juries of the counties of Sligo, and Mayo, followed the example set them by that of Roscommon; but the jury of the county of Galway was, by no means, so complying; and they suffered grievously on that account.

For, upon their refusing to find a title in the crown to the estates of their countrymen, Lord Wentworth made use of some of his just, and honourable means to convince them of their mistake (1). " We bethought ourselves," says he, on this occasion, " of a course to vindicate his Majesty's honour and justice, not only against the persons of the jurors, but also against the sheriff for returning so insufficient, indeed, we conceive, so packed a jury; and

(1) State Letters.

and therefore, we fined the sheriff in a thousand pounds to his Majesty." The mulct on the jurors was much greater (2). " They were fined *(a)* four thousand pounds each; their estates were seized, and themselves imprisoned, till the fines were paid." Such was the sentence pronounced against them in the castle-chamber, to which his Lordship had bound them over; and where (3), " he conceived it was fit, that their pertinacious carriage should be followed with all just severity."

What was then understood by " just severity," may be collected from an extract of the grievances which, towards the end of his administration, the Commons voted " real;" and which, in one article, seems to allude to this very case, viz (4). " Jurors, who gave their verdict according to their consciences, were censured in the castle-chamber in great fines: sometimes pillored with loss of ears, and bored thro' the tongue, and sometimes marked in the forehead with an hot iron, with other infamous punishments."

And although he had publickly promised, " That their counsel on this occasion should be freely, and willingly heard, in defence of their respective rights:" Yet he scrupled not to take severe vengeance on two eminent lawyers, who ventured to plead in their behalf; and all his Lordship's proceedings against them, and against the sheriff, and jurors before-mentioned, were afterwards (5) approved of by his Majesty.

Another of his just, and honourable means to attain this end (as he himself informs us) (6), " Was to enquire out fit men to serve upon juries; and to treat with such as would give furtherance to the King's title." He, besides, proposed the raising of four thousand horse (7), as good lookers-on, while the plantations were settling. And lastly, he prevailed upon the King to bestow four shillings in the pound, upon the Lord Chief Justice and Chief Baron, forth of the first yearly rent, raised upon the commission of defective titles; " which," as he afterwards says, " he had found, upon observation, to be the best given that ever was; for that by these means, they did intend that business, with as much care and diligence, as if it were their own private; and that every four shillings, once paid, would better his Majesty's revenue four pounds."

Against

(2) ib. (3) ib. (4) Common. Jour. Vol. i. (5) Straff. State Let. Vol. ii. fol. 465.
(6) Id. ib. Vol. i. fol. 339. (7) Id. ib. Vol. i. fol. 442. (8) Id. ib. Vol. ii. fol. 41.

(a) " The jurors of Galway were to remain in prison, till each of them paid his fine of four thousand pounds, and acknowledged his offence in court, upon his knees." Lel. Hist. Irel. Vol. iii. p. 32.

AGAINST the Deputy's predatory defigns, thus planned and executed, the natives were deftitute of all manner of defence (9). " No title in the fubject could ftand againft his claim. At firft none was held good, but that which was founded on letters patent; yet when even letters patent were produced, as in moft cafes they were, none were allowed *(b)* valid, nor yet fought to be legally avoided; fo that one hundred and fifty letters patent were fet afide in one morning; which courfe was continued, until all the letters patent in the kingdom, except a few, were declared void.

CHAP. V.

Further Diftreffes of the People of Conaught.

"THE gentlemen of Conaught," fays (1) Mr. Carte, " laboured under a particular hardfhip on this occafion; for their not having enrolled their patents, and furrenders of the 13th Jacobi, (which was what alone rendered their titles defective) was not their fault, but the neglect of a clerk entrufted by them. For they had paid near three thoufand pounds to the offices at Dublin, for the enrollment of thefe furrenders and patents, which was never made. There was an act of ftate made in Lord Grandifon's time, and dated May 14th, 1618, full in their favour, and confirming their poffeffions; and they had paid great fums of money for it into the Exchequer; they were quietly fettled in their lands, and paid the King his compofition better than any other part of the kingdom. It was hard, in thofe circumftances to turn them out of their eftates, upon a meer nicety of law, which ought to be tenderly made ufe of in derogation of the honour, and faith of the King's broad feal."

So general, and lafting, were the terrors arifing from thefe fevere proceedings of the Deputy, that in 1637, the whole body of the gentry of the county
of

---

(9) Remonft. from Trim.

(1) Life of Orm. Vol. i.

(b) The Deputy, and commiffioners of plantation, in their public difpatch to Secretary Cook, on this fubject, confeffed, " That in former plantations in Ireland, all men claiming by letters patent had the full benefit of them, either in enjoying the lands granted them, or other lands equivalent thereunto, whether their letters patent were valid, or invalid. And indeed," add they, " in thofe (former) plantations, that favour might better be yielded, where the lands claimed by letters patent, were not in any great, or confiderable proportion, than here, where almoft all the lands falling under plantation are granted, or mentioned to be granted, by letters patent." Straff, State Let. Vol. ii. fol. 139.

of Galway offered to make a furrender of their eftates to the crown, and, for that purpofe, fent a letter of attorney to the Earl *(a)* of Clanrickard, then at London (2), figned by an hundred and feventy-five perfons of the beft quality in the county. " At the fame time, the ftill imprifoned fheriff, and jurors, inftead of feeking redrefs, petitioned, but in vain, for pardon (3); offering to acknowledge the Deputy's juftice, and their own errors of judgment, upon condition only, that they and the reft, might be put upon the fame footing with the other planted countries;" for (4), in thefe cafes, the general rule was, that a fourth part of their land fhould be taken from the natives, with an increafe of rent upon the remainder; " but the county of Galway, on account of its former refractorinefs, was planted at a double rate, fo that they loft half."

For Lord Wentworth was fo far from being fatisfied with this fubmiffive petition, and offer, that he infifted upon a public acknowledgment from thefe jurors of their having committed, not only an error in judgment, but even actual perjury, in the verdict they had given; which being (5) refufed by them, he, befides planting their country at the rate before-mentioned, procured an order from the King, that their agents at London, fhould be fent prifoners to Dublin, to be tried before himfelf in the caftle-chamber, for having dared to patronife their caufe. Thefe feverities however, raifed no fmall apprehenfions in fome that were about the King, and even in the King himfelf (6), " left they might difaffect the people of Ireland; and difpofe them to call over the Irifh regiments, from Flanders, to their affiftance."

About this time, " the Bifhops, and their Chancellors, began (7) again to queftion the Catholics, and to lay heavy fines upon them, for their chriftenings and marriages." But the Deputy wifely confidered (8), " that it would be too much, at once, to diftemper them by bringing plantations upon them, and difturb them in the exercife of their religion; and very inconfiderate to move in the latter, till the former was fully fettled, and by that means, the Proteftant party become much the ftronger, which he did not then conceive it to be." Finding, therefore, that thefe proceedings of the Bifhops had very much difquieted the Catholics, and given them terrible apprehenfions of an

inftant

---

(2) Strafford's State Letters, Vol. ii. fol. 25.   (3) Id. ib.   (4) Id. ib. Vol. ii. fol. 35.   (5) ib. fol. 36.
(6) ib. fol. 39.   (7) Id. ib.   (8) ib. vol. ii. fol. 39.

(a) It was in Lord Clanrickard's houfe, that Wentworth held this court of inquifition ; " And the death of that Lord, (which happened foon after) enflamed the popular odium againft the Deputy. It was imputed to the vexation conceived by this nobleman at the attempts againft his property by an infolent governor, who poffeffed himfelf of the Earl's houfe at Portumna ; and, in his hall, held that court, which impeached his title to his Lands." Lel. Hift. Irel.

inftant perfecution, he wrote to England for orders, to put a ftop to them (9), " As," fays he, " 'tis a courfe which alone will never bring them to church; but is rather an engine to draw money out of their pockets, than to raife a right belief in their hearts."

C H A P. VI.

The Courts of Wards, and high Commiffion in Ireland.

ALL this while, complaints were every where heard of grievances, arifing from the court of Wards, and that of the high commiffion. The former was a new court, never known in Ireland till the 14th of James I. " It (1) had no warrant from any law or ftatute, as that in England had." Sir William Parfons, by whom it was firft projected, was appointed mafter of it, a man juftly, and univerfally hated by the Irifh. And fuch were the illegal and arbitrary proceedings of that court, that (2), " The heirs of Catholic noblemen, and other Catholics, were deftroyed in their eftates, bred in diffolution and ignorance; their parents debts unfatisfied, their fifters, and younger brothers, left wholly unprovided for; the antient appearing tenures of mefne Lords unregarded; eftates valid in law, and made for valuable confiderations, avoided againft law; and the whole land ·filled with frequent fwarms of efcheators, feudatories, perfuivants, and others, by authority of that court."

THE unlimited power, and great oppreffion of the high commiffion-court, which was ftill more recent in Ireland, than the court of wards, was not lefs grievoufly *(a)* complained of by the Catholics, on account of (3), " the incapacity thereby contracted, for all offices and employments; their difability to fue out livery of their eftates, without taking the oath of fupremacy; the fevere penalties of various kinds, inflicted by that court on all thofe of their religion (4), they being an hundred to one more than thofe of any other religion; in which refpect, the cafe of Ireland was very different from that of England, or Scotland, where there was fcarce one Roman Catholic to a thoufand Proteftants."

YET,

(9) ib.   (1) Carte's Orm. Vol. i.   (2) Remonft. from Trim.   (3) ib.   (4) Carte's Orm. Vol. i.

(a) " Thefe regulations in the ecclefiaftical ·fyftem were followed by an eftablifhment too odious, and therefore too dangerous to be attempted during the feffions of parliament, that of an high-commiffion court, which was erected in Dublin, after the Englifh model, with the fame formality, and the fame tremendous powers." Lel. Hift. Irel. Vol. ii. p 28.

Yet, in the midst of so many depredations, and pressures, the Catholics of Ireland gave such unquestionable proofs of their loyalty, and dutiful affection to the crown of England (and that at a very critical juncture,) as cannot, perhaps, be paralleled in the history of any other people, under the like circumstances.

These proofs were exhibited in that parliament, which met at Dublin, in 1640, in order to raise large supplies towards suppressing the rebellion in Scotland, which had then risen to a formidable height. Their zeal on this occasion, was honourably attested by several Privy-councellors, members of that parliament (5), " Persons," says Wentworth himself, " best able to satisfy, and in themselves most to be trusted." Among these, I find Sir William Parsons, Sir John Borlace, Sir Charles Coote, and others, whose malevolence, and enmity to the Irish in general, were well known, and confessed; and whose testimony, therefore, in their favour, as to this particular fact, cannot reasonably be suspected.

" After (6) the proposal of such acts of grace, and advantage to the subject," say these Privy-counsellors in their letter to Secretary Windebank, on this occasion, " as we conceived most fit to lead, in order to the propounding of the six subsidies; these six subsidies were demanded for his Majesty; whereupon, some of the natives declared that six, or more, were fit to be given; it being apparent, that the peace and safety of the kingdom, were become so nearly concerned. Some also of them said, that his Majesty should have a fee simple of subsidies in their estates on such occasions, for the honour of his person, and safety of his kingdoms; that it was fit to be done, though with leaving themselves nothing but hose and doublet. Some of them, with much earnestness, after forward expressions of readiness towards advancing the business, concluded that, as his Majesty was the best of Kings, so this people should strive to be ranked among the best of subjects.

" Thus," continues the Privy-counsellors letter, " every of them seeming in a manner to contend, who should shew most affection and forwardness, to comply with his Majesty's occasions; and all of them expressing, even with passion, how much they abhorred and detested, the Scotch covenanters; and how readily every man's hand ought to be laid on his sword, to assist the King in reducing them, by force to obedience, they desired that themselves, and others of this nation, might have the honour to be employed in this expedition;

(5) Straff. State Letters, Vol. ii. fol. 398.   (6) ib.

tion; and declared, with very great demonstration of chearful affection, that their hearts contained mines of subsidies for his Majesty; that twenty subsidies, if their abilities were equal to their desires, were too little to be given to so sacred a Majesty.

"In the end, considering how unable they were, without too much pressure to them, to advance more, at this time, they humbly besought, that by the Lord Lieutenant's interposition, four subsidies might be accepted from them; yet with this declaration, made by them with as much demonstration of loyalty, as ever nation, or people expressed towards a King, that if more than four subsidies should be requisite, and the occasions of the war continued, they would be ready to grant more; or to lay down their lives, and estates, at his Majesty's feet, to further his royal design, for correction of the disordered factions in Scotland. And this they did declare with general acclamations, and signs of joy and contentment, even to the throwing up of their hats, lifting of their hands."

CHAP. VII.

Some invidious Reflections on the foregoing Passage considered.

BUT we are told by some reputable historians, that, in the very next session, the untoward behaviour of these Commons discovered the *(a)* insincerity of their late professions; that they (1), "who had but just before devoted their lives, and possessions, to the service of the best of Kings, grew cold, querulous, and suspicious; objected to the rates of assessment though the same which had been used in the late parliament; and in short, that a general combination was formed, throughout the kingdom, to prevent the levying any money, until a new manner of taxation should be settled by the parliament; or in other words, until they should annul and rescind the late money-bill, enacted with such remarkable zeal and unanimity."

The late parliament here alluded to, was that which had met in Dublin, in 1634, under Lord Wentworth; who, as we have already seen, had formed, and

---

(1) Lel. Hist. of Ireland. Vol. ii.

(a) Lord Wentworth, who was certainly a more competent judge of that matter, than any historian that has since appeared, says on this occasion, " It is hardly to be believed, what a forwardness there is in this people to serve in this expedition (against the Scots) certainly, they will sell themselves to the last farthing, before they deny any thing, which can be asked of them, in order to that." State Let. Vol.

and managed it entirely for his own and his master's private purposes (2). "His Lordship regarded Ireland as a conquered kingdom, and from that conception deduced a consequence, at once rediculous, and detestable, that the subjects of this country, without distinction, had forfeited the rights of men and citizens, and for whatever they were permitted to enjoy, depended solely on the Royal grace." Agreeably to these sentiments, he exercised a despotic, and indeed, tyrannous power over that parliament (3). "With one voice the commons voted a grant of six subsidies, four for paying the debts of the establishment, two for buying rents and pensions; not that the uses were determined by a formal appropriation: they entrusted the management of their supply solely to the Deputy, requesting only by petition, that it might be appropriated to these purposes."

Such were the proceedings alluded to, as a proper precedent for the Commons, in 1640, to have followed, in the manner of rating their supplies. But these Commons thought very differently of that precedent; for Lord Wentworth, now Earl of Strafford, having been recalled into England, and having left directions with his Deputy, Wandesford (4), "His Lordship's friend and ally," to issue the same instructions, for settling the rates of taxation, with regard to the present subsidies, as had been formerly issued concerning those granted by parliament, in 1634, (which was accordingly done), the Commons thought fit to make use of the liberty, which they now were possessed of by his absence; and knowing that the former grants were (5) "exorbitant and oppressive," ventured to alter the mode of assessing three of these subsidies; declaring, at the same time (6), "that in consideration of his Majesty's many, and present occasions, the first of the four subsidies should be levied according to the instructions issued by the Deputy, and Council; not in deference to these instructions, but meerly by their own authority, and direction; and that neither these instructions, nor what was done in the late parliament, (1634) with respect to the subsidies then raised, should be a guide, or precedent, in levying the three other subsidies, which they ordered to be raised in a moderate, equal, and parliamentary way. They likewise ordered (7), "as the second subsidy was not payable till December, and as it might conduce to his Majesty's service, to hasten the payment of the third also, that both should be paid together, on the first of December 1640; six months earlier, than the third subsidy had been made payable by the original grant."

This

(2) Id. ib.   (3) Id. ib.   (4) Id. ib.   (5) Id. ib.   (6) Com. Journ. vol. i.   (7) ib.

This particular care, to haften the payment of the firft and third fubfidies indicated, one would imagine, in thefe Commons, fome attention to his Majefty's fervice. But his Majefty, it feems, was perfuaded to think otherwife; for we are told, that he looked upon this proceeding to be fo ridiculous and infolent, that he ordered (8), " with a peevifh impatience," the leaf, in which this refolution was inferted, to be torn from their journals; " which order was accordingly executed by the Deputy, on the 19th of November 1640."

But the King was foon brought to a right way of thinking, concerning this particular. For on the 4th of January following, he wrote to the Irifh Council, (and ordered his letter to be publickly read in the Houfe)(9), " that having, by a committee of the Commons of Ireland, received fatisfaction, both in their loyalty and affection unto him; and alfo in thofe matters, which induced him to require his Deputy to vacate an order made, concerning the levying of the fubfidies, granted in the fame parliament; he was then gracioufly pleafed, and did thereby authorize, and require them, to cauſe the inclofed (the vacated order) to be again inferted, and regiftered in the fame place, to continue, and be of equal force, as if the original had remained there."

From hence it appears, that thefe Commons were actuated by two very juft, and patriotic motives, viz. Oppofition to a meafure, confeffedly " exorbitant and oppreffive," and a laudable defire, to recover their antient conftitutional right of rating their own grants, which had been violently taken from them, in the preceding parliament. But how it could poffibly be inferred from fuch conduct, that they intended to annul, and refcind their late money-bill, or that they were united in a regular and determined fcheme of oppofition, for any difloyal, or unconftitutional purpofe, is, I think, very hard to be conceived.

(8) Lel. Hift. Irel. (9) Com. Journ. vol. i.

CHAP. VIII.

The Irish Commons' Encomium on the Earl of Strafford's Administration considered.

FOR the expedition against the Scottish rebels, Lord Strafford had raised an army in Ireland, consisting of about nine thousand men, eight thousand of which, were Irish Catholics. For his Lordship knew, and did attest, that in the support, or defence, of his Majesty's crown and dignity (1), " the Irish were as ready to venture their persons, as they were to open their purses."

" SIR (2) William St. Leger, Serjeant Major General of the army, having reviewed these troops at Carricfergus, saw such willingness and aptness in them, to learn their exercises; and that mettle and gallant appearance, which would recommend them to be chosen for a service where a crown lay at stake, made no scruple to pronounce, that considering how newly they had been raised, no Prince in the Christian world had, for their number, a better, and more orderly body of men in his service *(a)*."

LORD Strafford was extremely desirous to have the chief command of this army; but he was conscious, at the same time, that he was represented at court as a person odious to the people, of whom it was chiefly composed; in short (3), " as a Vizier, Bashaw, or any thing else, that might be worse; and as one hateful both to God and man." In order to remove that obstacle, he laboured, privately, to persuade the King (4), " that the Irish did not distaste him so much, as willingly to change him; or to desire any new Deputy in his stead; and, that if it were left to their choice, they would not have any other General but himself."

BUT his Lordship found means to procure a much more persuasive testimony, than his own, for this purpose; even a public and solemn attestation in his favour, from that House of Commons, which he had so often insulted and abused. For, in the preamble to the act of subsidies lately passed, we find the

---

(1) Straff. State Let. Vol. ii.   (2) Cart. Orm. vol. i. fol. 99.   (3) Straff. State Let. vol. ii.   (4) Id. ib.

(a) " The raising, cloathing, paying, and providing this army, by the latter end of September, 1640, when it was dispersed, cost 204057 l." Cart. Orm. vol. i. fol. 105.

the Commons [5], " returning thanks to his Majefty, for having placed over them, fo wife, juft, and vigilant a Governor; extolling his Lordfhip's fincere, and upright adminiftration of juftice, without partiality; his having increafed his Majefty's revenue, without the leaft hurt, or grievance to any of his Majefty's loving fubjects; and his care to relieve, and redrefs the poor and oppreffed."

" THERE could not be," fays Mr. [6] Carte, " an higher, and there has feldom been a jufter, elogium given of a Governor, and of his upright and impartial adminiftration, by any body of men, than was given of this Lord Lieutenant, and his adminiftration, by this Houfe of Commons; it was given nemine contradicente, and paffed with loud, and general acclamations of applaufe."

THUS we fee, that although this honourable teftimony had not, then, the wifhed for fuccefs, in faving his Lordfhip's perfon from the rage of his enemies, yet it has been fince more effectually made ufe of by hiftorians, to refcue his memory from that infamy, which his adminiftration of Ireland particularly, has brought upon it. But Mr. Carte has very imperfectly related another paffage, recorded in the fame journals of the Commons, from whence he took this elogium, viz. The folemn proteftation of thefe Commons againft it, (in which they were joined by the Lords) to this effect; that the [7] " aforefaid preamble to the act of fubfidies, was contrived, penned, and inferted fraudently, (without the privity of the Houfe,) either by the Earl of Strafford himfelf, or by fome other perfon, or perfons, advifers, procurors, or actors, of, and in, the manifold and general grievances, and oppreffions of his Majefty's kingdom of Ireland, by the direction and privity of the faid Earl, on purpofe to prevent and anticipate the juft, and univerfal complaints of his Majefty's faithful, dutiful, and loving fubjects, againft him." And they required their committee, then attending his Majefty, " to prefent unto him that their proteftation, and proofs thereof; and likewife, to prefent unto his Majefty, their humble requeft, that an act might be paffed in that parliament, for revoking, vacating, and taking from the records of parliament, the before-recited part of the preamble, concerning the Earl of Strafford."

THE reafon they affigned in that proteftation, for having fuffered this part of the preamble to pafs, when it was firft communicated to them, was [8], " that, before fuch time as that act, (having been formerly tranfmitted to England, and returned from thence,) was read, or known in the Houfe, the faid Earl of Strafford did declare, and fignify to both Houfes of parliament, his

[5] Com. Journ. vol. i.   [6] Orm. vol. i.   [7] Com. Journ.   [8] ib.

his Majesty's urgent and great occasions; and the near and approaching danger, that Ireland was suddenly to be invaded by the Scots; and thereupon, and not before, the said act was read, and made known in the House of Commons; and that their natural, and fervent zeal and devotion to his Majesty's service, and the fears of the said declared imminent danger, and the inconveniencies which they suspected might ensue, if they then had excepted against the said part of the preamble, concerning the Earl of Strafford, and had expected a new transmission, as a statute of force in this realm, doth require, did occasion, and enforce, their not then speaking, or protesting, against the said part of the preamble."

CHAP. IX.

Complaints of Grievances.

THE before-mentioned committee of parliament, attending the King in England, had presented a remonstrance of grievances which the Commons had voted (1), " of their own knowledge to be so clear, and manifest, that no place was left for denial of proof." These grievances were great, and numerous. Part of those recited in their journals, are " the scandalous extortions of the ecclesiastical courts, for old Popish rites and customs, condemned and renounced by those very persons, who then so greedily exacted the profits formerly annexed to them, which, it seems, they still deemed orthodox; great sums of money received by several Bishops, for commutation of penance, which they converted to their own use; the Lord Deputy's punishing the natives by fine, imprisonment, mutilation of members, pillory, or otherwise, arbitrarily, and without law; and making them forfeit their liberty, possessions, and inheritance, meerly for infringing an act of state, or proclamation; the sentencing the subjects to death, by martial law, in times of profound peace; the issuing quo warrantos out of the King's-bench, or Exchequer, against boroughs that antiently, and recently sent Burgesses to parliament; the censuring of jurors in the castle-chamber, that gave verdict according to their consciences, with mutilation of members, and other infamous punishments; the taking of the testimony of rebels, traitors, protected thieves, and other infamous persons, upon trials of men for their lives. And they particularly complained of the insecurity of their estates, by means of the enquiry into defective titles, which was still carried on with great rigour; humbly praying his Majesty, that he would be graciously pleased, to direct that bills might be drawn in the House of Commons, and transmitted from the Chief Governor, or Governors,

(1) ib.

vernors, and privy-council of Ireland, to be paſſed as acts of that parliament, for the redreſs of theſe grievances, and for the ſecurity of their eſtates, as their reſpective caſes, for their better aſſurance, ſhould require."

AFTER what has been now related, of the wretched condition of the Iriſh Catholicks, in this and the former reign, who can help wondering at Clarendon's ſtrange partiality, or ignorance, (which yet has been ſervily copied by all ſucceeding hiſtorians) when he confidently aſſerts (2), " That, at this very juncture of time, and for forty years before it, the ſtate of theſe Catholics affairs was as quiet and happy, as they themſelves could reaſonably wiſh it ; and that whatever their land, labour, and induſtry produced, was their own ; being free from fear of having it taken from them by the King, on any pretence whatſoever, without their own conſent."

IN compliance with the aforeſaid remonſtrance and petition of the Commons, his Majeſty ordered the Lords Juſtices, Parſons, and Borlace (3), " to aſſure his good ſubjects of Ireland, that his Princely promiſe, formerly paſſed unto them, (to redreſs theſe, and ſeveral other grievances) ſhould be ſpeedily performed ; and to that end, he required, that bills might be tranſmitted from their Lordſhips, and the Council, for ſecuring their eſtates, touching the limitation of his title, not to extend above three ſcore years."

CHAP. X.

The Remonſtrance of Grievances Vindicated.

IT has been of late objected, that this remonſtrance of grievances, was not fairly and deliberately voted in the Iriſh parliament ; but that, on the contrary, it was (1) " abruptly preſented to the Houſe, not ſuffered to be ſpoken to, and paſſed in the midſt of tumult and diſorder." But this objection ſhall be now proved to be nothing more than a partial and groundleſs ſurmiſe : for (2) " ſome of the grievances mentioned in it, had been preſented by parliament to the Deputy, in June preceding, as found real, and enormous, after many debates." And, as for thoſe now added, viz. the " tremendous powers" of the high commiſſion-court, the denial of the promiſed graces, &c. It is notorious, that they had been long before complained of, as intolerable, both in and out of parliament. It appears by the journals (3), " That

(2) Hiſt. of the Iriſh Rebel.   (3) Com. Journ. Vol. i.
(1) Lel. Hiſt. of Irel.   (2) Com. Journ. Vol. i.   (3) ib. vol. i.

" That a grand committee, was appointed to fit upon the grievances of the country, on the 12th of October, 1640; and that, on the 7th of the following month, an order was paffed, that the particular matters expreffed in the remonftrance in queftion, being thrice read, required prefent redrefs, and fhould be forthwith reprefented to the Right Honourable the Lord Deputy, by Mr. Speaker, and the whole Houfe." Another order was paffed on the 9th, " that Mr. Speaker, for the greater folemnity, fhould read the remonftrance twice, and that it fhould be afterwards prefented to the Lord Deputy." On the 11th, " a committee was appointed, confifting, among others, of the Vice-Treafurer, the Mafter of the Rolls, and the Chancellor of the Exchequer, to wait upon the Deputy, to know when he would give his anfwer to the remonftrance." And on the 12th, " a committee was again appointed, to attend his Lorfhip for his anfwer;" which appears then to have been, " that the Commons fhould confer with fome of the Lords of the Privy-council, (not, as has been (4) fuppofed, with the Houfe of Lords) concerning the nature of the grievances complained of." But to this conference, as being contrary to their privileges, the Commons refufed to confent (5); " in regard that the contents of their remonftrance, had been already voted in their Houfe, for grievances;" for which refufal, the Deputy prorogued them, on the fame 12th of November. And thus it evidently appears, that this remonftrance, inftead of being abruptly prefented to the Houfe, not fuffered to be fpoken to, and paffed in the midft of tumult and diforder, was agitated, for feveral days, with due deliberation and regularity, and at length agreed to, after many readings and debates.

C H A P. XI.

The immediate Caufe of the Infurrection, in 1641.

HAD his Majefty's commands before-mentioned, to the Lords Jufticcs, Parfons, and Borlace, to tranfmit bills for fecuring the eftates of the natives, and for confirming the other promifed graces, been duly executed, or rather not pofitively difobeyed, by their Lordfhips, the dreadful infurrection of the following year, either would not at all have happened, or would have been quickly fuppreffed. Such, at leaft, was his Majefty's opinion; as we find by his anfwer to a declaration of the Englifh Commons, on that occafion; for there he tells them (1), " that, if he had been obeyed in the Irifh affairs, before he went to Scotland, there had been no Irifh rebellion; or after it had begun, it would have been in a few months fuppreffed, if his directions

(4) Lel. Hift. Irel.   (5) ib.   (1) Reliq. Sac. Carolinæ, p. 273.

directions had been observed: for if the King had been suffered to perform his engagements to the Irish agents, and had disposed of the discontented Irish army beyond sea, there is nothing more clear, than that there could have been no rebellion in Ireland, because they had wanted both pretence, and means to have made one."

At this time, it was confidently reported in Ireland, that the Scottish army had threatened never to lay down their arms, till an uniformity of religion was established in the three kingdoms, and the Roman Catholic religion suppressed (2). "A letter was intercepted, coming from Scotland, to one Freeman of Antrim, giving an account, that a covenanting army was ready to come for Ireland, under the command of General Lesley, to extirpate the Roman Catholics of Ulster, and leave the Scots sole possessors of that province; and that, to this end, a resolution had been taken in their private meetings, and councils, to lay heavy fines upon such as would not appear at their kirk, for the first or second Sunday; and on failure the third, to hang, without mercy, all such as were obstinate, at their own doors."

The whole body of the Irish nobility and gentry, declared in their remonstrance at Trim, which was delivered, in due form, to his Majesty's commissioners, in March 1642, that previous to the insurrection (3), " certain dangerous and pernicious petitions, contrived by the advice and council of Sir William Parsons, Sir Adam Loftus, Sir John Clothworthy, and sundry others, of the malignant party in the city of Dublin, in the province of Ulster, and several other parts of the kingdom, directed to the Commons House in England, were at public assizes, and other public places, made known and read to many persons of quality; which petitions contained matters destructive to the said Catholics religion, lives, and estates (a)."

This dread of an extirpation, as appears from a multitude of depositions, taken before Doctor Henry Jones, and other commissioners, appointed by the Lords Justices, prevailed universally among the Catholics of Ireland, and was insisted upon, as one of the principal reasons of their taking arms (4). The Earl of Ormond, in his letters of January 27th, and February 26th, 1641, to Sir

---

(2) Cart. Orm. vol. i. fol. 160.   (3) See Append.   (4) Cart. Orm. vol. i. fol. 263.

(a) " It is evident," says Doctor Warner, " from the Lords Justices letter to the Earl of Leicester, then Lord Lieutenant, that they hoped for an extirpation, not of the meer Irish only, but of all the old English families also, that were Roman Catholics." Hist. of the Irish Rebel.

Sir William St. Leger, imputes the general revolt of the nation, then far advanced, to the publishing of such a design."

CHAP. XII.

The Romish Clergy of Ireland unjustly accused of stirring up the Irish to this Insurrection.

THE Romish clergy of Ireland at this period, are commonly charged with filling the minds of their votaries with such pernicious maxims, civil and religious, as could not fail to incite them to the most traitorous and bloody attempts. " They had," says (1) a modern historian, " that influence even over the gentry of their communion, with which they were invested by the tenets of their religion; the ignorant herd of Papists they governed at their pleasure. They had received their education, and imbibed their principles, in foreign seminaries of France and Spain; hence they returned to Ireland, bound solemnly to the Pope in unlimited submission; without profession, or bond of allegiance to the King. Full fraught with those absurd, and pestilent doctrines, which the moderate of their own communion profess to abominate, of the universal monarchy of the Pope, as well civil as spiritual, of his authority to excommunicate and depose Princes, to absolve subjects from their oaths of allegiance, and to dispense with every law of God and man, to sanctify rebellion and murder, and even to change the very nature and essential difference of vice and virtue. And, with this, and other impious trumpery of schools and councils, these ecclesiastics filled their superstitious votaries."

HORRIBLE, indeed, is this accusation; but, fortunately for the kingdom, wherein such a clergy is still suffered to exist, it is as erroneously stated, as it is groundless in itself. Nor is the injustice done to this clergy, by such shocking imputations, greater than that done to Walsh himself, the Irish Franciscan, whose sole authority is quoted in support of them. For there is no mention made in the place referred to, of these impious tenets having been taught, or maintained by any of the Romish clergy of Ireland, at, or about, the year 1641. All that appears there, relative to these tenets, is an indirect and angry charge and inference, against such of Walsh's brethren, as had opposed his remonstrance of loyalty, which was (2) not presented, nor even thought of, till

(1) Lel. Hist. Irel. vol. iii. p. 89. (2) See the dedication to the History of the Irish remonstrance, by Peter Walsh. (3) ib.

till more than twenty years after that period. Nay there too, Walsh confesses, that these tenets (3) " were quite different from what the Roman Catholics of England, Scotland, and Ireland, did believe;" and even asserts, " that many thousands of the most learned, most zealous, and most godly, Roman Catholic Prelates, Doctors, and Priests, besides laymen, cried down these tenets, as not only false, impious, and heretical, but also, as absolutely tirannical, and destructive of all government."

In order to explain this matter a little more fully, I must inform the reader, that in the year 1674, when Walsh's history of the remonstrance was first published, he had been provoked, by an excommunication newly denounced against him, to draw out this chain of blasphemous propositions, as the supposed consequences of the doctrine of the Pope's deposing power; and in the bitterness of resentment, to charge them on some of his adverse Roman Catholic brethren, (maintainers, perhaps, of that doctrine) whom he either knew, or suspected, to have been active in bringing that disgrace upon him. But that he was far from intending to charge such wicked principles upon the body of the Romish clergy of Ireland, incontestably appears, from his declaring, in the very same place, (with regard to the doctrine of the Pope's deposing power; and its supposed pernicious consequences) (4), " that he did not at all doubt, but rather was certain, that there were more than five hundred Priests, then in Ireland, who, if they were only permitted to live quietly there, would, by a public instrument, signed under all their hands, declare amply, clearly, and heartily, against the aforesaid doctrine, notwithstanding any declaration, precept, or censure of the Pope to the contrary."

As for those seminaries of France and Spain, where this Romish clergy is said to have imbibed these pestilent doctrines, I could not discover any of them in the place cited; but, on the contrary, I there found the author reckoning up eight seminaries in France alone, viz. " Those of Paris, Rheims, Caen, Tholouse, Potiers, Valance, Bourdeaux, and Bourges, together," adds he, " with the seven remaining universities of that kingdom; which had, on different occasions, publickly condemned the Pope's deposing power, as false, contrary to the word of God, seditious, and detestable."

(3) ib.   (4) ib.

CHAP. XIII.

The same Subject continued.

MR. Carte, who was no friend to the Romish clergy, and had better means of information, than any other writer on this subject, either before or since his time, has candidly owned (1), " that although this conspiracy was imputed to Roman Catholic Priests, yet not above two or three of them appeared to know any thing of it." Nay he even seemed to think, that had they all, to a man, afterwards concurred in it, they could not have been justly blamed on that account. For, not to mention the Lords Justices cruel injunctions to the officers of the army, to shew no mercy to that order of men (whom therefore, these officers promiscuously murdered, wherever they met them) (2), " The English House of Commons gave them reason to apprehend every thing that is dreadful to human nature. They had caused the laws against recusants to be put in execution all over England; eight Roman Catholic Priests had been taken up in London, for saying Mass; and the proof failing as to one, the other seven were condemned. The King, averse to the putting any man to death meerly for religion, had reprieved them; the Commons were offended at it, and made loud complaints on this subject against his Majesty. Nothing would satisfy them, till the King had left them to their mercy, to order the execution when ever they saw fit. When men," proceeds Mr. Carte, " have every thing to dread in peace, and much to hope from a war, 'tis natural for them to chose the latter, and use their utmost endeavours to make it successful. Nor is it any wonder, that those Priests, in such a situation of affairs, should have recourse to arms, for the safety of their lives; and despairing of indulgence in quiet times, should seek in troublesome ones for an establishment, never to be obtained but by the prevailing force of an insurrection."

Mr. Goodman, one of the above-mentioned condemned Priests, and who seems to have been particularly obnoxious to the parliament, made a voluntary offer of his life, as a sacrifice to the quiet of the King and kingdom, on that occasion; an instance of heroic loyalty, which can hardly, I fear, be paralleled by any of his opposites of the same order; who, nevertheless, are but too apt to represent Romish Priests as disloyal, through principle, to every Protestant government. That extraordinary person petitioned the King, to order his execution, in the following words.

" YOUR

(1) Life of Orm. vol. i.   (2) ib.

"Your Majesty's petitioner hath understood of a great discontent, in many of your Majesty's subjects, at the gracious mercy your Majesty was freely pleased to shew unto your petitioner, by suspending the execution of the sentence of death, pronounced against him. These are, therefore, humbly to beseech your Majesty, rather to remit your petitioner to their mercies that are discontented, than to let him live the subject of so great a discontent in your people against your Majesty; for it has pleased God, to give me grace to desire with the prophet, " that if this storm be raised for me, I may be cast into the sea, that others may avoid the tempest." This is, most sacred sovereign, the petition of him who should esteem his blood well shed, to cement the breach between your Majesty, and your subjects *(a)*."

CHAP. XIV.

Some Misrepresentations, concerning the Beginning of the Insurrection considered.

ON the 23d of October, 1641, the Lords Justices declared by proclamation (1), " that a discovery had been made of a most disloyal, and detestable conspiracy, intended by some evil affected Irish Papists, universally throughout the kingdom." This unfair representation has been either ignorantly, or maliciously adopted, by all the adverse writers on this subject. Sir John Temple, out of his abundant malice to these people, has so notably improved upon it, as to affirm (2), " that on the 23d of October aforesaid, an universal defection, and general revolt, broke out; wherein, not only all the meer Irish, but almost all the old English, that adhered to the church of Rome, were totally involved." And Mr. Hume, in a warm fit of declamation, confidently asserts (3), " that from Ulster, the flames of this rebellion diffused themselves, in an instant, over the three other provinces."

The above-mentioned proclamation gave a just alarm to the Catholic nobility, and gentry, of the kingdom; who knew themselves to be perfectly innocent, and entirely unconscious, of any such conspiracy. The Earl of

---

(1) Temple's History of the Irish Rebellion. (2) ib. (3) Hist. of England, Dub. ed. vol. iv. p 15.

(a) " But he escaped," says Mr. Hume, " with his life, rather because he was over-looked amidst affairs of greater consequence, than that such unrelenting severity would be softened by any consideration of his courage, or generosity." History of England.

of Clanrickard, who had arrived in Ireland some short time before, tells us, that. he (4) " was, at first, on a sudden surprised, with the fatal news of a desperate rebellion in the North, and a rumour of a general combination, and conspiracy, all over the kingdom. But we begin," adds his Lordship, " to recover our wits, scared away by the first reports; and do discern, that none appears in this detestable conspiracy, or enters into action, but the remains of the antient Irish rebels in the North, and some of the planted county of Leitrim."

In two or three days after the issuing of, this proclamation, the Lords, and gentlemen of the pale (5), " doubting," says Temple, " that by those general words of Irish Papists, they might seem to be involved," preferred a petition to the Lords Justices and Council, in behalf of themselves, and other old English of the kingdom; whereupon the Justices, on the 29th of the same month, sent forth another proclamation, in which (6) " they declared, and published, to all his Majesty's good subjects, that by the words " Irish Papists," they intended only such of the old meer Irish, in the province of Ulster, as had plotted, contrived, and been actors in that treason, and others, that adhered to them; and none of the old English of the pale, or other parts of the kingdom."

And although their Lordships, in this proclamation of the 29th of October, did " enjoin all his Majesty's subjects, whether Protestants, or Papists, to forbear upbraiding matter of religion on this occasion ;" yet certain it is, that all our adverse historians, preachers, and libellers, from that time to the present, seem to have thought themselves indispensably obliged, not only to upbraid matter of religion as the chief incentive to this insurrection, but also to represent the insurrection itself, as universal all over the kingdom, on the first day, or two, after its eruption.

These, and other misrepresentations, were no sooner devised, than transmitted to the Earl of Leicester, Lord Lieutenant in England; where they acquired still greater, and more extensive credit. Never, indeed, were fiction and calumny introduced to public notice with more pomp, and dignity, than they seem to have been upon that occasion.

" For (7) the Earl of Leicester, having received intelligence of this insurrection by the Lords Justices letter of the 25th of October, 1641, repaired, on

(4) Memoirs, Engl. ed. fol. 63.   (5) Irish Rebel.   (6) Id. ib.
(7) Warner's Irish Rebel. from Rushworth's collections.

on the firſt of the following month, to the Houſe of Commons, then ſitting; whither he was accompanied by the Lord Keeper of the great Seal of England, the Lord Privy Seal, the Lord High Chamberlain, the Lord Admiral, Earl March, Lord Chamberlain, Earl of Bath, Earl of Dorſet, Earl of Holland, Earl of Berkſhire, Lord Viſcount Say and Seal, Lord Goring, and Lord Wilmot, in grand proceſſion; when his Excellency communicated the papers and letters, ſent by the Lords Juſtices; and told them, that he had information of ſhedding much blood of the Proteſtants of Ireland; and that ſome of the rebels confeſſed, that all the proteſtants were to be cut off; and that they were not to leave any Britiſh men, women, or children alive: that the time for putting this bloody deſign in execution, was upon Saturday, the 23d of October, a day *(a)* dedicated to St. Ignatius, the founder of the Jeſuits; and in ſhort, that their deſign was to kill the Lords Juſtices, and all the King's Privy-council. The like information was given, by the Lord Keeper, and other Lords, and in the ſame ſolemn manner, to the Houſe of Lords.

THE falſehood of this repreſentation, with reſpect to the deſign of theſe inſurgents, is ſo very notorious, that even a writer, otherwiſe highly prejudiced againſt them, could not paſs it over uncenſured. " Both the Lord Keeper in the Houſe of Lords, and the Lord Lieutenant in the Houſe of Commons," ſays Doctor (8) Warner, " did exceed the informations that had been given, either in the letters, or in the examinations tranſmitted over. No hiſtorian," adds he, " hath taken notice of this falſification; and yet one cannot believe that it was owing in both to accident, or miſtake. The Lord Keeper hath ſaid, that the rebels had committed divers murders; and the Lord Lieutenant, beſides affirming that they had information of ſhedding much blood of the Proteſtants there, added moreover, that the deſign of the rebels was to kill the Lords Juſtices, and all the King's Privy-council; whereas neither in the letters, nor the examinations, is there a ſingle word of any murder being committed; nor was there the leaſt thought among the conſpirators, for any thing that appears, of killing, particularly, the Lords Juſtices and the King's Privy-council. And the Council in their letters, after having given an account of ſeveral robberies, burning houſes and villages, and ſeizing ſome forts and caſtles, expreſſ-

---

(8) Hiſt. of the Iriſh Rebel.

(a) This, like many other circumſtances of this pompous tale, is a well-known falſehood.

ly say, and this tho' too much, is all that we yet hear is done by them *(b)*."

THERE is but little wonder, that so shocking a calumny, thus solemnly delivered, by persons of honour, to an august assembly, should make a general and lasting impression, on a credulous, and prejudiced people; but the reader will please to reflect, that if so many persons of the first quality, living at a distance from the danger and mischiefs of this insurrection; and therefore, uninfluenced by fear or revenge, could, for their own *(c)* evil purposes, circulate such horrid falsehoods concerning it, how little stress ought to be laid on the evidence, or testimonies of some of the meanest of the adverse party at home, who were either exasperated by the injuries they themselves had suffered, or scared out of their wits by the shocking stories they had heard of those committed on others, when they were called upon to give such evidence. And yet, the testimony of persons so prejudiced, and otherwise unduly influenced, is the principal, if not only foundation, on which the belief of the Irish massacre has hitherto rested, and has so generally, not to say uncontrovertedly, prevailed.

(b) It is worthy of notice, that about this time, viz. before the end of October, 1641, Temple himself confesses, " that the rebels had got possession of all the towns, forts, castles, and gentlemens houses within the counties of Tyrone, Donegal, Farmanagh, Armagh, Cavan, Londonderry, Monaghan, and half the county of Down; except the cities of Londonderry and Colerain, the town and castle of Enniskillen, and some other places and castles. And that besides the above-mentioned, these rebels had taken a multitude of other castles, houses of strength, towns and villages, all abundantly peopled with British inhabitants." Hist. of the Irish Rebel. p. 34. Yet in none of those places does it appear, from this account, that any massacre, or murder, was committed by the insurgents, within that space of time.

(c) " The Irish rebellion," says Sir Edward Walker, " did fortify the designs in England, which then wanted matter to work upon. The parliament raised money for this war, and employed it in their own; and scandalised his Majesty, as not zealous in the suppression of it. Though to shew his odium of this rebellion, he proposed the going thither himself to suppress it; but his proposal was ill taken by the Commons, as fearing the rebels might submit to his Majesty, and so become his, in opposition to their designs." Hist. Discours. fol. 231.

AN HISTORICAL AND CRITICAL REVIEW OF THE CIVIL WARS IN IRELAND.

BOOK V.

CHAP. I.

The main Design of the Insurgents, not general, or premeditated.

IN order to set this tragical part of the history of Ireland in a true light, it is necessary to distinguish two insurrections, differing not so much in their causes, as their times. The first is that mentioned in the Lord Justices proclamation of the 29th October, 1641, of some of the meer old Irish only, in the province of Ulster. The other is that general defection, which happened some months after, in the other provinces; and was occasioned by a continuation, and increase of those grievances, and oppressions, which had produced the first. We will begin with the insurrection in Ulster, which (1) Sir (a) John Temple, and his numerous copiers, have represented as an horrible

(1) Hist. of the Irish Rebel.

(a) This gentleman published his history of the Irish rebellion in the year 1646; by the direction of the parliament-party, which then prevailed, and to which, tho' long before in actual rebellion, he was always attached. The falsehoods it contains, are so glaring, and numerous, that even the government, in the year 1674, seems to have been offended, and himself ashamed of the re-publication of it. This we gather from a letter of Capel Earl of Essex, then Lord Lieutenant of Ireland, to Mr. Secretary Coventry, of that date, wherein we find these words: "I am to acknowledge yours of the 22d of December, in which you

rible enterprife, long before concerted and refolved upon, by the generality of the Catholics of Ireland. But in this particular, and in truth in moſt others, that writer has fufficiently confuted himſelf; for he informs us, that feveral of the chiefs of thefe Ulſter infurgents, inſtead of providing men, arms, and other requifites for the execution of fuch a defign, did on the contrary, but a ſhort time before their rifing, taking even fuch meaſures, as had a manifeſt tendency *(b)* to prevent its fucceſs. For he tells us (2), " That Sir Phelim O'Neil, and many others of the prime leaders in this rebellion, did, not long before it broke out, turn their Iriſh tenants off their lands, even to ſtarve upon the mountains; while they took in Engliſh, who were able to give them much greater rents, and more certainly pay the fame." He has alſo informed us (3), " That thefe rebels, at their firſt rifing out, had not many better weapons, than ſtaves, fcythes, and pitchforks;" an indication furely, rather of a fudden unpremeditated eruption and tumult, than of any fettled fcheme of confpiracy, or rebellion.

Nay, fome weeks after their firſt rifing, fuch of thefe infurgents as appeared to the Earl of Ormond, feemed to him (4), " rather to be a tumultuous rabble, than any thing like a difciplined army;" and his Lordſhip was of opinion, that (5) " there were as many arms, within a few, in the hands of only fix hundred of the King's forces, as there were among all the rebels then in the kingdom."

But what puts this matter beyond all difpute is (6), " that the army of eight thoufand foot, and one thoufand horfe, (feven-eights of which were Roman Catholics,) that had been raifed, two years before, by the Earl of Strafford,

(2) ib. p. 14.   (3) ib. p. 79.   (4) Cart. Orm. vol. iii.   (5) ib.   (6) Carte's Orm. vol. i.

you mention a book that was newly publiſhed, concerning the cruelties committed in Ireland, at the beginning of the late war. Upon further enquiry I find, Sir J. Temple, Maſter of the Rolls here, (Ireland) author of that book, was, this laſt year, fent to by feveral ſtationers of London, to have his confent to the printing thereof; but he aſſures me, that he utterly denied it, and whoever printed it, did it without his knowledge. Thus much I thought fit to add to what I formerly faid upon this occafion, that I might do this gentleman right, in cafe it were fufpected, he had any ſhare in publiſhing this new edition." State Let. Dub. ed. p. 2. His Lordſhip was, at this time, foliciting a grant of three (he would have it five) hundred pounds a year on the forfeited eſtates, for Sir John Temple, which he at laſt obtained, (fee thefe letters,) and the Miniſtry feems to have made this re-publication of his hiſtory, an objection, which his Lordſhip thus endeavours to remove.

(b) " The difficulty which Moore found to prevail on the Ulſter-Iriſh, (to rife) ſhews there was no long-meditated fcheme of rebellion even among them." Lel. Hiſt. vol. ii. Lord Maguire, in his confeſſion, avers, that it was in May 1641, that he firſt heard the motion from Sir James Dillon, of taking the caſtle of Dublin. See Borl. Hiſt. of the Iriſh Rebel. fol. 34.

Strafford, was, in June 1641, entirely diffolved, without any inconvenience, or diforder, in the nation at that time."

"THE complaints of grievances made by the Roman Catholic members," fays (7) Mr. Carte, " in the Irifh Houfe of Commons, in fummer 1641, have been infifted upon, as a proof of their intention to raife a rebellion at that juncture; but, by all the obfervations I have been able to make, I do not find, that there was any formed defign of the body of the Roman Catholic party in that parliament, for an affair of that nature. The compiler of the Nuncios memoirs," adds the fame author (8), " (a fair writer, whatever his principles were, and who, on all occafions, feems to be well acquainted with his fubject, and to write what he believed to be true,) fays, " that the Englifh-Irifh of four hundred years ftanding, efpecially thofe of the Englifh pale, were extremely averfe to the rebellion, and offered their fervice very fincerely to the ftate againft the rebels; remembering their own origin, and chofing to adhere to the Englifh government, which they were apprehenfive would be thrown off by the natives. To which reafon he adds another, drawn from the nature of their eftates, a confiderable part of which was church-lands, which, he fays, they were afraid of lofing, if the old Irifh got the power of the nation into their hands."

CHAP. II.

The firft Caufes of the Infurrection of 1641, in Ulfter.

MEN, whofe minds are exafperated by the remembrance of former injuries (which was peculiarly the cafe of the *(a)* Ulfter gentry, on account of the feizure of the fix counties before-mentioned) are often fuddenly provoked to commit acts of violence, by a flight or inadequate caufe; but the immediate incentive to the infurrection of thefe Northerns was far from being fuch; it was nothing lefs, than a well-grounded fear of an intended extirpation of their religion, or perfons. The petitions already mentioned, which were calculated for that end, feem principally to have been levelled at them; and probably received moft furtherance from their malevolent neighbours, the puritan Scots. Nor will this in the leaft feem ftrange, if it be confidered, that

(7) ib. vol. i. fol. 152.   (8) ib. vol. i. fol. 256. Nunc. Mem. p. 392.

(a) " No great difficulty was apprehended in gaining the leaders of the Ulfter-Irifh, who had been fo feverely chaftifed by the arms of Elizabeth, and fo grievoufly defpoiled by the plantations of James." Lel. Hift. of Irel. vol. ii. p. 195.

that the Diffenters in that province, were audacious enough, about the fame time, to addrefs a petition to the Englifh Houfe of Commons (1), " figned by many thoufands in the county of Down, Tyrone, and others, againft epifcopacy, and the eftablifhed religion itfelf." In that petition they complain, " that the moft learned, and feemingly moderate and pious Prelates, did publickly, in fermons at Dublin, exclaim againft, and condemn the Scottifh covenant, and the religion profeffed in Scotland; and therefore, they moft humbly pray, that that unlawful hierarchical government, with all its appendixes, may be utterly extirpated."

These incentives to the infurrection in Ulfter are chiefly infifted upon in that impartial remonftrance of grievances from Cavan, which was drawn up by (2) Bifhop Bedel, a Prelate too wife to be impofed upon, and too juft and refolute, to advance any facts in excufe of thefe infurgents, of the truth of which he was not very-certain. As Bifhop Burnet, in his life, owns, that this remonftrance gives the beft colours to their proceedings of any of all their papers, that he ever faw, I will here tranfcribe it entire, from that Bifhop's copy.

" To the Right Honourable the Lords Juftices and Council, the humble remonftrance of the gentry, and commonality of the county of Cavan, of their grievances, common with other parts of this kingdom of Ireland.

" Whereas we his Majefty's loyal fubjects of his Highnefs's kingdom of Ireland, have, of long time, groaned under many grievances and preffures, occafioned by the rigorous government of fuch placed over us, as refpected more the advancement of their own private fortunes, than the honour of his Majefty, or the welfare of his fubjects; whereof, we, in humble manner, declared ourfelves to his Highnefs, by our agents, fent from the parliament, the reprefentative body of the kingdom; notwithftanding which, we find ourfelves of late threatened with far greater, and more grievous vexations, either with captivity of our confciences, or utter expulfion from our native feats, without any juft grounds given on our parts, to alter his Majefty's goodnefs, fo long continued to us. Of all which, we find great caufe of fears, in the proceedings of our neighbour-nations; and do fee it already attempted, by certain petitioners, for the like courfe to be taken in this kingdom, for the effecting thereof, in a compulfory way; fo as rumours have caufed fears of invafion from other parts, to the diffolving of the bond of mutual agreement, which hitherto, hath been held inviolable, between the feveral fubjects of

this

---

(1) See Pryn's antipathy to Bifhops, part ii.   (2) Burnet's life of Bedel.

this kingdom; and whereby all his Majesty's other dominions have been linked in one. For the preventing, therefore, of such evils, growing upon us in this kingdom, we have, for the preservation of his Majesty's honour, and our own liberties, thought fit to take into our hands, for his Highness's use and service, such forts, and other places of strength, as coming into the possession of others, might prove disadvantageous, and tend to the utter undoing of the kingdom; and we do hereby declare, that herein, we harbour not the least thought of disloyalty towards his Majesty; or purpose any hurt to his Highness's subjects, in their possessions, goods, or liberty; only we desire, that your Lordships will be pleased to make remonstrances to his Majesty for us, of all our grievances, and just fears, that they may be removed, and such a course settled by the advice of the parliament of Ireland, whereby the liberty of our consciences may be secured unto us, and we eased of other burdens in civil government. As for the mischiefs, and inconveniencies that have already happened, thro' the disorder of the common sort of people, against the English inhabitants, or any others, we, with the nobility and gentlemen, and such others of the several counties of this kingdom, are most willing and ready to use our, and their, best endeavours in causing restitution and satisfaction, to be made as in part we have already done.

" An answer hereunto is most humbly desired, with such present expedition, as may, by your Lordships, be thought most convenient, for avoiding the inconvenience of the barbarousness, and incivility, of the commonalty, who have committed many outrages, without any order, consenting, or privity of ours. All which we leave to your Lordships wisdom, and shall humbly pray, &c."

On the 10th November 1641, the O'Farrells of the neighbouring county of Longford, sent up also, to the Lords Justices, a remonstrance of their grievances; which was of much the same tenor with that from Cavan, intreating redress in a parliamentary way. " These gentlemen," says Mr. (3) Carte, " had deserved well of the crown, and were on that account, particularly provided for by King James, in his instructions for planting of that country. But the commissioners appointed for the distribution of the lands, more greedy of their own private profit, than tender of the King's honour, or the rights of the subject, took little care to observe these instructions; and the O'Farrells were generally great *(b)* sufferers by the plantations. Several persons were turned out of large estates of profitable land, and had only a small pittance, less

---

(3) Life of Orm. vol. i.

(b) " In a manuscript of Bishop Stearne, we find that in the small county of Longford, twenty five of one sept were all deprived of their estates, without the least compensation, or any means of subsistence assigned to them." Lel. Hist. Irel. vol. ii. p. 437.

less than a fourth part, assigned them for it, in barren ground. Twenty-four proprietors, most of them O'Farrells, were dispossessed of their all; and nothing allotted them for compensation. They had complained, in vain, of this undeserved usage many years; and having now an opportunity afforded them of redress, by the insurrection of their neighbours, had readily embraced it, and followed their example (for it does not appear that any of them were antecedently concerned in the conspiracy,) as they likewise did, in laying before the Lords Justices, a remonstrance of their grievances, and a petition for redress; which, like that from Cavan (4), came to nothing."

CHAP. III.

The Massacre in Island-Magee.

"THE report that his Majesty's Protestant subjects first fell upon, and murdered the Roman Catholics, got credit and reputation, and was openly and frequently asserted," says Jones, Bishop (1) Meath, in a letter to Doctor Borlace, in 1679. And, indeed, whatever cruelties may be charged upon the Irish, in the prosecution of this war, " their first intention, we see," says another Protestant (2) voucher, " went no further, than to strip the English and the Protestants of their power, and possessions." In a MS. journal of a Protestant officer in the King's service, quoted by (3) Mr. Carte. wherein there is a minute and daily account of every thing that happened in the North of Ireland, during the first weeks of this insurrection, there is not even an insinuation of any cruelties, committed by the insurgents on the English, or Protestants; although it is computed by the journalist, " that the Protestants of that province had killed near a thousand of the rebels in the first week or two of the rebellion." And, on the 16th of November, 1641 (4), " Mr. Robert Wallbank came from the North, and informed the Irish House of Commons, that two hundred of the people of Colerain fought with one thousand of the rebels, slew six of them, and not one of themselves hurt. That, in another battle, sixty of the rebels were slain, and only two of the others hurt, none slain." Nor do we find, in this account, the least mention of cruelties, then committed by the Irish; but much of the success, and victory of his Majesty's Protestant subjects, as often as they encountered them.

THAT

---

(4) Bishop Burnet's life of Bishop Bedel.

(1) See Preface to Borlase's Hist. of the Irish Rebellion. (2) Doctor Warner's Hist. of the Irish Rebellion, p. 47. Templ. Ir. Rebel. (3) Life of Orm. vol. i. (4) Appendix to the Journals of the Irish Commons.

THAT a great number of unoffending Irish were massacred in Island-Magee, by Scottish puritans, about the beginning of this insurrection, is not denied by any adverse writer, that I have met with. An apology, however, is made for it by them all, which even if it were grounded on fact, as I shall presently shew it is not, would be a very bad one, and seems, at least, to imply a confession of the charge. These writers pretend, that this massacre was perpetrated on those harmless people, in revenge of some cruelties before committed by the rebels on the Scots, in other parts of Ulster. But as I find this controversy has been already taken up by two able Protestant historians, who seem to differ about the time in which that dismal event happened, perhaps, by laying before the reader the accounts of both, with such animadversions, as naturally arise from them, that time may be more clearly and positively ascertained.

A LATE learned and ingenious author of an history of Ireland, has shifted off this shocking incident, from November 1641, (in which month, it has been generally placed) to January following, many weeks after horrible cruelties (as he tells us) had been committed by the insurgents on the Scots in the North (5). " The Scottish soldiers," says he, " who had reinforced the garrison of Carrickfergus, were possessed of an habitual hatred of Popery, and enflamed to an implacable detestation of the Irish, by multiplied accounts of their cruelties. In one fatal night, they issued, from Carrickfergus, into an adjacent district, called Island-Magee, where a number of the poorer Irish resided, unoffending and untainted with the rebellion. If we may believe one of the leaders of this party, thirty families were assailed by them in their beds, and massacred, with calm and deliberate cruelty. As if," proceeds the historian, " the incident were not sufficiently hideous, Popish writers have represented it with shocking aggravation. They make the number of the slaughtered, in a small and thinly inhabited neck of land, to amount to three thousand, a wildness and absurdity, into which other writers of such transactions have been betrayed; they assert, that this butchery was committed in the beginning of November 1641, that it was the first massacre committed in Ulster, and the great provocation to all the outrages of the Irish in this quarter. Mr. Carte seems to favour this assertion: had he carefully perused the collection of original depositions, now in the possession of the university of Dublin, he would have found his doubts of facts, and dates cleared most satisfactorily; and that the massacre of Island-Magee, as appears from several unsuspicious evidences, was really committed in the beginning of

(5) Lel. Hist. Irel. vol. ii.

of January, when the followers of *(a)* O'Neil had almost exhausted their barbarous malice."

BEFORE I examine the several particulars of the foregoing account, I must observe, that the objection taken from the smallness of the place, as if it were incapable of containing three thousand inhabitants, is grounded on a misapprehension of some circumstances in this event. For the Irish that were there destroyed, consisted not only of the inhabitants of the place, but also, and for the greatest part, of the country people residing in its neighbourhood; who, upon the (6) invitation of Colonel Chichester, and Sir Arthur Tyrringham, had fled to Carrickfergus for protection, on the first eruption of these tumults. "The town of Carrickfergus," says Mr. (7) Carte, "was then the place of the greatest strength in the North; and as Colonel Chichester and Sir Arthur Tyrringham, had, on the evening of the 23d of October, received intelligence of the insurrection, they immediately, by beat of drum and kindling of fires, apprised all the country people round them, of their danger; so that the poor country people, who had not yet stirred, flocked to that place continually, with all they could carry of their substance, in such multitudes of men, women, and children, that the town was overthronged." The same author also informs us (8), "That Colonel Chichester and Sir Arthur Tyrringham, invited several of the most eminent of the Irish thereabouts, who yet remained quiet in their houses, to come to Carrickfergus for security; who accordingly went thither, but were made prisoners on their arrival."

AND

(6) Cart. Orm. Vol. i. (7) ib. (8) ib.

(a) Sir Phelim O'Neal's. This assertion has no other foundation but the depositions now in the possession of the university of Dublin; what credit is due to these, we shall just now see; but if any regard at all is to be had to such of them, as have been carefully selected from the rest, and published by Temple and Borlace, in their histories of this rebellion, we shall find some of them vouching, that Sir Phelim O'Neal did not order the cruelties he is charged with, till many weeks after January, 1641. For by Captain Parkin's examination, "Sir Phelim began his massacres after his flight from Dundalk." Templ. Ir. Rebel. p 85. Now his flight from Dundalk did not happen till about the latter end of March following. Carte's Orm. vol. i. fol 288. Sir Henry Tichbourne's history of the siege of Drogheda. Mr. Carte, and most other adverse writers agree, " that it was Sir Phelim O Neal that first began, and encouraged these imputed massacres." Cart. ib. fol. 176. And Temple himself owns it, " to be a truth, that those British whom the rebels suffered to live among them, and such as they kept in prison, were not put to the sword by the Irish, until in their several encounters they had with his Majesty's forces, they suffered loss of their men, and so were enraged." ib. p. 126. Sir Henry Tichbourne, who had the chief command in that driving of O'Neil from Dundalk, performed that service, and afterwards pursued, it with such an amazing slaughter of the Irish, in them parts, that he himself boasts, that some weeks after, " there was neither man nor beast to be found, in sixteen miles, between the two towns of Drogheda and Dundalk; nor on the other side of Dundalk, in the county of Monaghan, nearer than Carrickmacross, a strong pile twelve miles distant." ib. It is, therefore, not strange, tho' absolutely inexcusable, if this incensed leader, or rather his savage followers, should be provoked to retaliate, in some measure, such cruelty and destruction on the unhappy English, whom they had in their power. Sir Phelim himself, in his last moments, declared, " that the several outrages committed by his officers and soldiers, in that war, contrary to his intention, then pressed his conscience very much." Dean Ker's testimony. Nalson's Hist. Collect.

AND because it is allowed, that Mr. Carte, seems to favour the assertion, "that near three thousand innocent Irish were massacred in Island-Magee, in the beginning of November, 1641," it is but just to produce the reasons, which appear to have inclined him to that way of thinking, by inserting the passage at large, wherein they are contained.

"On the 15th of November," says that (9) well-informed writer, "the rebels, after a fortnight's siege, reduced the castle of Lurgan; Sir William Bromlow, after a stout defence, surrendering it on the terms of marching out with his family and goods; but such was the unworthy disposition of the rebels, that they kept him, his lady, and children, prisoners; rifled his house, plundered, stripped, and killed most of his servants; and treated all the townsmen in the same manner. This," adds he, "was the first breach of faith, which the rebels were guilty of, at least in these parts, in regard of articles of capitulation; for when Mr. Conway, on November the 5th, surrendered his castle of Bally-aghie, in the county of Derry, to them, they kept the terms for which he stipulated, and allowed him to march out with his men, and to carry away trunks with plate and money in them. Whether," proceeds Mr. Carte, "the slaughter made by a party from Carrickfergus, in the territory of Magee, a long narrow island, in which it is affirmed, that near three thousand harmless Irish, men, women, and children, were cruelly massacred, happened before the surrender of Lurgan, is hard to be determined; the relations published of facts, in those times, being very indistinct, and uncertain, with regard to the time they were committed; though it is confidently asserted, that the said massacre happened in this month of November."

LET us now try these different accounts by the only sure test of dates, and facts. It is confessed on all hands, that the chiefs of the insurgents, through fear of the Scots in Ulster (10), ("who," as the Earl of Clanrickard informs us, "were forty thousand well armed men, when the rebellion commenced;" at the same time, that the rebels were, at least, by half less numerous, and furnished with few better arms than (11), "staves, scythes, and pitchforks,") (12) published a proclamation, "forbidding their followers, on pain of death, to molest any of the Scottish nation, in body or goods." Temple acknowledges, that this proclamation (13), "was for a time observed;" and from Mr. Wallbank's

---

(9) ib.   (10) Cart. Orm vol. iii. fol. 77.   (11) Templ. Irish Rebel. p. 79.   (12) Cart. Orm.
(13) Hist. Irish Rebel.

Wallbank's report, already mentioned, to the House of Commons, of the constant succefs of his Majesty's subjects against the insurgents, in different parts of Ulster, from the 23d of October, to the 16th of November following, we may reasonably suppose, that it was at least observed till that day; for it is surely in the highest degree improbable, that these chiefs would, at any time before, have wantonly provoked the resentment of so formidable a body of men, by any cruel outrage, or hostile act. But it is unquestionably evident, that the Scots in Ulster did some remarkable execution on the Irish, several days before the 15th of November, the day on which Lurgan was surrendered. For Sir William Parsons, in a letter from Dublin, of the 13th of that month, to the Earl of Clanrickard, acquaints him, as with a welcome piece of news (14), " that the Scots did hold the Northern Irish hard to it, having killed some of them." And *(b)* Sir William St. Leger, grudging, as it were, the Scots the honour of that action, told the Earl of Ormond, on the 14th, " that, had it pleased God that his Lordship had been there with his hundred horse, and himself to wait upon him, the Scots should never have had the honour to put such an obligation on Ireland."

From hence, I think, may be fairly deduced the only reason, why the behaviour of the insurgents to Sir William Bromlow, on the 15th, of November was so very different from that, which they had before shewn to Mr. Conway, on the 5th of the same month, viz. because the massacre in question was perpetrated on their innocent unoffending people, in that interval of time; which, no doubt, provoked them to the above-mentioned breach of articles at the surrender of Lurgan, and to several other acts of injustice and cruelty, in the prosecution of this war.

The deduction now made is so agreeable to dates, and facts, that I am surprised to find this first breach of articles by the insurgents, ascribed to any other cause; especially to one, which appears manifestly repugnant to both. This cause, we are informed, was the repulse, defeat, and slaughter, of a considerable body of the rebels at the siege of Lisburn, by a Scottish garrison stationed there; for thus the before-cited history relates the immediate effects, which that disaster produced in these rebels. " But (15) such succefs (of the Scots) was attended with consequences truly horrible; the Irish, incensed at resistance,

(14 Cart. Orm. vol. iii.   (15) Lel. Hist. Irel. vol. iii.

(b) This gentleman, who was Lord President of Munster, seems to have been very well qualified for acquiring such honour. For Lord Upper Ossory, in a letter to the Earl of Ormond about this time, informs him, " that he was so cruel and merciless, that he caused men, and women, to be most execrably executed; and that he ordered, among others, a woman great with child to be ript up, from whose womb three babes were taken out, through every of whose bodies, his soldiers thrust their weapons; which act, (says his Lordship) puts many into a sort of desperation." Carț. Orm. vol. iii. fol. 51.

resistance, carried on their hostilities without faith, or humanity. Lurgan was surrendered by Sir William Bromlow, on terms of security to the inhabitants, and permission of marching out with his family, goods, and retinue; but all was instantly seized, and the whole town given up to plunder." Thus have we a cause plausibly assigned, which did not exist until many days after its supposed effect was produced. For the defeat and slaughter of the rebels at Lisburn, or, as it was then called, Lisnegarvy, did not happen according to Borlace till the (16) 28th of November; but Lurgan, as we have seen, was surrendered to them, on the 15th of that month, thirteen days before.

Let us now see, upon what grounds this massacre in Island-Magee is transferred, from November 1641, to the beginning of January following. One would expect to find an assertion so singular supported by some solid, or at least plausible proof; but, instead of meeting with any such, in the place before quoted from this history, we are only there directed to look out for it (where certainly it never can be found) in the collection of original manuscript depositions, now in the possession of the university of Dublin. But we shall presently demonstrate the insufficiency, not to say futility, of proofs drawn from *(c)* these depositions. And, in truth, if they were to be admitted as proofs, or evidence in any degree, there is hardly any thing so incredible, or absurd, that might not, with equal reason, be obtruded upon us, for genuine history. " Every suggestion of phrensy and melancholy; miraculous escapes from death, visions of spirits chaunting hymns; ghosts rising from rivers, brandishing swords, and shrieking revenge," would have a just and rational title to our belief, having all of them received the sanction of these vouchers.

(16) History of the Irish Rebellion, fol. 57.

(c) " Any one," says Mr. Carte, " who has ever read the examinations and depositions here referred to, which were generally given upon hearsay, and contradicting one another, would think it very hard upon the Irish, to have all those without distinction, to be admitted as evidence." Orm. vol. ii. fol. 263.

CHAP.

CHAP. IV.

The original Depositions, now in the Possession of the University of Dublin, considered.

I SHALL now briefly confider the nature of that evidence, which has hitherto induced fo many people, learned and unlearned, to give, or at leaft, feem to give credit to thofe horrible relations of murders, and maffacres, which have been imputed to thefe infurgents. Evidence, that, in itfelf, is fo manifeftly futile, contradictory, or falfe, that, I am perfuaded, every perfon of common fenfe would be afhamed to produce the like, upon any ordinary occafion.

THE evidence I mean, is that huge collection of manufcript depofitions (confifting of thirty-two folio volumes) which are faid to have been fworn, on the fubject of the outrages and depredations committed by the infurgents, in this war, and are now in the poffeffion of the Univerfity of Dublin. From this enormous heap of malignity and nonfenfe, Temple and Borlace have felected fuch examinations, as appeared to them the leaft exceptionable, and confequently, the moft likely to obtain credit to their horrible narrations. To thefe, therefore, I fhall refer the reader, as a felect fpecimen of the reft; after I have fubmitted to his confideration, what Doctor Warner, (who, it feems, underwent the drudgery of perufing and examining this whole collection,) has left us, as his opinion of it. "Befides the examinations (1)," fays he, "figned by the commiffioners, there are feveral copies of others, faid to be taken before them, which are therefore of no authority; and there are many depofitions, taken ten years after, which are ftill lefs authentic. As a great ftrefs," adds the Doctor, "has been laid upon this collection in print, and converfation, among the Proteftants of Ireland; and as the whole evidence of the maffacre turns upon it, I fpent a great deal of time, in examining thefe books; and I am forry to fay, that they have been made the foundation of much more clamour, and refentment, than can be warranted by truth and reafon."

"THERE is one circumftance in thefe books, not taken notice of by any before me, which is, that though all the examinations, figned by the commiffioners, are faid to be upon oath, yet in infinitely the greateft number of them,

---

(1) Hift. of the Irifh Rebel.

them, the words being duly sworn, have the pen drawn through them, with the same ink, with which the examinations are written; and in several of those where such words remain, many parts of the examinations are crossed out. This is a circumstance, which shews that the bulk of this immense collection is Parole-evidence; and what sort of evidence that is, may be easily learned by those, who are conversant with the common people of any country, especially when their imaginations are terrified, and their passions heated by sufferings. Of what credit are depositions worthy," adds he, " (and several such there are,) that many of the protestants, that were drowned, were often seen in erect postures in the river, and shrieking out revenge *(a)* ?"

CHAP. V.

The original Examinations further considered.

AT the same time, that Doctor Warner rejects the depositions now in the possession of the university of Dublin, he informs us (1), " that he has, in his own possession, a choice and duly attested copy of such of these examinations only, as were taken on oath; which," says he, " demonstrates the falsehood of the relation, in every Protestant history of this rebellion." Had the Doctor favoured the world with a publication of these choice examinations, or even with an abstract of them, we should then be, in some measure, able to judge of their authenticity; whereas at present, we have only his bare word for it. However, from an anecdote, which he himself has related, concerning the first real and original examinations, we may fairly conclude, that his favourite copy of them, however well attested, deserves not a jot more credit, than those, which he has already so justly condemned. That anecdote imports (2), " that, soon after the restoration, when the claims, in favour of innocents,

(1) Hist. of the Irish Rebel.   (2) ib. see Cart. Orm. vol. ii.

(a) Doctor Maxwell, afterwards Bishop of Killmore, the most seemingly credible of these deponents; and, " who," says Borlace, " was a person, whose integrity and candour none ever dared to question," has given a kind of sanction to these fictions, having described, in his own prolix examination, the different postures and gestures of these apparitions; " as sometimes having been seen, by day and night, walking upon the river; sometimes brandishing their naked swords; sometimes singing psalms; and, at other times, shrieking in a most fearful and hideous manner." He adds, " that he never heard any man so much as doubt the truth thereof; but that he obliged no man's faith in regard he saw them not with his own eyes; otherwise he had as much certainty as could morally be required of such matters." Borlace's Hist. of the Irish Rebellion, Append. fol. 392.

innocents, were canvassed, and the *(a)* House of Commons desired, that none of those, whose names could be found in the depositions, might be heard, relating to such claims of innocency, the Duke of Ormond, though no friend to the Irish, for good reasons, *(b)* rejected the proposal. The Duke," adds he, probably knew too much of these examinations, and of the methods used in procuring them, to give them such a stamp of authority; or otherwise, it would have been the clearest and shortest proof of the guilt of such, as were named in them."

Upon this occasion, I submit it to the consideration of every candid and intelligent reader, whether depositions found insufficient to convict the persons, or confiscate the properties of the Irish, then living, ought to be now deemed proper, and competent evidence, to impeach the characters, or principles of their innocent descendents, at that time unborn? or, whether any person now existing, can be thought to be so well qualified, either by the want of partiality to the Irish, or by the knowledge of their case, to judge of the weight or futility of that evidence, as the Duke of Ormond was at that juncture? and, conscious of this material defect in the original examinations, with what probability of success, could Doctor Warner rely on his own copy of them, how well soever attested, as capable of ascertaining the facts, which he has too confidently related out of it *(c)* ?

(a) The whole House, with their Speaker, waited on his Grace the Duke of Ormond, with an address to that purpose; in which they proposed, among other things, " that all examinations and depositions, whatsoever, taken for discovery of the rebellion, or proceedings of the rebels and their adherents, as well during his late Majesty's reign, as in time of the usurped authority; and that all books, rolls, and writings, remaining in any offices, &c. should be taken for good evidence, in behalf of his Majesty, to bar such person or persons of their innocency." Journ. of the Irish Com. vol. ii. fol. 260.

(b) The Commons became so refractory on this refusal, that Lord Arlington in a letter to his Grace, in 1663, mentioning, " the distempers into which the House had fallen on that occasion, and the extravagant demands they had made to his Grace," tells him, " that he was commanded by his Majesty, to let his Grace know, that his Majesty expressed such an entire dislike and dissatisfaction on that account, that he was persuaded, nothing but their disavowing what they had done, and the restoring themselves to that duty and moderation, which became them, (and them especially, adds his Lordship, after so many acts of grace, and indulgence, on his Majesty's part towards them,) would keep them tolerable in his opinion; and hoped the insecurity of their condition there, and the support his Majesty might probably have from his English parliament, then sitting, in any thing that tended to their discountenance, would oblige them to retract what they had done." State Let. p. 281-2. This House of Commons consisted almost entirely of Anabaptists, independents, and levellers, partizans of the late usurpers. Cart. Orm. Some of them, afterwards, formed a dangerous conspiracy, on account of this refusal. See Cart. ib.

(c) Warner himself, confesses, " that so many of the rebels sayings to their Protestant, and English prisoners, which are recorded, even in the choice manuscript collection of depositions in his custody, are so ridiculous, incredible, or contradictory to one-another, as shew plainly, that they spoke what their own, or different passions of their leaders prompted them to." ib

CHAP.

CHAP. VI.

Concerning the Number of Murders.

DOCTOR Warner, after having established, as he thought, the authenticity of his select copy of depositions (1), " endeavours to ascertain from it, as near as may be, the number of British, and Protestants, that were destroyed out of war, by the Irish in this rebellion." And although he owns it " to be impossible, even from that authentic evidence of the murders, to come to any certainty, or exactness as to their numbers, from the uncertainty itself of some of the accounts that are given in; yet," he says, " it is easy enough, from thence, to demonstrate the falsehood of the relation of every Protestant historian." Upon the whole, he assures us, " that, setting aside all opinions and calculations in this affair, the evidence from the manuscript in his possession, stands thus (a).

" THE number of people killed upon positive evidence, collected in two years after the insurrection broke out, amounts only to two thousand one hundred and nine: on the report of other Protestants, one thousand six hundred and nineteen more; and on the report of some of the rebels themselves, a further number of three hundred; the whole, both by positive evidence, and by report making four thousand and twenty-eight.

" BESIDES these murders," adds he, " there is in the same collection, evidence on the report of others, of eight thousand killed by ill usage; and if we should

(1) ib.

(*a*) Many of the select original examinations, which Temple and Borlace have inserted in their histories of this rebellion, have only the marks, not the names, of the deponents set to them; many of these deponents were weak women, and illiterate men, not capable of reading their own depositions, and therefore apt to be imposed upon, and deceived by those who read them to them. A great number of them swore on meer heaisay; and some of those afterwards, touched by remorse, solemnly declared the contrary of what they had sworn; and they were all, at the time of swearing these depositions, either interested, or incensed enemies to those, against whom they swore. Hence we are told, that, " at the trial of qualifications at Athlone, (a court held by the regicides,) where the book, called the Black Book, being a collection of these examinations, being produced, the same was so falsified in most particulars thereof, as well by the witnesses pretended to be sworn, as also by some of the persons then, and now (1662) living, who were in the said book sworn to be murdered, that the same war, for shame, laid aside as no evidence; and several other persons, who have taken examinations touching murders, have, many times since, acknowledged the falsity of the matters published by them, as being had by the wrong information of others, who in the hurry of these times, and their own frights, were so transported, that they swore all their neighbours, whom they left behind them, were murdered, when all, or most of them, were afterwards found to be living." Collect. of Massac. and Murd. of the Irish, Pref.

should allow that the cruelties of the Irish, out of war, extended to these numbers, which confidering the nature of the feveral depofitions, I think in my confcience we cannot; yet to be impartial, we muft allow, that there is no pretence for laying a greater number to their charge."

"This account," continues the Doctor (2), " is corroborated by a letter, which I copied out of the council-books at Dublin, written on the 5th of May, 1652, ten years after the beginning of the rebellion, from the parliament-commiffioners in Ireland, to the Englifh parliament. After exciting," fays he, " the parliament to further feverity againft the Irifh, as being afraid their behaviour towards that people, might never fufficiently avenge their murders and maffacres; and left the parliament might fhortly be in purfuance of a fpeedy fettlement of that kingdom, and thereby fome tender conceffions might be concluded," thefe commiffioners tell them, " that it then appeared, that befides eight hundred and forty-eight families, there were killed, hanged, and burnt, fix thoufand and fixty-two."

After feeing this, in comparifon, exceedingly moderate charge, made even by the prejudiced Commiffioners of the Rebel-Englifh parliament, what are we to think of the accounts of thofe maffacres and murders, which have been left us by our moft feemingly impartial, and approved adverfe writers on this fubject? What, I fay, of Sir William Petty's cool calculation, that upwards of thirty thoufand Britifh were killed, out of war, in the firft year of this infurrection? Or, of Lord Clarendon's pathetic lamentation, that in the firft two or three days of it, forty or fifty thoufand of them were deftroyed? Or, of Sir John Temple's horrible affirmation, " that one hundred and fifty thoufand Proteftants were maffacred in cold blood, in the two firft months of the rebellion?"

There is no queftion, but that the defire of revenge, and the fear of tender conceffions upon a fettlement, caufed thefe commiffioners to heighten, and aggravate as much as poffible, this charge againft the infurgents; and yet we fee, that even their account of thefe cruelties during the whole time of this ten years war, falls infinitely fhort of that, which has been given us, I will not fay by Temple, or Petty, but by Clarendon himfelf, during the firft two or three days of it only. What fhame for the noble hiftorian, thus to have exceeded the very regicides, in calumny and mifreprefentation!

(2) ib.

CHAP.

CHAP. VII.

The Humanity of the Chiefs of the Insurgents.

MR. Hume, strangely misled by Temple's stupid legend, (for I will not suspect him of conscious misrepresentation,) asserts in a style better suited to romance than history, that, " an universal massacre of the English commenced with this insurrection (1); that no age, no sex, no condition, was spared,; that destruction was every where let loose, and met the hunted victims, at every turn; that all connections were dissolved, and that death was dealt by that hand, from which protection was implored, and expected." In short, " that, without provocation, without *(a)* opposition, the astonished English were massacred by their nearest neighbours, with whom they had long upheld a continued intercourse of kindness, and good offices." Not content with imputing these, and many other, if possible, greater barbarities, to the first insurgents, he confidently affirms, on the same exploded authority, " that the English Catholics of the pale, joining these old Irish, rivalled them in every act of cruelty, towards the English Protestants." Thus, the grossest, and most palpable fictions, which, when stupidly retailed by a noted and malicious libeller, have little or no chance to be believed by any, may yet be afterwards dressed out by a more artful writer, in such plausible colours, and with such semblance of truth, as will render them credible and affecting, even to some readers, of a moderate share of understanding. What pity it is, that in

(1) Hist. of England, Dub. ed. vol. iv.

(a) This demonstrates a strange unacquaintedness in this writer, even with those historians, some of whose prejudices he has all along adopted in this part of his history. For to omit other instances, Borlace has given us a journal of Sir William Cole's services against the insurgents, wherein it is boastingly asserted, " that, from the 23d of October, 1641, to some time in 1642, the said Sir William killed with his regiment of 500 foot, and one troop of horse, 2417 swordsmen of the rebels; and starved and famished, of the vulgar sort, (whose goods were seized on by the regiment,) 7000. And that he rescued and relieved 5467 Scotch and English Protestants." Borlace adds, " after this rate the English in all parts fought." Hist. of the Irish Rebel. fol. 112. Colonel Gibson having taken the strong castle of Caric-main, belonging to the Walshes, near Dublin, in which several hundreds of the Irish had taken refuge, " put them all to the sword, sparing neither man, woman, nor child." Id. ib. fol. 97. Numbers of such instances of barbarous, and indiscriminate oppression and revenge, are to be met with in all the adverse writers on this subject.

in all this historian's fine declamation on this tragical event, there is so very little of its true history to be found *(b)*.

In truth, the Irish engaged in this war, did not suffer more in their persons, by the swords of their enemies, while it was carrying on, than they have since done, in their characters, by the pens of some of those historians, who have either carelesly or maliciously commented upon it. The best, the noblest, and most loyal men in the kingdom, who, after having patiently endured numberless galling injuries and oppressions, were, at last, driven to the fatal necessity of taking arms in their defence, are confounded by these libellers, with the meanest of the Irish rabble, who followed them meerly for plunder. But I will now, from a motive of meer justice, produce a few signal instances, out of many, of the humane and christian behaviour of some of the chiefs of these insurgents, towards such of those English and Protestants, as happened to fall under their power. And this I shall do, not from writers of their own party, or persuasion, but from such adverse historians, as have otherwise too hastily condemned all their constrained efforts of natural self-defence, as so many overt acts of treason, and rebellion.

" THE (2) first thing that the new general of the Irish, Owen O'Neal, did, was to express his abhorrence of cruelties that had been committed on the English. He told Sir Phelim O'Neal, that he deserved himself to be treated in the same manner. In detestation of their actions, he burnt some of the murderers houses; and said, with a warmth unusual to him, that he would join the English, rather than not burn the rest."

" By

(2) Cart. Orm. vol. i.

(c) In the year 1764, a copy of the historical memoirs of the Irish rebellion, wherein all these calumnies are clearly refuted by unquestionable authority, was sent to Mr. Hume, when Secretary of the embassy at Paris, under Lord Hertford, in hopes of inducing him to correct these flagrant, and injurious mistakes, in a subsequent edition of his history. But the expected effect has not since appeared. He, indeed, returned a polite but evasive answer, on that occasion, in which he says, " I am here at such a distance from my authorities, that I cannot produce all the arguments which determined me to give the account you complain of, with regard to the Irish massacre. I only remember I sought truth, and thought I found it. The insurrection might be excused, as having liberty for its object. The violence also, of the puritanical parliament, struck a just terror into all the Catholics. But the method of conducting the rebellion, if we must call it by that name, was certainly such (and you seem to own it) as deserved the highest blame, and was one of the most violent efforts of barbarism and bigotry united." The authorities sent to him in the memoirs above-mentioned, demonstrating his mistakes, are by both parties confessed to be undeniable. And indeed, it appears from the softer style of this letter, that since the writing of his history, he has abated somewhat of his declamatory virulence with respect to those insurgents, probably from the perusal of these authorities.

" By (3) the humanity of Mr. Philip O'Reilly, one of the moſt confiderable chiefs of the rebels, ſcarce any murders were committed in the county of Cavan; ſuch of the Proteſtants as put themſelves under his protection, were ſafely conveyed into the Engliſh quarters; and thoſe that were ſtript and in neceſſity, he fed and cloathed, till they were ſent away. Among theſe, was Doctor Henry Jones, a nephew of Primate Uſher, and Dean of Kilmore, who, though he turned afterwards a noted partizan of Cromwell's, was promoted to the See of Clogher, and thence, after the reſtoration, to the See of Meath."

" Doctor (4) Maxwell, afterwards Biſhop of Kilmore, depoſeth, that Miſtreſs Catherine Hovenden widow, and mother to Sir Phelim O'Neal, preſerved four and twenty Engliſh and Scotch, in her own houſe; and fed them there for ſeven and thirty weeks, out of her own ſtore; and that, when her children took her away, upon the approach of an army, ſhe left both them, and the deponent, at their liberty. That Captain Alexander Hovenden, her ſon, conducted five and thirty Engliſh out of Armagh to Drogheda, whereof ſome were of good quality; when it was thought, he had ſecret directions to murder them. Twenty more he ſent ſafe to Newry, and he would truſt no other convoy but himſelf."

" There (5) are many honourable teſtimonies," ſays Warner, " of the care and preſervation of the Engliſh, by Lord Muſkerry and his Lady, not only in ſaving their lives from the enemy, but alſo, in relieving them in great numbers, from cold and hunger, after they had been ſtripped and driven from their habitations. Indeed," adds he, " all the gentlemen in that part of the kingdom, (Munſter) were exceedingly careful to prevent bloodſhed, and to hinder the Engliſh from being pillaged and ſtript, though it was many times impoſſible.

" In (6) the above-mentioned province of Munſter," ſays Mr. Carte, " Lord Mountgarret, by proclamation, ſtrictly enjoined all his followers not to hurt any of the Engliſh inhabitants, either in body or goods; and he ſucceeded ſo far in his deſign, for their preſervation, that there was not the leaſt act of bloodſhed committed. But it was not poſſible for him to prevent the vulgar ſort, who flocked after him for booty, from plundering both Engliſh and Iriſh, Papiſt and Proteſtant, without diſtinction. He uſed his authority, but

in

(3) Id. ib. (4) Id. ib. Borl. Hiſt. of the Iriſh Reb. App. (5) Hiſt. of the Iriſh Rebel.
(6) Ubi ſupra.

in vain, to put a ſtop to this violence; till ſeeing one of the rank of a gentleman, Mr. Richard Cantwell (deſcended from Mr. Richard Cantwell of Painſtown, a man much eſteemed in his country) tranſgreſſing his orders, and plundering in his preſence, he ſhot him dead with his piſtol."

" At (7) the ſame time the ſaid Lord Mountgarret's eldeſt ſon, Colonel Edmund Butler, taking poſſeſſion of Waterford, none of the inhabitants, of whatever country, or religion, was either killed or pillaged; and ſuch of the Britiſh Proteſtants, as had a mind to leave the place, were allowed to carry off their goods, wherever they pleaſed."

" Callan (8) and Gowran were ſeized at the ſame time, by perſons thereunto deſigned by Lord Mountgarret, without any bloodſhed; ſome plunder, however, was there committed, though with leſs violence for fear of complaints, it being confined to cattle of Engliſh breed, which were ſtolen as well from the Iriſh, who had any of that breed, as from the Engliſh."

" The (9) towns of Clonmell and Carrickmagriffit, in Tipperary, and Dungarvan, were ſeverally ſurprized by Mr. Richard Butler of Kilcaſh, ſecond brother to the Marquis of Ormond; and he had ſuch an influence over his followers, that he kept them not only from murder, but even from plunder; his great care and noble diſpoſition, being acknowledged even by his enemies."

James (10) Lord Dunboyne, hearing of the ſurpriſe of Feathard, by Theobald Butler, and being chief commander of the barony of Middle-thyrde, by ſpecial grants, made to ſome of his anceſtors, for ſervice performed to the crown of England, repaired thither the next day, and took on him the command of the town, diſperſing the rabble, and placing in it a garriſon, which he formed of the moſt ſubſtantial inhabitants of the place, and neighbourhood. He immediately ſet the Engliſh at liberty, reſtored them their goods, and ſent them away in ſafety to Youghall, and other places, which they choſe for their retreat. Two of theſe were clergymen, of whom Mr. Hamilton was, at his requeſt, ſent with his family to the Counteſs of Ormond *(d)*."

Mr.

(7) Id. ib.   (8) Id. ib.   (9) Id. ib.   (10) Id. ib.

(d) How different was the conduct of the pretended leaders of the Royal party, from that of the above-mentioned Chiefs of the Iriſh, when they got poſſeſſion of any place belonging to the latter. Among numberleſs inſtances of their unparalleled cruelty, I ſhall only mention two or three in Munſter, from their panegyriſt, Borlace. " Sir Frederic Hamilton," ſays he, " entering Sligo, about the firſt of July, 1642,

Mr. (11) Lowe, Vicar of Cloyne, having been barbarously murdered at Feathard, by one James M'Hugh, and some accomplices, Lord Ikerin, upon information given against him, committed him to prison, whence M'Hugh making an escape, fled the country for some time; but returning, was seized again, confessed the fact, and was hanged for it, with two of his accomplices."

" Sir (12) Richard Everet, Bart. in the beginning of the rebellion, sent the richest of the English planters in his country, with their stock and goods, into the English quarters. The poorer English, consisting of eighty-eight persons, he kept and maintained, at his own charge, till the middle of June, 1642; then conveyed them to Mitchels-town, and when that place was afterwards taken by the Irish, he sent for some of those families that were very poor, and maintained them for a long time. As soon as the cessation was made, some of the poor tenants came back to him, and he settled and protected them on his lands, till Cromwell came into the country."

When (13) Birr surrendered to general Preston, in January 1642, the articles were faithfully performed; and the Earl of Castlehaven, his Lieutenant General, conveyed the garrison and inhabitants, to the number of eight hundred persons, in a long march of two or three days together, thro' the woods of Irregan, and waste countries, safe to Athy."

" Sir Audley Mervin, a covenanter, Cromwellist, and Speaker of the Irish House of Commons after the restoration, in a speech," says (14) Sir Peter Pett, " glowing with anger enough against Papists, confessed, that in the barony of Inishoan, there were above two thousand papists, who could bring hundreds of Protestants to witness their civil demeanour. This," adds he, " I mention to give testimony to the heroic virtue of many of the church of Rome, at that dismal period."

But, not to dwell longer on particulars, the whole body of the Catholic nobility and gentry of Ireland, did, by their agents at Oxford, in 1643, petition his Majesty (15), " that all murders committed on both sides, in this war,

(11) Id. ib.   (12) Id. ib.   (13) Id. ib.   (14) Happy future state of England.
(15) Boil. Hist. of the Irish Rebel.

1642, burnt the town, and slew in the streets, three hundred of the Irish." Hist. of the Irish Rebel. fol. 112. " Lord Dungarvan and Lord Broghill, summoning the castle of Ardmore, in the county of Waterford, 21st of August, 1642, it was yielded upon mercy. Neverthelefs, one hundred and forty men were put to the sword." Id. ib. fol. 114. It is therefore no wonder, that this Lord Broghill declared, on another occasion, " that he knew not what Quarter meant." Id. ib. fol. 110.

war, might be examined in a future parliament, and the actors of them exempted out of all the acts of indemnity, and oblivion." But this proposal the Protestant agents, then also attending the King at Oxford, wisely declined; upon which it was justly observed, " that (16) if it should be asked, wherefore this offer of the accused Irish has been always rejected or evaded by their accusers, (for it was more than once repeated afterwards) there is no man of reason but understands it was, because the Irish were not guilty of those barbarous and inhuman crimes, with which they were charged; and because those who charged them so exorbitantly, found themselves, or those of their party, truly chargeable with more numerous, and more barbarous crimes and murders, committed on the stage of Ireland, whereon they had acted, and yet but partly, their own proper guilt; for many of them acted it on that of Great Britain too, even the most horrid guilt imaginable, by the most bloody, and most execrable murder, of the best and most innocent of Kings."

CHAP. VIII.

The Conduct of the Romish Clergy during the Insurrection.

BUT whatever cruelties these insurgents are supposed to have committed on the English and Protestants, either in or out of war, they are all said to have been perpetrated by the advice and instigation of their clergy. Mr. Hume, too confident of the truth of this imputation, on the sole credit of the depositions before-mentioned, has launched out into the most pathetic strains of invective on that occasion. " The English," says he (1), " as heretics abhorred of God, and detestable to all holy men, were marked out by the Priests, for slaughter; and of all actions, to rid the world of these declared enemies of Catholic faith and piety, was represented as the 'most meritorious." And thus, in consequence of these documents, " while death," adds he, " finished the sufferings of each victim, the bigoted assassins, with joy and exultation, still echoed in his expiring ears, that these agonies were but the commencement of torments infinite and eternal." This, indeed, might have appeared a pretty rhetorical flourish, but that the expression, " expiring ears," is somewhat of the boldest, and borders too closely on nonsense; but it never could have passed for real and genuine history, with any one, who had taken the least pains to inform himself, of the principles and conduct of these Priests, at that dismal

(16) Walsh's Reply to a Person of Quality.   (1) Hist. of Engl. Dub. ed. vol. iv.

dismal juncture (a). Mr. Hume might have learned, even from (2) Borlace, that, in a congregation of their Archbishops, Bishops, and inferior clergy, at Kilkenny, in May 1642, excommunication was denounced against all those of their communion, " who either had, from the beginning of the war, or should afterwards, in the course of it, murder, dismember, or grievously strike; all thieves, unlawful spoilers, or robbers of any goods; and such as favoured or received them." And they even included, in this censure, " all such as had invaded, or should invade, the possessions, or goods, spiritual or temporal, of any Irish Protestant, not being their adversary, and should detain them. They also, " commanded all and every of their clergy, as well regular as secular, not to hear the confessions of the aforesaid excommunicated persons; nor to administer to them the holy sacrament, under pain of excommunication ipso facto."

" This was, says (3) Doctor Warner, " a general synod of all the Popish Bishops and clergy of Ireland. Three of the titular Archbishops, six other Bishops, the Proxies of five more, besides Vicars Generals, and other Dignitaries, were present at this synod. And as these are the acts and ordinances purely of the Roman Catholic clergy of Ireland, represented in a general synod, I suppose it will be allowed, on all sides, that whatever proceedings are here condemned, are to be placed to the account of the follies and vices of particular people; and cannot fairly be charged on the Roman faith (b)."

Many instances might be produced, of the great beneficence and humanity, of these ecclesiastics, to the distressed English and Protestants, at that period

(2) History of the Irish Rebellion.   (3) ib. fol. 201.

(a) " If some Popish ecclesiastics," says Doctor Leland, " preached their horrid doctrines of blood and massacre, others were known equally zealous to moderate the excesses of war, to protect the English, and to conceal them from the fury of the enemy, even in their places of worship, and under their altars." Hist. of Ireland, vol. iii. p. 155.

(b) " How weak, how uncharitable, how unjust," exclaims the same writer, " is it in those, who charge such horrid impieties on the principles of the Roman Catholic religion, as were meerly owing to the accursed, hellish disposition of particular persons who gave a loose to them! The Protestants, I am sure, would take it ill, and very justly, if the barbarities of Sir Charles Coote, and Sir Frederick Hamilton were fastened on their religion. And why then should they charge those, of which Sir Phelim O'Neal, and others were guilty, on the principles of the Romish church, which hath disclaimed them? These considerations may be too candid and impartial, to please the ignorant and bigotted, of either side: but they will teach principles and practices more agreeable to christianity, than those which prevailed at that time, and which we now so much lament." Hist. of the Ir. Rebel. p. 202.

period (4). " At the taking of Cafhell, Doctor Samuel Pullen, Chancellor of that city, and Dean of Clonfert, with his wife and children, was preferved by Father James Saul, a Jefuit. Several other Romifh Priefts diftinguifhed themfelves on that occafion, by their endeavours to fave the Englifh; particularly Father Jofeph Everard, and Redmond Englifh, both Francifcan Friars; who hid fome of them in their chapel, and even under their altar. And foon after, thofe who had been thus preferved, were according to their defire, fafely conveyed into the county of Cork, by a guard of the Irifh inhabitants of Cafhell, who acted with fo much good faith, that feveral of the convoy were wounded, in defending them, from the violence of the rabble upon the mountains, in their paffage."

Doctor Bedel, Bifhop of Kilmore, when a prifoner with the infurgents, who doubtlefs had many Priefts among them (5), " was never interrupted in the exercife of his worfhip, although not only his houfe and all the out buildings, but alfo the church and church-yard, were full of people that flocked to him for fhelter. So that, from the 23d of October to the 18th of December following, he, and all thofe within his walls, enjoyed to a miracle," fays Bifhop Burnet, " perfect quiet. And when he died, at the age of feventyone, the titular Bifhop of that diocefs, although he had profelyted his brother, a Popifh Prieft, to the communion of the eftablifhed church, fuffered him to be buried in confecrated ground, the Irifh doing him unufual honours at his funeral. For the chiefs of the infurgents, having affembled their forces, accompanied his body to the church-yard, with great folemnity; and defired Mr. Clogy, one of his chaplains, to bury him according to the church-offices. At his interment, they difcharged a volley of fhot, crying out in Latin, Hic requiefcat ultimus Anglorum! May the laft of the Englifh reft in peace! Edmund Farilly, a Popifh Prieft, exclaimed at the fame time, O, fit anima mea cum Bedello! Would to God that my foul were with Bedel."

(4) Cart. Orm. vol. i.   (5) Burnet's life of Bedel.

CHAP.

CHAP. IX.

The first Cause of the Insurrection's increasing.

FOR almost (1) six weeks from its beginning, this insurrection *(a)* was confined to the province of Ulster, all the other parts of Ireland remaining quiet. Even in the conspirators first, and principal design to seize the castle of Dublin, not one of the Catholics of that city was any way concerned; although they were then (2) fifteen to one Protestant; and, what might have been an additional temptation (3), " there was not a company of the army, at that juncture, in the town." Nay so long after, as June 1642, the Lords Justices themselves testified (4), " that no particular crimes could be objected to them, and that they could not be charged with any thing, but bare suspicion."

Not less quiet, during the same space of time, were (5) the principal inhabitants of the county of Wicklow; although a great part of their territory had been taken from them, and planted, some years before. Nor was there yet any considerable commotion in Conaught, Clare, Tipperary, or Limerick (6), " which had been all lately found for the king, by several inquisitions, and were then ready to be disposed of to British undertakers." In short, it may, on very sure grounds, be asserted, that, for near two months after the 23d of October 1641, no formal insurrection appeared among the natives of any of the four provinces, except those of Ulster, who had been particularly threatened with extirpation, and were generally, says Lord Clanrickard (7), " haughty and ambitious spirits, the remains of the branches of antient rebels, and had lost large and great possessions." What occasioned the fatal change, that soon after ensued, in most parts of the kingdom, I shall now endeavour to demonstrate.

In August, 1641, the Irish parliament was in daily expectation of the return of their agents from England, with the Royal assent to two bills, that would

---

(1) Warner's Hist. of the Irish Rebel. p. 130. (2) Cart. Orm. vol. i.   (3) Id. ib.
(4) Temp. Hist. of the Irish Rebel.   (5) Id. ib.   (6) Id. ib.   (7) Memoirs, Engl. ed.

(a) " The rebellion," says Mr. Carte, " had been carried on till the month of December, by the meer Irish, and confined to Ulster, to some few counties in Leinster, and that of Leitrim in Conaught." Life of Orm. vol. i. fol. 243. He had before observed, " that no one nobleman of the kingdom, or any estated gentleman of English race, engaged in the rebellion, till the month of December." *ib.*

would have put an effectual ftop to thofe predatory fuits of enquiry into defective titles, which had been fo long and grievoufly complained of. "Never," fays (8) Mr. Carte, " were two acts better adapted to give general fatisfaction to any people, than thefe were to the gentlemen of Ireland." Even Temple owns (9), " that thefe bills had been long, and moft impetuoufly longed for by the Irifh." And although his Majefty had, in May preceding, fent pofitive orders to the Juftices (10), to pafs thefe bills, and the other promifed graces; and the Commons firft, and afterwards both Houfes, had moft earneftly, and repeatedly befought them (11), " that they might be fuffered to continue together for a further time; becaufe their agents were at the water-fide with thefe bills," yet thefe Lords Juftices (12), acting every thing in Ireland, by the influence of the puritan faction in the Englifh parliament, often in derogation of his Majefty's commands, caufed the parliament to be adjourned for three months." Which adjournment, the Catholic members, who were principally aggrieved by it (13), " afterwards aggravated againft the Juftices, as one of the chief moving caufes of the taking up of arms, generally throughout the kingdom."

Soon after this fatal and enforced adjournment, the parliament's agents arriving in Dublin (14), " prefently applied," fays Temple, " to the Lords Juftices, and Council, defiring to have thofe acts, and other graces, granted by his Majefty, made known to the people by proclamation." This was promifed, and an inftrument drawn up, and prefented to their Lordfhips for that purpofe; but (15), " they, as it feems, defiring rather to add fuel to the fire of the fubjects difcontents, than to quench the fame, did forbear to give any notice thereof to the people."

CHAP. X.

The fame Subject continued.

THIS general difguft was not removed, or leffened, by the next meeting of parliament, on the 16th of November following, the day to which it had been adjourned. On the contrary, by the manifeft reluctance, with which the Juftices fuffered it to meet even then, and by their fudden prorogation of it for two months longer, it was greatly increafed. This prorogation,

(8) Life of Orm. vol. i.   (9) Irifh Rebel.   (10) Commons Journal, vol. i.   (11) ib.
(12) Cart. Orm. vol. i.   (13) Temp. Irifh Rebel.   (14) Id. ib.
(15) Remon. from Trim.

gation, says (1) Mr. Carte, " gave a particular distaste to the Roman Catholics, who were like to be the greatest sufferers thereby, and to lose the benefit of those graces, which were intended for their particular relief (2). The Earl of Ormond, Lord Dillon of Costelloe, and some others, urged, among other things, against the prorogation, that all the nation was in expectation of the graces, and would be strangely uneasy, if they were not confirmed in parliament. But the Justices were deaf to all such remonstrances; for, as they had been with difficulty prevailed upon, by the importunate solicitations of the Lords and gentry of the pale, to suffer the parliament to meet even on the aforesaid 16th of November, so they then took especial care (3) to limit the session, in such a manner, that no act of grace, or any thing else for the people's quiet or satisfaction, might be propounded, or passed. For, well knowing that the members of both Houses, throughout the kingdom (a few in, and about Dublin, only excepted) would be absent from parliament, they published their proclamation for the meeting, but two days before the time; whereupon, only a few of the Lords and Commons appeared in the Houses; who, on their entrance at the castle-bridge and gate, and within the castle-yard, to the door of the parliament-house, were environed with a great number of armed men, with matches lighted, and muskets presented even to the breasts of the members of both Houses; none being admitted to bring one servant to attend him, or any weapon about him, within the castle-bridge. Yet how thin soever the Houses were, and how much soever overawed, they did both jointly (4) supplicate the Lords Justices and Council, that they might, for a time, continue together, and expect the coming of the rest of the members, to the end, they might quiet the troubles in full parliament; and that those acts of security, granted by his Majesty, and transmitted under the great seal of England, might be passed, to settle the minds of his Majesty's subjects. But, to these requests, conducing so much to his Majesty's service, and the settlement of the kingdom, a flat denial was given (5). Nay their Lordships dismissed the Houses, after only two days sitting, without saying a word of the graces from the King, or giving them any assurance, or even a faint glimmering hope, that they should be passed in another session."

The Earl of Castlehaven, who sate in that parliament, after having recited the loyal and unanimous protestation of both Houses (6), " that they would, if necessary, take up arms, and with their lives and fortunes, endeavour to suppress the rebellion;" informs us, " that in order speedily to bring the rebels to condign punishment, they fell immediately to consider of the most effectual

(1) Cart. Orm. Vol. i. fol. 222.   (2) Id. ib.   (3) Remon from Trim
(4) Castlehaven's Memoirs.   (5) Warner's Hist. of the Irish Rebel. Carte, &c.
(6) Memoirs.

effectual means to do the work. But this way of proceeding," adds his Lordship, " did not, it seems, suit with the Lords Justices designs, who were often heard to say, that the more there were in rebellion, the more lands would be forfeited; and therefore, in the very height of the business, they resolved upon a prorogation; which the parliament understanding, Viscount Costelloe, and myself, were sent from the Lords House, and others from the Commons, to desire the continuance of the parliament, till the rebels, then few in number, were reduced. But our advice was slighted, and the Parliament next day prorogued, to the great surprize of both Houses, and the general dislike of all knowing, and honest men."

CHAP. XI.

Further Misconduct of the Lords Justices.

AS it evidently appears, from divers circumstances, that the Justices, Parsons and Borlace, rather wished for, and promoted, than endeavoured to prevent this insurrection, so it is still more manifest, that all their subsequent proceedings tended only to *(a)* increase and extend it, for their own mercenary purposes (1). Sir Robert Talbot of Castle-Talbot, in the county of Wicklow, repaired to Dublin, in the beginning of the troubles; and offered to Sir William Parsons, in the presence of Dean Bulkely, who lived to attest it after the restoration, to secure the chief heads of the Byrnes, Tooles, and other septs, in that county, who, as their lands had been planted some years before, were the likeliest men to rise, and begin a rebellion in Leinster, if he would give him commission to do so; insisting, that they would not stir, while their chiefs were in custody, as so many hostages for their fidelity. But Sir William Parsons absolutely refused to give him a commission; and these septs, soon after breaking out into rebellion, Sir Robert engaged against them, in defence of the English in that, and the adjoining county of Catherlogh; and conveyed most of these English with their goods and stocks safe to Dublin. He had, indeed, the Lords Justices thanks for this service, but it cost him dear; for in revenge

(1) Cart. Orm. vol. i.

(a) " Had the Lords Justices," says Doctor Warner, " acquitted themselves like men of probity and understanding, there was time enough given them to suppress an insurrection, which for six weeks almost, was confined to the province of Ulster, without any chief that was so considerable, as Sir Phelim O'Neal. But it was the great misfortune of that unhappy country, to be then governed by a man (Sir William Parsons) that had not one qualification for such a post, at such a time; and to those defects, was added, great obliquity of heart towards both the King and the Irish. Hist. of the Irish Rebel. p. 130.

venge thereof, two of his beſt houſes, Cartan and Liſcartan, were burned by the Iriſh."

THE Earl of Ormond's early offer to ſuppreſs theſe tumults in their beginning, met with no better reception from their Lorſhips; for that nobleman, having undertaken to purſue the rebels, then in no reſpect conſiderable, if he might be allowed meat and drink for the ſoldiers in his march, his propoſal was rejected. "The only reaſon aſſigned by the Juſtices for this refuſal, viz. the want of arms, was," ſays (2) Mr. Carte, "a pretence ſo notoriouſly falſe, that it could only be made uſe of to cover motives, which they were aſhamed to confeſs; for there was, at this time, in the ſtores of the caſtle, a fine train of artillery, ammunition of all ſorts, in great quantities; arms for above ten thouſand men, tents, and neceſſaries of all kinds for the march, and proviſion, of an army; all which had been prepared, by the Earl of Strafford, for the Scots expedition."

WHAT theſe Juſtices real motives were, ſoon after appeared (3). "In the before-mentioned ſhort ſeſſion of November 16th, both Houſes had drawn up a letter to the King, which was ſent by the Lords Dillon and Taaffe; and in which they offered of themſelves, and without any aid from England, to put an end to this inſurrection." Immediately upon this, the (4) the Juſtices, and their party in the Council, privately wrote to the Earl of Leiceſter, Lord Lieutenant of Ireland; and after telling him, they expected and hoped for his ſecrecy, and that they could not open themſelves with freedom, at the council-board, they beſought his Lordſhip, that no ſuch overture ſhould be accepted; and among other reaſons, becauſe the charge of ſupplies from England, would be abundantly compenſated out of the *(b)* eſtates of thoſe, who were actors in that rebellion." From this information, the Lords Dillon and Taaffe, with their papers, were ſeized at Ware, by order of the Engliſh Houſe of Commons; and detained in cuſtody ſeveral months, till they made their eſcape to the King, then at York; but it was then too late to offer a remedy, as the inſurrection was become in a manner general.

(2) ib. vol. i. fol. 194.   (3) Id. ib.   (4) Id. ib.

(b) "Whatever," ſays Doctor Leland, "were the profeſſions of the Chief Governors, the only danger they really apprehended, was that of a too ſpeedy ſuppreſſion of the rebellion. Extenſive forfeitures was their favourite object, and that of their friends." Hiſt. Irel. vol. iii. p. 160-1.

CHAP.

CHAP. XII.

The Nobility and Gentry of the Pale banished from Dublin.

THE Lords Juſtices had lent a few arms to Lord Gormanſtown, and ſome gentlemen of the pale, for the defence of their houſes in the country; which, however, they ſoon after recalled (1), " thereby, renouncing all confidence in them, though nothing had happened to give occaſion to any further ſuſpicion of them, than when the arms had been entruſted to them. The arms particularly aſſigned to Mr. John Bellew, high ſheriff, and knight of the ſhire, for the county of Louth, were ſo quickly demanded back, that they were not delivered. Their habitations being thus rendered defenceleſs, they quitted the country and came up to Dublin, to put themſelves, as they thought, under the eye and protection of the government; but the Juſtices, inſtead of allowing them ſuch an aſylum (2), on the next day after ſending for the arms, publiſhed a proclamation requiring theſe noblemen and gentlemen, with others not having neceſſary cauſe of reſidence in the city, or ſuburbs of Dublin, and the places within two miles about the ſame, to be approved of by a council of war, to repair to their reſpective homes, in twenty-four hours, after the publication of the proclamation *(a)*, upon pain of death."

SIR Robert Talbot, whoſe houſes had been burned by the Iriſh, on account of the ſervice he had rendered the Engliſh (3), " found it neceſſary, at this time, to bring his lady and family to Dublin; where he again tendered his ſervice to the Lords Juſtices, offering to raiſe men, if they would furniſh him with arms, to fight againſt the rebels; but theſe were denied him, nor could either his offers, or his late ſervices, prevail for leave to continue in Dublin. He was forced, by the proclamation on pain of death, to leave the city in twenty-four hours; and having no ſure place of retreat, he was obliged to ſculk, and live privately, for a long time, for fear of the Iriſh, till

(1) Id. ib. vol. i. fol. 238.   (2) Id. ib.   (3) Id. ib.

(a) It appears from Borlace, that theſe Juſtices publiſhed two proclamations of that kind, even before the end of October, 1641. For that writer, after having ſaid that they had iſſued a proclamation, " in his Majeſty's name, commanding all perſons, not dwellers in the city and ſuburbs, to depart within an hour, on pain of death," adds, " that the ſtate, on the 28th of October, publiſhed a proclamation to the ſame intent with the former, with the penalty of death, to ſuch as wilfully harboured them." Ir. Reb. fol. 44. Another proclamation of the like tenour, and on the penalty of death, was iſſued by theſe Juſtices, on 11th of November following. Id. ib. fol. 49.

till the breach between the King and the Parliament of England, when he entered into the Roman Catholic confederacy; doing however, during all the time of the troubles, all the good offices in his power, sometimes with the hazard of his life, to preserve the English, and dispose the Irish to submit to the cessation, and afterwards to the peaces of 1646, and 1648, to which he constantly adhered."

CHAP. XIII.

The Justices invite the Lords of the Pale to a Conference.

NO signs of a formed insurrection had yet appeared in the provinces of Leinster, Conaught, or Munster, when, (on the 27th of November,) a report being spread of spoils committed on some of the English in the county of Wicklow, Sir Charles Coote was commanded from Dublin thither with a body of troops; where, in the town of Wicklow (1), he cruelly put to death several innocent persons, without distinction of age or sex (2). Among other instances, he is charged with saying, when a soldier was carrying about a poor babe on the end of his pike (3), " that he liked such frolicks." Upon his return to Dublin from this expedition, the Justices appointed him (4) governor of the city, in recompence for that service. At the same time, a rumour was spread, that he had made a proposal, at the council-board, for executing a general massacre on all the Catholics; which, from (a) the character of the man, was easily credited.

On the 3d of December, 1641, the Lords Justices directed letters to the Lords of the pale, whom they had lately driven from Dublin, acquainting them (5), " that they had immediate occasion to confer with them, concerning the present state of the kingdom." These noblemen knew, that the day before these letters were sent, the Catholics of Dublin had been disarmed; that they themselves, lying most exposed to the rebels, could not hinder their entrance

---

(1) Carte, Warner, &c. (2) Carte's Orm. vol. i. fol. 243. (3) Id. ib. (4) Id. ib.
(5) Cart. Orm. vol. i.

(a) " He was a stranger to mercy, and committed many acts of cruelty, without distinction, equal in that respect to any of the rebels." Warner's Hist. of the Irish Rebel. p. 135. " Sir Charles Coote," says Doctor Leland, " in revenge of the depredations of the Irish, committed such unprovoked, such ruthless, and indiscriminate carnage in the town of Wicklow, as rivalled the utmost extravagancies of the Northerns." Hist. of Irel. vol. iii. p. 146.

entrance into their houses in the country, to which they had been banished, from Dublin, by the proclamation on pain of death; or the paying of them contribution, which, in the eye of the law, was criminal, though unavoidable. They could not imagine, why these Lords Justices, who had, about a fortnight before, thought their abode in Dublin incompatible with the safety of the state, should now, by a sudden turn of sentiment, invite them thither, to be consulted with, on that subject. Hence it was natural for them to suspect, that the summons was only an artifice, to draw them to Dublin; and when they were there, to seize on their persons, and confine them to an irksome prison, and perhaps, prosecute them at law, with a severity which might end in the forfeiture of their estates, the ruin of their families, and the taking away of their lives by an ignominious execution.

Such were the reasons that hindered the Lords of the pale to pay obedience to the Justices' summons of the third of December, 1641. By appointment, however, they met together on the seventh; and then drew up a letter to the state, importing (6), " that they had, heretofore, presented themselves to their Lordships, and freely offered their advice, and furtherance towards the safety of the kingdom, which having been neglected, gave them cause to conceive, that their loyalty was suspected by their Lordships." They added, " that they had received certain advertisement, that Sir Charles Coote, at the council-board, had uttered some speeches, tending to a purpose to execute, upon those of their religion, a general massacre; by which they were deterred from waiting on their Lordships, not having any *(b)* security for their safety against those threatned evils; and rather thought it fit, to stand upon their best guard, until they heard from their Lordships, how they should be secured from those perils; protesting, nevertheless, that they were, and would continue, both faithful advisers, and resolute furtherers, of his Majesty's service, concerning the present state of the kingdom, and the safety thereof, to their best abilities." This letter was subscribed by the Earl of Fingall, the Lords Gormanstown, Slane, Dunsany, Netterville, Louth, and Trimblestown.

(6) Temple, Carte, &c.

(b) " Some," says Mr. Carte, on this occasion, " have not scrupled to furnish, that the Lords Justices never expected these noblemen would comply with their summons; and that all the measures they took at the same time, were taken expressly with a design to terrify them from trusting themselves in Dublin, and from thence to take some advantage for the forfeiture of their estates. It answered this end very well, that Sir Charles Coote, immediately after his inhuman executions, and promiscuous murders of people in Wicklow, was made governor of Dublin, at the very time of sending out the summons to the Lords of the pale." Life of Orm. vol. i. fol. 256.

CHAP.

CHAP. XIV.

The Gentlemen of the Pale assembled at Swords.

ON the same 7th of December, on which the abovementioned letter was drawn up (1), " a party of horse and foot being sent by the Justices, into the neighbourhood of Dublin, in quest of some robbers, came to the village of Santry, where they murdered some innocent husbandmen, (whose heads they brought into the city, in triumph,) on pretence, that they had harboured, and relieved the rebels, who had made inroads, and committed depredations in these parts. Hard (2), indeed," says Mr. Carte, " was the case of the country-people, at that time, when not being able to hinder parties of robbers, and rebels, from breaking into their houses, and taking refreshments there, this should be deemed a treasonable act, and sufficient to authorize a massacre."

THE next morning, complaint being made to the government of this outrage, no redress was obtained. Whereupon, some gentlemen of quality, and others, inhabitants of that part of the country, being justly alarmed at these proceedings, and mindful of the report of Coote's barbarous proposal at the council-board, forsook their houses, and prepared for their defence. For this massacre following so soon after (3), " the executions and murders, which Sir Charles Coote had ordered in the county of Wicklow; his being made governor of Dublin for that service; and the Catholics of that city being all disarmed, the day before the Lords of the pale were invited to a conference there, confirmed their belief of the truth of the report, that a general massacre of those of their religion was intended."

WHEREFORE, these gentlemen assembled together, on the 9th of December, at Swords, a village distant from Dublin about six miles; and on the 10th, the Justices issued their warrant (4), commanding them to separate, on sight of it; and that nine of the principal persons so assembled, should appear before them, at the council-board, by ten of the clock the next morning, to shew the cause of their assembling in that manner (5)." To this warrant, they returned an answer on the same day, to the following effect; " that they were constrained to meet there, for the safety of their lives, which they conceived

T 2

---

(1) Carte, Temple, Borlace. (2) Cart. Orm. (3) Id. ib. (4) Templ. Irish Rebels.
(5) Id. ib.

ceived to be in no small danger, having been forced to forsake their dwellings on the last Tuesday at night, by the rising out of horse-troops and foot-companies, who, on the said night, killed four Catholics, for no other reason, but because they bore the name of that religion; and that they had been before put into many fears, by certain intelligence given them of unexpected attempts against their lives. Wherefore, they desired ardently to be in some certain way assured by their Lordships of the safety of their lives, before they ran the hazard thereof; which was the only motive, that hindered them from manifesting that obedience, which they knew to be due to their Lordships commands."

C H A P. XV.

The Lords Justices violate the Public Faith.

THE Justices, seeming to comply with these gentlemens' ardent desire above-mentioned, issued a manifesto, dated the 14th of December, but not published *(a)* till the 15th (1); wherein they allowed them the space of two days, viz. until the 17th of that month, for their appearing before them in Dublin; and in order to induce them to appear then (2), " they gave them the word of the state, that they might safely and securely repair thither, without danger of any trouble, or stay whatsoever." And yet, on the same 15th of that month, they (3) detached a party of horse and foot to Clontarf, under the command of Sir Charles Coote, with orders " to fall upon, and cut off," the inhabitants, and burn the houses, of that village, which belonged to Mr. King, one of those gentlemen assembled at Swords, to whom, by name, the public faith had been given. " These orders," says Borlace, " were excellently well executed;" though it is confessed (4), that " no opposition was made." " Sir (5) Charles Coote, who by the Lords Justices special designation, was appointed to go on this expedition, as the fittest person to execute their orders, and one who best knew their minds, at this time pillaged and burned houses, corn, and other goods, belonging to Mr. King, to the value of four thousand pounds."

THE

(1) Remon. from Trim.   (2) Borl. Hist. of the Irish Rebel. fol. 61.   (3) Id. ib.
(4) Id. ib. Temple.   (5) Cart. Orm. vol. i.

(a) " This proclamation was sent, and delivered to Lord Gormanston on the 15th, by father Cahill, whom the Justices had lately employed in a treaty with the Ulster rebels." Carte's Ormond, vol. i. fol. 249.

THE pretended plunder of an English bark, by some of the common people of that village, (part of which plunder is said to have been put into Mr. King's house in his absence, and is made the sole pretence for this breach of public faith) must have happened, if at all, some time before this manifesto was published. For the Justices make express mention of it, in their letter to the Earl of Leicester of the 14th of December (6); on which day too, their order to pillage and burn Clontarf, is dated, altho' their manifesto was not published till the 15th. In that letter, their Lordships express their intention of ordering that expedition; and after betraying a guilty consciousness (7), " that the gentlemen of the pale would take new offence thereat;" they add, " but that we will adventure upon." From whence it evidently appears, that on the very day before that on which they published their manifesto, they had taken a resolution to violate it *(b)*.

C H A P. XVI.

The Order for a general Pardon limited by the Justices.

BUT, if even this perfidious order was not found sufficient to excite these gentlemen to any hostile, or disloyal attempt, the Justices had still in reserve, divers other means equally well calculated for that iniquitous purpose. Their Lordships had, about this time received (1) " an order of both Houses of the English parliament, dated November 30th, directing them, to grant his Majesty's pardon to all those, who within a convenient time, should return to their obedience." Yet, notwithstanding this order for *(a)* a general pardon, they still continued their former proclamation, which was so (2) limited, with respect to persons, places, and time; and clogged, besides,

(6) See Temp. Irish Rebel.   (7) Id. ib.
(1) See Temp. Irish Rebel.   (2) Id ib.

(b) " The Lords Justices, as soon as they were satisfied that the Lords of the pale would not trust themselves in the city in the hands of Sir Charles Coote, though they were ready to treat with commissioners sent from thence to any place out of his power, took measures in order to convict them of treason, and forfeit their estates." Cart. Orm. vol. i. fol. 275-6.

(a) " In another instance," says Doctor Leland, " the conduct of these wretched governors was still more suspicious; they received instructions for a general pardon to such rebels, as should submit within a certain time, to be limited by the Lords Justices. But no proclamation was published, no pardon offered, in consequence of these instructions.—A pardon offered in the name of the English parliament must have had greater influence, than any act of an Irish ministry, despised and suspected by the body of the nation. But the chief Governors, and their creatures, were experienced in the art of converting forfeitures to their own advantage." Hist. of Irel. vol. iii. p. 339-40.

besides, with such impracticable conditions, that they must have been themselves sensible, that it was apter to prevent, than to produce, submissions. For first, it absolutely precluded freeholders, from all hopes of pardon; "because," says Lord Castlehaven (3), " they had estates to lose." And on the other hand, the poorer Irish, who alone had been guilty of the depredations, and other mischiefs then committed, were to be pardoned upon such terms only, as it was not in their power to comply with. " For their pardon," says (4) Temple, " was to be granted only, on condition of restoring the goods, and chattels, taken from the British ;" which restitution, the same writer (5) confesses, " it was impossible for them to make." Besides this pardon, instead of being general, (as both Houses of the English parliament intended it should be) extended only to the lower people of four counties, viz. Meath, Westmeath, Louth, and Longford, (out of thirty-two that are in the kingdom,) " in (6) two of which four counties, no body of insurgents had yet appeared." And, the time allowed for their coming in, being stinted to ten days, it was hardly possible, as the nation was then circumstanced, for half the persons concerned to receive even notice of the proclamation, much less to surrender themselves, on so short a warning.

In like manner, when his Majesty afterwards sent these Justices his proclamation of January 1st, 1641, granting a general pardon to these insurgents, upon their submission (7); " they secreted the copies of it to such a degree, that the Lords and gentlemen of the pale, who lay nearest Dublin, could not get a sight of one of them." Nay, instead of pursuing such pacific and conciliating measures, they, on the 1st of February following, commanded out the Earl of Ormond, with a powerful army, on an expedition to the county of Kildare; where, " pursuant to his orders," says (8) Mr. Carte, " he burnt Newcastle and Lyons, and gave up Naas to his soldiers to plunder; having sent out parties, to burn Castle-Martin, Kilcullen-bridge, and in short, all the country for seventeen miles in length, and twenty-five in breath."

The Earl of Ormond was more implicitly obedient to these Lords Justices orders, than became either a true lover of his country, or a faithful subject of his King. He was not insensible of their Lordships criminal connection with the prevailing faction in the English parliament; nor of the flagrant iniquity of many of these orders: for although, while they remained in the government, he (9) " protested to Sir Henry Vane," who was one of the leaders of that faction, " upon the faith of an honest man, that he loved and honoured their persons,"

(3) Memoirs. (4) ib. p. 48. (5) ib p. 49. (6) Cart. Orm. vol. i. (7) Id. ib. vol. i. fol. 296.
(8) ib. vol. i. (9) Cart. Orm. vol. iii. fol. 43.

persons," yet, upon the disgrace of Sir William Parsons, he confessed to Lord Clanrickard, who, he knew, detested them (10), " that during their administration, the parliament's pamphlets were received as oracles, its commands obeyed as laws, and extirpation preached for gospel."

" The (11) Lords of the pale made no opposition to any of those parties, that were detached to make the above-mentioned general devastation. But it affected Lord Gormanstown, the principal mover of their union, to such a degree, that he died not long after of grief; and the rest of the Lords of the pale, grown desperate, laid aside all thoughts of pardon, or treaty; and joined all their forces, for the support of the common cause; in which many others, who had as yet stood out, soon joined, fearing that they should, at last, be involved in the others fate, since a total extirpation was intended *(b)*.

C H A P. XVII.

Lords Justices Orders concerning Roman Catholic Priests.

IN this expedition to the county of Kildare, " the soldiers found one (1) Mr. Higgins at Naas, who might, if he pleased, have easily fled, if he apprehended any danger in the stay. When he was brought before the Earl of Ormond, he voluntarily confessed, that he was a Papist, and that his residence was in the town, from whence he refused to fly away, with those that were guilty, because he not only knew himself very innocent, but believed, that he could not be without ample testimony of it; having, by his sole charity and power, preserved very many of the English from the rage, and fury of the Irish; and therefore, he only besought his Lordship, to preserve him from the violence and fury of the soldiers; and put him securely into Dublin, to be tried for any crime; which the Earl promised to do, and performed it; tho' with so much hazard, that when it was spread abroad among the soldiers, that he was a Papist, the officer in whose custody he was intrusted, was assaulted

(10) Id. ib.   (11) Id. ib. vol. i. fol. 303.

(1) Clarendon, Borl. Hist. of the Irish Rebel.

(b) " The favourite object both of the Irish government, and English parliament, was the utter extermination of all the Catholic inhabitants of Ireland.—— Their estates were already marked out, and allotted to their conquerors; so that they and their posterity were consigned to inevitable ruin." Lel. Hist. of Irel. vol. iii. p. 166.

ed by them; and it was as much as the Earl could do, to compofe the mutiny. When his Lordfhip came to Dublin, he informed the Lords Juftices of the prifoner he had brought with him, and of the good teftimony he had received of his peaceable carriage; and of the pains he had taken, to reftrain thofe, with whom he had credit, from entering into rebellion; and of many charitable offices he had performed; of all which there wanted not evidence enough, there being many then in Dublin, who owed their lives, and whatever of their fortunes was left, purely to him. Within a few days after, when the Earl did not fufpect the poor man's being in danger, he heard that Sir Charles Coote, who was Provoft-Marfhal General, had taken him out of prifon, and caufed him to be *(a)* put to death in the morning, before, or as foon as, it was light; of which barbarity, the Earl complained to the Lords Juftices; but was fo far from bringing the other to be queftioned, that he found himfelf upon fome difadvantage, for thinking the proceeding to be other, than it ought to have been *(b)*."

THE Earl of Ormond, tho' Lieutenant General of his Majefty's army, had it not, it feems, in his power, to fave the lives of any Popifh Priefts, however innocent, or meriting, whom he fhould happen to meet with in his march. For foon after (2), " his Lordfhip having promifed the Countefs of Weftmeath, to preferve her chaplain, Mr. White, whom he found at her houfe, from the fury of the foldiers, while he remained there; the poor man, having, on fome occafion, left it the next day, was taken abroad by them, and brought to the Earl, whom he reminded of the protection he had promifed him the night before; but he was only anfwered, that if he had ftayed in the houfe he was in, this would not have befallen him; and that it was then out of his power, to preferve him, himfelf being bound to purfue thofe orders,

(2) Clarend. Hift. of the Irifh Rebel.

(a) " It was certainly a miferable fpectacle, as Lord Caftlehaven obferves, in his manufcript vindication of his memoirs, to fee every day numbers of people executed by martial law, at the difcretion, or rather caprice of Sir Charles Coote, an hot headed and bloody man, and as fuch accounted even by the Englifh and Proteftants. Yet this was the man, whom the Lords Juftices picked out to entruft with a commiffion of martial law, to put to death rebels or traitors, that is (continues his Lordfhip) all fuch, as he fhould deem to be fo; which he performed with delight, and a wanton kind of cruelty; and yet, all this while the Juftices fat in council; and the Judges, in the ufual feafons, fat in their refpective courts, fpectators of, and countenancing, fo extravagant a tribunal as Sir Charles Coote's, and fo illegal an execution of Juftice." Cart. Orm. vol. i.

(b) Mr. Carte obferves, " that the hanging of this man, (deferving in many refpects, and exceptionable in none but that of his religion) by martial law, by Sir Charles Coote's authority, without a particular warrant from the ftate, feems perfectly well calculated to juftify the fears, which the Lords of the pale pretended to have of trufting themfelves in a place, whereof that gentleman was governor." Life of Orm. vol. i. fol. 280.

orders, which the Lords Juftices had given him. Neverthelefs," continues Clarendon, " he did endeavour to have faved him, at leaft, till he might be brought to Dublin; but the whole army, poffeffed with a bitter fpirit againft the Romifh clergy, mutinied upon it; and in the end, compelled his Lordfhip to leave him unto that Juftice, which they were authorifed to execute, and fo put him to death."

CHAP. XVIII.

The Caufe of the Infurrection in Munfter.

"IT (1) was the middle of December 1641, before any gentleman, in the province of Munfter, appeared to favour the infurrection. Many of them had fhewn themfelves zealous to oppofe it, and tendered their fervice to that end. Lord Mufkerry, who had married a fiftear of the Earl of Ormond's, offered to raife a thoufand men, at his own charge; and, if the ftate could not fupply them with arms, he was ready to raife money, by a mortgage of his eftate, to buy them; if when the fervice was ended, he might either keep the arms, or be reimburft what they coft him; nor did any figns of uneafinefs, or diffaffection, appear among the gentry, till Sir William St. Leger, Lord Prefident of that province, came to Clonmell; which was on the firft of that month. There had been, a few days before, fome robberies committed in the county of Tipperary, by a rabble of the vulgar fort, and a parcel of idle young fellows of the baronies of Eliogurty, Killemanna, Clanwillian, and Middlethyrde; who, as foon as they had got their prey, divided it, and retired to their feveral parifhes. Among other Englifh who fuffered, a great number of cows and fheep, were taken from Mr. Kingfmill of Ballyowen, brother-in-law to the Lord Prefident. Sir William St. Leger, upon Notice thereof, came in two or three days, with two troops of horfe, in great *(a)* fury, to Ballyowen; and being informed the cattle were driven to Eliogurty, he marched that way. As he fet forth, he killed three perfons at Ballyowen, who were faid to have taken up fome mares of Mr. Kingfmill's; and not far off, at Grange he killed, or hanged, four innocent labourers; at Ballymurrin fix, and at Ballygalburt eight;

---

(1) Cart. Orm. vol. i.

(a) " In Munfter the firft fymptoms of commotion appeared in fome petty ravages and robberies, which were punifhed by the Lord Prefident, Sir William St. Leger, with a barbarous feverity. The difaffected remonftrated to St. Leger on the rigour of his executions, were received with difdain and infolence, pleaded the neceffity of felf-defence, and declared for war." Lel. Hift. of Irel. vol. iii. p. 154.

eight; and burnt several houses. From thence, Captain Paisly, marching to Armail, killed there seven or eight poor men and women, whom he found standing abroad in the streets, near their own doors inoffensively; and passing over the river Ewyer, marched to Clonalta; where, meeting Philip Ryan, the chief farmer of the place, a very honest and able man, not at all concerned in the robberies, he, without any enquiry, either gave orders for, or connived at, his being killed, as appeared by his cherishing the murderer. The Captain went from thence, to meet the Lord President; where several of the chief nobility, and gentry of the country, being surprised at these rash and cruel proceedings, waited upon his Lordship, with their complaints, which were rejected, and the Captain applauded for what he had done. Among these gentlemen, was James Butler, Lord Baron of Dunboyne; Thomas Butler of Kilconnel, James Butler of Kilveylagher, Theobald Butler of Armail, Richard Butler of Ballynekill, Philip O'Dwyer, and several others of good quality.

" They observed to the Lord President, how generally the people were exasperated by these inconsiderate cruelties, running distractedly from house to house; and that they were upon the point of gathering together in great numbers, not knowing what they had to trust to, and what was likely to be their fate. They told him, that they waited upon his Lordship, to be informed how affairs stood, and that they coveted nothing more than to serve his Majesty and preserve the peace, and desired that he would be pleased to qualify them for it, with authority and arms; in which case, they would not fail to suppress the rabble, and secure the peace of the country. The President did not receive their representation and offer, in the manner they expected; but in an hasty furious way, answered them, that they were all rebels, and that he would not trust one soul of them; but thought it more prudent to hang the best of them. And in this extraordinary humour, he continued all the while these, and other persons of quality, their neighbours, were waiting upon him. This made them all withdraw, and return to their houses; much resenting his rudeness, and severity; as well as very uncertain about their own safety; some of them imagining, that this distrusting of their loyalty, and destroying of their reputations, was the preface to a design of taking away their lives. From Clonmell, Sir William St. Leger marched into the county of Waterford, and his soldiers in the way, as they went, and returned from the Wexford-rebels, killed several poor harmless people, not at all concerned in the rebellion, or in the plunder of the country; which also incensed the gentlemen of that county, and made them prepare for standing on their defence *(b)*."

CHAP.

(b) " In this sudden and violent commotion, the Southern leaders, however provoked by the cruelties of St. Leger, yet expressed a laudable sollicitude to preserve both the persons and the fortunes of the English from any outrage." Lel. ubi supra, p. 154. Temple informs us on this occasion, " that Sir William

CHAP. XIX.

The Cause of the Insurrection in Conaught.

THAT the like inhuman treatment of the natives in Conaught, by persons placed in authority there, occasioned the first rise, and subsequent extension of the troubles in that province, appears from the authentic testimony of the Earl of Clanrickard, who was governor of Galway, during the whole time of this war.

By his Lordship's great activity and vigilance, that province continued quiet, for many weeks after the insurrection commenced; " and did utterly mislike the proceedings of the insurgents (1)." The county of Galway, in particular, on the 6th of December 1641 (2), remained undisturbed." But on the 23d of the following month, the case seems to have been very different, which Lord Clanrickard imputes (in a letter of that date to the Duke of Richmond) to the mal-administration of the Lords Justices, as already related, both before and after the insurrection began (3). " All," says he, " are generally discontented with those, who manage the affairs of state here, whom they charge with secret practicing, in both kingdoms, before the commotions began, to raise parties to destroy their religion, and divert, and hinder the King's graces, intended towards them, and by that means, to put them into desperation, that they may forfeit their lives and fortunes. And since the distempers began, the same persons have disposed of affairs, as if the design was to put the whole kingdom into rebellion, as now it is."

His Lordship, in a letter to the Earl of Ormond in June following, grievously complained (4), " that insults offered to himself, within the limits of his government, were, at least, connived at; that one of his best manors was ravaged, by some of the army under Ormond's own command; and that outrages were committed on others, in that district, who had protections from the state;

---

(1) Minutes of Lord Clanrickard's letter in the council-books. (2) ib.
(3) Clanrick. Mem. Cart. Orm. vol. iii.   (4) Cart. Orm. vol. iii.

liam St. Leger gallantly pursued these rebels; and that after a long and tedious march, he came upon them unawares, and slew two hundred of them, besides several whom he took prisoners and hanged." Hist. of the Irish Rebel. p. 159. Sir William himself, in a letter to the Earl of Ormond, December 11th, 1641, acquainting him, with what sort of rebels he had been engaged, says, " never was the like war heard of; no man makes head; one parish robs another, go home and share the goods, and there is an end of it; and this by a company of naked rogues." Cart. Orm. vol. iii. fol. 47.

state, and who," says he, " fill these parts with their sad complaints, distracting most men's minds to desperation; which, he doubted not, would be of dangerous consequence to the whole province; as he then understood, that the people began to prepare for their defence, and gathered all the forces they could make."

THESE outrages were now so much increased, that his Lordship acquainted the Justices, that, since the time he made his former complaint, which was on the 27th of the preceding month (5), " Scarce any day passed, without great complaints of the Captain of the fort of Galway, and the *(a)* commander of a ship of war, then lying in the harbour, sallying out with their soldiers, and trumpet, and a troop of horse; burning, and breaking open houses, taking away goods, preying of the cattle, with ruin and spoil, rather then supply to themselves; and all this committed, not only upon those who were protected, but upon them who were most forward to relieve and assist them, not sparing mine," adds his Lordship, " frequently upon fancy, or rumour, without examining the occasion; the Captain of the fort shooting his ordinance into the town, or threatning to do it, keeping disorderly sentries at every gate, abusing those that offer to go out, threatening to take them prisoners to the fort, and to exercise martial law upon them; killing, and robbing, poor people, that came to market, burning their fisher-boats, and not suffering them to go out, and no punishment inflicted upon any that committed these outrages; and, as I am well informed," adds he, " acting most things without any regard to the King's honour engaged, or any respect at all to me, in action, though much in profession."

" THESE particulars, my Lords," proceeds Lord Clanrickard, " do so distemper and disquiet all men's thoughts, even those that have been most forward to do service, that it is like to be of most dangerous consequence at this time,

(5) Id. ib.

(a) Lord Forbes, who had brought along with him the famous Hugh Peters, as his chaplain, and was much governed by his advice." Cart. Orm. vol. i. fol. 347. This Peters and one Dell, another Presbyterian minister, seem to have afterwards, started the first hint of the project of the King's murder. An anonymous letter, of November 9th, 1647, to the following purpose, was privately handed to his Majesty, " In discharge of my duty, I cannot omit to acquaint you, that my brother was at a meeting last night, with eight or nine agitators; who in debate of the obstacle which did most hinder the speedy effecting their designs, did conclude it was your Majesty; and that as long as your Majesty doth live, it would be so: and therefore resolved, for the good of the kingdom, to take your life away; and that to that action, Mr. Dell, and Mr. Peters, they were well assured, would willingly bear them company; for they had often said to these agitators, your Majesty is but a dead dog. My prayers are for your Majesty's safety; but I do too much fear, it cannot be, while you are in those hands." Relig. Carol. Sacr. p. 207. In consequence of this information, his Majesty privately withdrew himself from Hampton-court, on the 11th of the same month, attended only by Sir John Berkley, Ashburnham, and Legg.

time, when Mayo, Sligo, Thomond, and other countries, have prepared forces, and are ready to fall upon my Lord President and myself. I must therefore, most humbly and earnestly intreat your Lordships to take a speedy course, that the country may be quieted and satisfied, that destruction is not intended against the well-affected; that I may be repaired in my honour, and preserved in my authority, now grown into contempt; or that your Lordships will be pleased to discharge me of the burden of this government, for, in this manner, I may not longer hold it, with disservice to his Majesty, and danger and dishonour to myself."

CHAP. XX.

Further Severities of the Lords Justices.

ABOUT this time (1), " Sir John Read, one of the gentlemen of his Majesty's privy-chamber, then in Ireland, being intrusted with letters to his Majesty, by the nobility and gentry of the pale, was invited by the Lords Justices to repair to Dublin, that they might confer with him, before his departure; but, at his coming to Dublin, he was committed close prisoner to the castle, notwithstanding they wrote for him, and though he told them, he brought letters to his Majesty. Soon after this, they put him to the rack (a)."

LORD (2) Dunsany, who lived quietly in his own house, doing all acts of humanity to the distressed English, even at the hazard of his life, came with his son to Dublin, and surrendered himself to the government, " where he was immediately imprisoned, and endited by a jury, which did (3) not consist of freeholders." At the same time, (4) Patrick Barnwell of Kilbrew, Esq; one of the most considerable gentlemen of the pale, a venerable old man, of the age of sixty-six, a lover of quiet, and highly respected in his country, " having surrendered himself to the Earl of Ormond, and received a (b) safe conduct from

(1) Cart. Orm. vol. ii. fol. 295. (2) Id. ib. (3) Brief Narrative. See Walsh's Reply to a Person of Quality. (4) Cart. Orm. vol. i.

(a) " The principal question put to him while on the rack, was, whether the King was privy to, or encouraged the rebellion? The Lords Justices, devoted to that party, (in the English parliament,) to whose disposition the government of Ireland was entirely left, endeavoured, in this detestable way, to serve their ends, by calumniating his Majesty; at the same time that they promoted their own scheme of an extirpation by racking these gentlemen, whose treatment could not fail of deterring every body from venturing themselves into their power for the future' Cart. Orm. vol. i. fol. 301.

(b) The Earl of Ormond, in a letter to Lord Justice Parsons, says, " Having received from your Lordship, a note intimating a safe-guard to Mr. Barnwell of Kilbrew, I suffered him to come along with me." Cart. Orm. vol. iii. fol. 68. " Patrick Barnwell of Kilbrew, Esq; endured the torture with so steady an avowal

from Sir William Parsons, was, nevertheless, upon his arrival in Dublin, imprisoned, and put to the rack; and he, (Lord Dunsany,) and Sir John Netterville, suffered great hardships afterwards, from the rigour of the Lords Justices, in their confinement in the castle of Dublin, for twelve or fourteen months; and being refused to be bailed, were ready to perish for want of relief."

BESIDES these, (5) Sir Andrew Aylmer, Girald and George Aylmer, Esqrs. Edward Lawrence, Nicholas and Stephen Dowdal, Esqrs. Sir Nicholas White, and his son, John Talbot, Gerald Fitzgerald, and William Malone, Esqrs. all gentlemen of the pale, had either submitted to the Lords Justices, or to the Earl of Ormond in this expedition to Drogheda. But, altho' it was certainly known, that they never were in any manner connected with the insurgents, but on the contrary, that they had greatly suffered by their depredations, " yet they were all committed prisoners to the castle, without being even admitted to the presence of the Lords Justices; after which, they were examined, some by menace, others by (c) torture, and most of them necessitated to subscribe to what the examiners pleased to insert. In consequence of those examinations, and perhaps (d) other kinds of management, they were all endited of high treason; in the space of two days, there were above three thousand such enditments upon record."

(5) Id. ib.

avowal of his innocence, and such abundant evidence was offered in his favour, that the Justices were ashamed of their cruelty; and to make some amends to the unhappy gentleman, he was permitted to reside in Dublin, and his estate protected from the general havock of the soldiery." Lel. Hist. of Irel. vol. iii. p. 165.

(c) " Preparations were made for their trials.—But, as they had never been engaged in any hostile action, proper facts were wanting to support a charge against them. To supply this defect, the Lords Justices had recourse to the rack, in order to extort such confessions, as these miscreants had a mind to put into the mouths of these unhappy men." Warner's Irish Rebel. p. 176.

(d) The Justices " had exerted themselves so vigorously, that enditments of treason were found against those, and above a thousand more, in the space of two days." Lel. Hist. of Irel. Ubi supra. " With a shameless outrage on decency, a memorial was publickly read at the council-board, from a friend of Sir William Parsons, representing his merits in expending sums of money for procuring witnesses on these enditments." Id. ib. p. 201.

CHAP.

CHAP. XXI.

The Gentlemen of the Pale petition the King and Parliament.

WHILE the gentlemen above-mentioned were confined in the caftle of Dublin, they addreffed to the Earl, now Marquis, of Ormond, the following petition; inclofing two others, one to his Majefty, and the other to the Englifh Houfe of Commons.

" MAY (1) it pleafe your Lordfhip to call to mind, how your petitioners, upon your Lordfhip's advancing into the country, with his Majefty's army, did come, and fubmit to your Lordfhip; not doubting but that they fhould thereby, partake of his Majefty's grace and mercy. And yet they have received as hard meafure fince, as if they had been taken prifoners, and committed the higheft acts of treafon. Your Lordfhip cannot forget, that we were then, out of danger of the army; and that, if we had fufpected any fuch hard, and extream ufage, as we have fince found, we might have means, and opportunity to fhift for ourfelves, and at leaft, to continue our former liberty. But we being confcious of no voluntary treafon, committed by us, did, of our own free will and accord, put ourfelves into your Lordfhip's hands; not doubting, but that this was an engagement upon your Lord fhip, in point of honour, (if not upon his Majefty, as we conceive it is) to intercede to his Highnefs, and to the parliament, for us; which your Lordfhip has not hitherto done.

" THEIR humble requeft unto your Lordfhip, is, that for the clearing of yourfelf, from having an hand in the proceedings, which, fince their fubmiffion, have been againft your petitioners; and for the vindicating your honour unto pofterity (which, in the opinion of many, doth in this much fuffer) your Lordfhip will be pleafed, by your letters, to tranfmit their petitions fubfcribed by them, unto his Majefty; and alfo to the honourable Houfe of Commons in England, which is the leaft right, and it is in the

main

---

(1) Carte's Orm. vol. iii.

main nothing but truth, which your Lordſhip is bound in honour to teſ-tify *(a)*."

THE Marquis of Ormond, in a letter to the Speaker of the Engliſh Houſe of Commons, after having made a kind of apology for ſending him theſe petitions, acquaints him (2), " that, indeed, what concerned theſe gentlemens' coming to him of their own accord, and the courſe that had been afterwards held with them, was very truly ſet forth; and that he had not heard of any hoſtile act, that had been done by any of them." But then he immediately ſubjoins, what certainly was never intended for their ſervice, viz. " and to enter into their hearts, and ſearch what is there, is only peculiar to God. I am not able," adds he, " to judge whether any treaſon was hatched there, or no." And, with this invidious inſinuation, " he ſubmitted it to the wiſdom of that great council (the Engliſh Commons) to adviſe when, and where, and to whom, to diſtribute mercy, for the moſt advantage of the preſent ſervice." The principal drift of which ſervice, he perfectly well knew, was by all manner of means, to attaint the perſons, and confiſcate the eſtates, of all the Roman Catholic nobility and gentry of the kingdom *(b)*.

(2) Cart. Orm. vol. iii.

(a) " The Lords Juſtices, who not only favoured the deſigns of their friends in England, but expected to have their own ſervices rewarded by a large portion of forfeitures, were reſolved to diſcourage pacific diſpoſitions. The gentlemen, who were ſent in cuſtody to Dublin, (on ſurrendering themſelves to Ormond) though men of reſpectable characters and families, engaged in no action with the rebels, ſome, ſufferers by their rapine, averſe to their proceedings, known protectors of the Engliſh, were all, indiſcriminately, denied acceſs to the Juſtices, cloſely impriſoned, and threatened with the utmoſt ſeverity." Lel. Hiſt. of Irel. vol. iii. p. 163.

(b) Mr. Carte informs us, " That he found in the Earl of Ormond's notes, written with his own hand, that in April, 1643, there was a letter read at the council-board, from an intimate friend of Sir William Parſons, who claimed a great merit to himſelf, in getting ſome hundreds of gentlemen endited; and the rather that he had laid out ſums of money to procure witneſſes to give evidence to a jury for finding their enditments." Orm. vol. i. fol. 423.

CHAP.

CHAP. XXII.

Barbarous Orders of the Lords Justices and Council to the Earl of Ormond.

WERE there any room to call in question the accounts hitherto given, of these Lords Justices cruel and rapacious administration, their own public orders, which were constantly and rigorously executed, would authenticate and confirm them, beyond all possibility of doubt. Out of these orders, I shall select two or three passages, (for more would be shocking to the reader's humanity,) with reference to the ends all along proposed by them, which evidently were, first to compel such of the Irish, as were still quiet, to rise in their own defence, and afterwards, to seize on their persons, and estates for having yielded to such compulsion.

On the 23d of February, 1641, the Earl of Ormond, when on his march towards the Boyne, received the following resolution of the Lords Justices, and Council (1). " It is resolved, that it is fit, that his Lordship do endeavour, with his Majesty's forces, to wound, kill, slay, and destroy, by all the ways and means he may, all the said (*a*) rebels, and their adherents, and relievers; and burn, spoil, waste, consume, destroy, and demolish, all the places, towns, and houses, where the said rebels are, or have been, relieved, or harboured, and all the corn and hay there; and to kill and destroy (*b*), all men there inhabiting, able to bear arms."

On the 9th of the following month, these Lords Justices and Council, dispatched another order to the Earl of Ormond, then marching into the pale, with an army of three thousand foot, and five hundred horse, to burn, spoil, and destroy the rebels of the pale, without excepting any. By this order, " those who offered to come in, were in no other manner to be taken in, than as prisoners, taken by the strength of his Majesty's army; and, if any of them should come to the army, the soldiers were to seize on them, before they

---

(1) Carte's Orm. vol. iii.

(*a*) Irish and Rebels were then synonimous terms.

(*b*) " Can any one think after this," says Doctor Warner, " that these Lords Justices had any reason to complain of the cruelties committed by the ignorant and savage Irish." Hist. of the Irish Rebel.

they had access to his Lordship; and afterwards, they were to be denied access to his person *(c)*."

In this manner, such of those unhappy noblemen, and gentlemen, as had been driven from Dublin by their Lordships' proclamation, on pain of death, had never offended the government, or were desirous to return to their duty, if in any respect they had offended, were delivered up, without distinction, to the mercy of soldiers, who thirsted after nothing more ardently, than the blood of the Irish; and whom their Lordships had before incensed, by all manner of ways, against the nation in general.

Doctor Nalson assures us (2), " that the severities of the Provost-Marshalls, and the barbarism of the soldiers to the Irish, were then such, that he heard a relation of his own, who was a captain in that service, relate, that no manner of *(d)* compassion, or discrimination, was shewn either to age or sex; but that the little children were promiscuously sufferers with the guilty; and that, if any, who had some grains of compassion, reprehended the soldiers, for this unchristian inhumanity, they would scornfully reply, why, nitts will be lice, and so would dispatch them."

" May (3) 28th, 1642, the Justices issued a general order to the commanders of all garrisons, not to presume to hold any correspondence, or intercourse, with any of the Irish or Papists dwelling, or residing in any place, near, or about their garrisons; or to give protection, immunity, or dispensation from spoil, burning, or other prosecution of war, to any of them; but to prosecute all such rebels, from place to place, with fire and sword, according to former commands, and proclamations. Such," says Mr. Carte, on this occasion, " was the constant tenour of their orders, though they knew, that the soldiers, in executing them, murdered all persons, promiscuously, not sparing, as they themselves tell the commissioners for Irish affairs, in their letter of the 7th of June following, the women, and sometimes, not children."

(2) Historic. Collect.   (3) Cart. Orm. vol. i.

(c) " In the execution of these orders, the Justices declare, that the soldiers slew all persons p omiscuously, not sparing the women, and sometimes not the children." Lel. Hist. of Irel. vol. iii. p. 172.

(d) " Among the several acts of public service performed by a regiment of Sir William Cole, consisting of five hundred foot, and a troop of horse, we find the following hideous article recorded by the historian Borlace, with particular satisfaction, and triumph: Starved and famished of the vulgar sort, whose goods were seized on by the regiment, seven thousand." Lel. ib.

CHAP.

CHAP. XXIII.

Orders of the English Parliament, relative to Ireland.

PREPARATORY to these destructive orders of the Justices and Council of Ireland, their partizans in the English parliament had procured a (1) resolution to be passed, on the 8th of December, 1641, never to tolerate the Roman Catholic religion in that kingdom; and, in February, or March following, the same parliament voted the confiscation of two millions and an half of acres, of arable, meadow, and pasture land, when very few persons of landed property were concerned in the insurrection. On occasion of this resolution concerning religion, Lord Clanrickard expostulated, with just and spirited resentment, in a letter to the Earl of Essex; who, it was then thought, would have come over Lord Lieutenant, with orders to execute it. " It is reported (2)," says he, " that the parliament hath resolved to make this a war of religion, that no toleration thereof is to be granted here; nor any pardons, but by consent of parliament, to send one thousand Scots into this kingdom, and yourself to come over Lord Lieutenant. If such be the resolutions of England, I should esteem it the greatest misfortune possible, to see you here upon such terms; but if you come over as becomes the person, honour, and gallant disposition of the Earl of Essex; and not as the agent of persecution, it may produce much happiness to your own particular, and to this kingdom in general. And, if I may presume to speak my sense, it will not agree either with the honour, or safety of England, to make use of such a power of Scots to destroy, or overrun us here. My Lord, recollect yourself, and draw together your best, and bravest thoughts; consider that, by this violent proceeding, contrary to the religion of the whole kingdom, you will put us into desperation, and so hazard the destruction of many noble families."

In consequence of the English vote, for the confiscation of two million and a half of Irish acres, " the Lords Justices, in a private (3) letter to the Speaker of the House of Commons in England, May 11th, 1642, without the rest of the Council, besought the Commons, to assist them with a grant of some competent proportion of the rebels lands. Here," says (4) Warner, " the reader will find a key, that unlocks the secret of their iniquitous proceedings; and here we find the motives to the orders they gave for receiving no submissions; for issuing no proclamation of pardon at first, as the parliament had suggested;

and

---

(1) Hughes' Abridgment. (2) Cart. Orm. vol. iii. (3) Id. ib. vol. i. (4) Hist. Irish Rebel.

and in short, for all their backwardness in putting an end to the rebellion, of which several opportunities offered; and consequently, for their sacrificing the peace and happiness of the country, and the lives of thousands of their fellow-subjects." " But (5) some kind of zeal," says a Royal author on this occasion, " counts all merciful moderation luke-warmness, and is, not seldom more greedy to kill the bear for his skin, than for any harm he hath done; the confiscation of men's estates being more beneficial, than the charity of saving their lives, or reforming their errors."

(5) Relig. Sacr. Carolin. p. 85.

AN HISTORICAL AND CRITICAL REVIEW OF THE CIVIL WARS IN IRELAND.

BOOK VI.

CHAP. I.

The Nobility and Gentry of Ireland unite in a regular Body.

THE Lords and gentlemen of the pale, who had seen their houses burnt, their lands destroyed, and their tenants murdered, without making any opposition, still renewed (1) their applications to government, to accept of their best assistance and endeavours, towards putting a stop to the insurrection, now daily increasing in every part of the kingdom. But these overtures were scornfully rejected, and even the proposers of them held worthy of punishment. The Earl of Castlehaven, who had presented one of their petitions, was (2) imprisoned; and had he not escaped by a stratagem, might have been racked for his officiousness, as Sir John Read was on a similar account. At the same time, Hugh Oge O'Connor, Sir Luke Dillon, and others of the principal gentry of the county of Roscommon, intreated the Lords Clanrickard and Ranelagh, to prevail with the Justices, to receive the like humble offer of their services, or, at least, to consent to a suspension of hostilities, for some short time. Lord Clanrickard transmitted their request to the government, with his humble wishes for its success; but Sir William Parsons was so much offended at the motion, that Clanrickard was obliged to apologize for having made

(1) Carte, Castlehaven.   (2) See his Memoirs.

made it, by telling him (3), " that his grounds for feconding that application were, that fire and fword having made a fharp difcovery of his Majefty's high indignation, fome part of his mercy might appear, by a diftinction of punifhment; which then, and fince, had fallen equally, not only on capital offenders, but even upon deferving fervitors. Thefe," adds his Lordfhip, " were the apprehenfions, which drew me into that error, which I muft now conceive to be fuch, as it ftands in oppofition, to fo able a judgment. But certainly, fome other way of moderation may be agreeable to his Majefty's goodnefs, and the deftruction and murders committed by the foldiers, thereby prevented; which are now acted upon thofe, who are protected by your Lordfhip, which, at prefent, puts all men into high defperation."

Thus, were the Catholic nobility and gentry of Ireland, at laft, compelled to unite in a regular body; and to put themfelves into that condition of natural felf-defence, which has been ever fince branded by their enemies, with the appellation of a moft odious and unnatural rebellion *(a)*.

The firft refult of this union was, an humble and dutiful addrefs from them to his Majefty, fetting forth (4), " that, having apprehended, with fulnefs of forrow, the condition to which the mifreprefentation of his Majefty's minifters in Ireland, united with the malignant party in England, had reduced them; and fad experience having taught them, that a refolution was taken to fupplant their nation and religion; they humbly conceived it neceffary, after long patience, to put themfelves in a pofture of natural defence; with intention, neverthelefs, never to difturb his Majefty's government, to invade any of his high prerogatives, or opprefs any of his Britifh fubjects, of what religion foever, that did not labour to opprefs them. Which intention in the beginning of the troubles, they had folemnly fworn to obferve; an oath, often fince reiterated, left the mifguided and unauthorifed motions of fome among them, fhould be conftrued to derogate from that faith and allegiance, which, in all humblenefs, they confeffed they owed, and fincerely profeffed unto his Majefty. That, before any act of hoftility committed on their parts, they had, with all fubmiffion, addreffed themfelves, by petition, to the Lords Juftices and Council, for a timely remedy againft the then growing evils; but that therein,

(3) Cart. Orm. vol. iii. (4) Id. ib.

(a) " To ftrengthen their party," fays Mr Carte, " as much as was poffible, they fent manifefts and declarations of the motives and reafons of their conduct, to all the Englifh Catholics throughout the kingdom. Nor did they find any great difficulty in engaging them; they being ready enough to confider it as a common caufe, and to imagine that the fame fnares, which they were perfuaded had been laid for the lives, and eftates of the Lords of the pale, would be made ufe of to deftroy them, by piece-meal, one after another: and that the only way to prevent the deftruction of each particular, was to unite all together as one man, to make a general affociation for their defence, and to depend upon the fate of war, to make the beft terms they could for themfelves." Orm. vol. iii. fol. 262.

therein, they had found, instead of a salve for their wounds, oyl poured into the fire of their discontents, which occasioned such intemperance in the common people, that they acted some unwarrantable cruelties upon puritans, or others suspected of puritanism, which cruelties they *(b)* really detested, had punished in part, and desired to punish with fulness of severity, in all the actors of them, when time should enable them to it; though (added they) the measure offered to the Catholic natives here, in the inhuman murthering of old decrepit people in their beds, women in the straw, and children of eight days old; burning of houses, and robbing of all kind of persons, without distinction of friend from foe, and *(c)* digging up of graves, and there burning the dead bodies of our ancestors, have not deserved that justice from us."

In the conclusion of this address, we find the following zealous obtestation. " We therefore, with hearts bent lower than our knees, do humbly beseech your sacred Majesty, timely to assign a place, where, with safety, we may express our grievances, and you may, with freedom, apply a seasonable cure unto them; and there you shall find our dutiful affections, attended with just cause of security in our faithfulness, and manifest arguments of our earnest desire to advance your service."

(b) They kept their word religiously in this respect. For, in the two peaces concluded afterwards with the Marquis of Ormond, viz. those of 1646 and 1648, they expressly excepted, from pardon, all those of their party that had committed such cruelties. And long before either of these peaces, Lord Clanrickard testified, " that it was the desire of the whole nation, that the actors of these cruelties should, in the highest degree, be made examples to all posterity." Carte's Orm vol. iii. And the Marquis of Ormond himself, confessed, " that those assuming power among the Irish had long disclaimed them, and professed an earnest desire that they might be brought to punishment." Id. ib.

(c) That they did not exaggerate in this particular, is plain from a letter of Lord Clanrickard's, who says, " that while he was at Tyrellan in treaty with Lord Forbes, (the commander of a parliament ship of war,) tho' Lord Ranelagh, president of Conaught, was then in the fort of Galway, he saw the country on fire, his tenants houses and goods burnt, and four or five poor innocent creatures, men, women, and children, inhumanly murdered by Forbes's soldiers; who having taken possession of Lady's church in Galway, the antient burying place of the town, did, upon their departure, not only deface it, but digged up the graves, and burnt the coffins and bones of those that were buried there." Carr. Orm. vol. iii. fol. 109. Lel. Hist. of Irel. vol. iii p. 174.

CHAP. II.

The King consents to hear the Grievances of the Insurgents.

THE King (1), considering the occasion and circumstances, which had caused such a body of nobility and gentry, most of them of English race, to have recourse to arms; the apparent moderation of their demands, their earnest desire of laying their grievances before him, and submitting them to his determination, resolved to issue out a commission, under the great Seal of England, to empower certain persons to meet with the principal of those, who had sent the petition; to receive, in writing, what the petitioners had to say, or propound; and to transmit the same to his Majesty.

" This commission was dated January 11th, 1642, and directed to the Marquis of Ormond, the Earls of Clanrickard and Roscommon, the Lord Viscount Moore, Sir Thomas Lucas, Sir Maurice Eustace, and Thomas Bourke, Esq; any three, or more, of them being authorised to meet, and act for the purpose aforesaid. It was sent over to Ireland by the last of these commissioners, who delivered it to the Marquis of Ormond, on the 30th. He at the same time, brought the Lords Justices a letter from the King, notifying the purport of it."

" But these Lords Justices, taking," says the Marquis of Ormond (2), " this commission for a step towards the peace of the kingdom, and their own ruin;" and (3), " being displeased that even a wish, or consent, should be discovered in any man, that the war, from which so many promised themselves revenge, and fortunes, should be any other way ended, than with the blood and confiscation of all those, whom they could propose to be guilty of the defection," sought many different expedients to hinder, or delay the execution of it; and at length hit upon one, that, for a while, produced the wished for effect (4). There came a trumpet to the supreme council of the confederate Catholics, then sitting at Rofs, with a safe conduct from their Lordships for such of their number, as that council would employ to represent their grievances to the King's commissioners above-mentioned. In the commission, there happened to be the words " odious rebellion," applied to the proceedings of these Catholics; which the Lords Justices not only inserted in their safe conduct,

(1) Carte's Orm. vol. i. (2) Ormond's Letter in Cart. Orm. vol. iii.
(3) Clarend. Hist. of the Irish Rebel. (4) Belling's MSS. History.

duct, but also, added other words of their own of the same provoking tendency; hoping thereby to prevent the intended pacification. But the confederates, looking upon the whole to be the Lords Justices' contrivance, and neither knowing, nor expecting, that any such language was in his Majesty's commission, sent the trumpet back, with a spirited answer, giving their Lordships to understand, " That they were not, they thanked God, in that condition, as to sacrifice their loyalty to the malice of any; and that it would be a meanness beyond expression in them, who fought in the condition of loyal subjects, to come, in the repute of rebels, to set down their grievances. We take God to witness," added they, " that there are no limits set to the scorn and infamy, that are cast upon us; and we will be in the esteem of loyal subjects, or die to a man."

THE confederate Catholics did undoubtedly believe, that in taking arms against (a) this administration, which was entirely influenced by the prevailing faction in the English parliament, they were actually serving his Majesty. This appears evidently from Lord Clanrickard's letter to the King, October 26th, 1642, wherein he acquaints him (5), " That neither intreaties, threats, or protestations, could draw most men from the belief, that those did really serve his Majesty, who were in that commotion. And if vows and protestations, (proceeds his Lordship) may gain belief, I should be followed by thousands to serve your Majesty, in any other place. But, as the state of this kingdom stands, such is their sense of the opposition given to your Majesty by some faction of your parliament of England; of the injustice done them by those that govern here; and of the general destruction, conceived to be designed against the natives, that almost the whole nation are united into one resolute body, to gain their preservation, or sell their lives, at the dearest rate."

(5) Cart. O.m. vol. iii. Clanrick. Mem. Eng. ed. fol. 180.

(a) The Earl of Castlehaven, among other reasons for having joined the confederates against this administration, assigns the following. " I began to consider," says he, " the condition of this kingdom, as that the state did chiefly consist of men of mean birth and quality; that most of them steered by the influence and power of those, who were in arms against the King; that they had by cruel massacring, hanging, and torturing, been the slaughter of thousands of innocent men, women, and children, better subjects than themselves; that they, by all their actions, shewed that they looked at nothing but the extirpation of the nation, the destruction of monarchy, and by the utter suppression of the antient Catholic religion, to settle and establish puritanism. To these," adds his Lordship " I could be no traitor." Desid. Curios. Hibern. vol. ii. p. 132. See Append.

CHAP.

CHAP. III.

Another Contrivance of the Justices to hinder the Cessation.

BUT the confederate nobility and gentry being soon after made sensible, that the words " odious rebellion" above-mentioned, were taken from the King's commission, and inserted in the safe conduct for the aforesaid evil purpose, were resolved to disappoint so iniquitous a design; and therefore, immediately wrote to the commissioners appointed by the King, " that (1) they were ready to appear before them, with a representation of their grievances." Accordingly, the time and place of meeting, proposed by the confederate Catholics, which was the 18th of March, at Trim, were agreed to by these commissioners. But the confederates still resenting the imputation of rebellion, though taken from the King's commission, thought it necessary to " protest at the same time (2), in the presence of the God of truth, that they had been necessitated to take arms, to prevent the extirpation of their nation and religion, threatened and contrived by their enemies; to maintain the rights and prerogatives of his Majesty's crown and dignity, and the interests of his royal issue, and for no other reason whatever." And, indeed, of the sincerity of this protestation, we shall presently find them giving unquestionable proofs.

THE Justices now perceiving, that abusive appellations could not provoke the confederates to absent themselves from the intended meeting, resolved to try what cruel and perfidious actions would do (3). " For, on the 13th of March (five days before the appointed time) they gained the consent of the council to an act, which," says Mr. Carte, " could only serve to exasperate the confederates, and produce a retaliation, that might inflame matters to such a degree, as to put a stop to all further treaty. Sir Richard Greenville had taken, at Longwood, Mr. Edward Lisagh Connor; and in the battle of Rathconnel, on February the 7th, he had also taken one Dowdal, another gentleman named Betagh, and one Aylmer, son of Garret Aylmer, a lawyer eminent in his profession, all gentlemen of considerable families. Sir Richard, though very severe in the prosecution of the war, was a man of great spirit and honour, and not likely to violate the quarter he had given. The Lords Justices, therefore, wrote to him, that they had occasion to examine said prisoners,

(1) Belling's MSS. Hist. of the Wars of Ireland.   (2) Cart. Orm. vol. iii. Belling, ib.
(3) Cart. Orm. vol. i. fol. 407.

ners, and ordered him to send them for that purpose to Dublin, under a safe guard. They signed, at the same time, another order to *(a)* Sir Henry Tichbourne, to examine only, if these prisoners were so taken, and to cause them immediately to be executed by the martial law."

But even this detestable expedient to prevent the appointed meeting, proved as unsuccessful, as the former. For, " on the before-mentioned 18th of March 1642, by virtue of his Majesty's commission (4), the Earl of St. Albans and Clanrickard, the Earl of Roscommon, Sir Maurice Eustace, and others, the King's commissioners, met the commissioners of the confederate Catholics at Trim." These latter were Lord Gormanstown, Sir Lucas Dillon, Knight, Sir Robert Talbot, Bart. John Walsh, Esq; and others; at which time, they produced a remonstrance, by the title of a *(b)* Remonstrance of the Grievances presented to his Majesty, in the name of the Catholics of Ireland (5). Which remonstrance was, accordingly, received in due form, by his Majesty's commissioners, and by them transmitted to his Majesty.

The Marquis of Ormond, though first named in the commission, seems to be the only commissioner, that did not assist at this meeting. His Lordship, instead of going to Trim on that pacific business *(c)*, marched towards (6) Ross, with an army of about two thousand five hundred foot, and five hundred horse. In his way thither, he took the Castle of Timolin; and although he had promised quarter to the garrison, on account of their gallant defence, yet

---

(4) Carte ubi supra.   (5) See Append.   (6) Belling's MSS.

(a) Sir Henry Tichburn, soon after made Lord Justice on Parsons' removal, informs us, " that the cessation intended was so disagreeable to the Irish Privy-council, that most of them desired to run any fortune, and extremity of famishing, rather than yield unto it." Hist. of the siege of Drogheda.

(b) This remonstrance has been already quoted, in this review, and will hereafter be quoted as authentic evidence, as well on account of the solemnity of its delivery and acceptance, as because of the severe examinations it underwent in the Irish House of Commons, (from which all the Roman Catholic members had been expelled) from the 8th to the 12th of April, 1644, and then dismissed without the least disproof, or even contradiction, of any of the numerous grievances it complains of; and without any resolution, or motion, after a debate of so many days, that bears the slightest appearance, either of a censure, or denial of the facts it contains. See Append. to the Journals of the Commons.

(c) This expedition was undertaken by Ormond, at the desire of a committee of the English parliament, then sent to direct and superintend the affairs of Ireland, expressly against the King's command. See Borl. Ir. Rebel. fol. 142-3. " It being desired by the officers of the army, on a certain occasion, that Major Wodowes might repair to his Majesty to express their service, this committee demonstrated, that the parliament would certainly withdraw their supplies, on notice of such an address, upon which the ships were stayed; yet the business was so argued, as the Major had licence to proceed in his journey " Id. ib. fol. 144. " But with this the English parliament was so much displeased, that they for some time, withheld those scanty supplies which they before used to send them." Id. ib. fol. 145.

yet he suffered them to be (7) cut in pieces by the soldiers, after they had surrendered their arms. And, in his return from Rofs to Dublin, on the 18th of March, (the day on which the other commiffioners were receiving the remonftrance at Trim) having met and attacked an army of the confederates, under General Prefton, he entirely routed it; (8) killing above five hundred of their men, among whom were many officers and gentlemen (d). The (9) Juftices, in a letter to the Speaker of the Englifh Houfe of Commons, take particular notice of this action, as a fatisfactory proof, " that the King's commiffion for hearing the complaints of the confederate Catholics, gave not the leaft interruption to the proceedings of the war (e) againft them."

CHAP. IV.

Sir William Parfons *difplaced from the Government.*

IN confequence of the remonftrance delivered at Trim, his Majefty informed the Lords Juftices (1), " That he had given command, and authority to the Marquis of Ormond, to treat with his fubjects of that kingdom, who had taken arms againft him; and to agree with them on a ceffafion of arms for one year; which, as it was a fervice of very great concernment to his Majefty, and his prefent affairs in both kingdoms, fo he willed and commanded, that they would therein give the moft effectual affiftance and furtherance to advance the fame, by their induftry and endeavours, as there fhould be occafion."

Not

(7) Id. ib.   (8) Id. ib.   (9) Carte's Orm. vol. iii.
(1) Id. ib.

(d) " And in his return to Dublin," fays Mr. Carte, " he burnt and fpoiled the enemy's country, without the leaft oppofition." Orm. vol. i. fol. 407.

(e) They obferve, however, in the fame letter, that their poverty, and want of all things, was fuch, " that although the rebels were not able to overcome his Majefty's army, and devour his other good fubjects, yet both his army and good fubjects were in danger to be devoured by the wants of needful fupplies forth of England. And that the miferies of the officers and foldiers for want of all things, even of food, were unfpeakable; that, by the infupportable burthen then laid on the city of Dublin, for their maintenance, many houfekeepers were daily breaking up houfe, and fcattering their families, leaving ftill fewer to bear the burden. In the end, therefore," add they, " we were enforced to fix on our former way, and to fee who had any thing left him, untaken from him, to help us; and, although there were but few fuch, and fome of them poor merchants, whom we have now by the law of neceffity utterly undone, and difabled from being hereafter helpful to us, yet we were forced to wreft their commodities from them." Bor. Hift. of the Irifh Rebel. fol. 146-7.

Not long after the arrival of this order (2), Sir Francis Butler landed from England, with a superfedeas for Sir William Parsons's government, on account of his being a principal opposer of the intended cessation, and with a commission to Sir John Borlace, and Sir Henry Tichbourne, to be Lords Justices; who, accordingly, on the 1st of May, 1643, were instituted in the government. And on the 12th of the same month, Major Warren and Sir Francis Butler, came to the council, the Lords sitting, and presented a petition to the Lords Justices, accusing Sir William Parsons of high misdemeanors, and other treasonable matters, and requesting that his person and goods might be secured."

After many needless delays, and a second command from the King, the Lords Justices appointed the Marquis of Ormond to meet the commissioners of the confederate Catholics at Castle-Martin, on the 23d of June, and to enter upon a treaty with them for a cessation of arms. The Marquis, as we have seen, had shewn but little inclination to be concerned at all in such a treaty; and he discovered less to be instrumental in concluding it. For (3), on the day before he set out for Castle-Martin, having caused the principal Citizens of Dublin to be summoned before the council-board, he delivered a motion in writing, that " if ten thousand pounds might be raised, the one half in money, the other in victuals; and to be brought in within a fortnight, he would, in that case, proceed in the war, endeavour to take Wexford, and break off the treaty for the cessation."

But the principal citizens of Dublin, not being able to advance that sum, (such was their (*a*) extreme poverty at that juncture) Sir Henry Tichbourne, who, upon the supposition of his favouring the cessation, was appointed Lord Justice in Parsons' room (4), " moved the board, (there being then one and twenty counsellors present,) that every one for himself, out of his peculiar means and credit, should procure three hundred pounds, which, among them all, would raise six thousand three hundred pounds; for even with that," says Sir Henry himself, " he (the Marquis) offered to undertake the work, and, that there should be no further mention of a cessation among them. But this motion of mine,"

---

(2) Id. ib. vol. i. (3) Carte's Orm. vol. i. (4) Hist. of the siege of Drogheda.

(*a*) Temple informs us, " That when, in the beginning of the insurrection, the Justices sent for the Mayor and Aldermen of Dublin, and laid before them the high necessities of the state, desiring to borrow a considerable sum of money for the present, which they undertook to repay out of the next treasure, that should arrive from England, they returned this answer, after a most serious consultation, and very solemn debate among themselves, that they were not able to furnish above forty pounds, and part of that was to be brought in in cattle." Hist. of the Irish Rebel. p. 47.

mine," proceeds he, " finding no (b) place, the cessation began to be treated on, and was in sincerity of heart, as much hindered, and delayed by me, as was in my power." Such was the zeal and fidelity of one of his Majesty's chosen, and principal ministers, then in the government of Ireland!

CHAP. V.

His Majesty's Commissioners meet those of the Confederate Catholics, to treat of the Cessation.

ON the 23d of June, 1643, the (1) commissioners of the confederate Catholics presented themselves before the Marquis of Ormond in his tent, near Castle Martin, in the presence of divers Colonels, Captains, and other officers of his Majesty's army, his Lordship sitting in his chair covered, and the Irish commissioners standing bare-headed. After several passages between them, all tendered in writing, the latter gave his Lordship a copy of the authority they had received from the supreme council of the confederate Catholics at Kilkenny, in these words.

" WHEREAS (2) his Majesty's most faithful subjects, the confederate Catholics of Ireland, were enforced to take arms, for the preservation of their religion, for the defence of his Majesty's just prerogatives and rights, and for the maintainance of the rights and liberties of their country, laboured to be destroyed by the malignant party; and whereas his Majesty in his high wisdom, and in his Princely care of his said subjects, welfare and safety, and at their humble suit, that his Majesty might be graciously pleased to hear their grievances, and vouchsafe redress therein, did direct there should be a cessation

---

(1) Borl. Hist. of the Irish Rebel.   (2) Id. ib.

(b) There is an odd passage in Borlace, which shews the extremely necessitous condition of the Protestants of Ireland, about this period, more than any thing else I have any where met with. Upon the English parliament's neglecting to send them any part of the money which had been subscribed, and paid in, in England, solely for their relief (and which, as we have seen, they perfidiously employed against the King himself) " Yet," says my author, " that something might seem to be done, there was an order of the Commons house of parliament, the 3d of August, 1642, that the ministers about the city of London should be desired to exhort the people to bestow old garments, and apparel, upon the distressed Protestants in Ireland; in reference to which, the 19th of September following, the Lord Mayor of London ordered, that those cloaths should be brought to Yorkshire-hall in Blackwell-hall, to be ready for shipping them for Ireland, and a vast supply was brought in; (charity never so much manifesting its compassion, as in that case,) which afterwards was entrusted to a reverend person, who discharged his trust with singular prudence and integrity, though, as to the army, these cloaths never reached, or were intended." Hist. of the Irish Rebel. fol. 120.

tion of arms, and thereupon did direct the Right Honourable the Marquis of Ormond, to treat of, and conclude, the said cessation with the said confederate Catholics; know ye, that the supreme council, by the express order and authority of the said Catholics, by them conceived and granted in their general assembly at Kilkenny, on the 20th day of the last month of May; and in pursuance of the said order and authority, reposing special trust and confidence, in the wisdom, circumspection, and provident care, honour, and sincerity of our very good Lords, Nicholas Lord Viscount Gormanstown, Donogh Lord Viscount Muskerry, and our well-beloved Sir Lucas Dillon, Knight, Sir Robert Talbot, Bart. Terlagh O'Neal, Esq; Geoffry Brown, Esq; Ever Macgennis, Esq; and John Walsh, Esq; have constituted, appointed, and ordained the said Nicholas Lord Viscount Gormanstown, Donogh Lord Viscount Muskerry, &c. our commissioners, and do, by these presents, give and grant to our said commissioners, or any five, or more of them, full power and authority to treat, with the said Lord Marquis of Ormond, of a cessation of arms, for one whole year, or shorter, and to conclude the same for the time aforesaid, upon such terms, conditions, or articles, as to the commissioners aforesaid, in their judgments, consciences, and discretions, shall be thought fit, and expedient; by these presents ratifying, and confirming whatever act, or acts, our said commissioners shall do, or execute, concerning the said cessation. Given at Kilkenny, the 23d of June, 1643.

    MOUNTGARRET,
    CASTLEHAVEN, AUDLEY,
    MALACH, Archiepisc. Tuamens.
    FLEMING, Archiepisc. Dubliniens.
    MAURIT de RUPE et FERMOY,
    NETTERVILLE,
    NICHOLAS PLUNKETT,
    EDMUND FITZMORRICE,
    PATRICK DARCY,
    ROBERT LYNCH,
    RICHARD BELLING."

CHAP. VI.

The Cessation at last concluded.

BUT a difference arising upon two points, viz. (1) the dissolution of the present Irish parliament, and liberty to use hostilities against all such persons, as should appear in arms against either party, (which, the commissioners of the confederate Catholics were ordered to insist upon, and the Marquis of Ormond peremptorily refused,) caused the treaty to be adjourned to the following month.

ONE reason, among many others for insisting on the dissolution of that parliament, was (2), " its having expelled, by an arbitrary order, all those members who had been indicted in the illegal manner, and by the iniquitous means already mentioned; and its afterwards having passed another order, that no persons should sit either in that, or any future parliament, till they had taken the oath of supremacy." By the the first of these orders, forty-six members were expelled, and their places supplied (3), " by clerks, soldiers, serving men, and others not legally, or not at all chosen or returned; and by the last, a much greater number, unexceptionable (4)," says Warner, " in all respects, but that of their religion *(a)*."

THE other point was insisted upon, from a well-gounded suspicion, that the Scottish forces in Ulster, that had taken the covenant, and received their pay from the English parliament now in open rebellion against the King, would reject the cessation, as they soon after actually did. And of the reasonableness of that suspicion, the Marquis of Ormond himself, was then, probably convinced, from his knowledge of their disposition, and circumstances; at least, on the 8th of March following, he certainly was so, when he told Lord Digby (5), " that the soldiers and common people in that quarter, were so deeply infected, that he had little hopes they could be unanimously, or in any considerable number, drawn to serve the King against the rebels in England or Scotland;

(1) Cart. Orm. vol. i.   (2) Warner's Irish Rebel. p. 211.   (3) Remonst. from Trim.
(4) Ubi supra.   (5) Cart. Orm. vol. iii. fol. 256.

(a) " His Majesty on this occasion, afterwards ordered the Lord Lieutenant to call before him the Speaker and members of the house, and require them to vacate that order, there being no law or statute in force in Ireland to support the same. This was an act necessary to vindicate his own prerogative, which had been invaded by that order, as well as to give some satisfaction to the Roman Catholics, who were thereby aggrieved in a point which they had most at heart, and on which depended all their hopes of redress either of present, or future grievances." Carte's Orm. vol. i. fol. 523.

Scotland; of the "new Scots," adds he, "your Lordſhip ſees there is no hope," and yet, even at this juncture (as we ſhall hereafter ſee) when theſe forces were guilty of frequent breaches of the ceſſation then concluded, and did at laſt openly reject it, he refuſed to join with the confederates, or even to countenance them by his authority, to make juſt repriſals upon them.

During this adjournment of the treaty, a ſmall, but ill intended, incident had like to have fruſtrated all hopes of its ſucceſs (6). One Captain Farrer, in the goverment's ſervice, had been taken priſoner by the confederates; while one Synott, a Captain among the confederates, was in the ſame condition with the government. The Lords Juſtices and Council deſiring to have Farrer exchanged for Synott, directed the following notice to the ſupreme council of the confederates. "We, the Lords Juſtices and Council, do declare, if Captain Farrer be forthwith releaſed by the rebels, and ſafely ſent hither, that forthwith, upon his coming ſo releaſed, we will give order for the releaſing Synott, lately employed as captain among the rebels, out of priſon, the jailor's juſt dues being firſt paid; and will then permit him to depart freely, without interruption."

The following ſpirited anſwer ſhews, how highly the confederates reſented this, (as they deemed it) new inſult on their loyalty.

"We (7) do not know to whom this certificate is directed; for we avow ourſelves, in all our actions, to be his Majeſty's loyal ſubjects. Neither ſhall it be ſafe, hereafter, for any meſſenger to bring any paper to us, containing other language, than ſuch as ſuits with our duty, and the affections we bear to his Majeſty's ſervice; wherein ſome may pretend, but none ſhall have more real deſires, to further his Majeſty's intereſts, than his Majeſty's loyal and obedient ſubjects,

MOUNTGARRET, MUSKERRY, &c."

Shortly after the ſending of this anſwer (8), Sir William Parſons, Sir Adam Loftus, Sir Robert Meredith, and Sir John Temple, Privy-counſellors, were charged before the council, by the Lords Dillon and Wilmot, Sir Faithful Forteſcue, and others, with having by divers ways and means, abuſed the truſt repoſed in them by his Majeſty, in their ſeveral offices and employments; and with having traiterouſly endeavoured to withdraw his Majeſty's army in Ireland, from his obedience, to ſide with the rebels in England. "Upon this charge, they

(6) Belling's MSS.   (7) Id. ib. Borl. Ir. Rebel.   (8) Carr. Orm. vol i.

they were all imprisoned in the castle of Dublin. But we find (9), "That they were so dear to those English rebels, and so highly valued by them, that they avowed them for theirs, by offering in exchange for them, three of the King's chief commanders, whom they had prisoners at London."

THE King had often and earnestly pressed the Lords Justices, to conclude this cessation, as the only visible means, by which his distressed army in Ireland could be relieved, or himself supplied in England, or Scotland, with those additional forces, of which he then stood in the greatest need; but, not till after the receipt of his (10) fifth letter of September 7th, 1643, were his commands, in that respect, obeyed. And thus, at length, on the 15th of that month, the Marquis of Ormond, and the Irish commissioners (11), signed the instrument of the cessation at Sigginstown; which, being confirmed by the Lords Justices and Council, was notified, by proclamation, to the whole kingdom; the commissioners of the confederate Catholics insisting, all along, on their title of dutiful and loyal subjects, which no consideration whatever could make them forego.

C H A P.   VII.

The Advantages of the Cessation to his Majesty's Army.

AND, in truth, the confederates, by consenting to this cessation, (as both armies were then circumstanced,) gave an undeniable proof of their having highly merited that title. Sir Philip Percival, Commissary General of the provisions of the King's forces, declared, in a memorial which he afterwards gave into the English parliament, " that (1) both the state, and the army were, at that juncture, in the greatest distress; that the stores in Dublin had no manner of victuals, many times for one day; that the soldiers would not move without money, shoes, and stockings; for want of which, many had marched barefooted, and had bled much on the road; and that others, through unwholsome food, had become diseased and died.

" THAT

(9) Id. ib. vol iii. fol. 271.
(11) Carte's Ormond, vol. i.
(10) Borlace Irish Rebellion.

(1) Carte's Ormond, vol. i. fol. 156.

" THAT the Irish, all this while (a), subsisted very well, carrying their cattle, especially their milch-cows, with them into the field.

" THAT the state at Dublin had no money in the treasury; sometimes wanting means even to bury their dead commanders; that, before the cessation was concluded, the government's army was so oppressed with wants, and their necessities were so great, besides the discontent of the officers, that there was no need of any other enemy, than hunger and cold, to devour them suddenly.

" THAT the confederate Catholics had, all this time, three armies on foot in Leinster, well furnished with necessaries, and ordnance; and that they had perfect intelligence of this distress of the state, and the condition of the English forces, knowing the prevailing strength of their own armies."

THE Lords Justices and Council, in a letter of the 8th of May, 1643, confessed, " that they then, found the royal army suffering under unspeakable extremities of want of all things necessary to the support of their persons, or maintenance of a war; and that they had no visible prospect, by sea or land, of being able to preserve the kingdom for his Majesty, from utter destruction of the remnant of his good subjects there."

BUT they were now to be relieved from this extreme distress, by those very men, whom they had hitherto considered, and treated, as their worst and most implacable enemies. For the confederate Catholics freely (b) obliged themselves on the conclusion of this treaty, to pay to the Marquis of Ormond thirty thousand pounds, for the present subsistence of his Majesty's army. And, in order to " vindicate (2) themselves from the calumny, that was raised against them, as if they were rebels, and had resolved to throw off the King's government,

(2) Cart. Orm. vol. i.

(a) Sir Philip Percival was so far from being inclined to favour the Irish in this representation of their circumstances, or in any other respect, that he was one of those agents, that had been sent to the King by the Protestants of Ireland to oppose the cessation. And he did so virulently oppose it, that Sir George Ratcliff told the Marquis of Ormond on that occasion, " that, had he not been recommended by his Lordship, he would have passed at court for a round head." Carte's Orm. vol. iii. fol. 316. This Sir Philip Percival soon after joined the English rebels.

(b) " Ormond's demand for a supply for maintenance of the King's forces, was not warranted by his commission to hear their grievances; the confederates refused to bind themselves by any previous stipulation, but declared their intention to grant his Majesty a free gift, on the conclusion of the truce." Ld. Hist. of Ireland. vol. iii. p. 205.

government, they further engaged, to transport several thousands of their best men to Scotland, to re-inforce his Majesty's army there; which engagement they afterwards performed, with great honour to themselves, and not less advantage to his Majesty's service.

CHAP. VIII.

The Cessation violated by his Majesty's Forces in Ulster.

THE cessation was scarce sooner published, than rejected by the Scots in Ulster, still, nominally at least, under the Marquis of Ormond's command. For, upon the first notice of it, the English parliament (1), " sent them fresh supplies of money, arms, and provisions, with orders, on their arrival, to denounce fire and sword to all that should embrace it, and to march in a body, with all necessary provisions, towards Dublin."

But these Scots did not, it seems, wait for the parliament's orders. For we find the supreme council complaining to the Lords Justices, on the 15th of October, that (2) " the Scots, who, not long before, had come over in great numbers to Ireland, had, by the slaughter of many innocents, without distinction of age, or sex, possessed themselves of large territories in the North; and that, since the notice given them of the cessation, they had continued their former cruelties, upon the persons of weak, and unarmed multitudes." Wherefore, they humbly proposed to their Lordships, " that these violators of the cessation, and secret enemies of his Majesty, might be prosecuted by the joint power of all his Majesty's good subjects, of what nation soever; and that, while the succours for his Majesty were in preparation, their own proceedings against them, might no way be imputed, as a desire to violate the cessation."

But this proposal being rejected by their Lordships, and the hostilities of the Scots still continuing and increasing, a stop was, for a while, put to those supplies, which the confederate Catholics had engaged to send to the King; a great part of them now becoming absolutely necessary for their own defence. Lord Inchiquin was sensible of this impediment, when he told the Marquis of Ormond, in a letter from Oxford, February 1643 (3), " that tho' the

(1) Lord Digby's Let. to the Marquis of Ormond, Cart. vol. iii.   (2) Belling's MSS. Botl. Ir. Reb. f. 176. (3) Carte's Orm. vol. iii. fol. 244.

the Irish were extremely relied on, yet he feared, they were unable to do more than defend themselves from the Scots, who, he doubted, would prove dangerous rebels to his Majesty." And Lord Digby also, writing to the Marquis about the same time (4), " made no question, but that the Irish, in case they were rid of their apprehensions of the Scots in Ulster, would engage thoroughly, numerously, and entirely in his Majesty's service."

THE Marquis of Ormond was himself conscious, that the increasing hostilities of the Scots, for a while prevented the confederates from sending the promised supplies to his Majesty; though he afterwards charged them with their delay in the performance, as a breach of their engagement. For, excusing himself to Prince Rupert (5), " touching the procuring of arms, and ammunition from them, for the service of his Majesty's ships under his command, he told him, that he had little hopes of prevailing with them; and that they were not very much to blame, the Scots being yet in Ireland in great numbers, and fresh reports coming daily, that they would not only begin the war with them in England afresh, but endeavour to impose the taking of their covenant on the people of Ireland, by force of arms (a)."

CHAP. IX.

The Covenant brought into Ireland; further Breaches of the Cessation by the Scotch and English Forces.

THE English parliament having, on the 25th of September, 1643, with great solemnity, taken the covenant, dispatched on the 4th of November following, Captain Owen O'Connolly, the famous discoverer of the Irish rebellion, with letters to all the British Colonels in Ulster, " recommending to them the taking of the same (1), and the carrying on the war against the Irish; and assuring them of sufficient supplies for their maintenance, upon complying with these conditions." And this commission did O'Connolly undertake to execute, altho' he knew, that the King had on the 9th of the foregoing

(4) Id. ib. (5) Cart. Orm. vol. iii. (1) Cart. Orm. vol. i. fol. 487.

(a) In another letter he says, " I have with much earnestness pressed the Irish for some considerable payment of their arrears; but their preparations for their own defence, and the poverty of the kingdom, wasted and exhausted by war, makes me doubt their supplies will be slow and small." Carte's Orm. vol. iii. fol. 315.

going month, declared by proclamation, " that covenant to be a traiterous, and seditious combination against him, and against the established religion and laws of the kingdom." This man had now entered into all the measures of the English rebels *(a)*; and was (2) soon after made a Colonel by them; but, about the year 1649, he was killed in an engagement, by Colonel John Hamilton.

AFTER the landing of O'Connolly, " all the Scotch, and most of the English officers in Ulster, took the covenant; altho' the Marquis of Ormond had, by the King's command, sent down a proclamation against it, which the Colonels of the regiments under his command there did not publish, for fear, as they pretended, of Major General Monroe. The inhabitants of the North were now become so violent for the covenant, that they even *(b)* refused maintenance to such of the soldiers, as would not take it."

AND now, even those English officers, and soldiers in Ulster, (who had submitted to the cessation) were prevailed on to promise Major General Monroe, that, whenever he marched out against the Irish, they would join him in the expedition (3); and of the justice of this union, against such an enemy, they declared themselves satisfied in their consciences. " Accordingly (4), on the 30th of June, the two combined armies, making about 10,000 foot, and 1000 horse, (tho' neither Owen O'Neil, nor the Earl of Castlehaven, the two Irish Generals in that province, did suspect in the least, that either the old Scots, or the English under the Marquis of Ormond, would march against them, in breach of the cessation,) sent out several parties into Westmeath, and Longford, which burnt the country, and put to the sword all the country people that they met."

Major General Monroe's ingratitude and perfidy were, in every respect, equal to his cruelty. This appeared by his behaviour to the Earl of Antrim, soon after his arrival in Ireland. " Mr. Archibald Stuart, chief agent to that Earl, had (5) raised, in the beginning of the troubles, about eight hundred men, a great part of them the Earl of Antrim's tenants and dependents, near Ballymenagh; and with them secured that part of the county of Antrim; notwithstanding

---

(2) Id. ib. (3) Id. ib. fol. 495. (4) Id. ib. (5) Cart. Orm. vol. i. fol. 188.

(a) He had gotten, for the first discovery of this conspiracy, 500l. and 200l. per ann. from the English parliament. Borl. Hist. of the Rebel. fol. 55.

(b) " They, whoever appeared most attached to the Royal cause, now caught the popular contagion," (of the covenant.) Lel. ubi supra, vol. iii. p. 203.

notwithstanding which, this Major General, with two thousand five hundred Scots, marched about the middle of April, 1642, into that country, where he made a prey of above five thousand cows, burnt Glenarm, a town belonging to the Earl of Antrim, and wasted that nobleman's lands. The Earl came, in the latter end of April, to his seat at Dunluce, a strong castle by the sea side; and after his arrival there, found means to supply Colerain, which had been blocked up by the Irish, and was reduced to extremity, with an hundred beeves, sixty loads of corn, and other provisions, at his own expence. He had offered Monroe his service and assistance for securing the country; in the peace of which, he was greatly interested, by reason of his large estate, the rents of which he could not otherwise receive. Monroe made him a visit at Dunluce, where the Earl received him with many expressions of gladness, and had provided for him a great entertainment; but it was no sooner over, than the Major General made him a prisoner, seized the castle, and put the rest of the Earl's houses into the hands of the Marquis of Argyle's men."

THE continuation of the before-mentioned outrages of the Scots in Ulster, in breach of the cessation, caused Lord Digby to write to the Marquis of Ormond, in July 1644, " That (6) the growing disorders of the kingdom imported a greater necessity of peace with the Irish, and of an union against those traitors of the covenant, so much more dangerous, than any other, as they were firmly linked with the rebels in England."

CHAP. X.

The Revolt of Lord Inchiquin.

ABOUT this time, died Sir William St. Leger, Lord President of Munster; and the King having (1) appointed the Earl of Portland to succeed him in that charge, Lord Inchiquin, who was married to Sir William's daughter, and had solicited, and expected that Presidentship after his father-in-law's decease, was now so much incensed by the disappointment, that he was easily persuaded by (2) Lord Broghill, to reject the cessation, and receive the English parliament's commission for the Presidentship of Munster, in opposition to the King's appointment. " In (3) this capacity, he performed many considerable services for that parliament, taking great store of plunder from the Irish, and not

(6) Id. ib. vol. iii. fol. 335. (1) Id. ib. vol. i. fol. 512. (2) Ludlow's Mem. vol. i.
(3) Id. ib.

not sparing," says Ludlow, " his own kindred; but if he found them faulty, hanging them up, without distinction."

But one of his most memorable services on this occasion, was, his barbarous exploit at Cashel (4); " where, having brought together an army, and hearing that many priests and gentry thereabouts had retired with their goods into the church of that city, he stormed it, and put three thousand of them to the sword, taking the Priests even from under the altar."

At the same time, that he himself deserted the King's service (5), he persuaded his brother, Lieutenant Colonel Henry O'Brien, to deliver up Wareham to the English parliament, and to come away, with his whole regiment, to Ireland. This Lieutenant-Colonel was, afterwards (6), taken prisoner by the confederates, and in great danger of an unhappy end, in revenge for a Roman Catholic Dean, whom his brother had lately caused to be hanged, and for his own crime in delivering Wareham to the parliament. But Lord Castlehaven, alleging that for this very reason he ought, for a testimony of their own loyalty, and of their detestation of his breach of trust, to be sent as a present to the King, to be punished as his Majesty should see fit, he was saved from present execution, and afterwards exchanged."

Though Inchiquin's disappointment was the real cause of his defection, yet he pretended another, and more extraordinary, reason for it to the Marquis of Ormond, viz. " An (7) information he had received, from some English women, of a common talk of some of the Irish, that they designed to seize Cork," and, upon this frivolous pretence, he drove all the magistrates, and Catholic inhabitants out of that city; as also out of Youghall, and Kinsale, allowing them to take no more of their goods with them, than (8) what they could carry on their backs, seizing all the provisions, and effects in their houses." Lord Digby, by his Majesty's command, recommended these distressed people to the Marquis of Ormond's care. " The King," says he (9), " is very sensible of their sad condition, and will not soon forget the inhumanity of that Lord."

But Inchiquin, in order to engage his officers and soldiers in the same measures he had embraced himself, caused an (10) oath to be administered to them, by which they obliged themselves to endeavour the extirpation of Popery, to carry on the war against the Irish, notwithstanding any command, proclamation,

(4) Id. ib. Castlehaven's Memoirs. (5) Cart. Orm. vol. i. fol. 513. (6) Id. ib. fol. 529.
(7) Id. ib. vol. iii. (8) Id. ib. vol. i. (9) Id. ib. vol. iii. fol. 353. (10) Belling's MSS.

tion, or agreement, to the contrary; and to submit to no peace, or conditions with them, but by confent, and allowance of King and parliament. This was then a favourite mode of expreſſion with thoſe who fought, in the King's name, againſt his perſon.

CHAP. XI.

The Confederates ſend Supplies to the King.

HOW much ſoever the King has been cenſured *(a)*, for employing his Iriſh Catholic ſubjects, againſt his Engliſh and Scottiſh rebels, (even by thoſe, who had actually reduced him to that neceſſity) his Majeſty's good opinion of their courage and fidelity, was certainly well grounded. Lord Byron, in a letter from Cheſter, to the Marquis of Ormond, January 30th 1643, requiring ſupplies from Ireland (1), " wiſhed they were rather Iriſh, than Engliſh; for that the Engliſh he had already, were very mutinous; and being," ſays he, " for the moſt part this countrymen, are ſo poiſoned by the ill-affected people here, that they grow very cold in this ſervice." And, indeed, that this preference, in favour of the Iriſh, was juſt, and reaſonable, appears from hence, that ſuch of the Engliſh Proteſtant forces, as were commanded over on that duty (2), " went with ſuch reluctance," ſays Borlace, " as the ſharpeſt proclamations, of which there were ſeveral, hardly reſtrained them from flying their colours, both before and *(b)* after their arrival in England." But with how much ſpirit and alacrity, the Iriſh crowded into that ſervice; and what wonders they performed in it, ſhall be preſently related, from unqueſtionable authority.

But there now aroſe a new, and more ſubſtantial impediment to the tranſmiſſion of theſe ſupplies by the confederates (3), " from the Iriſh coaſts being infeſted

(1) Carte, Leland, &c.   (2) Hiſt. Iriſh Rebel. fol. 177.   (3) Cart. Orm. vol. i.

(a) " It was Lord Inchiquin above-mentioned, that firſt moved the King to ſend for the forces of Ireland into England." Borl. Hiſt. Iriſh Rebel. fol. 203.

(b) " They deſerted to Sir Thomas Fairfax, notwithſtanding their ſolemn oath; and numbers of them were perſuaded to take arms for the parliament." Lel. Hiſt. Irel. vol. iii. p. 216.

infefted by fwarms of *(c)* rebel-fhips," whofe commanders fhewed no mercy to fuch of the Royal party, as had the misfortune to fall into their hands. For " of (4) one hundred and fifty men, whom the Marquis of Ormond had about this time fent to Briftol, and who happened to be taken by Captain Swanley, commander of a parliament fhip, feventy, befides two women, were inhumanly thrown over board, on pretence that they were Irifh." This ftruck a juft terror into all the neighbouring ports, and fcarce a fhip durft ftir out of the harbour. Shortly after, however, feveral hundred Irifh ventured off to his Majefty's affiftance; "and on the third day of their failing (5), having taken a Scotch veffel, with about fifty Kirk-minifters, deputed to preach up, and adminifter, the covenant in Ulfter, inftead of retaliating Captain Swanley's late inhumanity, they contented themfelves with only making them prifoners."

On the 16th of May, 1644, the Earl of Antrim acquainted the Marquis of Ormond, that (6) " he had then, for three months paft, maintained by his own credit, and that of his friends, at leaft two thoufand men, ready to be fhipped off, waiting for their arms and provifions; which, he feared, would not come fo foon as expected, while the parliament fhips were fo thick on that coaft *(d).*"

Yet fo great was that Lord's zeal for his Majefty's fervice, and fo little did the Irifh fear the danger then attending it, that on the 27th of the following month, he wrote again to the Marquis (7), " that he had fent off about fixteen hundred men, being as many as the fhips could conveniently hold, completely armed by his own fhifts, befides fifteen hundred pikes; and that he had difcharged feven, or eight, hundred men, for want of fhipping." But his Lordfhip feems to have fhifted fo well afterwards, that we find, by a letter of the Marquis of Ormond, July 17th following, " that (8) the number of men then embarked by him (Antrim) from Waterford and other places,

---

(1) Ormond's Let. Cart. Collect. of his Papers, vol. i. p. 48.   (5) Cart. Orm. vol. i.   (6) Id. ib. vol. iii.
(7) Id. ib.   (8) Id. ib. vol. iii. fol. 328.

(c) The Marquis of Ormond himfelf, in a letter to the Archbifhop of York, May 27th, 1644, mentions thefe two great impediments to the tranfmiffion of the Irifh fupplies. " In addition to other difficulties," fays he, " we are here threatened with an invafion of the Scots out of the North, who have treacheroufly furprifed Belfaft, and attempted other Englifh garrifons; fo that, until thefe feas be cleared, and the danger of the Scots over, Anglefey can expect little indeed, or no fuccour out of Ireland." Cart. Collec. of Orig. Papers, vol. i. p. 48.

(d) " I am forry," fays Secretary Nicholas, in a letter to the Marquis of Ormond, May 20th, 1644, " that the paffage to and from Ireland, is, by the Englifh rebels' fhipping on that coaft, rendered fo difficult; and that there is no poffibility for the King fuddenly to fet forth and maintain fuch a guard upon the Irifh coaft, as to fupprefs their forces by fea." Carte's Collect. of Orm. Orig. Papers.

places, amounted to two thousand five hundred, well armed, and victualed for two months."

Lord Clarendon's high encomiums on this nobleman's zeal, and activity in the King's service; and on the valour, fidelity, and wonderful success, of these Irish in promoting it is the more remarkable, as it is well known, that his Lordship was not at all biassed, by any partial affection to either of them (9). "It cannot be denied," says he, " that the levies the Marquis of Antrim made, and sent over to Scotland under the command of Colkitto, were the foundation of all those wonderful acts, which were performed afterwards by the Marquis of Montrofs. They were fifteen hundred men, very good, and with very good officers; all so hardy, that neither the ill fare, nor the ill lodging, in the Highlands, gave them any discouragement. They gave the first opportunity to the Marquis of Montrofs of being in the head of an army, that defeated the enemy, as often as they encountered them. After each victory, the Highlanders went always home with their booty; and the Irish only staid together with their general. And from this beginning, the Marquis of Montrofs grew to that power, that after many battles won by him, with much slaughter of the enemy, he marched victoriously with his army, till he made himself master of Edinburgh, and redeemed out of the prison there, the Earl of Crawford, Lord Ogilvy, and many other noble persons, who had been taken and sent thither, with a resolution that they should all lose their heads; and the Marquis of Montrofs did always acknowledge, that the rise and beginning of his good success, was due, and to be imputed, to that body of the Irish, which had in the beginning been sent him by the Marquis of Antrim; to whom, the King had acknowledged the service, in several letters of his own hand-writing."

It is therefore no wonder, that we find Lord Digby so frequently importuning the Marquis of Ormond (10), " to use all possible means to assist, and encourage, the Earl of Antrim, and his forces, in the service of Scotland; whereof the King's party," says he, " find such admirable effects in England." nor, on the other hand, is it at all strange, that in order to prevent their coming into England, the parliament of that kingdom passed that cruel ordinance of the 24th of October, 1644 (11), " that no quarter should be given to any Irishman, or Papist born in Ireland, that should be taken in hostility against the parliament, either upon the sea, or in England, or Wales."

(9) Clarendon's Life written by himself, vol. ii. p. 246. See Append.   (10) Carte's Orm. vol. iii.
(11) Borl. Ir. Rebel. fol. 178. See Hughe's Abridgment.

CHAP. XII.

The Confederates prefs the Marquis of Ormond *to take the Command of their Forces.*

THE hostilities daily committed on the confederates by Monroe in Ulster, Sir Charles Coote in Conaught, and by Inchiquin in Munster, in breach of the cessation, caused them to repeat their most earnest request to the (a) Marquis of Ormond, now (b) Lord Lieutenant of Ireland, that he would condescend either to take the command of their forces upon himself, or to permit them to employ them against those, now his Majesty's open and declared enemies. They were the more importunate in this request, as they were privately assured, that orders of that kind had been already sent to his Excellency; for his Majesty had promised, that the (c) Marquis should join with them, particularly against the Scots in Ulster, when a peace, or cessation, was concluded (1); " It being understood," says Lord Digby on this occasion, " that, if the Scots submitted not to it, they should then be declared against, as common enemies."

THE Marquis himself was fully sensible of the rebellious disposition of these Scots. He even owned (2), " that he doubted not, but that, when they were all able, they would endeavour to be masters of all the harbours, and other places of consequence, in the kingdom, on pretence of securing them against Papists, and malignants." Soon after this, he acquainted the Earl of Clanrickard

---

(1) Carte's Orm. vol. iii. fol. 346. Letter to Ormond. (2) ib. vol. iii. fol. 327.

(a) Who was fully sensible of the heinousness of that breach. For, in a letter to Colonel Mathews, so soon after its conclusion, as December 14th, 1643, he says, " his Majesty having agreed thereunto (the cessation) and published to the world by his proclamation, that the same should be kept, is bound by honour, and all laws, to maintain it with all his power; from whence it doth follow, that all who shall oppose it, must oppose themselves against his power and authority." Carte's Orm. vol. iii. fol. 218.

(b) " On the 21st of January, 1643, James Marquis of Ormond was solemnly in Christ-church, Dublin, sworn Lord Lieutenant, with general acceptance." Borl. Hist. of the Irish Rebel. fol. 180.

(c) The King himself in the postscript of a letter to Ormond, in December 1644, says on this occasion, " I have thought to give you this further order (which, I hope, will prove needless) to seek to renew the cessation for a year; for which you shall promise the Irish, if you can have it no cheaper, to join with them, against the Scots, and Inchequin." Relig Sacr. Carol.

Ch. XII. CIVIL WARS IN IRELAND. 181

rickard (3), " that he had difcovered a confpiracy, whereby Drogheda firft, and by confequence, Dublin, was to have been put into their hands." On the other fide, he confeffed, that by accepting the command of the confederates' army (4), " he might have drawn their dependance upon him, and been able to difpofe of their forces, according to his Majefty's pleafure, for the advantage of the fervice, either in Ireland, or elfewhere; that he was affured, the confederates, in cafe of his compliance, would provide the King's army then in his charge; but that, if he refufed, they might conceive they were not obliged to it, having, as they alleged, paid *(d)* all that was promifed, or been damnified by his party, in more than remained due, fince the ceffation." He (5) knew, that actually, at that very juncture, thefe confederates were preparing fix hundred barrels of corn, and four hundred beeves, for his army; and in fhort, that all his hopes of fubfiftence then depended upon them, and that a breach with them, for which they did not want a colour, might have ftopt that fupply."

YET, in oppofition to all thefe motives of duty, neceffity, and convenience, his Excellency alleged, as his principal reafon for not complying (6), " that if he agreed to either of the ways defired by the Irifh; that is," fays he, " if I take the charge of their army upon me, or denounce immediately an offenfive war againft the Scots, not ten Proteftants will follow me; but rather rife as one man, and adhere to the Scots (7)." Nay " he was confident, he fhould, in that cafe, be fuddenly and totally deferted by the Proteftants."

AFTER fuch a reprefentation of the different difpofitions of the Proteftants and Catholics of Ireland at that diftracted period, and by fo impartial and competent a judge and witnefs, who can entertain the leaft doubt, but that the latter were really, and the former only nominally, his Majefty's loyal fubjects.

AND indeed, not only the confederate Catholics, but even feveral other noblemen of the kingdom, entirely unconnected with them, preffed earneftly,
for

---

(1) Carl. Orm. vol. ii. fol 370.   (4) Id. ib vol. iii fol. 322.   (5) Id. ib. vol. i.
(6) Id. ib. vol. iii. fol. 323.   (7) Id. ib. vol. iii. fol. 323.

(d) The confederates had affured Daniel O'Neal, a Colonel in the King's fervice, whom Ormond had fent to them on this occafion, " that though by the agreement in writing, his Excellency was to receive 30,000l. yet, to their agents, or commiffioners, who treated with him, he engaged his honour, that 15,000l. fhould make fatisfaction." Carte's Orm. vol. iii. fol. 308. On occafion of this Gentleman's death, in 1669, King Charles in a letter of that date, to his fifter, the Dutchefs of Orleans, fays, " Poor O'Neal died this afternoon of an ulcer in his guts; he was as honeft a man as ever lived: I am fure I have loft a good fervant by it." Sir John Dalrymp. Mem Append. vol. ii. p. 32.

for a declaration of hostilities against these violators of the cessation. The Earls of Thomond and Clanrickard, and the Lords Dillon, Taaffe, Ranalagh, Fitzwilliams, and Howth, jointly urged the necessity of that measure in an affecting memorial, addressed to his Majesty; wherein, after having represented (8) " their distracted condition, exposed to the mercy of two powerful armies, the one of the confederate Catholics, (if," say they, " they were disposed to make any invasion upon us) and the other of the Scotch-covenanters, and such as adhered unto them, who by burning, spoiling, and committing of cruel, and hostile acts, had broken the cessation, and cast off all obedience to his Majesty's government; they humbly proposed, that the Lord Lieutenant, and Council, might be commissioned to proceed in the articles, and conditions of (e) peace, with the moderate and well affected, on both sides; and that, in regard the Scotch-covenanters, and their adherents, did refuse to pay obedience to his Majesty's government, they might be speedily declared enemies, and his Majesty's power employed for the suppressing of them; to which the confederate party," added they " who kept the cessation, would doubtless give their best assistance."

CHAP. XIII.

The King sends Ormond a Commission to conclude a Peace with the Confederates.

ON the 26th of July, 1644, the Marquis of Ormond received a commission from his Majesty, to conclude the peace mentioned in the above memorial with the confederate Catholics, upon such conditions, as should appear to him just and honourable. In the treaty for that purpose, which was not begun till the 6th of September following, the confederates insisted, as they had before done in the treaty for a cessation, upon (a) the dissolution of the present

(8) Cart. Orm. vol. iii. fol. 322.

(e) The Marquis of Ormond had before this time, received a commission to conclude a peace with the confederate Catholics.

(a) " On account of its being determined by the death of Lord Deputy Wandsford, in 1640, and of the illegal order made by it since, August 7th, 1641, excluding Roman Catholics from the House." Carte's Orm. vol. i. fol. 517. In this treaty also, the Irish commissioners proposed, " that the Scots in Ulster, who had violated the cessation, and all those that adhered to them, should be proclaimed traitors; but this proposal was likewise rejected." Id. ib. vol. iii. fol. 519.

present parliament, and the calling of a new one; and upon the repeal of the penal statutes against the exercise of their religion.

For their first demand, they had now much better grounds, than when they treated for a cessation of arms, for they had since learned, that his Majesty, in a letter of the 2d of July, 1643, directed to the Lords Justices, and Marquis of Ormond himself, had commanded them (1), to "assure the Irish, in his name, that he was graciously inclined to dissolve the present parliament, and call a new one, between that and the 20th of November following; and to take a course to put all those, that should be chosen members of said parliament, into such a condition, as that they should not be prejudiced of their liberty of assisting, sitting, and voting, in said parliament."

And, with respect to the repeal of the penal statutes, the Marquis of Ormond himself owned (2), "that the confederates had been assured, by divers, and by some as from the King, that his Majesty would not stick at it; Lord Taaffe and Mr. Brent affirming, that they had command from the King to give them that assurance: And that generally, all who came from court, declared, that it was not only his Majesty's sense, but held reasonable by most of his servants on that side, whether of the army, or others."

To these two points, however, his Excellency could, by no means, be persuaded to agree. Their first proposal of calling a new parliament, he absolutely rejected, tho' he knew, that the present parliament was irregular and illegal (3). "Their new parliament," says he, in a letter to Lord Digby, on this occasion, "is to be, at no hand, admitted." And how obstinately he persisted in refusing the repeal of the penal statutes, notwithstanding his enlarged powers to grant it, will hereafter appear. In short, he seems to have, all along, concealed his own settled aversion to the peace, under the pretence (4) "of taking with him, in that great work, the advice of the Privy-council;" in which, nevertheless, he owned, "that his Majesty had not a ruling number;" it being, as we have seen, composed of men, already predetermined against even a cessation with the confederate Catholics, almost upon any terms.

(1) Borl. Hist. of the Irish Rebel. (2) Carte's Orm. vol. iii. fol. 450. (3) Id. ib.
(4) Id. ib. vol iii. fol. 340.

CHAP. XIV.

The Treaty of Peace adjourned.

THUS was the treaty adjourned, from the 6th of September to the 10th of January following; and afterwards, by means of the same disagreement in the two points above-mentioned, to the 10th of April, 1645.

On occasion of this last adjournment, Lord *(a)* Clanrickard told his Excellency (1), "that if the confederates' commissioners should then depart in that unsettled condition, he was confident, it would not be in the power of any, the best affected, to prevent a sudden and irrecoverable breach. And freely," adds his Lordship, " to declare my own opinion, if these commissioners have so moderated their propositions, as is reported, that they will insist on no material demand, but that, without which neither themselves, nor any of that religion, can securely enjoy the liberty of conscience, or live either with honour, or safety; to break upon such a point, may prove much to the disservice of his Majesty."

As a further incitement to the speedy conclusion of this peace, Lord Digby had informed his Excellency, in February 1644 (2), " that the Scottish commissioners at London, having gained a tyranny over the English, were the only hinderers of peace, and most fierce in the point of Ireland, as," adds he, " they had reason; for in this treaty, a clear discovery is made, that Ireland is wholly given up to them, by the close committee of state."

His Majesty, in a letter to the Marquis of Ormond of the 18th of the same month, thus emphatically expresses himself, on the subject of this treaty (3). " A peace with the Irish is most necessary to my affairs in England; wherefore, I command you to dispatch it out of hand. And I do hereby promise them, and

(1) Id. ib. vol. iii. fol. 351.   (2) Id. ib. vol. iii. fol. 382.   (3) Carte's Orm. vol. iii.

(a) The very extraordinary merit and services of this Lord, tho' a Roman Catholic, are universally allowed. The Marquis of Ormond, in a letter to Lord Digby, says, " the Earl of Clanrickard's merits and abilities are such, that I cannot readily advise of any proportionable reward and encouragement for them. But it shall be my work, and an hard one it will be, his Majesty and the present times considered, to find out what will best fit and please him." Carte's Orm. vol. iii. fol. 285.

and command you to see it done, that the penal laws against the Roman Catholics shall not be put in execution, the peace being made, and they remaining in their due obedience. And further, when the Irish give me that assistance, which they have promised, for the suppression of this rebellion, and I shall be restored to my rights, I will consent to the repeal of them by a law."

In short, so impatiently did the King desire and urge the conclusion of this peace with the confederates upon the terms above-mentioned, that he dispatched another letter to the Marquis of Ormond, on the 27th of the same month of February, wherein we find these remarkable words. " I (4) do, therefore, command you to conclude a peace with the Irish, whatever it cost. And tho' I leave the management of this great and necessary work entirely to you, yet I cannot but tell you, that if the suspension of Poinings act for such bills as shall be agreed on between you there, and the present taking away the penal statutes against the Papists by a law, will do it, I shall not think it a hard bargain, so that freely, and vigorously, they engage themselves in my assistance against my rebels in England and Scotland; for which no conditions can be too hard, not being against conscience."

Yet, notwithstanding these enlarged powers, and repeated commands, to gratify these confederates in a matter so reasonable in itself, and, in its consequences, so essential to his Majesty's service, the Marquis, at his next meeting with their commissioners in April 1645, thought fit to dismiss them, not only discontented, but altogether hopeless, in that respect. For, besides his persisting in the refusal of these conditions, and his denying that he had received any such instructions, as are contained in his Majesty's letter of the 27th of February now mentioned (of (5) which instruction, however, Lord Taaffe, Mr. Burke, and Mr. Brent, who had lately seen the King, had given them intelligence) he was hardy enough, even to tell his Majesty, in his answer to that letter (6), " that he treated with these commissioners, in such a manner, and gave them such answers, as might let them conjecture, that he had directions to the contrary (b)."

(4) Id. ib.   (5) Cart. Orm. vol. iii. fol. 430.   (6) Id. ib.

(b) The reason assigned by him for this proceeding, is pretty extraordinary, and seems to have added the sin of ingratitude to that of disobedience. " If I had not done this," says he, in the same letter, " the treaty would immediately have been broken, and the greatest part of our subsistence, (which is from their quarters by traffic, and by connivance at the shifts I make) would have been taken from us; which might have produced so great and sudden inconvenience, as would have denied me the short time now left me most humbly to beg, and receive his Majesty's commands." Cart. Orm. vol. iii.

CHAP.

CHAP. XV.

The Earl of Clanrickard *expostulates with* Ormond *upon his last answer to the Confederates' Commissioners.*

BUT his Excellency being now conscious, that he had raised some ill humours in the general assembly at Kilkenny, by his late answers to their commissioners in Dublin, prevailed on the Earl of Clanrickard to make a journey thither, in order to appease them. That nobleman was a Roman Catholic, and, therefore, supposed to have some influence on the members who composed that assembly. In his letter from Kilkenny, May 26th 1645, he told the Marquis of Ormond (1), " that the answers he was pleased to give in Dublin, to the propositions of the confederates' commissioners, had been reported to the assembly, and, as he was informed, very favourably represented, and all entertained with appearance of good satisfaction; but that the part which concerned religion, being reserved for the last, was very sadly received. And, indeed, my Lord," adds he, " the truth is, I find little probability of persuading a settlement of peace, if the penal laws, for so much as lays a penalty, or incapacity, upon them for the exercise of their consciences, be not repealed; and I must freely acknowledge, I do not apprehend where lies the difficulty of that work, or why men of judgment of the King's party in either kingdom, that desire or expect assistance from them, should be offended at it; and this I am very probably assured of, that if the repeal of these laws was now granted, a peace might be suddenly concluded, with the ready and sincere affections of the best of the whole nation, to hazard the uttermost of their lives and fortunes in his Majesty's service."

But to all such representations, counsels, or commands, from whatever quarter they came, his Excellency's constant answer was (2), " that the Irish Privy-council would never agree to such concessions; and that it would be very dangerous, if possible, to make a peace without, or against, the advice of that council; that the English, and Protestants in Ireland, would certainly disobey it, if the council disallowed it; that he found by experience, that further than they saw his Majesty's directions for it, they would not consent to any thing of favour to the Irish; and in short, that some of them were negative in things reasonable, and consented to by the King in England." But how

(1) Id. ib. vol. iii.   (2) Id. ib. vol. iii. fol. 430.

how frivolous, and inexcusable must this apology appear, when it is considered, that so long before as [3] "December 1644, his Majesty had sent him a power, to sequester from the council-board, such members of it, as he did not approve of." And (a) certainly, if his Excellency ever made use of that power, it was only, by what now appears, in an exchange of bad Counsellors for worse.

But, in order to remove this, and all other pretended obstacles to the conclusion of the peace, the King, in a letter of October 22d 1645, told his Excellency [4], "that if he could procure the concurrence of the council, it would be so much the better; but that the Irish peace was of such absolute necessity, that no compliments, or particular respects whatever must hinder it. Wherefore," adds his Majesty, "I absolutely command you, and without reply, to execute the directions I sent you the 27th of February last; giving you leave to get the approbation of the council, so as, and no otherwise, than by seeking it you do not hazard the peace, or so much as an affront, by their foolish refusal to concur with you." But even this last peremptory command of his Majesty proved equally ineffectual with all the former.

CHAP. XVI.

Ormond treats privately with the Scots in Ulster.

STRANGE as this conduct of his Excellency may appear to those, who have been always taught to consider him as a mirror of loyalty to Charles I. even in his most deprest, and forlorn state; their wonder will certainly increase, when they know, that he was, all this while, privately soliciting that King's greatest enemies in Ireland, to join all their forces with his, in order to renew the war against those confederate Catholics, with whom he was, by his Majesty's reiterated commands, publickly negociating a peace. This appears evidently from a secret correspondence between his Excellency and one Galbraith, a Major

in

---

[3] Cart. Orm. vol. i. fol. 522.   [4] Id. ib. vol. iii. fol. 431.

(a) "A power was at that time sent him, not only to sequester from the Council-board disaffected persons, but also, to remove and change the governors of counties, cities, castles, and forts at his pleasure." Carte, ib.

in the Ulster army, which had commenced, and was carrying on *(a)*, ever since the month of January 1644. The Marquis's secret proposal of this new alliance [1], "was joyfully received by the chiefs of both the Scotch and the English armies, in that province; and Monroe himself was *(b)* fully affected that way." [2] This Monroe had just before received a commission from the English parliament, under their new broad seal, to command in chief all the English as well as Scotch forces in Ulster; and, in virtue of that commission, had taken Belfast by surprise, turned out his Majesty's garrison, and replaced them with one from the parliament.

But, as these officers had, it seems, been told [3], "that his Excellency had an innate malice against the Scots in general, his friend Galbraith," in order to accelerate this new alliance, "advised him [4], to write a letter with his own hand, directed to Colonel Monroe now mentioned, in which he was to take notice, that he understood there were some evil instruments, who laboured to possess all Scots, that he entertained an implacable prejudice against them; and that he sent that his just and necessary apology, to vindicate himself, against such secret wounds; and that all of them might be persuaded of the sincerity of his affection for that nation, and of his endeavours to serve every of them, with his best offices of friendship."

We have already observed, that his Excellency had discovered a conspiracy, "whereby Drogheda first, and, by consequence, Dublin, was to be put into the power of those Scots, or at least, into the obedience of the English parliament." It seems, this conspiracy was "concerted, and carried on, by some ill-affected persons, active in intelligence with *(c)* Monroe." On that occasion, the

[1] Id. ib. vol. iii. fol. 385.   [2] Cart. Orm. vol i.   [3] Id. ib. Galbraith's Letter.
[4] Id. ib.

(a) Ormond had received a letter on this subject from Galbraith, dated the 29th of January, 1644. See Carte's Orm. vol. iii. fol. 385.

(b) Galbraith, in one of his letters to the Marquis of Ormond, on this occasion, says, "That he had met most of the officers of the old British, and found in all an earnest desire, that the war should be carried on, with the Marquis's allowance, and concurrence; whereof," adds he, "when I gave them hopes, as from the mouth of a confident of your's, they were overjoyed, and approved the cautions I shewed them." Carte, ib. vol. iii.

(c) The conspirators' agreement with Monroe, was, "That they should seize the town, and plunder and turn out all the Papists, and such as would not adhere to them; and that they would keep the entire command of the place to themselves. But that, if he would assist them with his forces, till they received succours from the parliament, he should have half the plate, jewels, money, and goods, of the Papists, that were to be plundered, except bedding, corn, and other things necessary for the garrison. Monroe readily closed with this proposal." See Carte's Orm. vol. i. fol. 525.

the Marquis told Galbraith (5), "that by letters from Ulster, he found it was misunderstood, that all the Scots, serving in Ireland, were in that conspiracy, or so far mistrusted, that they were under a great cloud of suspicion." But after having observed, how difficult it was to stop the mouths of the common people, " he confidently affirmed, that their nation had lost no jot of esteem or trust, in the more considerate sort, by it; and that it should be found, that no rigour, beyond necessity, in order to his preservation, had been, or should be used." This shewed an apt disposition in his Lordship, to follow his friend Galbraith's advice, to acquit himself to the Scots in the manner prescribed. Whether, or no, he actually did so, does not appear; but certain it is, that in all his letters to the King's friends, he expressed very different sentiments of these people, from what are here recited; and, particularly, in one written to the King himself, in January 1645, while this secret treaty was carrying on, he told his Majesty (6), " That, through an almost general defection in the Northern army, Colonel Chichester was no longer able to serve him there *(d)*."

On the other hand, he was frequently and positively assured by his noble friend, Lord Clanrickard, that the loyalty of the confederate Catholics was such, (at the very time that he was thus negociating their ruin) (7), " That, if the impediments to the peace were once removed, they would soon satisfy his Excellency of their real, earnest, desire, to be employed in his Majesty's service; and that the difficulty would be rather, to keep back the multitude of forward spirits, that would press into that expedition."

(5) Id. ib.   (6) Cart. Orm. vol. iii. fol. 442.   (7) Id. ib. fol. 413.

(d) And so long before, as July 1644, he told Lord Digby, as we have already observed, " that he could not doubt, but that, when the Scots in Ulster were able, they would endeavour to be masters of all the harbours, and other places of consequence in the kingdom." Cart. Orm. vol. iii.

CHAP.

CHAP. XVII.

The Earl of Glamorgan *arrives in Ireland.*

THE King, finding that the Marquis of Ormond would not conclude a peace with the confederate Catholics, upon those equitable terms, which he had so often ordered him to grant them, dispatched the Earl of Glamorgan to Ireland, with a private commission for that purpose; a nobleman, whose zeal for his Majesty's service could be exceeded by nothing, but his attachment to his religion, which was the Roman Catholic [a].

Upon this Earl's first arrival at Kilkenny, Lord Muskerry acquainted the Marquis of Ormond, from thence, with the business he came about, in general terms. To which his Excellency answered (1), " That he knew no subject in England, upon whose favour, and authority with his Majesty, and real, and innate, nobility, he could better rely, than upon Lord Glamorgan's; nor any person, whom he (Ormond) would more endeavour to serve, in those things, which that Lord should undertake [b] for his Majesty's service."

This answer Lord Muskerry communicated to the general assembly, then sitting at Kilkenny; as an indication, that his Excellency was disposed to support, or at least, would not disavow any agreement they should make with Glamorgan. Upon which presumption, the assembly resolved to conclude a public peace, for civil matters, with the Marquis of Ormond on his own terms; after they had made a private one with that Earl, for matters of religion;

(1) Carte's Ormond, vol. iii.

[a] " The Earl of Glamorgan had spent one hundred thousand pounds, in raising, providing, and maintaining forces for the King, in the first year of the rebellion." Cart. Orm. vol. i fol. 553.

[b] " If the particular instructions, or commissions granted to Glamorgan," says Doctor Leland on occasion of this answer to Lord Muskerry, " were not communicated to the Lord Lieutenant, it appears, at least, from this warmth of recommendation, that he considered the Earl as a person duly authorised to treat with the Irish. The Irish considered Ormond as secretly disaffected, and in conjunction with the Presbyterian council, (as they called them,) determined to defeat the King's hopes of succour, by obstructing the Irish peace. To this they attributed every delay, and when the seizure of the King's cabinet at Naseby, discovered his private instructions to Ormond to conclude a peace, whatever it might cost, they were enraged, and printed the letter with severe animadversions on the Marquis." Hist. of Ireland, vol. iii. p. 253.

religion; which last they soon after did, about the latter end of August, 1645.

The government's determined opposition to a peace with the Irish, on any tolerable terms, made it absolutely necessary, to keep this last transaction secret. But a copy of Glamorgan's treaty having been [c] accidentally found, soon after its conclusion, it was transmitted to the English parliament, and by them made public. And Lord Digby, who was then in Dublin, fearing that the [d] large concessions, in point of religion, which the confederate Catholics had obtained by that peace, might alienate the affections of his Majesty's Protestant subjects in both kingdoms, did, in concert with the Lord Lieutenant, summon the Earl of Glamorgan before the council; where they confidently accused him of having either forged, or surrepticiously obtained his Majesty's commission; upon which, on the 26th of December, that Earl was committed [e] close prisoner to the castle of Dublin. About the same time, the King was prevailed upon, publickly to disavow, in a message to both Houses of the English parliament, Glamorgan's commission, and thereby, made void the peace, lately concluded with the confederate Catholics, in virtue of it.

In what light we are to consider his Majesty's public disavowal of Glamorgan's commission, may, I think, partly be gathered from his dispatch to the Lord Lieutenant and Council of Ireland on that occasion; wherein, among other things, he says (2), "The truth is, that the pressing condition of my affairs,

(2) Carte ubi supra.

[c] "In the pocket of Malachias O Kelly, Titular Archbishop of Tuam, when he was killed near Sligo." Carte's Orm. vol. i. fol. 553.

[d] "The confederates, for the present, had receded from the demand of an act of parliament for securing the possessions of the clergy, as difficult, and prejudicial to his Majesty." Lel. Hist. of Irel. vol. iii. p. 268.

[e] "When Glamorgan's imprisonment was known to the confederates at Kilkenny, that event put them into a terrible consternation. Some cried out to arms and were immediately for besieging Dublin, to set him free. The council laboured to cool the flame, but were forced to submit to the calling of a new assembly in an inconvenient time. They wrote to the Lord Lieutenant, pressing Glamorgan's release, as absolutely necessary for the relief of Chester, then besieged, and in great distress; for which service, three thousand men were ready to embark, and nothing wanting but the ships, for which Glamorgan had contracted, to transport them. That all was at a stand by his imprisonment; and neither that expedition, nor the treaty of peace (with Ormond) could go on, till he was at liberty." Cart. Orm. vol. i fol. 562. But, it seems, Chester was lost by the delay of sending these three thousand Irish to its relief, occasioned by Glamorgan's imprisonment; for Sir Edward Walker informs us, " that, had not the designed relief from Ireland been stopt, by the accusation and imprisonment of the Earl of Glamorgan, that place had not so soon fallen into the rebels hands; and might possibly have been the basis of a new fortune to his Majesty." Hist. Discours. fol. 151.

affairs, obliging me to procure a peace in Ireland, if it might be had on any terms safe to my honour, and conscience, and to my Protestant subjects there; and finding also, that the said peace could not be gained, but by some such indulgence to the Roman Catholics, in point of freeing them from the penalties imposed upon the exercise of their religion, as although justly, and duly, I might grant, yet haply, in a public transaction, could not be without some scandal to such of my good subjects, as might be apt to be wrought upon by their arts, who did continually watch all opportunities to blast the integrity of my actions; I thought fit, over and above my public power, to assure the said Roman Catholics, in a less public way, of the said exemptions from the penalties of the laws; and of some such other graces, as might, without blemish to my honour and conscience, and without prejudice to my Protestant subjects, be afforded them. With the knowledge of these secret instructions to the Marquis of Ormond, I thought fit to acquaint the Earl of Glamorgan, at his going to Ireland; being confident of his hearty affection to my service; and withal, knowing his interest with the Roman Catholic party to be very considerable, I thought it not unlikely, that the Marquis of Ormond might make good use of him, by employing that interest, in persuading them to moderation, and to rest satisfied upon his (Glamorgan's) engagement also, with those above-mentioned concessions; of which, in the present condition of affairs, Ormond could give them no other but a private assurance; and to that end, it was possible, I might have thought to give unto the said Earl of Glamorgan such a credential, as might give him credit with the Roman Catholics, in case Ormond should find occasion to make use of him, either as a further assurance of what he (Ormond) should privately promise; or, in case he should judge it necessary to manage these matters, for the greater confidence, a part by him (Glamorgan) of whom, in regard of his religion and interest, they might be less jealous [*f*]."

[*f*] "At the very time of the King's public letter to the Lord Lieutenant and Council, ordering among other things, Lord Digby's charge against Glamorgan should be thoroughly, and diligently prosecuted; he by another letter to the Marquis of Ormond, privately directed, that the execution of any sentence against him should be suspended. And he still contrived to convey secretly to Glamorgan, repeated assurances of his confidence and friendship." Lel. Hist. of Irel. vol. iii. p. 274.

CHAP.

CHAP. XVIII.

Glamorgan now freed from his Confinement, treats with the Nuncio Renuccini; Ormond's Opinion of that Proceeding.

"ON (1) the 30th of the same month of December, the Earl of Glamorgan, having sent to the Lord Lieutenant, the original counter-part of the articles of his peace with the confederate Catholics, was set free from his close confinement, but still remained a prisoner in the castle, having only the liberty of the house, until his Majesty's further pleasure was known. And shortly after, his Lordship was enlarged, upon his own recognizance of twenty thousand pounds, and that of (2) the Earl of Kildare, and the Marquis of Clanrickard, of ten thousand pounds each, to appear on thirty days notice. Soon after his enlargement, he went to Kilkenny, where he shewed (3) the utmost zeal to bring the confederate Catholics to agree to the terms of peace offered by the Marquis of Ormond, the defects of which, in the article of religion, were to be supplied by himself."

THE Nuncio Renuccini, who some short time before, had (*a*) arrived from Rome, and had gained considerable influence on the Irish soldiery, the common people, and even on the general assembly, was then at Kilkenny. With him the Earl of Glamorgan had chiefly negociated, when he wrote to the Marquis of Ormond from thence (4), " that since the high post his Excellency held, and the difference of religion, would not permit him to engage openly, he was of opinion, it would not be improper to delegate that office to others, to whom if he would join himself, he doubted not, but in a few days, and even hours, he should obtain whatever should be thought reasonable and honourable."

(1) Carte's Orm. vol. iii. fol. 562.   (2) Id. ib.   (3) Id. ib.
(4) Id. ib. vol. iii.

(*a*) Lord Castlehaven tells us, that, " coming near the coast, he was chaced by a parliament frigate, commanded by one Plunket; and that, as he was ready to lay him on board, to the great misfortune of the confederate Catholics, Plunket's frigate took fire, to quench which, he was forced to lye by, and in the main time, the Nuncio got to shore." Memoirs.

In anſwer to this letter, his Excellency told him (5), " that his affections, and intereſts, were ſo tied to his Majeſty's cauſe, that it would be madneſs in him to diſguſt any man, that had power, and inclination to relieve his Majeſty, and the ſad condition he was in; and therefore, that his Lordſhip might ſecurely go on, in the way he propoſed to himſelf, to ſerve the King, without fear of interruption from him, or ſo much as enquiring into the means he worked by (b)." Such encouragement to proceed in his treaty with a perſon, who thought he could not make too high demands, in the article of religion, is ſurely an authentic proof, that his Excellency was, by this time at leaſt, convinced, that Glamorgan's commiſſion was not either forged by himſelf, or ſurreptitiouſly obtained.

But, leaſt any doubt ſhould remain on that head, I ſhall produce part of two letters from his Majeſty to that Earl, which clearly demonſtrate the reality of his commiſſion, and which are ſtill to be ſeen in the Britiſh muſeum, in his Majeſty's own hand-writing (6). In the firſt of theſe letters, which is dated February 3d, 1645-6, a ſolicitude is plainly expreſſed, leſt reſentment of the ill uſage that had been given to his Lordſhip, ſhould provoke him to diſcover the whole ſecret. " In a word," ſays his Majeſty, " I have commanded as much favour to be ſhewn to you, as may poſſibly ſtand with my ſervice, or ſafety; and, if you will yet truſt my advice, which I have commanded Digby to give you freely, I will bring you ſo off, that you may be ſtill uſeful to me, and I ſhall be able to recompence you for your affection. If not, I cannot tell what to ſay; but I will not doubt your compliance, ſince it ſo highly concerns the good of all my crowns, my own particular, and to make me have ſtill means to ſhew myſelf your aſſured friend,

CHARLES R.

The other letter is dated the 28th of the ſame month, when his Majeſty knew, that the Earl either was, or would ſoon be, at liberty; and was ſent by Sir John Winter, his Lordſhip's couſin-german, and a Roman Catholic.

" Herbert,

---

(5) Id. ib.   (6) See Warner's Hiſt. Iriſh Rebel.

(b) " This anſwer of the Marquis of Ormond ſeems inconſiſtent with a real perſuaſion, that Glamorgan was not duly authoriſed to treat with the confederates." Lel. Hiſt. Irel. vol. iii. p. 276.

"HERBERT,

I AM confident, that this honeſt, truſty bearer, will give you good ſatiſ-faction, why I have not, in every thing, done as you deſired. The want of confidence in you being ſo far from being the cauſe thereof, that I am every day more and more confirmed in the truſt that I have of you. For believe me, it is not in the power of any, to make you ſuffer in my opinion by ill offices. But of this, and divers other things, I have given Sir John Winter ſo full inſtructions, that I will ſay no more, but that I am your moſt aſſured friend (c),

CHARLES R.

I SHALL add nothing more on this ſubject, but that we find in the Nuncio's memoirs (7), " that the Earl of Glamorgan left with the confederate Catholics, the original of his commiſſion to treat with them, in his Majeſty's own hand."

CHAP. XIX.

Peace concluded with the Marquis of Ormond.

THE impriſonment of the Earl of Glamorgan, and the King's diſavowal of his commiſſion, were two incidents, that greatly favoured Renuccini's deſigns. That prelate had brought to the confederates pretty large ſupplies, and much larger promiſes (1). His entrance into Kilkenny on horſeback under a canopy, was as ſolemn and magnificent, as both clergy and laity could make it. When he came to the place, where the council ſate, he was placed in a chair not far from Lord Viſcount Mountgarret, preſident of the council. After ſome pauſe, he preſented the Pope's brief to the preſident; which being publickly read, he made an oration to the aſſembly, and concluded it with letting them know three things, which were principally given him

---

(7) Enquiry into the ſhare which Charles I. had in Glamorgan's treaty, p. 107.
(1) Belling's MSS.

(c) " That Glamorgan did ſtill enjoy the Royal favour and confidence in a very high degree, there is direct, and poſitive proof in thoſe letters extant among the Hulſian manuſcripts, in which Charles aſſures him of the continuance of his friendſhip, and promiſes to make good all his inſtructions to him, and the Nuncio." Lel. Hiſt. of Irel. vol. iii. p. 285. Note.

him in command by his Holiness. The first was, to endeavour the propagation of the Catholic religion, the second to conserve the Catholics in union among themselves, and the third, to cherish in them the allegiance due to their lawful sovereign. He could not," adds my (2) author, who was present, " have ended his discourse more to the satisfaction of all that heard him, than by mentioning the subjects' duty towards their King, and his having it in charge to cherish it. For it was collected from thence, that he was willing they should bury the memory of their past sufferings in the blessings of an happy peace. But in the sequal, we shall find, how little conformity there was between his proceedings and his professions."

At this time, however, he was held in the highest esteem, and veneration, by the confederate Catholics; and, as their hopes of obtaining liberty of conscience, which were all centered in Glamorgan's peace, were now at an end, by the King's disavowal of it, they readily accepted the Nuncio's offers, of what he then called aid and protection, but what was soon after changed into dominion and controul. That this acceptance was a matter rather of necessity, than choice, appears from their conduct towards a former agent from Rome, in which they shewed little inclination to submit their temporal concerns to a spiritual superintendency. For when, soon after the cessation was concluded, Petrus Franciscus Scarampi, sent upon the same business by Pope Urban VIII. (3), " came to Limerick, attended by some twenty horse, the gates were shut against him, and a compliment sent him by the magistrates, that they were sorry he had undertaken so tedious and troublesome a journey, at so unseasonable a time, when all the city were busily employed in matters of great consequence, in chosing of magistrates for the ensuing year, and in app'otting their first payment of the thirty thousand pounds, with which, upon the cessation, they had agreed to supply his Majesty's army, on which account, they could not give him fit attendance; but they offered to lodge him a mile off the city, and to let him know the next day their resolution concerning his admittance. But the agent replied, that if they were not at leisure to receive him then, he would not attend their leisure the next day, and so went away (*a*)."

But

(2) ib.   (3) Clanrick. letter to Ormond, Mem. Engl. ed. Carte's Orm. vol. iii.

(*a*) Lord Orrery, in his answer to Peter Walsh, cites a bull of Pope Urban VIII. dated the 28th of May, 1643 (the time Scarampi arrived in Ireland,) encouraging, and exciting the confederates, by pardons, indulgences, &c. to continue the war against the King's forces, as a proof of the dangerous influence which Popes have had, in such cases, on Roman Catholic subjects living under Protestant governments. Walsh, with good reason, suspects this bull to have been forged, as he could not find upon enquiry, that the original was ever seen by any one. But, even supposing it real and genuine, it proves the direct contrary of what his Lordship has produced it for, as it did not in the least hinder, or retard the trea-

ty

But the confederates growing weary, soon after, of Renuccini's haughtiness, and despotism; and being assured besides, that the King would, when he had it in his power, make good his engagement to them by Glamorgan, privately resolved to conclude the peace with the Marquis of Ormond, which related chiefly to civil matters, on his own terms; in order to enable his Majesty, by sending him powerful supplies, to renew, and confirm Glamorgan's treaty with them, concerning matters of religion. "But (4) although the Nuncio was extremely averse to Ormond's peace, as containing no satisfactory concession in spirituals; yet he was far from desiring that the promised supplies should be withheld from his Majesty. The method he proposed was (5), "That the cessation should be still continued, and assistance sent to the King, in the same manner, as if the peace had been concluded *(b)*."

Pursuant to the above resolution, the general assembly, which met on the 6th of March 1645 (6), dispatched Lord Muskerry, and other commissioners, to Dublin, to conclude the peace with the Marquis of Ormond; and accordingly, it was there concluded on the 28th of the same month.

At the same time, with the articles of peace, was signed a conditional obligation, or defeasance (7), "whereby the confederates engaged to transport ten thousand foot into England or Wales, well armed and provided, by April the 1st; and four thousand more by May 1st following, to be mustered, viewed, and allowed, by such persons, as the Marquis of Ormond should appoint. And, in case the said forces were not sent, at the times appointed (unless hindered by the blocking up of harbours, contrary winds, or other reasonable cause, to be allowed, as such, by the Marquis of Ormond) these articles were to be of no effect, and each party disengaged, as if they never had been agreed upon."

(4) Cart. Orm. vol. i. (5) Id. ib. (6) Id. ib. (7) Id. ib.

ty of cessation, which the confederates cheerfully concluded with the Marquis of Ormond, in September following; although they very well knew the great wants and distresses of his Majesty's army at that juncture; while their own was in good condition, and enjoyed great plenty.

(b) The Nuncio, though he opposed Ormond's peace, yet exhorted the confederates in the mean time, to prolong the cessation, and to send their forces for the relief of Chester. Lel. ubi supra, p. 275.

CHAP.

CHAP. XX.

The Conclusion of the Peace too long deferred.

THUS was the peace at length concluded; but too late for the principal end of it, his Majesty's affiftance in England, or Wales. For the Englifh rebels were, by this time, grown fo powerful in all thofe places, where the fupplies from Ireland might propofe to land, that there was not a fecure fpot left (1) for their defcent, nor any horfe on that fide, to countenance their landing, nor even a fafe retreat for them, after they were landed; fo that to fend them away, as matters then ftood with the King, would be only expofing fo many men to inevitable deftruction (2). " The fupreme council, however, immediately *(a)* iffued warrants, to have four thoufand men drawn out of the ftanding forces of Leinfter and Munfter, and two thoufand more from the other provinces; prefixing a day for their being at Ballyhafke, and Paffage, places commodious for their embarkation. And they gave out commiffions for levying the remaining four thoufand, which were to be tranfported in a fecond miffion; having laid embargoes on all veffels in the river of Waterford, and in the harbours of Wexford, and Dungarvon. And as no induftry," proceeds Mr. Belling, " was omitted on their part, fo there was not any occafion, fince the beginning of the war, wherein the council found more prompt obedience to their commands, or more hearty willingnefs in the people, to bear any charge, that might conduce to the advancement of it."

But the King himfelf, on account of the unhappy fituation of his affairs, in the places now mentioned, thought fit to countermand this embarkation. For, in a letter to the Marquis of Ormond, March 26th, (two days before the conclufion of the peace) he told him (3), " that his condition was then very fad and low, by the late difbanding of his army in the Weft; which," adds his Majefty, " if fuccours of foot had arrived in time out of Ireland, might have been prevented, to our moft certain advantage. That he thought fit

(1) Id. ib. Belling's MSS.   (2) Belling's MSS.   (3) Cart. Orm. vol iii. fol. 451.

(a) Lord Digby, in a letter, from Ki'kenny, to the Marquis of Ormond, April 3d, 1646, affured him, " That the fupreme council of the confederate Catholics undertook, with great chearfulnefs, to furnifh his Lordfhip with all he defired, and in the way he defired; but that the men and officers were daunted, as apprehending themfelves fent to facrifice, unlefs there might be fome more certainty of a fecure landing place for them, on the other fide; wherein," adds his Lordfhip, " as we have reafon to believe things ftand on the other fide, i cannot fay but they have reafon." Cart. Orm. vol. iii. fol. 456.

fit to advertife him thereof, that he might ftop the fending over foot, which would be loft, if they fhould come, he having no horfe, nor ports in his power to fecure them." And in another letter to Lord Digby, of the fame date, which he defired him to communicate to Ormond, he fays (4), " forces from Ireland, unlefs they were much greater than, he believed, could be fent him from thence, would do him more harm than good; yet that he much defired that the peace there was made. But that Ormond fhould ftop any forces from coming over, and employ them for the reducing of that kingdom into a perfect obedience; by which," fays he, " it is poffible, it may pleafe God to reftore me to the other two; or be a fafe retreat for myfelf."

(4) IJ ib. fol. 45c.

AN

HISTORICAL AND CRITICAL

REVIEW

OF THE

CIVIL WARS IN IRELAND.

BOOK VII.

CHAP. I.

The Confederates still press the Marquis of Ormond to take the Command of their Forces upon him against the Violators of the Cessation.

THE Marquis of Ormond still continued the cessation with the confederate Catholics, as a measure absolutely necessary for the subsistence of his army; and the confederate Catholics, in hopes that the peace would be soon (a) proclaimed, patiently bore that army's frequent breaches of it. But these breaches now became so very grievous, and extensive, especially in Ulster, that the supreme council renewed their intreaties to his Excellency, " to (1) unite his forces with theirs, in order to resist the attempts of the Scots of Tyreconnel, and other parts of Ulster, his Majesty's now open and avowed enemies; and so to manage the war, that the service might not suffer, thro' the want of due correspondence, for the little time the entire settlement of the kingdom was suspended. They informed him, that they had received intelligence,

(1) Belling's MSS. Carte.

(a) " It was privately affirmed to me with some confidence," says the Earl of Clanrickard, in a letter to Ormond, May 11th, 1646, " that upon your Lordship's publication of the peace, the generality of the whole kingdom would declare themselves to be solely and entirely under your Lordship's government." Cart. Orm. vol. iii. fol. 466.

intelligence, that Monroe, with a numerous army, was going to fall upon Newry, Dundalk, and other maritime towns within his Excellency's quarters; and that the Scots of Tyreconnel, were gathering in a body of three thousand foot, and five hundred horse, to invade Conaught, where they were sure to be joined by Sir Charles Coote's forces." They added, " that if his Excellency would agree, that they might, on all sides, fight to clear the kingdom of the *(b)* common enemy, their councils in civil and military matters, should be managed by his advice. And the council having understood, that the want of money to prepare for the field, was what chiefly retarded this conjunction, they promised to send his Excellency (2) three thousand pounds; two thousand of which, they soon after sent him."

On the conclusion of the peace (3), " promises of mutual assistance, (in case either of their quarters were attacked before the time appointed for the publication of the articles) had passed between the confederates and the Lord Lieutenant, who promised to engage in actual service, where it was necessary, and, as he should find himself enabled, would further prosecute those, that should not submit to the peace, as enemies and rebels to his Majesty, in such a way, as he should judge most for his Majesty's service." But he now told them, in answer to their above-mentioned solicitations (4), " that, indeed, he understood very well the necessity of an union; but that he might not join with any party not deriving authority from his Majesty; that nothing further could be done towards a union, till the articles of peace were published, about which, he had not yet received his Majesty's pleasure, nor had they performed the engagements made at signing them."

The chief of these engagements was, as we have already seen, the sending off ten thousand of the confederates' forces to the King's assistance in England, or Wales; which was, on many accounts, impracticable, precisely within the time stipulated by the articles. If his Excellency had not yet received his Majesty's *(c)* order of the 26th of March before-mentioned, for stopping these forces, he certainly could be no stranger to the reasons, which induced him to send it. With these reasons, Lord Digby had acquainted him *(d)*, five or six days
after

(2) Belling's MSS. Cart. Orm. vol. i. fol. 567.   (3) Cart. Orm vol. i.
(4) Id. ib vol. i. fol. 571.

(b) " It is true," says Lord Digby, in a letter to Ormond on this occasion, " that his Majesty did promise, that you should join with them (the confederates) against the Scots, when a peace, or cessation, should be concluded." Cart. Orm. vol. iii. fol. 346.

(c) He received it April 25th, 1646. Carte's Orm. vol. i. fol. 567.
(d) April 3d, 1646.

after the conclusion of the peace; and the Marquis of Ormond himself, four [e] days after that, informed the King [5], "that he had sent to Lord Byron, to know the state of North-Wales, and whether three thousand men, for whom there was shipping, might be useful, and safely disposed of there. And that, although the time for sending off the supplies was elapsed, for want of shipping, yet he was confident, the men had been, and were still ready." And Lord Digby, at the same time, assured the Marquis [6], " that he found in these men, such an universal, not only disposition, but passion, to be under his Excellency's government, that he thought it would be impossible for any to hinder them from it, almost upon any terms."

CHAP. II.

Lord Clanrickard *expostulates with the Marquis of* Ormond, *on his Refusal to join the Confederates, and to proclaim Sir* Charles Coote *a Rebel.*

HIS Excellency's justly admired friend, the Earl of Clanrickard, once more acquainted him, about this time [1], " that he was privately importuned, to second the speedy publication of the peace, with his humble addresses and persuasions to his Lordship; that he was himself of opinion, that if some such course was not soon taken, the kingdom would be suddenly, and totally ruined; that all access to his Majesty, to know his further pleasure, or to give him a right information of the state of his affairs, was then made impossible; that the confederates, in order to what was required of them, had provided shipping for transportation, and drawn a considerable body of men to the sea-side, whether to the just number, was, he thought, too nice a scrutiny in them distracted times; that it then appeared, there was no army of the King's to join with them near those places, to which they were to guide their course; nor any harbour left, to secure their landing; and that their going would only be the destruction of so many men, and nothing of assistance or preservation to his Majesty."

ALL this while, hostilities were daily committing on the confederates, by the parliamentarian forces in Ulster and other parts, and even by those of his
Majesty's

[5] Id. ib. vol. iii. fol. 459. [6] Id. ib. vol. iii. [1] Id. ib. vol. iii. fol. 465.

[e] April 7th, Cart. Orm. vol. iii. fol. 559.

Majesty's army, in breach of the cessation. Lord Clanrickard himself had been frequently assaulted by Sir Charles Coote, within the limits of his government, without being able to obtain redress from the Lord Lieutenant, and Council. In a letter to his Excellency, on that occasion, he told him [2], " that it did somewhat disturb and perplex his thoughts, to observe those, whom he conceived himself bound in duty to oppose, having all, or most of them, taken the covenant, assumed power and government, contrary to his Majesty's authority, and quite opposite to his Royal grants to others, constant violators of the cessation, and frequent invaders of his, and his adherents estates; and, if he was not much mistaken, such as rather expected submission from their sovereign, than shewed any inclination to submit to him, did still seem to be accounted loyal subjects, and within the compass of obedience to his Excellency's government; and that, by implication, the breach of the cessation did seem to be allowed them, at least, not corrected." After which, his Lordship proceeds to say, with a spirit suitable to his great integrity, and honour [3], " being now reduced into the condition I am, give me leave to call upon your Excellency and the state, even in the King's behalf, and for justice sake, that Sir Charles Coote, who commands in chief the forces here, under the title of Lord President of Conaught, may be, forthwith, declared and proclaimed a rebel and a traitor, according to his deserts, and all such, as hereafter assist, or adhere unto him; for the matter hath now proceeded so far, as, certainly, these attributes must be fixed either upon him or me; pardon me, if I should further affirm, upon your Excellency."

But with neither of these just requests of his truly noble friend, could the Marquis of Ormond be persuaded to comply; not with that for proclaiming the peace, because, as he pretended [4], " having received intelligence, that the King was gone to the Scots' army, he conceived that change of things there might occasion some alteration in his resolutions, as to the manner he should propose for his Majesty's service, and the settlement of the kingdom." But as his Excellency had been apprized, long before, by Lord Digby, secretary Nicholas, and by the King himself [5], " that the Scots were the greatest opposers of the Irish peace, having all along entertained hopes, that Ireland should be given up to them," what else could he have expected from " that change of things," but that they would compel his Majesty, as they soon after did, to send him positive orders, to forbear all further proceedings in it? And, what further demonstrates the weakness, and insincerity, of that excuse is, that his

[2] Carte's Orm. vol. iii. fol. 463.   [3] Id. ib.   [4] Id. ib. vol. iii. fol. 468.
[5] Cart. Orm. vol. iii. Collect. of Orm. Orig. Papers.

Excellency was, at the same time *(a)*, " well satisfied," as Lord Clanrickard told him (6), " that the King was still desirous of the peace, though he failed of the supplies at the time appointed."

As for his proclaiming Sir Charles Coote and his adherents, traitors and rebels, his Excellency would not venture to do it, without the consent of the council (7), " by whose advice, he affected to be guided throughout, in carrying on the work of peace;" though Lord Digby had before informed him, " that the King understood, and did promise, that his Excellency should join his forces with those of the confederates, when a peace, or cessation should be concluded, against all those, who violated or opposed either." But his Excellency knew, that the Majority of that council were Sir Charles Coote's real, though secret, adherents; and therefore could not expect, that they would consent to an act, implicitly condemning themselves.

CHAP. III.

The King is prevailed on by the Scots to forbid Ormond to proceed in the Peace with the Confederates.

THE Scottish army having, by many deceitful promises, gotten the King into their hands, kept him under the closest, and most irksome restraint. Lord Digby, in a letter from Paris, June 17th, 1646, told the Marquis of Ormond (1), " that the Scots were likely to make use of the King's person, only to force him to what they aimed at with the parliament; insomuch, that he was to consider his Majesty among them, in shew and formality, treated as a King, but really worse than a prisoner; for that, besides the guards about him, and strict observation of his person, he had no kind of liberty of mind, as all power of expressing any thing, but what they would have him, was taken away; not a person being permitted about him, by whom he could either receive, or transmit any thing, to, or from, those whom he would have to

---

(6) Cart. Orm. vol. iii. fol. 474.
(1) Id. ib. vol. iii.

(7) Carte's Orm. vol. iii.

(a) That he was then satisfied that the King was still desirous, that the peace with the confederates, should be be concluded, appears from Ormond's having received his Majesty's letter, wherein he expresses that desire, on the 25th of April, 1646. Carte's Orm. vol. i. fol. 567. And Clanrickard's letter to him, telling him that his Excellency was satisfied that such was his Majesty's desire, is dated the 3d of June following. Id. ib. vol. iii.

to know his mind. This only," adds his Lordship, " we have had the happiness to know from him, when he foresaw the condition he was likely to be in, that he desired, that the Prince his son, the Queen, and all his faithful servants, should jointly govern themselves, according to what they should judge to be the true interests of his crown and posterity; and not according to what, from his forced condition, might outwardly be made appear as his pleasure. And I am confident," proceeds his Lordship, " if there be a possibility of conveying any thing of secret to you, your Lordship will receive his express pleasure to this effect."

After this, as if he dreaded an event, which, though unknown to him, had then recently happened, he adds (2), " My greatest fear is, least before my return to you, the King should have been forced by the Scots, to set an embargo upon the peace of Ireland; but, tho' he have, I hope you will be able to keep things fair, till I come; and that then, having received such further assurances, as I shall be able to give you, of the King's condition, of the Queen and Prince's resolutions, and of the grounds laid to carry them through, no such embargo will be any hindrance to you, to pursue vigorously that course, which you shall judge prudent, just, and honourable."

If the Marquis of Ormond did not receive this letter on the 24th of that month, when the King's order, forbidding him to proceed in the peace (3), arrived; (which might, I own, have been the case) yet he certainly knew, from his own recent experience, that his Majesty was, then, in the condition of a prisoner with the Scots, and not suffered to send to, or receive from, his friends any dispatches, but such as they had both seen and approved of. For his Excellency and the Council, having some time before (4), twice demanded a safe conduct, from Major General Monroe, for one of their messengers, who was to pass by way of Scotland, with letters to the King, they were both times peremptorily refused. This refusal was given about the 7th of June, and on the 11th of the same month, the Scots in England compelled his Majesty to sign an order to the Marquis of Ormond, to forbear all further proceedings in the peace with the confederates; which order was transmitted to his Excellency, by the Scots committee in Ulster, with evident marks of an intended affront to his Majesty's authority in his Lordship's person; for they not only sent him the King's letter with (5) the seal broken, declaring in their own, which inclosed it, that no dispatch from his Excellency and the Council, should be permitted to pass, unless they were made acquainted with it's contents,

(2) ib.　　(3) Cart. Orm.　　(4) Cart. Orm. vol. iii. fol. 480.　　(5) Id. ib

tents, but they also omitted giving the *(b)* Marquis of Ormond his title of Lord Lieutenant, either in the body, or superscription of their letter. Yet this so grossly affronted the Lord Lieutenant, and Council, who had frequently disobeyed his Majesty's free and positive commands, to conclude this peace with the confederates, did now, all at once, most readily comply with this constrained order, so disrespectfully sent them, to forbear all further proceedings in it.

C H A P. IV.

Lord Digby *arrives in Dublin and causes the Peace with the Confederates to be proclaimed.*

BUT that visible alacrity, with which the Lord Lieutenant and Council obeyed this inhibiting order, was suddenly damped, by the arrival of Lord Digby in Ireland, on the 4th of the following month; who, upon hearing of it, and of their prompt compliance with it, wrote to his Excellency (1), " that having received, by an express, the knowledge of his Majesty's condition, and of his positive pleasure in the weightiest of his affairs, and particularly, those of the kingdom of Ireland, he was commanded to signify the same, as Secretary of State, to his Excellency. Your Excellency therefore," proceeds he, " is to take notice, that his Majesty, having upon most positive engagements of the Scots, both unto himself and the crown of France, by the French agent residing with the Scots, received assurances from them in three points, namely, that they would not endeavour to force his conscience; that they would give a sure retreat among them to all his faithful servants, and adherents; and lastly, that they would endeavour, by treaty, or by force, to restore him to, and establish him in, his just rights; put himself voluntarily into their hands: but since, he hath found them so far from performing any part of their engagement, that they have used him, according to his Majesty's own expression, barbarously; and have made him, from the time of his last said dispatch, which was the 2d of June, a prisoner of the strictest kind; having

not

(1) Id. ib.

(b) The Lord Lieutenant and Council, in their answer to the cots committee in Ulster on this occasion, observe, " that they found so little hope of receiving his Majesty's free pleasure, touching his affairs and servants in Ireland, that they had great cause to fear even the safety of any messenger of trust they should send; that, as soon as it should please God to give them clear, and unintercepted ways of address to his Majesty, they hoped to give him fit accounts of all his commands directed to us the Lord Lieutenant; which title, by the way, we hold fit to observe unto you, his Majesty is pleased to give us, though you, in the several letters directed by you unto us, are not pleased so to stile us." Cart. Orm. vol. iii. fol. 450.

not only chaced from him the only person that accompanied him thither, but also set forth a proclamation of death against any who had served him during these troubles, that should presume to come amongst them; insomuch, that his Majesty declares, that he hath no possibility left him, either of receiving any knowledge of his own affairs, but as his enemies shall represent them, or any advices from his faithful servants; much less to express his pleasure to them, in any way, but what they shall force from him. And that, having with much skill and difficulty, obtained that secret means of expressing, in short, his sad condition, and his will and pleasure thereupon, the Queen and Prince, and all his faithful servants were to understand that, as the last free direction they were to receive from him; and that they should, in all things, pursue, and cause to be pursued steadily, those orders, that he had given before this time of his unfree condition; and that, in all things wherein he had not given directions, while he judged himself free, the Prince his son should give, from time to time, such orders, as should be judged best for the advantage of his crown, and interests, without being diverted from it by any thing, that, in his present restraint, might be either surreptitiously, or violently got from him. That particularly, for the business of Ireland, he had, while he was free, redoubled unto his Excellency such positive orders, for the conclusion of the peace, upon the terms expressed to him by his Excellency, since the mutual signing of the articles, that he was confident it would be proclaimed, before his Lordship could be back in Ireland."

CHAP. V.

Lord Digby *insists on the proclaiming of the Peace.*

ON the 28th of July 1646, to satisfy the council on this occasion, Lord Digby drew up and signed a declaration, wherein after repeating what has been mentioned in the above letter, concerning his Majesty's having redoubled his positive orders to the Marquis of Ormond to perfect the peace with the confederates, and his own expectation, that it would, therefore, have actually been proclaimed before his arrival in Ireland; he added, that (1), " finding, instead thereof, a stop set upon the same, by occasion of a letter dated from Newcastle the 11th of June, supersigned Charles Rex, and attested Lanerick; and knowing, by his Majesty's free expression of his will and pleasure, and of his resolutions and designs in the whole state of his affairs, how

(1) Cart. Orm. vol. iii. fol. 491.

how contrary to his free judgment and will, the fame letter of the 11th of June is, and how deſtructive to all the foundations laid by his Majeſty, for the recovery of his own, his crown's and poſterity's rights, whether by way of a good accommodation, or of war, any obedience to the ſaid letter in putting a ſtop to the peace of this kingdom, expected by his Majeſty, would be; I do, according to my duty, and as Secretary of State, upon certain knowledge of his Majeſty's reſolution, and as I will anſwer it with my life,

"DECLARE unto his Excellency, the Lord Lieutenant, and Council of his Majeſty's kingdom of Ireland, that the ſaid letter of the 11th of June, is either a ſurreptitious letter, or a forced one from his Majeſty; procured by ſome falſe information of the ſtate of his affairs, and moſt contrary to what I know to be his free reſolution, and unconſtrained will and pleaſure. And I do further declare, with the ſame ſolemnity, and engagement of my life, that, if the peace of Ireland ſhall not be preſently concluded, the hinderers of it are the occaſion of ſubverting, and deſtroying, the main foundation reſolved, and laid, by his Majeſty, for the recovery of his own, his crown's, and poſterity's rights, as aforeſaid, whether by way of accommodation, or war; for the preventing of which irreparable miſchief, if there ſhould be the leaſt danger thereof by the ſcruples of any, I will freely take the whole matter upon myſelf, to anſwer to his Majeſty, as his Secretary of State, with my life for this declaration of his will. And I do offer myſelf to be detained as a priſoner, where the Lord Lieutenant ſhall appoint, until ſuch time as his Majeſty ſhall be at liberty to expreſs freely, and publickly, unto the Marquis of Ormond (after private letters received from the Marquis of Ormond and myſelf) his unconſtrained will: and then, if his Majeſty ſhall not juſtify me to have declared it faithfully, I ſubmit myſelf to ſuffer death. And I deſire, that this declaration of mine be entered in the council-book, for my juſtification, that I have diſcharged my duty, in caſe the miſchiefs here ſet down, ſhall be occaſioned by deferring the peace of this kingdom, upon the aforeſaid letter of the eleventh of June. In witneſs whereof, I have hereto ſet my hand, July 28th, 1646.

DIGBY."

This declaration was accordingly (1) regiſtered in the council-book; and, upon the ſame day, a proclamation was publiſhed ratifying, and confirming, the articles of the peace; and enjoining all perſons to obſerve, and pay due obedience to it.

(1) Carte's Orm. vol. i.

CHAP.

CHAP. VI.

Owen O'Neal and the Nuncio reject the Peace.

THE Marquis of Ormond seemed not more unwilling to have the peace proclaimed, after it was agreed to, than desirous of an occasion to dissolve it, after it was proclaimed. Unhappily for both sides, such an occasion soon presented itself. The peace had been generally received by the confederate nobility and gentry, and by the greatest and best part of their clergy, conformable, in that respect, to the established clergy of Ireland; who, in a remonstrance to the Lord Lieutenant on that occasion, signed by two Archbishops, nine Bishops, and seventy-seven clergymen (1), " did most heartily acknowledge, that by his Excellency's very great pains and labour, he had, at last, concluded a most necessary peace; which they humbly conceived to be the only means to continue the blessings of religion and loyalty among them; and to be the only hopeful way to reduce the kingdom, wholely to his Majesty's obedience."

But the Nuncio Renuccini, and General Owen O'Neal, absolutely refused to submit to it; the former, because there was no provision made for, what he deemed *(a)*, the free exercise of religion; without which, the confederates were engaged by their oath of association, never to conclude a peace; and the latter, though on the same pretence, yet in reality, because no stipulation was made for restoring him, and his numerous followers, to their *(b)* forfeited estates in Ulster. The Nuncio alledged besides, that the commissioners, who had concluded the peace, did not, according to their instructions, insist upon the repeal of the penal statutes against the Roman Catholic religion. The Marquis of Ormond could not deny the fact; but he maintained (2), " that the peace, which the confederates' commissioners had concluded, by virtue of

---

(1) Borl. Hist. of the Irish Rebel.   (2) Cart. Orm. vol. ii.

(a) Yet, " The Pope himself," says Doctor Leland, " had declared, that a connivance was all that could at present be reasonably demanded." Hist. of Irel. vol. iii. p. 277.

(b) " Over and above those demands, which concerned religion, to which they seemed to adhere with more than ordinary zeal, and thereby drew a dependency of the clergy to them, they insisted upon the restitution of the great estates in Ulster, which was not in the power of the crown to make." Do. Hist. of the Irish Rebel. fol. 313. Clarendon.

an authority derived from their general assembly, whether advantageous, or prejudicial to those that trusted them, ought to have been inviolably stuck to, how blame-worthy soever they might be pretended, for transgressing instructions." This manner of reasoning, however, seems to have been taken up by his Excellency, only for present convenience; for he argued very differently on the same topic of instructions, when, in a former treaty with the confederates, the case was to be his own; and when, in order to justify his rejecting some of their propositions, he told them (3), " that if he had exceeded his instructions, he would have deluded those he treated with, with the shadow of concessions; for that the substance would be lost, by his transgressing the rules given him, in any one particular."

But however that might have been, the Nuncio's casuistry differed materially from that of his Excellency on this occasion; and therefore, that prelate resolved to enforce his opinion by such means, as, in truth, neither belonged to, nor *(c)* became his character, or mission. For, having called together, at Waterford, such of the Irish Bishops and other clergy, as were mostly under his influence, on pretence of forming a synod to settle ecclesiastical matters, they entered all at once on a debate concerning the lawfulness of the late peace; and having soon determined, that all those who were instrumental in making it, were for the reasons before-mentioned, guilty of a formal breach of their association-oath, they issued an excommunication against them; as also, against those of their communion, who should afterwards adhere to it; forbidding, under the same penalty, any public dues to be collected by, or paid to such persons as were formerly appointed to receive them; and giving encouragement, at the same time, to the people to resist any force that might be used for that purpose. This," says Mr. Belling (4), " of all their commands, met with the promptest obedience; and men were so pleased with the observance of it, that; when the clergy themselves had, soon after, formed a new government, by the name of the Council and Congregation, they found much difficulty to bring the people to open their purses."

[3] Id. ib. vol. iii. fol. 424. [4] Bell'ng's MSS.

(c) " The Nuncio's violent measures were, it seems, contrary to the instructions he had received from Rome, and made it necessary for him to send an apology to the Pope." Lel. hist. of Irel. vol. iii. p. 292. Note.

CHAP.

CHAP. VII.

The bad Effects of the Clergy's Proceedings.

BY this spiritual weapon alone, the Nuncio and his clergy, contributed more, in one week, towards the defeat of the confederate army, than the Marquis of Ormond, with all his forces, had been able to effect, during the whole preceding time of the war. The cause of religion, which is said to have first moved them to take arms, and, afterwards, to have united them in a regular and formidable body, was now made an instrument to split them into parties more exasperated against each other, than they were before against their common enemy. The titular Bishop of Ossory shut up, by an interdict, all their churches, and houses of prayer, in Kilkenny, the place where their general assembly, and supreme council, usually met; upon which the Marquis of Ormond sarcastically observed (1), " that they were a strange sort of people, who, after fighting so long for liberty to open their churches, and having got it, shut them up again, of their own accord, and hindered their people to resort to them."

THE Nuncio's violent measures, as I have already observed, were contrary to the instructions he had received from the court of Rome. By these, he was (2) directed, in case peace was made, to do nothing, either by word or deed, to shew that he either approved, or disliked the same. Nay, there was great reason to believe, that the peace concluded with the Marquis of Ormond, was agreeable to his Holiness's sentiments. For some time before, when Mr. Belling had an audience of him on that subject, the Pope told him (3), " It was no wonder, if the King thought it unsafe publickly to grant the Irish the conditions they demanded, lest it might disoblige his Protestant subjects, and that, therefore, a connivance ought to content them for the present."

THE terror, however, of this excommunication drew off great numbers of the common soldiers; and it so far scared General Preston and his officers, who had submitted to, and proclaimed, the peace at the head of his troops, that he and his whole army, went over to these militant ecclesiastics. Their plea

(1) Cart. Orm. vol. iii. (2) Id. ib. vol i. fol. 578.
(3) Belling's MSS. Carte, vol. iii. fol. 564.

plea of the breach of their (a) affociation oath, and of the failure of their commiffioners to infift on the public exercife of their religion according to their inftructions, was indeed plaufible; but they had a much better excufe, in the infecurity of that peace from the King's before-mentioned order of the 11th of June to the Marquis of Ormond, to proceed no further in it; and in that order's not having come to their knowledge, till after it was proclaimed. But notwithftanding this defection of fome of the commanders, foldiers, and common people (4), " all the confederate nobility, and gentry (except a very few of the latter) and all the old Bifhops, and regulars, whofe miffionary powers were not fubordinate to the Nuncio's authority, ftill adhered to the peace, in defiance of the cenfures denounced againft them (5); and the Nuncio himfelf, foon after, received a fevere reprimand from Rome, for having acted in the matter contrary to his inftructions."

C H A P. VIII.

The Marquis of Ormond *goes to Kilkenny, but returns fuddenly to Dublin.*

THE Marquis of Ormond, having had notice of thefe practices of the Nuncio and clergy at Waterford, went to Kilkenny (1), " being invited thither, and informed, that his prefence would foon remove the caufes, or fupprefs the effects, of the clergy's difcontent. His Lordfhip confeffes (2), " that he was received there with many expreffions of joy in the people, and with the refpect due to his Majefty's Lieutenant;" but adds, " that upon his further march into the country, being refufed admittance into Clonmell, and befides, informed that General O'Neil, leading an army of Ulftermen, was invited, and drawn towards Kilkenny, to hinder his retreat, and cut off the guards

(4) Clarend. Ir. Rebel.
(1) Id. ib. vol. iii.
(5) Carl. Orm. vol. i. fol. 570.
(2) Id. ib.

(a) In that oath, the following, among other propofitions, was agreed to, viz. " That they would not confent to lay down arms, until all the laws and ftatutes, made fince the time of King Henry VIII. whereby any reftraint, penalty, mulct, or incapacity, or other reftriction whatfoever, is, or may be, laid on any of the Roman Catholics, either of the clergy, or laity, for the exercife of the Roman Catholic religion within this kingdom, and of their feveral functions; fhould be repealed, revoked, and declared void in the next parliament, by one, or more acts of parliament to be paffed therein." Unkind Deferter, &c. p. 53. The fame author adds, " Now, if the faid committee of treaty for concluding the peace, fwerved from any of the rules, and inftructions given them (as, indeed they have done) what they acted, can no way oblige either the clergy or the people, to their own overthrow, and deftruction. It were a hard cafe for a Common-wealth, if perfons by her impowered with truft, could bind it to acts prejudicial, and deftructive to their prefervation, interefts, and liberty." Ib. p. 60.

guards he had brought with him, he haftily returned to Dublin, full of indignation, and refentment at this inftance of treafon, perfidy, and ingratitude."

Such was the Marquis of Ormond's declared fenfe of this matter, which has been generally, adopted by all our hiftorians. I fhall, however, take the liberty to examine, whether the information his Excellency fpeaks of was grounded on fact; or whether it was not rather contrived, or at leaft, countenanced by himfelf, in order to juftify a defign, which he then entertained, of renewing his treaty with the Scots in Ulfter; and with their now only acknowledged mafters, the rebels in the Englifh parliament.

WHATEVER faults General O'Neil might have had, ingratitude, and *(b)* perfidy were not, certainly, of the Number. Mr. Carte himfelf, one of his accufers on this occafion, informs us, in relation to a tranfaction fubfequent to this (3), " that the Marquis of Ormond had a very advantageous opinion, as well of his honour, conftancy, and good fenfe, as of his military fkill; from which, he propofed as much advantage to the King's affairs, as he did from the force of his troops; and that he always ufed great franknefs, in his treaties with him."

His Excellency knew, that O'Neil had publickly rejected the peace, and was ftill in hoftility againft him; fo that, fuppofing the information true, and that he really defigned to cut off his retreat to Dublin, fuch a defign could not be properly deemed perfidious; or, indeed, fo difhonourable, in any refpect, as thofe frequent acts of rapine and cruelty, committed on the confederate party by forces under his Lordfhip's obedience, during the ceffation; which acts, inftead of being punifhed, or reftrained, were conftantly connived at, if not encouraged, by his Lordfhip and the council; a proceeding very different from that of the general affembly of the confederate Catholics, with regard to O'Neil; whom, on account of his oppofition to the peace, while it was in agitation, they neglected, in their appointment of generals, after its conclufion. And refentment of that neglect was thought to have been the chief caufe of his hoftile, and too fuccefsful, endeavours, to fruftrate all their fubfequent undertakings for the fettlement of the kingdom.

UNDER

(3) ib.

(b) " O'Neil," fays one of his moft inveterate enemies, " was a man of an haughty and pofitive humour; and rather hard to be inclined to reafonable conditions, than eafy to decline them, or break his word, when he had contented." Borl. Hift. of the Irifh Rebel. fol. 233. " Owen O'Neil," fays Mr. Carte, " obferved the ceffation fo religioufly, that when fome of the garrifon of Ennifkillen made him an offer of betraying the place, he would not embrace it, altho' great great preys had been taken from the Irifh, in the excurfions made by that garrifon." Orm. vol. i.

UNDER colour of juſt indignation at O'Neil's ſuppoſed deſign, the Marquis of Ormond, in concert with the council, (ſoon after his *(c)* return to Dublin from Kilkenny,) addreſſed the Britiſh parliament, and renewed his treaty with the Scots in Ulſter, with compliments to theſe latter, which, whether ſincere or not, reflected no ſmall diſhonour on his Excellency (4). " There now goes," ſays he, in a letter to Sir James Montgomery, September the 18th, " from me and the council, a diſpatch to the old and new Scots, and Britiſh officers, (in Ulſter,) acquainting them, that for the preſervation of the kingdom to the crown of England, we have made an addreſs to the parliament, and deſiring, in the mean time, there might be, betwixt us here, ſuch a correſpondence, as befits men, that are certainly of one mind, however, through the diſtemper of the times, we may have differed in our ways."

CHAP. IX.

The Marquis of Ormond *purſues his Treaty with the Covenanters in Ulſter.*

IN vain did his Excellency's noble friends, the Lords Clanrickard and Digby, aſſure him, on this occaſion (1), " that they ſtill found the generality of the Iriſh nobility and gentry, and others of inferior rank, very well diſpoſed to peace; that General Preſton, and his officers, were ſtill well inclined; that Preſton's compliance with the Nuncio was only to preſerve himſelf, and to get ſuch a body together as might make him as conſiderable as O'Neil; that this body conſiſting of all thoſe forces, which the Marquis had moſt reaſon to hope well of, if he might have but private ſatisfaction for the ſecurity of religion, ſo far as he did underſtand it to be ſecured by the articles of the peace, but found it indeed not to be, he would join heartily with his Excellency." Theſe remonſtrances, I ſay, made no change in the Marquis's, and council's ſettled purpoſe, to proſecute their treaty of alliance with his Majeſty's declared enemies in both kingdoms.

As the Biſhops, and clergy aſſembled at Waterford, found themſelves ſuſpected of having put O'Neil on the ſuppoſed deſign of cutting off his Excellency's retreat

(4) Cart. Orm. vol. iii. fol. 566.   (1) Id. ib. vol. iii. fol. 507.

(c) He arrived in Dublin from Kilkenny, on the 13th of September. Cart. Orm. vol. iii. fol. 566.

retreat to Dublin, one of their body thought it incumbent upon him to wipe away that afperfion (2), " by protefting folemnly, before God and his Angels, that they were utter ftrangers to any fuch defign; and that they neither knew, nor expected, that his Excellency would have fo fuddenly returned to Dublin." And General Prefton affured the Earl of Clanrickard (3), " That, (inftead of the Nuncio and clergy's having given encouragement to O'Neil's advance) he himfelf had been the bearer of two different orders from them, upon notice of his advancing with his army, to oblige him to retire. But that O'Neil's anfwer was, " that the Nuncio was but a young foldier, and that, for his part, he muft, and would go, where his army might be beft kept together, and provided for."

GENERAL Prefton himfelf, was not altogether unfufpected by the Marquis, of having confpired with the Nuncio and clergy, in the defign of intercepting him. His Excellency, however, even in his hafty retreat to Dublin, met with fufficient reafon to acquit him of any fuch defign (4), " for, having difpatched Major General Sir Francis Willoughby, with a confiderable party, to prepare his way, the Major General underftood, when he came to Leighlin-bridge, that Colonel Bagnal, under General Prefton's command, was pofted in the fort there, with an hundred men; and as he was to pafs by that fort, he fent two officers to Bagnal, to know whether he might expect him a friend, or an enemy. Colonel Bagnal returned a very civil anfwer, that the paffage over the bridge fhould be open, and that he might command any accommodation the caftle could afford. The Major General found it fo at his coming, and marching over the bridge, rendevouzed his men in the plain field, where he refted till Lieutenant Colonel Flower joined him in the evening, with the Lord Lieutenant's own regiment."

(2) Unkind Deferter, &c.   (3) Carte's Orm. vol. iii. fol. 497.   (4) Cart. Orm. vol. ii

CHAP.

CHAP. X.

A new General Assembly and Council.

IN the mean time, the Nuncio's party increased daily, and his opposition to the peace in proportion; insomuch, that, after having formed a new general assembly of such persons, ecclesiastics and others, as he knew to be most attached to him, he had the hardiness to cause several eminent members of the former assembly, who had been active in concluding the peace, to be imprisoned in the castle of Kilkenny. Among these (1), were Lord Mountgarret, with his two sons, and all the members of the supreme council, except Plunket and Darcy. Sir Robert Talbot, Sir Pierce Crosby, Doctor Fennel, Colonels Bagnal and Wale, with several others, underwent the same fate (2). This assembly assumed the entire government to themselves; and, by a solemn decree, on the 26th of September, appointed a new supreme council, consisting of four Bishops and eight laymen, commanding all the generals to be subject to their orders. The Nuncio took upon him to be president of this council.

It is, nevertheless, certain, that the Irish clergy did not by these rash proceedings, deviate in the main, from their real and fixed sentiments of duty, and allegiance to the King. This appears from a letter of the Nuncio's to Cardinal Pamphilio, wherein he tells him (3), " that the oath of allegiance was sworn by all the Bishops without any scruple, and that it was so thoroughly rooted in the minds of all the Irish, even the clergy, that, if he had in the least opposed it, he would presently have been suspected of having other views besides those of a mere Nunciature; which without any such handle, (adds he) have been already charged upon me by the disaffected."

Yet, even in this new-modelled confederacy, there wanted not some strenuous advocates for the observance of the late peace. Part of those honest reasons produced by Colonel Walter Bagnal, in support of it, at one of their meetings, I shall here transcribe from Mr. Belling, who was present.

" I ap-

(1) Carte, ib. Belling's MSS. (2) Cart. vol. i. fol. 584. Belling's MSS.
(3) Carte's Orm. vol. i. fol. 579. From the Nuncio's Memoirs.

"I APPEAL," said he, "to the consciences of all that hear me, if when we were first compelled (for compelled we were) to take arms for the safety of our lives and fortunes, and for the defence of our religion, and our King's rights; and when his Majesty had power to dispute his cause, with probability of success, against his rebel-subjects of England; if, I say, we had been then offered less advantageous conditions, than those granted by the late peace, whether we should not have accepted them, with a thankful submission to his Majesty's gracious pleasure? And truly, I cannot see that improvement in our condition, if we prudently weigh all circumstances, which should make us now less willing to acquiesce. We have plenty of arms, you will say, which we then wanted; our armies are formed, and our affairs directed by a constant way of government. Certainly, it cannot be denied, if we make the comparison only between us and ourselves, without having a prospect on our enemy, and upon the change of his condition, between the then tumults, and now confederate Catholics, that we have manifold advantages, which we then wanted. But when we consider likewise, that the party in the parliament of England, which had vowed the extirpation of our religion, and was then seconded but by the confused clamours of the multitude in London, hath armies at present, and the Royal fleet at their command; and that, of the two contending parties, whose conflict and hostility against each other gave us respite to advance thus far in our work, that party is likely to prevail, which threatens our destruction; when, I say, we shall maturely weigh this change to the better in our enemies, we cannot be so partial to ourselves, as to think our present estate so much improved beyond theirs, that we should now reject those conditions, which we would have chearfully embraced at first. And it is very manifest, that if we would have inclined to such resolutions, at a time when our King was in a situation to keep the parliament-forces employed, and so to divert this storm from falling on us, both regard to our own interest, and dutiful compassion of our sovereign's present condition, ought now, in all reason, to move us, by endeavouring to relieve his Majesty from his heavy pressures, to lay everlasting obligations of gratitude upon him; and, by assisting his party in England, to lift up a shield for our own defence; which can no otherwise be done than by accepting this peace, concluded, and published by authority of the kingdom; and by avoiding those severe punishments, which never fail to attend the breach of public faith."

AFTERWARDS, addressing his speech to the Bishops there present, "My Lords," proceeds he, "there was a time, when our ancestors, at the peril

peril of their fortunes, and with the danger of their perſons, ſheltered ſome of you, and your predeceſſors, from the ſeverity of the laws; they were no niggardly ſharers with you in your wants; and it cannot be ſaid, that the ſplendor of your preſent condition hath now added any thing to the ſincere and filial reverence, which was then paid you. We, their poſterity, have with our blood, and at the expence of our fortunes, aſſerted this advantage, which you have now over them, have redeemed the exerciſe of your functions from the penalties of the law, and your perſons from the perſecution to which they were ſubject. We are upon the brink of a formidable precipice, reach forth your hands to pull us back; your zeal for the Houſe of God will be thought no way leſs fervent, that you have preſerved the Iriſh nation; reſcue us, we beſeech you, from theſe imminent miſeries, that viſibly environ us. Grant ſomewhat to the memory of our fore-fathers, and to the affection we bear you ourſelves. Let a requeſt find favour with you, made to prevent the violation of public faith, and to keep the devouring ſword from the throats of our wives and children *(a).*"

Mr. Belling informs us (4), " that this ſpeech moved compaſſion in ſome of the Biſhops; but that a reſolution taken in their ſynodical congregation was held too ſacred to be revoked, or changed, upon any conſideration."

C H A P. XI.

The Nuncio, O'Neal, and Preſton, advance towards Dublin, with a conſiderable Army.

THE Nuncio's lay-eccleſiaſtical confederacy, tho' much elated with their newly acquired power, were ſuddenly alarmed, by certain, and undoubted intelligence of the Marquis of Ormond's having advanced ſo far in his treaty with the Engliſh parliament, that commiſſioners were appointed to paſs over to Ireland on that occaſion, and orders iſſued for two thouſand foot, and three hundred horſe, to be tranſported from Cheſter to Dublin. This intelligence

(4) Ubi ſupra.

(a) This loyal gentleman having been afterwards ſent by confederates to the Cromwellians, as a public hoſtage for the performance of articles agreed on between them, was executed at Kilkenny by order of the latter, for having formerly ſigned a warrant, as was pretended, to hang one John Stone, a known, and convicted ſpy. See Collect. of Maſſacres committed on the Iriſh. Append.

intelligence made the new confederates imagine, that his Excellency was no longer entitled to their obedience, they now confidering him in the fame hoftile light, with thofe declared enemies of his Majefty, whofe alliance, and afliftance againft them, he was then folliciting. Purfuant to this Idea, they unanimoufly refolved, to march their whole army to Dublin, in order to prevent it's being delivered up to the Englifh parliament. Accordingly, about the latter end of October 1646, the two Generals, O'Neal and Prefton, fet out, at the head of fixteen thoufand foot, and fixteen hundred horfe, together with the Nuncio, his congregation of clergy, and new fupreme council, towards that capital; and, on the fecond of the following month, they fent the Marquis of Ormond certain propofitions, which, in effect (1), contained the fame demands, that they had all along made, and the King was willing to grant them, but which his Excellency had ftill obftinately refufed.

THE Marquis of Ormond was, at this time, ill provided with the Means of defence, againft fo numerous and powerful an army. There was great fcarcity of victuals in the city; and not more (a) than fourteen barrels of powder in the ftores; yet, relying on the hopes of affiftance from the Englifh parliament, he rejected the confederates propofitions, with derifion and difdain. At the fame time, he privately follicited the aid of the covenanters in Ulfter (2), with previous offers to them of thofe very terms, which he now refufed to the confederates, namely, the free exercife of their religion, and the reception of their forces into his garrifons; and, not having then prevailed, he afterwards, of his own accord, as we fhall prefently fee, furrendered the Royal authority to their mafters, the independents in the Britifh parliament, to the ruin of the King, and of the eftablifhed religion and government, in both kingdoms.

(1) See Carte, Borlace.   (2) Carte's Orm. vol. iii.

(a) "In the fenfe of his weaknefs," fays Mr. Carte, on this occafion, "his Lordfhip had defired the commander of a veffel belonging to the parliament to carry his wife and children to the Ifle of Man, but was refufed. And tho' the captain offered to tranfport them to Chefter, or any place in the parliament's obedience, he chofe rather to expofe them to the fame hazards with himfelf in Dublin, than to accept of that offer. For," adds my author, "he had reafon to fufpect the good faith of the parliament." Carte's Orm. vol. i. fol. 568. Yet to that very parliament he, within a few months after, delivered up all the King's delegated authority in Ireland.

CHAP. XII.

The Sentiments of the Catholic Clergy of Dublin on this Occasion.

BUT his Excellency and the council, being (1) doubtful, how the Catholics of Dublin, who was by far the greatest part of its inhabitants, would behave, in case that city were assaulted by so great an army, fighting under the title of so specious a cause, and under the authority of so extraordinary a minister of the Apostolic See, ordered the following questions to be proposed to such of the Roman clergy, as then resided there.

1st, " If the Pope's Nuncio, and the rest of the Roman Catholic clergy in a synod, should excommunicate those, who adhere to the peace lately made, whether such an excommunication would be in itself void, or sufficiently grounded on the Doctrine of the church of Rome?"

2dly, " In case this city shall be besieged, or assaulted, by the advice, consent, direction, or command, of the said Nuncio or clergy, or both of them, whether, in such case, are the Roman Catholics of this kingdom obliged, in conscience, to resist such siege or assault, with the peril of their lives, and fortunes?

" To the above questions the undernamed Roman Catholic clergy of Dublin, in obedience to his Excellency's and the council's commands, with all humility, return the following answers.

To the first question. " We conceive, and hold for void, and in no wise grounded on the doctrine of the Roman Catholic church, any excommunication, that hath no other ground, but the adhering to the peace lately concluded, or to any other point of true and cordial loyalty to our gracious sovereign King Charles.

To the second, " As we really, in our hearts and consciences, hold our sovereign Lord, King Charles, to be true and lawful King of this city, and kingdom of Ireland, and of all other his Majesty's dominions; so we do conceive, that the Roman Catholics of this kingdom, in case of a siege or assault made,

(1) Belling's MSS. Carte's Orm. Vindic. Catholic.

made, or intended, for the taking of this city from our said sovereign, the King, or from any deriving lawful authority from him, and holding it for him, are obliged in conscience to resist, with the peril of their lives and fortunes. This being our answer, we thereunto put our hands,

> F. MARCUS ROCHFORT,
> F. PETER DARCY,
> ADRIAN CARDAN,
> WILLIAM BROWN,
> THOMAS QUIN,
> F. JAMES FLEMING,
> F. GREGORY LAWLESS,
> RICHARD OSBURNE."

C H A P. XIII.

The Marquis of Ormond proceeds in his treaty with the Parliament.

"ON (1) the 14th of November 1646, commissioners from the English Parliament arrived in Dublin, with men, ammunition, and provisions of all kinds; who, seeing the weakness of the place, and knowing his Excellency stood in need of every thing necessary for its defence, made no doubt of his receiving the supplies they had brought, upon any terms. The Lord Lieutenant expected the commissioners had brought specific answers to the propositions, which he had sent to England; but they had brought no such answers, nor any instructions about them. And when he offered them a copy of the propositions, they would not receive it, nor enter into any debate upon the subject; their instructions confined them to treat only for the sword, and garrisons; for which they offered to take the Protestants of Ireland under their protection, on condition of their submitting to the ordinances of parliament (2). But no Protestant," continues Mr. Carte, " that would not renounce his allegiance to the King, could depend upon that protection for his security." His Lordship, on his part, proposed, until their instructions from the parliament could be enlarged, to distribute their forces into his garrisons,
if

(1) Cart. Orm.   (2) Id. ib. vol. i. fol. 591.

if they would submit to his orders, and to martial law, and if they would lend him three thousand pounds, to support the army; but these proposals were refused. So resolving to break off the the treaty, his Excellency told them, that he could not, consistent with his duty, part with so great a trust, without his Majesty's command, and asked them, whether they could produce it? But the commissioners, wondering with good reason, that he should expect any such authority from them, embarked on board their ships, with all their men, whom they carried into Ulster."

CHAP. XIV.

Clanrickard's *Engagement with* Preston.

THE Marquis of Ormond, with a view of gaining time to better his conditions with the English parliament, to prevail with the Scots in Ulster to march to his assistance, and to avert the impending storm from Dublin, sent the Lords Clanrickard and Digby to Leixlip, where, agreeably, as they thought, to his Excellency's sentiments, they entered into a private *(a)* engagement with General Preston and his officers, that (1), upon their submitting to the peace, sufficient security should be given to the Roman Catholics, for the free exercise of their religion; that part of Preston's army should be admitted into the King's garrisons; that the Marquis of Ormond should obey his Majesty's free commands, the Queen's, and those of the Prince of Wales, and Lord Digby's signification of them; and that his Excellency should not, for the future, obey such commands, to the prejudice of what was undertaken, as should be procured, by the advantage of his Majesty's want of freedom."

But this not being consented to, or rather being peremptorily (2) refused by his Excellency, Lord Digby wrote to him on the 18th of November, " that the utmost that was expected by Preston and his officers was, a declaration from his Excellency to the following effect, which being granted, they would immediately submit to the peace, viz. (3), " That, whereas it is well known,

(1) Id. ib. vol. iii.   (2) Id. ib. vol. iii.   (3) ib.

(a) " This engagement," says Mr. Carte, " was of eminent service in a time of the greatest danger, and the means of saving Dublin." Orm. vol. i. fol. 592.

known, even by his majesty's printed letters, that his Majesty's gracious intentions were to secure his Catholic subjects of this kingdom in the free exercise of their religion, by the repeal of the penalties of the laws against them; which in the last articles of the peace was left out, by the subtilty of some of their own party, who intended to found this late mischief upon it; that it was far from his Majesty's or Excellency's intention, to take advantage of that omission; but that they may rest as secure of his Majesty's favour, in the repeal of the said penalties, as if it had been positively expressed in the articles."

The Marquis of Ormond having, in his answer to this letter, given a (4) positive denial to every part both of the above-mentioned engagement, and this declaration, not without some indecent reflections on General Preston and his officers, who had already signed the engagement, and expected nothing but his Excellency's commands, to prosecute, in action, what they had thereby promised; Lord Digby replied (5), "that he could not consider these answers of his Excellency, without such an heart-breaking amazement, as rendered him almost unable to make any reply." He, however, reminded him, as did Clanrickard also (6), "that they had entered into that engagement with General Preston, not without sufficient grounds given them by himself; that by such variance of his Excellency, or mistake of their own, not only the business, wherein they had laboured all that time, so essential to his Majesty's present service, and all his future hopes; but the honour and personal safety of his faithful servants, was upon the point of being made absolutely desperate."

As for the admission of Preston's forces into his Excellency's garrisons, which was the article chiefly objected to, Lord Digby declared, in his own and Clanrickard's name (7), that, "upon a full examination of the whole proceedings of Preston, and his army, they were most confident, that, upon this engagement of theirs, they deserved to be trusted, as having, originally, never had any intention of hostility against his Excellency; but, on the contrary, that they had purposely delayed and kept off from him, the mischief, that would otherwise, long before have overwhelmed him. That, if his Excellency had expressed a confidence even in words, without engagement, he might have employed Preston's forces instantly, upon what other design he thought best; and have deferred the admitting any of them into his garrisons, until their service against the Nuncio's party, had confirmed his confidence in them. In short, that he could not, but with astonishment, receive the

strange

(4) ib. vol. iii.   (5) ib.   (6) ib.   (7) Id. ib.

strange invective against them in his Excellency's letter; wherein," adds his Lordship, " all the reason of your dislike to the whole business seems to be founded."

CHAP. XV.

Ormond *consents to the Engagement.*

THE Marquis of Ormond, thus warmly and frequently importuned, and, perhaps, ashamed totally to reject an expedient, first moved by himself, condescended at last, to write (1) two letters; one to General Preston, ratifying and confirming the engagement, made by him with Clanrickard; and the other, to Clanrickard himself, which was to be shewn to Preston's officers, and contained, likewise, his Excellency's agreement to the engagement now mentioned, with some flattering expressions of his confidence in the valour and fidelity of these officers.

Soon after this, Ormond and Digby found means to inform the King, of the conclusion of this engagement with General Preston; and of the breaking off of the late treaty, with the English parliament. On which occasion, his Majesty sent his Excellency the follow letter, of the 27th of December.

" ORMONDE, (2)

" THIS is chiefly to confirm that which I wrote to you the *(a)* 5th of this month, whereby I approved of what you have done, both concerning your London-treaty, and that with General Preston; shewing you, also, the great necessity of my affairs, that you should repiece the peace with the Irish."

BUT the Marquis of Ormond, instead of endeavouring to repiece his peace with the Irish (by which, the Nuncio's and O'Neil's party only can be understood,

(1) See Carte, ib. vol. iii. fol. 332.   (2) Carte's Orm. vol. ii. Append. fol. 13.

(a) In his letter of the 5th of that month, here referred to, his Majesty says, " I really and heartily approve of all you have done hitherto, and in particular concerning Preston. But, for further directions, I can only say, that, upon no terms, you must submit to the C. W. C. K. and that you endeavour what you can, to repiece your peace with the Irish. Warn. Irish Rebel. Nothing else can possibly be meant by the above cypher, consistently with the context, but the English parliament. Warn. ib.

stood, because they alone were then unengaged) soon found out a plausible pretext for breaking his engagement with Preston himself. We have already seen, that his obstinate refusal of the free exercise of religion to the confederates, was what principally delayed the conclusion of the peace, until it became both useless to his Majesty, and insecure to them. The case was much the same, with respect to his engagement with General Preston; his delay, and unwillingness, to ratify that engagement; Preston's knowledge, perhaps, that he was still carrying on his treaty with "those traitors of the covenant," the Scots in Ulster; but above all, his not having received any of Preston's forces into his garrisons, as he *(b)* promised he would, caused that General to suspect the sincerity of his professions of trust and confidence in him and his officers. These motives coinciding with the Nuncio's threatened censure, of which he was too scrupulously fearful, made him relapse, in shew at least, into his former connection with that turbulent ecclesiastic. He, however, immediately apprised the Marquis of Ormond of this change in his resolution, by several letters and messages (3), "left his Excellency (as he told him) who was then on his march to join him, might, by advancing too far, expose himself to some insult from the Nuncio's party." On this occasion, he assured his Excellency (4), "that he would not have failed to meet him, according to their appointment, but that his commanders, and the rest in general, were wholly withdrawn from their first resolution; that, however, he had caused notice to be given to his Excellency in a second letter, two hours after the former, by an express messenger, that his Excellency might not advance further, on doubtful uncertainties; whereby (adds he) your Excellency may perceive, how right my intentions have ever been, and how studious I was to give you the means of avoiding inconvenience, by that intelligence." And, indeed, of the rectitude of his intentions, and of his sincere and zealous attachment to his Majesty's service, he soon after gave unquestionable, but melancholy, proof. For the Marquis of Ormond, having (as we shall presently see) shamefully surrendered his out-garrisons to the parliament-commissioners, began to repent of what he had done; and, in concert with Lord Digby, entered into a new, but secret, treaty with the confederates, in order, by their assistance, to recover the possession of them; to which the confederates having readily agreed (5), "dispatched immediate orders to General Preston, to march his whole army, consisting of between seven and eight thousand men, into the English

(3) Cart. Orm. vol. iii.   (4) ib. vol. iii.   (5) Layburn's Memoirs, p. 60.

(b) In the before-mentioned letter to General Preston, he, among other things, "desires him and his officers to believe that he would employ him and them in all truths, both in the field, and in his garrisons, with as much freedom, and assurance, as he would any whatsoever." Cart. Orm. vol. iii. f. 332.

English quarters; which he accordingly did, took Naas and Maynooth by assault; and afterwards sat down before Trim; where, being attacked by Michael Jones, with superior forces from Dublin, he was totally defeated; having had four thousand men killed on the place, and almost all his commanders taken prisoners, himself hardly escaping *(c)*."

C H A P. XVI.

Ormond resumes his treaty with the English Parliament.

HIS Excellency either was, or affected to be, so much provoked by Preston's seeming tergiversation (for Lord Digby was (1) confident it was not real), " that (2) he publickly resumed his treaty with the English parliament, (notwithstanding the King's late order forbidding him to submit to them, " on any terms,") offering to put his Majesty's garrisons into their hands, upon the same conditions they had formerly proposed; which," as we have already observed from Mr. Carte, " no Protestant could accept without forfeiting his allegiance." And, in order to induce them, for the present, to give him the command of some of their men, provisions, and ammunition in Ulster, 'till they could send him more, he promised to deliver hostages, for the performance of what he had undertaken; and (3) accordingly, on the 16th of March, 1646, he sent over as such, the Earl of Roscommon, Colonel Chichester, Sir James Ware, and Sir Richard Butler, afterwards Earl of Arran, one of his own sons.

ABOUT this time, Mr. Leyburne, under the assumed name of *(a)* Winter Grant, arrived in Ireland, with letters from the Queen and Prince, to the Lord Lieutenant. " After I had delivered (says that (+) gentleman) such letters, as I had for the Marquis of Ormond, I said, I was sure they expressed civilities from the Queen and Prince, much better than I could; that, by my instructions, when decyphered, his Lordship would find the confidence her Majesty

---

(1) Cart. Orm. vol. iii. (2) Cart. Orm. vol. iii. Id. ib. vol. i. (3) Id. ib. vol. i. fol. 603. (4) Memoirs.

(c) " General Preston had, after the restoration, conferred upon him by the King, the title of Lord Viscount Taragh, with 800 l. a year in lands, to support the honour." Cart. Orm. vol. ii. fol. 64.

(a) Concerning this gentleman's arrival, Lord Digby wrote to Ormond from Leixslip, May 12th, 1647, at two o'clock in the morning, what follows. " Mr. Grant is come hither this night with such dispatches to your Excellency, as makes me think it necessary, that I should wait upon you presently; but I think it not fit that he should come to you." Cart. Orm. vol. iii. fol. 553.

Majesty and the Prince had in him; which was so great, as no reports could shake, though we had, weekly, news of treaties with the parliament, for delivering up those places, which were under his command. To which his Lordship replied, "that confidence shall never deceive them;" and added, "that he, who had ventured himself, his wife, and all his children in the King's service, would make no scruple of venturing, or casting away, one *(b)* son, when there should be cause. Yet, that if there should be a necessity, he would rather give up those places under his command, to the English, than the Irish, rebels; of which opinion, he thought every good Englishman was." To this, adds Mr. Leyburne, I answered nothing."

His Excellency had (4) then with him in the city, two thousand of the parliament forces, and expected many more in a few weeks. But his cessation with the confederates being now to expire in three days, he endeavoured to renew it for three weeks longer; within which time, he had good reason to expect, that the remainder of his supplies from the parliament would arrive. Mr. (5) Leyburne, whom he employed to go on that occasion to Kilkenny, "desired to know from his Excellency, what he should say, in case the confederates should object, that his Lordship proposed so short a cessation, only that he might gain time, to receive more forces from the parliament? To which he was answered, that he should receive orders for that on the way, if, on consideration, there was cause." Accordingly, the next day a post over-took him, with a letter from the Lord Lieutenant, in which he gave him power, " to undertake to the confederates that, if a cessation should be agreed upon, he would not receive into the garrisons under his command, forces from the parliament, during three weeks; but Mr. Leyburne was to use his utmost endeavours to procure a cessation without that condition; or at least, that it should be kept private; which last he was to engage them in, before he consented to the said condition."

But the general assembly, having pregnant causes of fear, that his Excellency sought that short cessation *(b)*, only with a view of obtaining succours from

---

(4) Cart. Orm.   (5) Mem. p. 34-5.

(b) He meant Sir Richard Butler, one of the hostages sent to the English parliament, mentioned above.

(b) The Lord Lieutenant and council in their answer to the King's constrained order of the 11th of June above-mentioned, or rather to the English rebels with whom he was then a prisoner, says on this occasion, " that they were desirous on the one hand, not to make a cessation for too long a time, left in case their supplies should arrive sooner than they expected, it might prevent the going on with the war that summer; and on the other side, not to make it for too short a time, lest the many preparations requisite for a full supply, and other intervening accidents, might retard it so, as not to arrive so speedily as they desired." Cart. Orm. vol. vol. iii. fol. 485.

from the parliament, refused to agree to it. At the same time, such was their inclination to peace, and zeal for his Majesty's service, that they proposed to lengthen out the cessation (6) for six months, provided his Lordship would, in the mean time, admit no more of the parliament's forces into his garrisons. But he absolutely refused to accept of a cessation for any longer term, than three weeks." His reason for rejecting the offer of a six months cessation, evidently was, that all his hopes of agreeing with the parliament would have been thereby defeated.

CHAP. XVII.

Ormond delivers up the King's Authority to the English Parliament.

UPON (1) the hostages before-mentioned having been received in England, one thousand English foot and four hundred horse, were ordered to march out of Ulster to Dublin; and on the 7th of June following, the parliament-commissioners arriving with six hundred horse, and fourteen hundred foot more, the treaty between them, and the Marquis of Ormond, was concluded, and (2) signed on the 19th of that month; by which his Excellency was to quit the sword, on the 28th of the following month, or sooner, upon four days notice." Thus did his Lordship deliver up the King's authority to men, who soon after became, as he himself has described them (3), " murderers of his Royal person, usurpers of his rights, and destroyers of the Irish nation; by whom the nobility and gentry of it, were massacred at home, and led into slavery, or driven into beggary abroad *(a)*."

His

---

(6) Id. ib.　　(1) Cart. Orm. vol. i. fol. 603.　　(2) Id. ib.　　(3) Id. ib. vol. ii. App.

(a) " I am told," says the Earl of Essex Lord Lieutenant of Ireland in 1674, " that when the Lord Ormond delivered up the sword to the parliament-commissioners here, Alderman Smith, then Mayor of Dublin, aged near four-score years, and always reputed a man of great integrity and loyalty, came to the council table, and acquainted my Lord of Ormond, that it was generally reported in town, and spread so far, as no man doubted it, that his Excellency intended to deliver up the government to the parliament, that he came to acquaint his Lordship, that himself was entrusted with the King's sword of the city, and that he would not resign it to rebels. Whereupon, my Lord of Ormond gave him some check, and ordered him to withdraw; but upon further consideration, his Lordship and the council thought fit to call him in again, and to commend him for the resolution he had shewed in maintaining his Majesty's authority; and withal read the letter from his Majesty, requiring the Lord Lieutenant to deliver up the sword to the commissioners impowered by the parliament of England; whereupon, he said he would submit." State Let. p. 344. This letter from his Majesty could be no other, than that of the 11th of June, the preceding year, extorted from the King by the Scots, when he was their prisoner, and forbidding the Marquis of Ormond to proceed in the peace with the confederates, as we shall hereafter see.

His Lordship, through this whole transaction with the English parliament, was sufficiently careful of his own private concerns; having stipulated, that a large sum of money should be paid him on the conclusion of it; and (4) that his estate, which was heavily incumbered at the beginning of the insurrection, " should not be subject to any debts contracted before that time." But there appears no reason to believe, that he was equally, or at all, anxious in this agreement, for the interests or preservation of that church and government, for whose support and dignity, in all his negociations with the confederates, he had affected to be thought so scrupulously zealous. For (5) on the 24th of June 1647, five days after the treaty with the parliament was signed, and a month before he delivered up the sword, he suffered the parliament-commissioners to publish an order, requiring all ministers of congregations, and others officiating in the several churches and chapels in Dublin, to observe the directory, and for the discontinuance of the Liturgy and Common Prayer; altho' the act of uniformity was still in force in Ireland, and not so much as suspended by any order of either, or both, Houses of parliament. Accordingly, the established clergy ceased to officiate, and the Liturgy was left off, in all the churches of the city, except that of Trinity-College, where Anthony Martin, Bishop of Meath, and Provost of that college, continued to use it.

These consequences, the Marquis of Ormond must have certainly foreseen; because one of his first propositions to the English parliament, (which were rejected) was (6), " that the covenant should not be imposed, nor the Liturgy suppressed at present; lest it should divide the Protestants, and hinder their joint prosecution of the war (against the Irish) and that nothing should be done in relation to either, but by act of parliament." Now, even supposing this proposition had been granted, what else could his Lordship have expected, from an act of either the Irish or English parliament, at that juncture, but a more certain and rigorous imposition of the covenant, and suppression of the Liturgy and Common Prayer in both kingdoms?

Both Houses of the Irish parliament had, with great solemnity, presented an address of thanks to his Excellency, on occasion of this treaty with the English parliament. In that address, they set forth, " that (7) his proceedings therein, being such a free earnest of his Excellency's love to their religion, nation, and both Houses, did incite them to come unto him, with hearts filled with his love, and tongues declaring how much they were obliged to

his

---

(1) Borl. Hist. of the Irish Rebel. fol. 235.   (5) Carte's Orm. vol. i. fol. 605;
(6) Id. ib. vol. iii. fol. 586.   (7) Com Journ. Append. Borl. Hist. of the Irish Reb.

his Excellency. And that, in order to perpetuate unto posterity, the memory of his Excellency's merits, and their thankfulness, they had appointed that instrument to be entered into both Houses, and under the hands of both Speakers, to be presented to his Lordship." To which address, his Lordship politely answered (8), " that this acknowledgment of theirs was unto him a *(b)* jewel of very great value, which he should lay up among his choicest treasures; it being an antidote against the virulency of those tongues, and pens, that, he was well assured, would be busily set on work, to traduce and blast the integrity of his present proceeding for their preservation." The reader will easily perceive, that those, for whose preservation he entered into measures so destructive of monarchy, and of the established religion in Ireland, were generally a rabble of sectaries, who conspiring with their brethren in the British parliament, prepared the way for, and at last, effectually brought about, the murder of their King in England.

CHAP. XVIII.

The Marquis of Ormond *ordered to leave the Castle.*

ON (1) the 16th of July, 1647, the parliament-commissioners gave notice to the Marquis of Ormond, to remove, with his family, from the castle; and to deliver the regalia within four days, according to his agreement. But, it being inconvenient to his Lordship to embark so soon, he compromised the matter with them, by quitting the castle immediately, and deferring the ceremonial of the sword, till the day first agreed upon (2). "Yesterday," says his Lordship, " I was summoned to leave the sword and castle, according to the direction of the committee of Derby-house; which, by the way, I note as no good sign, that committee consisting of all independents."

MR. Leyburne justly remarks, that this circumstance might have furnished his Lordship with a good excuse for breaking off the agreement, as matters were then greatly altered (3), " for," says he, " the parliament, with whom he

(*b*) ib.   (1) Cart. Orm. vol. i. fol. 605.   (2) Id. ib. vol. iii.   (3) Memoirs, p. 37.

(*b*) Alluding to a jewel of 500l. value, which he had some years before got from the English parliament, as a reward for his service in prosecuting the war against the Irish, in the manner we have seen.

he had held his treaty, were Presbyterian; but now it became independent, quite another thing; so that I was confident, My Lord of Ormond would be very wary of parting easily from his government, without fresh commands from the King."

But his Lordship, instead of making use of such an argument, would have parted from his government some weeks sooner, had not Lord Digby, as principal secretary of state, resolutely interposed (4). "For his Excellency being pressed by the parliament-commissioners, to perform his engagement, he was *(a)* resolved to do it, and writ so to Lord Digby, who had in several letters, persuaded his delay. But finding that nothing but a personal interview, and most serious conference, was able to hinder him any longer from accomplishing the work, Lord Digby, notwithstanding the most imminent hazard of the attempt, ventured by night, to steal into Dublin-castle, to prevent the surrender the next day intended; where, upon his arrival, which procured a very great disturbance, he wrought so effectually with the Marquis of Ormond, that he brought him the next day to declare to the commissioners (under pretence of doubting the authority of their powers, and in expectation of the parliament's solemn engagement of the faith of both Houses for the security of himself, and all his party, whether perhaps, excepted, or not excepted) that, unless they would yet give him five weeks time to hold the sword and castle, in order to his satisfaction in these particulars, he would rather die in the gate, with an halbert in his hand, than give it up. In which resolution, the commissioners finding him positive, at last assented, that, if he would surrender into their hands the militia forthwith, they would permit him the sword and castle, together with any three companies he should chuse for his guard, for the fore-mentioned time."

On the 26th of July, his Excellency moved these commissioners that (5), " in regard his servant was not come with his money to discharge his debts,

(4) Id. ib.   (5) Carte's Orm.

(a) How indifferent both Digby and Ormond were about the future fate of Ireland, at this juncture, appears from the following passage in a letter of the former to the latter. Digby, after strongly advising Ormond, that, on quitting the Kingdom, he should have liberty from the parliament-commissioners to carry off with him five thousand five hundred men, to any other kingdom in amity with England, adds, " that he ought to value that condition above all the others, not only as most honourable, but far more profitable to him, than if they should give him five times the sum they offered. But that, if the parliament would not give him such conditions, then he conceived Ormond's course must be, by temporizing with the Irish, by renewing other treaties with the parliament: upon lower conditions, in fine, by any art to prolong his possession of the garrisons and forces, till he (Digby) could procure him shipping and money for the said transportation. And then," says he, " let who will take the carcass of what you shall leave." Cart. Orm. vol. iii. fol. 544.

debts, and other neceffary payments, they would permit his Lady to remain in the caftle, till he came." But even that requeft was refufed him. In fhort, as his Lordfhip had, over and above the hoftages, put all the power into their hands before any performance on their part, it is no wonder, that they (6) did not afterwards keep within the bounds of common decency in their dealings with him. And when he complained of feveral breaches of honour, which they were guilty of, they did not pretend to affign a reafon for their proceedings, but told him plainly, " that they were competent judges of them, and would not allow others to direct their actions *(b) (c)*."

CHAP. XIX.

Reafons affigned for the Marquis of Ormond's Surrender confidered.

TWO reafons are commonly affigned by hiftorians, in order to juftify, or excufe, Ormond's delivering up the King's authority at this juncture, to the Englifh Rebels. Firft, his Majefty's verbal order, or, at leaft, permiffion, privately fent him for that purpofe by Sir George Hamilton. And fecondly, a defign of the confederate Catholics, then newly difcovered, to tranfer their allegiance from their natural fovereign to fome foreign Prince. The former of thefe reafons, I fhall prove to be groundlefs from his Lordfhip's own words; the latter has been always denied by the accufed, nor ever yet,

(6) Id. ib. vol. i. fol. 605.

(b) The Marquis of Ormond had obtained from thefe commiffioners a pafs, for Lord Digby to tranfport himfelf to France. But " all their fea-men fent his Lordfhip word, that let him have what pafs he would, they would either throw him over-board, or bring him prifoner to London, and the parliament-foldiers at Dublin declared refolutions of no lefs violence againft him, if he came that way, in fpight of any protection." Cart. Orm. vol. iii. fol. 571. " Thefe foldiers foon after threatened the parliament-commiffioners themfelves, and plundered the houfes of the inhabitants, Proteftants as well as Papifts. Money was fent over for their pay, but that could not reftore difcipline among them; they continued their diforders, and beat their officers, if they offered to reprimand them." Id ib vol ii fol. 9. Borlace informs us, that thefe foldiers had received fuch a tincture of mutiny, that Mr. Annefly, and Sir Robert King, two of the parliament-commiffioners, for fear of violence, privately quitted the Kingdom." Hift. of the Irifh Rebel. fol. 235.

(c) Sir Maurice Euftace, afterwards Lord Chancellor of Ireland, in a letter to the Marquis of Ormond, October 8th, 1647, acquainted him, " that Sir William Parfons (formerly Lord Juftice of that kingdom) had by late letters, advifed Jones (then governor for the parliament) to the burning of corn, and to put man, woman and children to the fword; and that Sir Adam Loftus had written in the fame ftrain." Carte's Collec. of Orm. Orig. Papers, vol. ii. p. 550.

yet, in any manner proved by their accusers, though frequently called upon for that purpose.

Mr. Belling, one of the Marquis of Ormond's earliest, warmest, and most intelligent apologists, owns (1), " that this surrender of Dublin, and the other garrisons, did, indeed, pave the way, not only to the destruction of the people of Ireland, but also, to the King's murder in England." But he, at the same time, insists, " that his Majesty had sent the Lord Lieutenant, by Sir George Hamilton, private orders to make it." The same is affirmed by Clarendon, Hume, Carte, and, generally, by all succeeding *(a)* writers on this subject. But the Marquis of Ormond himself, in all his letters to the Queen and Prince, at that juncture, not only apologizes, with great submission, for this surrender (which, certainly, he would not have done, had he received the King's order, or permission, for it) but also, in that long and laboured state of the affairs of Ireland, which he afterwards laid before the King himself, he represents (2), " that act of his, as done on presumption, that it was more for his Majesty's honour and service, and consequently more agreeable to his pleasure, which he had neither means, nor time, to consult."

But the following letter from his Lordship, to the King, which was sent soon after he resigned the government, leaves not the least room to doubt the falsity of this assertion.

" May (3) it please your Majesty,

" I know not how my last actions, or present condition, have been represented to your Majesty; the latter your Majesty finds in the Public articles with the parliament-commissioners; but upon what grounds, or advices, these articles were agreed to, I must reserve for a time, when by the grace of God, and your Majesty's good pleasure, I shall be admitted to cast myself at your feet. I should, in the mean time, beg the suspension of any thought, that may be suggested into, or arise in your Majesty, in prejudice

---

(1) Vindiciæ Cathol. et MSS.   (2) Carte's Orm. vol. iii. fol. 569.
(3) Id. ib. vol. iii. fol. 558.

(a) Doctor Leland has made a proper distinction on this occasion. " Ormond," says he, " was assured, his Majesty had signified his pleasure, that in case of extreme necessity, he should submit rather to the English, than the Irish. The King's private letters afforded Ormond abundant reason to doubt the truth of these assurances; yet they (these assurances) served to justify the resolution, he had now taken to the public." Hist. of Irel. vol. iii. p. 307.

dice to thofe fincere affections, wherewith I have endeavoured to ferve you. But that were to mifdoubt your juftice, and fo to make myfelf unworthy of your pardon, if, deprived of your directions to guide me, I have erred in the way to your fervice."

Sir George Hamilton was fo far from bringing fuch private Orders from the King, that he did not even fee his Majefty on that occafion; for altho' his Lordfhip had fent him to wait on the King for fome fuch purpofe, yet, he tells us himfelf (4), "that Sir George fell fick at Dundalk; and that, hearing there of the refolution taken by the parliament of Scotland, and by their army, to deliver him up to the two Houfes of parliament, he proceeded no further in his journey, but returned, with that fad affurance, to Trim, where the Marquis then was."

C H A P. XX.

Ormond's *fecond Reafon confidered*.

TO the fecond reafon affigned for this furrender, viz. the difcovery of a defign of the confederate Catholics at that juncture, to transfer their allegiance to a foreign Prince; their anfwer always was, that they never entertained fuch a defign; and that the only application made by them, for obtaining the aid and affiftance of any foreign power, was *(a)* fubfequent to, and occafioned by, this furrender of Dublin, and the other garrifons, to the Englifh rebels. For thus they related that tranfaction, when it was firft objected againft them, appealing for the truth of the relation, to their affembly's inftructions concerning it, which were then in the hands of their enemies.

" The (1) power of thofe who were in arms in England againft the King, was," faid they, " in the year 1647, confiderable in Ireland; they being then free from any oppofition in the former kingdom, and at entire liberty to difpofe

(4) Id. ib. vol. iii. fol. 563.   (1) Walfh's reply to a perfon of quality.

(a) This appears plainly from the date of the injunction, which the confederate Catholics at Kilkenny gave to their agents on that occafion, viz. January 18th, 1647; feveral months after Ormond's agreement with the parliament-commiffioners; and even after his departure from Ireland. See Borlace's Hift. of the Irifh Rebel. fol. 227.

dispose of their forces for carrying on their designs in the latter. Wherefore, the confederate Catholics, perceiving the danger they were in, met in the winter of that year in a general assembly at Kilkenny, where they took into consideration, that his Majesty was in restraint; that all addresses to him were forbidden; and that some members of parliament, who spoke in his favour, were expelled.

" In that sad extremity, there being no access to his Majesty for imploring either his justice or mercy, all laws, human and divine, did allow the said Catholics to take some other course, in order to their defence and preservation; not against his sacred Majesty, but against those who had laid violent hands on his person, who designed to abolish the Royal authority, and resolved to destroy, or extirpate, the said Catholics.

" These Catholics, therefore, in January 1647, did, in the said assembly, conclude, that the Marquis of Antrim, Lord Viscount Muskerry, and Geoffry Browne, Esq; should be employed into France; the Bishop of Ferns, and Nicholas Plunkett, Esq; to Rome; and some others to Spain. Those sent to France, were by their applications to the Prince of Wales, and the Queen, to declare the danger the said Catholics apprehended; and humbly to beseech them to find out some expedient, by which these dangers might be averted. They were likewise commissioned, in case of absolute necessity, to implore the aid and Protection of some foreign Prince; but they were limited not to act any thing, in order to such foreign protection, but by the direction of those persons, who were employed to receive his Majesty's commands. Upon the said application made to his Majesty through the Queen and Prince, the Marquis of Ormond's commission was afterwards renewed, and his Excellency qualified with power to conclude a peace with the said Catholics. Whereupon, all further proceedings, concerning the protection of any foreigner, were stopt, and the agents recalled; neither they, nor any of them, having ever moved, or acted any thing further, relating to the protection of any foreign power. Those agents, who were employed to Rome, did, on their return in 1648, before the general assembly then sitting, give such an account of their negotiation, that it (b) encouraged the assembly

---

(b) " The account these agents gave to the general assembly, from his Holiness was, that if the Nuncio did engage, that the confederate Catholics should be supplied by his Holiness in the maintenance of their war, he did it without any commission from him; his Holiness being resolved to give no money upon the event of a war; and that as it was not proper for him to appear, in expressing his sense of the conditions fit to be demanded in matters of religion, so he left them at liberty to proceed, as best suited with the good of the Kingdom. This account," adds Mr. Carte, ' putting an end to all expectations of foreign succours, set every body upon reflecting on their own condition, and disposed the confederates to moderate their propositions for a peace, which was become absolutely necessary for their preservation." Orm. vol. ii. l. l. 48.

to haften the conclufion of the peace with the Marquis of Ormond, then in agitation.

"And the faid Catholics are fo confcious to themfelves of the refolution they took, from the beginning, to perfevere irremoveably faithful, through all extremities, to his Majefty's interefts, that they are well affured, though thofe who poffefs their eftates, have now the books of faid general affembly in their hands; yet can they not make it appear, that there was any actual treaty, or offer, for transferring the fubjection, naturally due from them to his Majefty's dominion over them, to any foreigner whatfoever, or any thing tending thereunto, but what is here acknowledged."

It happens unluckily for this part of Ormond's apology, that about the time of this tranfaction, the confederate Catholics gave new, and very fignal proofs of their unalterable duty, and attachment to his Majefty's fervice. For, upon the Nuncio's publifhing a declaration againft the ceffation of arms, which the affembly, in order to haften the intended peace, then found it neceffary to conclude with Inchiquin (2), " they appealed, in form, againft that declaration, and were joined by two of their Archbifhops, twelve Bifhops, and all the fecular clergy in their dioceffes; by all the Jefuits, Carmelites, and five hundred of the Francifcans. And the number, learning, zeal, and diligence of thefe religious, in preaching, and other applications, in a great degree defeated the Nuncio's meafures, and brought his party into difcredit. Lord Taaffe had fo modelled his army, that all his officers were excommunication-proof. The Marquis of Clanrickard had a body of three thoufand men of the fame temper; and if Prefton and his officers were not fo hardened, they were better united than they had been, and were refolved to carry their point. In anfwer to the Nuncio's folicitations to ftand by him, they defired he would not trouble them with any more letters; becaufe they had determined to obferve no orders, but what came from the fupreme council, whom they were fworn to obey."

(2) Warner's Irifh Rebel. p. 424 Lel. Hift. of Irel. vol. iii. p. 325.

CHAP.

CHAP. XXI.

Ormond prepares to leave the Kingdom. Is preſſed by the Confederates to remain a while in it, but refuſes.

WHEN General Preſton and his forces heard, that the Marquis of Ormond intended to leave Ireland in the following week, there appeared (1) an incredible conſternation among them; inſomuch, that Preſton ſent to conjure Lord Digby, as he valued the preſervation of thoſe, whom he believed yet well affected to his Majeſty, that he would afford him, and ſome he would appoint, an opportunity of conferring with him. Accordingly, by his Lordſhip's appointment, Sir Robert Talbot, Mr. Oliver Darcy, Mr. Belling, and Sir Thomas Dungan, met Lord Digby privately at Leixſlip, and earneſtly preſſed him to beg it of the Marquis of Ormond, as the only teſtimony and proof, that he was not willing to ſacrifice the good men of his country with the bad, to remain in the kingdom, ſomewhere out of Dublin, but for one month, his conditions with the parliament allowing him to ſtay ſix. In which time, they made no doubt, but Preſton's army joined with that under Lord Muſkerry in Munſter, would ſo awe the new ſupreme council, as to prevent that deſtruction, which they foreſaw the nation would undoubtedly ſuffer, if the Marquis, by leaving, ſhould break them; for that they could no longer hold united, than while they had their eyes upon his Lordſhip."

LORD Digby, from whoſe letter to the Marquis of Ormond this account is taken, ſeemed to approve of the propoſal as the beſt thing the Marquis could reſolve upon, as he was then circumſtanced (2), for his own credit. "My reaſons," ſays he, " principally are, that your Lordſhip having been forced to an act, which how juſt ſoever, muſt needs make you infinitely odious, you will have ſo eaſy a means of redeeming the hatred, and obloquy, with all thoſe of the country, whoſe affections are to be valued; and becauſe, if there were nothing elſe in the caſe, it would be worth your running a very great hazard, to purchaſe ſuch an acknowledgment of the neceſſity and juſtice of your proceedings with the parliament, ſo ſubject to calumny, as would, by that means, be procured, even from thoſe, who are likely to undergo the greateſt ruin by it; and whoſe ſacrifice, if you have not a juſtification of your actions from them, will be the heavieſt part of the work."

BUT

(1) Cart. Orm. vel. iii. fol. 561.   (2) Id. ib.

But the Marquis of Ormond abfolutely declined the overture (3), "becaufe," as he faid, " he held it, by no means fafe." At the fame time, he told Lord Digby, " that he could not conceive what ufe they could make of his ftaying in the kingdom, which would, while it feemed for their prefervation, ferve likewife for his deftruction. That however, he cared not if it were known to the world, that he would ufe all his powers and induftry, to difpofe his Majefty, and all others, to have good thoughts of thofe, he had found faithful, or that he believed to be rightly inclined to the Englifh government; and that he would improve all opportunities of procuring advantageous conditions for them, according to the peace." How diametrically oppofite to thefe foothing promifes, his fubfequent conduct was, at a time when he had it abfolutely in his power to perform them, will hereafter appear. Thus, the Marquis of Ormond, after having fhamefully furrendered his high truft and dignity, left the kingdom, and went to England, about the end of July, or beginning of Auguft, 1647; where, on his arrival at London, he waited on his Majefty; but was foon after obliged to make a kind of efcape to France, having had notice fent him (4), " that a warrant was actually iffued out to feize his perfon," by thofe very men, into whofe hands he had juft before delivered up Ireland. But, in a fhort time after, we fhall find him return to that kingdom, in quality of Lord Lieutenant.

(3) Id. ib.   (4) Id. ib. vol. ii. fol 16.

AN HISTORICAL AND CRITICAL REVIEW OF THE CIVIL WARS IN IRELAND.

BOOK VIII.

CHAP. I.

The Marquis of Ormond *returns to Ireland.*

HIS Excellency having arrived at Cork, on the 29th of September, 1648, was there received with general acclamations of joy; and on the next day, the general assembly sitting at Kilkenny, gave a very signal proof of their real desire to be again received under his government (1), by fixing a public brand on the two principal opposers of the late peace, the Nuncio Renuccini, and General Owen O'Neal. For they proclaimed the latter a rebel and a traitor; and upon entering into a treaty of peace, with the Marquis, they drew up a charge against the former (2), " representing the manifold oppressions, transcendent crimes, and capital offences, which he had been continually, for three years past, acting within the kingdom, to the unspeakable detriment of their religion, the ruin of the nation, and the dishonour of the See of Rome." This heavy accusation met with no opposition, even from such ecclesiastics as were present in that assembly (3). " It seems exceedingly strange to me," says the Nuncio himself in a letter to Cardinal Panzirolo on this occasion, " that, although there were eight Bishops present in this assembly, which offered such violence to my authority, and passed an order, that none should hereafter obey

(1) Cart. Orm. vol. ii. fol. 42. (2) Id. ib. vol. iii. (3) Nuncio's Memoirs.

obey my commands, not one of them did proteſt, or declare, againſt it, or depart from the place, in which it was held; or even make an apology, by a letter to his Holineſs, or myſelf, for their conduct; affirming only, that therein, they followed the example of thoſe of Portugal, who drove Cardinal Palotto out of the kingdom, and impriſoned his auditor."

WITH the above-mentioned charge, Sir Richard Blake, chairman of the aſſembly (4), ſent him notice, by their order, that there was a declaration, and proteſtation preparing againſt him, which were to be ſent to his Holineſs, to the end that his Lordſhip might prepare for his journey, and for his defence; and that, in the mean time, he ſhould not intermeddle, by himſelf, or any of his inſtruments, directly, or indirectly, with the affairs of the nation, on the penalty which might enſue, by the law of God and nations."

THE Nuncio accordingly *(a)*, left Ireland on the 23d of February following, to the great joy of the principal nobility and gentry, and the moſt reſpectable eccleſiaſtics, of the kingdom. Yet while he was preparing for his departure, the Lord Lieutenant ſent him a private meſſage, by two of his particular friends, the Biſhop of Ferns and Nicholas Plunkett, Eſq; (5), " that, if he would then, at parting, take off his excommunication, and diſpoſe the people to an abſolute obedience to the peace, and the King's authority, he ſhould not only receive all poſſible civility from him, at his departure from Ireland; but that he would make a very advantageous mention of him to the Queen, whoſe diſtreſſed condition," he ſaid, " would certainly gain ſome credit to her at Paris, if it was not worſe than London." But the Nuncio did not wait their coming; for, on the night before, he went to ſea in his own frigate, and, on the 2d of March, landed at St. Vaaſt, in the Lower Normandy.

AT his return to Rome, he was but coldly received by the Pope; and, after having been told (6), " that he had carried himſelf raſhly in Ireland," inſtead of being honoured with a Cardinal's hat, as he expected, he was baniſhed to his biſhoprick, and principality of Fermo; which he found in a diſtracted condition, by juſt ſuch another inſurrection of the people againſt their Viceroy, as he had himſelf raiſed and fomented, againſt the King's Lieutenant in Ireland. Theſe diſappointments of his own, and the diſtractions of his people, affected him ſo ſenſibly, that he ſoon after died of grief.

To

---

(4) Cart. Orm.   (5) Id. ib. vol. ii. fol. 55.   (6) Walſh's Hiſt. of the Ir. Remonſtrance.

(a) " The court of Rome," ſays Mr. Carte, " though it was contrary to their maxims to fix a public mark of cenſure on the conduct of their miniſters, diſapproving his conduct, ſent him orders to make haſte thither." Orm. vol. ii. fol. 56.

To what *(b)* desperate courses, General O'Neal was driven by the assembly's proclaiming him a rebel, and a traitor, shall be hereafter related.

CHAP. II.

His Excellency treats of a Peace with the Confederate Catholics.

"THE (1) Lord Lieutenant being invited to Kilkenny, by the general assembly, October the 28th, in order to a more expeditious settling of the points in dispute, made his entry into that city in a splendid manner; having been met at some distance from it, by the whole body of the assembly; and by all the nobility, clergy, and gentry, in the neighbourhood. He was received into the town, by the Mayor and Aldermen, with all those ceremonies, and honours, which such corporations used to pay to the supreme authority of the kingdom, and was lodged in his own castle, with all his own guards about him."

THE next day after his arrival at Kilkenny, his Excellency entered into a treaty of peace with the general assembly; and, after he had advanced so far in it, as that (2), " he thought, he had good grounds to hope it would be speedily concluded, upon the conditions he was empowered to give them, he found it suddenly interrupted, by a very dangerous mutiny, raised by some leading officers in Lord Inchiquin's army, who endeavoured, not only to hinder the conclusion of the peace, but also to incline those under them to a treaty, and submission to the English parliament."

ON this occasion, it was thought necessary by his Excellency and Lord Inchiquin, to suspend the conclusion of the peace (3), " in such a manner, as might induce the mutineers to believe it would be wholly laid aside for their satisfaction." On the other hand, the article concerning the free exercise of religion, was not yet adjusted to the satisfaction of the assembly; some of the clergy having much higher expectations, in that respect, than others thought fit to be insisted on (4). " This was the only point, in which there was

(1) Carte's Orm. vol. ii. fol. 45. (2) Id. ib. vol. iii. (3) ib.
(4) Id. ib. vol. ii. fol. 43.

(b) " The Malice, and headiness of Owen O'Neal and his party afterwards, was as much, and in truth more, against the confederate Irish, than the King." Borl. Irish Rebel. fol. 269.

was danger of the treaty's breaking up unfinished, it being very difficult to give content therein to the Roman Catholics without, at the same time, difgusting the Protestants." But an incident happening at this juncture, united the differing parties in that assembly, and greatly accelerated the peace. Some copies of the remonstrance of the independent army in England, which had publickly avowed their design of subverting every thing, that had been hitherto known for government in these nations, were then brought to Kilkenny, and read with universal abhorrence. This (5) immediately removed all the difficulties, which some of the Roman Catholics, in zeal for their religion, had thrown in the way of the peace. The general assembly receded from their demands in that point. And, on the 28th of December, upon consideration of his Majesty's present condition, and their own hearty desires, says Mr. Carte, of spending their lives and fortunes, in maintaining his rights and interests, they resolved unanimously, to accept of the Marquis of Ormond's answer to their propositions for religion (6). " That desperately wicked remonstrance," says the Marquis himself, " whatever mischief it may do, hath yet done this good, that it put us quite from all disputes upon the necessity of conditions, and was no small cause of the speedy, and I hope, happy conclusion of the peace."

C H A P. III.

The Peace of 1648 concluded and proclaimed.

ON (1) the 17th of January 1648, the general assembly repaired to the presence of the Lord Lieutenant in his castle at Kilkenny, and there, with all solemnity imaginable, presented to him, sitting on a throne of state, the articles of the peace, by the hands of Sir Richard Blake, their chairman, which he received; and, having confirmed them, on his Majesty's behalf, caused them to be publickly proclaimed. Nine Roman Catholic Bishops, present in the assembly, joined, the next day, in a circular letter, which they sent to all the cities and corporations of their party, exhorting them to receive, and obey the peace now concluded; which was in substance, that which had been made in 1646, but rejected by a former assembly."

(5) Id. ib. vol. ii. fol. 49.   (6) Id. ib. vol. iii. fol. 602.
(1) Id. ib. vol. ii. fol. 50.

The Lord Lieutenant, in a letter to Lord Digby, January the 22d, after telling him, that the peace was concluded, adds (2), " I muſt ſay for this people, that I have obſerved in them, great readineſs to comply with what I was able to give them; and a very great ſenſe of the King's ſad condition." And in another letter, of the ſame date, to the Prince of Wales, he takes notice (3) " of the very eminent loyalty of the aſſembly, which was not," ſays he, " ſhaken by the ſucceſs, which God hath permitted to the monſtrous rebellion in England; nor by the miſchievous practices of the no leſs malicious rebels in Ireland."

AFTER the ſigning of the articles, his Excellency made a ſpeech to the aſſembly, wherein he congratulated them, not only on the ſcore of what they had already obtained by that peace, in point of freedom of Worſhip, abatement of penalties, and other advantages; but alſo on the hopes of further indulgence and favour in all theſe reſpects, according to their future merits." For he told them (4), " that, beſides the proviſion made againſt their remoteſt fears of the ſeverities of certain (penal) laws; and beſides many other freedoms, and bounties conveyed to them, and their poſterity, by theſe articles; there was a door, and that a large one, not left, but purpoſely ſet open, to give them entrance to whatever of honour, or other advantage, they could reaſonably wiſh." And yet, about the ſame time that his Lordſhip made this public and ſolemn declaration to the aſſembly, he, in a private letter to Sir Charles Coote, a parliamentarian rebel (5), " averred with much confidence, (they are his own words,) that the advantages, which the Romiſh profeſſors were ſuppoſed to have, in religion or authority, by that peace, were no other but pledges for his Majeſty's confirmation of the other conceſſions, and that they were to determine therewith *(a);*" as in truth they did.

(2) Id. ib. vol. iii. fol. 600.   (3) Id. ib. fol. 601.   (4) Id. ib. vol. iii.   (5) ib. vol iii.

(a) Yet the King himſelf, in a letter to the Marquis of Ormond, March the 9th, 1649. told him on this occaſion, " that he had lately received from Lord Byron the articles of the peace, which he had made in Ireland, together with a copy of his letter to him; that he was extremely ſatisfied with both, and would confirm wholly, and entirely, all that was contained in the articles." Cart. Collect. of Orig. Papers, vol. ii. p. 363.

CHAP. IV.

The happy Effects of this Peace. Ormond's Defeat at Rathmines. Cromwell's Arrival in Ireland.

THERE was, for some time, great union and harmony between the English and Irish forces, now joined, under the Marquis of Ormond's command. His Excellency in a letter to the King, June 28th, 1649, acquainted him (1), " that the ground of his greatest confidence of future success was their present cordial conjunction against the rebels, their former disaffection to each other appearing, then, only in an emulation rather of advantage, than hinderance (a), to his Majesty's service." To this union it was certainly owing, that their first operations were extremely successful; for, in the space of a few months, they became masters of Sligo, Drogheda, Dundalk, Waterford, Trim, Newry, and in short of all the strong holds and towns in the kingdom, except Londonderry and Dublin. Towards this latter city therefore, his Excellency marched the combined armies; hoping to repair the mischiefs he had done by his late surrender of it to the English rebels, and to reduce it once more under his Majesty's obedience. His Excellency's excessive confidence in these united forces, though now in want of almost every necessary for his enterprise on Dublin, is one of the supposed causes of his fatal disappointment in that attempt. That this confidence was indeed excessive, appears by his letter of July 18th, to the King, from his camp at Finglas; for there he tells him (2), " that, which only threatens any rub to our success, is our wants, which have been, and are such, that soldiers have actually starved by their arms, and many, of less constancy, have run home: many of the foot are weak; yet I despair not to be able to keep them together. and strong enough to reduce Dublin, if good supplies of all sorts come not speedily to relieve it. I am confident, I can persuade one half of this army to starve outright;

(1) Id. Carte's Orig. Pap. vol. ii. p. 387.   (2) Id. ib. vol. ii. p 389.

(a) And yet Borlace confidently asserts, from Clarendon, " that from the first Iour of the peace (of 1648) these English and Irish had not been without the prejudice towards each other, as gave the Marquis much trouble; and that they were rather incorporated by their obedience and submission to the authority and pleasure of their chief commanders, than united by the same inclinations and affections to any public end." Hist. of the Ir. Rebel. fol. 287.

outright; and I shall venture far upon it, rather than give off a game, so fair on our side, and so hard to be recovered if given over."

But while his Excellency was thus securely making preparations for that enterprise at Rathmines, a place three miles distant from Dublin, his whole army was surprised and routed, by Michael Jones, governor of that city for the parliament, on the 2d of August 1649. " Jones (3), according to the Marquis of Ormond's account, slew six hundred in that engagement; some upon the spot, and in the pursuit; but the greatest part, after they had *(b)* laid down their arms, upon promise of quarter, and had been, for almost an hour *(c)*, prisoners; and divers of them were murdered, after they were brought within the works of Dublin." This sudden and unaccountable defeat at Rathmines *(d)*, renewed, in the Irish, all their former suspicions, that his Excellency had still some private understanding with the English rebels; and these suspicions were increased, by the constant ill success of all his subsequent undertakings against their partizans in Ireland. To these misfortunes, was soon after added a general panic, occasioned by the unparalleled cruelties of Oliver Cromwell, who landed at Dublin (4), on the 15th of that month, with eight thousand foot, and four thousand horse, two hundred thousand pounds in money, and a vast quantity of ammunition, and all kind of necessaries for war. " With these forces, he on the 3d of September, besieged, and took Drogheda by storm. And although all his officers, and soldiers, had (5) promised quarter to such of the garrison, as would lay down their arms, and performed it, as long as any place held out, which encouraged others to yield; yet when they once had got all in their power, Cromwell, being told by Jones, that he had now the flower of the Irish army in his hands,

gave

(3) Id. ib. vol. ii. p. 397.
(4) Cart. Orm. vol. ii. fol. 83.
(5) Id. ib. vol. ii. fol. 44. Lel. Hist. vol. iii. p. 350.

(b) " Fifteen hundred private soldiers, and three hundred officers, were made prisoners; about six hundred slain; many of these, to the disgrace of the conquerors, when they had accepted quarter, and laid down their arms." Lel. Hist. of Ireland, vol. iii. p. 346.

(c) " Soon after this defeat," says Borlace, " Jones was writ to by his Excellency, to have a list of the prisoners he had taken from him, to whom it was replied, " My Lord, since I routed your army, I cannot have the happiness to know where you are, that I may wait upon you. Michael Jones." Irish Rebel. fol. 280.

(d) Borlace informs us, " that this defeat at Rathmines altered the result of councils at court, till then very strong for his Majesty's repair into Ireland, the the Scots having given ill proof of their integrity and faith. And certainly," adds he, " the Irish were, at that time, so disposed, as properly they would have submitted to his Majesty, whatever afterwards might have been the result of their compliance." Hist. of the Irish Rebel. fol. 280.

gave orders, that no quarter should be given; so that many of his soldiers were forced to kill their prisoners."

THE Marquis of Ormond, in a letter to Lord Byron on this occasion, says (6), " that Cromwell exceeded even himself, for any thing he had ever heard of, in breach of faith, and bloody inhumanity; and that the cruelties exercised there, for five days after the town was taken, would make as many several pictures of inhumanity, as are to be found in the book of martyrs, or the relation of Amboyna." In this carnage, out of three thousand, he left only about thirty persons alive; and these he sent to Barbadoes.

CHAP. V.

Cromwell's *Policy to reduce Ireland.*

CROMWELL having soon after repeated the same cruelties in the town of Wexford, which was betrayed to him by one *(a)* Stafford, increased the general terror to such a degree (1), " that towns fifty miles distant from him, declared against the Marquis of Ormond;" which provoked his Excellency to say, probably with more anger, than truth (2), " that the Roman Catholics, who stood so rigidly with the King upon religion, and that, as they called it, in the splendor of it, were then, with difficulty withheld from sending commissioners to intreat him to make stables and hospitals of their churches." But if, indeed, these people were at first so much terrified by this monster's unparalleled cruelties, they soon resumed sufficient courage, to reject several more advantageous conditions from his favourite, and confident, Ireton, even in point of religion, than the Marquis of Ormond could ever be prevailed upon, by the most urgent necessity of his Majesty's affairs, to allow them. For, when that regicide, in his march to munster, sent proposals to the citizens of Limerick (3), offering them the free exercise of their religion,
enjoyment

---

(6) Cart. Collect. of Orig. Papers, vol. ii.   (1) Id. ib.   (2) ib.
(3) Cart. Orm. vol. ii. fol. 123. Lel. Hist. vol. iii. p. 370.

(a) Stafford was governor of the Castle of Wexford; " which Cromwell having thus gained, advanced his flag upon it, and turned the guns against the town. Fear seized the townsmen, and the soldiers in confusion quitted their posts. Cromwell's soldiers perceiving this, presently clapped scaling-ladders to the walls, and entered without resistance into the town; wherein all found in arms were put to the sword, to the number of two thousand." Borl. Irish Rebel fol. 284.

enjoyment of their estates, churches and church-livings, a free trade and commerce, and no garrison to be pressed upon them, provided they would only give a free passage to his forces into the county of Clare, these citizens absolutely rejected the overture."

But Oliver Cromwell, besides his execrable policy of facilitating the conquest of Ireland, by the fame of his cruelties, had taken care, before he left Dublin, to publish a (4) proclamation, forbidding his soldiers, on pain of death, to hurt any of the inhabitants, or take any thing from them, without paying for it in ready money. This was so strictly executed, that even in his march from Dublin to Drogheda, where he was guilty of that horrid butchery, and breach of faith before-mentioned (5), he ordered two of his private soldiers to be put to death, in the face of the whole army, for stealing two hens from an Irishman, which were not worth sixpence."

Upon this strict observance of the proclamation, together with positive assurances given by his officers, " that they were for (6) the liberties of the commons, that every one should enjoy the freedom of his religion, and that those who served the Market at the camp, should pay no contribution, all the country people flocked to them, with all kind of provisions; and due payment being made for the same, his army was much better supplied, than even that of the Irish ever had been."

On this occasion, a congregation of (7) twenty Catholic Bishops and Archbishops, having on the 4th of December 1649, assembled, of their own accord, at Clanmacnose, published a declaration, wherein " they admonished all their people, not to delude themselves with vain expectations of conditions to be obtained from that merciless enemy. And they besought the gentry, and the rest of their countrymen, for God's glory, and their own safety, to contribute, with patience, to the utmost of their power, towards the support of the war against him. They, particularly, exhorted those, who were enlisted in the army, to persevere constantly in their opposition to the common enemy, as they expected the blessing of God upon their endeavours." The Marquis of Ormond, in a letter to the King, observed (8), " that, in this assembly, there were divers speeches made, tending to the satisfaction of the people; and to incline them to obedience to his Majesty, and amity among themselves, in opposition to the rebels." Let it be here observed, in justice to these Bishops, that it was in this letter to the King, that the Marquis first asked his Majesty's

(4) Cart. Orm. vol. ii. fol. 90.   (5) Doctor Gorges' Letter to Colonel Hamilton. Append. to Lilly's Anfw. to King's state of the Protestants under K. James.
(6) Carte, ubi supra.   (7) Borl. Ir. Rebel. fol. 290.   (8) Cart. Collect. of Orig Papers.

jesty's permission to leave the kingdom, as being absolutely indefensible against the rebels, by what powers he could then command. So very distant from truth, is that general assertion of our historians, that it was the refractoriness, disobedience, and even rebellious disposition of the Irish clergy, that first made him resolve upon quitting the government of Ireland at that juncture.

CHAP. VI.

Owen O'Neil submits to the peace; Inchiquin's Forces revolt to the Rebels.

OWEN O'Neil, who commanded an army of five thousand foot, and five hundred horse, having been incensed, beyond measure, at the assembly's proclaiming him a traitor; and at the same time, flattered by Sir Charles Coote and Colonel Monk, with hopes of a toleration of his religion, and the restitution of his estate, had entered into a treaty with the latter, and (1) relieved the former when closely besieged in Derry, the only place of strength that was then in the rebels possession in the province of Ulster. But the English parliament soon after condemned his treaty with the Monk, and rejected his further service. This is commonly thought to have been the *(a)* cause of his quitting that party, and seeking an alliance with the Marquis of Ormond (2), " to whom two blanks had been sent, about that time, under his Majesty's hand and seal, to be made use of, in any treaty or transaction with him."

Wherefore, thro' the agency of Colonel Daniel O'Neil, that General's nephew, whom the Marquis of Ormond sent to solicit him for that purpose, " Owen (3) O'Neil, on the 12th of October 1649, concluded and signed an agreement, on certain conditions, with his Excellency; which though himself

(1) Cart. Orm. vol ii. fol. 77.   (2) Cart. Collect. of Orig. Pap. vol. ii. p. 317.
(3) Cart. Orm. vol. ii.

(a) 'There is a very different cause assigned for this accommodation of O'Neil with Ormond in a letter from Secretary Nicholas to Ormond himself, which he says came from a very good author, Lord Brudenell. It is there expresly said, " that O'Neil had written to Cromwell to thank him for the care he had taken of himself and his army; but desired him withal to consider, that his promise (to assist him) was but conditional, as presupposing the Pope's approbation, which he could never obtain; but, on the contrary, had received a peremptory command from him, to do nothing prejudicial to the crown of England." Cart. Collect. of Orm. Orig. Papers, vol. i p. 298.

self lived not to accomplish, dying at Cloughouter-castle in the county of Cavan, in the beginning of December, was shortly after performed *(b)*."

The Marquis of Ormond had received frequent warnings of the infidelity of Inchiquin's officers; and some probable reasons for withdrawing his confidence from Inchiquin himself. His Excellency, in a letter to that Lord, November 16th, 1648, on occasion of the before-mentioned mutiny of these officers, told him plainly, "that (4) he was very unwilling to have any thing to do with them; and seemed to think that they had but delayed their design, waiting for a more hopeful opportunity to accomplish their end, which he understood to be, to betray his Lordship, and himself to the independents."

The defection of these officers soon after to the parliament, to which Lord *(c)* Broghill's treachery and artifice not a little contributed, sufficiently justified these suspicions. For in this favourable conjuncture of the accession of O'Neil's forces, the distress of Cromwell's army, and the probability there was, by the advantage of a pass, of cutting off his provisions, and of making his retreat to Dublin very difficult, without losing a good part of his men; in these circumstances, I say (5), " on a sudden, and altogether, all the considerable places in the province of Munster, as Cork, Youghall, Kinsale,

K k Bandon-

(4) Id. ib. vol. iii.   (5) Clarend. Carte.   (6) Lel. Hist.-vol. iii. p. 357.

(b) Mr. Belling informs us, " that when the news came, of Ormond's being routed by Jones, O'Neil assembled the chief officers of his army, and addressed them thus. " Gentlemen, to demonstrate to the world, that I value the service of my King, and the welfare of my nation, as I always did, I now forget and forgive the supreme council, and my enemies, their ill practices, and all the wrongs they did me from time to time, and will now embrace that peace, which I formerly rejected out of a good intent." MSS. History. He sent his forces to Ormond, under Ever M'Mahon, Bishop of Clogher, to whom the Marquis had given a commission to command them. " It must be acknowledged," says Borlace, from Clarendon, " that this Bishop performed, and observed the conditions very justly, as he was punctual in what he promised, and applied himself with all dexterity, and industry to the advancement of his Majesty's interest; so that, during his time, he restrained the clergy from making any acts, which might discourage the people from their obedience to the King's authority." Hist. of the Irish Rebel. fol. 313. This Bishop was afterwards taken prisoner in an engagement near Enniskillen, after having received many wounds; and ignominiously put to death, by the positive order of Sir Charles Coote, whom, within less than a year, he had relieved when in great extremity." Id. ib. fol. 512. Clarend. Irish Rebel.

(c) In an engagement near Clonmell, " this Lord Broghill had taken the titular Bishop of Ross prisoner, and promised to spare his life on condition that he should use his spiritual authority with the garrison of a fort adjacent to the field of battle, and prevail on them to surrender. For this purpose he was conducted to the fort; but the gallant captive, unshaken by the fear of death, exhorted the garrison to maintain their post resolutely against the enemies of their religion and country, and instantly resigned himself to execution. His enemies," adds my author, " could discover nothing in his conduct but insolence and obstinacy; for he was a Papist, and Prelate." Lel. Hist. of Irel. vol. iii. p. 362-3.

Bandon-bridge, Moyallo, and other garrisons, under Lord Inchiquin, revolted to the English parliament; and thereby gave them a safe retreat, free passage, and necessary provisions of all they wanted; as likewise harbours for their ships, to bring every thing to them they could desire. This defection, in so fatal a juncture of time, when the streights Cromwell was in by the winter, and want of provisions, had raised the spirits of men; and when they looked upon themselves as like to have, at least, some hopeful encounter with him, was not (adds my author) a loss, or a blow; but a dissolution of the whole frame of their hopes, and designs; and confirmed that spirit of jealousy and animosity, in the army, which no dexterity, nor interest, of the Lord Lieutenant could extinguish, or allay *(d)*."

This general defection of Inchiquin's forces seems to have given the first rise, and occasion to the proceedings of the congregation of Bishops at Jamestown, they looking upon it, as a new, and corroborating proof of Ormond's being privately connected with the English rebels. For, although his Excellency had been fully (7) apprised, by the confederates, of the ill affections, and actual revolt, of several of the officers of these garrisons, before the general treachery now mentioned; yet he readily agreed to Inchiquin's suspicious stipulation, " that (8) these garrisons should be entirely left to his own disposal; nor could Inchiquin ever after be prevailed upon, to admit any of the Irish forces, though actually in the King's service, into them."

(7) Carte's Ormond, vol. ii. fol. 101-2.   (8) Id. ib. vol. ii.

(d) Yet, " the above-mentioned revolting garrisons had been supplied by the Irish, during the whole preceding summer, to their excessive charge." Orm. Let. to the King. Carte's Collect. of Original Papers, vol. i. p. 419.

CHAP.

CHAP. VII.

The Marquis of Ormond desires Leave to quit the Kingdom.

HIS Excellency, so early as December 24th, 1649, requested, and shortly after obtained, the King's permission (1), "to withdraw both himself, and his Majesty's authority, out of the Kingdom, if he should see occasion." And the better to secure his retreat on all sides, from a people whose losses under him, and jealousies of him, were daily increasing, his friend (2) Dean Boyle, privately procured him a pass from Oliver Cromwell; which being afterwards discovered by the ungenerous use that regicide made of it, his Lordship returned it by a trumpet, with a letter informing him, that it was officiously sought for and obtained by the Dean, without either his consent, or privity."

His Excellency's desire to withdraw himself out of the kingdom proceeded not, as has been already hinted, from the supposed refractory and disloyal behaviour of the Irish clergy, but from his own conscioufness of the people's great mistrust of him, and their consequent aversion to his government. For, as he himself justly observed on that occasion (3), "these people believing themselves betrayed, would think it vain to be persuaded into action, which might render them incapable of conditions from the enemy. Or if they should be got forth, perhaps with church-censures, it would be with despair, not hope, of success; whilst they suspected their leader of having made conditions for himself, upon their ruin."

ANOTHER of his reasons for desiring that permission was (4), "that it appeared every day more evidently than other, and would soon be visible to those of the shortest foresight, that upon any thing Ireland could afford, it would not be possible to make any resistance against the rebels; who then had the whole coast towards England, Waterford excepted, ready to receive their forces;

---

(1) Carte. (2) Carte, Orm. vol. ii. fol. 121.
(3) Carte's Collect. of Orig. Pap. vol. ii. p. 450. (4) Ib.

forces; commodious harbours for their shipping, and garrisons, from whence they would immediately be in the heart of his best countries, and at the walls of his remaining towns." After which he thus proceeds, " what thoughts of submission (to the rebels) this may produce in these people, or the greater number of them, I know not; I therefore humbly desire that your Majesty would be pleased to send me your commands to withdraw myself hence."

Nay, his Excellency seemed in some measure, to apologise for these people's aversion to his government, and their desire to get rid of it (5); " for many of the Irish," says he, " having promised themselves many advantages by their coming under his Majesty's obedience, as the assistance of the army formerly under Lord Inchiquin's command, and the advantage of trade with the towns possessed by him; that his Majesty would be able, in part, to ease them of the burden of the war, by supplies of money, arms, and ammunition; and that whilst the rebels forces were bent against them, occasion would be taken to raise some diversion in England, or out of Scotland; and finding Lord Inchiquin's forces, which, to their excessive charge, they had supplied all the summer, now turned against them, and the towns become garrisons to their enemies, from whence to annoy them by sea and land; no supplies at all from abroad, and no diversion in England, though Cromwell and Ireton, the supposed heads of the rebels, were removed from thence; all these disappointments of their hopes, aggravated by the enforced spoil of a successless army, began to breed in them such aversion," says he, " to his Majesty's authority, and to myself, to whom all their misfortunes, the negligence, cowardice, and treachery of others,- are attributed, that I am told, it was in agitation with the violent party of the clergy, and others set on by Lord Antrim, to procure a protestation against my government."

(5) Ib. p. 419.

CHAP.

CHAP. VIII.

The King is invited to go to Scotland.

ABOUT this time, the King was proclaimed in Scotland; and commissioners were sent from thence, to invite him over to that kingdom; but upon such conditions, as were utterly inconsistent, not only with the dignity, and good faith, of a King, but even with the honour and integrity of a gentleman. "These (1) commissioners were the Earl of Castels, two burgesses, and four Presbyterian divines. To give the better assurances of their good intentions to his service, immediately before their coming out of Scotland, the Marquis of Huntly was put to death, for no other crime but his loyalty to the King."

The Marquis of Ormond, still in Ireland, was consulted upon this, as indeed, he was upon every other important concern of his Majesty. But that he did not always deliver his opinion, with such candour and sincerity, as were suitable to the confidence reposed in him, is but too apparent, from his own letters on that occasion. In one of them to Secretary Nicholas, who, he knew, was averse to that measure, he seems to have clearly foreseen all the evils that were likely to attend it; for he tells him, that, " Unless (2) his Majesty was resolved to deliver up both himself, and his people, to the Covenant, and Presbytery, he would not go into Scotland; and that the covenant was inconsistent with the peace he had concluded with the Irish, and which his Majesty had confirmed." But from what we find in a private letter of Lord Byron's, who was then with the King at Breda, to his Excellency, it appears that he secretly abetted, and promoted, that design. For Lord Byron told him (3), " that, in order to what he found was his Lordship's opinion, concerning his Majesty's conjunction with the Scots, he had contributed his best endeavours to the effecting of it; and that his Majesty would begin his journey in a few days, and had commanded him (Byron) to attend him thither." And the King himself, in a letter to the Marquis, January 16th, 1649, says (4), " you will perceive by my public letter, that I have resolved of a treaty with my subjects of Scotland, whereunto I was principally induced by that

relation

---

(1) Ib vol. i. p. 268.   (2) Carte's Orm. vol. iii. fol. 607.
(3) Cart. Orig. Papers, vol. i. p. 333.   (4) Ib. vol. ii. p. 423.

relation which Harry Seymour made to me, from you, of the state of things in Ireland."

Accordingly, his Majesty, having agreed with the Scotch commissioners, left Breda, and arrived in Scotland, on the 23d of June 1650, O. S. but before they suffered him to land (5), they obliged him to sign both the covenants, national, and solemn. And, in about two months after, he was prevailed upon to publish a declaration, " That he would have no enemies but the enemies of the covenant; and that he did detest, and abhor, all Popery, superstition, and idolatry, together with prelacy; resolving not to tolerate, much less to allow, those, in any part of his dominions, and to endeavour the extirpation thereof, to the utmost of his power." And, with regard to the peace lately concluded with the confederates, and confirmed by himself, he expressly pronounced it *(a)* null and void, adding, " that he was convinced in his conscience of the sinfulness and unlawfulness of it, and of his allowing them (the confederates) the liberty of the Popish religion; for which he did, from his heart, desire to be deeply humbled before the Lord; and for having sought unto such unlawful help, for the restoring of him to his throne."

WHAT opinion one of his Majesty's own secretaries had of this declaration, appears from his letter to the Marquis of Ormond, January 25th, 1650. " When (6) I consider," says he, " this infamous declaration, which the Scots compelled the King to publish, and are still resolved to have his Majesty make good (though not only all the King's party, but even strangers that have any sense of honour, or conscience, declaim against it) I cannot so much as hope, that they intend any good, or safety, to his Majesty, whom they have so wickedly and notoriously abused." Most certain it is, that after this declaration was known in England (7), " many people there, who were before averse to the parliament's measures, freely and voluntarily enlisted in their armies, to fight against the Scots."

(5) Sir Edward Walker's Historic. Discour.
(7) Id. ib. p. 417.

(6) Cart. Orig. Pap. vol. i. p. 400.

(a) " Nothing could be more convenient for the congregation of prelates, (soon after assembled at James-town) and their purpose of enflaming the people, than this virulent declaration. They imputed it entirely to the representations of the Marquis of Ormond." Lel. Hist. of Irel. vol. iii. p. 376.

CHAP.

CHAP. IX.

The King secretly regrets this Measure.

HIS Majesty did not become guilty, all at once, of this open violation of the public faith (1). " Before he left Breda, he yielded thus far to the Scotch commissioners, that if a free parliament in the kingdom of Scotland should so think fitting, he would then find some way, how with honour, and justice, he might make void the Irish peace. In the mean time, his Majesty would by no means permit, that any such thing should be inserted in the body of the articles of agreement; and it was concluded, that, that business should remain in a distinct paper in the Earl of Cassell's hands, in regard of the dishonour it might bring on the Marquis of Ormond, and his Majesty's friends in Ireland. No sooner was this done, but his Majesty laboured immediately to inform Ormond of what had passed; and Mr. Richard Weston was dispatched, on the 16th of May, from Breda, and one hundred and fifty pounds given him to defray his charges. But when his Majesty came into Scotland, he found him there, alledging (2), " that he was not permitted by the Scots to proceed in his journey; at which his Majesty was exceedingly troubled, but saw plainly, it was a contrivance between him (Weston) Lord Wilmot and the Scots.

" AFTER his Majesty had put to sea, the Scotch commissioners shewed him new, and higher, propositions from the kingdom of Scotland; which were, that unless his Majesty would immediately take the covenant, and, *in terminis*, break the peace with the Irish, he was not to be received into Scotland; at which he was so much disgusted, that he resolved to lay aside all thoughts of going thither, upon such terms. But, overcome with the intreaties of his servants, he yielded, in terminis, to the breach of the peace with the Irish, conditionally, that it should not be published, until his Majesty had acquainted the Marquis of Ormond, and his friends in Ireland with it."

AT the same time, that the Scots detained Weston in Scotland, and, by that means, prevented Ormond's earlier and particular knowledge of this transaction,

(1) Id. ib. vol. i. p. 391.   (2) Ib.

faction (3), " they dispatched several of their ministers to the Laggan, and Clanboys, in the North of Ireland;" who, doubtless, proclaimed aloud, the news of the King's having consented to take the covenant, and to declare the late peace void; being assured, that nothing could more effectually alienate the affections of the Irish from his Majesty, or set them at greater variance among themselves, than such intelligence. In May 1650, the Marquis of Ormond had (4) " heard by reports, which he thought probable, that the King had agreed with the Scots." And he afterwards expressed his apprehension (5), " that great advantage was left to such, as were industrious to draw the Irish from their allegiance, by infusing into them a belief, that his Majesty, having taken, or approved, the covenant, they were deprived of the benefit of the peace, and left to the extirpation, which the covenant proposes, of their religion and persons."

CHAP. X.

Proceedings of the Bishops at James-town.

THE confederates being now alarmed by repeated accounts of the King's having taken the covenant, not without a well grounded suspicion, that Ormond had approved of, and advised, that measure; several of their Bishops met at James-town, in order to consult what was fit to be done on so important an emergency; where, taking into consideration the sad condition, to which their nation and religion must necessarily be reduced by such an event; and mindful of a resolution they had formerly *(a)*, with good reason, entered into, that, in case of a breach, or disavowal of the peace on the part of his Majesty, or Lord Lieutenant, they would return to their original confederacy, as the likeliest means to hinder their people from closing with the parliament, " they now fell to deliberate on the most effectual way of putting that resolution in practice; and, at length, determined to recall, and withdraw, on the peril of ecclesiastical censure, all those of their communion, from under the Marquis of Ormond's command (1)." Wherefore, on the 12th of August 1650, they drew up,

and

(3) Carte's Orm. vol. ii.   (4) Cart. Collect. of Orig. Papers.   (5) Ib.
(1) Clarend. Carte.

(a) On account of the King's disavowal of Glamorgan's peace, and his being prevailed on, by the Scots, to disavow that, which had been concluded with the Marquis of Ormond in 1646, by his own reiterated commands.

and signed, an excommunication againſt all ſuch Catholics, "as ſhould enliſt under, feed, help, or adhere to, his Excellency; or aſſiſt him with men, money, or any other ſupplies whatſoever."

To this excommunication (which, tho' thus haſtily drawn up, was not publiſhed till the 15th of the following month) a limitation was annexed (2), "that the next general aſſembly, which was ſoon to meet at Loughrea, ſhould diſpoſe of it as they thought proper." But that aſſembly not having met at the appointed time; and freſh, and undoubted, intelligence arriving daily, that his majeſty had taken the covenant, and made void the peace, (the only ſecurity that was left them, for their religion, liberty, lives, and fortunes) theſe Biſhops, on the 15th of September 1650, publiſhed their excommunication in the uſual form. At the ſame time, they unanimouſly reſolved, purſuant to their aſſociation-oath, ſtill faithfully to ſerve the King againſt the regicides, and to uſe all the means in their power to hinder their people from aſſiſting them in any reſpect whatſoever. The ſincerity of this reſolution appears, by their including, in the ſame eccleſiaſtical cenſure (3), "all thoſe unnatural patriots, and others of their own flock, that ſhould adhere to theſe common enemies of God, King, and country; or ſhould any ways help, aſſiſt, abet, or favour them, by bearing arms for, or with them; or by otherwiſe contributing to them, without urgent neceſſity." So little foundation was there for the injurious reflection made by a late (4) hiſtorian, "that, it having been propoſed to theſe Biſhops, to iſſue their excommunication againſt thoſe, who were guilty of ſuch compliances they had reſerved this engine of theirs, for more factious purpoſes, and could not be prevailed upon to employ it in the King's ſervice."

On the very next day, however, after this excommunication was publiſhed, theſe Biſhops iſſued an order for ſuſpending the effects of it in the Earl of Clanrickard's army, which conſiſted chiefly of Roman Catholics, the only perſons that could be affected by it. Upon which irreſolution of theirs, the Marquis of Ormond failed not to obſerve (5), "that, ſuppoſing them to have proceeded on juſt grounds, yet their raſhneſs was not excuſable, as appears in that as they haſtily denounced their excommunication on the 15th of September, ſo it was more wiſely ſuſpended by the ſame men on the 16th following."

(2) Id. ib.
(1) Lel. Hiſt. of Ireland.
(3) Append. to Walſh's Hiſt. of the Remonſ. fol. 70.
(5) Cart. Orm.

CHAP. XI.

Ormond approved, and advised, the King's Agreement with the Scots.

LORD Clarendon, Doctor Borlace, Mr. Carte, and generally all our historians affirm, " that, when the Marquis of Ormond first heard of the King's declaration at Dumferling, he did really *(a)* believe it a forgery, contrived either by the English rebels, or the Irish congregation, to seduce the people from their loyalty, and affection to his majesty." However that might be, his Lordship certainly knew long before that declaration was published, (what was equally destructive to the Irish peace) that the King had agreed to take the covenant, and thereby engaged his solemn promise to endeavour the utter extirpation of these people's religion, or persons. For, so (1) early as March 5th, 1648, we find, that " he understood the Kingdom of Scotland had invited his Majesty thither to be crowned; but that he was to secure religion, according to the covenant, before he was to be admitted to govern." After which he says, " if his Majesty resolves to consent to that condition, in the most rigid construction of it to himself, and his subjects, I doubt not but his immediate going thither is most counselable." But he, at the same time (2), " questioned not, but it would be considered, how inconsistent the covenant was with the peace concluded with the Irish, by virtue of the power given him; and that there would be care taken, to give that people no apprehension, that they would be broken with, which might drive them to take desperate ways for their safety." In November 1649, he declared (3), " that he was, at no time, against the treaty with Scotland; and that much less was he then." In July 1650 (4), " he believed it then appeared, that the treaty was ended, he hoped, in an agreement with the Scots, so that," adds his Lordship, " in place of arguments to dispose his Majesty to an accord so necessary, as without, or besides, it, I see no near hope of his restitution, I shall apply myself to the use to be made of such an accord, in this kingdom," (Ireland.) And then he proposes (5), " that himself may be fortified with some gracious declaration

(1) Orm. Let. to Sec. Nicholas. Cart. Orig. Pap. vol. ii. p. 361.   (2) Ib.
(3) Id. ib. p. 415.   (4) Id. ib. p. 436.   (5) Append. to Walsh's Remonstrance.

(a) Doctor Leland more cautiously, and indeed, more truly, says, " that Ormond affected to believe it a forgery; but that he soon received a private letter from the King, acknowledging that he had really subscribed the declaration, apologising for this shameful transaction, as the effect of fear, or force." Hist. of Irel. vol. iii. p. 376.

claration from his Majesty, subsequent to the agreement of Scotland, in favour of all those (Irish) that had been, and still continued, loyal, and affectionate, to his service; and he conceived, that, without such a declaration, and purpose as to those, his Majesty could not acquit himself with honour towards that people; whereof," adds he, " many have perished, and more are likely to do so, for their loyalty to the crown."

CHAP. XII.

The real Cause of the Clergy's Proceedings at James-town.

AT the same time that the King's declaration at Drumferling was notified in form to the Irish congregation, the Marquis of Ormond proposed to make good the peace, upon certain conditions; one of which was the revoking their excommunication. But that they refused to consent to, because, as they alleged among other reasons, " they understood from his Lordship's letter to them on that occasion, that he had suggested matter unto his Majesty for making that declaration, by which for ought appearing unto them, the King had withdrawn his *(a)* commission from him, and had cast away the nation, as rebels, from his protection. Nor could they understand (they said) the mystery of preserving his Majesty's authority with them, or over them, in such a case; or how it could be done." They added, " that they believed, the King's authority being thus taken from them, the best remedy for hindering the people to close with the parliament, was to return to their former confederacy, as it was intended by the nation, in case of the breach of the peace, on the part of his Majesty."

THAT the King's agreement with the Scots, and the shameful conditions of it, were early known to the Irish in general, is manifest, not only from what has been already mentioned, but also from the following instance of the insincerity of his Majesty's more recent promises to them. When his Majesty first took the resolution of entering into a personal treaty with the Scotch commissioners at Breda, he wrote to the Marquis of Ormond, January 23d, 1649.

(a) In the declaration at Drumferling, the King " acknowledged his sorrow for making peace with the Papists, and recalled all the commissions granted by him in Ireland." Cart. Orm. vol. ii. fol. 131. Hence the Earl of Clanrickard, in a letter to Lord Muskerry, confesses, " that the King, by that act (declaration) disavowed the peace with the Irish, and took away his protection from them." Clanrick. Mem. Dub. ed. p. 108.

1649 [1], " to affure him, that though he would endeavour to oblige that nation (the Scots) by all juft, and honourable, condefcenfions, to engage themfelves to enter England in the fpring, with a confiderable army, for his fervice; yet he would not, either in the faid treaty, or upon any other occafion whatfoever, confent to any thing, that fhould be contrary to the agreement made with the Roman Catholics of Ireland; but would fulfil, and perform all grants and conceffions, which he had either made, or promifed them, according to the full extent of that grace, he had always intended that nation; which, as he had new inftances of their loyalty and affection to him, he fhould ftudy rather to enlarge, than to diminifh, or infringe, in the leaft degree." He, at the fame time, defired the Marquis " to give thefe affurances to all the Irifh Roman Catholics." But this letter, it feems, did not reach his Lordfhip, till Midfummer following; and [2], " that delay," fays Mr. Carte, " brought an irreparable mifchief upon the King's fervice; the Marquis's continued ignorance of the King's condition, and pleafure, difabling him to refute the malicious reports raifed, and the afperfions thrown on the King, for breach of faith, and for having abandoned, and given up the Irifh;" fo that as his Excellency complains in his difpatches by Lord Taaffe, " the venom of the forgery had wrought very near a deadly effect, before the remedy came." Thus we fee, that before Midfummer 1650, the King's agreement with the Scots, and its ruinous confequences, were not only generally known in Ireland, but alfo had wrought an almoft deadly effect upon the affections of that people towards him.

AND fo groundlefs is the pretence, that the Marquis of Ormond was furprifed, and puzzled at thefe proceedings of the Bifhops at James-town, as at an event, of which he was at a lofs to divine the caufe, that it is manifeft, from a letter of his to Secretary Long, that he was fully apprifed of them, and the motives that produced them, at leaft, fourteen days before they were made public. For, having mentioned, in that letter, an anfwer he had fent to a requeft of theirs, which he judged would be ill taken, he adds [3], " which anfwer, whether it will produce a direct declaration againft me, and an excommunication of all thofe that fhall adhere to me, or not, is more than I am certain of, though I be told it will." This letter is dated the 2d of September; and the clergy's declaration, and excommunication, were not publifhed till the 15th of that month.

[1] Cart. Orm. vol. ii. fol. 129.   [2] Id. ib.   [3] Cart. Collect. Orig. l'ap. vol. ii. p. 443.

CHAP.

CHAP. XIII.

The Generality of Irish Catholics condemned the Clergy's proceedings at James-Town.

THESE violent proceedings of the Irish clergy, though not unprovoked, were far from being approved of by the generality of the Catholics of Ireland. "All (1) the sober professors of the Catholic religion," says Clarendon, "abhorred them; and most of the commissioners of trust, and the principal nobility, and most considerable gentry remained firm in their particular affection, and duty to the King; and in their submission to the authority of his Lieutenant, notwithstanding the excommunication. And not only the whole nobility, and gentry of fortune and interest, some very few of the latter excepted, but also many pious and learned men, of the secular and regular clergy, and even some of the Bishops, did abhor, and abominate, the proceedings of that congregation, and the doctrine they infused into the people; the same being disowned by some of those Bishops, as being obtruded upon them by the major vote; or done by their procurators, without their assent or knowledge. And even others of them, who were present at the congregation, and subscribed the excommunication, disclaimed their having consented to it, though they were obliged to sign it for conformity."

It has been mentioned above, that this congregation had annexed to their censure a restriction, by which the next general assembly was empowered to dispose of it in what manner they thought proper. That assembly met, by the Marquis of Ormond's appointment, at Loughrea, on the 15th of November 1650; "it was very full, and (besides the clergy) (2), consisted of the principal nobility, and gentry of fortune and interest in the kingdom." "The Bishops there present, for the removing of those jealousies, which were occasioned by their proceedings at James-town (3), declared and protested, of their own accord, that by their excommunication, and declaration, they had no other aim, but the preservation of their religion and people; and that they did not purpose to make any encroachment upon his Majesty's authority, or the liberty of their fellow subjects; confessing that it did not belong to their jurisdiction so to do."

WHEN

(1) Hist. of the Irish Rebel.   (2) Cart. Orm. vol. ii. Clarend.   (3) Cart. Orm. vol. ii. f. 139. Clarend

When this assembly understood the Marquis of Ormond's resolution to leave the kingdom, they (4) sent four o their members, viz. the Lords Dillon and Clanrickard, and others, to his Lordship at Kilcolgan, with an instrument bearing date the 7th of December; in which, after reciting what the Bishops had protested in the assembly, concerning their excommunication and declaration, they added (5), " that they, the Lords spiritual and temporal, and the gentry met in that assembly, conceived, that there was no better foundation, or ground, for their union, than the holding to, and obeying, his Majesty's authority, to which they owed and ought to pay all dutiful obedience. And they did thereby declare, and protest, that there was not any power in the Lords spiritual or temporal, gentry or people, clergy or laity, of the kingdom, to alter, or take away, his Majesty's authority; they holding that to be the chief flower of the crown, and the support of the people's liberty; and they unanimously beseeched his Excellency, in his hearty desire of the nation's preservation, to leave that authority with them in some person, faithful to his Majesty, and acceptable to the nation; to which person, when he should be made known to them, they would not only afford all due obedience, but would also offer, and propose the best ways and means they could devise for the conservation of his Majesty's right, and the people's liberties, and interests; and for the begetting a ready obedience in all places and persons, to his Majesty's authority."

In answer to this request, his Excellency told them (6), " that he was resolved to make use speedily, of the liberty the King had given him as to his own person; which he found was unacceptable to the people. Yet that, if they could propose to him any way how he could deposit the King's authority in such a manner, as that it might not be exposed to the same affronts it had received in him, and might be applied to the preserving of the people, and the recovery of the kingdom, he should readily agree to it; and he heartily wished they might receive that happiness by his absence, which they could not receive by his presence."

His Excellency was (7) resolved to trust the royal authority in no body, but the Earl of Clanrickard, the only person in the kingdom fit for so high a trust; and on the 7th of December aforesaid, after he had embarked, he wrote to the assembly, " that he had left authority with his Lordship,

(4) Borlace Hist. of the Irish Rebel. fol. 339.   Clarend. Carte.   (5) Ib.   (6) Clarend. Carte.
(7) Cart. Orm. vol ii. fol. 137.

ship, to govern the kingdom, provided their declaration were so far explained, as to give the Marquis of Clanrickard full satisfaction, with regard to the expressions they made use of to declare their duty of obedience."

An instrument was hereupon drawn up, wherein (8) the assembly declared, that neither the Lords spiritual or temporal, gentry or people, clergy or laity had power to discharge the people from that due, and perfect obedience to his Majesty's authority vested in the Marquis of Clanrickard; and that, in case of any such act or endeavour, no persons should, or ought to be led thereby; but that, for their disobedience, on any such grounds, they were subject to the heavy censures, and penalties, of the laws of the land. But to this, a proviso was added, that this obedience was not intended to be paid to any person, that should be appointed chief governor, who had joined in the covenant, or should violate the articles of the peace *(a)*. Upon this declaration, Lord Clanrickard was prevailed upon to accept the government; and Ormond departed for France..

CHAP. XIV.

The Presbytery of Bangor's *Proceedings on the Peace.*

NONE censured the congregation at James-town more severely, than the Presbyterians in Ulster; yet none had so little right to censure it. For that congregation only followed the example, that was set them the year before, by the Presbytery of Bangor; with this difference, that the former, as we have seen, had some provocation given them, which the latter could not pretend.

For on the conclusion of the peace in 1648, the King having sent a commission to Hugh Lord Viscount Montgomery of Ards, to command all the forces within

---

(8) Id. ib.

(a) That proviso was expressed in these words. " And inasmuch as his Majesty is at present in the hands of a Presbyterian party of the Scots, who have declared themselves enemies to this nation, and vowed the extirpation of our religion, we declare, it is not hereby intended, to oblige ourselves to receive, obey, or observe any governor, that shall come unduly nominated by, or procured from his Majesty, by reason of, or during his being in, an unfree condition, that may raise a disturbance in the present government, established by his Majesty's authority, or cause the violation of the articles of peace." Borl. Hist. of the Irish Rebel. fol. 339.

within that province, his Lordship thought it neceſſary to ſignify to his Majeſty's ſubjects of Ulſter his inveſtiture with that commiſſion, and accordingly publiſhed a declaration, July 4th, 1649, for that purpoſe.

A PRESBYTERY was thereupon convened at Bangor, July 7th, in which a declaration was drawn up, containing ſeveral virulent reflections on his Lordſhip. He is therein charged, among other things (1), "with lifting up his hand againſt them; with betraying the covenant; with owning King Charles the ſecond; with cloathing himſelf with a commiſſion from him; with receiving commands from the Marquis of Ormond, and joining with malignants, who blaſphemed the covenant. For this cauſe," ſaid they, "as embaſſadors of Chriſt, we beſeech the people not to join hands to ſuch a courſe; not to join in executing ſuch a commiſſion, by ſerving either as officers, or ſoldiers, or they ſhall wring the dregs of the cup, which the malignants have been drinking, theſe many years paſt. We do alſo, in the name of Jeſus Chriſt, warn the people of our charge, from all compliance with their ungodly courſe, either by ſpeaking favourably of them, acknowledging the authority of the preſent command under the Marquis of Ormond, and the Lord of Ards; by impoſing ceſs for the maintenance of their unlawful power; or by obeying their orders, or paying ceſs to their army, or ſupplying them with that, which is the ſinews of war, money and victuals."

I HAVE ſaid, that the Preſbytery at Bangor could not pretend ſuch provocation for this outrage on the Royal authority, as the congregation at Jamestown really had; for, by the King's having taken the covenant, the latter were threatened openly with the utter extirpation of their religion; but the Preſbytery were promiſed, and aſſured of the preſervation, and extenſion, of theirs. Lord Montgomery, (a) who was himſelf a zealous Preſbyterian, ſolemnly engaged in his declaration (2), "in the preſence of God, that he would uſe his uttermoſt endeavours, while he was entruſted with power, to countenance and aſſiſt the exerciſe of their religion, as it was then practiced; and likewiſe, that he would ſolicit his Majeſty, and, (as he had good grounds to hope) with ſucceſs, for a confirmation under his hand." And, two days before that declaration iſſued (3), Lord Inchiquin wrote to the ſame Preſbytery, "that he, being a well-wiſher to the Preſbyterian government, and honoured with a public truſt by his Majeſty, knew, that his Majeſty was reſolved, for their ſatisfaction,

(1) Preſbyterian Loyalty. (2) ib. p. 409. (3) Id. ib.

(a) "In April following, 1650, this ſame Lord of Ards, Lord Moor, and Col. Trevor, came from the Iriſh quarters, to Oliver Cromwell at Clonmell, ſoon after he had taken that town, to render themſelves to him, being perſons of great note and eminency in the kingdom, and the firſt of quality of the Proteſtant party, that came from the Iriſh army unto them." Borl. Hiſt. of the Iriſh Rebel. Append. fol. 22.

satisfaction, to establish the Presbyterian government in them parts; and, he believed, in other parts also of the kingdom. And no man knows," adds his Lordship, " whether the whole number of Protestants may not agree to embrace it."

CHAP. XV.

The total Defection of the Protestant Forces.

SHORTLY after the Presbytery's declaration was published, there was such a general defection in the Northern army, that the Marquis of Ormond told the King. in December 1649 (1), " that his Majesty might account that province, if not wholely lost, yet in a low, and desperate condition; and that he expected to be strongly invaded from thence next summer." In that letter it was, that he desired his Majesty's permission to withdraw himself out of the kingdom (2), " because it was unable of itself, and without powerful aids from abroad, to resist the growing power of the rebels." Yet, when his Lordship did withdraw himself, some months after, he greatly increased these rebels power, by permitting, or rather transmitting, the forces then under his immediate command to join and assist them. For, when he was preparing to leave the kingdom, and had designed Lord Clanrickard for his deputy, " he permitted," says the Earl (3) of Orrery, " all those worthy Protestants, who, till then, had served under him, to come off to the rest of the Protestants, though then headed by Ireton himself, esteeming them safer with that real regicide, so accompanied, than with those pretended antiregicides, so principled." How these (as he is pleased to call the confederates) pretended antiregicides were principled, with respect to his Majesty's service, sufficiently appears, from what has been already related. Nor, indeed, was Ormond himself unconscious, that both their attachment to his Majesty, and opposition to these rebels, were real and permanent. For when, upon a (4) former occasion, he solicited leave from the English parliament, to transport 5000 foot, and 500 horsemen, together with himself, out of the kingdom into France, in order to obtain their consent, he observed (5), " that it would be a sure means of ridding their partizans in Ireland of many unsure friends, among the King's party, as well as many certain enemies among the Irish;" and thereby facilitate the reduction of the kingdom under their power. Thus were many of those Protestant forces, under his Excellency, whom he calls the King's party

(1) Cart. Orm. vol. ii. p. 422. (2) Ib. (3) Answer to Walsh. (4) In the year 1647.
(5) Carte's Orm. vol. i. fol. 603.

party acknowledged by himself to be friends to the English rebels, though unsure, and the confederate Irish Catholics to be their certain enemies.

By this great accession of forces, permitted to these real regicides, the ruin of Ireland was quickly completed. Such permission, however, was perfectly consonant to his Excellency's former agreement in 1647, when he delivered up all his power and authority to the same party. And in fact, had any comment been wanting to explain the motives of that agreement, this permission would be a very full, and clear one; for, as the same Lord Orrery observes, and seems to appeal to Ormond himself, then Lord Lieutenant of Ireland, for the truth of the whole passage (6), " certainly, he esteemed those less ill, to whom he sent his friends, than those, from whom he sent them;" and consequently, was more solicitous for the interests and success of the former, than for those of the latter; which, surely, was, besides, an unpardonable imposition on his truly noble friend, the Marquis of Clanrickard; with whom, in appearance, he left the government of the kingdom, but, in reality, by that permission, deprived him of the means of defending and preserving it.

CHAP. XVI.

Treaty with the Duke of Lorrain.

DISTRESSED as the confederate Catholics now were, and deserted by all the Protestant forces of the kingdom, their fidelity and zeal for his Majesty's service remained unaltered. While the general assembly was still sitting at Loughrea, very favourable offers of accommodation were sent them by the regicides, which they not only rejected, but prevailed on the deputy (1) to issue a proclamation, declaring all those of their communion, guilty of high treason, and punishable with death, who should aid or assist them; and such as were already with them, and did not quit their service in fourteen days, were by the same proclamation, made liable to the same punishment (2). The Bishops likewise, present in that assembly, denounced excommunication against all Catholics, who either served under the regicides, or entered into any treaty of pacification with them.

YET

---

(6) Orrery, ubi supra.   (1) Cart. Orm. vol. ii. fol. 144.   Borl. Irish Rebel. fol. 340.
(2) Carte, ib.

YET loyal as this perseverance of the Irish clergy was, (not lessened by the daily desertions of the Protestant royalists, or by the increasing power and success of the regicides,) it has not hindered party-malice to suggest, that they were, even at this juncture, instilling such sentiments into the minds of their people, as were utterly incompatible with their allegiance to the King, or due submission to his Lieutenant (2). " The Irish," we are told, " had still as much of Ireland in their power, as could maintain a war against all the English rebels there; that his Excellency the Marquis of Clanrickard, had argument enough to hope, if he could be confident of the union of the nation; that he might have reasonably promised himself an union of the nation, if he could have been confident of the affection, and integrity of the clergy; but that the greatest part of the Irish ecclesiastics had no mind to have any relation to the English nation, and as little to return to their obedience to the crown; that it was by the advice and influence of these ecclesiastics, that the confederate Catholics were first inclined to treat with the English rebels for conditions; and that afterwards, such offers were made to the Duke of Lorrain by commissioners of their chosing, as in effect transferred the whole right, and sovereignty of that kingdom to his Highness."

BUT, besides what has been already related of the temper, and disposition of these ecclesiastics, and of the state of the nation at that dismal juncture, the whole of this charge is incontestibly proved to be false, from that " state of his Majesty's affairs, and the condition of his faithful subjects in Ireland, which the Marquis of Clanrickard himself transmitted to the Marquis of Ormond, on occasion of the above-mentioned treaty with the Duke of Lorrain."

FOR therein his Lordship sets forth (3), " that the power, and success of the rebels were such, as that the whole nation was in their possession, or subject to their contribution, except the province of Conaught, and county of Clare, his Majesty's city of Limerick, and town of Galway; and that the said province of Conaught, and county of Clare were, for the most part, waste; that the inhabitants thereof were utterly impoverished; that no considerable forces could be brought together, to maintain a defensive war against the rebels, much less an offensive; that the city of Limerick, and town of Galway, had of a long time, out of a feel-

---

(2) Clarend.   (3) Clanrick. Mem. Dub. ed. p. 56.

a feeling fenfe they had of their own deftruction, being inclined to treat for conditions with the rebels; that the fame was the refolution of moſt of the other people of Ireland, who could not humanely fee how they could be otherwife preferved; and that many of the officers of his Majefty's army did, from feveral parts of the kingdom, reprefent their fenfe that it was abfolutely neceffary for the people's prefervation to treat with the rebels for conditions, feeing there was no power to refift them."

From hence it is manifeft, that whatever inclination thefe deferted Irifh had to treat with the rebels, was not at all owing to the advice, or influence, of their clergy; but naturally arofe from that irremediable diftrefs, to which they then found themfelves reduced, and from the difmal profpect of its daily increafe, until it fhould end in their total deſtruction.

" But no fooner," proceeds (4) Lord Clanrickard, " had thefe Irifh underftood, that the Duke of Lorrain's embaffador had arrived in Ireland, with offers of powerful affiance for the prefervation of the Catholic religion, and of his Majefty's fubjects' interefts, than they took much comfort and encouragement thereby, hoping that the rebels power might be oppofed. And foon after, the towns of Limerick and Galway, and all other places yet in his Majefty's obedience, feemed more chearfully, than before, to affift his Majefty's authority, in oppofing the rebels; and to difavow, and difclaim, any treaty with them, though formerly inclined, if not refolved."

Upon this change in the temper of the people, the deputy (5) " authorifed fome of the Roman Catholic prelates, and commiffioners of truft, to treat with the faid embaffador; who being accordingly called together, with feveral officers of the army, after a long and ferous debate, weighing the unavoidable danger the nation was in of falling into the hands of the rebels, did therefore advife, that it was abfolutely neceffary to accept of his faid Highnefs's protection. But the faid embaffador's propofitions being fuch, as Lord Clanrickard could not confent to, the treaty, and conclufion for farther fupplies, were put over to be determined by his Highnefs, or fuch as he fhould depute; and by fuch as fhould be authorifed by the deputy in his Majefty's behalf."

(4) ib.   (5) ib.

His Lordship concludes with his own opinion upon the then situation of affairs thus (6), " It is very evident, how great the evils are that will happen, if immediately great aids are not haftened to this nation; for the kingdom will, by the forefloing thereof, be entirely in the enemies power and poffeffion, and the people univerfally enforced to fubmit unto them."

CHAP. XVII.

The Treaty with the Duke of Lorrain confidered.

IT muft be confeffed, that this imminent danger of the whole kingdom's falling under the power of the Englifh rebels, did induce Sir Nicholas Plunket and Geoffry Brown, Efq; (commiffioners on that occafion appointed by Lord Clanrickard) to yield to the folicitations of fome private agents of the Irifh clergy, then at Bruffels, to agree to the terms propofed by the Duke of Lorrain, rather than break off the treaty; for which the deputy feverely reprimanded, and threatened to proclaim them. But even that ftep they did not take without previous encouragement from the Queen, the Duke of York, and the Marquis of Ormond himfelf.

" FOR (1), their commiffion being accompanied with inftructions for application to be made to the Queen, the Duke of York, and the Lord Lieutenant, upon their landing; in accomplifhment thereof, Lord Taaffe repaired to Paris, and prefented to her Majefty, the Duke of York, and Lord Lieutenant, all the papers, and inftructions, which they had received concerning that treaty; among which were the propofitions, agreed to and advifed, by the general affembly, for obtaining the protection, and future fuccour, of the kingdom; which were in effect the fame with the articles afterwards concluded with the Duke of Lorrain. And the faid papers having been confidered, by her Majefty, the Duke of York, and Lord Lieutenant, her Majefty directed her letters to Sir Nicholas Plunket, and Geoffry Brown, Efq; willing them to give credit to Lord Taaffe, in what he fhould relate unto them, concerning that affair. By Lord Taaffe
they

(6) ib.   (1) Clanrick. Mem.

they underſtood, that her Majeſty, the Duke of York, and Lord Lieutenant wiſhed his Highneſs would undergo the charge; and that he ſhould meet with no oppoſition from any of them: yet that, by any inſtrument under their hands, they could not conſent to it, leſt it might draw danger on the King's perſon, being then in the power of the Scots; and, in purſuance of this letter of credence, Lord Taaffe adviſed, that they ſhould proceed to a concluſion of the treaty."

THE Marquis of Ormond, after having been informed by Lord Taaffe of the particulars of this tranſaction, wrote back to his Lordſhip (2), " that, touching the buſineſs of Ireland, and the Duke of Lorrain, for ought appearing to him, there was nothing done, that were to be wiſhed undone; and for what remained to produce new, and further ſupplies, it was left to the agreement that ſhould be made with his agent by the Marquis of Clanrickard, aſſiſted by ſuch as the late general aſſembly had appointed; who, as they were beſt judges of their own condition, ſo they had free liberty from his Majeſty, in caſe of high neceſſity, to endeavour their own preſervation, even by receiving conditions from the rebels, which muſt be much more contrary to his intereſts, than to receive them from any other, almoſt upon any terms." He afterwards reminds his Lordſhip (3), " that he had already made his application, where the King (a) commanded he ſhould, and that ſo he was fairly quit of the matter (b)."

THIS

(2) Id. ib. p. 77.   (3) ib.   (4) To the Queen, and Duke of York.

(a) The King himſelf, in a letter to Lord Clanrickard, condeſcended to apologize for theſe commiſſioners. For, after having told that Lord, " that they excuſed their having conſented to this treaty with the Duke of Lorrain, only by the remedileſs neceſſities they then conceived Ireland to be in, and the abſolute deſpair they had to procure a preſent ſupply by any other means," he informs him, " that they kept both parts of the articles in their hands, till his pleaſure ſhould be known; and that they had not, in that tranſaction, any purpoſe of undutifulneſs or diſreſpect, towards him," adds his Majeſty, " we are willing to believe, and graciouſly accept their future ſervice; and we recommend them to your good opinion and favour, to the end, that upon their application to you, you may receive them into the ſame place of confidence, and eſteem, you have formerly had of them, and uſe their advice, and ſervice, as heretofore." Clanrick. Mem. Dub. ed. p. 120.

(b) The King in a letter to Lord Taaffe, from Johnſtone, January 2d, 1650, uſes theſe words, relative to this treaty with the Duke of Lorrain. " The ways here for my affairs in Ireland being obſtructed, I have heretofore intreated the Queen to take that care upon her; and if therefore ſhe ſhall direct you in any thing, you may ſafely follow her advice and direction, and have my conſent to it." Clanrickard's Memoirs, Dub. ed. p. 76.

THIS is the true state of that negociation for the Duke of Lorrain's assistance, and protection. But we will suppose, for a moment, the common invidious representation of it to be just, namely, " that the Catholics of Ireland, when theirs and the King's forces were almost entirely reduced, invited the Duke of Lorrain over, engaging, upon his appearing among them with his forces, to deliver up the whole Island into his hands, and declare him their sovereign." I say, even supposing this to have been the case, let the candid and impartial judge, from the dismal situation of these Catholics at that juncture of time, whether a better, or more justifiable, project could have been thought of (5). " They were then reduced to slavery, and beggary, by the English rebels; many thousands of them murdered, and the rest deprived of their estates. So that the question will turn upon this, whether the Catholics of Ireland, in this wretched situation, and in utter despair of ever seeing the monarchy restored, for the preservation of which they had suffered so much, were to be blamed for calling in a foreign prince of their own religion, who had a considerable army to support them, rather than submit to so infamous an usurper as Cromwell, or such a bloody, and ignominious conventicle, as the rump-parliament. Many Protestants, both Dissenters and Conformists, who have been conversant in the history of those times, have freely confessed, that, considering the miserable condition the Irish were then in, they could not have thought of a braver, or more virtuous, attempt; by which they might have been instruments of restoring the lawful monarch, at least, to the recovery of England and Scotland, from those betrayers, and sellers, and murderers, of his royal father."

AND, indeed, his Majesty's affairs were then so absolutely desperate, in every part of his dominions, that, after this treaty with the Duke of Lorrain was entirely broken off, the Marquis of Ormond himself, abhorrent as he always seemed to be, from any connection with the Irish Catholics, and especially with their clergy, advised, that speedy recourse might be had to their supreme spiritual head, the Pope himself, as the only visible means of retrieving them; which he seemed to think might be happily effected by his Holiness's mediation, and influence, with other Catholic Princes and states. " To come shortly," says he (6) in a letter to the Marquis of Clanrickard on that occasion, " to what I would be at, wherein you may be concerned, I conceive some one must be found, that hath power, if not with all, yet with most Christian Princes, and states. Among the Protestants

(5) Swift's Works.   (6) Carte's Col. of Orm. Original papers vol. i. p. 461.

testants there is none such; and among the Roman Catholics, it is visible, that the Pope has most of authority, and persuasion; and it shall be, without scruple, my advice, and that speedily, that fitting Ministers may be sent, and apt inducements proposed, to him for his interposition with all Princes and states."——Here the sentence is left thus abruptly broken off, with what view, if done designedly, may be easily conjectured, from the foregoing fragment.

AN

AN

HISTORICAL AND CRITICAL

REVIEW

OF THE

CIVIL WARS IN IRELAND.

BOOK IX.

CHAP. I.

The Marquis of Clanrickard *leaves Ireland, now entirely subject to the English Rebels.*

THE affairs of the confederate Catholics being now absolutely irretrievable, the Marquis of Clanrickard, in 1652, left Ireland, carrying with him the royal authority (1). " And within a twelvemonth after, Mortogh O'Brien, the last of the Irish commanders, submitted to the parliament, on the usual terms of transportation; by the favour of which," adds (2) my author, " twenty-seven thousand men had been that year sent away." "Cromwell (3)," says a late historian, " in order to get free of his enemies, did not scruple to transport forty thousand Irish from their own country, to fill all the armies in Europe with complaints of his cruelty, and admiration of their own valour."

This, together with the multitudes destroyed by the sword, during the war, and by famine and pestilence after it, caused a prodigious scarcity of people

---

(1) Borl. Irish Rebel.   (2) ib.   (3) Dalrymp. Mem. of Great Brit. vol. i. part 2. p. 267.

people in the kingdom. But to supply that defect (4), Fleetwood, deputy for the parliament, invited over several colonies from England; offering good conditions to such families, as would settle in Ireland; whereupon great numbers of all sorts, and sexes, flocked to that kingdom."

"It (5) cannot be imagined, in how easy a method, and with what peaceable formality, that whole great kingdom was taken from the just owners and proprietors, and divided among those, who had no other right to it, but that they had power to keep it. In less than two years after Lord Clanrickard left Ireland, this new government seemed to be perfectly established; insomuch that there were many buildings erected for ornament, as well as use; orderly and regular plantations of trees and fences, and enclosures raised throughout the kingdom; purchases made by one from the other, at very valuable rates; and jointures settled upon marriages; and all the conveyances, and settlements executed, as in a kingdom at peace within itself, and where no doubt could be made of the validity of titles."

On the 26th of September 1653, the English parliament declared, that the rebels in Ireland were subdued, and the rebellion ended; and thereupon proceeded to the distribution of their lands, in pursuance of the act of subscriptions 17° Caroli. "This being notified to the government of Ireland (6), Lord Broghill, afterwards Earl of Orrery, proposed at a council of war of all the chief commanders for the parliament, that the whole kingdom should be surveyed, and the number of acres taken, with the quality of them; and then, that all the soldiers should bring in their demand of arrears; and so to give every man, by lot, as many acres as should answer the value of his demand."

This proposal was agreed to, and all Ireland being surveyed, the (7) best land was rated only at four shillings an acre, and some only at a penny. The soldiers drew lots in what part of the kingdom their portions should be assigned them (8). Great abuse was committed in setting out the adventurers satisfaction for the money they had advanced, at the beginning of the war; for they had whole baronies set out to them in gross; and then they employed surveyors of their own, to make their admeasurements (9). "No men had so great shares as they, who had been instruments to murder the King. What lands they were pleased to call unprofitable, (which were thrown in gratis,) they returned as such, let them be never so good, and profitable (10). The lands held by the soldiers, as unprofitable, and as such, returned into the

(4) Borl. ubi supra.   (5) Life of Clarend. vol. ii. p. 117.   (6) Morris's Life of Orrery.
(7) Id. ib.   (8) Cart. Orm. vol. ii. fol. 301.   (9) Id. ib.   (10) Id. ib.

the surveyor's office, amounted to 605,670 acres. In this manner was the whole kingdom divided between the soldiers, and the adventurers of money (d).

CHAP. II.

The Transplantation of the Irish into Connaught.

"CROMWELL (1) and his council, finding the utter extirpation of the nation, which they had intended, to be in itself very difficult, and to carry in it somewhat of horror, that made some impression upon the stone-hardness of their own hearts, after so many thousands destroyed by the sword, fire, famine, and the plague; and after so many thousands transported into foreign parts, found out the following expedient of transplantation, which they called an act of grace. There was a large tract of land, even to the half of the province of Connaught, that was separated from the rest, by a long and large river, and which, by the plague, and many massacres, remained almost desolate. Into this space, and circuit of land, they required all the Irish (a) to retire by a certain day, under the penalty of death; and all who after that time, should be found in any other part of the kingdom, man, woman, or child, might be killed, by any body who saw or met them. The land within this circuit, the most barren in the kingdom, was out of the grace and mercy of the conquerors, assigned to those of the nation, who were enclosed in such proportions, as might with great industry, preserve their lives. And to those persons, from whom they had taken great quantities of land in other provinces, they assigned greater proportions within this precinct. And that they might not be exalted with this merciful donative, it was a condition that accompanied this their accommodation, that they should all give releases of their former rights and titles to the land that was taken from them, in consideration of what was now assigned them; and so they should for ever bar themselves, and their heirs, from laying claim to their old inheritance. What should

---

(1) Clarend. Life, vol. ii. p. 116.

(d) Lord Antrim's estate, consisting of 107,611 acres, was allotted to Sir John Clothworthy, afterwards Lord Massareen, and a few others, in consideration of their adventures, and pay, which did not in all, exceed the sum of 7000l. Cart. Orm. vol. ii. fol. 278.

(a) "Whom Cromwell had declared innocent of the Rebellion." Lel. Hist. of Irel. vol. iii. p. 409. Carte, &c.

should they do," continues my author, " they could not be permitted to go out of this precinct, to shift for themselves elsewhere; and without this assignation, they must starve here, as many did daily die of famine."

" In (2) this deplorable condition, and under this consternation, they found themselves obliged to accept, or submit to, the hardest conditions of their conquerors; and so signed such conveyances, and releases, as were prepared for them, that they might enjoy those lands, which belonged to other men. And by this means, the plantation of Conaught, as they called it, was finished, and all the Irish nation was inclosed within that circuit; the rest of Ireland being left to the English. Some few estates were left to the old Lords, and just proprietors, who being all Protestants (for no Roman Catholics were admitted) had either never offended them, or had served them, or had made composition for their delinquencies, by the benefit of some *(b)* articles."

CHAP. III.

High Courts of Justice in Ireland.

ABOUT this time, a new tribunal, under the title of an high court of justice, was erected in different parts of both kingdoms, for the trial of rebels, and malignants, that is to say, of those who were still found faithful to the King. That, which sat at Dublin in 1652, was besides, authorised (1), " to hear and determine, all massacres and murders, done or committed, since the first day of October 1641; that is to say, the actors, contrivers, promoters, abettors, aiders, and assisters, of any of the said massacres, or murders, or killing after quarter given." From the iniquitous, and bloody, sentences frequently pronounced in these courts, they were commonly called
Cromwell's

(2) Id. ib.   (1) Borl. Irish Rebel.

(b) This transplantation, grievous and shocking as it appears in this authentic description of it, has been represented by a late historian, rather as a piece of necessary, and useful policy at that time, than as an act of severity, and injustice to the Irish. " Conaught," says that writer, " was reserved entirely for the Irish, under the qualifications determined by parliament. Here they were to confine themselves, and to enjoy their several proportions of land; that so the new English planters might proceed without interruption, and without that danger of degenerating, which former ages had experienced from an intercourse with the Irish; and the natives, divided by the Shannon from the other provinces, and surrounded by English garrisons, might be restrained from their old barbarous incursions." Lel. Hist of Irel. vol. iii. p. 396.

Cromwell's (2) slaughter-houses; "for no articles were pleadable in them: and against a charge of things said to be done twelve years before, little or no defence could be made: and the cry that was made of blood, aggravated with expressions of so much horror, and the no less daunting aspect of the court, quite confounded the amazed prisoners, so that they came like sheep to the slaughter *(a)*."

AND indeed, what else could be expected at a time, when all distinctions of right and wrong were confounded, and lost in those of power, and impotence (3); "when the noblest acts of loyalty, (says the Marquis of Ormond himself,) received the judgment due to the foulest treason; due to the unrighteous judges that pronounced it, without authority in the persons, or justice in the sentence; when the benches were crowded, and oppressed, with the throng, and wicked weight of those, that ought rather to have stood manacled at the bar; when such was the bold contempt, not only of the essentials, but also of the very formalities of justice, that they gave no reason for taking away mens estates, but that they were Irish Papists; when all men were liable to the entanglements of two-edged oaths, from the conflicts raised by them in mens breasts, between conscience and conveniency; between the prostitution of their consciences, and the ruin of their fortunes; than which an harder, and more tyrannical, choice could not be obtruded on christians. For here the election was not swear thus against your conscience, or you shall have no part in the civil government, no office in the army, or benefice in the church; but swear thus, or you shall have no house to put your head in, no bread to sustain yourselves, your wives, and your children *(b)*."

MANY instances might be produced of the barbarous iniquity of these courts; but I shall mention only one, which was exhibited at the trial of Sir Phelim O'Neil, in February 1652, when an infamous attempt was made by his judges to blacken the memory of their deceased King, with the same mock-appearance of justice, though not with the same success, with which their masters in England had lately murdered his royal person.

SIR

(2) Hist. of Independency. (3) Ormond's speech to parliament. Borl. Ir. Rebel.

(a) Such was the indiscriminate, and glaring injustice of these courts, that, although in different parts of Ireland, they contrived to condemn about two hundred persons, as guilty of murder, on forged, corrupt, or no evidence; "yet in the Northern province, which had been the great scene of barbarity, not one was brought to justice but Sir Phelim O'Neil." Lel. Hist. vol. iii. p. 394.

(b) Is not this the case, at this day, of many Irish Roman Catholics, with respect to the operations of the present Popery-laws?

Sir Phelim O'Neil, one of the principal leaders in the infurrection of 1641, confcious that nothing would more effectually induce the Irifh to join in his confpiracy, than their belief that it was approved of, and authorifed, by the King, counterfeited his Majefty's commiffion for that evil purpofe; and having furprifed the caftle of Charlemount, he there found an old patent, the feal of which he ordered to be torn off, and affixed to that commiffion. The Irifh infurgents believed the authority real, and, therefore, entered heartily into his meafures. The Englifh rebels, for a while, either believed, or pretended to believe, the fame; and from thence had taken occafion to heap infinite reproaches on the King, who thereby loft the affections of many of his otherwife well-difpofed fubjects. Thus the fame credulity, real, or affected, of thefe two contending parties, by increafing their numbers, equally anfwered their different purpofes. But the motives, by which it operated in each, were very different; that of the infurgents being an honeft, though mifguided, intention of ferving his Majefty againft a factious, and difloyal adminiftration; and that of the others, an avowed defign to carry on, and foment the rebellion againft himfelf.

But the regicides, having now gotten into their hands the known author of the forgery, and imagining that he would not hefitate to accept of any conditions, that might extricate him from his prefent dangerous fituation, expected to be able to convince the world, by his own teftimony, that he had levied, and carried on that war by a real commiffion from his Majefty; hoping, by that means, to wipe away, or at leaft, extenuate, their own guilt, in the late King's murder, as if they had only by that act, rid the world of the author and abettor of a rebellion, which they every where reprefented as moft odious, and deteftable. Full of thefe hopes, they privately offered him his pardon, and the reftitution of his eftate *(c)*, if he would make public confeffion, and proof of the genuinenefs and authenticity of this commiffion; but they being anfwered, " that it was impoffible for him to do fo," refolved to try, what the terror of their high court of juftice would do; and therefore brought him to his trial (4), where his judges publickly repeated the fame tempting offer, and enforced it with fhamelefs importunity; but he perfifting refolutely in his denial of the fact, his fentence was deferred till the next day; and then again, for

---

(4) Nalfon's Hiftoric. Collect.

(c) " He had been frequently folicited thereunto by fair promifes, and great rewards, while he was in prifon." Cart. Orm. vol. ii. fol. 181. " Sir Richard Kennedy, made Baron of the Exchequer of Ireland by King Charles II. who attended Sir Phelim in prifon, as his council, ufed frequently to mention this as told him there by Sir Phelim, with great deteftation of the offer." Id. ib. Note.

for the same reason, postponed to the third, in order, as his judges told him, (d) to give him time to reflect on their friendly proposal. But Sir Phelim still acquitting his Majesty of having any hand in that commission, and even calling witnesses to prove, that he had himself fixed the seal to it, in the manner before-mentioned, sentence of death was pronounced against him. But even then, they did not cease to tempt him; for at the very place of execution, and after he had mounted the ladder, Ludlow sent him an offer of his life, and estate, if he would then accuse his Majesty of having sent him that commission. But he calmly answered, " I thank the Lieutenant General for his intended mercy; but I declare, good people, before God and his Angels, and all you that hear me, that I never had any commission (e) from the King, for what I have done, in levying, and prosecuting this war." More of his speech, says (5) Dean Ker, who was present at both his trial, and execution, " I could not hear, the guards beating off those, that stood near the place of execution."

SIR Phelim O'Neil is never mentioned in any history of this insurrection, but as a monster of cruelty, perfidy, and rebellion: I mean not to represent him as quite innocent in any of these respects; but I am inclined to think, that these charges have been greatly aggravated in his particular, as we find, they have certainly been, with regard to his associates in this war (6). At his trial he fervently declared, " that divers outrages, committed by his officers and soldiers, though contrary to his intention, pressed his conscience very much (f)." And, indeed, his whole conduct, on this occasion, seems to

(5) ib. (6) ib. Carte.

(d) " His trial," says Mr. Carte, " was drawn out into a length of several days, in hopes that the criminal, might in that time be wrought upon to save his life, by blackening the memory of the late King." Orm. vol. ii. fol. 181.

(e) " Lord Maguire, also, who was privy to all the transactions of the insurgents, denied it to the last, (in 1644) with more sense of conscience, (saith his Majesty in his answer to the parliament's two last papers concerning Ireland,) than they who examined him expected." Borl. Irish Rebel. fol. 45.

(f) " He declared, that his conscience was already oppressed by the outrages of his followers, and that he could not add to the severity of his present feelings by an unjust Calumny of the King. Even at his execution, he was again tempted; and returned the answer above-mentioned aloud." Lel. Hist. of Irel. vol. iii. p. 395.
He is generally accused of having given orders for the killing Lord Caufield, on seizing his castle of Charlemount; but he was, on the contrary, so highly provoked at that villainy, committed by some of his brutal followers, that, in February 1642, having discovered six of the murderers, he ordered them to be first hanged, and afterwards beheaded." MSS. Irish Journ. written by his Chaplain.

to ascertain the sincerity of that declaration. In this charitable light, I am apt to consider that unfortunate gentleman, with respect to his past life; but when I compare his behaviour in this last scene of it, with that of his judges, I am at a loss to determine, which should be deemed greatest, the heroism of the former, or the villainy of the latter *(g)*.

CHAP. IV.

Henry Cromwell's *Administration in Ireland.*

HAD Henry Cromwell, second son to Oliver Cromwell, been placed earlier in the government of Ireland; or when he was so placed, had he been suffered to follow the bent of his own humane disposition, the Irish of that period would have had much fewer, and less grievous, causes of complaint than were then given them; for to his favourable *(a)* representation, and

---

(g) Notwithstanding the confessed truth of the above relation of the trial of Sir Phelim O'Neil, a late learned historian censures Mr. Carte, as rather uncharitable for saying, " that they would have pardoned and rewarded him, if he had been profligate enough to have falsely accused the late King." And he even asserts on this occasion, that Sir Phelim " was not tempted to accuse the King: and that his pardon was not promised on any such condition, but that he was to purchase it by producing a material, and authentic proof of his guilt," Lel. Hist. of Irel. vol. iii. p. 395. Now I can't comprehend, what, or whose guilt is here to be understood. Sir Phelim O'Neil had already confessed himself guilty of the insurrection, but still denied that the King had given him a commission for commencing it. It is not to be supposed, that they would have pardoned, and rewarded him, for " producing material and authentic proof of that guilt, which he had already confessed; it therefore remains, that they wanted him to confess, and produce proof, that the King had granted him the commission in question, which he could not do, because no such com-

mission had been granted. And it is sufficiently evident, from all the circumstances of his trial and execution, that had he been profligate enough to yield to their importunity, by producing any proof, however immaterial and unauthentic, or even by simply avowing that calumny in any public manner, it would have gone very far towards contenting them."— Dean Ker, who was present, testifies expressly, " that on the second day of his trial, some of the judges told him, that if he could produce any material proof that he had such a commission from Charles Stewart (for so they called his late Majesty,) to declare and prove it, before sentence of death was passed against him, and that the said Sir Phelim should be restored to his estate and liberty." See Nals. Hist. Collect.
" Doctor William Sheridan, formerly Bishop of Kildare," says Mr. Carte, " and the late Mr. Locke, a very worthy man, and member of parliament, were present at the same time; and have to many gentlemen now living confirmed the truth of Dean Ker's relation." Life of Orm. vol. ii.

(a) " The assessments which the Irish paid were above a fourth as much as those of all England and Wales; which, he told his father in one of his letters, was ten times more than in due proportion they ought to be; and that they paid incomparably more other charges, owing to the devastations in the civil war, than any other of three nations." Warn. Irish Rebel. p. 567.

Ch. IV.   CIVIL WARS in IRELAND.   281

and influence, it was entirely owing, that the Protector's council did not add new grievances, and oppressions, to those they already suffered. His letters in Thurloe's collection shew his abilities and skill in governing (1). As Chancellor of Trinity College, he took that seminary into his particular care, and patronage, instituting anew all the literary exercises, together with the long neglected degrees in arts, and the several professorships; and presented the college with Primate Usher's noble library, which he had purchased with his own money. He was easy of access, and affable to all; often entertaining at his table, even sequestered persons, and remitting to them one half of those large sums with which they were taxed for their loyalty. Far from being maddened with the enthusiasm of the times, he restored religion to some sort of decency; gave back some churches, which were occupied by the Anabaptists, to the former incumbents; and even had a new-born child of his own publickly baptized in the cathedral of Dublin, a ceremony not seen there of a long time before."

HAD he been endowed with fortitude, equal to his justice, and benevolence, his government would have been signalized by an act, that would have made some atonement for his father's usurpation, and parricide. He once (2) promised to declare for the King; the city of Dublin had undertaken to stand by him, and the Lord of Ards engaged to draw 20,000 men together in the North, in support of that design; but, upon the receipt of letters from England, the very next day after he had made the promise, his spirits failed him. The King's friends in Dublin justly complained on that occasion (3), " that no commissions had been sent them, nor any persons appointed to command them in such an attempt. If these precautions had been used, they could have easily, at that juncture, seized upon the castle."

OF his integrity, and disinterestedness, he gave many signal proofs, during his administration; but none so signal, or indeed so unprecedented, as that which appeared at the conclusion of it. " For upon his (4) recall from Ireland, altho' he had held the government of that kingdom four years, he was not master of money enough after all, to carry him back to England; and was, therefore, under the necessity to crave some from thence for that purpose."

WHAT pity it was, that such a man as this, should be placed at the head of a nation without any other power, but merely that of executing designs planned,
O o   for

(1) Bates' Elenchus Motuum Nuperor. in Angliâ, part ii. p. 57.   (2) Sir Ed. Hyde's Let. to the Marquis of Orm Cart. Collect. vol. ii. p. 242.   (3) Id. ib.   (4) Warn. Irish Rebel.

for its destruction, in another kingdom! To enforce ordinances, by which those who dared to profess the religion of their consciences (5), or had not manifested their constant good affections to the usurpation; and also the constant good affections of those ancestors, from whom any estates descended to them, and had not already proved the same, and obtained judgment thereof, were adjudged rebels convict, attainted of high treason, and to have forfeited all their honours, estates, and preferments. With what regret must such a chief governor have beheld those numerous rapines, and *(b)* murders, that were daily committed by his soldiers on that miserable people, not only with impunity, but even by his own constrained order, or connivance. But injustice and cruelty had then the sanction of law; and, in so dismal a conjuncture, it is not, perhaps, less meritorious to employ power to prevent the increase of evil (as he often did his) than it is, in better and more equitable times, to exert its authority and influence, for the promotion of actual good.

(5) Hughes' Abridgment, p. 33.

(b) In those days, the name of Irishman and rebel was thought to signify the same thing. For whenever the Cromwellians met any of the poor country people abroad, or discovered them lurking from their fury in dens and caverns, they killed them on the spot, if some unusual, or whimsical circumstance did not happen to save them. Thus Ludlow tells us, "that being on his march, an advanced party found two of the rebels; one of whom, says he, was killed by the guard before I came up; the other was saved, and being brought before me, I asked him, if he had a mind to be hanged? And he only answered, if you please. So insensibly stupid, adds he, were many of these poor creatures." Mem. vol. i. At another time he tells us, he found some poor people retired within a hallow rock; "which," says he, "was so thick that he thought it impossible to dig it down upon them, and therefore resolved to reduce them by smoak. After some of his men had spent most part of the day in endeavouring to smother those within, by fire placed at the mouth of the cave, they withdrew the fire; and the next morning, supposing the Irish to be made incapable of resistance by the smoak, some of them crawled into the rock; but one of the Irish, with a pistol, shot the first of his men, by which he found the smoak had not taken the designed effect; because tho' a great smoak went into the cavity of the rock, yet it came out again at other crevices: upon which he ordered those places to be closely stopped, and another smother to be made; and the fire was continued till about midnight; and then taken away, that the place might be cool enough for his men to enter the next morning; at which time they went in armed with back, breast, and head-piece, found the man, who had fired the pistol, dead; and put about fifteen to the sword; but brought four or five out alive, with the priests' robes, a crucifix, chalice, and other furniture of that kind (but no arms.) Those within," says he, "preserved themselves, by laying their heads close to a water, that ran thro' the rock. We found two rooms in the place, one of which was large enough to turn a pike." Such were the enemies, whose lives these gallant regicides were incessantly hunting after. A score of poor despoiled people, lurking in caverns from the fury of their pursuers, and furnished but with one pistol to guard the entrance of their hiding-place! From the character of these barbarians, we may well believe (tho' Ludlow does not mention it) that those four or five wretches, whom they brought alive out of the rock, soon after met with the fate of their companions.

CHAP. V.

Contrivances of Sir Charles Coote, *and Lord* Broghill.

"THE (1) King's intereſt had been ſo totally extinguiſhed in Ireland, for many years paſt, that there was no perſon of any conſideration there, who pretended to revive it. At the death of Cromwell, and at the depoſition of his ſon Richard, Henry Cromwell was inveſted with the full authority in Ireland; the two preſidents of Munſter, and Conaught, were Lord Broghill, and Sir Charles Coote, both equally depending on the Lord Lieutenant; and they the more depended upon him, and courted his protection, by their not loving one another, tho' ſtill agreeing in a long averſion to the King, by multiplications of guilt. Amidſt the many ſucceeding changes in the government, the two preſidents remained in their ſeveral provinces, with full power; either becauſe they had not deſerved to be ſuſpected, or becauſe they could not be eaſily removed." Some ſuſpicion, however, there was of Lord Broghill, which he took uncommon pains to remove; for, but a few months before the King was reſtored, he wrote to ſecretary Thurloe (2), " that he had heard, he and his friends were miſrepreſented in England, as perſons, that intended to ſet up for themſelves, and to make Ireland a back door to let Charles Stewart into England; and thereby, at one blow, to cut up by the roots, the precious rights, they had been ſo long contending for. But he profeſſed, that he knew nothing further from the thoughts of all his acquaintance and friends; for that intereſt, as well as duty, would keep them from ſo ruinous a wickedneſs."

In the confuſion that now aroſe, from different revolutions in the ſtate, Sir Charles Coote took an opportunity to ſend an expreſs to the King, with a tender of his obedience, and with great cautions, as to the time of appearing; only deſiring (3), " to have ſuch commiſſions in his hands, as might be applied to his Majeſty's ſervice, in a proper conjuncture; which were ſent to him, and never made uſe of by him. He expreſſed great jealouſy of Broghill, and unwillingneſs that he ſhould know of his engagement. Coote found aſſiſtance to ſeize upon the caſtle of Dublin, and the perſons of thoſe that were in

---

(1) Clarendon's Life, vol. ii. p. 107.   (2) See Warner's Hiſt. of the Iriſh Rebel.
(3) Clarend. ubi ſupra.

in authority, who were imprisoned by him; and the government was settled in such a manner, as was thought most agreeable to the Presbyterian humour; until, upon the King's restoration, General Monk was declared Lord Lieutenant of Ireland; soon after which, the King was proclaimed at Dublin, and in every other part of the kingdom."

CHAP. VI.

Commissioners sent from Ireland; their Characters and Designs.

AS soon as the King was proclaimed, Sir Charles Coote and his associates sent (1) commissioners to his Majesty, whom they called commissioners from the state; and a present of money from the same, accompanied with all those professions of duty, which could be expected from the best of subjects.

These commissioners were the Lord Broghill, Sir Audley Mervin, Sir John Clothworthy, and several other persons of quality, much the greater number whereof (2) had been always notorious for the disservice they had done the King. All these commissioners from the state had instructions, to which they were to conform, in desiring nothing from the King, but the settling of his own authority amongst them, the ordering the army, the reviving the execution of the laws, and the settling the courts of justice, and such other particulars, as purely related to the public; and their public addresses were to this, and no other purpose. But then (3), to their private friends, and such as they desired to make their friends, most of them had many pretences of merit, and many expedients by which the King might reward them, and out of which they might be able liberally to gratify their patrons. And by these means, all who served the King were furnished with suits enough to make their fortunes, in which they presently engaged themselves, with very troublesome importunity to the King himself, and all others, who, they thought, had credit, or power, to advance their desires."

Lord (4) Broghill appeared so very generous, and to be without the least pretence to any advantage to himself, that he quickly got himself believed;
and

(1) Clarendon's Life.   (2) Id. ib.   (3) Id. ib.
(4) Id. ib. vol. ii. p. 110.

and having free accefs to the King, by mingling apologies for what he had done, with promifes of what he would do, he made himfelf fo acceptable to his Majefty, that he heard him willingly, becaufe he made all things eafy to be done and compaffed; and gave fuch affurances to the bed-chamber men, to help them to good fortunes in Ireland, which they had reafon to defpair of in England, that he wanted not their teftimony on all occafions, nor their defence, and vindication, when any thing was reflected upon to his difadvantage or reproach."

The Ground-work of the before-mentioned expedients, propofed by thefe commiffioners for the public fervice of the kingdom, was (5) the calling a new parliament, confifting only of Proteftant Peers, and Commoners; a general pardon, and indemnity to all the Proteftants: and that nothing fhould be done to the prejudice of the adventurers, or foldiers; or towards qualifying the Irifh for recovering poffeffion of their eftates.

CHAP. VII.

The Irifh excluded out of the General Act of Oblivion.

IT was apprehended that the act of oblivion, and general pardon, which the Englifh parliament had been drawing up to be prefented to the King at his landing, might be fo extenfive as to comprehend the Roman Catholics of Ireland (1). To prevent this, other agents were fent over by perfons concerned in the new purchafes; all thefe attended the Houfe of Commons, fuggefting continually, that they never could be fecure in any parliament, that could be called in Ireland, if it did not exclude out of that act of general indemnity, all perfons who had any hand in the rebellion; under which notion, they comprehended promifcuoufly all thofe of the Roman Catholic religion, who had been fequeftered, or in arms.

Reports alfo were induftrioufly fpread by thefe agents, that the Irifh were ready to rife in a new rebellion. But this was a thing (2) impoffible to be conceived by any body, that knew the miferable condition of thefe people (3). There were, indeed, fome perfons, who had been deprived of their eftates, fo tranfported with the thoughts of regaining them upon the King's being
proclaimed,

(5) Cart. Orm. vol. ii.   (1) Id. ib.   (2) Id ib.   (3) Id. ib.

proclaimed, that they endeavoured to take poffeffion of them immediately, without having recourfe to thofe methods, which the law prefcribes, in cafe of being unlawfully dif-feized. Thefe were chiefly of thofe Irifh gentlemen, who had been found innocent (4), when in Cromwell's time, inquifition was made into the guilt of perfons concerned in the rebellion; and who were afterwards by him forced to quit their antient eftates, and accept other lands in Conaught, or Clare, in lieu thereof. They had fuffered grievoufly in the exchange, and having been tranfplanted by an ufurped power, eafily imagined, they might warrantably re-enter upon their former poffeffions, and eject the intruders, as all in England did, whofe eftates had been taken from them (5) by the ufurpers. Hence arofe feveral riots, and difturbances, which the convention at Dublin taking hold of, publifhed on May 20th, a declaration for preferving the peace, and quieting poffeffions; and the fevere laws and ordinances, lately made by the ufurpers againft the Irifh, were hereupon put in execution. They were not allowed to go from one province to another, to tranfact their bufinefs; abundance of the eftated men were imprifoned, all their letters to and from Dublin intercepted, and the gentry forbid to meet, and thereby deprived of the means of agreeing upon agents, to take care of their interefts, and of an opportunity to reprefent their grievances."

CHAP. VIII.

A Proclamation publifhed againft the Irifh.

THE members of both Houfes of the Englifh parliament thus clofely folicited by the convention-agents, and too apt of themfelves to believe the worft things that could be fuggefted concerning thefe people, joined in a reprefentation to his Majefty, as foon as he came to London (1), " that many of the natives of Ireland, who had been deeply guilty of the late rebellion, had broke out of late into new acts of force and violence, fome of them robbing, defpoiling, and murdering, feveral of the Proteftants there planted, and others by force entering upon, and difquieting the poffeffions of the adventurers, and foldiers, to the great and manifeft difturbance of the Englifh plantation; and they defired, that a proclamation might be iffued to reprefs thefe attempts."

THE

(4) Id. ib. (5) Id. ib. (1) Carte, Borlace.

The King accordingly, on the 3d of June, 1660, issued a proclamation, wherein (2), taking notice, by the information of the Lords and Commons, that many of the natives of Ireland had broken out into the above-mentioned acts of violence, and bloodshed, " did, by the advice of said Lords and Commons, hold it his duty to God, and the whole Protestant interest, to command, publish, and declare, that all Irish rebels, other than such as by articles had liberty to reside in his dominions, and had not forfeited the benefit thereof, that should resort to England, or Ireland, should be forthwith apprehended, and proceeded against as rebels, and traitors; and that the adventurers, soldiers, and others, who were on the 1st of January last past, in possession of any of the manors, castles, houses, or lands, of any of the said Irish rebels, should not be disturbed in their possessions, till either legally evicted by due course of law, or till his Majesty, by the advice of parliament, had taken further order therein."

This proclamation was not more injurious to many of the loyal Irish, whom it caused to be imprisoned, or driven out of both kingdoms, than it was fortunate to all those, whom the late usurpers had left masters of their estates. For, by being thus preserved in the enjoyment of the freeholds, they were enabled to chuse representatives to their mind, in the ensuing parliament, who, they knew, would confirm, and perpetuate, their unjust possessions.

C H A P. IX.

The Irish Parliament.

LORD Chancellor Eustace, (a) Lord Broghill, now Earl of Orrery, and Sir Charles Coote, now also Earl of Montrath, were appointed Lords Justices of Ireland. They had procured instructions to be sent them from England (1), " to tender the oaths of allegiance, and supremacy, to all his Majesty's subjects; to proceed according to law against those, that should refuse

---

(2) Borlace, Carte.   (1) Carte's Orm. vol. ii.

(a) " These two (new) Earls," says Clarendon, " had been eminently against the King; but upon this turn, when all other powers were down, were eminently for him. But the King had not then power to chuse any, against whom some as material objections might not be made. With them there were too many others, upon whom honours were conferred; upon some, that they might do no harm, who were thereby enabled to do the more." Clar. Life, vol. ii. p. 219.

fuse them; and to prepare such bills, as by them and the Privy Council (which was then likewise appointed) should be thought to be for the good of the people, in order to a parliament.

THAT parliament met on the 8th of May 1661. The House of Commons consisted of two hundred and sixty members, of which number all but sixty-four were burgesses. And (2) Cromwell having filled all the corporations throughout the kingdom with a set of people of his own stamp, it is easy to account for the strength and prevalency of that party in the House, which laboured to make good all the estates of the adventurers, and soldiers, how guilty soever, and refused to hearken to any reasonable proposal, in favour of the old proprietors, however innocent."

BUT even this favourable *(b)* composition of the House of Commons did not content these state-harpies. In order to have the dividing the spoil of the nation entirely among themselves, and for ever to preclude the Catholics from having any share, even in their debates about it, one of their first illegal resolutions was (3), " that no members should be qualified to sit in that House, but such as had taken the oaths of allegiance, and supremacy." With the same view of banishing the Catholic Peers from the House of Lords, Primate Bramhall, their Speaker, procured an order to be passed there (4), " that all the members thereof should receive the Sacrament of the Lord's Supper from his Grace's own hands." To such vile, and predatory purposes, was one of the most awful institutions of religion prostituted at that juncture! But in no other parliament but one so constituted, and perverted, could acts, alienating the just properties of almost all the Catholics in the kingdom, be expected to pass.

(2) Id. ib.   (3) Orrery's State Letters, vol. i. p. 35.
(4) Borl. Reduct. of Irel. p. 34.

(b) " That House of Commons consisted chiefly of adventurers and soldiers." Carte's Orm. vol. ii. fol. 263.

CHAP. X.

False Reports of a Conspiracy among the Irish continued. The Effects of these Reports.

BUT the Commons, not satisfied even with these advantages, in order to have some colourable pretext for the injustice intended, resolved to render the party to be injured as obnoxious as possible. For this purpose they left no means unattempted, however *(a)* wicked or absurd, to countenance, and diffuse the calumny, lately raised by their emissaries, as if the Irish had actually entered into a new conspiracy. They (1) had with great industry, called before them several witnesses to prove that the Papists were sometimes seen attending divine service in their own way, and that considerable numbers of people were gathered together on such occasions; that a cutler's apprentice had new furbished an old sword for one of them; and that another was detected buying a horse for his necessary occasions. Such proofs of a conspiracy, says Mr. Carte, might have appeared good, and sufficient, to the two new Earls; but did not satisfy Sir Maurice Eustace, and a few others. Recourse was, therefore, had to an old expedient for realizing imaginary plots, which had been formerly found successful (2). A letter supposed to have been written by one Irish priest to another, upon somewhat that was deemed treasonable, because dark, and unintelligible, was somewhere found, and laid before the parliament, by one Jephson, a member; who, with several other members, was himself about two years after, convicted of a real conspiracy against the government. In consequence of this pretended discovery, a proclamation was issued, and executed with great rigour (3), " by which all artificers, and shopkeepers, who had been left in their habitations by the usurpers, at the time of the transplantation, were now banished from Kilkenny, and other great towns. Horses and arms, being no where else to be found, were sought for in trunks and cabinets; and silver cups were defined to be chalices. The letter above-mentioned was transmitted into England with a representation of the insolence of the Papists, for whose suppression

---

(1) Cart. Orm. vol. ii.   (2) Id. ib.   (3) Id. ib.

(a) " The enemies, and competitors of the Irish," says Doctor Leland on this occasion, " were indefatigable in endeavouring to load their whole party with the guilt of new conspiracies; and even manifest forgeries were received as solid proofs." Hist. of Irel. vol. iii. p. 426.

sion, in order to prevent the threatened danger, his Majesty's directions were desired."

" BUT (4) Chancellor Euſtace ſuſpected the injuſtice, as well as deſign, of this charge againſt the Iriſh; and to diſcover what ground there was for it, he directed the judges, in their circuits, to cauſe the matter to be enquired into by the grand juries of the ſeveral counties, through which they paſſed. The finding of theſe juries was alike every where; there being a great calm in all places; no preparations for a riſing, nor ſo much as a rumour of any new troubles. Nothing could be more frivolous, and void of proof, than the paper, which the Commons drew up on this occaſion, and preſented to the Lords Juſtices; who yet thought fit to ſend it, incloſed in their letters, to Secretary Nicholas, ſignifying at the ſame time their opinion, that it would be deſtructive to the Engliſh intereſt, to admit the Iriſh to trade, and ſettle in corporate towns; or to allow the Roman Catholic lawyers to practice in their profeſſion; both which, however, had been poſitively allowed, by his Majeſty's letters."

CHAP. XI.

The Parties principally ſuſpected of this Conſpiracy voluntarily appear before the Lords Juſtices, in order to detect the Forgery.

THIS imputation of a new conſpiracy was (1) matter of great conſequence to the whole body of the Iriſh Roman Catholics; all their fortunes depending on the pleaſure of his Majeſty, who was likely to be eſtranged from them, by unjuſt repreſentations of their diſpoſitions, and deſigns. Wherefore, the ſuperior of their clergy was prevailed upon, to ſend for the two prieſts, whoſe names were in the letter (2); the Earl of Fingall waited upon the Lords Juſtices, to deſire a protection with regard to their function, but not to extend to the letter, or any other crime, with which they might be charged. But the Lords Juſtices would not grant ſuch a protection; and ſome of the council told Lord Fingall, that they were no friends to the King, who made any objections, or took meaſures to prove it a forged letter. Dermott, however, the ſuppoſed writer of this letter, came to Dublin; as did Phelan, the other prieſt, to whom it was directed. Soon after the (3) former preſented a petition to the council, complaining of the injury done him, by

this

(4) Id. ib. vol. ii. fol. 231.   (1) Id. ib.   (2) Id. ib.   (3) Id. ib.

this imposture, desiring leave, notwithstanding his function, to appear before them, to justify his innocence, being ready to suffer any punishment, if he should be found criminal as to that letter, or any thing else, that might tend to sedition, and the disturbance of his Majesty's government. After a long examination, he was committed to the custody of an officer; and the next day Phelan appearing, Mr. Belling went with him to the council, who having examined him, committed him in the like manner, upon his denying he had ever received any such letter."

" It was very improbable, continues (4) Mr. Carte, that the Irish should, at a time when their all depended on the King's good-will to them, be forming against him designs of an insurrection, which, if they were never so unfaithful, they were in no condition to execute."

CHAP. XII.

Loyalty of the Catholic Nobility and Gentry of Ireland, at this Juncture.

ON account of a severe persecution at this time raised against them, and in hopes of removing all future pretence for the same, the Catholics of Ireland, having agreed upon a remonstrance, and protestation of their loyalty, which was couched in the strongest and most explicit terms (1), sent it by the Earl of Fingall to *(a)* Mr. Walsh, an Irish Franciscan, then at London, who

was

---

(4) ib.   (1) Walsh's Hist. of the Irish Remonstrance, fol. 9.

(a) " This Religious," says Mr. Carte, " had always been very cordial and sincere in all his professions, and zeal for the Duke's service. And his Grace, having the post of Seneschall, or Steward to the Bishop of Winchester (it being usually given, in antient times, to some of the most powerful of the nobility, who were thereby engaged in the protection of the See) by a patent from Bishop Morley, with the fee of one hundred pounds a year, had settled it upon him for his subsistence. This was all Walsh had to live on. He received it duly, and enjoyed it till his death, which happened a little before the Duke of Ormond's. Orm. vol. ii. fol. 548. The same historian informs us, " that Walsh having urged his Grace to turn Roman Catholic towards the latter part of his life, the Duke told him, among other things, " that he wondered, if the condition wherein he was appeared so dangerous to him, why so good a friend did not admonish him sooner thereof." Walsh soon saw there was no good to be done, and did not venture on a second attempt." Ib.

The following passage from Lord Castlehaven, further illustrates this Irish Friar's character. His Lordship after having told us, " that he had received a long letter by a trumpet from Ireton, setting forth the great value he had for his person, and offering him, if he would retire from the King's service and live in England privately, he should not only enjoy his estate,

but

was an humble confident of the Duke of Ormond: by whom it was immediately prefented to his Majefty, and moft gracioufly received.

WALSH, having foon after come to Ireland, in order to get this remonftrance figned by all the Roman Catholic clergy, nobility, and gentry of the kingdom (as many of them as were at London, when it was prefented, having figned it there) fucceeded fo well, as to obtain, in a fhort time, the fignatures (2) " of fixty-nine of the clergy, fecular and regular; five Earls, fix Vifcounts, two Barons, twenty-four Colonels and Baronets, and fixty Efquires and Gentlemen."

BUT the Duke of Ormond, now returned to his government, and but too well acquainted with the late diffentions, and animofities. Among the Irifh clergy, (which, it will, hereafter appear, he then intended to revive) affected to believe, that there could be no certain reliance on any declaration of loyalty from the Catholic laity, until the whole body of their clergy had firft unanimoufly fubfcribed it. He therefore wrote a letter to Walfh, which was to be fhewn to all thofe, ecclefiaftics who were backward in fubfcribing, wherein he told him (3), " that, confidering how well his Majefty received the fubfcriptions to the proteftation, prefented to him in England, he did not a little wonder, that the example had not been more readily, and frequently followed in Ireland. That he had no other end in wifhing it fhould, than that thofe of loyal and peaceable difpofitions might thereby be diftinguifhed from others, for their own advantage; that the fubfcribers were more likely to find fuch advantage than the refufers; and that he defired to know who had already fufcribed, and who had refufed."

His Grace already knew, that as this Proteftation had been cenfured by fome minifters of the court of Rome, on account of its fomewhat entrenching on the Pope's fpiritual authority, it would be hardly poffible to prevail on fuch of the Irifh clergy, as had expectations from that court, to fubfcribe it, in the fame offenfive terms, in which it was conceived. For their chief, if not only, objection was to thefe terms; as Walfh himfelf owns (4), " that none at all fcrupled

(2) ib.   (3) Id. ib fol. 94.   (4) ib.

---

but remain in fafety with the efteem, and favour of the parliament;" adds, " I immediately fhewed this letter to Father Peter Walfh, my then ghoftly father, whom I had always found faithful to the King, and a lover of his country. With his advice, by the fame trumpet, I anfwered all his points, and rejected his propofition concerning my own perfon: defiring him withal to fend no more trumpets with fuch errands, if perhaps, he would not have the meffenger illtreated. From this time, there was an end of all meffages, and letters between us." Memoirs, p. 127.

scrupled about what he calls the *(b)* Catholicness of it;" and that these non-subscribers had repeatedly offered to draw up, and sign, a protestation of their own, equally loyal to his Majesty in point of civil obedience, and less liable to misconstruction, with respect to their spiritual subjection to the Pope. But all their proposals of that kind were constantly rejected.

But the Irish nobility and gentry were not quite so scrupulous in this respect; for in order to convince the Duke of Ormond, that the refusal of any number of their clergy should be no hinderance to their subscribing, in terminis, to the first remonstrance, "they (5) assembled together at Lord Clanrickard's house in Dublin; where, after Lord Tyrconnell had declared, that their agreement to, and concurrence in, that address was wholely and solely their own act; that it was originally proposed by the Earls of Clancarty, Carlingford, and himself; and seconded, in very good earnest, by the Earl of Inchiquin, as many noblemen and gentleman as were then present, and had not subscribed at London (6), in number thirty-three, put their names to it; which number being joined to the London subscribers made, in all, one hundred and twenty-one, whereof twenty-one were Earls, Viscounts, and Barons."

Not content with this, they at the same time drew up a letter, praying and inviting the unanimous, chearful, and speedy subscriptions of all the rest of the Catholic noblemen and gentlemen of the kingdom. This letter was signed by the Earls of Castlehaven, Clancarty, Clanrickard, Fingal, Tyrconnel, and Carlingford; and expressed (7) " their hopes, that the same prudential, christian, catholic, and obvious reasons, which had induced themselves to sign that remonstrance, would prevail upon them also to do the like, as these reasons imported no less than the clearing of their holy religion from the imputation of most unholy tenets; the assuring his Majesty ever more of their loyal thoughts, hearts, and hands, in all contingencies whatsoever; and the opening of a door to their own liberty, and future ease, from those rigorous penal laws, under which they, and their predecessors, had sadly groaned, during an hundred years past. That as they hoped they could not think, they would even for these desirable ends, swerve in the least tittle from the true, pure, and unfeigned, profession of the Roman Catholic faith,

nor

(5) Id. ib.   (6) Id. ib. fol. 95.   (7) Id. ib.

(b) " I must desire the reader," says he, " to take notice here, that since the year 1661, till this present, about the end of the year 1666, there was not, among such a number of pretences and excuses, any one alleged, by any at all, of unlawfulness, unconscionableness, or uncatholickness in point of faith, religion, or morality, in the subscription of that remonstrance, or declaration of allegiance." Hist. of the Irish Remonst. fol. 42.

nor from the reverence and obedience due unto his Holiness the Bishop of Rome, or the Catholic church in general; so they believed, that they would rest satisfied, that nothing contained in this remonstrance reflected at all on the spiritual jurisdiction, power, or authority of the Pope, or church; the whole tenor of it asserting only the supreme temporal power in the Prince to be independent of any but God alone, and the fidelity, and obedience due to him, in temporal affairs, to be indispensable by any power on earth, spiritual or civil."

Two (8) and thirty copies of this letter (one for each county in the kingdom) were signed by these noblemen. "And (9) questionless," says Walsh, "had they been sent away, as designed, the hands of all the Catholic noblemen, and gentlemen of Ireland would have been subscribed to the remonstrance, in less than six months." But the Duke of Ormond, who had been made acquainted with the drawing up, and signing, of this letter, affected to have it believed, that, as there was then lately discovered a plot of the fanatics to seize the castle of Dublin, if any papers were known to be carried about by Catholics for getting subscriptions, their good intentions might be easily misinterpreted, and even a conspiracy imputed to them on that account; so, "his Grace was pleased," says (10) Walsh, "to countermand, for that time, and to suspend ever since, the sending about of these letters, expecting it might be done more seasonably, when the clergy had signed first."

CHAP. XIII.

The Irish Clergy's Remonstrance of Loyalty.

HIS Grace still persisting in his demand of a general and uniform subscription of all the Irish clergy to the remonstrance first delivered by Walsh (which he was privately assured, would not be *(a)* obtained) procured his

(8) Id. ib. fol. 96.   (9) ib. fol. 97.   (10) ib.

(a) One of the reasons, among many others, assigned by the non-subscribers, was, " that none of either the laity, or clergy, who had subscribed, were more favoured, or more at liberty, than others; the lay-proprietors not, therefore, restored to their estates, tho' several of them could, besides, according to the laws, plead innocency; and all of them, public articles both of war and peace, for their said estates, and for the public, and free exercise of their religion too.

" Nor were the clergy, who had subscribed, suffered to enjoy even one chapel, without daily hazards

his Majesty's consent, to suffer them to meet in a national synod at Dublin; which, notwithstanding its favourable appearance, he clearly foresaw, would only serve to increase those dissentions already sprung up among them, on that subject. For, notwithstanding all Walsh's prolix, and learned harangues at this meeting, to prove the great expediency, and even absolute necessity, of their general compliance, the majority of the Synod still refused to subscribe to that particular address; not, as they all declared, that they thought it contained any thing repugnant to the Roman Catholic faith; nor yet, " that they meant thereby to decline, or disavow the substance of it; but because they believed it more becoming the dignity of that meeting, and more respectful to his Majesty and his Grace, to present a remonstrance of their own framing, which, at the same time that it expressed as much loyalty as the other, should be so unexceptionable in point of language, that not only the Bishops, and other clergy there present, but every Roman Catholic priest in the kingdom, both secular and regular, would chearfully subscribe it. Wherefore, after mature deliberation and debate, the following remonstrance of loyalty was drawn up, and signed by this congregation; and on (1) the 16th of June 1666, delivered to the Duke of Ormond by two of their Bishops, together with a petition, praying his Grace, to accept that remonstrance from them, and to present it to his Majesty, the rather that it was so unanimously agreed to, as there was not one dissenting voice in all their number."

" To the King's most excellent Majesty Charles the Second, King of Great Britain, France, and Ireland, &c.

" WE your Majesty's subjects, the Roman Catholic clergy of the kingdom of Ireland together assembled, do hereby declare and solemnly protest before God and his holy angels, that we own, and acknowledge your Majesty to be our true and lawful King, supreme Lord, and undoubted Sovereign, as well of this realm of Ireland as of all other your Majesty's dominions; consequently we confess ourselves bound in conscience, to be obedient to your Majesty in all civil and temporal affairs, as any subject ought to be to his Prince, and as the laws of God and nature require at our hands. Therefore we promise, that we will inviolably bear true allegiance to your Majesty, your lawful heirs, and
successors;

(1) ib. fol. 683.

zards of imprisonments, and even men's lives, as appeared by a late persecution, when both on St. Stephen's, and new year's day, in 1662, the chapel of the Franciscans in Dublin, who had all been subscribers, and wherein Walsh himself did officiate, was by guards of soldiers, and whole companies with naked swords, assaulted, the altar rifled, the priests carried prisoners to Newgate, and many both men and women grievously hurt, some flashed and wounded sorely, even to the great endangering of their lives." Walsh's Hist. of the Irish Remonst. fol. 26

successors; and that no power on earth shall be able to withdraw us from our duty herein; and that we will even to the loss of our blood, if occasion requires, assert your Majesty's rights against any that shall invade the same, or attempt to deprive yourself, or your lawful heirs and successors of any part thereof. And to the end this our sincere protestation may more clearly appear, we further declare, that it is not our doctrine that subjects may be discharged, absolved, or freed from the obligation of performing their duty of true obedience, and allegiance to their Prince; much less may we allow of, or pass as tolerable any doctrine that perniciously, and against the word of God maintains, that any private subject may lawfully kill or murder the anointed of God, his Prince; wherefore, pursuant to the deep apprehension we have of the abomination and sad consequences of its practice, we do engage ourselves to discover unto your Majesty, or some of your ministers, any attempt of that kind, rebellion, or conspiracy, against your Majesty's person, crown, or royal authority, that comes to our knowledge, whereby such horrid evils may be prevented. Finally as we hold the premisses to be agreeable to good conscience, so we religiously swear the due observance thereof to our utmost, and will preach and teach, the same to our respective flocks. In witness whereof we do hereunto subscribe the 15th day of June 1666."

But the Duke of Ormond not only rejected the petition, and remonstrance of this clergy, but also ordered them immediately to disperse; and soon after, banished them out of the kingdom; insomuch that when his Grace quitted the government, there were not more than three Catholic Bishops remaining there, two whereof were bed-rid, and the third had absconded. *(b)*.

(b) His Grace expected their subscriptions to that very remonstrance, which had been presented to the King; and would accept of no other. See Walsh's Remonst. fol. 489. Although the non-subscribers alleged, and Walsh himself owns, in several parts of his history, that his remonstrance seems to assert all that is contained in the oath of supremacy itself.

CHAP. XIV.

The Duke of Ormond's *Design in permitting this Meeting of the Irish Clergy.*

PETER Talbot, titular Archbishop of Dublin, and one of the most powerful opponents of Walsh's remonstrance, observed, afterwards, to that religious, that he had been, all along, only made use of as a tool, and a dupe, in that business (1). "The ministry," says he, "for reasons best known to themselves, were willing to let you preach, and press a formulary, which they foresaw would divide the Catholics among themselves, discredit their religion, and give the government the colour, and advantage of excluding from their estates, many meriting gentlemen, for not professing that allegiance, which learned men of their own religion maintained to be absolutely necessary in a faithful subject." That there were sufficient grounds for such an observation, can be now proved by unquestionable authority; for about the end of the year 1666, after the before-mentioned synod of the Irish clergy had been dispersed, Lord Orrery, taking advantage of that incident, wrote thus to the Duke of Ormond (2). "I humbly offer to your Grace, whether this may not be a fit season, to make that schism, which you have been sowing among the Popish clergy, publickly break out, so as to set them at open difference; as we may reap some practical advantage thereby." And, when, some years after, his Grace's enemies had strangely accused him of having countenanced, and encouraged, Popery in Ireland, during his administration, and instanced his permission of this synodical meeting of the Irish clergy, as a proof of it; the Duke himself frankly declared (3), "that his aim in permitting that meeting was to work a division among the Romish clergy; and that he believed he had compassed it, if he had not been removed, and, if contrary councils, and courses had not been taken, and held by his successors in the government; of whom, says he, some were too indulgent to the whole body of Papists, and others not much acquainted with any of them; not considering the advantages of the division designed."

SOME hopes, it appears, had been given, (which his Grace's before-mentioned letter to Walsh seemed to confirm) that the subscribers to the first remonstrance would be restored to their estates. But Archbishop Talbot calls upon

(1) Friar disciplined, p. 92.   (2) State Let. vol. ii.   (3) Cart. Orm. vol. ii. Append.

upon Walsh (+), " to name but one, who had been the better for his subscription. A man," says he, " would think that my Lord of Iveagh's extraction, innocency, and merit, his breaking General Owen O'Neil's army, his raising, and losing two or three regiments, in the King's service, his venturing himself, and his nearest relations, in the towns besieged by Cromwell, his constantly following his Majesty's person, and fortune in exile, needed no further remonstrance of his loyalty; but, however, that nothing might be objected against him, he signed yours: and yet is nothing the nearer his estate. I know you pressed my Lord Duke of Ormond very much in Sir Robert Talbot's behalf, saying it would be a great scandal if the only gentleman in Ireland, who never would reject the peace of 1646, and suffered so much on that account, were not restored to his estate; and yet you see he was, and his son *(a)* is, in the same condition with the rest of your subscribers."

CHAP. XV.

The King confesses his Obligation to make good the Peace of the Year 1648.

HIS Majesty had, at several times, acknowledged himself bound to fulfil his engagements to the Irish by the peace of 1648. We have already observed, that in a letter from Breda, in 1650, he desired the Marquis of Ormond (1), " to assure them, that he would perform all grants and concessions which he had either made, or promised them by that peace; and which, as he had new instances of their loyalty and affection to him, he should study rather to enlarge, than diminish, or infringe, in the least degree."

In his speech to both Houses of parliament, July 1660, when a general act of oblivion was intended to be passed, his Majesty knowing that means had been used to exclude the Irish from the benefit of that act, told them, " that he hoped the Irish alone would not be left without the benefit of his mercy; that they had shewn much affection to him abroad; and that he expected the parliament would have a care of his honour, and of what he had promised them." And in his declaration of the 30th of November following, (which was intended

(1) Friar discipl. p. 87.   (1) Carte's Collect. of Orm. Orig. Pap.

(a) This book was published in the year 1674.

intended to be the ground-work of the acts of settlement,) he again acknowledged this obligation, and said (2), " he must always remember the great affection a considerable part of the Irish nation expressed to him, during the time of his being beyond seas; when, with all chearfulness, and obedience, they received, and submitted to, his orders, though attended with inconvenience enough to themselves; which demeanour of theirs," adds he, " cannot but be thought very worthy of our protection, justice, and favour."

But the commissioners from Ireland, fearing that if the Irish were included in the general pardon, they would be of course restored to their estates (of which, by the bounty of the late usurpers, these commissioners, and their adherents, were then actually in possession) (3) petitioned both houses, that they might be excluded by an express clause, to be inserted in the act. And upon a motion being made in the House of peers, that this petition should be rejected, and the Irish included in the general indemnity, the Duke of Ormond opposed it, alleging (4) that, " his Majesty had reserved the cognizance of that matter to himself;" *(b)* though it was notorious, that his Majesty in his speech to parliament, but a few days before, had acquainted them, " that he expected (in relation to his engagement to that people) they would have a care of his honour, and of the promise he had made them." Excluded however they were, to the astonishment of all honest men; who now perceived, what powerful instruments their enemies made use of, to accomplish their wicked purposes.

(2) Irish Statutes.   (3) Carte ubi supra.   (4) Sale and settlement of Ireland.

(b) I shall hereafter have frequent occasion to quote this small tract. It was commonly called the Coventry-letter, because it was dated from Coventry. It was written by Mr. Nangle, Attorney General in Ireland in 1685. The Earl of Clarendon, when Lord Lieutenant of Ireland, often mentions it in his letters to England, as a piece much taken notice of. " I have received," says he, in one of them, " a copy of a letter, written by Mr. Nangle, to the Earl of Tyrconnel, from Coventry, 'tis a notable letter." St. Let. vol. i. p. 156 Elsewhere, he says, " I gave my Lord Chief Justice Keating a copy of Mr. Nangle's letter, and desired his thoughts upon it." ib. His Excellency mentions Mr. Nangle, in several of his letters, as " a person of undoubted abilities, and integrity, in his profession."

CHAP. XVI.

Ormond's Reasons for his Opposition to the Irish, considered.

THE Duke of Ormond assigned two reasons, in excuse of his ungenerous conduct in this particular. First he said (1), " if he had not opposed the motion for including the Irish in the general pardon, others undoubtedly would; who, by exaggerating their former misconduct, would have excited rather the parliament's indignation against, than commiseration for, their case." But this reason has no manner of force. For although the English had heard nothing of the insurrection in Ireland, but what gave them horror, and possessed them with the worst opinion of the whole Irish nation, yet his Grace could have easily set them right, as to that matter (2): for, " besides his being a witness of every man's behaviour during the troubles, he was well acquainted with all the circumstances of their case; he knew what early attempts the most considerable of their nobility and gentry made to return to their duty; the difficulties they had to struggle with in that work, the perseverance with which they pursued their design, till they had accomplished it; and the zeal with which, in the late King's distress, they had embraced the peace of 1648. All this, I say, his Grace could have easily made known to their Lordships, in case of the supposed exaggeration of their misconduct, and would have been bound in honour and justice to do so; whereas, by his opposition to the motion for including them in the general pardon, he gave occasion to their Lordships to consider them, as the most criminal of all his Majesty's subjects in that respect, and as meriting peculiar and exemplary punishment."

His second reason was still weaker than the first, and is refuted by his own experience. He pretended (3), "that he did not think, that the Protestant Peers, or Commons of Ireland; or even the very Catholic Irish, would be concluded by, or content with, an act of the English parliament." viz. An act granting their pardon, and thereby putting them in a capacity to be restored to their estates! His Grace could not, seriously, have meant, that either the Protestant Peers or Commons, or the Catholic Irish, would have deemed an act of the English parliament

---

(1) Walsh's letter to the Bishop of Ferns, p. 24. (2) Carte's Orm. vol. ii.
(3) Walsh, ubi supra.

parliament infufficient for the purpofe of their reftitution; becaufe it was notorious (4) that he himfelf was reftored to his lands in Ireland, by an act of the Englifh parliament; and particularly (5), that one Blackwell was difpoffeffed of his Grace's large eftate of Killcafh, in virtue of it."

CHAP. XVII.

The Earl of Orrery abufes the King's Confidence, with refpect to the Settlement of Ireland.

HIS Majefty's declaration before-mentioned, for the fettlement of Ireland, (which comprehended every foot of land in the kingdom) ordained, that about five hundred Irifh gentlemen therein named, who had faithfully ferved him abroad, fhould be reftored to their eftates; but not until land of equal value was found *(a)*, to reprize the Cromwellian adventurers, and foldiers, who then had poffeffion of them. It alfo ordained, that fuch of the Irifh, as had never infringed the articles of the peace, concluded between the Marquis of Ormond and them, in 1648, fhould be reftored, upon the fame conditions. But the King had already difpofed of fo great a part of the kingdom, in gifts to Englifh and Irifh favourites (fome of whom had been acceffaries in his father's murder,) that the order for reprifals was abfolutely *(b)* impracticable; on which account the adventurers and foldiers ftill continued their

(4) Carte's Orm. vol. ii. fol. 398.   (5) Id. ib. vol. ii. fol. 392.

(a) The claim of the adventurers was founded on an Englifh act of parliament 17° Caroli, by which all thofe, who had lent money towards carrying on the war againft the Irifh, fhould upon their being fubdued, have a certain portion of their forfeited eftates conveyed to them. By the fame act, it was provided that the money fo lent fhould not be applied to any other ufe but that of the Irifh war. Yet, "fcarce was there one hundred thoufand pounds thus raifed, when the fame parliament, contrary to its own act and engagement, caufed it to be laid out for the fetting forth their army under the command of the Earl of Effex, then ready for its march, againft the King at Nottingham." Borl. Hift. of the Irifh Rebel. fol. 121.

The foldiers, who were to be reprized with lands of equal value, had conftantly fought for the ufurpers againft the King; and were thus to be rewarded for that fervice. "They were," fays Mr. Carte, "for the moft part, Anabaptifts, independents, and levellers." Orm. vol. ii.

(b) "If," fays Ormond on this occafion, "the adventurers and foldiers muft be fatisfied to the extent of what they fuppofe intended for them by the declaration; and, if all that accepted, and conftantly adhered to the peace (of 1648) muft be reftored, as the fame declaration feems alfo to intend, there muft be new difcoveries made of a new Ireland; for the old will never ferve to fatisfy thefe engagements." Carte's Orm. vol. iii. fol. 340.

their usurped possession (1); " altho' many of them, in respect of their notorious, and opprobrious actions against the crown, throughout their whole employment; and of their expressing, even after his Majesty's return, how little they were satisfied with the revolution, were universally odious, both in England and Ireland."

The Earl of Clarendon, who was thoroughly acquainted with the conduct, and intrigues, of this settlement, informs us (2), "that his Majesty was led into this mistake by a very positive assurance from Lord Orrery, who was believed to understand the state of that kingdom very exactly, that there was land enough to satisfy all the soldiers and adventurers; and that there would be a very great proportion left for accommodating the Irish very liberally." But his Lordship, at the same time, made use of every sinister means, for his own private advantage, to reduce that proportion to nothing.

For (3), " believing he could never be well enough at court, except he had courtiers of all sorts obliged to him, who would therefore speak well of him in all places, and companies, he recommended to many of them divers suits for such lands, as by forfeiture, or otherwise, should come to his Majesty; altho' he knew, that his Majesty had resolved, (and that by his Lordship's own advice) to retain those lands in his own power, to the end that, when the settlement should be made, he might be able to gratify those of the Irish nation, who had any thing of merit towards him, or had been least faulty (4). His Lordship often, even sent certificates to these courtiers under his own hand, of the value those suits might be to them, if obtained; and of the little importance, the granting them would be to his Majesty; which having been shewed to the King, disposed him to those concessions, which otherwise he would not so easily have made."

(1) Clarend. Life.   (2) ib.   (3) Id. ib.   (4) Id. ib.

CHAP.

CHAP. XVIII.

The Affairs of Ireland brought before the English Council.

ABOUT this time, a warm dispute was carrying on at London, between the agents for the late confederate Catholics, and the commissioners from the council and the two Houses of the Irish parliament, in several memorials presented by them to the King, in justification of their respective claims, and pretensions. " But (1) the Irish agents pleaded their cause under great disadvantages (2). The commissioners from the council and parliament differed a little among themselves, about their private and personal interests; but they were all united in one unhappy extreme, that is (says Lord Clarendon who was present in council, during these disputes) in their implacable malice to the Irish; insomuch, that they concurred in their desire, that they might gain nothing by the King's return; but be kept with the same rigour, and under the same incapacity to do hurt, which they were then under. And though eradication was too foul a word to be uttered in the hearing of a Christian Prince, yet it was little less, or better, that they proposed, in other words, and hoped to obtain. Whereas the King thought that miserable people to be as worthy of his favour, as most of the other party; and that his honour, justice, and policy, as far as they were unrestrained by laws, and contracts, obliged him more to preserve them, at least as much as he could. And yet it can hardly be believed, how few men, in all other points very reasonable, and who were far from cruelty in their nature, cherished that inclination in the king; but thought it in him, and more in his brother, to proceed from other reasons, than they published. Whilst others, who pretended to be only moved by christian charity, and compassion, were more cruel towards them, and made them more miserable by extorting great engagements from them for their protection, and intercession; which being performed, would leave them in as forlorn a condition as they were found."

BESIDES these impediments to their success, from the malice of their enemies, the ignorance and prejudice of some about the King, and the fraud and cruelty of others, these agents from the confederate Catholics had another obstacle in their way, which was still more unsurmountable; and that was,

the

---

(1) Carte's Orm. vol. ii. (2) Clarend. Life.

the great poverty of those who sent them. "The (3) new Earls of Orrery and Montrath had taken care to raise *(a)* privately among the adventurers and soldiers twenty or thirty thousand pounds, to be disposed of properly, without any account, by way of recompense to such as should be serviceable to the what was called English interest. The Irish had no such sums to command; few friends about the court, and no means of procuring any. Those of the English council, before whom they were to plead their cause, were highly prejudiced, and incensed against the whole nation, knew little of the conduct of particular persons, who deserved favour; but were willing to involve every body, in the general guilt of the massacre, as well as the rebellion."

C H A P. XIX.

The Sufferings of the Irish set forth by their Agents before the King and Council.

IN vain did the Irish agents urge (1), "the great and long sufferings of their countrymen; the loss of their estates, for five or six and twenty years, the wasting and spending of the whole nation in battles, and transportation of men into the parts beyond seas; whereof many had the honour to testify their fidelity to the King by real services; many of them returned into England with him, and were still in his service; the great numbers of men, women, and children, that had been massacred, or executed in cold blood, after

(3) Carte's Orm. vol. ii.   (1) Clarend. Life.

(a) And as much more publickly, for " the Irish Commons, on the 4th of March 1661, ordered, nem. con. thirty thousand pounds English to be raised throughout the kingdom, and presented to his Grace the Duke of Ormond, with a clause, that they intended not that present of theirs should be interpreted as an exclusion of his Grace, from any other just favour his Majesty might think fit to confer on him, or his." Com. Jour. vol. i.

This order was procured by his Grace's friend, the Earl of Orrery, then one of the Lords-Justices; for thus that Earl wrote to his Grace, the day after it was past. " Yesterday the parliament met in this city. I had engaged the Speaker, and much the most, if not all, the members, that their motion for their humble present for your Grace might be the very

first business gone upon.—It passed without one negative." Orrery's State Let. vol. i. p. 99.

The same Orrery having acquainted Ormond, that the first act of settlement was sent to England, adds, " All this kingdom looks upon your Grace as their great patron, to whom they in a high degree, owe those hopes, which his Majesty's gracious declaration has given them." State Let. p. 37. This declaration was the basis, and ground-work of the acts of settlement. Again, he tells him, " your Lordship's favour to this poor kingdom in hastening the bill of settlement, is so signal and great, that I know not one man concerned in the good settlement of this kingdom but must, and does, own himself your Grace's servant, for your eminent pains and care in that desired work." ib. p. 90.

after the King's government had been driven from them; the multitudes that had been destroyed by famine, and the plague, these two heavy judgments having raged over the kingdom for two or three years; and at last, as a persecution unheard of, the transplanting of the small remainder of the nation into a corner of the province of Conaught, where yet much of the lands were taken from them, which had been assigned with all those formalities of law, which were in use, and practice under that government."

" In vain did they claim the benefit of the two treaties of peace, the one in the late King's time, and confirmed by him; the other confirmed by his Majesty, who was present (2); by both which, they alleged, they stood indemnified for all acts done previously by them in the rebellion, and insisted upon their innocence since that time; and that they had paid so entire an obedience to his Majesty's commands, while he was beyond the seas, that they betook themselves to, and withdrew themselves from, the service of France or Spain, in such manner as his pleasure was they should do."

It was deemed strange indiscretion and folly in them, even by some of the least prejudiced of their judges, to mention, in that conjuncture (3), " the unworthiness and incapacity of those, who for so many years had possessed themselves of their estates, and sought then a confirmation of their rebellious title from his Majesty; or to insinuate, that *their* rebellion had been more infamous, and of greater magnitude, than that of the Irish, who had risen in arms, to free themselves from the rigour and severity that was exercised upon them, by some of the King's ministers, and for the liberty of their consciences, without having the least intention or thought of withdrawing themselves from his Majesty's obedience, or declining his government (a); whereas

(2) Id. ib.   (3) Id. ib.

(a) Lord Clarendon's life, and memoirs, from which these passages are cited, is a posthumous work, written by himself, but not published till within these few years past. In this place, he seems to exhibit some symptoms of remorse for that Machiavilian advice, which the Irish ever accused him of having given the King, while the settlement of Ireland was under consideration, viz. " to provide for his enemies, who might otherwise be troublesome, and to overlook his friends, who would always stick to him;" and this advice they ever considered, as one of the principal causes of their ruin. That his Lordship did give his Majesty some such counsel, on that occasion, and that, after his disgrace, he was heartily sorry for it, appears from the following certificate, which was lately printed in one of the public papers. Memorandum. " The Rev. Mr. Cock, of Durham being at his kinsman's, Sir Ralph Cole at Burspeth castle, about the time that Lord Chancellor Clarendon was disgraced, Sir Henry Brabant of New castle, came thither, in his way from London, and told Sir Ralph, and him, this passage. That he, Sir Henry Brabant, having been to wait on Lord Clarendon just after his disgrace, his Lordship after telling him how kindly he took that piece of friendship, express'd himself to this effect. " That there were grievous things laid to his charge;

whereas the others had carried on an odious rebellion againſt the King's ſacred perſon, whom they had horridly murthered in the fight of the ſun, with all imaginable circumſtances of contempt, and defiance; and, as much as in them lay, had rooted out monarchy itſelf, and overturned, and deſtroyed, the whole government of church and ſtate. And therefore they obſerved, whatever puniſhment the Iriſh had merited for their former tranſgreſſions, which they had ſo long repented of, and departed from, when they had arms and ſtrong towns in their hands, (which together with themſelves, they put again under his Majeſty's protection,) that ſurely this part of the Engliſh, who were poſſeſſed of their eſtates, and had broken all their obligations to God, and the King, could not deſerve to be gratified with their ruin, and total deſtruction. " It was," I ſay, " deemed unpardonable indiſcretion in the Iriſh agents, to inſiſt upon theſe, and other well known topics; and not leſs ſo, to give the moſt diſtant intimation of their humble hope (4), " that when all his Majeſty's other ſubjects were, by his clemency reſtored to their own eſtaes, and were in full peace, mirth, and joy, the Iriſh alone ſhould not be exempt from all his Majeſty's grace, and left in tears, and mourning, and lamentation; and be ſacrificed, without redemption, to the avarice, and cruelty of thoſe, who had not only ſpoiled, and oppreſſed them, but had done all that was in their power, to deſtroy the King himſelf, and his poſterity; and who now returned to their obedience, and ſubmitted to his government, when they were not longer able to oppoſe it."

To this juſt, and affecting ſtate of the caſe, with reſpect to both parties, the commiſſioners from the council and parliament of Ireland, anſwered only by a falſe, or exaggerated, imputation of the crimes of particular perſons among the Iriſh to the generality of that people (5); and by an impudent revival of former ſelf-refuted calumnies; which, though at this day, they are well known to be ſuch, were then believed, or pretended to be believed, as ſo many certain, and unqueſtionable truths, by their corrupt, malicious, or ill-informed judges.

(4) Id. ib.

(5) See Clarendon's Life.

charge; but that he could bear up againſt all the reſt, if his majeſty would forgive him but one thing, which was, that he was the perſon, who adviſed him " to prefer his enemies, and neglect his friends; ſince the principles of the latter would ſecure them to him;" adding, "that he took that for the cauſe of his own ruin, and wiſhed it might not occaſion that of many others, and at laſt the King's." This is teſtified by H. Bedford, who had it from the above Mr. Cock. London Chronicle, Decem. 2d, 1773.

CHAP.

CHAP. XX.

A Court of Claims appointed in Ireland.

"THE (1) King found, that if he deferred settling the government of Ireland, till a perfect adjustment of all particular interests could be made, it would be very long; he saw, that there must be some examination taken there, before he could make his determination upon those particulars, which purely depended upon his own judgment; and so he past that which is called the first act of settlement; and was persuaded to commit the execution thereof to commissioners, recommended to him by those who were most conversant in the affairs of that kingdom, though none, or very few of them, were known to his Majesty."

"These commissioners constituted what was commonly called the Court of Claims in Ireland (2), "but were very ill qualified for such a trust. They were for the most part engaged, by their interests, in the party of the adventurers and soldiers; very many of them were in possession of those lands, which others sued for before them; and they themselves bought broken titles, and pretences of other men, for inconsiderable sums of money, which they supported, and made good, by their own authority. Thus the judges themselves were both parties and witnesses, in all causes that were brought before them."

"Such scandalous practices could not be suffered to continue long (3). These commissioners were removed; and seven gentlemen, of very clear reputations, appointed in their room; some of them lawyers in very much esteem; and others, persons of very good extractions, excellent understandings, and above all suspicion for their integrity, and generally reputed to be superior to any base temptation."

It was imagined, however, by the same noble historian, whom I have hitherto cited, and who has honoured them with this very reputable character, that these new commissioners decided somewhat too partially in favour of the

Irish

---

(1) Id. ib.
(2) Clarend. Life, vol. ii. p. 231. Carte's Orm. vol. ii. fol. 220.
(3) Clarend. Life.

Irish on this occasion (4); " that there was reason to believe, that the observation they had made of the great bitterness, and animosities, from the English, both soldiers and adventurers, towards the whole Irish nation, of what kind soever; the scandalous proceedings of the first commissioners, together with the very ill reputation many of the soldiers and adventurers had for extraordinary malice to the crown, and to the Royal family; and the notable barbarity they had exercised towards the Irish, who without doubt, for many years, had undergone the most cruel oppressions of all kinds, that can be imagined (many thousands of them having been forced, without being covered under any house, to perish in the open fields (5) for hunger;) the infamous purchases that had been made by many persons, who had compelled the Irish to sell their remainders, and lawful pretences, for very inconsiderable sums of money; these, I say, and many other particulars of that kind, his Lordship imagined, might probably dispose these commissioners to such a prejudice against many of the English, and to such a compassion towards the Irish, that they might be much inclined to favour their pretences, and claims, and to believe, that the peace of the kingdom might be better provided for by their being settled in the lands of which they had been formerly possessed, than by supporting the ill-gotten titles of those, who had manifested all imaginable infidelity, and malice against his Majesty, whilst they had any power to oppose him." But certainly, every candid person will allow, that men of such distinguished integrity, and understanding, as his Lordship admits these commissioners to have been, were not likely to be biassed even by the motives he has recited, to any unjustifiable partiality in favour of a people, with whom they had no manner of connection, and against whom, it is probable, they had imbibed some part at least of those unreasonable prejudices, which prevailed but too generally at that juncture of time.

(4) Id. ib. (5) Id. ib.

CHAP.

CHAP. XXI.

The Conditions of the Innocency, or Nocency of the Claimants.

BUT although the commissioners of the court of claims were thus happily changed, the rigorous conditions of the innocency, or nocency, of the claimants, that had been first resolved upon, were still continued. According to these conditions, to prove a person innocent (1), it was not enough to shew, that he had never taken arms in the late insurrection, or entered into any treaty, or association, with those who had; no: for, if such a person chanced but to dwell, however inoffensively, in any of the places occupied by the insurgents, he was to be judged nocent.

This was, surely, a very hard condition; "for abundance of Roman Catholics," as (2) Mr. Carte observes, "well-affected to the King, and very averse to the rebellion of their countrymen, lived quietly in their own houses, within the quarters of the rebels; who out of reverence to their virtues, or favour to their religon, allowed them to do so; such of them as had offered to take shelter in Dublin, were by the Lords Justices banished thence on pain of death by publick proclamation, and ordered to retire to their own houses in the country, where they could not help falling under the power of the rebels; and if these suffered them to live there in quiet, an equitable man, who considers the circumstances of those times, and the condition of all countries that are in a state of war, will hardly see any iniquity in the receiving that mercy, or in the unavoidable necessity they were under of living in their own houses, as should bring upon those persons the forfeiture of their estates."

But of all the marks of nocency established on this occasion, that of having taken the engagement to Cromwell, was the most extraordinary; for that engagement was primarily contrived, during the usurpation, by those very *(a)* persons, who, after the King's return, had acquired authority and influence enough to have the modelling and imposing of these rigid conditions.

From

---

(1) Sale and Settlement of Ireland, Carte's Orm. vol. ii.   (2) Orm. vol. ii.

(a) The new Earls of Orrery and Mountrath.

From whence resulted this very shocking injustice and absurdity, peculiar, certainly, to the policy of these times (3), that the original framers and promoters of that engagement, who had themselves voluntarily taken and signed it, and had compelled others to take it, were not only held innocent, but rewarded with great honours, and employments of the highest authority in the state; while those who abhorred it, when it was forced upon them, and never took it but at the last extremity, and to avoid a violent and shameful *(b)* death, were condemned, as nocent, not only to the loss of their estates, but also to the mortification of seeing them bestowed upon the very authors, and imposers, of that engagement.

CHAP. XXII.

The Time limited for holding these Courts found too short, and not suffered to be enlarged.

THE time limited for holding the court of claims was a twelvemonth; but it sat (1) only " from February to August following; during which space, the claims of near a thousand innocents were heard; whereof half were declared innocent, notwithstanding the many difficulties they had to encounter, as well from the rigorous conditions before-mentioned, as from a swarm of corrupt witnesses, that were daily employed against them. For the suborning of witnesses at these trials, was so frequent, and barefaced, that their perjuries were sometimes (2) proved in open court, by the testimony of honourable persons, who happened accidentally to be present. Sir William Petty boasted, when he had evicted the Duke of Ormond out of some lands before this court, that he had gotten witnesses, that would have sworn through a three inched board."

THE

---

(3) Sale and Settlement, &c.   (1) Cart. Orm. vol. ii.   (2) Cart. Orm. vol. ii. fol. 393.

(b) " This engagement was, during the usurpation, forced upon the Irish in so violent and barbarous a manner, that those who refused it, were not only excluded from all benefit of the laws, but were also in imminent danger of their lives from the public orders given to Cromwell's soldiers to allow quarters to no person, whom they should meet in their way, that could not produce a certificate of his having taken it; orders, which were cruelly executed, even on poor peasants, when thro' ignorance, or forgetfulness, they had left their certificates behind them." Sale and Settlement of Ireland.

THE time limited for the trial of innocents being now expired (3), Sir Richard Rainsford, one of the commissioners, and a man of great probity, thought it reasonable to sue for more time, in order to try the claims of those, who could not be heard within the period above-mentioned, and who certainly, had as much right to demand the restitution of their estates, until they were heard and found nocent, as those who had undergone their trials, and being adjudged innocent. " But these (4), says Mr. Carte, were left to be ruined, merely for want of that common justice of being heard, which is by all nations allowed to the worst of malefactors *(a)*. The Duke of Ormond," adds he, " did not think it proper, to insert a clause in the bill, in the draught of which he was obliged to have the concurrence of the council, for relief of these unheard innocents." The Duke himself seemed conscious of the injustice of this omission; for in a letter to the Earl of Clarendon on that occasion, he says (5), " if you look upon the composition of this council, and parliament, you will not think it probable, that the settlement of Ireland can be made with much favour, or indeed reasonable regard, to the Irish. If it be, it will not pass; and if it be not, we must look for all the clamour, that can be raised by undone men."

THE King had committed the drawing up of that bill *(b)*, chiefly, if not solely, to the Duke of Ormond's discretion. His Grace therefore was certainly blameable for not inserting the above-mentioned clause, even supposing him to have been merely passive in the omission; but that he was equally active with those of the council, in hindering his Majesty to grant further time for trying the claims of so many unheard innocents, will, I fear, be found too evident for the credit of his impartiality, or honour.

(3) Sale and Settlement.   (4) Ubi supra.   (5) Carte's Ormond, vol. iii.

(a) " Of four thousand claims of innocents, entered in that court of claims, the commissioners had not time to hear above six hundred, by the 22d of August, when their commission ended. Id. Life of Ormond, vol. ii. fol. 297.

(b) There was hardly any step taken in England, with respect to the settlement of Ireland, wherein his Grace's advice was not sought for, and followed. His friend the Earl of Orrery told him, " that he was assured by good hands, that most of the persons to be restored by name, would be nominated by his Grace, though afterwards inserted in the act by his Majesty." State Let. vol. i. p. 184. Lord Orrery's information was very right; for Lord Arlington had before acquainted Ormond, " that his Majesty had promised willingly to harken to his Grace's representations from Ireland, concerning the qualifications of those whose merit he should desire to recompense." And in another letter, he expresly told him, " that his Majesty had bid him write to his Grace to know, what persons he would advise him to nominate to be restored to their estates." And soon after, the same Lord sent him a warrant. " Which," he said, " he drew up as near as he could to his Grace's sense, by which his Majesty empowered him to send a list of the names." State Let. by Brown.

CHAP.

CHAP. XIII.

An Enlargement of Time for hearing all the Claimants, by whom hindered.

HIS (1) Majesty, by a letter of February 21st, 1662, to the Duke of Ormond, had, probably at Sir Richard Rainsford's request, granted an enlargement of time for the trial of those innocents, who could not be heard within the year. But he afterwards revoked that grant, at the request of his Grace, and the Irish council. This appears from a letter of Lord Arlington to his Grace, of the 7th of March following, wherein he tells him (2), "that his Majesty was surprised at reading a letter from him and the council, of the preceding month, relating to the period that ought to be put to the commissioners sitting and determining claims, on account of the contradiction, which that letter contained to what himself had judged, upon hearing that point debated in the (English) council;" but that, "however, his Majesty would resume the consideration of it." And accordingly, on the 25th of July following, the same Lord Arlington informed his Grace and the council (3), "that the king had actually revoked his grant of the 21st of February at their request, and solicitation." For after having told them, that upon receipt of their dispatch concerning his Majesty's letter of the 21st February directed to his Grace the Lord Lieutenant, for receiving, and admitting, in general, all such persons to put in their claims before his Majesty's commissioners in Ireland, as his Grace should judge fit, notwithstanding the time limited by the act of parliament was elapsed, he adds (4), " that he had acquainted his Majesty with their opinion thereupon, and that his Majesty had accordingly commanded him, to signify to their Lordships, that it was his Majesty's pleasure, that his said letter of the 21st of February should be wholely suspended, and laid aside; finding that said letter was gained upon grounds, seemingly equitable, tho' now, by their Lordships found to be *(a)* inconsistent with the act of settlement." And thus above three thousand persons, who

(1) State Let. (2) State Let. Collect. by Brown, p. 356. (3) Id. ib. (4) ib.

(a) " The King referred the preparing of this bill to Ormond, and the Irish council." Lel. Hist. of Irel. vol. iii p 435. " But the Lieutenant and Council were empowered to explain any difficulties, and amend any defects in it." Id. ib. p 442. " Ormond promised to explain and amend, agreeably to the wishes of the Commons." Id. ib. These Commons, as we have seen, " were, for the most part, Cromwellian rebels, independents, anabaptists, and levellers; and, by the appointment of the regicides, actually possessed of the estates of the Irish.".

who had entered claims of innocency, were not heard, and yet were left to be utterly ruined.

For the court of claims being now at an end, that which was called the explanatory bill, put an absolute period to all future hopes of these unheard claimants. By that bill, it was enacted (5), " that no person or persons, who by the qualifications in the former act of settlement, had not been adjudged innocent, should at any time after, be reputed innocent, so as to claim any lands, or tenements thereby vested ; or be admitted to have any benefit, or allowance of adjudication of innocency ; or any benefit of articles *(b)* whatsoever (6)." This bill (which the Irish called the *(c)* black act) was brought over to Ireland, signed and sealed, by the Duke of Ormond himself.

The articles above-intended, of which the Irish were to receive no benefit, were those of the peace of 1648; on the conclusion of which, Ormond himself, then Lord Lieutenant, declared by proclamation, in his Majesty's name, " that all persons rendering due obedience to the said peace should be protected, cherished, countenanced, and supported, according to the true intent, and meaning of the said articles."

I must here observe, that the King was so sensible of his obligation to perform his part of the articles of that peace, that mentioning it in his declaration for the settlement of Ireland, which was to be the foundation and ground-work of these acts, he used the following remarkable words. " We (7) cannot but hold ourselves obliged to perform what we owe, by that peace, to those who have honestly and faithfully performed what they promised to do, though both we and they were miserably disappointed as to the effects of those promises." Nor did any of the dispossessed Irish then claim the benefit of it, but such as were conscious, and could produce authentic and undeniable proof (some of them by appealing even to his

S s   Grace's

---

(5) See Acts of Settlement. Lel. ubi supra. p. 440.
(7) See that declaration. Acts of Settlement.

(6) Walsh's Hist. of the Irish Remon. fol. 568.

(b) " Thus every one remaining of those numerous claimants, whose causes had not been heard, was entirely cut off. They complained of perjury and subornation in the causes that were tried before the court of claims; but their great, and striking grievance was, that more than three thousand persons were condemned without the justice granted to the vilest criminals, that of a fair, and equal trial." Lel. Hist. of Irel. vol. iii. p. 440.

(c) " By this act, Ormond is said to have got the city of Kilkenny, and six other corporate towns, together with their lands and liberties, valued by himself, and his friends of the council but at 60,000 l. though they are well worth 120,000 l." Unk. Desert. p. 165.

Grace's knowledge) that they had all along faithfully obferved the conditions of it. And thefe, furely, had an inconteftable right to the benefits of a peace, "which, as Lord Caftlehaven witneffeth (8), they had fealed, and confirmed, with the blood of more than twenty thoufand of their beft men; who loft their lives to maintain it, refufing, in the mean while, all offers of peace, and that to the very laft, from the Englifh parliament *(d).*"

C H A P. XXIV.

Some Reflections on the foregoing Acts.

BUT matters were now fo ftrangely altered, that the very claiming the benefit of that peace, was made ufe of as an argument againft their having any right to obtain it (1); "becaufe," fays Mr. Carte, "fuch claim was deemed a plain confeffion of former offences;----in (2) fhort the King now declared for an Englifh intereft to be eftablifhed in Ireland; and confidered the fettlement of that kingdom, rather as a matter of policy, than juftice. He faw, that one intereft or other muft fuffer, and he thought it moft fit, for the good of the nation, the advantage of the crown, and the fecurity of the government, that the lofs fhould fall upon the Irifh."

THE Duke of Ormond's confolatory argument, with refpect to thefe defpoiled people, in his fpeech to parliament on paffing the firft act of fettlement, is fomewhat remarkable (3). "Thofe," fays he, "that fhall be kept out of their antient eftates, the inheritance of their fathers, through the defect of their qualifications, and by the all difpofing providence of God, who was not pleafed to make them active inftruments in this happy change, are delivered from tyrannous confinements, caufelefs imprifonments, and a continual fear

---

(8) Memoirs, firft ed. (1) Orm. vol. ii. Lel. ubi fupra. (2) Carte, ib.
(3) Id. ib. vol. ii. Append. fol. 25.

(d) i. e. While they could keep any confiderable number of their people together; for even Borlace "confeffes, that while their affembly continued, fuch terms were tendered to, and refufed by, the confederates, as were agreeable to a conquering army to give (fuch as that of the ufurpers then was) to a broken fcattered party, as the confederates were." But being then (1652) reduced to bogs and woods, as their beft holts, the terms fo offered, and rejected by the affembly, when together, were foon after embraced by all of them, when fcattered and divided into parties; on which they fubmitted, and laid down their arms; having by the conditions, liberty to tranfport themfelves into foreign parts, or to ftay in the kingdom." Hift of the Irifh Rebel. fol. 385-6.

fear of their lives. The (a) good land lies afore them; their induſtry is at liberty, and they are reſtored to the freedom of ſubjects, and the protection of the laws; if an Iriſh Papiſt be oppreſt, they ſhall relieve him; if the blood of the meaneſt of them be ſhed, it ſhall be ſtrictly enquired after. Let this ſtate be compared with that they were in before the King's reſtoration, and it will be found that the greateſt loſer has got ſomething." But this cajoling amounts to no more, than an oſtentatious ſuppoſition, that his Grace's adminiſtration of Ireland was not, altogether, ſo unjuſt, tyrannous, and bloody, as that of the regicides, his now favoured predeceſſors in the government of that kingdom. And the difference will appear ſtill leſs, when it is conſidered, that the innocent ſufferers under Cromwell, had at leaſt the comfort of a remote, but reaſonable hope, that juſtice might be one day done them on his Majeſty's reſtoration; but of this, their only remaining proſpect, they were then totally deprived, under Ormond, by this explanatory bill.

"It (4) will be difficult," ſays a contemporary writer, "to perſuade thoſe, who were not eye-witneſſes of the fact, that the royal authority of a chriſtian King, which in one part of his dominions maintained the Peer in his dignity, the commoner in his birth-right and liberty; which protected the weak from the oppreſſion of the mighty, and ſecured the nobility from the inſolence of the people; and by which, equal and impartial juſtice was diſtributed to all, ſhould, at the ſame time, be made uſe of, in another part of his dominions, to condemn innocents before they were heard, to confirm unlawful, and uſurped poſſeſſions, to violate the public faith, to puniſh virtue, and countenance vice, to hold loyalty a crime, and treaſon worthy of reward; in a word, to exempt ſo many thouſands of faithful and deſerving ſubjects, from a general pardon, which, by a mercy altogether extraordinary, was extended to ſome of the murderers of his royal father."

"Colonel (5) Talbot, afterwards Duke of Tyrconnel, ſuſpecting the Duke of Ormond to have done ill offices to the Iriſh on this occaſion, expoſtulated with his Grace in ſo huffing a manner, that it looked as if he meant to challenge him; and his Grace, waiting upon his Majeſty, deſired to know if it was his pleaſure, at this time of day, that he ſhould put off his doublet to fight

---

(4) Sale and Settlement of Irel. (5) Carte's Orm. vol. ii.

(a) Before the year 1641, "the Iriſh," ſays Col. Laurence, "were proprietors of ten acres to one that the Engliſh had in Ireland; but, after the act of ſettlement, theſe Engliſh were in poſſeſſion, by that act, of four millions, five hundred ſixty thouſand thirty-ſeven acres.——So that," adds my author, "if the majority of proprietors may give the denomination to a country, which uſually it doth, Ireland is become Weſt-England." Intereſt of Irel. part ii. p. 50-51.

fight duels with Dick Talbot; for so he was usually called. Talbot hereupon, was sent to the tower, but after some time was released upon his submission."

CHAP. XXV.

A dangerous Conspiracy of the Puritans.

THE consciousness of having done a wrong is ever attended with some fear of resentment from the party injured. Such was the Duke of Ormond's situation at this juncture, with respect to the despoiled Irish (1). " He had spies and intelligencers in every part of Ireland, who served him so well, that there was not the least motion among them, but it came to his knowledge." Complaints, indeed, that wretched privilege of sufferers, were heard from all parts; but no traces of a conspiracy, nor even endeavours for redress were any where discovered. The case was very different with those rebellious sectaries, who had got possession of *(a)* their estates. For upon the restoring of a few innocents, legally adjudged such (2), " they conceived such resentment against the government, for not having divided the spoil of the whole nation among them, that they entered into two dangerous conspiracies on that account; first, in 1663, to surprise the castle of Dublin, and afterwards in 1665, for a more desperate purpose. For, at this later period, there was a general design concerted in England, Ireland, and Scotland, to rise at one time, and to set up the long parliament, of which above forty members were engaged. Measures had been taken to gather together the disbanded soldiers of the old Cromwellian army; and Ludlow was to be general in chief. They were to rise all in one night, and to spare none, that would not join in the design; which was to pull down the King, with the House of Lords; and, instead of Bishops, to set up a sober, and painful ministry." In these conspiracies several (4) Presbyterian ministers, and

---

(1) Id. ib.   (2) Id. ib.   (3) Orrery's State Let. vol. i. p. 225.
(4) Carr. Orm. vol. ii.

(a) " I confess," says Lord Arlington in a letter to Ormond on this occasion, " It will be a hard matter to be very secure of those, who see their estates enjoyed by other men, till time hath accustomed them to such digestion." State Let. by Brown. p. 408.

" This country (Ireland)," says the Earl of Essex, Lord Lieutenant in 1675, " has been perpetually rent and torn, since his Majesty's restoration. I can compare it to nothing better, than the flinging the reward, upon the death of a deer, among a pack of hounds, where every one pulls and tears, where he can, for himself; for, indeed, it has been no other than a perpetual scramble." State Let. p. 334.

and seven members of the Irish parliament, were found to be (5) engaged. The prisons of Dublin were (6) crowded with these ministers; and the members of parliament were ignominiously expelled.

LORD Orrery, from whom this account is mostly taken, has confessed a truth on this occasion, which he certainly never intended should be made public. In a private letter to the Duke of Ormond, he tells him (7), " that he had brought over Captain Taylor, one of the leaders in the latter conspiracy, to make confessions to him; and that he had, as well as he could, laid open to him, the inexpressible mercy of his Majesty to that vile party he had engaged himself with; not only in pardoning to them their past crimes, but also giving them the lands of many, who had served under his royal ensigns abroad, to pay the arrears, which had been contracted against his service at home." Such, in those days, were confessedly the rewards of loyalty, and the punishment of rebellion, in Ireland!

CHAP. XXVI.

The Duke of Ormond apologizes for the Favour he had shewn to the Cromwellian Party in Ireland.

THE Duke of Ormond's (a) strange partiality in favour of the partizans of the late usurpers, to the ruin of so many thousands of his Majesty's loyal, innocent, and meriting subjects, is thus more strangely accounted for by himself. Having, in his speech to parliament on passing the first act of settlement,

(5) Com. Jour. vol. i.   (6) Carte ubi supra.   (7) State Let. vol. i. p. 226.

(a) A remarkable instance of this partiality we find in one of his Grace's letters to John Walsh, Esq; one of h's commissioners. " You know," says he, " what my instructions have always been to my commissioners and servants; to give up, even whilst I might legally do otherwise, whatever I was possessed of, which was but set out to adventurers, or soldiers, though they had not cleared their title in the court of claims." Cart. Orm. vol ii. Append. fol. 34.
 This partiality will appear still more strange, when it is considered, " that his Grace was the first of that family of the Butlers, that was educated a Protestant; that his mother Lady Thurles, his brothers, sisters, and all his relations continuing Roman Catholics, still remained in the Irish quarters, during the late insurrection; and such of them as were able to bear arms, as Lord Muskerry, Colorel Fitzpatrick, his brother-in-law, his brother Colonel Butler of Kilcash, and Colonel George Mathews, and other his relations, as the Lord Mountgarret, Dunboyn, and divers other Lords and gentlemen of his name and family, were generals, or commanders of lower quality in the army of the confederates." See Earl of Anglesea's Let. to the Earl of Castlehaven, p. 62.

settlement, given a most odious, and shocking *(b)* description of these usurpers, he thought fit in a subsequent speech to the same parliament, on passing the explanatory act, to observe, " that it might seem liable to some objection, that whilst he declaimed against the proceedings of these men, he yet undertook to see them ratified." After which, he ludicrously, and as if he were sporting with the destruction of a whole people, adds, " to this I shall only, for the present, say, that unjust persons may sometimes do justice; and for instance, I will assure you, that Ireton, at Limerick, caused some to be hanged, that deserved it almost as well as himself."

Thus, according to the Duke of Ormond's casuistry, Ireton's supposed merit in hanging up some Catholics, (obnoxious perhaps to his Grace, though otherwise, *(c)* good subjects) entitled that Regicide's vile adherents to be legally invested with the estates, and properties, of so many thousands of the innocent, and loyal natives; and that too in breach of articles, by which his Grace had solemnly engaged, to see these natives restored.

But leaving this frivolous apology to the contempt it deserves, let us now see, if we cannot assign more probable causes of this partiality from the constant tenuor of his Grace's conduct, during the whole time of the preceding war, and for some years after his Majesty's restoration.

(b) viz. As " murderers of his Majesty's father, and usurpers of his inheritance; whose endeavours were incessant to destroy his person, and to blast his fame; who drove him into exile, and all the afflicting circumstances of that miserable state of a King, &c." See Borl. Hist. of the Irish Rebel.

(c) The chief of those executed at Limerick, by Ireton's order, were the titular Bishop of Emely, Major General Purcell, Sir Geoffry Baron, Sir Geoffry Gallaway, and the mayor of that city. These Ireton caused to be put to death, in revenge for their noble perseverance in defending that city, tho' infected with the pleague, against him, for his Majesty. " Ireton had sent in articles of surrender, in which he insisted that about seventeen of the principal persons of the place, who were still for holding it out, should be excepted (from mercy).—But these made so strong a party, that the treaty was broke up, without any agreement. But the town being afterwards surrendered (by the treachery of Col. Fennel) the Bishop of Emely, Major General Purcell, &c. were taken in the Pest-house, where they were hid." Ludlow's Memoirs, vol. i. p. 370, &c. Ireton himself, a few days after he had taken Limerick, caught the infection, and died of it there. N. B. Ludlow, from whom the above is cited, was one of the judges of that court-martial, which condemned these gentlemen.

" Colonel Fennel," says Lord Castlehaven, " having cowardly, or treacherously left the defence of the pass at Killaloe, fled into Limerick, with all his party; where, upon the rendition of the town, which was not long after, Ireton, with more than his ordinary justice, hanged him." Mem. p. 128.

CHAP.

CHAP. XXVII.

The probable Motives of the Duke of Ormond's *paſt and preſent Conduct, with reſpect to the Iriſh.*

" TWO (1) grants were made to the Marquis of Ormond by the King, ſoon after the breaking out of the war in 1641; one was the veſting in him all the ſecurities, and mortgages, upon his eſtate, formerly made, and belonging to ſuch perſons, as were, or had been, in the inſurrection. The other grant, was that of the lands held under him, and forfeited to him for breach of conditions. This grant was confirmed by a clauſe in the firſt act of ſettlement, and the eſtates thus granted contained *(a)* a prodigious quantity of land, which had been granted to gentlemen upon fee-farm, or quit-rents, and military tenures; by which they were obliged to follow their Lord, the head of that family, upon any occaſion of hoſting, into the field; and upon failure thereof the lands were forfeited to their Lord."

From his Grace's early application for theſe grants, it is evident enough, what uſe he intended to make of them; as alſo what were the true motives of his backwardneſs to conclude the ceſſation in 1643; and of his frequent diſobedience to his Majeſty's urgent commands to haſten the peace of 1646; of his carrying on, at the ſame time, a private correſpondence, and treaty with the Scotch covenanters in Ulſter, in oppoſition to that peace; and of his hindering the Iriſh to be included in the general act of indemnity, after the reſtoration, or to be indulged with the neceſſary enlargement of time, for proving their innocence, in the court of claims. From all this, I ſay, it is manifeſt, that his Grace foreſaw, that a different conduct, in any of theſe conjunctures, would have precluded him from ſome part of that vaſt emolument, which he expected from theſe grants, and which he knew, was in the end, to be proportioned to the extent, duration, and heniouſneſs, of the inſurrection.

" And

(1) Carte's Orm. vol. ii. fol. 306.

(a) It is affirmed, that he got as many gentlemen's eſtates, upon the pretence of a grant of enjoying all lands that he could prove (by witneſſes) to have paid him any chiefry, as were worth at leaſt 150,000 l." Unkind Deſert. &c. p. 166.

"And thus we find, his noble *(b)* friend, the Earl of Anglesey, acknowledging in print, in 1681 (2), " that it was then apparent, that his Grace and his family, by the forfeiture and punishment of the Irish, were the greatest gainers of the kingdom, and had added to their inheritance, vast scopes of land, and a revenue *(c)* three times greater than what his paternal estate was, before the rebellion; and that most of his increase was out of their estates, who adhered to the peaces of 1646, and 1648, or served under his Majesty's ensigns abroad." From whence his Lordship justly concluded, that " his Grace could not have been very sincere, in making either of these peaces with the Irish; but that, whatever moved him thereto, whether compassion, natural affection, or any thing else, he was in judgment, and conscience, against them; and so," adds he, " he has since appeared, and hath advantage by their laying aside *(d) (e)*."

(2) Letter to the Earl of Castlehaven. Castlehav. Mem. 1st. ed.

(b) When the Duke of Buckingham was endeavouring to supplant Ormond in the King's favour, and made overtures to the Earl of Anglesey to join him for that purpose, the " Earl rejected these overtures with indignation, and gave Ormond notice of the designs formed against him." Lel. Hist. of Ireland, vol. iii. p. 453. See Carte's Orm. vol. ii. fol. 482.

(c) A knowing contemporary writer asserts, " that the annual rents of Ormond's estate before the war, were but seven thousand pounds sterling, (his antient estate being then encumbered with annuities and leases, which otherwise was worth forty thousand pounds sterling per annum,) and at present (1674) it is upon eighty thousand. Now the first part of his new great revenues is the King's grant of all those lands of his own estate, which were leased, and mortgaged; the rest were grants of other men's estates, and other gifts of his Majesty " His gifts and grants are thought to amount to 630,000l. Unkind Desert. p. 161-2. See Queries. ib. Appen. p. 168.

(d) It is, therefore, no wonder, that his Grace's noble brother-in-law, Lord Muskerry, when on his death-bed, declared to himself, " that the heaviest fear that possessed his soul, then going into eternity, was for his having confided so much in his Grace, who had deceived them all, and ruined his poor country, and countrymen." Unkind Deserter, &c.

(e) " My Lord Duke of Ormond," says the Earl of Essex Lord Lieutenant of Ireland in 1674-5. " has received above 300,000l. in this kingdom, besides all his great places, and employments; and I am sure the losses in his private estate have not been equal to those I have suffered (in the preceding civil war) and yet he is so happy, as no exception is taken to it." State Let. p. 213-14.

CHAP.

CHAP. XXVIII.

The Duke of Ormond *befriends the Irish.*

HISTORICAL juftice has hitherto obliged me to exhibit the Duke of Ormond, as acting very unfuitably to that character of eminent loyalty, integrity, and honour, which the generality of our hiftorians have beftowed upon him. But we are now come to a period of our hiftory, wherein, more willingly complying with the fame hiftorical juftice, we fhall be able to reprefent his Grace's conduct in a far different light, in all thefe refpects.

In the year 1679, when fo much innocent blood was fhed in England, by means of the perjuries of Titus Oates, and his flagitious affociates, encouraged and patronifed by the Earl of Shaftfbury (1), "the peace and quietnefs of Ireland was a great difappointment to that Earl, and his party; and they took all poffible methods to provoke, and exafperate the people of that kingdom, already too much difcontented. For that end, they procured orders from the council of Ireland, to tranfmit fevere bills againft the Irifh Catholics in matter of religion, in hopes to drive them into a new rebellion. It was now propofed to introduce the teft-act, and all the Englifh penal laws, into Ireland; and that a proclamation fhould be forthwith iffued for encouraging all perfons, that could make any further difcoveries of the horrid Popifh plot, to come in, and declare the fame *(a).*

The Duke of Ormond, then Lord Lieutenant of Ireland, and luckily, at that juncture, in England, employed all his intereft with the King, to prevent the calling a parliament for thefe cruel purpofes (2). "I will venture," fays his Grace, in a letter to the Earl of Arran on that occafion, " to tell you, without

---

(1) Cart. Orm. vol. ii. fol. 494.   (2) Cart. Orm. vol. ii. fol. 535.

(a) On the firft report of the Popifh plot, "Peter Talbot, Archbifhop of Dublin, in a dangerous fit of the ftone, was imprifoned in the caftle. Orders were iffued, that all officers fhould repair to their refpective garrifons; that Popifh ecclefiaftics fhould depart from the kingdom, Popifh feminaries, and convents, fhould be fuppreft. Informations quickly multiplied, and directions were received from England to feize Richard Talbot, (afterwards Duke of Tyrconnel) Lord Mountgarret and his fon, and a Colonel of the name of Peppard. Lord Mountgarret, reprefented as a dangerous confpirator, was of the age of eighty years, bed-ridden, and in a ftate of dotage; and, to the further difcredit of the evidences, no Colonel Peppard was known, or could be found in Ireland." Lel. Hift. of Irel. vol. iii. p. 474.

out a cypher, that the reason why the calling of a parliament in Ireland sticks, is the severity of two bills transmitted against the Papists; the one taking away the votes of Peers, whilst they are Papists; and the other inflicting death upon a certain sort of Popish clergy, if found in Ireland; the one seeming unjust, and the other cruel, and neither necessary. For my part, I confess, if I had been here, when the expelling of the Popish Lords passed, I should have voted against it in conscience, and prudence; in conscience, because I know no reason why opinion should take away a man's birth-right; or why his goods, or lands may not be as well taken away; since money misapplied is, for the most part, a more dangerous thing in disaffected hands, than a word in his mouth. And I think no less of the other bill, for upon serious, and cool thoughts, I am against all sanguinary laws, in matters of religion purely, and properly, so called."

"It (3) was a terrible slur upon the credit of the plot in England, that after it had made such an horrible noise in a nation, where there was scarce one Papist to an hundred Protestants, there should not, for a year, be found one witness from Ireland, to give information of any conspiracy of the like nature in that kingdom, where there were fifteen Papists to one Protestant. But the proclamation above-mentioned, which was published according to the order sent from England, supplied that defect. For upon the encouragement given in it, Tories, and other criminals, confined in jails, pretended to have great discoveries to make on that head, and obtained their liberty, and had money given them by the government of Ireland, to transport them to England for that purpose; though these wretches knew nothing of the matter, till they were instructed by Mr. Hethrington, Lord Shaftsbury's agent in managing and providing for them."

It may not be unentertaining to the reader, to find here an exact description of these witnesses, left us by the Lord Lieutenant himself, after his return to Ireland (4). "At council," says he, "there is little more to do than to hear witnesses, some come out of England, and some producing themselves here, and all, I doubt, forswearing themselves. Those that went out of Ireland with bad English, and worse cloaths, are returned well-bred gentlemen, well-caronated, periwigged, and cloathed. Brogues and leather straps are converted into fashionable shoes and glittering buckles; which, next to the

---

(3) Id. ib.   (4) Carte's Orm. vol. iii.

the zeal Tories, Thieves *(b)*, and Friars have for the Proteſtant religion, is a main inducement to bring in ſhoals of informers. They find it more honourable, and ſafe, to be the King's evidence, than a cowſtealer, though that be their actual profeſſion; but as they have not the honeſty to ſwear truely, they want the wit to ſwear probably *(c)*."

Jones (5), Biſhop of Meath, who was both the procurer, and examiner, of theſe witneſſes in Ireland, had been Scout-maſter General to Oliver Cromwell's army.

Yet, upon the bare teſtimony of theſe notorious miſcreants, ſeveral of the Iriſh nobility, clergy, and gentry, were at that juncture, either thrown into jails, or forced to quit the kingdom. Primate Plunkett, (as Biſhop Burnet informs us, on the report of the Earl of Eſſex, who had been Lord Lieutenant of Ireland, and knew him perſonally) (6), " was a wiſe and ſober man, fond of living quietly and in due ſubjection to the government, without engaging in intrigues of ſtate;" yet he was brought over to England, and condemned, and executed at Tiburn, on the accuſation of theſe ſuborned witneſſes. But the *(d)* Duke of Ormond, by his reſolution, and

---

(5) Id. ib. vol. ii. fol. 498.

(6) Hiſt. of his own times, vol. i. fol. 230.

(b) " I dare not," ſays his Grace in another letter, " ſay, though it be manifeſt, that moſt of our diſcoveries give more diſcredit, than confirmation, to the plot. It is well that I am not like to be charged for a plotter, or a Papiſt." Carte's Orm. vol. ii. Append.
" There were too many Proteſtants then in Ireland," ſays Mr. Carte, " who wanted another rebellion, that they might increaſe their eſtates by new forfeitures. And letters were perpetually ſending into England, miſrepreſenting the Lord Lieutenant's conduct, and the ſtate of things in Ireland. The Earl of Angleſey gave the Duke of Ormond, a friendly advertiſement of thoſe miſrepreſentations and ſuggeſtions againſt his proceedings, made by one of the greateſt perſons in the kingdom, tranſmitted to ſeveral perſons in London, and particularly to ſome members of parliament, and of the privy council." Orm. vol. ii. fol. 482.

On the other had, " ſome perſons to whom the Duke of Ormond's moderation was not agreeable, imagining that he might be driven out of it by the danger of an aſſaſſination, dropped letters in the ſtreets of Dublin, inſinuating a conſpiracy formed for murdering his Grace; and ſeveral pretended to give an account of what they had heard, or ſuſpected of ſuch a deſign. Divers examinations were taken, and the Duke could not well tell at firſt what to think of the matter; as it ſeemed to agree, with what was mentioned in general by Oates, and Dugdale, whoſe depoſitions it was calculated to countenance. But he had too much firmneſs of mind to be moved by ſuch dark and inexplicable informations as were given, to alter a conduct founded on ſo much reaſon, as what he had hitherto obſerved." Id. ib. vol. ii. fol. 481.

(c) Alluding to two Friars that informed againſt the titular Primate Plunkett.

(d) His Grace in one of his letters to England on this occaſion, ſays, " Here is one Owen Murphy authoriſed to ſearch for, and carry over witneſſes, I ſuppoſe to give evidence againſt Oliver Plunket (the Primate.) He has been as far as the county of Tipperary, and brought thence about a dozen people, not like

and activity, put a stop to this spreading mischief, not without exposing himself to the danger of being represented by the faction in England, as a plotter, or a Papist, on that account.

like to say any thing material as to Plunket." Carte's Orm. vol. ii. Append.

His Grace was urged to imprison all the principal Roman Catholics of Ireland at this juncture; but he refused to do it, because, as he said," " it could not be known, how many might be thus driven to desperate courses. It was well known," adds my author, " how much the imprisonments, and other severities of Sir William Parsons had contributed to hurry numbers into the last rebellion ; and neither the Duke, nor the privy council, deemed it prudent to make another experiment whether the same measures might not be attended with the same effects." Lel. Hist. of Irel. vol. iii. p. 547.

AN HISTORICAL AND CRITICAL REVIEW OF THE CIVIL WARS IN IRELAND.

BOOK X.

CHAP. I.

Archbishop King's *State of the Protestants of Ireland, under King* James II. *considered.*

MANY, and foul, are the misrepresentations of Irish Catholics, exhibited in Archbishop King's state of the Protestants of Ireland under King James II. and although Mr. Lesley, a learned contemporary Protestant divine, has demonstratively proved most of his charges to be either absolutely false, or greatly exaggerated, (without any defence, or reply, from his Grace, or his friends) yet the Archbishop's book has passed, with applause, through several editions since Mr. Lesley's decease; and is generally quoted, as of unquestionable authority, by all writers, foreign and domestic, who have since treated of that part of Irish history; while Mr. Lesley's refutation of it, is hardly any where to be met with, having been suppressed by authority, in the first edition of it; and it was then so far stifled in its birth, that it has never since been re-printed.

INSTEAD

INSTEAD of taking pains to extol Mr Lefley's character for (a) veracity, or to depreciate that of Doctor King for the want of it, I shall make use of no other argument, for either purpose, but such as will naturally arise from the plain and certain evidence of facts, alleged and vouched by the former writer, but never disproved, nor so much as contradicted, by the latter.

"No (1) man," says Mr. Lefley, "was, or could be, an higher assertor of passive obedience, than Doctor King had been all his lifetime. Even at the beginning of the revolution, he told a person of honour, from whose mouth I had it, "that if the Prince of Orange came over for the crown, he prayed God might blast his designs." In a letter to a person of undoubted credit, in the year 1686, he said, " the principle of non-resistance, was a steady principle of loyalty; that it was intolerable for the members of any state, to flee to foreign succours, on pretence that their own governors had made laws against reason, conscience, and justice; yet this is one of his principal arguments, in the book above-mentioned, for justifying the revolution. "What I have above-written," adds Lefley, " I have from the person to whom he wrote it, and if he desires it, his letters shall be produced." But it does not appear, that he ever did desire it.

By such feigned assurances of loyalty, which he had often given to King James, after his arrival in Ireland (2), " that King had once so good an opinion of him, that he had him frequently in private, and trusted him in his affairs; until at last, he found he was holding correspondence with his enemies in England, and in the North of Ireland, and he, thereupon, imprisoned him. But his old friend, Chief Justice Herbert, was so far mistaken in

(1) Answ. to King, p. 113.   (2) Id. ib. p. 106.

(a) It will, probably, be objected to this writer's testimony, that he was a non-juror. But to this objection I shall only answer in the words of Bishop Burnet, on a similar occasion. " I never," says that Prelate, " think the worse of men for their different sentiments in such matters; I am sure I am bound to think much better of them, for adhering strictly to the dictates of their consciences, when it is so much to their loss, and when so sacred a thing as an oath is in the case. I wish all, who had the same persuasions, had acted with the same strictness, and tenderness." See Defence of the Bishop of Worcester's Vindication of the church of England, p. 63.

Doctor Swift's testimony of this writer's merits, in his preface to Bishop Burnet's introduction to his history of the Reformation, is worthy of notice. "Without doubt," says he, " Mr. Lefley is unhappily misled in his politics; but he has given the world such a proof of his soundness in religion, as many a Bishop ought to be proud of. I never saw the gentleman in my life: I know he is the son of a great and excellent Prelate, who, upon several accounts was one of the most extraordinary men of his age. I verily believe, that he acted from a mistaken conscience, (in refusing to swear allegiance to K. William,) and therefore I distinguish between the principles, and the person. However, it is some mortification to me, when I see an avowed nonjuror contribute more to the confounding of Popery, than could ever be done by an hundred thousand such introductions." Works, Dub. ed. vol. viii. p. 240.

in him, that he vouched for him at the council-table, with so much zeal, as to say, that he was as loyal a man (to King James) as any that sate at the board; which did retrieve the Doctor from some inconveniences, and continued him, for some time longer, in King James's good opinion."

CHAP. II.

The same Subject continued in general.

SUCH is Lesley's untroverted account of Doctor King, as a subject, and a man. His judgment of him, as author of the book in question, is partly as follows.

" I (1) CAN'T say," proceeds he, " that I have examined into every single matter of fact, which this author relates; I could not have the opportunity; but I am sure I have looked into the most material, and by these you will easily judge of his sincerity in the rest. But this I can say, that there is not one I have enquired into, but I have found it false in the whole, or in part; aggravated, or misrepresented, so as to alter the whole face of the story, and give it perfectly another air, and turn; insomuch, that though many things he says, are true, yet he has hardly spoken a true word, that is, told it truely, and nakedly, without a warp." Mr. Lesley adds this particular caution, for those who peruse that book (2), " that where Doctor King seems most exact, and sets his quotations in the margent, that the reader might suspect nothing, there he is to suspect most, and stand upon his guard."

THESE are heavy accusations, of which, and several others, Mr. Lesley has exhibited many convincing proofs; and more shall be added in the sequel, from undeniable authority. His Grace's continued silence under them, for more than thirty years, that he survived the publication of this answer, is the more wonderful, on account of his solemn attestation of the sacred name of God, in the conclusion of his book, " that he had not misrepresented, or aggravated, any thing therein, in prejudice to any body, or out of favour or affection to a party; or insisted on such particulars, as might seem to serve no other purpose, but to make his adversaries odious."

(1) Id. ib. p. 105.   (2) Id. ib. p. 175.

CHAP. III.

Particular Facts related in Archbishop King's *Book, proved false, concerning Popish Judges and Juries.*

BUT to come now to the test of this solemn attestation; I mean his relation of particular facts. Doctor King tells us (1), "that no sooner had the Papists of Ireland got judges and juries, that would believe them, but they began a trade of swearing, and ripping up what they pretended their Protestant neighbours had said of King James, whilst Duke of York, in the time of the Popish plot; and that of these Protestants, many were found guilty, and excessively fined; and some of them imprisoned for their fines, not being able to satisfy the King, who seized both their body and estates."

THE Doctor likewise informs us (2), " that these Popish judges, and juries, connived at a wicked contrivance, which was discovered to the very bottom, in the county of Meath, to carry on this trade of swearing against all the Protestant gentlemen in the country."

BUT unfortunately for Doctor King's credit, as an historian, that eminent, and zealous *(a)* Protestant nobleman, Henry Earl of Clarendon, Lord Lieutenant of Ireland in 1685, has left us a very different account of the behaviour

---

(1) State of the Protestants, &c. p. 75.   (2) ib. p. 76.

(a) " All the Irish Protestants," says Mr. Lesley, " speak exceeding good things of Lord Clarendon. They never parted with any chief governor with so much regret; and, as I have been told, none courted him more than Doctor King, who was admitted one of his chaplains." Answ p 132. His Lordship himself suspected, that he was recalled from the government of Ireland, on account of his religion " If," says he, " my being a Protestant be the cause of my ill usage, I am so far from being troubled, that I look upon it as a great honour, to be found worthy to suffer for my religion." State Let. vol. ii. p. 158. Harris informs us, " that he was so much depended upon by the Protestants of Ireland, that after the Prince of Orange's arrival in England, they made all their applications to him, through his Lordship." Life of King William, fol. 187 That the Roman Catholics of Ireland did not think him partial in their favour, appears from one of his Excellency's letters from Waterford, Sept. 12th, 1686, wherein he says, " Lord Tyrone came to see him there, and had continued with him all the time of his being there; but that not one of the other Roman Catholic gentlemen had been with him. And that none of the Roman Catholic inhabitants of that city (tho' there were there some pretty considerable merchants,) had taken notice of him." State Let. vol. i. p. 402.

viour of these Popish judges and juries, on that occasion. He tells us, " that, when these Popish judges went to the assizes in the county of Down and Londonderry, where many considerable persons were to be tried for words formerly spoken against King James (3), they took as much pains, as it was possible, to quiet the minds of the people, wherever they went; and that they took care to have all the juries mingled half English, half Irish." And particularly with respect to the county of Meath, where Doctor King tells us, they principally connived at this wicked trade of swearing, his Lordship adds (4), " that Judge Daly (one of these Popish judges) did, at the assizes of that county, enlarge much on the unconscionableness of indicting men upon words spoken so many years before; that he told the jury, that most of those then charged before him in court, could give a good account of themselves, and were well known in the countries where they lived, and that thereupon the juries, the major part of whom were Irish, acquitted them;" that Mr. Justice Nugent (another Popish Judge) (5), " made the same declaration at Drogheda, where several persons were tried for words, upon bills found at the former assizes; and that they were all acquitted, except one man, who was found guilty, and fined five pounds*(b)*."

But who would suspect this impartial writer to have known, while he was committing these falsehoods to the press, that Lord Clarendon had, by King James's express command, published a (6) proclamation, so early as July 1686, (the Popish judges were made (7) only in April preceding,) " forbidding all prosecutions of that kind; and ordering, that no person should be accountable for any words spoken against his Majesty, at any time before his accession ;" which proclamation his Excellency immediately sent off to the judges, then on their circuits. Yet these known facts, Doctor King has disingenuously suppressed; for nobody, I think, will have the hardiness to pretend, that he, who was one of his Lordship's chaplains, and a busy enquirer into all the transactions of that time, could possibly be ignorant of a matter so notorious as this proclamation must have then been, in every part of Ireland.

(3) State Let. Dub. ed. vol. i. p. 326.   (4) ib.   (5) ib.   (6) Id. ib. p. 324.
(4) Id. ib. vol. i. p. 162.

(b) That Lord Clarendon was no way partial in his account of the Irish judges, appears from a letter of his March 20th, 1685-6, wherein we find this passage: " Some letters say, there will be an alteration among the judges (in Ireland) but that men will be sent out of England to fill their places; and that none of the natives will be admitted; I wish it may be true." State Let. vol. i. p. 108.

CHAP. IV.

The Execution of Captain Afhton.

THE execution of one Captain Afhton for murder, is another of Doctor King's inftances of the cruelty and injuftice, of thefe Popifh judges and juries. "The Papifts," fays he (1), "might kill whom they pleafed, without fear of the law, becaufe they had Popifh judges and juries on their fide; but if any killed, or hurt them, they were fure to fuffer *(a)*." And then he complains, that Afhton was hanged for killing a Papift; who, he fays, "abufed his wife in the ftreet." What the nature of the abufe was, or whether it was by words or actions, he does not inform us; from whence we may probably conclude, that it was not of a very heinous nature; and that the Doctor would infinuate, that the killing of a Papift, tho' but upon a flight provocation, ought not to be punifhed, as a capital offence.

BUT we find that Lord Clarendon, in whofe time it happened, thought very differently of this affair. For his Lordfhip informs us, that, at that gentleman's trial (2), "care was taken to have a good jury; but that they brought him in guilty; that great interceffion was made with himfelf in his behalf; but that, in good earneft, the fact was fo horrid, and fo fully proved, and the Captain had fo little to fay for himfelf, that he did not think him a fit object of the King's mercy." His Lordfhip adds (3), "that the pannel was made up of the beft men in the city; that is," fays he, "men of the beft reputation, and credit, without regard to religion; and that there were as many of the one perfuafion, as of the other returned; that the Captain excepted

against

(1) State of the Proteft. p. 47.   (2) State Let. p. 196.   (3) ib.

(a) There is a paffage in Lord Clarendon's letters, which demonftrates a very different difpofition in thefe Popifh judges towards Proteftants, from what Doctor King has imputed to them. "Upon a full hearing," fays his Lordfhip, "at the council-board, there was a complaint of the commiffioners of the revenue proved againft a juftice of peace, who had difcountenanced a collector of the excife in the execution of his office. When the board came to deliberate what to do, "This," adds his Lordfhip, "is remarkable, that feveral of our new Roman Catholic counfellors, tho' the juftice was an Englifhman, and a Proteftant, were for putting off the bufinefs, and particularly the three new (Popifh) judges faid the gentleman would be more careful for the future." State Let. vol. i. p. 292. His Excellency alfo takes notice of the fingular modefty of thefe Popifh judges, when they were made privy counfellors; and fays, "they were almoft out of countenance on that occafion; that they thought it would bring envy upon them, when it was not needful; they being, every way, as well qualified to do the King all poffible fervice, without the burden of that honour." ib. 231.

against as many of the jury, as the law allowed him, who were all Roman Catholics; but that the rest, who were very honest men, regarded nothing but the evidence and their oaths."

EVEN Chief Justice Nugent, a Papist, and one of the judges before whom this unhappy man was tried, and to whom Doctor King has been pleased to give a most profligate character (4), " had been with his Excellency, and desired he might intercede with his Majesty, that he would be pleased to bestow the Captain's estate upon his wife and children." Which, for any thing I have found to the contrary, appears to have been done.

CHAP. V.

The Affair of the Quo Warrantos against the Corporations not truly stated by Doctor King.

BUT these Popish judges, not content with taking away the lives and properties of Protestant individuals, conspired, it seems, with the Popish lawyers, to destroy whole corporate bodies, by issuing quo-warrantos against their charters; although, (if we believe Doctor King,) (1) " there was not one of these corporations found to have forfeited, by a legal trial, so that all the corporations in the kingdom were dissolved without any reason, or pretence, of abuse of privilege."

" BUT (2) will any man believe, that lawyers, (and some of them, this author acknowledges, understood their profession) would, bring a quo-warranto against a charter, and not so much (a) as pretend any abuse,

---

(4) Id. ib. p. 204.   (1) State of the Protest. p. 68.   (2) Lesley's Answ.

(a) " The several corporations in Ireland having forfeited their charters by miscarriages, misdemeanors, and other offences during the rebellion in 1641, and since, Charles II. had empowered his chief governor of that kingdom to grant new Charters to such of these corporations, as he should think fit; and for such of them as should not make application for renewing their charters, to issue quo-warrantos against them for avoiding the same. And King James being informed that very few had made such application, directed his deputy Tyrconnel to cause these quo-warrantos to be issued, by which their former charters were made void, and new ones given them with additional franchises." See Harris's Life of King William. It appears from Lord Clarendon, " that King James's intention in all this was nothing more than that religion should be no hinderance to the natives from enjoying the benefit of being freemen, and holding offices, as the rest of his subjects did." State Let. But Dr King would have that benefit monopolized in the hands of Protestants alone, excluding the papists from freedom, and votes in the corporations." State of the Protest. p. 66.

abuse *(b)*, or forfeiture? Of Mr. Nangle, the then Attorney General, who was chiefly employed in that business, Lord Clarendon makes very honourable mention in several of his letters (3), " as a man of great knowledge, very able in his profession, and of the best reputation for learning, as well as honesty, amongst that people."

But Doctor King's precipitate passion, or prejudice, against these Popish judges and lawyers, seems to have so far transported him, that he has entirely mistaken, or misrepresented, this transaction. " Lord (4) Tyrconnel *(c),*" he tells us, " knowing that the Protestants would not give up their charters, did endeavour to prevail with them, to admit Papists to freedom and offices, in their corporations, that, by their means, he might have their charters surrendered; but," adds he, " the resolution of the Lord Mayor of Dublin spoiled that design, and forced the King to bring quo-warrantos against them." Harris, in his life of King William, has retailed this story from King, and dates it in the year 1686, in the mayoralty of Sir John Knox. But it is manifest, from Lord Clarendon's authentic account of these matters, that the Lord Mayor and Aldermen of Dublin, and many other corporations, had been prevailed upon, long before Tyrconnel's time, to admit Papists to freedom and offices among them (5); " for his Lordship had himself dispensed with no less than fifteen Roman Catholic merchants of Limerick, according to the King's order, from taking the oath of supremacy, when admitted to the Common-council of that city; and, in a letter to Lord Sunderland, July 6th, in this very year, his Excellency says (6), " that he had sent letters to all the corporations for giving their freedoms to all the Roman Catholics, as to his Majesty's other subjects, without tendering them the oath of supremacy; and for presenting

(3) vol. i. p. 72. vol. ii. p. 373.   (4) State of the Protest. p. 67.   (5) State Let. vol. i.
(6) ib. vol. i. p. 304.

(b) Upon much less provocation, Capel Earl of Essex, Lord Lieutenant of Ireland, (that celebrated champion for liberty, and who was said to have fallen a martyr to it) thought the bringing of quo warrantos against the charter of Dublin necessary. That chief governor, in a letter to Secretary Coventry, in 1674-5. on occasion of a trifling dispute between the Aldermen and Commons of that city, says, " in my own thoughts, I am of opinion, and have been long so, that nothing will reduce this city to a due composure, unless it be the avoiding their charter by quo-warranto, and granting them a new one ; for the body of the Commons are so numerous,—and most of them being extreme poor men, are continually mutinous and factious ; whereas, if they had a new charter, and the number reduced to fewer, and those named out of the most substantial chief trading men of the city, whose interest it is to be quiet, I am confident, it would be the only way to bring them into order and peace." Essex's Letters, p. 114.

(c) Doctor King was so ridiculously prejudiced against such natives of Ireland, as were afterwards appointed to city-offices, under Tyrconnel's government, that not content to represent them, as poor and unworthy, (the contrary of which can be proved,) he tells us, " their very names spoke barbarities." State of the Protest. p. 69. So much, it seems, were the Doctor's delicate ears offended with the harsh sound of Irish firnames.

senting to him such as should be chosen into offices, that he might dispense with their taking the said oath according to the rules; that he had then received returns from about twenty of the corporations, all full of duty and obedience; and that, in some places, where they had two bailiffs, which are there the chief magistrates, they had, without any contest, chosen one of each religion."

And although, in the year 1686, some seeming opposition, in that respect, was made by the Lord Mayor and Aldermen of Dublin; or rather as Lord Clarendon expresses it (7), " not so speedy a compliance given to the King's commands as he expected ;" yet it is by no means true, that they were so very resolute, or uncomplying in that particular, as King and Harris have represented them. On the contrary, it appears, that they afterwards not only complied with the King's orders, but also made a proper, and reasonable apology, for their not having done so sooner. For his Excellency, having (8) sent for the Lord Mayor of Dublin to come to him, he, with the Aldermen, expressed great readiness to obey the King in any thing he should command them; but said, that it being their constitution, that freemen should be elected only at certain terms, they could not prevail with the Commons (without whose consent that rule could not be altered) though they tried twice, by his Lordship's positive directions, to admit any freemen, till the usual time; and when that time came," adds his Lordship, " all the Roman Catholics, who made application, were admitted *(d)*."

CHAP.

(7) ib.   (8) ib.

(d) The following extracts from papers relating to the admitting of Papists into corporations, and sent by Secretary Coventry to Lord Essex, in 1674, chief governor of Ireland, may throw some light on this affair.

" In most of the corporations of Ireland, the freemen were generally papists in the year 1641, and so continued till about the year 1652; and although most of the persons who were then free, may now be presumed to be dead, yet there being a custom in most corporations, that all the sons of freemen are also free of the corporations, whereof their fathers were free, there cannot but be now very many Papists living, who are entitled to their freedoms in their several corporations. In the Usurper's time, all the Papists, that were freemen, were hindered from enjoying the benefit of their freedom.

" Since the King's restoration, many disputes have happened concerning the Papists (in Ireland) who were formerly free, being admitted again into the corporations.

" By a letter from the King, dated the 22d of May, 1661, his Majesty declared his pleasure, that the respective former inhabitants, natives and freemen, and such as had right to be freemen in any of the cities or towns in this kingdom (Ireland) should be forthwith restored to their accustomed privileges and immunities, and admitted to trade, in the said respective cities and towns, as freely as heretofore, without making any national distinction, or giving any interruptions, upon pretence of difference of judgment, or opinion, in matters of religion. Notwithstanding this letter, many of the antient freemen, that were Papists, were kept out of several of the corporations.

" His Majesty afterwards, by his letters bearing date 26th February, 1671, in the time of Lord Berkley's government, did again declare his pleasure that all

CHAP. VI.

The Behaviour of the Irish Priests, and new Recruits, under King James, impartially considered.

HAD Doctor King been as candid in his relation of facts, as he ought, and as he solemnly professed to be; at the same time that he reproached the Papists of Ireland, with the forwardness of some of their clergy, and the insolence of the new recruits, at this period, in Dublin; (neither of which shall I undertake to justify) he would have given us, at least, some intimation of the provocations, which both of them had received from the Protestant inhabitants of that city; which indeed were so great and notorious, that Lord Clarendon takes frequent notice of them in his dispatches into England. In one of these, he complains (1), " that the new recruits were often affronted by the boys in Dublin, and that the soldiers, that were put out, did rap them soundly at fisty-cuffs." From another of these dispatches it appears, that these insults and disorders of the inhabitants of Dublin towards these recruits had risen so high, that his Lordship was obliged, " to send to the (2) Lord Mayor, to let him know, that he expected he would keep the town in order, and not suffer any rudeness to be committed." And, as for the forwardness of the Popish priests, at that juncture, such provocation was really given them from the pulpit *(a)*, and otherwise, not only by the inferior

(1) Ib. vol. i. p. 295. (2) Ib. vol. i. p. 294.

all the antient freemen of the respective corporations should enjoy their former freedoms, and privileges.— Yet in some of the corporations, in which the number of Protestants is great, many of the Papists are still kept out, and hindered from their freedoms. If they should be hindered from their freedoms, they will complain that there is no law to take that benefit from them; that it is against the King's pleasure

(a) On this occasion his Excellency " assured some of the Roman Catholic Bishops, that he would give effectual orders, that whatever should happen of that kind, the parties should not be countenanced, and that their superiors should have notice of them. For that he was too well acquainted with the mischief that sort of loose clergy had done, who would submit to no authority; of which," adds he, " there are

expressly declared in his several letters, and since made public by proclamation; that by the rules, Papists, who are foreigners, may be admitted to be free in the corporations, and that it will be hard to bar Papists, who are natives, from enjoying that freedom, which has been already granted them." Lord Essex's Letters, p. 185-6-7. &c.

too many in all religions." State Let. vol. i. p. 136-7. In this letter to Lord Sunderland, his Excellency acquaints him, " that he was then giving the necessary orders, which Lord Sunderland had directed, to all Archbishops, Bishops, Sheriffs, &c. that the Roman Catholic clergy might not be molested in the exercise of their functions." ib.

rior Proteſtant clergy, but even by the Biſhops (3), "that his Excellency thought himſelf bound to ſend for the Biſhop of Meath to rebuke him, on that account; and to let him know his mind on that head, which that Biſhop promiſed to obſerve." And (4) although he had reſolved " to hold the ſame courſe with other Biſhops, and had even ſuſpended ſome of the turbulent preachers (5)," yet, he ſays, "he could not anſwer, but ſome impertinent things would be ſaid even before himſelf; and that he durſt not undertake to keep the inferior clergy of Dublin within the bounds of duty and good manners."

C H A P. VII.

The Conduct of the Iriſh and Engliſh Army compared.

IF the new Iriſh recruits were inſolent and flagitious, their officers, according to Doctor King's account of them, were infinitely more ſo. Theſe officers were, in truth, the ſons of ſome of the beſt, but deſpoiled, families of the kingdom. But, if we *(a)* believe the Doctor (1), " they were the ſcum, and *(b)* raſcality of the nation, who ruined all the Proteſtant inns; and might have killed whom they pleaſed, without fear of the law." In ſhort, there was no irregularity, vice, or villainy, which he has not repreſented them capable of, and diſpoſed to commit.

Mr.

(3) Id. ib. vol. i. p. 84.   (4) ib.   (5) ib.
(1) State of the Proteſtants, p. 47.

(a) Lord Chief Juſtice Keating, ("whom," as Lord Clarendon teſtifies, "all parties owned to be a good man," State Let. vol. i. p. 140.) in a letter dated 1688, ſays, "that the Roman Catholic nobility and gentry of Ireland were univerſally concerned both in the Iriſh army then raiſed, and in that, which was afterwards to be raiſed." Append. to King's ſtate of the Proteſtants, &c. Lord Clarendon himſelf,

(b) This ſcurrility ſeems leſs indecently applicable to King William's officers in Ireland; for Marſhal Schomberg, in a letter to his Majeſty from Liſburn, January 1689, tells him, "that moſt of the Iriſh officers under him, particularly thoſe of the Enniſkilleners and Derry-men, were Peaſants." Dalrymple's Mem. vol. ii. p. 72. part ii. The ſame Marſhal Schomberg mentioning the Iriſh army, ſays, "the enemy are not only ſtrong in numbers, but alſo well-diſ-

when in the government, had recommended ſeveral of theſe Roman Catholic officers to be provided for, as Lord Brittas, Captain Butler, Major M'Carthy, Colonel Lacy, and others. State Let. paſſim, and vol i. p. 4. The firſt and laſt of the above-named officers, he ſays, were almoſt ruined by Oates's villainy. ib.

ciplined, and the ſituation of their camp as well choſen as the ableſt generals could contrive." ib. p. 51. Of his own officers he ſays, "I never was in an army, where there were ſo many new and lazy officers. The officers of the artillery are ignorant, lazy, and timorous. I diſcovered that in the artillery, there has been a great deal of roguery." ib. p. 60, 27, et paſſim.

Mr. Lefley has juftly obferved on this occafion, " that there never was, and perhaps never will be, a war, wherein there were not fome diforderly and wicked perfons; and that, that army is beft conducted and difciplined, wherein fuch crimes are feweft and leaft. Now," fays he, " whether the Proteftant army, then in Ireland, was not much more mifchievous and ungovernable, than the Popifh, I appeal to the teftimony of an enemy then on the fpot."

That enemy was Doctor Gorge, fecretary to Marfhal Scomberg, who in a letter to Colonel James Hamilton (2), (after having told him, " that the foldiers in the Proteftant army under King William, robbed and plundered at pleafure, that fome of its *(c)* leaders ridiculed, fcorned, and condemned, all motions for its good government, and order, and faid, that religion was nothing but canting, and debauchery the neceffary practice of a foldier) takes notice, by way of contraft, of the good difcipline, principles, and practices, of the Popifh army under King James, the ftrict proclamations publifhed by that King, for the obfervance of good order, and how the penalties enjoined by them, were feverely and impartially executed." Doctor Gorge adds, " that too many of the Englifh, as well as French and Danes, in King William's army, were highly oppreffive to the poor country-people, whereas," fays he, " their enemies (the Irifh) had reduced themfelves to that order, that they exercifed violence on none, but the properties of fuch as they knew to be abfent, or as they phrafed it, in rebellion againft them; whofe ftock, goods, and eftates, were feized, and fet by the civil government, and the produce applied towards, and for, the charge of the war."

(2) See Append. to Lefley's Anfwer to King.

(c) Marfhal Scomberg, in a letter to King William, in February 169°, informs him, that " the Ennifkillen and Londonderry regiments were upon a footing of licence both to rob and fteal." Dalrymp. Mem. vol. iii. p 78. In another letter, he tells his Majefty, that, " one muft count upon the troops raifed in Ireland, (for his Majefty's fervice,) only as fo many Cravats. That, in the day of battle, they will always throw themfelves upon the firft plunder. That Mr Harbord (Pay-mafter General of his army) had experience of this. For that, having gone one night with his fowling-piece, upon a party with Count Scomberg, and having fallen from his horfe, five or fix Ennifkillen-troopers began to ftrip and rob him, although he cried out that he was Pay-mafter, and that he would give them money to carry him to the camp; but that a French officer, in paffing, having known him, the Ennifkilleners brought him back." Id. ib. p. 66. " I don't love to pillage." adds the Marfhal, " I do what I can to prevent others from doing it, who think of nothing elfe." Id. ib. " Your Majefty," fays the fame, " had need of officers of juftice to reprefs the diforders among thefe people (officers) who are lazy, and live only by theft and pillage." ib. p. 59.

CHAP.

CHAP. VIII.

Irish Rapparees.

ALTHOUGH Doctor King confesses (1), "that the hearts of the Irish soldiery were generally sunk, and that they openly declared themselves to be desirous to lay down their arms, proposing to themselves no other conditions, but to return to the station in which they were in at King James's accession;" yet, he at the same time, represents that whole army as a band of furious freebooters and robbers *(a)*, " plundering the Protestants in every part of the country; and its new commissioned officers, under the denomination of rapparees, as committing so many depredations and outrages, on their Protestant neighbours, that they could not be safe in their houses." This conscious untruth, I say, he was not ashamed to assert, in the body of his book, though, in his appendix to it, he has published a letter of Lord Chief Justice Keating already cited, which testifies (2), " that the thefts and robberies, then committed, were done in many places, by the cottiers and idlers in the country, and often by King William's soldiers, though generally fathered on King James's army." And even Burnet has owned, that (3) " many of King William's army were suspected of robbing in their turns, though the rapparees carried the blame of all *(b)*."

(1) State of the Protest. p. 82.   (2) See Append.   (3) Hist. of his own times, vol. ii.

(a) This the Doctor asserts without proof; but if we may rely on what Marshal Scomberg says of the officers under his command, we shall find them much worse than those of King James. " The troops of Londonderry, and Enniskillen," says he, " (as well as the French) pillage on their side.—I must, however, tell your Majesty, that if our Irish Colonels were as able in war, as they are to pillage the country, and not to pay the soldiers, your Majesty would be better served by them. I have worked all this week to regulate what the captains should give their soldiers, to prevent their cheating the men." Dalrymp. vol. iii. p. 50. In another letter to the King, wherein he censures one Major Broadnax, he says, " there are many other officers whom I could wish in England. I never saw any more wicked, and more interested." ib. p. 33.

(b) " They (among the Irish) who received protections from King William's generals, and were yet plundered by his soldiers, ran with particular animosity to swell the number of these ravagers." Lel. Hist. of Irel. vol. iii. p. 589. " The people exclaimed, in the bitterness of grief, that the (English) army were worse than the rapparees." Id. ib. p. 590.

The following passage from Bishop Burnet, is applicable on this occasion. " The King's (William's) army in Ireland was almost as heavy on the country, as the rapparees were. There was a great arrear due to them; for which reason, when the King settled a government in Ireland, of three Lords Justices, he did not put the army under the civil authority, but

THE accounts, seriously given us of these Irish rapparees, by some British writers, are really as ridiculous, as their treatment by the English soldiers, was cruel and unjust. We are told (4), "that they carried the locks of their muskets in their pockets, and hid them in dry holes of old walls; and that they laid their muskets charged, and closely corked up at the muzzel, and touch-hole, in ditches, with which they were acquainted; that their retreat was safe; for that they hid themselves in the unequal surfaces formed by boggrafs; or laid themselves all along in muddy water, with nothing but their mouths, and nostrils above it."

BUT Mr. Lesley's account of them, who had much better means of information, is both piteous and shocking. He relates it as a well-known fact, "that (5) those, who were then called rapparees, and executed as such, were for the most part, poor harmless country people; that they were daily killed, in vast numbers, up and down the fields; or taken out of their beds, and shot immediately; which," adds he, "many of the Protestants did loudly attest; and many of the country gentlemen, as likewise several officers of King William's army, who had more bowels, or justice, than the rest, did abhor to see what small evidence, or even presumption, was thought sufficient to condemn men for rapparees; and what sport they made to hang up poor Irish people by dozens, almost without pains to examine them; they hardly thought them human kind." In Dean Story's list of persons, who died in this war, there are (6), " of rapparees killed by the army, or militia, one thousand nine hundred and twenty-eight; of rapparees killed and hanged by the soldiers, without any ceremony, one hundred and twenty-two."

(4) Sir John Dalrymp. Mem. of Brit. and Irel. part. i. p. 176.   (5) Answ. to King.
(6) Sir John Dalrymp. ubi supra, p. 176.

kept them in a military subjection to their officers; for he said, since the army was not regularly paid, it would be impossible to keep them from mutiny, if they were put under strict discipline, and punished accordingly. The under officers finding, that they were only answerable to their superior officers, took great liberties in their quarters; and instead of protecting the country, they oppressed it. The King had brought over an army of 7000 Danes, but they were cruel friends, and though they were masters; nor were the English troops much better,—but the pay, due for some months, being now sent over, the orders were changed, and the army was made subject to the civil government. Yet it was understood, that instructions were sent to the Lords Justices, to be cautious in the exercise of their authority over them; so the country still suffered much by these forces." Hist. of his own times, vol. ii. fol. 39. Even Harris confesses, " that the disorders, and robberies committed by King William's army, afforded matter for infinite complaints, that it was found by experience, that that army was almost as heavy on the country as the rapparees; that they took vast liberties in their quarters, and, instead of protecting the country, oppressed it. And that, notwithstanding the orders of the Lords Justices, extravagant outrages were daily committed by it." Life of King William, fol. 295-6.

CHAP.

CHAP. IX.

A Conspiracy of the Protestants of Dublin against the Government.

DOCTOR King must have entertained a very mean opinion of his readers' understanding, if he expected to be believed when he said (1), " that the government of Ireland, during Tyrconnel's administration, purposed to ruin the trade of both Protestants and Papists, in order to make King James absolute and despotic; that, for the same end, it had formed a scheme, to hang up one half of the Protestants, and starve the other *(a)*." These notions are so perfectly burlesque, that they do not deserve a serious answer; and yet the Doctor has so gravely set about proving the latter assertion, from the circumstance of disarming the Protestants of Dublin, on the 24th of February 1688, and on the 20th of July 1689, that, I hope, I shall be excused for taking some notice of it.

As for the first disarming (2), " this author himself knew, (and probably at that time, avowed) that the necessity of it was very great, and urgent; as Derry had before *(b)*, on the 7th of December 1688, shut its gates against the King's army; and as the Enniskilleners *(c)* had marched, attacked and defeated,

---

(1) State of the Protest. p. 71, 74.

(2) Lesley's Answ. p. 77.

(a) He is guilty of still greater extravagance in saying, " that the Protestants could not but conclude, that King James was so intent upon destroying them,

that so he compassed that design, he cared not if he enslaved himself, and the kingdoms." State of the Protest. p. 59.

(b) " By an order of the Irish Commons, December 7th, 1695, the Lord Lieutenant was acquainted, that it was the unanimous opinion of that house, that the late rebellion in this kingdom could not be thought to have begun before the 10th of April 1689, being the time given by his Majesty's (King William's) declaration to the Irish to lay down their arms. But that it should seem more reasonable to have its first beginning from the time Duke Scomberg landed with with his army in the kingdom; that till Duke Scomberg's landing, the late King James's authority was

submitted to, almost through the whole kingdom; and that what was taken from the Protestants, before that time, was disowned by the late King James, as may appear by several proclamations declaring, that whoever should plunder any Protestant, should be answerable for the same, and undergo the penalties of the law." Com Jour. vol. ii. fol. 801. N. B. August 13th. 1689. Duke Scomberg landed at Bangor in the North of Ireland, with about 10,000 men. Which, then, of the two parties in arms so long before that time, ought to be deemed rebels?

(c) These Enniskilleners were merciless enemies. At the battle of Lisnilkea, they " defeated, and pursued the Irish with great slaughter, granting quarter to none but officers. About two thousand fell by the

weapons of an enemy, transported by zeal, and resentment. Above five hundred plunged into lake Earne, and but one of that multitude escaped." Lel. Hist. of Irel. vol. iii. p. 534.

defeated, a party of his Majesty's forces. He knew, that the Protestant gentlemen in Ulster had sent a deputation to the Prince of Orange, December the 8th 1688; that they had received commissions from him (and they actually proclaimed him in the beginning of March following) that, by reason of a *(d)* villainous forged letter, found in Cumber, setting forth, that the Papists intended to massacre all the Protestants, the whole North of Ireland appeared of a sudden in one blaze, though the Protestants then were so far from having any reason to fear the poor Irish there, as they pretended they did fear them, that they had them panting under their feet, in as much submission, as ever a hawk had a lark."

Doctor King himself confesses, that, before King James left England, the Protestants of Dublin had entered into a plot, to (3) seize the Lord Deputy with the castle, where the stores of arms and ammunition (*e*) lay (4); " he knew, that these Protestants (and himself among the rest) had a private understanding, and connection with the Northern rebels, as they were then called; that when they were disarmed, February 24th, 1688, all the Protestants, generally, in Ulster, Munster, and Conaught, and in all Ireland, except Dublin, and other parts of Leinster, (which the Lord Deputy kept in awe, with what forces he had) were then actually, in arms in opposition to the government, and had entered into associations, to carry on their war. And he has even owned (5), " that King James's army was but an handful to the Protestants, there being even after the disarming, men and arms enough in Dublin, says he, to have dealt with them." And yet this impartial writer has represented the government's disarming the Protestants, at such a critical juncture, as nothing less than a design to massacre them.

(3) State of the Protest. p. 82. (4) Lesley, ubi supra, and p. 189. (5) King, ib. p. 82.

(d) Chief Justice Keating, says, " Copies of that letter were dispersed all over the Kingdom." Append. to state of the Protest. " That letter caused the Protestants of the North to meditate the design of rising against the government." Lel. vol. iii. p. 513.

(e) " When the news," says he, " came to Ireland, that King James had sent commissioners to treat with the Prince of Orange, it was proposed by some to seize the castle of Dublin. The success was extremely probable; considering that the Papists, besides the four thousand of the army, were generally without arms; and that those who were in arms, were raw and cowardly. To do it effectually, there needed no more, than to seize the Deputy Tyrconnel, &c. King's State of the Protest. p. 83.

CHAP.

CHAP. X.

The disarming of the Protestants further considered.

AS for the second disarming of the Protestants, on the 20th of July, 1689, (1) " It was in the very heat of the war, between King James, and the Northern associators, when Kirk had came from England, and was riding with his ships in Loughfoil, for the relief of Derry; which, with the before-mentioned conspiracy of the Protestants of Dublin, to seize the Lord Deputy and castle, will surely justify the suspicion which the government entertained of these Protestants, from the beginning."

WITH respect to the scheme of starving one half the Protestants of Dublin, which Doctor King has imputed to King James, Mr. Lesley observes (2), " that the hanging two of his Irish soldiers before a Protestant baker's door, for stealing two loaves, not worth a shilling; and the leaving them to hang there forty-eight hours (which Doctor Gorge testifies) to terrify others, did not look like starving the Protestants of Dublin; but rather like feeding them, by letting them have bakers of their own, and protecting them in that manner." And as for that King's design of hanging the other half of the Protestants, Mr. Lesley also observes, " that in all the time the Protestants of Dublin were in King James's power, viz. in summer 1689, he did not hang one of them, though some of them deserved it by the law then, as Doctor King —— could witness."

(1) Lesley, ubi supra.   (2) Ubi supra. See Doctor Gorge's letter. Append

CHAP. XI.

General De Rosen's *Cruelty before Derry.*

AFTER Derry had shut its gates against King James, and several times refused to submit to his authority upon any conditions whatever, General De Rosen, a foreigner, was sent to besiege it; who made use, indeed, of a barbarous, tho' not unusual, expedient to reduce it under his Majesty's obedience. For, finding that the town was in extream want of provisions, he purposed to increase their distress, by adding to their number; for which purpose, he issued orders for a general driving of all the Protestants, protected, and unprotected, within thirty miles round; who were brought to his camp, and placed before the walls of the town, in hopes that their friends within would receive them into it, rather than suffer them to remain in so perilous a situation. On account of this inhuman order of De Rosen, Doctor King thought himself entitled to brand the whole Irish army under him, with the decent appellation of (a) murderers," because (1), " he did not remember to have

(1) State of the Protestants, &c.

(a) " Had Doctor King," says Mr. Lesley, " such a story as that of Glenco, to tell of any of King James's officers in Ireland, O! what declamations we should have of the bloody Irish cut-throats, massacrers, &c. And what use would he have made of their giving it under their hands, that what they did, was by the King's express command, and none punished for it?" Answ. to King, p. 184.

That shocking story of Glenco is thus briefly related by a late intelligent and unprejudiced writer. " A proclamation was published in Autumn, 1691, which declared that all rebels who took the oaths to the government, before the first of January ensuing, should be pardoned All the 'attainted chieftains of the Highlands, except M'Donald of Glenco, took the oaths before the time prefixed Upon the last day of December, he went to Fort William, and desired the oaths to be tendered to him by the governor of the fortress, who, as he was not a civil magistrate, refused to administer them. M'Donald then went to Inverary, the country town, to take them; but by bad weather was prevented from reaching it, till the term prescribed by the proclamation was elapsed. The

Sheriff scrupled at first, but was prevailed upon at last, to receive his allegiance. Advantage was taken of M'Donald's not having complied literally with the terms of the proclamation, and a warrant for proceeding to execution was procured from the King, which was signed both above and below with his own hand. Sir John Dalrymple, the secretary, gave orders that the execution of it should be effectual, and without any previous warning. For this purpose, in the month of February, two companies went, not as enemies, but as friends, to take quarters in the valley of Glenco, where all the clan lived. To conceal the intention the better, the soldiers were of their own lineage. Highlanders of Lord Argyle's regiment. They were all received with the rude, but kind, hospitality of the country. They continued in the valley near a fortnight, and then, in the night-time rose to butcher their hosts! Captain Campbell of Glenlyon, who was uncle to the wife of one of M'Donald's sons, and had supped and played cards with M'Donald's family the night before, commanded the party. Thirty-eight men were slain. The rest would have shared the same fate, had not the alarm been given by one of M'Donald's

have met any thing like it in history." Had the Doctor been a little more conversant with, or mindful of the history of his own country, he would have found, that in the reign of Queen Elizabeth, and since also, many orders of equal, or greater cruelty had been issued, by some of the most celebrated English commanders of those times, in their several expeditions against the Irish. In the year 1602, Lord Deputy Mountjoy boasted, in a letter to the English council [2], " that with his army, he had destroyed their corn, and caused a famine; that being the only sure way," adds he, " to reduce, or root them out." And his Secretary, Morrisson [3], " thought the war was then no way so likely to be ended, as by a general famine." Which, as we have already seen, they did, at last completely effect. In the list of Sir William Cole's boasted exploits against the insurgents in 1641, we find [4], " that within a few months, he had starved and famished, five thousand four hundred and fifty seven of the Irish." And when the garrison of Limerick, which was besieged by Ireton, in 1650, and like that of Derry, was in great want of provisions, had turned out several useless persons [5], " that barbarous commander caused some of them to be executed, and the rest to be whipped back into the town (b)."

In September 1690, the Lords Justices of Ireland issued a proclamation, which actually produced a greater famine among the Irish, than that which De Rosen's driving was only intended to produce [6]. By that proclamation, " the wives, children, and families of all those, who were in arms against King William, and of all those who had been killed in the same cause, and of all absentees, were ordered to quit all places under his Majesty's obedience, upon pain of being treated as spies and enemies; by which means, great multitudes, especially of women and children, were driven into the Irish

[2] Morris Hist of Ireland, fol 115.   [3] Id. ib. fol. 68.   [4] Borl H'ss. of the Ir Reb.
[5] Ludlow's Memoirs.   [6] Lesley, ubi supra.

nald's sons, who over-heard one of the soldiers say to another, " He liked not the work; he feared not to fight the M'Donald's in the field, but had scarcely courage to kill them in their sleep; but that their officers were answerable for the deed, not they." This

(b) The celebrated Mr. Spencer, after having mentioned, that Lord Deputy Gray (whose Secretary he was) in carrying on the war against the Irish in Munster, in 1580, " had driven them to such an extremity of famine, that they digged dead carcasses out of the graves for food," was not ashamed to conclude in these shocking words, " therefore, by all means it must be assured, that

execution made the deeper impression, because the King would not permit any of those, who were concerned in it, to be punished, conscious that in their case his own was involved." Sir John Dalrymple's Memoirs, vol. i. p. 213. Dub ed.

after once entering into this course of reformation, there be afterwards no remorse, nor drawing back, for the sight of any such rueful objects, as must thereupon follow, nor for compassion of their calamities; seeing that by no other means it is possible to cure them." State of Irel. p. 166.

Irish quarters, which haſtened that famine, that was afterwards among them."

"But to ſpeak impartially," ſays Mr. [-] Leſley on that occaſion, "is not the ſtarving of a country, or province, as barbarous as ſtarving a city? And was not crowding all the Iriſh, men, women, and children, over the Shannon in this war, done on purpoſe to reduce them to famine? And it had that effect. Many of theſe wretches died, many women miſcarried, and numbers were ſtarved in that driving over the Shannon; inſomuch that ſome of the (c) Proteſtant officers, who were employed in that expedition, expreſſed the greateſt regret to ſee ſuch lamentable ſpectacles, and were aſhamed of their commiſſions; and thoſe, who were thus driven, had King William's protections in their pockets."

CHAP. XII.

King James countermanded De Roſen's Order as ſoon as he heard of it.

I AM far from vindicating, or even meaning to extenuate the cruelty of De Roſen's order, from any former examples of the ſame kind; though many more than thoſe I have mentioned might be produced, in the commanders of armies, on ſuch occaſions [1]. King James himſelf expreſſed the higheſt reſentment of it, and put a [a] ſtop to its execution, on the firſt notice; and in his circular letters to the governors of towns, and to the officers commanding in chief in the North, he commanded them by no means to obey it; and accordingly, that order was not executed in moſt parts of that province. This, adds [2] Mr. Leſley, I had from the officers, to whom theſe orders were ſent, and from ſeveral Proteſtants who have ſeen them, and can produce them."

[7] Anſw. to King, p 185.   [1] Leſley, ubi ſupra.   [2] Id. ib.

(c) The Iriſh officers likewiſe, who were employed in De Roſen's driving, "executed theſe orders againſt their countrymen," ſays Sir John Dalrymple, "weeping, and obeying; and many of them owned, that the cries they then heard rang for ever after in their ears." Memoirs, part. ii. p. 40.

(a) "It would be inhuman to the memory of the unhappy, to impute the diſgrace of this action to King James. He revoked the order as ſoon as he heard of it, becauſe his own ſufferings had probably taught him to feel for thoſe of others." Dalrymple's Mem. part. ii. p. 41.

them." Mr. Lesley also (3) appeals to the Earl of Granard, then living, " whether the same day, that the news of this order of De Rosen's came to Dublin, his Lordship did not tell King James of it, and whether his Majesty did not answer, that he was grieved for it, that he had sent immediate orders to discharge it, and that none but a barbarous Muscovite, (for such, it seems, De Rosen was,) could have thought of so cruel a contrivance." This Earl was accounted very (4) zealous for the Protestant interest; his Lady was a Presbyterian, and he had constantly received five hundred pounds a year from King Charles the second, to be distributed among the Presbyterian clergy in the North of Ireland, even when he permitted a cruel persecution of their brethren in England."

After all, the garrison of Londonderry was, it seems, resolved not to be hind-hand in cruelty with De Rosen himself (5). " For they erected gibbets, and had determined to hang some Irish gentlemen, who were prisoners in the town, had not De Rosen's order been so soon countermanded. And some add, that they even threatened to eat them after they were hanged;" which, from the extreme want of food, which they then laboured under, seems not to be very improbable.

CHAP. XIII.

The Protestants of Ireland were not deprived of their Churches by King James, as Doctor King sets forth.

KING James, when in Ireland, was not actuated by that intemperate *(a)* zeal for the re-establishment of the Roman Catholic religion, which he had before, on some occasions, discovered in England; probably because he had experienced the unhappy effects of it in the latter kingdom. Even when he

---

(3) ib. p. 100. (4) Har. K. William, fol. 105. Note. (5) Id. ib.

(a) The true cause and motive of King James's endeavours to re-establish the Roman Catholic religion in England, seems not so much to have been any bigoted attachment to that religion, (as is commonly thought) as, " his sufficiently knowing, that he could never be in entire safety, till the Catholic religion was established in England, in such a manner as not to be ruined, or destroyed." These were his own words in a private conference with Barillon, the French embassador. And whoever considers his recent and alarming remembrance of his father's murder, and of his brother's incessant troubles during his whole reign, which were both caused, principally, by those very men, who were the greatest enemies of that religion, and who impudently called themselves the only true Protestants; will abate somewhat of their wonder at these his unconstitutional endeavours to give some establishment to his R. C. subjects. See Sir John Dalrymp. Mem. vol. iii. p. 37.

he sent the Earl of Clarendon Lord Lieutenant of Ireland, one of his instructions to him was [1], " to consult the *(b)* Archbishop of Canterbury in all the religious affairs of that kingdom." And Doctor King [2] confesses, that when he was there in person, he turned out the Popish Mayor of Wexford, for not restoring a church of which the Protestants of that city had been dispossessed; and that he expressed himself with more passion on that occasion, than was usual to him." This was a fact so notoriously true, that the Doctor was ashamed to deny, or conceal it; but he was not ashamed to affirm and publish what was as notoriously untrue, viz. [3] " that in the diocess of Dublin alone, twenty-six churches and chapels were by him taken from the Protestants; and that his Majesty could not, or rather would not, prevent the demolishing, defacing, or seizing of nine churches out of ten."

KING James had published a proclamation, December 13th, 1689, against meddling with any of the Protestant churches in Ireland, as a violation of the act of liberty of conscience [4]. But " his promises to protect the Protestants of that kingdom," says Doctor King, " were meer pretences; the Popish Priests having taken possession of most of the churches there, by his private permission *(c) (d)*."

MR.

[1] Clarend. State Let. vol. i. p. 50. [2] Ubi supra. [3] State of the Protest. &c p. 177. [4] ib. p. 174.

(b) The Earl of Clarendon, in a letter to Lord Sunderland, having informed him, " that a Printer in Dublin had petitioned for liberty to reprint the papers, that were found in the late King's closet, shewing his reasons for becoming a Roman Catholic, as they had been before printed in England; and that he thought it not fit to grant such liberty, till he knew his Majesty's pleasure; soon after wrote to the same Lord, " that he was very glad his Majesty was pleased to approve of what he had done, concerning printing, and stopping of books, from beyond seas." State Let. vol. i. p. 136. and vol. ii. p. 204. His Lordship mentions two parcels of Roman Catholic books, which he stopped, one of religious controversy, called Pax Vobis; and the other, a tract justifying the

(c) King James was hardly ever noted for duplicity of conduct; this can't be said of his competitor for the crown. The Prince of Orange, in a letter to the Emperor, acquainting him with his intended expedition into England, says, " I assure your Imperial Majesty, by this letter, that whatever reports may have been spread, and notwithstanding those, which may be spread for the future, I have not the least intention to do any hurt to his Britannic Majesty, or to those who have a right to pretend to the succession of

insurrection in 1641, and condemning the acts of settlement, under the title of the Bleeding Iphigenia. ib.

King James, in a private letter to the Prince of Orange, Jan. 26, 1686, exhibits a laudable spirit of toleration. " I do easily believe," says he, " you are not for prosecuting any meerly for their religion: I always was, and will be of that mind; and am of your opinion, that it was the very hard usage the Hugonots had, and have still in France, which made that affair of the regulars (Friars, whom the states were then going to banish) be talked on where you are; and hope, as to that, you will continue of the same mind you are." Sir John Dalrym. Mem. vol. iii. p. 72.

his kingdoms, and still less to make an attempt upon the crown." . And a little after; " I ought to intreat your Imperial Majesty to be assured, that I will employ all my credit to provide, that the Roman Catholics of that country may enjoy liberty of conscience, and be put out of fear of being persecuted on account of their religion " Sir John Dalrymp. Mem, vol. iii. p. 170. See Append. Not only the Emperor, but the Pope himself, was cajoled by these deceitful assurances.

(d) And yet Doctor King, at the same time, confesses, " that the Protestants, in their application to government for the recovery of some churches, had

the luck to gain several of the Popish nobility to favour their suits." Ubi supra, p. 176.

Mr. Lefley treats this whole accusation, as a notorious untruth and calumny [5]; he calls upon Doctor King, to shew one Protestant church in Ireland, that was taken away, either by King James's order, or connivance. He affirms that his Majesty was so very careful of the Protestants, in that point, that even at Dublin, where he kept his court, neither the cathedral, nor any parish church in the whole city was taken from the Protestants; he owns, that he took Christ-church for his own use, because it was always reputed the King's chapel. But Doctor King himself," adds he, " and others, then preached passive obedience in their own pulpits in Dublin; and that to such a degree, as to give offence to some of their Protestant hearers, who thought they stretched even to flattery [*e*]."

These positive assertions, publickly and grievously impeaching Doctor King's veracity, having never since been contradicted, or even questioned by him or his friends, afford the strongest presumption, that they were, at that time, generally known and acknowledged to be undeniably true.

CHAP. XIV.

King William's Treatment of the Episcopal Clergy in Scotland, compared with King James's Behaviour towards the Protestant Clergy of Ireland.

Mr. Lefley has drawn a parallel between King William's behaviour to the episcopal clergy of Scotland, and King James's to those of the established church of Ireland, at the same time, viz. in the year 1689; by which it appears, that the former did actually effect in Scotland, what the latter was only suspected to have designed in Ireland.

" When [1]," says he, " the states of Scotland were convened by King William's circular letter of March 1689, the oaths required by the law to be taken by all members of parliament, or any judicature, before they can sit and

[5] Answ. to King.

[1] Pref. to his Answer to King.

(*e*) " Doctor King then used to say, that persecution never hurted religion, but that rebellion destroyed it; and that it would be a glorious sight to see a cartful of clergymen going to the stake for asserting the principles of religion." Lefley, Answ. Pref.

and vote there, being laid afide, the antimonarchical, and fanatical, party were admitted into the houfe; and thereby, becoming the greater number (when the major part of Scotland, and much the greater part of the nobility and gentry, were epifcopal) did afterwards frame an act of grace, pardoning, and acquitting all thofe, that had been concerned in the open and public rebellions of Pentland-hills, and Bothwell-bridge; and thus thefe furies incarnate, the affaffinates of the Lord Archbifhop of St. Andrews, as many of them as were then alive, were enabled to become members of parliament. The fanatical mob, that had rabbled the epifcopal clergy, were armed, and made the guard of this meeting of the eftates, and refolved to facrifice any, who durft oppofe their defigns. They attacked the Archbifhop of Glafcow in the ftreets of Edinburgh, where the convention fate."

" On the 31ft of May, 1689, King William fent inftructions to Duke Hamilton, commiffioner, in thefe words, " you are to pafs an act, turning the meeting of the eftates into a parliament, and the three eftates are to confift of the noblemen, barons, and burgeffes.". Accordingly, the meeting, where the Bifhops formerly fate, was on the 5th of June, 1689, turned into a parliament, the Bifhops being firft excluded. Two days after, that parliament paffed an act fettling Prefbyterian church-government, and on the 22d of July following, abolifhed epifcopacy. This was done in confequence of new inftructions, fent to Duke Hamilton in thefe words, " You are to touch the act abolifhing epifcopacy, as foon as you can; and to refcind all acts inconfiftent therewith." Thefe (a) inftructions were figned by King William, at White-hall, July 17th, 1689, and the act was touched at Edinburgh, on the 22d of the fame month; and thus fell epifcopacy in Scotland, two months and eleven days, after King William and Queen Mary took upon them the crown of that kingdom, which was the 11th of May, 1689."

(a) " They were printed at London, by order of King William, an. 1689; and the Scots acts of convention, and parliament above quoted, are collected and extracted from the regifters, and records of the meeting of eftates and parliament there by the commiffioner, then exercifing the office of Clerk-regifter, and printed Cum Privilegio at Edinburgh, an. 1690." Lefley, ib.

CHAP.

CHAP. XV.

The true Cause of the Decline of the Protestant Religion in Ireland, in the Reign of King James.

THE decline of the Protestant religion in Ireland, in the reign of King James, was not owing, as Doctor King supposes, either to the violence of his government, or the artifice, or industry of his priests; but to the (a) negligence at first, and afterwards, to the self-interestedness, of its own clergy. Of their negligence (1), Lord Clarendon himself (b) frequently complained, in his letters to the Archbishop of Canterbury, whom, as I have already observed, the King had ordered him to consult, in all the religious affairs of that kingdom. And the effects of that negligence, together with the ensuing war, (for which religion was the pretence) were such, that Mr. Lesley says, " he (2) was himself a witness, that Atheism, contempt of all religion, debauchery, and violence, were more notorious and universal, in the Protestant army in Ireland, from the year 1688 to 1692, and more publickly owned, than since he knew the world. That to his knowledge, several had turned Papists, on account of the lewdness of the army, and the apostacy of the clergy. And that, however it might seem a paradox, it was nevertheless true, that there had been more converts to Popery, in England also, and from the same causes, within the

---

(1) State Let. vol. i. p. 215.   (2) Ubi supra, p. 36-7 8.

(a) " I do not find," says Marshal Scomberg, in a letter to King William, from Lisburn, Decem. 1689. " that the ministers apply themselves enough to their duty; whilst the Romish Priests are passionate to exhort the people to die for the church of Rome, and in putting themselves at their head." Dalrymp. Mem. vol. iii. p. 59.

(b) In one of these letters, he tells his Grace, " that very few of the clergy resided in their cures: but employed pitiful curates, which necessitated the people to look after a Romish Priest, or a non-conformist preacher, of both which there was plenty. That he found it an ordinary thing in Ireland for a minister to have five or six, or more cures, and to get them supplied by those, who will do it cheapest. When," adds he, " I discourse with my Lords the Bishops on these things, I confess I have not satisfactory answers." ib. vol. i. p. 215. Even Marshal Scomberg himself complained to King William in 1690, " that the (established) clergy of Ireland were people, that were little attached to their parishes." Dalrymp. Mem. vol. ii. Append. p. 79.

Lord Clarendon complained in 1685-6, " that several of the clergy were absent in England; and among these the Archbishop of Tuam; and the Bishop of Down and Connor: that the former, after three years absence, was resolved to come home; but that the latter, who had been absent from his charge six years, desired to have his licence of absence renewed; and that yet, it was really a shame to think how his diocess lay." State Let. vol. i. p. 215.

the four years above-mentioned, than in four years before that period." That is to say, more in the four years after King James's abdication, when he could make use of neither force nor allurements, to gain converts to his religion, than in all the time, that he had it so amply in his power, to employ both these means of seduction, for that purpose.

Bishop Burnet has accounted for this sudden growth of irreligion and immorality, at that juncture, in the same manner. " A disbelief," says he (3), " of revealed religion, a profane mockery of the christian faith, and the mysteries of it, became scandalous and avowed; and it must be confessed, that the behaviour of many clergymen gave Atheists no small advantage. They had taken the oaths to, and read the prayers for, the present government; they observed the orders for public fasts and thanksgivings; and yet they shewed, in many places, their aversion to our establishment too visibly. This made many conclude that the clergy were a sort of men, that would swear, and pray, even against their consciences rather than lose their benefices; and by consequence, that they were governed by interest, not by principle. Upon the whole matter, the nation was falling into a general corruption, both as to morals, and principles; and that was so much spread among all sorts of people, that it gave us great apprehensions of heavy judgments from Heaven *(c)*."

C H A P. XVI.

The Perplexity of the established Clergy of Ireland after the Coronation of King William.

THE strange versatility, and trimming behaviour, of the Irish clergy on this occasion, is thus freely described by Mr. Lesley (1). " Before the association in the North, they prayed for King James; in the beginning of March following, they proclaimed the Prince of Orange King, and prayed for him; on the 14th of that month, King James's army broke their forces at Dromore, in the North of Ireland; then they prayed again for

King

---

(3) Hist. of his own times, vol. ii.   (1) Answ. to King, p. 108.

(c) Queen Mary, in a letter to King William July 1690, has these remarkable words. "I must put you in mind of one thing, believing it now the season, (the King was then in Ireland,) which is, that you would take care of the church in Ireland. Every body agrees, that it is the worst in Christendom." Dalrymp. Mem. vol. iii. p. 154.

King James, that God might strengthen him to vanquish and overcome all his enemies; in August following, Schomberg came over with an English army; then, as far as his quarters reached, they returned to pray the same prayer for King William, the rest of the Protestants still praying for victory to King James. And yet they say, that, all that while, they all meant the same thing; four times, in one year, praying backward and forward, point blank contradictory to one another. The (2) Bishop of Meath in his speech at the head, and in the name, of the Protestant clergy of Dublin, took pains to clear himself, and them, to King William, from having been so much as trimmers to King James, while he was among them; that is, they were his inveterate enemies. Yet his Lordship was one of the Lords Spiritual mentioned in the address of the parliament of Ireland to that King, on the 10th of May, 1689; in which they abhor the unnatural usurpation of the Prince of Orange, and the treason of those who joined with him in England, and Ireland; and profess to King James with their tongues and hearts, that they will ever assert his rights to his crown, with their lives and fortunes, against the said Usurper, and his adherents, and all other rebels and traitors whatsoever (3)."

C H A P. XVII.

The established Clergy of Ireland laboured under a particular Difficulty on this Occasion.

AFTER King James's abdication, the parliament of England abolished the declaration, viz. (1) " that it was not lawful upon any pretence whatsoever, to take up arms against the King." But this, by some neglect, was still left upon the Irish Protestant clergy, under the penalty of forfeiting their livings, and as many of them as came into livings, after the revolution (among whom Doctor King was one) read the said declaration publickly, in time of divine service, and were to continue so to do, until some parliament took it away. Notwithstanding which, they preached against it, disputed against it, and instructed their congregations against it. And yet, to save their livings, they continued still to subscribe this hated declaration, before their ordinaries; and took certificates under their hands and seals, that they had subscribed it; and openly and publickly read the same, on the Lord's day, in their parish churches,

(2) Id. ib. p. 103.   (3) Id. ib. p. 103.   (1) Lesley's Answ. to King, p. 112.

churches, in the prefence of the congregation there affembled. They read it in the defk, and preached againſt it in the pulpit; and when they came out of the church, railed at the parliament, that impofed it, and wondered and curfed their hard fate, that this declaration was not taken out of their way in Ireland, as it was in England, and wifhed it was done. In the mean time they would lofe nothing by it, they could fwallow."

Nor was their embarraffment much lefs, upon taking the new oaths, that were afterwards framed [2]. " There never was, proceeds Mr. Lefley, fo fudden, and fo fhameful, a turn of men profeſſing religion; and their manner of doing it fo impolitic, as to make it evident, that they took the oaths, at leaſt, with a doubting and *(a)* fcrupulous confcience. For they did not take them freely, but haggled, and kept off, fome to the laſt day, roaring againſt them all the while; and then coming about, all at once, with new-coined diftinctions and declarations, point-blank contrary to the declared fenfe of the impofers; they differed among themfelves; every one had a falvo for his own confcience; fome pretended they kept paſſive obedience ſtill, others that they were never for it. It was a fevere jeft, that the common people had got up, againſt the clergy, that there was but one thing formerly, that the parliament could not do, that is, to make a man a woman; but that then, there was another that is, to make an oath the clergy would not take."

[2] ib. p. 123.

(a) The Irifh Roman Catholics, " made no fcruple to take the oath of allegiance to King William and Queen Mary, which was agreed to in the articles of Limerick; and it was generally taken by them all over the kingdom, by the direction of their clergy." Lefley's Anfw. p. 125. The Englifh Roman Catholics, in their chapels at London, prayed publickly, at the fame time, for King William and Queen Mary. Lefley, ib. p. 126.

CHAP.

CHAP. XVIII.

The good Faith of King William's and King James's Officers compared.

DOCTOR King was not ashamed to affirm [1], " that among all the articles into which King James's officers entered, they never kept any to the Protestants." Yet these Protestants themselves [2] spoke, at the same time, with commendation and honour, of Sarsfield's punctual observation of his articles, when he took Sligo, to omit other instances [3]. General Ginckle owned to Major General Dorington, in the presence of the Prince of Wirtemberg, Monsieur Marquis de la Forest, and several other general officers, the good usuage their Prisoners had received at Limerick, and other Irish garrisons; and most of the Protestants, that belonged to the North of Ireland, did then confess, that the Irish, while among them in the summer of 1689, kept their protections better to the Protestants, than the Protestants kept theirs to them. Even some of the most zealous sticklers for King William's government have complained much, that the articles entered into with the Irish at Carrickfergus, by Marshal Schomberg, were not *(a)* punctually observed. For when that general first landed, he issued proclamations of protection and encouragement to the Irish, who would return to their habitations, and follow their labour; which many accepted, and a great part of the country was thereby planted, some places in as full a manner as before the revolution; but notwithstanding these protections, the Protestant army fell upon them, and wasted their whole country; and when the Irish held out their protections, they tore them, and bid them wipe their a——e with them, and none were punished for this breach of protections."

[1] State of the Protestants, &c.   [2] Lesley, ubi supra.   [3] Id. ib.

(a) " Upon the garrison of Carricfergus being allowed to march out with their arms, and some baggage, and to be conducted to the next Irish garrison, such was the resentment of the Ulster-Scots, for the outrages they sustained from these men, and such their virulent enmity to Popish troops, that, without regard to faith, they fell furiously upon the garrison, wrested their arms from them, plundered the more helpless, and were restrained from murder, only by the more vigorous interposition of the general." Lesl. Hist. of Irel. vol. iii. p. 547.

Notwithstanding General Ginckle's proclamation (4), printed at Dublin, February 4th, 1690, wherein he affured the Papifts in their Majefties names, " that all of them, who would fubmit to their Majefties government, fhould be protected as to their religion, eftates, and liberties ; yet that did not (b) hinder the multitude of out-lawries, and other forfeitures, proceedings againft thofe Irifh Papifts, who fubmitted to the government, on that affurance. As to their religion," adds Mr. Lefley, " they did not complain, for King William was very gracious to them in that refpect; but as to their perfons, eftates, and liberties, they cried out heavily of breach of public faith, and great oppreffion."

Mr. Lefley had before attempted to prove that thefe forfeiting Irifh were not guilty of rebellion (5 , " how could they," fays he, " who adhered to King James, be made rebels to King William, before they had fubmitted to him? If you fay he had a title to Ireland, by being King of England, becaufe Ireland is an appendix to the crown of England; I anfwer, from the beginning it was not fo; and the government of England being diffolved, as Doctor King fays, by abdication, and returned back to the fuppofed Original contract, or firft right of mankind, to erect government for their own convenience, of confequence the tye which England had upon Ireland was diffolved, and Ireland left, as well as England in its fuppofed original freedom, to choofe what government and governors they pleafed; befides all this, Doctor King's principles freed them from King William ; becaufe of the prefumptions they had to think, that King (c) intended to invade their property, lives, and religion."

(4) Lefley's Anfwer.   (5) Id. ib.

(b) " The impatience of William's Englifh adherents only ferved to confirm the Irifh in their averfion to the new government. And by a fhameful difregard, and almoft perpetual violation of his protections, granted to the peafantry, they forced this order alfo, to croud to their old leaders, and to take arms for their fecurity." Lel. Hift. of Irel. vol. iii. p. 574.

(c) The Irifh " faw their religion on the point of being utterly extinguifhed, and their remains of property ready to be feized by ftrangers ; no fecurity in fubmiffion, no reliances on any promifes of pardon." Lel. ubi fupra, p. 576. At Chapel-Izod, " William was employed in receiving petitions and redreffing grievances, arifing from the perpetual violations of his protections." Id. ib.

CHAP.

CHAP. XIX.

A short Sketch of the Cruelties inflicted on the Irish Prisoners in this War.

MR. Lesley, after having shewn, that the foregoing charge of breach of articles made by Doctor King against King James's officers, was groundless and wicked, has, by way of contrast, produced several notorious and uncontroverted instances of the perfidy and cruelty of King William's officers, towards their Irish prisoners, in the course of this war. Out of these instances, I shall select the few following; and with them conclude this tedious and melancholy narrative of the state of the Irish at different periods, for the space of more than one hundred and fifty years.

" WHEN (1) Drogheda surrendered to King William, after the defeat at the Boyne, the sick and wounded soldiers were, by the capitulations, to be taken care of, and to be sent with passes to their own army, as they recovered. But they were not only neglected, and might have starved but for the charity of some of their own poor countrymen, who sold their beds, and cloaths to relieve them, but they were also kept as prisoners after they recovered, contrary to their articles."

Upon (2) the surrender of Cork, the Irish army, though prisoners of war, were by the conditions to be well used. Notwithstanding which, even those Protestants, who were most zealous for King William, owned, that the Irish *(a)* General narrowly escaped being murdered by the inhabitants; that he had no justice done him, nor any satisfaction, upon his complaint to the English General; and that the garrison, after laying down their arms, were stripped; and marched to a marshy wet ground, where they were kept with guards four or five days; and not being sustained, were forced by hunger to eat dead horses, that lay about them; and several of them died, for want even of that, when they were removed from thence. That they were afterwards

---

(1) Answ. to King.   (2) Id. ib.

(a) General M'Carthy, of whom when colonel, Lord Clarendon, Lord Lieutenant of Ireland, reported to the English ministry, " that he was a man of quality, and a soldier; and that he behaved himself extremely well, wherever he was quartered, with great easiness, and moderation." State Let. vol. i. p. 45. His Excellency soon after recommended him to the King to be made a Major General, ib. p. 47.

wards so crouded in houses, jails, and churches, that they could not all lie down at once, and had nothing but the bare floor to lie upon; where the want of sustenance, and the lying in their own excrements, with dead carcasses lying whole weeks in the same place with them, caused such infection, that they died in great numbers daily. The Roman Catholics of Cork, though promised safety, and protection, had, on this surrender, their goods seized, and themselves stripped, and turned out of the town soon after."

" In (3) December 1690, one Captain Lauder, of Colonel Hale's regiment, being ordered with a Lieutenant, Ensign, and fifty men, to guard about two hundred of the Cork prisoners to Clonmell, as they fainted on the road with the above said bad usage, shot them to the number of sixteen, between Cork and Clonmell; and upon Major Dorington's having demanded justice against this officer from General Ginckle, Lauder got a pardon for the murder, and was continued in his post."

" King (4) William's army, after being entire masters of *(b)* Athlone, killed, in cold blood an hundred men in the castle, and little out-work on the river, And at Aughrim above two thousand, who threw down their arms, and asked quarter; and several who had quarter given them, were afterwards killed in *(c)* cold blood; in which number, were the Lord Galway and Colonel Charles Moore. The Major of Colonel Epingham's dragoons owned to Major General Dorington, that Lord Galway was killed after quarter, and when the battle was over. More vouchers," adds Mr. Lesley, " might be produced if needful."

" In short, many hundreds of the poor Irish prisoners were sent at a time (5) into Lambay, a waste, deserted Island in the sea, near Dublin; where their allowance for four days might, without excess, be eaten at a meal; and being thus out of the reach of their friends, (all (6) persons being prohibited to pass into it with boat, or other vessel, under the penalty of forfeiting the same) they died there miserably, and in heaps."

Thus

(3) Id. ib. (4) Id. ib. (5) Id. ib. Harris's King William, fol. 318. (6) Id. ib.

(b) " Douglas, in his expedition to Athlone, marched as through an enemy's country, his men plundering, and even murdering, with impunity, in defiance of the Royal proclamation, or the formal orders of their General. As he advanced, the Irish peasantry appeared, successively, in considerable bodies, to claim the benefit of King William's declaration; and were successively ensnared by assurance of protection, and exposed to all the violences of the soldiers." Lel. ubi supra, vol. iii. p. 576.

(c) " In the battle of Aughrim, and in a bloody pursuit of three hours, (stopped only by the night's coming on) seven thousand of the Irish army were slain. The unrelenting fury of the victors, appeared in the number of their prisoners, which amounted only to four hundred and fifty." Lel. ubi supra. p. 606.

THUS publickly, were thefe, and many other facts, attefted by Mr. Lefley, in his anfwer to Doctor King's ftate of the Proteftants of Ireland under King James, in refutation of the numerous falfehoods contained in that book. The truth of which anfwer is ftill further confirmed, by the Doctor's *(d)* confcious filence, under fuch heavy accufations, for more than thirty years, that he furvived the publication of it; being moft of that time, in the exalted ftations of Bifhop of Derry, and Archbifhop of Dublin; to which fucceffive dignities, he was thought to have been raifed, chiefly on account of the great merit and fervice of that performance.

(d) One can't help fmiling to find an affertion in his life, lately prefixed to Dean Swift's letters to his Grace, that, notwithftanding this long filence both of his Lordfhip and friends, " his Grace had by him at his death attefted vouchers of every particular fact alleged in his ftate of the Proteftants of Ireland, which are now in the hands of his relations." Swift's Works, vol. viii. If this be not a ridiculous boaft of his biographer, as moft probably it is, thefe relations of his Grace are now again thus publickly called upon to produce thofe attefted vouchers.

THE END.

APPENDIX.

No. I. From the MSS. Trinity College, Dublin.

A brief Declaration of the Government of Ireland; opening many Corruptions in the same; difcovering the Difcontentments of the Irifhery; and the Caufes moving thofe expected Troubles: and fhewing means how to eftablifh Quietnefs in that Kingdom honourably, to your Majefty's Profit, without any Encreafe of Charge.

[Wrote in the Government of Sir William Fitz-Williams, who was fix Years Lord Deputy in Ireland; that is, from the Year 1588 to the Year 1594.]

By Captain THOMAS LEE, 1594. Anno Regni Reginæ 37°.

To the Queen's moft excellent Majefty.

UNDERSTANDING, moft gracious fovereign, the proud and infolent terms the lords of the North of Ireland do now ftand upon, it maketh me bold to fet down my knowledge of thofe parts to your Majefty, becaufe I have debated often with the chiefs of them, what was fit they fhould yield unto your Majefty; and that it was unmeet for them in any fort to condition with your Highnefs: in the end (after long debating) they feemed fomewhat to like and allow of that which I demanded, as hereafter fhall appear. And becaufe your Majefty may the better judge the caufes of their difcontentments, I have here fet down the unconfcionable courfes which have been held towards them, which being remedied, and that they may fee your Majefty doth no way allow of the fame, there is no doubt (notwithftanding all their proud fhews of difloyalty) but that they may be brought to dutiful obedience, and to yield you that profit which neither your Majefty now hath, nor any of your progenitors ever had; fo as they may likewife have that which they demand, being nothing unfit for your Majefty to grant. In which difcourfe, if any thing fhould feem unpleafing to your Majefty, I humbly befeech you to pafs it over, and to perufe the reft, whereof I

doubt

doubt not, but something will content your Highness, for that it tendeth to your Highness's service and commodity.

My meaning, whereby your Highness's profit may arise, is by O'Donnel, Maguire, Bryan Oge, O'Rorke, and Bryan Oge M'Mahon.

THE demands I made for your Majesty were these, that they should receive your Majesty's forces into their countries: and your laws to go current, as they did in other places; and some part of their countries to be reserved for your Majesty, to dispose unto them who should govern them, and they to charge themselves with that proportion that was fit for them to bear.

To those demands they all yielded, so that they might have such gentlemen chosen, as they knew would use no treachery nor hard measures towards them, but to live upon that which your Majesty would allow; and that which they would give of their free consents, and to be no further charged; and they would be as dutiful as any other country in Ireland now is. And how this may be performed, I have made bold with your Majesty's favourable liking, here to set down upon my knowledge, both how your Majesty's forces may be received with their consent, and they to yield great profit in discharge of that which your Majesty allows to the soldiers, and the soldiers to be well satisfied.

THE cause they have to stand upon those terms, and to seek for better assurance, is the harsh practices used against others, by those who have been placed in authority, to protect men for your Majesty's service, which they have greatly abused and used in this sort.

THEY have drawn unto them by protection, three or four hundred of these country people, under colour to do your Majesty service, and brought them to a place of meeting, where your garrison soldiers were appointed to be, who have there most dishonourably put them all to the sword; and this hath been by the consent and practice of the Lord Deputy for the time being. If this be a good course to draw these savage people to the state, to do your Majesty service, and not rather to enforce them to stand upon their guard, I humbly leave to your Majesty.

WHEN some one who hath been a bad member (pardoned by your Majesty) hath heard himself exclaimed upon to be a notable thief after his pardon; and hath simply come in without any bonds, or any other enforcement, to an open session, to take his trial, by your Majesty's laws, if any could accuse him: notwithstanding his coming in after this manner, and without any trial at the time (because he was a bad man in times past) there hath been order given in that session for the execution of him; and

APPENDIX.

so he has lost his life, to the great dishonour of your Majesty, and discredit of your laws.

There have also been divers others pardoned by your Majesty, who have been held very dangerous men, and after their pardon have lived very dutifully, and done your Majesty great service, and many of them have lost their lives therein; yet, upon small suggestions to the Lord Deputy, that they should be spoilers of your Majesty's subjects, notwithstanding their pardon, there have been bonds demanded of them for their appearance at the next sessions. They knowing themselves guiltless, have most willingly entered into bonds, and appeared, and there (no matter being found to charge them) they have been arraigned only for being in company with some one of your Highness's servitors, at the killing of notorious known traitors; and for that only have been condemned of treason and lost their lives: and this dishonest practice hath been by the consent of your deputies.

When there have been notable traitors in arms against your Majesty, and sums of money offered for their heads, yet could by no means be compassed, they have in the end (of their own accord) made means for their pardon, offering to do great service; which they have accordingly performed, to the contentment of the state, and thereupon received pardon, and have put in sureties for their good behaviour, and to be answerable at all times, at assizes and sessions, when they should be called; yet, notwithstanding, there have been secret commissions given for the murdering of those men. They have been often set upon by the sheriffs of shires, to whom the commissions were directed, in sundry of which assaults, some of them have been killed, and others have hardly escaped. And after all this, they have simply come without pardon or protection, to an open place of Justice, to submit themselves to your Majesty's laws, where they have been put to their trial upon several indictments, of all which they have been acquitted, and set at liberty. If this be a course allowable, for poor men to be handled in this manner, and to be at no time in safety of their lives, I humbly leave to your Majesty.

When many notorious offenders have submitted themselves to your Majesty's mercy, and have been accepted, and have had their pardons, and have put in good assurances to be at all times answerable to your laws; the chiefest rebel (whose followers they were) hath been countenanced and borne out by your state, to rob and spoil, burn and kill these poor men, who did thus submit themselves. When they have very pitifully complained against that arch-rebel and his complices, of these outrages, they have been sharply rebuked and reproved for their speeches, and left void of all remedy for their losses; so as when in the end they have made petition to have licence by their own means, and help of their friends, to recover their goods from the rebels, they have been rejected, and utterly discomforted; yet, nevertheless, remained dutiful subjects, although

although they see, that such as continue notorious malefactors, are in far more safety than they who depend upon your Majesty's defence.

For it is well to be proved, that in one of your Majesty's civil shires, there lived an Irishman peaceably and quietly, as a good subject, many years together, whereby he grew into great wealth, which his landlord thirsting after (and desirous to remove him from his land) entered into practice with the sheriff of the shire, to dispatch this simple man, and divide his goods between them. They sent one of his own servants for him, and he coming with his servant, they presently took his man, who was their messenger, and hanged him; and keeping the master prisoner, went immediately to his dwelling, and shared his substance (which was of great value) between them, turning his wife, and many children to begging. After they had kept him fast for a season with the sheriff, they carried him to the castle of Dublin, where he lay by the space of two or three terms; and having no matter objected against him, whereupon to be tried by law, they by their credit and countenance, being both English gentlemen, and he who was the landlord (the chiefest man in the shire) informed the Lord Deputy so hardly of him, as that without indictment, or trial they executed him, to the great scandal of your Majesty's state there, and impeachment of your laws. For if this man had been such an offender as they urged, why was he not tried by ordinary course of law, whereby good example of justice might have been shewed, and your Highness benefited by his wealth, which they shared; but to cut him off by martial law, who was a good householder, inhabiting a civil country always liable to law, and last imprisoned in Dublin (where all the laws of that land have their head) was in my conceit rather rigour than justice; for as martial law is very necessary, and (in my opinion) ought to be granted to all governors of remote and savage places, where your Majesty's laws are not received, with all other authority and power severely and sharply to cut off, or punish offenders, according to the quality of their offence, until such time as the people shall become civil, and embrace the laws, and peaceable living (for till then they are not to be governed without the like measure of justice) so to use the same where the people are civil and obedient to other laws, is very indirect, and favours of cruelty; and yet this, and the like exemplary justice, is ministered to your Majesty's poor subjects there, who, if they have once been offenders, live they never so honestly afterwards, if they grow to any wealth, are sure by one indirect means or other to be cut off.

When there have been means made to an aged gentleman (never traitor against your Majesty, neither he nor any of his ancestors, and dwelling in one of the remotest parts of your kingdom) to come into your state; and that the hard courses used to others, made him demand security for his coming in, which hath been sent unto him by great oaths and protestations, delivered by the messenger, whereof he hath accepted, and thereupon come in: yet, notwithstanding all these promised safeties, this aged gentleman

man hath been detained prisoner six years, and so yet remaineth. And his imprisonment is the only colour to satisfy your Majesty for a wonderful great charge, which your Majesty and your subjects were then put unto. But his detaining contrary to promise, hath bred great fear in all or most of his sort (in those parts) of crediting what your state there shall promise.

When upon the death of a great lord of a country, there hath been another nominated, chosen, and created, he hath been entertained with fair speeches, taken down into his country, and for the offences of other men, indictments have been framed against him, whereupon he hath been found guilty, and so lost his life; which hath bred such terror in other great lords of the like measure, as maketh them stand upon those terms which now they do.

When there hath been a stratagem used for the taking into your Majesty's hands a young * youth, the heir of a great country, by whose taking his whole country would have been held in obedience, the practice whereof was most good and commendable; yet (after the obtaining of him) his manner of usage was most dishonourable and discommendable, and neither allowable before God nor man. My reasons are these: he being young, and being taken by this stratagem, having never offended, was imprisoned with great severity, many irons laid upon him as if he had been a notable traitor and malefactor, and kept still among those who were ever notorious traitors against your Majesty; having no other council or advice, or company, but theirs, what good could come to this young man for his education among such, I humbly refer to your Highness.

The taking of him as aforesaid, was most commendable, and for the good of that country, so he had been brought up in this manner, presently to have been sent to your Majesty, to have been instructed in the fear of God, to have known his duty to your Majesty, and to have been furnished with all necessary parts for a gentleman. And as your Majesty should have found his disposition, so either to have detained him here or sent him home into his country, whose good example (by his virtuous training up) might have done God and your Majesty much good service in those parts.

I have been the more bold to discover unto your Majesty the dishonourable managing of your service there, by the indirect cutting off of sundry your Majesty's poor subjects, because it pleased your Highness (many years since) to impart unto me, how much you abhorred to have your people there dealt withal, by any practice, but only upright justice, by your Majesty's laws, and forces, which being otherwise handled, I desire to make known unto your Majesty, and your most honourable council, for redress thereof.

* The Earl of Tyrconnel.

APPENDIX.

But I fear, that they who have well liked that courſe, and have been practiſers of the ſame, will inform your Majeſty, that thoſe people are ſo bad, as it is no matter of conſcience to cut them off any way howſoever, which is (in my opinion) for none but tyrants and beggarly princes to imitate. But your Majeſty being of ſo great power to offend the mightieſt Kings of the world, and to revenge yourſelf upon them, may with much honour ſuppreſs your own vaſſals, by your Highneſs's laws and forces, wherewith you are at charge in thoſe parts for that purpoſe.

Theſe principal inſtruments, as the Lord Deputy, and they who have been his aſſiſtants in thoſe diſhoneſt practices, have not only uſed theſe bad means againſt thoſe poor remote and ſavage people, but have done all their endeavours (ſo far as in them lay) to diſcomfort and diſcredit your Majeſty's beſt ſervitors, living under their commands, becauſe they miſliked to execute ſuch unjuſt practices and devices, and to allow of their covetous, unconſcionable and diſhonourable gettings.

I am emboldened, moſt gracious ſovereign, to declare thus much, becauſe, not only my poor ſelf (one of the meaneſt in that place of ſervice) have been partaker of it ; but ſome of your Majeſty's chief officers alſo have taſted the indiſcreet bitterneſs of the two laſt Lord Deputies, as namely, Sir Robert Gardiner, in his place of juſtice, a moſt worthy man, and void of all manner of corruption ; and Sir Richard Bingham, in his place of government, againſt whom (even within his own juriſdiction) traitors have been ſuborned and countenanced by them ; and the like in nature, though not in quality, hath been done againſt myſelf ; and as for Sir Richard, there was never man in his place that hath done your Majeſty like honourable ſervice, without increaſe of charge. For my own part, I leave the report of my ſervice, to ſuch as know it, and have ſeen it ; yet have they not only done me injuſtice there, but have alſo uſed their beſt friends and credit here, to obſcure my good deſerts, and to make (as far as in them lieth) me a man to be hated of your Majeſty, depreſſing me with all their might and authority there, and croſſing me with all their ability and malice here, not becauſe I have ſlacked or not performed your Majeſty's ſervice at any time, but for that I have afore time, and now, diſcovered unto your Highneſs their diſhonourable dealings, and intolerable corruptions.

And I deſire not that your Majeſty ſhould either ſimply credit me in this my plain detecting them, nor them in excuſing themſelves ; but, if it pleaſe your highneſs, to appoint commiſſioners in that realm for the trial, if I prove not directly all that ever I have here declared, let me loſe your gracious favour for ever.

Thus far of the diſordered courſes there held, all which notwithſtanding, your Majeſty's profit, may ariſe in thoſe parts, in ſort, as followeth :

First,

APPENDIX.

FIRST, for O'Donnel's country, it may please your Majesty to send thither fit gentlemen, against whom O'Donnel nor his country can take any exceptions; nor your state there think unfit for judgment or ability; namely, Captain Anthony Brabazon, to be seneschal of that country, and to have under his charge 25 horse; Captain Nathaniel Smith, to have 100 foot; Captain William Warren, to have his 5 horsemen restored to him (which Sir William Fitz-Williams bestowed upon others) and added to the 20 which he hath, to strengthen his band, and to be sent thither to be sheriff of that county. And for the settling of your Majesty's forces there, to reserve these lands to be inhabited by those, whom those gentlemen shall take with them, viz. one small barony belonging to Tyrconnel, on that side of the river towards Connaught, called, as I take it, the barony of Carbery; the castle of Ballyshannon to be reserved still in your Majesty's hands, for him who shall command there; the abby of Tashiroe to be bestowed upon the seneschal; the abby of Donegal, and the abby of Derry, are two abbies, that have no lands belonging to them; so much land, therefore, to be laid unto them, as shall be thought sufficient for their habitations, who shall be drawn thither.

AND the remain of the whole country to be given to O'Donnel and the chief men under him, so as they will contribute to this charge, which is only the diet of the hundred foot, which they may pay in meal, butter and beef, according to their usual manner, and your Majesty's chief rent besides, which is 200 l. yearly, to be the seneschal's fee; which 200 l. your Majesty seldom or never hath. This I believe O'Donnel will submit himself unto and perform, if he may be handled thereafter.

THIS garrison once settled in that place, will procure great quietness in your province of Conaught, and stop the only passage which they have to go to and fro to assist any traitor that may rebel there.

FOR Maguire's country called Farmanohan, Sir Dudley Loftus with his 25 horse (whereof he also wanteth five, taken from him as aforesaid is mentioned, to be restored to him,) and he to be sent seneschal of that country; Henry Warren his brother-in-law, to be sent as sheriff and assistant unto him, and to have 100 footmen under his charge, your Majesty to bestow upon those two gentlemen (to be inhabited by them and their friends) all those islands which are upon the lough, and that one abby which is in the country and the lands belonging to it, and the castle of Enniskillen, lately taken from Maguire; and the rest of that country, to remain to the chief men inhabiting there, so as they defray the seneschal's fee and the charge of the 25 horse, to be levied in butter, meal and beef, both for the diet and wages of the horsemen, and their horse-meat, in such sort as the Irishery themselves shall set down, which will be a greater proportion than your Majesty would demand.

APPENDIX.

For the county of Monaghan, called Macmahon's country, in respect of the great dislike which the Irishery have of the now seneschal there, it may please your Majesty to let him be removed, and in his place (for that it is next to the Earl of Tyrone's country, and the chief place of the Earl's abode) that Sir George Bourchire may be sent thither as seneschal, because of the companies of horse and foot, which are under his charge, and for that he is a gentleman of good worth, who will with some good show live in the place, which will be a great comfort to the Earl to have such a neighbour; and to assist Sir George in that service, to send Sir Henry Duke as sheriff of that country, to be placed in the abby of Cloonis (which is your Majesty's, and himself your farmer there) with his own company of light-foot, and a band of 100 foot more to be there in garrison.

This place of Cloonis is the only passage from M'Guire's country, and those parts, whereby the rebels may be stopped from doing your Majesty's good subjects any great damage in the English pale.

Your Majesty may supply those places with 200 foot and 25 horse without any increase of charge, taking them from such of the old garrisons as may very well spare them; for some one of the commanders of them is not worthy of a company, because (in the last conflict with the rebels) he lost his colours, and all his men ran away; and he who receiveth such dishonour by such base traitors, it is a pity ever he should carry colours or credit any more.

The aforenamed 200 foot and 25 horse are to be placed in Tyrconnel and Farmanohan, and the 100 foot to be under Sir Henry Duke in Monaghan; at the abby of Cloonis may be also one of the companies of the old garrison, and yet all other places of service very well furnished within.

Within short time after Sir William Fitz-Williams his receiving the sword he (finding many of your Majesty's garrison-bands of soldiers in the hands of divers of your Highness's counsellors there) had an intent to take them from them, and to dispose them to such gentlemen as were more fit to follow your Majesty's service, and often said it was no reason but rather a great shame that such as were assistants to him at the council board (having great offices and great entertainments belonging to them, and being otherways men of good living, and yet unable to lead men and follow the fury of the wars) should have bands of your Majesty's soldiers remaining in their hands; adding moreover, that it was unfit and unsafe for your Majesty's men and service to be trained by and trusted to their officers discretion, but rather to be bestowed upon gentlemen of worth, ability, and skill to follow the wars, which purpose of his, if it had taken effect, would (no doubt) have advanced your Majesty's service in that kingdom very much;

much ; but when he better confidered his own eftate, and his coming to that place, and what peril he fhould draw unto himfelf to hinder all his purpofes of gaining, if he fhould ftrive with thefe great ones, he thought it more fafe to let thofe bands remain as they were, than to pluck fuch a danger upon himfelf; for he knew if he fhould difpleafe them (being men of great friends and abilities) he could not have lived there fix years to have made his commodity of that your Majefty's poor kingdom, deferving the place fo little as he did.

But your Majefty being free from fuch doubt as troubled him, may difpofe thofe bands (as he had purpofed) unto men of good deferts, who have been long trained in your Majefty's fervice there without reward, and many of them live difcontented to fee men of no worth accounted of, and themfelves being men of value neglected.

Whereby alfo your Majefty fhall encourage many others to offer themfelves freely to your Highnefs's fervice, when they fhall fee good deferts rewarded.

If thefe counfellors had been heretofore themfelves employed with their bands in the remoteft parts there, to do your Majefty's fervice in perfon, where great need ever was, there is no doubt but it had much availed ; but to hold their bands of foldiers as they have done, and yet do, there is no reafon why they fhould have them.

But to return to my purpofe ; thefe bands being well difpofed of, and the forenamed garrifons placed in manner before expreffed, and the fame accepted of by the Irifhery, becaufe they fhall fee that it tendeth to their good, and that nothing fhall be taken from them more than is compounded for, fhall win them to honour, love and obey your Highnefs, and your officers and laws.

Your Majefty (to have this good fervice effected) may be pleafed, that as well the chief commanders of thefe garrifons, as alfo the foldiers, may be fully paid all their entertainment every month, whereby your Majefty fhall be freed from the charge of their victualling, and they fhall have no caufe to exact upon the poor people for want of victuals, or other provifion.

It may likewife pleafe your Majefty, in refpect thefe late and prefent wars, and troubles have greatly impoverifhed them, to grant unto the inhabitants of thofe countries of Tyrconnel, Farmanohan, and Monaghan, two whole years refpite before they fhall pay any of the aforefaid contributions; and that for thofe two years they may not have any affizes or feffions within their countries, but that the feneschals of thofe places may have full and abfolute authority over them, together with martial law (as hath been accuftomed) to cut off all malefactors, and ftraggling traitors; in which time thofe countries may be quietly inhabited, and grow to fome competent means to live upon, and be able to pay your Majefty.

And

AND likewise it may please your Majesty, to appoint them such a judge for the circuit as will use them with all clemency and mercy, and not to take such slender advantages against them as many of their own countrymen have done; for, I assure myself, if the choice of a justice was left to themselves, they would never choose an Irishman, because none are so corrupt as they.

WHEREAS young O'Roirke is also out, and a great disquiet of your Majesty's province of Connaught, he will in like sort yield himself a subject, and receive a sheriff into his country, and pay all duties appertaining, so as he may be accepted into grace and restored to all that was his father's. This I think he verily will perform, because I have been moved to be a dealer between Sir Richard Bingham and him.

AND whereas I have taken upon me to nominate certain gentlemen as fit men for the places aforesaid, without any of their privities, yet I am well assured (if it please your Majesty to appoint and command them) they will with all their abilities and endeavours be ready; but if any of them shall mislike, in respect of the dangers of the places, and smallness of their companies, there be others who will undertake it.

A GREAT part of that unquietness of O'Donnel's country came by Sir William Fitz-Williams, his placing of one Willis there to be sheriff, who had with him three hundred of the very rascals, and scum of that kingdom, which did rob and spoil that people, ravish their wives and daughters, and made havock of all; which bred such a discontentment, as that the whole country was up in arms against them, so as if the Earl of Tyrone had not rescued and delivered him, and them, out of the country, they had been all put to the sword.

THE profit which shall redound to your majesty by placing these garrisons aforesaid in this sort, will (after the first two years) amount yearly to 6000 marks, that is to say 3000 marks to be saved, and 3000 marks to be gained.

CONCERNING Tyrone, as your Majesty hath bestowed it upon the Earl, so for the better furtherance of the aforesaid services, it may please your Highness to accept of his own offers, which were that all Tyrone might be but one county, which granted, he would (upon his own charge) build a goal and a session-house, and receive a sheriff into his country, whereby your laws might be observed there.

AND where the Earl's adversaries have, in times past, incensed your Majesty against him, for the hanging and cutting off one Hugh Gavelock, a notable traitor, and son to Shane O'Neale, informing your Majesty that the said Hugh was your Majesty's subject, it shall be well proved that he was ever a traitor against your majesty, a daily

practiser

practiser with foreigners (as the Scots and others) for the disturbances of that kingdom, and one who fought by all means to overthrow the Earl, who by martial law (which he then had) did cut him off for his offences. For the doing whereof, he did incur your highness's displeasure; and the said martial law, which kept that whole country in awe, was taken from him; the want whereof has made his country people grow insolent against him, and careless of observing any humanity or duty, which hath bred the outrages now in practice, so that (in my poor opinion) it were requisite to restore the same authority unto him, provided it should not extend to the cutting off of any but such malefactors, as shall be of his own country, his tenants and followers: and I dare say, he may every year hang 500 false knaves, and yet reserve a great stock to himself: he cannot hang amiss there, so he hangs some body.

For the performance of the service in those aforesaid countries, it is not O'Donnell, Maguire, Brian Oge Macmahon, nor Brian Oge O'Roirke, nor any of those four who must be dealt withal, for they are all traitors and villains, and most obstinate against your majesty. But the foundation must be laid upon the earl of Tyrone, to draw him by any reasonable conditions unto your majesty, that you may have conference with him, and as he is made by your majesty a great man there, so may he be also a special good member in that commonwealth, to redress and remedy many great disorders, which no doubt he would faithfully do, if he might be trusted, for what maketh a man honest but trust.

And whereas some affirm that he standeth upon a pardon for himself and his followers, I think not so, for he and they hold themselves in less safety thereby, than they were before, because they have seen pardons serve (in their conceit) rather for traps to catch others in, than for true and just remission and acceptance into the free benefit of subjects, which maketh him fear the like practice towards himself.

For whom, although I have undertaken at my first coming, that he should have performed as much as I then delivered on his behalf to your majesty, now I dare not engage my credit so far from him, because it is long since I saw him.

But if it please your majesty to send me unto him, with encouragement and protection immediately from your majesty, that he shall come to your lord deputy there, and to your highness here in safety, to come and go without impediment or stay of his person, I doubt not but to bring him and his son (whom I would wish to be detained, but as himself shall like of) and whatsoever he undertaketh to the lord deputy, coming in after this manner, there is no doubt of his performance: I know his adversaries, who never were such friends as they might have been to the commonweal of that kingdom, will be earnest with your majesty against this, and that it is a great dishonour to you to grant it; but it will be proved, by their testimony who live there, how greatly it shall advance your majesty's service in this dealing with him, who hath heretofore served faithfully and valiantly, and hath therefore well merited, and shall save the lives of your highness's subjects, and the expence of much of your treasure.

They who will be against this, have those many years suffered notorious traitors, namely, Feagh M'Hugh, and the bastard Geraldines, mightily to dishonour your majesty, in the very view of your state; and with that base rebel and his adherents they will deal, as it were by way intreaty, to accept of protections, which is as much dishonour to a prince of your excellency and greatness as may be, so to condition with such beggarly objects, as have neither power nor wealth, and yet are noted here to be great and dangerous men to your state there.

If there go not some speedy contentment to the earl, to stay all this expected fury, which is very like to happen, but that there must be present wars made upon him and his adherents your majesty shall take them in hand at a very unfit time, when they are thoroughly provided to do great mischief, and your majesty, not so provided to defend your poor subjects from their sudden force and fury.

Your majesty, since you were queen, never had so great cause to bethink you of the service of that place, as now you have. Your highness shall not get so great honour in cutting off him, and thousands of those bare people that follow him, as you shall to win him and them, to be good and loyal subjects, and to live and serve your highness, for good offices. As the case now standeth with the earl, he hath small encouragements to be otherwise than now he is.

For where it was your majesty's pleasure he should have great encouragement given him, by thanks for his last good service against Maguire, it was held from him, and instead of that, they devised all means and policies to aggravate matters against him to your majesty, which is credibly made known unto him; and more, that upon what security soever he should come in, your majesty's pleasure is to have him detained. How he hath these advertisements from hence, I know not, but your majesty is, or shall be informed that he and his lady are papists, and foster seminaries, &c.

True it is, he is affected that way, but less hurtfully and dangerously than some of the greatest in the English pale: for when he is with the state, he will accompany the lord deputy to the church, and home again, and will stay and hear service and sermon; they, as soon as they have brought the lord deputy to the church door, depart as if they were wild cats, and are obstinate; but he, (in my conscience) with good conference, would be reformed; for he hath only one little cub of an English priest, by whom

whom he is feduced, for want of his friends accefs unto him, who might otherwife uphold him.

THERE hath been an old dunfical demand in taking pledges of fuch as are held dangerous men to your majefty's ftate there. I make bold to give it that term, becaufe there is no one who hath known your fervice of Ireland longeft, who can fet down and prove that ever Irifhman was held in obedience by his pledge: if any can, let me lofe my credit for ever. I am able to fet down of my own knowledge, almoft by 20 years experience, in which time I have feen many pledges taken for the Irifhery, for retaining them in obedience, the father for the fon, the fon for the father, the brother for the brother, and many other of like nature; when they have taken their times, neverthelefs, without any regard of pledge, to play the traitors againft your majefty at their pleafure. For when they neither fear God, nor be careful of their duty towards your majefty, nor fear your force to reform them, your majefty may be affured, it's not their pledges that can hold them in obedience. Your majefty, therefore, may (in my opinion) do well to let no fuch demand be made of them, but when they fhall give caufe of offence, let them be thoroughly followed with your forces, and plagued in fuch fort, as may make them afraid to offend you. For the lefs your majefty fhall efteem them, the more obedient you fhall have them; and by this courfe your majefty fhall fave a great deal of charge for the diet of fuch as they put in for pledge.

AND where there was a credible report made, that the earl of Tyrone came into the now lord deputy, without pardon or protection, I affure myfelf, your majefty fhall find he came in upon the credit of your ftate, altho' in policy he might be willed to give out otherwife, and no doubt, but fuch as have often miftaken his actions, and intents, would make an open demand of him, how? and he perhaps anfwer them, without protection; and upon this his anfwer, they might be very importunate with the lord deputy and the council, that he might be detained for great matters of treafon, wherewith they had to charge him, which demand of theirs being refufed, it is not unlike but they would either write to your majefty, or to their friends here, to inform your majefty how provident they were to have him fafe kept, and yet their cares and offers were neglected.

LET thofe devices of theirs take effect, or otherwife, to have him cut off, your majefty's whole kingdom there would moan it moft pitifully; for there was never man bred in thofe parts, who hath done your majefty greater fervice than he, with often lofs of his blood upon notable enemies of your majefty's; yea, more often than all the other nobles of Ireland. And what quietnefs your majefty had thefe many years paft in the northern parts of that kingdom, it's neither your forces there placed, (which have been but fmall) nor their great fervice who commanded them, but only the honeft difpofition and carriage of the earl, hath made them obedient in thofe parts to your majesty. And what pity it is that a man of his worth and worthiness shall be thus dealt withal by his adversaries (who are men who have had great places of commandment) and neither they, nor their friends for them, are able to set down they ever did your majesty one good day's service, I humbly leave to your majesty.

If he were so bad as they would fain enforce (as many as know him and the strength of his country, will witness thus much with me) he might very easily cut off many of your majesty's forces which are laid in garrison in small troops, in divers parts bordering upon his country; yea, and overrun all your English pale, to the utter ruin thereof; yea, and camp as long as should please him even under the walls of Dublin, for any strength your majesty yet hath in that kingdom to remove him.

These things being considered, and how unwilling he is (upon my knowledge,) to be otherwise towards your majesty than he ought, let him (if it so please your highness) be somewhat hearkened unto, and recovered (if it may be) to come in unto your majesty to impart his own griefs, which no doubt he will do, if he will like his security. And then, I am persuaded, he will simply acknowledge to your majesty how far he hath offended you; and besides (notwithstanding his protection) he will, if it so stand with your majesty's pleasure, offer himself to the marshal (who hath been the chiefest instrument against him) to prove with his sword, that he hath most wrongfully accused him. And because it is no conquest for him to overthrow a man ever held in the world to be of most cowardly behaviour, he will, in defence of his innocency, allow his adversary to come armed against him naked, to encourage him the rather to accept of his challenge.

I am bold to say thus much for the earl, because I know his valour, and am persuaded he will perform it; and what I have spoken of him, over and above this, these reasons have led me to it.

Being often his bedfellow, he hath divers times bemoaned himself, with tears in his eyes, saying, if he knew any way in the world to behave himself (otherwise than he hath done) to procure your majesty's assured good opinion of him, he would not spare (if it pleased you to command him) to offer himself to serve your highness in any part of the world against your enemies, though he were sure to lose his life.

And as he hath in private thus bemoaned himself unto me, so are there many eye-witnesses here in your highness's court, who have seen him do no less openly; which tears have neither proceeded from dissimulation, nor of a childish disposition, (for all who know him will acquit him thereof) but of meer zeal unto your highness, and grief and fear to lose your favour, whom he desireth with life, and all he hath, most dutifully and loyally to serve.

Whereas

APPENDIX.

WHEREAS I have taken upon me to nominate certain gentlemen as fittest to be employed in the above mentioned services in those remote places, I know there will be great exceptions against them, because they are thought to be too near friends to the earl. But I will prove, that none can ever do your majesty such good service there, as they who have been always trained up in those parts in service, and are best acquainted with the earl, and the other lords of those countries. And I am of opinion, if it were demanded of the earl and the rest, they had rather have strangers placed in those places, than those gentlemen of their acquaintance: because there, in any outrages in these countries, dare trust the earl with themselves and their small troops, to be aided by him, whereof they should not fail; when strangers would be loth, and fear so to do: for their trust will procure the earl and his followers to undertake and perform with them whatsoever they shall require for your majesty's service.

AND what is it to your majesty, to lay upon the earl the trust and credit of settling your majesty's forces in those parts, and to give him your majesty's free protection to come in, without fear, from time to time, to answer to any thing that shall be objected against him, and to retire home again? And if it shall at any time happen that he shall so offend, as to deserve punishment, then your majesty is to prepare your princely forces, and make royal war upon him, letting him sharply taste what it is to offend so gracious and great a prince.

AND likewise, the rest of the lords of those countries are (upon the receiving in of your majesty's garrisons, and paying the duties and compositions before specified) to have the like measure afforded them.

I AM the bolder, most gracious sovereign, to set down this my opinion for managing those remote places, and preventing these present expected troubles; because I have been an eye-witness of a needless and a chargeable war held against one of the lords of the North, namely, Surleboy, a Scot, which war ended not by your majesty's forces, but by the loss of that rebel's chief instrument, his son Alexander; yet were the said traytors intreated to accept of their pardon, and had more bestowed upon them for playing the traytors, than they demanded before. And my fear is (if this expected fury shall follow to be wars) it will fall out to the like or a worse issue: for he who doth now oppose himself against the earl, was the chief commander then, and did most dishonourably perform it, as shall be apparently proved, when it shall please your majesty to appoint.

I HAVE heard, many think much that the earl performed not his promise with the now lord deputy, but they little consider what slender encouragement he had given him at his coming in to do it. If he found, as like he did, in what great peril he was

to

to be detained, as, notwithstanding the assurance whereupon he came in, if his adversaries credit would have place, he had been restrained. There was no likelihood of his performance of any thing he then undertook, because he saw himself in so great peril, neither is it like he will hereafter hazard the like. But if his promise be expected to be performed, then, I think, he desireth good assurance, first, of his own safety, whereupon there may be hope he will effect all promises, good offices, and services, for the good of that poor kingdom; and till then there is nothing to be expected from him but doubt, and preparation to defend himself, and offend greatly.

WHEN your majesty's garrison soldiers were first planted in the county of Monaghan, there was great service offered to Sir William Fitzwilliam by Sir Henry Duke, for his sitting down at the abby of Cloonis (whereof he is farmer) with his own company of light foot, and fifty of your highness's garrison soldiers, and to have discharged your majesty of all manner of victualling charge, only to have been monthly fully paid their entertainment; and at that time there were at the same abby good and defensible buildings to succour your majesty's garrison, which are defaced and pulled down by the traytors, for fear they should serve for that purpose. If this offer had then been accepted, it had greatly furthered your majesty's service now, and peradventure had prevented, or at least hindered the troubles now expected, because it is so near upon Maguire's country, and the stay of his passage to the English pale.

NOTWITHSTANDING it much imported that this service should have been hearkened unto, yet Sir William Fitzwilliam his malice at that time was so extreme against Sir Henry Duke, who no doubt would have performed it as effectually as he offered it, as he utterly rejected it; even as he did the like and many greater services, offered by other your majesty's good servitors there.

HIS greedy desire at that time, in respect of his own gain, made him careless of these offers, and of those good servitors, who would freely offer themselves; he esteemed best of the baser sort, as of one Willis, and such as he was, whom he made captains and officers in the Irish countries, who with their great troops of base rascals, behaved themselves so disorderly, as made the whole country to rise in an uproar, and to drive them out, which advantage given by those bad and lewd fellows to the ill-disposed Irishery, hath emboldened them ever since to stand in no fear or subjection of your highness state, or forces there. These, and many the like services, as bad or worse, did Sir William Fitzwilliam, whilst he had authority in that place.

ALTHOUGH many needless journies were made by Sir William Fitzwilliam, which were both chargeable to your majesty, and troublesome to your poor subjects, yet was there one into the province of Conaught, which was very necessary, and grounded

upon

APPENDIX.

upon probable reason, determined for the cutting off and utter banishing of the traytor O'Roirke, and all his confederates; which service could not be performed without the affiftance of the earl of Tyrone, who was fent unto before the journey was undertaken. The meffenger was one belonging to your highnefs's council there, a friend of Sir William Fitzwilliam, and one well-affected by the earl, who declared to him the caufe of his coming down, to be for preparation againft O'Roirke, and what the lord deputy's demand was, that the earl fhould perform therein. The earl moft honourably (as he had oftentimes before) undertook to perform as much as the lord deputy then required, returning the faid meffenger very well fatisfied, for he fent the lord deputy word, he would be ready to attend the fervice with 1000 men at the place appointed, and more he would have brought, if he had more time, or fooner warning. The place to him affigned was on the border of Tyrconnel, on that fide of Lougherne towards Conaught, there to ftop the paffage, that O'Roirke with his companies and creatures fhould not that way efcape into thofe parts, which he well liked of, and promifed fo to do, adding further (if it pleafed the lord deputy to command him) he would break a ferry with his forces into O'Roirke's country, and either drive him out of it, or deprive him of life, and prey his whole country, and do great fervice upon all O'Roirke's adherents. This anfwer of the earl's feemed to fatisfy the lord deputy very well, who prepared your majefty's forces forthwith, and fent word to the earl to be in readinefs upon fix days warning.

The lord deputy took with him all your highnefs's garrifon, the raifing out of the pale as many as he thought fit, and went onward his journey, giving out (becaufe the rebels fhould not fufpect) that it was only to fee feffions and affizes duly kept in Conaught, and fat in divers places accordingly, infomuch as at length he came to Sligo, which joins upon O'Roirke's country, where he abode four or five days with all his forces, being fufficient to execute upon O'Roirke, and the other traytors, as much as he had before determined; the earl all this while expecting when he fhould be called to that pretended fervice, kept all his forces ready together for the purpofe, which was no fmall charge for him. But as it fell out afterwards, Sir William (as it feemed) had no fuch intention; for upon a fudden he departed from Sligo, journeying quite crofs the whole province of Limerick, leaving O'Roirke's country at his back, doing no fervice, but charging the poor country (whereof as then it had little need) impofing the performance of all this expected ftratagem on Sir Richard Bingham, with fome of the garrifon to affift him, who moft honourably and painfully profecuted the faid proud traytor upon his feet, to the great endangering of his life by the difeafe of the country, which caught him in the purfuit of that traytor, whom he then drave out of his country, by which means he was afterwards fent to have his deferts here in England. Which exploit (if it had been performed as it was plotted by Sir William Fitzwilliam) O'Roirke had perifhed there, and all thofe traytors, which are now affiftants to his fon, had then been cut off.

And

APPENDIX.

And if it shall seem to your majesty, that the time will be over long to have all these (and those other notes by me before delivered to your majesty) tried by commission, it may please your majesty to let him presently be called before your honourable council here, to see how he can answer, first, the leaving off of this so great and necessary a service by himself complotted; secondly, why he placed not your highness's garrison (lying then idle, and doing no service) in Tyrconnel for the respects aforementioned; and thirdly, why he refused the many great offers of those your well known and experienced servitors there, which was to do several services, and put your majesty to no charge for the effecting of them; and to make choice of such base men as Conell, Fuller, and Willis, whose behaviour I have partly touched before, being such as a well advised captain of that kingdom would not admit into any office in his company.

His answering in these three points, and as many of the rest as shall please your majesty, will, I don't doubt, be so gross, as your majesty and honourable privy council may the more easily judge of the rest. It may be, most gracious sovereign, that he will frame answers to all my objections, or else be persuaded by some of his friends, not to esteem them worth answering, in respect of the inequality of my estate to his, chiefly for the place which he held. For this I appeal to your majesty, how much it importeth. And I do further affirm, that until he can disprove these my allegations, or some of them, I ought to be credited as well or better than he; because he hath avouched to your highness's most honourable council monstrous and apparent untruth, which I can as well prove as any of these aforesaid articles, namely, about the buying and getting of imprest bills into his hands, which he hath sworn and forsworne that he never did; but for the proof hereof, if it be your highness's pleasure, that Sir Henry Wallop and his men be called, they can testify what great sums of money they had paid him for imprest bills in the time of his government, whereof most of them came to him better cheap than buying: for some were given him for cows, which he took in bribes, upon base conditions, of the Irishrie; other for placing men in sundry offices. And he that will make no conscience to forswear such a thing before so honourable personages, is hardly to be credited in excusing greater matters.

It may be also upon demand, why he did not place your majesty's garrison soldiers in those Irish countries? He will answer, that they could not be spared from other places; wherein your majesty may well reprove him thus; for those were the places where the foot-bands were then bestowed; Sir George Bourchier's at the Dingon in Ophalie, captain St. Leger's at the fort in Leafe, captain Dowdall's band at Youghall, fifty of Sir Henry Wallop's band at Eniskorthy, the Marshall's company at Newry. And in all those places there was no need of garrison, because there were no enemies

out

out to do service upon, but they might very well have been bestowed in other places, as some of them are now, when it is too late.

And for the fifty soldiers under my charge, they did your majesty as little service in all the time of his government, as the rest, although they lie in a place of great service, which is at Knockfergus; he having appointed such base commanders over them to direct them, as deserved not the pay of one of the soldiers. And although it was your majesty's pleasure that I should command them, as captain over them; and notwithstanding that I often made petition to him, and used all the means I could besides, to go down to my company, and to have that authority he gave to others, undertaking to do your majesty great service in that place, yet did he, (for what cause I know not) utterly refuse to grant my request; as he rejected many other great services by me offered unto him, holding me, to my great charge, to live upon the borders of Feagh M'Hugh's country, where I was fain to retain many men upon my own purse, to defend myself, and do your majesty some service upon those traitors; whereby, though it were to my cost, I took many notable rebels, who were commanders of men, and brought them in to abide the censure of your majesty's laws, which cut them off. For these, and many other services done in his time, he rewarded me with all hinderance that ever he could do me, not only by his authority and power, but by obscuring my deserts.

As it is the custom and manner, most gracious sovereign, of some to darken and disgrace the deeds of the well deserving, thereby to countenance and grace their own favourites, tho' they merit nothing; which manifestly appeareth in the plotting down of that service done upon that traitor Maguire the last year, which, as I understand (by Sir George Carew) was first delivered to my lord treasurer, and by his lordship shewed unto your majesty, wherein captain Dowdall is portrayed on foot, wading the ford in the fore front, arm and arm with myself, which is most untrue, as one Sadler, who was then his ensign bearer, and divers other gentlemen, and others of credit, who are now in your majesty's court, can testify; for he came not in the ford at all to wet his foot, but forsook his place, both he and his lieutenant behaving themselves, as in my other notes I have declared to your highness already. But when he saw the rebels defeated off their place, and driven to flight, then he came over the ford upon his horse, and so on horseback offered to lead the battle, which he ought to have done on foot, having no reason to ride, except he meant (if the enemy should make head again) to shift for himself. These and the like untruths (as the case now standeth) serve to grace such servitors, and to obscure and hinder the merits of such as deserve well. Although it would be too tedious to your majesty to hear of all the needless journeys made by Sir William Fitzwilliams in the time of his government, yet can I not omit (besides that one before rehearsed) his last journey into the county of Cavan, by the which your majesty may judge of all the rest.

APPENDIX.

WITHIN short time after the overthrow to that traitor Maguire, wherein your majesty's soldiers were worn out, of all manner of reparations, he sent for them to meet him 100 miles from their garrison places, which was at the Cavan. The time limited for their repair was but short, yet came they thither the day appointed. He carried with him many horsemen thro' the English pale, to the great prejudice and impoverishment of the same, by reason of his many needless journeys before. And he ought in conscience at that time have forborne coming into the county of the Cavan, because it was charged with 200 soldiers, which were newly erected for the service against Maguire, and paid only by the inhabitants of that country; yet nevertheless he made his journey thither, and there remained many days, to the great charge of that poor country, having no other cause but only to see a boat launched; which was so needless a journey undertaken and performed, that many a gentleman then under his command might (with his men) as well have effected, as it was by his presence; which course if he had taken, it had saved the great charge whereat your majesty then was, the extream and needless labour of your poor soldiers, and given the poor people of that country no cause of exclamation, who came before him in great troops with their plow-irons in their hands, ringing them together with pitiful moans, saying they were undone by his coming amongst them, because they were not able to bear the soldiers already put upon their charge. But so little was he moved with this their complaint, that he assessed them with more soldiers, horsemen and boys. In his return towards Dublin, he was met by many of the said poor country people with the like lamentable outcry, which he regarded as much as the former.

HE commanded your majesty's soldiers back again to their places of garrison, as little respecting their long journey, and the relief of their wants, as he did the poor peoples outcry whom he had oppressed. It was then near Christmass, when the soldiers to whom (against that good time) he would not allow one penny of imprest, he seeing them all very poor and greatly turmoiled.

MOREOVER he was so miserable, as he refused to lend one of your majesty's captains 20 l. to imprest amongst his soldiers, he promising upon his credit, to pay the same within six days next after his coming to Dublin: such was his honourable mind, as he never respected no man's necessity in comparison of his own commodity. This needless journey, although it did not benefit him much, yet it served his turn another way; for he coming home to Dublin in the deadest time of the winter, a little before Christmass, it caused him to lie so close, and to keep so miserable a Christmass, as was never there seen in representation of the state.

HE

APPENDIX.

As he hath had neither care nor conscience in sundry sorts, to dishonour so gracious a prince as your majesty (who did most bountifully enable him to do your majesty good and honourable service, and to spend liberally in his house) but to turn all those your majesty's bounties to his own private gain, preferring that before your majesty's service and the good of those your people; your majesty (in my opinion) being advertised by those notes by me delivered, and the same proved true, may with safe conscience benefit yourself with that which he hath dishonestly gotten both by your majesty and your highness's subjects in that poor kingdom; which example will (no doubt) cause others hereafter to prefer your majesty's service and profit before their own, and to beware of the like trespass for fear of the like justice.

It may please your majesty likewise to be advertised, that divers persons having been for their offences pardoned by your majesty, and thereby emboldened to frequent all places without fear, having been apprehended and committed straightway to prison, without any cause given (since their pardoning) whereof law might take hold: they have offered very sufficient bail which hath been refused, and they detained, because they, in times past, were bad (for which they were pardoned) or for fear they should be bad in time to come. And being thus kept severely in prison many years, they have at length made friends there, and by great sums of money here, purchased their pardon from hence, whereby they have been enlarged; now when they obtain their liberty by these money-means, and not by the justice which your majesty's laws allow them, they think themselves very hardly used, and others thereby become doubtful, and afraid to trust to their pardons; supposing, if they want such friends and such means, they should either be indirectly cut off, or else for ever kept in prison, upon suggestion or surmise. But if they might perceive, that it is not your majesty's pleasure to have them thus handled, and that none should lie in prison without receiving trial by your highness's laws, if their cause so required, or else upon good sureties to go at liberty, by either of which means, they may enjoy the benefit of your gracious laws, even as your good subjects which never offended, no doubt it would free them of great fear and suspicion, and make them more dutiful than ever they were.

There is one prisoner in the castle of Dublin, an aged and impotent gentleman, of whom (if it be your highness's good pleasure) I desire your majesty shall take notice; his name is Sir Owen Mc Tool, one who was never traitor against your majesty, nor ever in any traiterous action, but so good a subject, and so faithful a servitor as (for his deserts) he had a pension from your majesty, whereof Sir John Perrott bereft him.

This gentleman was sent for by promise and assurance from the state, that he should not be abridged of his liberty; contrary whereunto he was committed unto prison, where he hath remained these eight years; for whose enlargement all bail hath been refused, yet is the gentleman of so great years, as he is not able to go, and scarcely able to ride; for which respects and for the states, promise (methinks) he ought to find favour. Moreover he is pledge for no man; if he were, pledges profit nothing, as before I have rehearsed. He is father-in-law to the earl of Tyrone, and if the earl recovers your majesty's favour, how highly your majesty shall honour yourself by bestowing this old gentleman's liberty upon the earl, and how much your majesty shall provoke the earl to acknowledge your highness's favour therein, your majesty may easily judge, and they who know the state of that kingdom can inform. But if the earl be not so happy as to obtain such grace at your majesty's hands, yet it may please your majesty graciously to regard the poor aged gentleman, that upon good sureties he may have his liberty; for which I know there would be five hundred pounds given, tho' he can by no means steed them in any bad practice against your majesty's state there, neither in body nor council, neither can his imprisonment stay any of his friends from doing evil, if they be badly disposed. If therefore your highness would be pleased to release him of your own princely motion, he putting in sufficient sureties within the English pale to be ever ready within twenty days to answer to whatsoever may be objected, you shall bind him (as his bounden duty) always to pray for your highness, and mightily increase the affection of your majesty's people there.

And if he or any other, of whom such security shall be taken, shall afterwards offend as traitors, your majesty's coffers are to be enriched by the forfeitures of their sureties bonds (which are in no case to be remitted) and the traitors to be honourably cut off by your majesty's forces at your pleasure; which justice will be an example to traitors how they offend, and to their sureties how they become bound.

There have been (these many years past) divers traitors suffered, I might rather say, suborned, in all their bad and traitorous actions who (if matters had been discreetly and uprightly handled) might either have been utterly overthrown or cut off, or else drawn to subjection and due obedience to your majesty and your laws, without any other, or more charge unto your highness, than you have been at continually: for your majesty's soldiers were not at all employed, and yet those traitors were suffered to go uncorrected for all their murders and treasons;. nay more, they were suffered to use your highness unreverently, which caused your majesty's good subjects with grudge and heart's grief, often times to complain.

APPENDIX.

The principal rebels and arch-traitors whom I mean, are Feagh Mc Hugh, and the baftard-Geraldines, who are by marriage linked in affinity with that grand traitor; and becaufe I would have your majefty underftand how you have been long abufed by untrue informations concerning this traitor and his complices, I proteft they neither are of that ability to offend, nor of that power to defend, nor fo hardly to be conftrained to yield their due obedience, as hath been reported; yea, and that without the employing of great troops of foldiers againft them, or charging the near bordering fubjects extraordinarily: for they will now with more willingnefs afford all their helps of provifion in the traitors country, than they have done heretofore, becaufe then they were greatly charged, and no whit defended. But if they might have fuch a one chofen and appointed for that fervice as they know would never ceafe until he had quite deftroyed that den of mountain-thieves, the poor fubjects would neither fpare charge nor trouble to affift him. The means how to reform thefe difobedient rebels, and to perform this fervice are thefe:

First, Let no protection be granted to any, fave only to fuch as fhall come in unto him who fhall be appointed to follow that fervice, and offer themfelves to do offices againft the chief traitors: which when they have performed, and that fpecial good hath fucceeded their draught, then let them have pardon for their former faults, and fafe protection (without any traitorous practice which hath too commonly been ufed towards them) fo long as they fhall behave themfelves as good and loyal fubjects, living in duty and obedience unto your highnefs, your officers, and laws.

And if any who be, or fhall be, in authority to protect, do fend for any offender upon promife that the fame fhall fafely come and go, and then fhall (contrary to that promife) take away the life of that offender, be his tranfgreffion never fo heinous, let that man in authority (be he never fo mighty) lofe his credit in that place, and be punifhed to the uttermoft that law will afford, for fo difhonouring your majefty, when your highnefs's word is paft: for fuch ufage is the caufe why they will not now come to the lord deputy upon protection, and much lefs will they truft any other, except they have had long experience of his upright and juft dealing.

Furthermore, whofoever hath a country or a feignory, which your majefty hath beftowed upon him, let him be bound that all his tenants fhall be anfwerable to your laws, or himfelf to fatisfy all fpoils and trefpaffes which they, or any to whom they give maintenance fhall commit againft your majefty's good fubjects.

I know

APPENDIX.

I know there will be great exceptions taken against this; they affirming, that many dwell upon their lands whether they will or not; let this (if it please your highness) be no excuse, for if they know how to receive their rents and customs, let them likewise pay the spoil done to the good subjects, or bring in the offenders to answer to the law; especially if they have the commandment of any of your majesty's soldiers, by whose assistance they may enforce them to obedience.

And whosoever shall be appointed to serve upon the aforesaid traitors Feagh Mc Hugh and his adherents, shall not need to have more than 100 foot and some 20 or 25 horse, which horsemen it were requisite (for good respects) should be strangers to that border; and with this small number may he do very great service.

But if it be objected, that this proportion of soldiers is too weak to do service against so strong a traitor, if it may please your majesty to give me the leading of these soldiers, and the credit of the service, I will either lose my life, or effect as much as I have here set down. And where I will venture my life to perform such a service as this, I trust your majesty will venture your soldiers, and give me in charge to lie upon those borders, to see your majesty's subjects live in safety, and to give those traitors, and the inhabitants of those parts to understand, that henceforth they are no more to expect protection, but to submit themselves as subjects, and so continue, or else to feel the sharp punishment due to obstinate rebels. And to such as shall submit and do service upon the rest, there is pardon to be granted, and to him who shall do the best service, shall not only be given pardon, but also maintainance for him to live upon. By which means I am assuredly persuaded, I shall find instruments among themselves, that shall serve effectually to cut off the rest; so shall your highness be honourably served, and those parts of your kingdom, so near the state, be reduced to obedience, for the example of those countries which are more remote.

If this traitor Feagh Mc Hugh should be made more strong by his friends (as I see not how they should) and that further force should be required against him, your majesty's subjects in the English pale would willingly yield to your highness 600 soldiers, horse and foot, at their own charge for six months, and longer if need required, so as they might see your majesty would once take him in hand: thus much, many of the best of them, willed me to deliver to your highness.

There is no cause, why these expected troubles in the North should hinder the present proceedings against these traitors in the south, who are persuaded they are spared, but till such time as your majesty have settled the North, and then they expect to be followed by your highness's forces for their cutting off: all things therefore
considered,

APPENDIX.

confidered, they fhould not be forborne till then; for tho' there be wars in the North, thofe in the South will offend your majefty's fubjects as much as they can, and thereby keep the ftate the more bufied and troubled. And if they happen to be over hardly diftreffed, then will they fly to the North, there to be fafe from your majefty's forces; which refuge, if they be once driven unto, it's great odds they fhall never come back to annoy the fouth, which I pray God I may once fee, and that fome of your majefty's good fubjects may dwell where that traitor Feagh Mc Hugh's forefathers and followers have remained thefe 100 years, to the great difhonour of the ftate and hurt of the poor fubject.

For the due reformation of all the diforders in that poor realm of Ireland, and the execution of what worthy action foever fhall be by your majefty, and your honourable council here determined, and for recovering the honour of that ftate, which former governors there have loft; your majefty, in my judgment, hath made a moft excellent choice of the now lord deputy, a man accomplifhed with all neceffary parts both in body and mind, as I doubt not but his fervice fhall hereafter give good teftimony, altho' he have received the fword in a far more troublefome and dangerous time than any of his late predeceffors ever did. For neither the laft Defmond's wars, nor thofe of Connor's and the Moore's, being both put together, are comparable to that which is now expected if it prove wars; which I defire (if it be God's will and your majefty's good pleafure) may be otherwife, not for my private affection for any in the North, but for the publick good which I wifh to that poor kingdom.

For the benefit whereof, and for the performance of all fuch honourable fervices as are now expedient to be done, and all the reft before in this declaration mentioned, it's your majefty, who muft not only direct him, but alfo thoroughly enable his lordfhip, that he may give better encouragement to your majefty's foldiers to take pains in your highnefs's fervice, than they have had, or yet have; becaufe they daily fee that he who never ferved your majefty in thofe fervices, fhall come to far better preferment in that place, than the beft commander or ferving fervitor there. Befides you cannot get that done, which they do, who painfully, and faithfully ferve.

What encouragement then can a man have to offer himfelf freely in the wars of that country, who fhall neither get honour, reward, nor payment for his labour; I fpeak by experience of myfelf, who (upon my credit) have not had ten crowns impreft of my own private pay, thofe ten years, to furnifh me towards your majefty's fervice, when I was called upon, and yet I have made one at all times.

When fuch hard meafure then is offered unto captains, I humbly refer to your majefty, what encouragement they can have to go to the field. Although without

money

money or any thing elſe, they will do their beſt endeavour, with their ſubſtance, and themſelves, to do your highneſs ſervice; becauſe I know (and ſo do all the reſt) that it's not your majeſty's pleaſure to have them ſo diſcouraged, but the fault is in them, who have been thither ſent as deputies, who have preferred their own gain before your highneſs's honour and ſervice, or the juſt rewarding of ſuch as have moſt truly and and painfully ſerved: and for that they would pleaſe ſuch cowardly captains, as were their inſtruments to bring them in cows, to convert into angels, to cram their greedy purſes; whom I have a better will particularly to name, than thus generally to write of, if I were perſuaded, your highneſs would thereupon diſcard them: and I know they would not challenge me, becauſe I do them no wrong.

To encourage therefore your majeſty's ſoldiers, and to furniſh the lord deputy againſt all accidents that may happen, if it may pleaſe your majeſty, that all the treaſure which is ſent over into that realm at ſundry times, may be intirely ſent at one time, with commandment, that your majeſty's whole garriſon may be fully paid every month, your majeſty ſhould be moſt honourably ſerved, and the ſoldiers well contented, and the ſubjects not occaſioned to exclaim for want of payment for the ſoldiers diet, when both captains and ſoldiers ſhould have in their purſes to ſatisfy that, and to furniſh themſelves with all other neceſſaries.

For notwithſtanding your highneſs's garriſon hath been ſo ſlenderly paid theſe many years, your majeſty hath not ſaved any thing thereby, but it hath enriched a ſort of baſe clerks, and beggarly merchants, who will not credit a captain now for a groat upon his bill; but all the commodity goeth to the lord deputy, the clerks, and the merchants, ſo as the captain, to furniſh his company, can get no money unleſs he will give 400 for 200 or 200 for 100, and after the like rate; and in this prowling manner your ſoldiers are paid.

Forasmuch as your majeſty doth pay all in the end, you may (if it be your highneſs's pleaſure) as well benefit your captains, and ſoldiers as other men's clerks, by ſending an overplus of treaſure to the lord deputy, to pay the old debt due only to captains, and ſoldiers, which few thouſands will diſcharge; except it be one man, unto whom your majeſty oweth five or ſix thouſand pounds, which (if it be your highneſs's pleaſure) may with ſafe conſcience be detained in your hands, becauſe he hath ſo ill deſerved, thro' the diſhonouring your majeſty in the place wherein he ſerveth.

And now (moſt gracious ſovereign) for that (as I have heard) it hath been credibly reported to your majeſty, that the laſt Deſmond's wars did coſt but 40,000 pounds, thereby the rather to induce your highneſs to make wars upon the north, I have thought it
my

my duty (under your majesty's protection) to set down the truth thereof, whereby it may the more easily be judged what the charge of these expected northern troubles may stand your highness in, by comparing the said Desmond's wars and these together.

The charge of those wars (notwithstanding the great supplies then had of your subjects, and the great succour and assistance of sundry castles and good towns, which held firm and faithful to your majesty, to receive and aid your soldiers upon all extremes; which towns and castles stood in most commodious places, not only to annoy, but utterly, in a manner, to overthrow the traitor, and all his co-partners. And where it cost your majesty then one pound, it cost your subjects three, during all the time of those wars, which charge of your subjects I can well make out; for the chief lord of one small village, who had but eight pounds yearly rent for the same village, paid for one year's cess to your highness's soldiers thirty-eight pounds sterling, whereof I was also an eye-witness. These wars I say did stand your majesty in four thousand pounds at the least, for the monthly charge was 7000l. besides the victualling by sea. And yet after all this, your majesty afforded pardon to the basest rebel who then took arms against you, who yet liveth in view of your state.

The cause of those Desmond's wars, was even like to this in the north, through the great mistaking of the Desmond's adversaries; and that it cost your majesty no less than I do here set down, Sir Henry Wallop can well testify.

Moreover, there are no helps to be hoped for in the north, either of castles or towns, wherein to garrison, or once lodge your majesty's soldiers, for the following, and suppressing of those traitors; for those parts are merely void of such refuge. Again, all the friends to your highness in those countries are but two, O'Hanlon and Maginnes, and they uncertain, as your majesty may thus judge: for O'Hanlon is married to the earl of Tyrone's sister, and merely enriched by the earl; Maginnes, his eldest son is to marry the earl's daughter. And this affinity, in the manner of the Irish, is always to the party they see strongest; and when your majesty (as there is no doubt) shall prevail, they will then seek favour and make offer of much service, but seldom or never perform any; whereof myself have been too often a witness. These things considered, it may please your majesty, and honourable council, to be rightly and thoroughly advertised, before there be wars made in the north parts, whatsoever by sinister informations may be suggested to the contrary.

For it is not the north only your majesty shall now have to deal withal, but your highness's whole province of Conaught shall be in great peril of losing, except Sir Richard Bingham be more strongly enabled or assisted than he is now, trusting to only one band of 100 foot and 50 horse, wherewith I confess he hath done great service. Knockfergus, and the Clanboyes, which are now garrisoned only with 100 foot and 25 horse (who have done your majesty no service by reason of such bad commanders as have been appointed over them) cannot but be lost without a very great garrison, and exceeding great charge; so that your highness's realm of Ireland being now (as it were) divided into four parts, viz. Leinster, Munster, Conaught, and Ulster, will be in very great danger to be half lost, for Ulster is the earl's already: And in Conaught there are divers who have been traitors not long since (and yet scarce good subjects) who watch but such an opportunity. And in Leinster there are many, who now stir not, who will then arise in arms, namely, the Birns, the Tools, the Moores, the Connors, and the Cavanaughs; and many other as false traitors as those, who (if they once perceive troubles to increase in the north) will seek to molest and offend the English pale, as they have done in times past.

And one special matter more is to be thought upon, where your majesty in all the wars of Shane O'Neale, had Tyrconnel faithful, and ready to do your highness service, and to assist your soldiers, giving the traitor many overthrows (being then an utter enemy to all the Neals) now it's not so, for O'Donnel is married to the earl of Tyrone's daughter, and is thereby so linked to him, that no place of succour is left to your majesty's forces in all the north; for Sir John O'Dogherty (who was well affected to your majesty's service) is now in hold under O'Donnel, so as no aid is to be expected from him. This poor gentleman hath been hardly used on both sides; first, by Sir William Fitzwilliams, who imprisoned him, in hope to have had of him some Spanish gold; and now by O'Donnel, because he shall not in these troubles annoy him.

To write of all other particularities belonging to the north, would be over tedious. To conclude therefore (with your majesty's pardon) there are but two ways, either to accept of their own offers of submission, and contribution for defraying of the charge, in this discourse, especially before mentioned, and so to place your majesty's garrisons in their countries, thereby to hold them in continual obedience to your highness's profit, or else to make royal war upon them, and so utterly to overthrow, and root them up thro' all the whole north of that kingdom, and plant others in their room or places. I may in no wise omit humbly to acquaint your majesty, what great hinderance unto your present service the stay of Sir Robert Gardiner his coming over is like to be, because that he can best truely report to your highness the state of Ireland, who (as he was specially chosen by your majesty to be a chief instrument for the good of that poor kingdom, where he ever did, and doth minister such upright justice, as is void of bribery, affection, intreaty of friends, or fear of authority to over-rule him, thereby to do any thing unfit for a man of his place) can very hardly be spared from thence; yet, as the necessity of this time importeth, it were (under pardon) most meet

he

he were sent for with all speed; for that (as he can) so he will, without fear of any, inform your majesty truly how the state of that your kingdom now standeth, and shew good means how to stay this expected present fury, that is like to happen, to the utter ruin and cutting off many of your majesty's subjects, and the exceeding expence of your highness's treasure. There will be (no doubt) many reasons alledged to your majesty to stay him there, but I humbly beseech your highness not to hearken to them, for the authors of these troubles are afraid of his coming hither. But his instant repair over, will more avail him than his stay there, although it's well known he doth (as far as his authority extendeth) afford the people justice, without begging it or buying it, which hath been too often bought and sold there. And your majesty may at your pleasure return him hither again when he hath done exceeding good service there: although I fear he will be loath (if either his own credit or friends may prevail) to go back thither any more, because he seeth he is not able to do your majesty such good service as he would and might, if he were more strongly assisted; moreover good deserts there, procure scarce good opinion, or friends here.

What mean I to say thus much, when it is not to be amended? nay what pity it is that so gracious a prince, as is your majesty, cannot help it! For these many years past your poor subjects have been crying out for justice, and could never get it; besides it's grown to such gain by corruption, that unless your majesty vouchsafe to take it upon yourself, or make special choice of some of your honourable council here to look into it, it will not be holden; for if it be referred (as it hath been) there will be such shuffling, and so much time spent, to save the credit of some one, that thousands of your majesty's good subjects shall perish the while. And the rather because advice is chiefly required of him, who is causer of all those troubles; and that your majesty may the better judge what good can follow by his directions, let him set down what service he did you when he had the whole authority in his own hands, whereby your highness may discern the rest. I know (and thereon dare pawn my life) he cannot prove any one honourable, or profitable service he did your majesty therein at the time of his government.

Opinion is likewise required of some other counsellors now here, who can say as little of those northern parts, as he who was never there.

This being most true, let not (I humbly beseech your majesty) your poor realm of Ireland be trusting to the advice of such blind advisers: but vouchsafe your highness to be advised by those who know your service there, by their own experience, and eye witness of that, whereof they shall yield their opinion; and no one (of a counsellor) can do it better than Sir Robert Gardiner, because his circuit is northward, whereby he doth hear the griefs, and discontentments of those people.

APPENDIX.

MOREOVER I most humbly beseech your majesty to be no longer abused by lip-labour, and paper and ink; which have, these many years gone for current payment, instead of good servce; and in show of discovering great and weighty causes, when in truth they seldom tended to any such purpose; but seeing your majesty doth pay them so well, it may please you to require better service at their hands, whom your highness doth there put in trust.

If I have in these my plain and simple discourses offended your majesty any way, I most humbly ask pardon for the same.

As the physician cannot cure the disease of his patient, until he both know, and take away the cause thereof, so neither are the calamities of your majesty's kingdom of Ireland to be remedied, until your majesty be both rightly advertised of the same, and put in practice the redress of the great abuses there; which can't be better done (in my simple skill) than by making an example of some one, who has served your majesty corruptly in that place; and the greater the personage is, the greater the justice, and the more your honour in making a precedent of such a one: for your inferior officers can punish small offenders, but it is in your majesty only to correct the mighty transgressors.

AND so may your majesty (if so you will vouchsafe) look down by degrees, and in time survey your highness's captains, who serve you there; discerning, by a little observation, the good from the bad; which is easily done, if every one be called to account, what service he hath done you, what traitors he hath cut off, having full authority for it, or else how your highness's subjects have been defended by him and his soldiers. He who hath not performed one of these two, is unworthy to have command, or have pay.

FURTHERMORE, when some experienced captain shall make offer of his best endeavours, let him (if it please your highness) be hearkened unto, and especially when it tendeth greatly to the advancement of your majesty's service, without encrease of charge: and let them not (I beseech your highness) be put off so grossly as they have been, with saying, it is too small a proportion of soldiers to perform so great a service. For that is not the cause (most dread sovereign) but this; if they should allow of those services, when they are offered, it would discover, as many think, some of their great abuses, which your majesty may perceive, when you shall see great services done with, 100 where 500 have been employed, and your highness's subjects no whit the better defended.

THERE is no well advised captain will make offer of service, but he hopeth to perform, or lose his life; and especially when he shall not gain thereby; for his soldiers must be paid, or else they will not serve; besides he must keep them, or else he cannot effect the service undertaken, so that his only hope of gain resteth in reputation, reward, and preferment from your majesty, as he shall deserve, and not in polling and pilling the soldiers and your majesty's subjects.

THESE good services then being accepted, and the abuses reformed, there is no doubt but your majesty's kingdom of Ireland shall quickly flourish in true subjection, and due obedience, to your majesty's honour and comfort, which I beseech the Almighty to grant, and continue.

THE consideration (most gracious sovereign) of my own estate, who have engaged myself and my friends very far, for means to live, and do your majesty service, hath many times (in the penning of this discourse) sought to withhold me from discovering to your highness these causes of discontentments of your poor people in that kingdom, and the bad managing of your majesty's affairs there, with the means of quieting them, of advancing your majesty's service, and advantaging your revenues, assuring myself that the doing of such an office would neither procure me any friends, nor pay any of my debts: besides it's against my profession (being a soldier) to be a penman, or so earnestly to seek for peace. Yet nevertheless, when I considered what due honour may be done unto God, what true service to your highness, and what good to that poor common weal, it made me utterly neglect my own fortune, and respect of my private benefit, and emboldened me to discharge my duty to God and your majesty, and disclose my zeal for benefiting that poor realm. And if these my labours shall be rightly conceived of by your majesty, and your most honourable council, I shall think my time happily spent, and enjoy as much as I desire.

AND thus, most humbly beseeching pardon for this my bold and rude discourse, and praying on my knees to Almighty God, the director of all princes' hearts, that it may please him to move your majesty's mind duely to consider of the premises, and pitifully to regard the present state of that your poor kingdom, and beseeching him to bless your highness with all honour, health, and princely happiness, long to reign over us, I most humbly conclude with this my petition.

I HUMBLY beseech your majesty, if it be your gracious pleasure to accept the earl of Tyrone into your highness's protection that he may safely come in unto your majesty, or to your lord deputy, and hither at your pleasure, that I may be the messenger; because at my coming over, he reposed great trust in me, to deliver unto your majesty those things, wherewith he found himself grieved, wherein I doubt not but to do your

highness

highness acceptable service, by reason of the poor credit I have with him. But if your majesty be minded to deal otherwise with him (because it hath been reported by those who are adversaries both to him and me, that I am a great friend unto him) to show what manner of love mine is towards him, there is none of them, nor any other, who shall do greater service than I will, if it please your majesty to command me, and enable me fit for it; if not, my service, and myself rest at your highness's command to be disposed, as it shall please you, for whom, as is my bounden duty, I will daily pray, &c.

Your majesty's faithful

and obedient servant,

THO. LEE.

Numb. II.

[From Desid. Curios. Hibern.]

Remonstrance of divers Lords of the Pale to the King, concerning the Irish Parliament in 1613.

[See Review, p. 48, &c.]

MAY it please your majesty, such is the excessive grief and anxiety of mind and conscience, which we, the nobility of this your highness's kingdom, whose names are here under-written, do conceive, by the more preposterous courses holden in parliament, as we must be inforced, before we descend further, most humbly with tears, to implore your gracious favour, that if the due regard of your majesty's sacred honour, the careful consideration of the good peace and tranquility of this your realm and country, the tender and feeling respect of our bounden and obliged duty to both, do carry us in aught beyond the limits of a well-tempered moderation, your highness will be graciously pleased to pardon our excess herein, so far as *pius dolor* and *justa iracundia*, do in themselves deserve. It would far pass the compass of a letter, if we should insist to particularize the manifest, old, precedent disorders, and such as still do accompany this intended action; only your highness shall understand, that many knights from counties, and citizens and burgesses from cities and towns, have, contrary to the true election, been returned; and in some places force, and in many others fraud, deceit, and indirect means have been used for effecting of this so lawless a course of proceeding. Neither can we but make known unto your majesty, that under pretence of erecting towns in places of the new plantation, more corporations have been made since the beginning of last month, or a little more, than are returned out of this whole kingdom; besides, the number thereof (as we conceive it) contrary to your highness's highness's intended purpose, is dispersed throughout all parts of this kingdom; and that in divers places, where there be good ancient boroughs, not allowed to send burgesses to the parliament; and yet these new created corporations, for the most part are so miserable and beggarly poor, as their *tuguria* cannot otherwise be holden than as *tituli fine re, et figmenta in rebus*; for divers of which, (their extreme poverty being not able to defray the charges of burgesses, nor the places themselves, to afford any one man fit to present himself in the poorest society of men) and for others, we must confess, that some of great fashion have not sticked to abase themselves to be returned: the lord deputy's servants, attornies, and clerks, resident only in the city of Dublin, most of them having never seen or known the places for which they were returned, and others of contemptible life and carriage. And what outrageous violence was offered yesterday to a grave gentleman, whom men of all sorts, that know him, do and will confess to be both learned, grave, and discreet, free from all touch and imputation, and whom those of the lower house, to whom no exceptions could be taken, had chosen to be their speaker, we leave, for avoiding tediousness to your highness, to their own further declaration. And forasmuch as, most renowned and dread sovereign, we cannot in any due proportion of reason expect redress in these our distressed calamities, where many of those, who represent the body of your estate, were the chief authors of them, upon the knees of our loyal and submissive hearts, we humbly pray, that it would please your majesty to admit some of us to the access of your royal presence, where, if we fail in the least point of these our assertions, and declarations of other evils, which do multiply in this estate, we willingly submit ourselves to any punishment, as deserved, which it shall please your highness to lay and inflict upon us. For we are those, by the effusion of whose ancestors blood, the foundation of that empire, which we acknowledge your highness by the laws of God and man to have over this kingdom and people, was first laid, and in many succeeding ages preserved. To us it properly appertaineth, both in the obligation of publick duty and private interest, to heed the good thereof, who never laid the foundation of our hopes upon the disturbance of it, garboils and dissentions being the downfal of our estate, as some of us now living can witness; and therefore, we cannot, but out of the consideration of our bounden duty and allegiance, make known unto your highness the general discontent which those strange, unlooked for, and never heard of courses particularly have bred; whereof, if the rebellious and discontented of this nation abroad do take advantage, and procure the evil-affected at home, which are numbers, by reason of that already-settled, and intended plantation, in any hostile fashion to set disorders on foot, and labour some underhand relief from any prince or estate abroad, who peradventure might be inveigled, and drawn to commiserate their pretended distresses and oppressions, however, we are assured the prowess and power of your majesty in the end will bring the authors thereof to ruin and confusion; yet it may be attended with the effusion of much blood, exhausting of masses of treasure, the exposing of us, and others your highness's

well-

well-affected subjects, to the hazard of poverty, whereof the memory is very lively and fresh among us; and finally, to the laying open of the whole commonalty to the inundation of all miseries and calamities, which garboils, civil war, and diffentions, do breed and draw with them, in a rent and torn estate. For preventing whereof, we nothing doubt but your majesty will give redress, by the equal balance of your highness's justice, which we beseech the Almighty, with your royal person, ever to maintain and preserve,

Your majesty's most faithful subjects,

David Buttevant. Gormanston. Da Roche. Fermoy. Montgarret. Killine. Delvin. Christopher Slane. Robert Trymbleston. James Dunboyne. Matthew Louth. Thomas Cahyr.

May 19, 1613.

N u m b. III.

[From Desiderat. Curios. Hibernic.]

To the Right Honourable the Lords of his Majesty's most Honourable Privy Council.

The humble Petition of the Knights, Citizens, and Burgesses of the Counties, Cities, and ancient Boroughs of Ireland.

[See Review, p. 49, &c.]

MOST humbly declaring to your lordships, that the assurance of his majesty's most princely inviolable justice, whereof your lordships, in matters of state and government, are the high and supreme distributors, doth embolden us, in our oppressions, to address these our submissive lines to your honours; wherein our purpose is, not to be pleaders, the strangeness of our extremities finding no fit words to express them; and therefore, in declaration of the naked truth, your lordships shall understand, that we, the knights, citizens, and burgesses of the counties, cities, and ancient boroughs of this realm, coming, according to our bounden duties, into the parliament house, we find there 14 counsellors of state, 3 of the judges, having before received writs to appear in the higher house, all his majesty's council at law; and the rest of the number, for the most part, consisting of attornies, clerks in courts, of the lord deputy's retinue, and others his houshold-servants, with some lately come out of England, having no abiding here; and all these, save very few, were returned from the new corporations erected, to the number of 40, or thereabouts, not only in places of the new plantation, but also in other provinces, where there be corporations of antiquity; few or none of them having been ever resident, and most of them having never seen these places: the rest, who possessed the rooms of knights of shires, save 4 or 6, came in by practice, and dishonest devices, whereunto themselves were not

strangers;

strangers; and some there were from ancient boroughs, who intruded themselves into their places, by as undue and unlawful means; as the knights and burgesses duly elected were ready at the parliament door to prove and avouch. For redress whereof, we of the ancient shires, cities, and towns, to whom no exceptions could be taken, being desirous to take the usual and accustomed course, what outrageous violence ensued, by the fury of some there, we humbly leave to your lordships to be informed by our declarations; whereunto a schedule, by direction of my lord deputy, subscribed with our hands, is annexed. And forasmuch, right honourable, as the strangeness of these proceedings, in a Christian commonwealth is such, as we think his majesty, and your lordships will hardly be induced to believe; they being, in the likelihood of impossibility, equal to that of Messalino unto the emperor Claudius in ancient Rome; or to any other accident, how rare soever, transmitted to posterity in modern or ancient shires, we humbly pray, that your lordships, in commiseration of our distress, will be a mean to his highness, that some of us, with some of our nobility, may be licensed to present ourselves there, for the proof of our assertions; wherein if we fail in any one point, we utterly renounce all favour; and that in the mean time his majesty will be pleased to suspend his gracious judgment, in the apprehension of what to our prejudice may be informed here; those from whom his highness doth usually receive information, being the authors of the carriage of what is done amiss.

Numb. IV.

[From Desiderat. Curios. Hibernic.]

Abstract of the Report and Return of Commissioners sent by the King to Ireland, to enquire into the Grievances and Complaints of the Irish, in 1613.

[See Review, p. 50.]

UPON our arrival in Dublin the 11th of September, we caused his majesty's commission and instructions to be enrolled, and presently directed our letters to the governors of Munster and Conaught, as also to divers lords, archbishops, and bishops, and to several of the sheriffs of counties, and others, concerning the articles of the said instructions, whereby our arrival, and the cause of our employment were made known to the people in most parts of the kingdom. Yet during the space of one month at the least, after our landing, no one petition was exhibited to us complaining of any grievances. Nevertheless afterwards, upon the coming over of the lord Killeene and Sir Christopher Plunket, two of the late petitioners to his majesty, they exhibited unto us particular instances of oppression and exactions by soldiers, provost-marshals, and some others, specially those that reside nearest the state; out of which particulars, being many,

APPENDIX.

we selected three-score or thereabouts, as meetest to be examined; whereby we might discern, what were the several kinds of the soldiers' oppressions towards the people; for proof of which selected articles, divers days were assigned to them to produce their witnesses: at which time, some of the captains of horse and foot, provost-marshals, and some of their soldiers we warned to appear before us, and thereupon we proceeded in presence of the lord Killeene and Sir Christopher Plunket, and some of the parties grieved, and we proceeded to a summary examination of those disorders; and by these examinations, and by other means, it doth appear unto us, that the soldiers, both horse and foot, have extorted upon his majesty's subjects in manner following: first, in all their journies and thorough-fairs, where, by their warrant from the lord deputy, they are commanded to take meat and drink in the country, paying ready money, or giving tickets, for the same; the soldiers nevertheless, for the most part, neither pay money, nor give tickets, as they ought to do; and in cases where the collectors receive tickets for the payment of the country for victualling of soldiers, they, and sometimes persons authorised by the principal gentlemen of the country, do get these tickets into their hands, and obtain payment from his majesty's treasurer, and seldom make distribution thereof to the poorer sort to whom it is due.

THE soldiers, where they are cessed, do extort money from the poorer people (besides meat and drink) for every night's lodging three shillings for a horse-man, and two shillings for a foot man, sometimes more, and sometimes less; and certain petty sums are also taken for their boys and attendants, besides victuals; and it happeneth sometimes, that the soldiers that take cess, take money, as well for themselves as for other soldiers absent, which the country call Blackmen, because they are not seen; and sometimes soldiers in pay, and others discharged out of pay, and divers vagrants in the name of soldiers, take meat and money of the people without warrant, or after the date of their warrant is expired, in extortious manner, by two or three or more in a company. And in all these cases, when the people have not money to pay them, they take divers times, forcibly, either some of their cattle, or some of their household stuff for pawns in lieu thereof, whereby breach of peace, and affrays are occasioned.

LIKEWISE the soldiers, although they be always enjoined by the lord deputy's warrant to pass to and fro the direct way in their journies, yet do they sometimes make a circular and long course in their thorough-fair, whereby they cess, and hurt the people, more days than is limited unto them, or is requisite for their journey.

ALSO the soldiers in journies, being cessed in small numbers in villages by the collectors, according to the ability of the places, they do sometimes take money in the towns, wherein they are assigned to take their lodgings, and victuals, and depart the same fame, and lodge themfelves, without warrant, near the fame place, whereby the people bear a double charge.

Moreover it appeareth, that fome officers of bands have taken monies of townfhips, to forbear to cefs upon them in their journies, and have ceffed upon the towns not far diftant from thence; and thefe exactions are committed by foldiers in counties where the compofition in lieu of cefs is paid, as in other other places; wherein is to be obferved, that by the tenor of the compofition, the counties are to victual the foldiers in their paffage at ufual rates, a matter referved for neceffity of ftate.

The foldiers do not only commit thefe abufes in their thorough-fares, but when they are fent into the country upon other employments.

The provoft-marfhal (whereof there is one at the leaft in every province) has likewife certain men to attend him, who do exact victuals and money in their paffage up and down the country from the people, and commit other diforders as foldiers do; which extortions have been committed by the foldiers and the reft of themfelves, without any warrant at all, or connivance of any, fo far as hath appeared unto us.

And notwithftanding the oppreffions in thefe kinds are very many (as may be feen by their informations to us exhibited from divers parts of the kingdom) yet, for any thing appearing unto us, very few have complained thereof to the lord deputy; who, upon their complaints, hath given order for redrefs of fuch grievances, as hath been manifefted unto us.

The reafons wherefore the people pretend to have forborne to make their complaints, is the fear they have had to be worfe ufed by the foldiers complained of at other times, and that the charges of the complaint would far have exceeded their damages and loffes, although they cannot deny but the lord deputy hath given as eafy accefs, and as fpeedy remedy, as hath been given by former governors.

The names of fome few foldiers that are offenders in thefe kinds, and are yet in pay, appear in our examinations, others are dead or difcharged, and in many of the complaints againft foldiers, their names are not known to the parties, neither have the foldiers, or others complained to us for want of pay by their captains, although fome of them have been by us required publickly to deliver us their knowledge therein.... There be divers complaints againft fheriffs in general, namely, that fundry fheriffs have no freehold, or habitation, in the counties for which they ferve, as they ought to have by the laws of the kingdom; alfo that divers of them have no fettled eftates of land or freehold in other places; and having gathered rents, and other duties for his majefty, they depart without paffing their accounts, which appeareth to be true: and the reafon son thereof is affirmed to be, that in the civilest countries in the English pale, and in other counties within the kingdom, there are found very few protestants that are freeholders of quality fit to be sheriffs, and that will take the oath of supremacy, as by the laws they ought to do; and by the lord deputy's order, no sheriff is admitted till he enter into sufficient bond for answering his accounts.

It is likewise a grievance complained of, and found true, that many sheriffs, especially those of the meaner sort, do suffer their men, bailiffs, and followers to take victuals of the country for themselves without money, and sometimes both money and victuals; and that in gathering in his majesty's rents, and the fines for using the short ploughs, and other impositions, as building of bridges, and such like, they do take of the people, besides the principal duties twelve pence in the pound, and sometimes greater sums, for their private uses, for which the sheriffs give no reason, but that the same is taken towards their charges in collecting those duties, in regard of the little benefit which their office otherwise yieldeth, &c.

Numb. V.

[From Carte's Orm. vol. iii.]

The Remonstrance of the Catholicks of Ireland, delivered to his Majesty's Commissioners at Trym, 17th March, 1642.

[See Review, p. 166, &c.]

To the King's most excellent Majestie.

Most gratious Soveraigne,

WEE your majestie's most dutifull and loyall subjects, the Catholiques of your highness kingdome of Ireland, being necessitated to take armes for the preservation of our relligion, the mainetenance of your majestie's rights and prerogatives, the naturall and just defence of our lives and estates, and the liberties of our country, have often since the beginning of these troubles attempted to present our humble complaynts unto your royall view; but we are frustrated of our hopes therein by the power and vigilance of our adversaryes, (the now lords justices and other ministers of state in this kingdome) who by the assistance of the malignant partie in England, now in armes against your royall person, with less difficultie to attain the bad ends they proposed to themselves, of extirpateing our religion and nation, have hitherto debarred us of any access to your majestie's justice, which occasioned the effusion of much innocent blood, and other mischiefs in this your kingdome, that otherwise might well bee prevented. And whereas of late notice was sent unto us of a commission granted by your majestie

to

APPENDIX.

to the right honorable the lord marques of Ormond, and others, authorizing them to heare what we shall say or propound, and the same to transmitt to your majestie in writeing, which your majestie's gratious and princely favour, wee finde to be accompanied with these words, viz. (albeit wee doe extreamly detest the odious rebellion which the recusants of Ireland have without ground or colour rayfed against us, our crowne, and dignitie) which words wee doe in all humilitie conceive to have proceeded from the misreprefentations of our adverfaries; and therefore doe proteft, we have been therein malicioufly traduced to your majestie, haveing never entertayned any rebellious thought against your majestie, your crowne, or dignitie; but allwayes have beene, and ever will continue, your majestie's most faithfull and loyall subjects; and doe most humbly befeech your majestie foe to owne and avowe us; and as fuch we prefent unto your majestie thefe enfueing grievances, and caufes of the prefent diftempers.

IMPRIMIS, The Catholiques of this kingdome, whome no reward could invite, no perfecution inforce, to forfake that religion profeffed by them and their anceftors for thirteen hundred years, or thereabouts, are fince the fecond yeare of the reigne of queene Elizabeth, made incapable of places of honour or truft, in church or commonwealth; their nobles become contemptible, their gentry debarred from learning in univerfities, or public fchools within this kingdom; their younger brothers put by all manner of imployment in their native country, and neceffitated (to their great difcomfort, and impoverifhment of the land) to feeke education, and fortune abroad; misfortunes made incident to the faid Catholiques of Ireland only, (their numbers, qualitie, and loyalltie confidered) of all the nations of Chriftendome.

2. SECONDLY, That by this incapacitie, which in respect of their religion was impofed upon the faid Catholiques; men of meane condition and qualitie, for the moft part were in this kingdome, imployed in places of greateft honour and truft, who being to begin a fortune, built it on the ruines of the Catholique natives, att all tymes lying open to be difcountenanced, and wrought uppon: and who (becaufe they would feeme to be carefull of the government,) did, from tyme to tyme, fuggeft falfe and malitious matters againft them, to render them fufpected and odious in England; from which ungrounded informations, and their many other ill offices, thefe mifchiefes have befallen the Catholiques of Ireland. Firft, the oppofition given to all the graces and favours that your majestie, or your late royall father, promifed, or intended to the natives of this kingdom; Secondly, the procuring of falfe inquifitions, upon faigned titles, of their eftates, againft many hundred years poffeffion, and no travers, or petition of right, admitted thereunto, and jurors denying to find fuch offices were cenfured even to publique infamie, and ruine of their eftates, the findeing thereof being againft their confciences, and their evidences; and nothing muft ftand againft fuch offices taken of great and confiderable parts of the kingdome, but letters pattents under the great feale; and if letters pattents were produced, (as in moft cafes they were) none muft be allowed valid,

valid, nor yet fought to be legally avoyded: foe that, of late tymes, by the underhand working of Sir William Parſons knight, now one of the lords juſtices heere, and the arbitrary illegal power of the two impeached judges in parliament, and others drawen by their adviſe and counſell, one hundred and fifty letters pattents were avoyded in one morning; which courſe continued untill all the pattents of the kingdome, to a few, were by them and their aſſociates declared void; ſuch was the care thoſe miniſters had of your majeſtie's great ſeale, being the publique faith of the kingdome. This way of ſervice, in ſhew only pretended for your majeſtie, proved to your diſſervice; and to the immoderate, and too tymely advancement of the ſaid miniſters of ſtate, and their adherents, and nearly to the utter ruine of the ſaid Catholiques.

3. That, whereas your majeſtie's late royall father, king James, having a princely and fatherly care of this kingdome, was gratiouſly pleaſed, to graunt ſeverall large and beneficiall commiſſions, under the great ſeale of England, and ſeverall inſtructions, and letters under his privie ſignett, for the paſſing and ſecuring of the eſtates of his ſubjects here by letters pattents under the great ſeale, and letters pattents accordingly were thereof paſſed, fynes payed, old rents increaſed, and new rents reſerved to the crowne. And the ſaid late king was further gratiouſly pleaſed, att ſeverall tymes, to ſend divers honorable perſons of integritie, knowledge and experience, to examine the grievances of this kingdome, and to ſettle and eſtabliſh a courſe for redreſs thereof. And whereas your majeſtie was gracioufly pleaſed, in the fourth yeare of your raigne, to vouchſafe a favourable heareing to the grievances preſented unto you, by agents from this kingdome; and thereupon did graunt many graces and favours unto your ſubjects thereof, for ſecuritie of their eſtates, and redreſs for remove of thoſe heavie preſſures, under which they have long groaned; which acts of juſtice, and grace extended to this people by your majeſtie, and your ſaid royall father, did afford them great content, yett ſuch was, and is yett, the immortall hatred of ſome of the ſaid miniſters of ſtate, and eſpecially of the ſaid Sir William Parſons, the ſaid impeached judges and their adherents, to any welfare and happineſs of this nation, and their ambition to make themſelves ſtill greater and richer, by the totall ruine and extirpation of this people; that under pretence of your majeſtie's ſervice, the publique faith involved in thoſe grants was violated, and the grace and goodneſs intended, by two glorious kings ſucceſſively, to a faithful people, made unprofitable.

4. The illegall, arbitrary, and unlawfull proceedings of the ſaid Sir William Parſons, and one of the ſaid impeached judges, and their adherents and inſtruments, in the court of wards, and the many wilfully erroneous decrees, and judgments of that court, by which the heirs of Catholique noblemen, and other Catholiques, were moſt cruelly and tyrannically dealt withall, deſtroyed in their eſtates, and bred in diſſolution and ignorance, their parents debts unſatisfied, their ſiſters and younger brothers left wholly unprovided for, the auncient and appearing tenures of meſne lords unregarded, eſtates

valid

APPENDIX.

valid in law, and made for valuable confiderations, avoyded againſt law, and the whole land filled upp with the frequent ſwarmes of eſcheators, feodaryes, purſuivants, and others, by authoritie of that court.

5. The ſaid Catholiques, notwithſtanding the heavy preſſures beforementioned, and other grievances, in part reprefented to your majeſtie by the late committees of both Houſes of parliament of this kingdom, (whereunto they humbly deſire that relation be had, and redreſs obtained therein,) did readyly, and without reluctance, or repineing, contribute to all the ſubſidies, loanes, and other extraordinary grauuts made to your majeſtie in this kingdome, ſince the beginning of your raigne, amounting unto well neere one million of poundes, over and above your majeſtie's revenue, both certain and caſuall : and although the ſaid Catholiques were in parliament, and otherwiſe, the moſt forward in graunting the ſaid ſummes, and did beare nyne parts of ten in the payments thereof, yett ſuch was the power of their adverſaryes, and the advantage they gained by the opportunitie of their continuall addreſs to your majeſtie, to increaſe their reputation in getting in of thoſe moneys, and their authoritie in the diſtribution thereof to your majeſtie's greate diſſervice, that they aſſumed to themſelves to be the procurers thereof, and reprefented the ſaid Catholiques as obſtinate and refractory.

6. The army raiſed for your majeſtie's ſervice here, at the greate charge of the kingdome, was diſbanded by the preſſing importunitie of the malignant partie in England, not giving way that your majeſtie ſhould take adviſe therein with the parliament here; alledging the ſaid army was popiſh, and therefore not to be truſted; and although the world could wittneſs the unwarrantable and unexampled invaſion made by the malignant partie of the parliament in England, uppon your majeſtie's honour, rights, prerogatives, and principall flowers of your crowne; and that the ſaid Sir William Parſons, Sir Adam Loftus knight, your majeſtie's vice-treaſurer of this kingdome, and others their adherents, did declare that an army of ten thouſand Scotts was to arrive in this kingdome, to force the ſaid Catholiques to change their religion, and that Ireland could never doe well without a rebellion, to the end the remaine of the natives thereof might be extirpated; and wagers were laid at generall aſſizes and publique meetings, by ſome of them then, and now imployed in places of greate profitt and truſt in this kingdome, that within one yeare no Catholique ſhould be left in Ireland; and that they ſaw the ancient and unqueſtionable privileges of the parliament of Ireland unjuſtly and againſt law enchroached uppon, by the orders, acts and proceedings of both Howſes of parliament in England, in ſending for and queſtioning, to, and in, that parliament, the members of the parliament of this kingdome, ſitting the parliament here; and that by ſpeeches, and orders printed by authoritie of both Houſes in England, it was declared that Ireland was bound by the ſtatutes made in England, if named, which is contrary to knowen truth, and the laws here ſettled for fowre hundred yeares, and upwards; and that the ſaid Catholiques were thoroughly enformed of the proteſtation

made

APPENDIX.

made by both Houses of parliament of England against Catholiques, and of their intentions to introduce lawes for the extirpation of Catholique religion in the three kingdomes; and that they had certain notice of the bloody execution of priests there, only for being priests, and that your Majestie's mercy and power could not prevaile with them to save the lyfe of one condemned priest; and that the Catholiques of England being of their owne flesh and blood, must suffer, or departe the land, and consequently others not of so neere a relation to them, if bound by their statutes, and within their power. These motives, although very strong and powerfull to produce apprehensions and feares in the said Catholiques, did not prevaile with them to take defensive armes, much less offensive; they still expecting that your majestie in your high wisdome might be able in a short tyme, to apply seasonable cures, and apt remedies unto those evills, and innovations.

7. That the committees of the lords and commons of this kingdome, having attended your majestie for the space of nyne months, your majestie was gratiously pleased, notwithstanding your then weightie and urgent affayrs in England and Scotland, to receive, and very often with great patience to hear their grievances, and many debates thereof at large; during which debates, the said lords justices, and some of your privy councill of this kingdome, and their adherents, by their malitious and untrue informations conveyed to some ministers of state in England, (who since are declared of the malignant partie,) and by the continuall solicitation of others of the said privy councill, gone to England of purpose to cross and give impediment unto the justice, and grace your majestie was inclined to afford to your subjects of this realme, did, as much as in them lay, hinder the obtayning of any redress for the said grievances, and not prevailing therein with your majestie as they expected, have by their letters, and instruments, laboured with many leading members of the parliament there, to give stopp and interruption thereunto, and likewise transmitted unto your majestie, and some of the state of England, sundery misconstructions and misrepresentations of the proceedings and actions of your parliament of this kingdome, and thereby endeavoured to possess your majestie with an evill opinion thereof; and that the said parliament had no power of judicature in capitall causes, (which is an essentiall part of parliament) thereby aymeing at the impunitie of some of them, and others, who were then impeached of high treason; and at the destruction of this parliament: but the said lords justices and privie councell, observing that no art or practice of theirs could be powerfull to withdraw your majestie's grace and good intentions from this people, and that the redress graunted of some particular grievances was to be passed as acts in parliament; the said lords justices, and their adherents, with the height of malice, envieing the good union long before settled, and continued between the members of the House of commons, and their good correspondence with the lords, left nothing unattempted, which might rayse discord, and disunion in the said House; and by some of themselves, and some instruments of theirs in the said commons house, private meeteings of greate numbers of the said
House

Houſe were appointed, of purpoſe to rayſe diſtinction of nation and religion, by meanes whereof a faction was made there, which tended much to the diſquiet of the Houſe, and diſturbance of your majeſtie's and the publique ſervice; and after certain knowledge that the ſaid committees were by the water ſide in England, with ſundry important and beneficial bills, and other graces, to be paſſed, as acts in that parliament; of purpoſe to prevent the ſame, the ſaid faction, by the practiſe of the ſaid lords juſtices, and ſome of the ſaid privy councill and their adherents, in a tumultuous and diſorderly manner, on the ſeventh day of Auguſt 1641, and on ſeverall days before, cryed out for an adjournement of the Houſe, and beinge over-voted by the voices of the more moderate partie, the ſaid Lords Juſtices and their adherents told ſeverall honourable peers, that if they did not adjourne the lords Houſe on that day, being Saturday, that they would themſelves prorogue or adjourne the parliament on the next Munday following, by meanes whereof, and of great numbers of proxies of noblemen, not eſtated, nor at any tyme reſident in this kingdome, (which is deſtructive to the libertye and freedom of parliaments here,) the lords Houſe was on the ſaid ſeventh day of Auguſt adjourned, and the Houſe of Commons by occaſion thereof, and of the faction aforeſaid, adjourned ſoone after, by which meanes thoſe bills and graces, according to your majeſtie's intention, and the great expectation and longing deſires of your people, could not then paſs as acts of parliament.

Within few dayes after this fatal and enforced adjournement, the ſaid committees arrived at Dublin, with their diſpatch from your majeſtie, and preſented the ſame to the ſaid lords juſtices and councill, expreſſing a right ſence of the ſaid adjournment, and beſought their lordſhips, for the ſatisfaction of the people, to require ſhort heads of that part of the diſpatch wherein your majeſtie did appeare in the beſt manner unto your people, might be ſuddainely conveyed unto all the partes of the kingdome, atteſted by the ſaid lords juſtices, to prevent deſpaire, or miſunderſtanding. This was promiſed to be done, and an inſtrument drawen, and preſented unto them for this purpoſe, and yett, (as it ſeemes deſireing rather to add fuell to the fire of the ſubjects diſcontents, than quench the ſame,) they did forbeare to give any notice thereof to the people.

8. After this, certaine dangerous and pernitious petitions, contrived by the adviſe and councell of the ſaid Sir William Parſons, Sir Adam Loftus, Sir John Clotworthy, knights, Arthure Hill, Eſq; and ſundry others malignant partie, and ſigned by many thouſands of the malignant partie in the citty of Dublin, in the province of Ulſter, and in ſundry other of the partes in this kingdome, directed to the commons Houſe in England, were at publique aſſizes and other publique places made known and read, to many perſons of quallitie in this kingdome, which petitions contayned matters deſtructive to the ſaid Catholiques, their religion, lives, and eſtates, and were

F f f

the more to be feared by reason of the active power of the said Sir John Clotworthy in the commons Howse in England in oppostition to your majestie, and his barbarous and inhumane expressions in that Howse against Catholique religion, and the professors thereof. Soone after an order conceaved in the commons House of England, that no man should bowe unto the name of Jesus, (att the sacred sound whereof all knees should bend) came to the knowledge of the said Catholiques, and that the said malignant partie did contrive and plott to extinguish their religion and nation. Hence it did arise that some of the said Catholiques begun to consider the deplorable and desperate condition they were in, by a statute law here found among the records of this kingdome, of the second yeare of the raigne of the late queen Elizabeth (but never executed in her tyme, nor discovered till most of the members of that parliament were dead) by which no Catholique of this kingdome could enjoy his life, estate, or lyberty if the said statute were executed; whereunto no impediment remayned but your majestie's prerogative and power, which were endeavoured to be clipped, or taken away, as is before rehearsed; then the plott of destruction by an army out of Scotland, and another of the malignant partie in England, must be executed; the feares of those twofold destructions, and their ardent desire to maintaine that just prerogative, which might encounter and remove it, did necessitate some Catholiques in the North, about the 22d of October 1641, to take armes in maintenance of their religion, your majestie's rights, and the preservation of life, estate, and libertie; and immediately thereuppon tooke a solemn oath, and sent several declarations to the lords justices and councill to that effect; and humbly desired they might be heard in parliament, unto the determination whereof, they were ready to submitt themselves, and their demands: which declarations being received, were slighted by the said lords justices, who by the swaying part of the said councill, and by the advise of the said two impeached judges, glad of any occasion to put off the parliament, which by the former adjournment was to meete soone after, caused a proclamation to be published on the 23d of the said month of October 1641, therein accuseing all the Catholiques of Ireland of disloyaltie, and thereby declareing that the parliament was prorogued untill the 26th of February following.

9. Within few dayes after the said 23d day of October 1641, many lords and other persons of ranke and qualitie, made their humble addres to the said lords justices and councill, and made it evidently appeare unto them, that the said prorogation was against law, and humbly besought the parliament might sit according to the former adjournment, which was then the only expedient, to compose or remove the then growing discontents and troubles of the land; and the said lords justices, and their partie of the councill, then well knowing that the members of both Houses throughout the kingdome, (a few in and about Dublin only excepted,) would stay from the meeteing of both Houses, by reason of the said prorogation, did by proclamation two dayes before the time, give way the parliament might sitt, but so limitted, that no act of grace, or any

thing

thing elſe for the people's quiet or ſatisfaction, might be propounded or paſſed. And thereuppon, a few of the lords and commons appeared in the parliament Houſe, who in their enterance at the caſtle-bridge and gate, and within the yard to the parliament Houſe doore, and receſs from thence, were invironed with a great number of armed men with their match lighted, and muſkets preſented even to the breaſts of the members of both Houſes, none being admitted to bring one ſervant to attend him, or any weapon about him within the caſtle-bridge. Yet how thin ſoever the Howſes were, or how much overawed, they both did ſupplicate the lords juſtices and councill, that they might continue for a tyme together, and expect the coming of the reſt of both Houſes, to the end they might quiet the troubles in full parliament, and that ſome acts of ſecuritie graunted by your Majeſtie, and tranſmitted under the great Sale of England, might paſs to ſettle the minds of your majeſtie's ſubjects. But to theſe requeſts, ſoe much conduceing to your majeſtie's ſervice, and ſettlement of your people, a flatt denyall was given; and the ſaid lords juſtices and their partie of the councill, by their workeing with their partie in both Howſes of parliament, being then very thyn as afforeſaid, propounded an order ſhould be conceaved in parliament, that the ſaid diſcontented gentlemen tooke armes in rebellious manner, which was reſented much by the beſt affected of both Howſes; but being awed as afforeſaid, and credibly informed, if ſome particular perſons amongſt them ſtood in oppoſition thereunto, that the ſaid muſketteeres were directed to ſhoote them att their goeing out of the parliament Houſe, thorough which terror, way was given to that order.

10. NOTWITHSTANDING all the beforementioned provocations, preſſures, and indignities, the farr greater, and more conſiderable parte of the Catholiques, and all the cittyes and corporations of Ireland, and whole provinces, ſtood quiet in their howſes; whereupon the lords juſtices and their adherents, well knowing that many powerfull members of the parliament of England ſtood in oppoſition to your majeſtie, made their application, and addreſſed their diſpatches full fraught with calumnies and falſe ſuggeſtions againſt the Catholiques of this kingdome, and propounded unto them, to ſend ſeverall great forces to conquer this kingdome; thoſe of the malignant partie here were by them armed; the Catholiques were not only denyed armes, but were diſarmed, even in the citty of Dublin, which in all ſucceſſions of ages paſt continued as loyall to the crowne of England as any citty or place whatſoever: all other auncient and loyall cittyes and corporatt townes of the kingdome, (by meanes whereof principally the kingdome was preſerved in former tymes) were denyed armes for their money to defend themſelves, and expreſs order given by the ſaid lords juſtices to diſarme all Catholiques in ſome of the ſaid cittyes and townes: others disfurniſhed were inhibited to provide armes for their defence; and the ſaid lords juſtices and councell having received an order of both Houſes of parliament in England to publiſh a proclamation of pardon unto all thoſe who were then in rebellion (as they tearmed it) in this kingdome, if

they

they did submitt by a day to be limited, the said Sir William Parsons, contrary to this order, soe wrought with his partie of the councill, that a proclamation was published of pardon only in two countyes, and a very short day prefixed, and therein all freeholders were excepted; through which every man saw that the estates of the Catholiques were first aymed att, and their lives next. The said lords justices and their partie haveing advanced their designe thus far, and not finding the success answerable to their desires, commanded Sir Charles Coote, Knight and Baronet deceased, to march to the county of Wickloe, where he burnt, killed, and destroyed all in his way, in a most cruell manner, man, woman, and childe; persons that had not appearing wills to doe hurt, nor power to execute it. Soone after, some foote companies did march in the night by direction of the said lords justices, and their said partie, to the towne of Sauntry in Fingall, three miles off Dublin; a country that neither then, nor for the space of four or five hundred yeares before, did feele what troubles were, or war meant; but it was too sweet and too near, and therefore fitt to be forced to armes. In that towne innocent husbandmen, some of them being Catholiques, and some Protestants taken for Catholiques, were murdered in their inn, and their heads carryed tryumphant into Dublin. Next morning, complaint being made of this, no redress was obtayned therein; whereupon some gentlemen of qualitie, and others the inhabitants of the country, seeing what was then acted, and what passed in the said last march towards the county of Wickloe, and justly fearing to be all murthered, forsooke their howses, and were constrayned to stand together in their owne defence, though ill provided of armes or ammunition. Heereupon a proclamation was agreed upon at the board, on the 13th of December 1641, and not published or printed till the 15th of December, by which the said gentlemen, and George Kinge by name, were required to come in by, or upon the 18th of the said month, and a safetie was therein promised them. On the same day another proclamation was published, summoning the lords dwelling in the English pale near Dublin to a grand councill on the 17th of the said month; but the lords justices and their partie of the councill, to take away all hope of accommodation, gave direction to the said Sir Charles Coote, the said 15th day of the said month of December, to march to Clontarffe, being the house and towne of the said George Kinge, and two miles from Dublin, to pillage, burne, kill, and destroy all that there was to be found; which direction was readily and particularly observed, (in a manyfest breach of publick faith) by meanes whereof, the meeteing of the said grand councill was diverted: The lords not dareing to come within the power of such notorious faith-breakers: the consideration whereof, and of other the matters aforesaid, made the nobilitie and gentry of the English pale, and other parts of the province of Leinster, sensible of the present danger, and put themselves in the best posture they could for their naturall defence. Wherefore they imployed lieutenant Collonel Read to present their humble remonstrance to your sacred majestie, and to declare unto you the state of their affayres, and humbly to beseech relief and redress; the said lieutenant Collonell, though your majestie's servant, and

and imployed in publique truſt, (in which caſe the law of nations affords ſafety and protection) was without regard to either, not only ſtopped from proceeding in his imployment, but alſo tortured on the rack at Dublin.

11. The lord preſident of Munſter, by direction of the ſaid lords juſtices, (that province being quiet) with his accomplices, burnt, preyed, and put to death men, women and children, without making any difference of qualitie, condition, age, or ſex in ſeveral parts of that province; the Catholique nobles and gentlemen there were miſtruſted and threatened, and others of inferior quality truſted and furniſhed with armes and ammunition. The province of Connaught was uſed in the like meaſure; whereupon moſt of the conſiderable Catholiques in both the ſaid provinces were inforced (without armes or ammunition) to look after their ſafety, and to that end did ſtand on their defence; ſtill expecting your majeſtie's pleaſure, and allways ready to obey your commands. Now the plott of the ſaid miniſters of ſtate and their adherents being even ripe, applications were inceſſantly by them made to the malignant partie in England, to deprive this people of all hopes of your majeſtie's juſtice or mercie, and to plant a perpetual enmity between the Engliſh and Scotiſh nations, and your ſubjects of this kingdome.

12. That whereas this your majeſtie's kingdome of Ireland in all ſucceſſions of ages, ſince the raigne of King Henry the ſecond, ſometime King of England and Lord of Ireland, had parliaments of their owne, compoſed of lords and commons in the ſame manner and forme qualified with equall liberties, powers, priviledges and immunities with the parliament of England, and onely depend of the king and crowne of England and Ireland: And for all that tyme, no prevalent record or authentique preſident can be found, that any ſtatute made in England could or did bind this kingdome, before the ſame were here eſtabliſhed by parliament; yet upon untrue ſuggeſtions and informations, given of your ſubjects of Ireland, an act of parliament, entituled, an act for the ſpeedie and effectual reduceing the rebells in his majeſtie's kingdome of Ireland to their due obedience to his majeſtie and the crowne of England; and another act, intituled, an act for adding unto and explayneing the ſaid former act, was procured to be enacted in the ſaid parliament of England, in the eighteenth yeare of your majeſtie's raigne; by which acts, and other proclamations, your majeſtie's ſubjects unſummoned, unheard, were declared rebells, and two millions and a halfe of acres arrable, meadow, and profitable paſture, within this kingdome, ſold to undertakers for certain ſummes of monie; and the edifices, loghs, woodes, and bogges, waſtes and other their appurtenances, were thereby mentioned to be granted and paſt gratis. Which acts the ſaid Catholiques doe conceave to have beene forced uppon your majeſtie; and allthough void, and unjuſt in themſelves to all purpoſes, yett containe matters of evill conſequence, and extreame prejudice to your majeſtie, and totally deſtructive to this nation. The ſcope ſeemeing to aime att rebells only, and at the diſpoſition

of a certaine quantitie of land; but in effect and substance all the landes in the kingdome, by the words of the said acts, may be distributed, in whose possession soever they were, without respect to age, condition, or qualitie; and all your majestie's tenures, and the greatest part of your majestie's standing revenue in this kingdome, taken away; and by the said acts, if they were of force, all power of pardoning and of granting those lands, is taken from your majestie; a president that no age can instance the like. Against this act the said Catholiques do protest, as an act against the fundamentall lawes of this kingdome, and as an act destructive to your majestie's rights and prerogatives, by collour whereof, most of the forces sent hither to infest this kingdome by sea and land, disavowed any authoritie from your majestie, but do depend upon the parliament of England.

13. ALL strangers, and such as were not inhabitants of the citty of Dublin, being commanded by the said lords justices, in and since the said month of November 1641, to depart the said citty, were no sooner departed, than they were by the directions of the said lords justices pillaged abroad, and their goods seized uppon and confiscated in Dublin; and they desireing to returne under the protection and safetie of the state, before their appearance in action, were denied the same; and divers other, persons of rank and qualitie, by the said lords justices imployed in publique service, and others keeping close within their doores, without annoying any man, or siding then with any of the said Catholiques in armes, and others in severall parts of the kingdome liveing under, and having the protection and safetie of the state, were sooner pillaged, their howses burnt, themselves, their tenants and servants killed and destroyed, than any other, by direction of the said lords justices. And by the like direction, when any commander in chiefe of the army, promised, or gave quarter or protection, the same was in all cases violated; and many persons of qualitie, who obtained the same, were ruined before others; others that came into Dublin voluntarily, and that could not be justly suspected of any crime, if Irishmen or Catholiques, by the like direction were pillaged in Dublin, robbed and pillaged abroad, and brought to their tryall for their lives. The cittyes of Dublin and Corke, and the ancient corporatt townes of Drogheda, Yeoghal and Kingsale, who voluntarily received garrisons in your majestie's name, and the adjacent countryes who relieved them, were worse used, and now live in worse condition than the Israelites did in Egypt; so that it will be made appeare, that more murders, breaches of publique faith, and quarter, more destruction and desolation, more crueltie, not fitt to be named, were committed in Ireland, by the direction and advise of the said lords justices and theire partie of the said councill in less than eighteene months, than can be parallelled to have beene done by any Christian People.

14. THE

14. The said lords justices and their adherents have, against the fundamentall lawes of the lande, procured the sitting of both Howses of parliament for severall sessions, (nyne parts of ten of the naturall and genuine members thereof being absent, it standing not with their safety to come under their power) and made upp a considerable number in the Howse of commons of clerkes, souldiers, serveing men, and others, not legally, or not chosen at all, or returned, and having no manner of estate within the kingdom; in which sitting, sundry orders were conceived, and disn̄sies obteyned of persons before impeached of treason in full parliament; and which passed or might have passed some acts against law and to the prejudice of your majestie, and this whole nation. And dureing these troubles, termes were kept, and your majestie's court of cheefe place, and other courts sate at Dublin, to no other end or purpose, but by false and illegall judgments, outlawries, and other capitall proceedings, to attaint many thowsands of your majestie's most faithfull subjects of this kingdome, they being never summoned, nor haveing notice of those proceedings; and sheriffs, made of obscure meane persons, by the like practice, appointed of purpose; and poore artificers, common soldiers and meniall servants, returned jurors, to pass upon the lives and estates of those who came in upon protection, and publique faith.

Therefore the said Catholiques, in the behalfe of themselves and of the whole kingdome of Ireland, doe protest and declare against the said proceedings, in the nature of parliaments, and in the other courts aforesaid, and every of them, as being heynous crimes against law, destructive to parliaments and your majestie's prerogatives and authoritie, and the rights and just liberties of your most faithful subjects.

Forasmuch, dread sovereigne, as the speedy applycation of apt remedyes unto these grievances and heavie pressures, will tend to the settlement and improvement of your majestie's revenue, the prevention of further effusion of blood, the preservation of this kingdome from desolation, and the content and satisfaction of your said subjects, who in manifestation of their duty and zeale to your majestie's service, will be most willing and ready to imploy ten thousand men under the conduct of well experienced commanders in defence of your royal rights and prerogatives; they therefore most humbly beseech your majestie, that you will vouchsafe gratious answers to these their humble and just complaints, and for the establishment of your people in a lasting peace and securitie, the said Catholiques doe most humbly pray, that your majestie may be further gratiously pleased to call a free parliament in this kingdome, in such convenient tyme as your majestie in your high wisdome shall think fitt, and the urgencie of the present affayres of the saide kingdome doth require; and that the said parliament be held in an indifferent place, summoned by, and continued before, some

person

person or persons of honour and fortune, of approved faith to your majestie, and acceptable to your people here, and to be timely placed by your majestie in this government, which is most necessary for the advancement of your service, and present condition of the kingdome: in which parliament, the said Catholiques doe humbly pray these or other their grievances may be redressed, and that in the said parliament, a statute made in this kingdome in the tenth yeare of king Henry the Seventh, commonly called Poyning's Act, and all acts explayning, or inlarging the same, be by a particular act suspended during that parliament, as it hath beene allready done in the eleventh yeare of queen Elizabeth, upon occasions of far less moment than now doe offer themselves; and that your majestie, with the advice of the said parliament, will be pleased to take a course for the further repealing, or further continuance of the said statutes, as may best conduce to the advancement of your service here, and peace of this your realme; and that no matter, whereof complaint is made in this remonstrance, may debarr Catholiques, or give interruption to their free votes, or sitting in the said parliament, and as in duty bound they will ever pray for your majestie's long and prosperous raigne over them.

WEE the undernamed being thereunto authorised, doe present and signe this remonstrance in the behalfe of the Catholiques of Ireland, dated this 17th day of March, 1642.

      GORMANSTON.   LUCAS DILLON.
      ROBERT TALBOTT.   JOHN WALSH.

ACCORDING to your majestie's commission to us directed, we have received this remonstrance, subscribed by the lord viscount Gormanstown, sir Lucas Dillon, knight, sir Robert Talbott, bart. and John Walsh, Esq; authorised by, and in the behalfe of the recusants of Ireland, to present the same unto us to be transmitted to your sacred majestie, dated the 17th day of March, 1642.

      CLANRICKARD and ST. ALBANS.   ROSCOMMON.
      MOORE,   MAU. EUSTACE.

APPENDIX.

Numb. VI.

Extract of a Collection of some of the Massacres, and Murders committed on the Irish in Ireland, since the 23d of October 1641.

[See Review, p. 121, &c.]

This collection was first published in London in the year 1662. The author's frequent, candid, and public appeals to things openly transacted, and to * enemies themselves, then living, and well known, is a strong proof, that what he relates is real matter of fact; and there is yet a stronger inducement to think it so, because it has never yet been proved to be otherwise: nor, as far as I have learned, even attempted to be proved.

County of ANTRIM.

1641. ABOUT the beginning of November, the English, and Scotch forces in Knockfergus murdered in one night all the inhabitants of the territory of the Island Magee, to the number of about 3000 men, women, and children, all innocent persons, at a time when none of the Catholics of that country were in arms, or rebellion. Note, that this was the first massacre committed in Ireland of either side.

Mr. Mac. Naghten having built a small fortress in the said county, to preserve himself, and his followers, from outrages, until he understood what the cause of the then rebellion was; as soon as Colonel Campbell came near with part of the army, he sent to let him know, that he would come to him with his party, which he did; and they were next day murdered to the number of 80, by Sir John Clotworthy, now lord Masareen's, soldiers.

About the same time, 100 poor women, and children, were murdered in one night, at a place called Balliaghiun, by direction of the English, and Scotch officers commanding that county.

* Sir Audley Mervyn, Sir Robert Hannah, (lady Mountrath's father,) several general, and other officers, then, and many years after, alive.

County of DERRY.

1641. Some 300 men, women, and children of the Irish, having freely come under the protection of the garrison of London-Derry, were stripped, plundered, and killed by the said garrison.

1644. Mr. Morris Mac. Daniel, natural son of the late earl of Antrim, was hanged at Coleraine, by the governour's orders, notwithstanding he had colonel Michael Jones's pass.

County of DOWN.

1641. The burgesses, and inhabitants, of the town of Newry, meeting the English army on their march to besiege the castle of the said town, were received into protection; and, after quarter given to the garrison of the said castle, the said inhabitants, and the soldiers of the said garrison, to the number of 500, and upwards, men, women, and children, were brought on the bridge of Newry, and thrown into the river, and such of them, as endeavoured to escape by swimming, were murdered.

County of DONEGALL.

1641. About the 20th of November, Sir William Steward commanded the gentry, and inhabitants of that county to join with his forces in opposition to the rebels, and accordingly they came to the place appointed, where captain Cunningham, with a party of the said Sir William's regiment, under pretence of incorporating with them, fell upon the inhabitants with his armed soldiers, and killed very many of them; among whom were Owen Mac Sweeny, Morris O'Farey, and Donagh O'Callan, gentlemen of quality, and estates.

About the same time captain Fleming, and other officers of the said regiment, commanding a party, smothered to death 220 women and children, in two caves. And about the same time also the said captain Cunningham murdered about 63 women, and children, in the isles of Ross.

1641. The governour of Letter-kenny gathered together on a Sunday morning 53 poor people, most of them women, and children, and caused them to be thrown off the bridge into the river, and drowned them all.

1641. In November, one Reading murdered the wife and three children of Shane O'Morghy in a place called Ballykenny of Ramaltan, and after her death cut off her breasts with his sword.

1641.

1641. 1642. The garrisons of Rapho, Dromho, Lifford, and Castle Raghaen, slaughtered no less than 1500 of the poor neighbouring inhabitants never in arms; and three persons were chiefly noted among them for their barbarous cruelty, by name James Graham, Henry Dungan, and Robert Cunningham, commonly called the killer of old women.

1641. 1642. About 2000 poor labourers, women and children, of the barony of Tirbu, were massacred by the garrisons of Ballashany, and Donegal; and lieutenant Thomas Poe, an officer among them, coming under colour of friendship to visit a neighbour that lay sick in his bed, and to whom he owed money, carried a dagger under his cloak, which, whilst he seemed to bow towards the sick man in a friendly manner, asking how he did, he thrust it into his body, and told his wife her husband should be no longer sick.

1650. In the month of June, about 3000 horse and foot of his majesty's army being defeated near Letter-kenny by the English rebels, adhering to Cromwell, most of the principal officers of the said party taken prisoners in the battle, were killed in cold blood, by order of Sir Charles Coote, late lord of Mountrath, notwithstanding they had quarter from the officers who took them prisoners.

County of MONAGHAN.

1641. CAPT. Townsley, governour of Magherneckle, killed four labourers, and a woman, being under protection. Captain Bromwell, governour of Clunes, meeting upon the road with Marc Charles O'Conolly, a gentleman living under his protection, caused him to be shot to death. The soldiers of the garrisons of Dundalk and Trim, killed no less than 500 innocent persons, women and children in that county.

1641. 1642. The armies of Monroe, and the Lagan, in their several marches through that county, slaughtered about 2000 poor old men, women and children.

1652. COLONEL Barrow of Cromwell's army, having taken an island defended by lieutenant colonel Patrick Mac Mahon for his majesty, after killing the said lieutenant colonel, and his soldiers, put all the women and children to the sword, to the number of 80, among whom a child of six years old, being spared by the soldiers, was killed by order of the said colonel Barrow.

County of CAVAN.

1642. MARC de la Pool, an English gentleman, having taken lands in that county some years before the war, invited several of his friends to come out of England, and live with

with him, who were all murdered in their houses by the army, (only the said de la Pool who was brought into the town of Cavan,) and there hanged for no other reason, but their being Roman Catholicks, and living among the Irish. Sir Alexander Godren, and his lady, both Scotch, but Roman Catholicks, each of them above 70 years. old, were plundered of their goods, and stripped naked; and all their tenants, servants, and all their sons murdered. In the same year the English forces in this county drowned 600 men women and children, in and about Butler's bridge, no murders having been committed on any Protestants there, altho' in the pamphlet lately printed, several murders are said to have been committed in that place.

County of MAYO.

In this county few murders were committed by either side, tho' the libel saith, that about 250 Protestants were murdered, whereof at Bellicke 220; whereas not one person was murdered there, which the now lady of Mountrath can witness; her ladyship, and Sir Robert Hanna, her father, with many others, having retreated thither for security, were all conveyed safe to Mannor-Hamilton; and it is observable, that the said lady and the rest came to Mr. Owen O'Rorke's, who kept a garrison at Drumaheir, for the Irish, before they came to Mannor-Hamilton, whose brother was prisoner with Sir Frederick Hamilton; and the said Mr. Rorke, having so many persons of quality in his hands, sent to Sir Frederick to enlarge his brother, and that he would convey them all safe to him: but Sir Frederick, instead of enlarging his brother, hanged him the next day, which might have well provoked the gentleman to revenge, if he had not more humanity than could be well expected upon such an occasion, and in times of so great confusion; yet he sent them all safe where they desired.

There was a murder committed near the Moyn on 27 Protestants, which was all (and that too many) that was committed in that county. Buchannan, said to be buried alive, was killed in a private quarrel, and he cut off his adversary's hand, before himself was killed.

County of GALWAY, and Province of CONNAUGHT.

1642. Serjeant Redmund Bourke, of the lord of Clanmorris's foot-company, and two more were hanged by the then governour of the fort of Galway, the said lord being then of his majesty's army; for which action no reparation being given to his lordship, he alleged it to be the occasion of his revolt from the lord marquis of Clanriccard. A party of the garrison of the said fort murdered six people in Rinveel, among whom one Geffery Fitz-Thibot, aged about 70 years, and in a burning fever, with his wife, who was old, were murdered in their beds; which action provoked many of the neighbours to stand on their guard against the said fort.

RICHARD

1652. RICHARD Bourke, a colonel in his majesty's army, had quarter given him by some of colonel Coote's men, he being taken in a Skirmish between colonel Grace, and some of Cromwell's party, and being prisoner for some time, colonel Henry Ingoldsby caused his head to be cut off.

1652. 1653. It was a usual practice with colonel Stubbers, then governour of Galway, and others commanding in said county, to take the people out of their beds at night, and sell them for slaves to the Indies; and by computation he sold out of said county above 1000 souls.

Murders committed in the said County of GALWAY on Protestants.

1642. It is confessed, that two Protestants were murdered in that county, whereof one was a minister, as the libel says; but it is most certain the lord marquis of Clanriccard caused the three men, who murdered one of them, to be hanged in gibbets in three several places; and, by his lordship's orders, Sir Roger O'Shaghnesy hanged the two cow-herds who murdered the other. Lord Clanmorris having declared against the said fort for hanging his serjeant, as above expressed, took serjeant Rowlright, and two or three more of the soldiers of said fort, pillaging a village near Galway, and hanged Rowlright, and the other three.

A BARBAROUS murder was committed by one Edward Alta, an irreligious prophane fellow of the county of Mayo, and his accomplices, on some Protestants at Shruel, a place meeting Galway, on about 30 persons; and the pamphleteer might well remember, that the neighbouring gentry came with all expedition to rescue the said Protestants; and that they did rescue the bishop of Killala (who by the pamphlet seems to have been murdered) and his wife and children, with most part of the said Protestants; and Bryan Kilkenny, a fryar, then guardian of the abby of Ross, near Shruel, was of the first that made haste to that rescue, and brought the said bishop's wife and children, with several others of the said distressed Protestants, to his monastery, where they found as much civility as was in the said fryar's power to give them for several nights; until Mr. Burke of Castle-Hacket brought the said bishop, his wife, and family, to his own house, where they wanted nothing he could afford them for some weeks: the like being done by several other neighbouring gentlemen to the rest of the said Protestants, until they were sent to places of security by the lord marquis of Clanrickard's order; yet the said fryar hath been these eight years past kept a prisoner for his function or calling, without any other crime laid to his charge, now being above 80 years old. And it is observable, that in this county of Galway all the war time, several Protestant ministers, viz. Dean York, Mr. Corroyn, Mr. Kelly, and other ministers, had their Protestant flocks and meetings without interruption, living among the Irish.

County of ROSCOMMON.

No murders were committed by any party in this county, only five perfons at Ballanafada by one Roger O'Connor; and no murders were committed at Ballaleague during the war, altho' in the pamphlet the contrary is expreffed; nor was any fuch man as William Stweart known in that county, nor to have been murdered there; tho' the Abftract fets forth his being murdered in a moft barbarous manner as is pretended.

County of LEITRIM.

1641. It was commonly known to all fides how cruel the governour of Mannor-Hamilton (fir Fred. Hamilton) was in that county, how he ufually invited gentlemen to dine with him, and hanged them after dinner, and caufed their thighs to be broke with hatchets before execution. Alfo the faid governour, being in Ulfter when the rebellion broke forth, defired one Mr. Iraght (a gentleman who profeffed much friendfhip to him) to do him the favour to guide him in fafety to Mannor-Hamilton aforefaid, which the gentleman did, and came near 100 miles with him; but after being friendly treated for fome days by the faid governour, he was hanged without the leaft occafion; neither was the gentleman in the rebellion, but was hanged leaft he fhould. The libel fays three Proteftants were murdered in this county; but on due examination it will be found, there was none.

County of SLIGO.

Here is none at this time who can give any exact account of the murders committed in this county, but one remarkable murder in Creane's-caftle in the town of Sligo. The Irifh had a party commanded by major Richard Burke, (who after obtaining quarter to march away) to the number of about 200 were murdered, rendering the caftle. This Sir Audley Mervyne knoweth to be true.

County of DUBLIN.

1641. About the beginning of November * 5 poor men (whereof two were Proteftants) coming from the market of Dublin, and lying that night at Santry, three miles from thence, were murdered in their beds by one captain Smith, and a party of the garrifon of Dublin, and their heads brought next day in triumph into the city; which occafioned Luke Netterville and George King, and others of the neighbours, to write to the lords jufticcs to know the caufe of the faid murder; whereupon their lordfhips iffued forth a proclamation, that within five days the gentry fhould come to Dublin

---

* See Sir John Temple's Apology for this maffacre in his hiftory of the Irifh Rebellion.

to receive satisfaction, and in the mean while (before the five days were expired) old Sir Charles Coote came out with a party, plundered and burned the town of Clontarffe, distant two miles from Dublin, belonging to the said George King, nominated in the proclamation, and killed 16 of the townsmen and women, and three sucking infants. Which unexpected breach of the proclamation (having deterred the gentlemen from waiting of the lords justices) forced many of them to betake themselves to their defence, and others to abandon their houses.

In the same week 56 men, women and children, of the village of Bulloge (being frighted at what was done at Clontarffe) took boats and went to sea, to shun the fury of a party of soldiers come out of Dublin, under the command of colonel Crafford; but being pursued by the soldiers in other boats, were overtaken, and thrown overboard. One Russel, a baker in Dublin, coming out of the country in company with Mr. Archbold of Cloghram, (who went to take hold of the proclamation of the lords justices) were both hanged and quartered. In March a party of horse, of the garrison of Donsoghlin, murdered 7 or 8 poor people in protection, tenants of Mr. Dillon of Hunstowne, having quartered in their houses the night before, and receiving such entertainment as the poor people could afford. About the same time a party of the English, quartered at Mallahyde, hanged a servant of Mr. Robert Boyne's at the plough, and forced a poor labourer to hang his own brother; and soon after they hanged 15 of the inhabitants of Swords, who never bore arms, in the orchard of Mallahyde; they likewise hanged a woman bemoaning her husband hanged among them.

In the same year, after quarter given by lieutenant colonel Gibson to those of the castle of Carrigmain, they were all put to the sword, being about 350, most of them women and children; and colonel Washington, endeavouring to save a pretty child of 7 years old, carried him under his cloak, but the child against his will was killed in his arms, which was a principal motive of his quitting that service.

1642. In April one Nicholas Hart, and 14 labourers, going with corn to the market of Dublin, and having a pass, were all murdered on the road by a party commanded abroad by lord Lambert. The same day Mr. Sarsfield of Lucan sent his groom to guide the lord of Gesil's troop, which the fellow having performed, was knocked on the head for his labour. The same day 18 villages in protection, the farthest within six miles to Dublin, were plundered and burned, and to the number of 400 men, women and children, were cruelly massacred. About the same time a party of the garrison of Swords, having brought in 30 poor labourers, forced them to dig their own graves, and then killed them: much about that time one Bennet, Sheriff of the county, killed 16 men and women, coming from the market of Dublin. A party under

der the command of colonel Crafford murdered 140 women and children in Newcastle, and Coolmain, being under protection. Many thousands more of the poor innocent people of that county, shunning the fury of the soldiers, fled into thickets of firs, which the soldiers would usually set on fire, killing as many as endeavoured to escape; or forced them back again to be burned, and the rest of the inhabitants, for the most part, dyed of famine.

Note, That no less than 12000 of the poor inhabitants of that county were cruelly massacred the first year of the war.

County of KILDARE.

1641. Captain Thomas Hues, having summoned thirty three contributors to meet him at Hedgestowne, caused them all to be murdered. The said Hues murdered Mrs. Eustace, aunt to Sir Robert Talbot, 90 years old, with two gentlewomen that waited on her, after she entertained him friendly in her house. The soldiers of Clongow's wood, and Rathcoffy, yielding upon quarter, were conveyed to Dublin, and hanged there, and upwards of 150 women and children were found in the said places murdered. It is well known, that the commons of that county were, for the most part, destroyed, and slaughtered by the English, in so much, that there were not so many left living as could gather the twentieth part of the harvest.

County of MEATH.

1642. IN April Mrs. Elinor Taaffe of Tullaghanoge, sixty years old, and six women more, were murdered by the soldiers of the garrison of Trim; and a blind woman aged 80 years, was encompassed with straw by them, to which they set fire, and burned her. The same day they hanged two women in Kilbride, and two old decrepid men that begged alms of them. In the same year Mr. Walter Dulin, an old man, unable to stir abroad many years before the war, was killed, in his own house by lieutenant colonel Broughton's troopers, notwithstanding the said Broughton's protection, which the old man produced. Mr. Walter Evers, a justice of the peace and quorum, an aged man, and bedrid of the palsie long before the rebellion, was carried in a cart to Trim, and there hanged by the governour's orders.

MANY plowmen were killed at Philbertstowne. Forty men, women, and children in protection, reaping their harvest in Boneftown, were killed by a troop of the said garrison; who upon the same day killed Mrs. Alson Read at Donsaghlin, being 89 years old, and 40 persons more, most of them women and children, shunning the fury of the said troop, were overtaken and slaughtered. About 70 men, women, and children, tenants to Mr. Francis Mc Ovoy, and under protection, were killed by Greenvill's vill's foldiers, and 160 more in the parifh of Rathcoare, whereof there was one aged couple blind 15 years before. Captain Sandford, and his troop, murdered in and about Mulhuffey upwards of 100 men, women, and children, under protection, and caufed one Connor Breflan to be ftuck with a knife into the throat, and fo bled to death: And one Eleanor Cufack, 100 years old, was tied about with lighted matches, and fo tortured to death in Clonmoghon. James Dowlan, about 100 years old, Donagh Comen, Darby Dennis, Roger Bolan, and feveral other labourers, and women, to the number of 160, making their harveft, were flaughtered by the garrifon of Trim.

Mr. Barnwell of Tobertinian, and Mr. John Huffey, innocent perfons, were hanged at Trim by old Sir Charles Coote's party. Gerrald Lynch of Donower, aged 80 years, was killed by troopers of Trim, being in protection. Mr. Thomas Talbott of Crawly's-town, about 80 years old, being protected, and a known fervitor to the crown, was killed at his own door by fome of captain Morroe's troop. About the month of April the foldiers under the faid Greenvill's command killed in and about the Navan 80 men, women, and children, who lived under protection. Captain Wentworth and his company, garrifoned at Dumo, killed no lefs than 200 protected perfons in the parifh of Donamora, Slane, and barony of Margellion, and Ovmorein, the town of Ardmulchan, Kingftown, and Harrifton, all protected perfons.

Sir Richard Greenvill's troop killed 42 men, women, and children, and 18 infants at Doramftown. A woman under protection was by captain Morroe's foldiers put into the ftock of a tuck-mill, and fo tucked to death in the town of Steedalte. Lieutenant Ponfonby put two aged protected perfons to death at Downaftone, each of them about 80 years old. Captain Morroe caufed about an hundred protected perfons, men, women, and children to be put to death in the barony of Dooleek, and lieutenant John Tench killed a protected perfon 70 years old, near Dooleek. Mr. Patrick White, fon and heir of Mr. White of Clangill, in protection, was taken out of his bed, and knocked on the head by lieutenant Luaton of the garrifon of Trim. Many thoufands of the poor inhabitants of this county were deftroyed in the firs, as thofe in the county of Dublin, and the reft for the moft part perifhed with famine.

County Westmeath.

1642. About the latter end of March Mr. Chriftopher Mc. Gawly, notwithftanding the protection of the Duke of Ormond, was killed in his own houfe, with two of his fervants, by a party of the Englifh army marching to Athlone, who laying the protection on the faid Mc. Gawly's breaft, fhot him through his protection, to try whether it was proof againft a bullet. Mrs. Ellis Dillon of Killenennin, having the lords juftices protection for herself and tenants, their wives and children, they were all killed by soldiers under Sir Michael Earnley's command.

County of Lowth.

1641. In the month of February about 300 poor people, men, women and children, were cruelly slaughtered in the wood of Derruer by a party of the garrison of Dundalk, and Tredath. About the beginning of March about 300 farmers and labourers, never in arms, with their wives and children, were massacred by a party of the garrisons of Dundalk, and Tredath in the Redmoore of Bragamstown. About the same time captain Charles Townsly, and lieutenant Faithful Townsly, with a part of the English army, and garrison of Dundalk, slaughtered at Dunmogham 220 inhabitants of several villages, commanded by the officers of the said army to live in that place for their greater security. A party of the said garrison of Tredath and Dundalk killed above 200 persons in the castle of Reaghstown after quarter given. One Anthony Townsly hanged Mr. Dromgole of Dromgolestown at his own gate. The said Townsly hanged upwards of 30 poor men and women, going to the markets of Dundalk and Tredath, on a tree, commonly called Eight Mile Bush, midway between the said towns.

1642. A party of horse and foot of the garrison of Tredath, killed and burned in the firs above one hundred and sixty men, women and children, of the inhabitants of Termorfeighlin, within three miles of Tredath: no less than one thousand of the poor inhabitants of that county, tho' they were not taxed with any murders committed on the Protestants, according to their own abstract, were massacred.

County of Wicklow.

October, 1641. Three women, whereof one gentlewoman big with child, and a boy, were hanged on the bridge of Neuragh by command of Sir Charles Coote in his first march to that county; and he caused his guide to blow into his pistol, and so shot him dead. He also hanged a poor butcher on the same march called Thomas Mac William. Mr. Dan. Conyam of Glanely, aged, and unable to bear arms, was roasted to death by captain Gee of Colonel Crafford's regiment: and in the marches in 41, 42, and 43, the English army killed all they met in this country, tho' no murders are charged in the said county to be committed on Protestants by the abstract. In the Usurper's time captain Barrington, garrisoned at Arklow, murdered Donagh O'Dayle of Killearrow, and above 500 more protected by himself; and it is well known that most of the commonalty were murdered.

County of KILKENNY.

1641. The English soldiers of the garrison of Ballenakil burned an old woman of 90 years old in her own house in Idough. 1642. The said soldiers massacred one hundred and eighty men, women, and children, who were cutting their corn, near the said garrison. They dragged Mr. Thomas Shee, an innocent person, out of his own house, with five of his servants, and hanged them all at Ballenekill.

County of TIPPERARY.

1641. On the 24th of October one Browne and Captain Peasely murdered eleven men, women, and children, in their own houses at Golden Bridge, before any of the Catholics took up arms in that county. About the same time the said captain Peasely going through Clonculty, Philip Ryan, a peaceable gentleman, and owner of the said town, came out of his house to salute the captain; who pulled out his pistol and shot the poor harmless gentleman dead at his own door.

Note, That these two murders occasioned the rising of the gentry and inhabitants of that county.

One John Wife of Ballyowen, an English soldier, came several times in woman's attire upon the road, and committed divers murders upon simple country people coming from the market.

County CLARE.

1644. Forty families in protection were murdered by the garrison of Inchicronan. 1646. Several residing near Bunratty were murdered by the soldiers of that garrison under command of lieutenant Adams.

County CORK.

1641. In Condon's country above 300 labourers, women, and children were murdered by some of the now Earl of Orrery's soldiers. In the said county, among others, they gelded one Denis Downy, and pulled out one of his eyes, and sent him in that posture to his wife. Fifty-six persons, or thereabouts, were brought prisoners to Castle Lyons, (most of them labourers, who did never bear arms) were put into a stable, and the women in that garrison at night fired their beards, and the hair of their heads, which so disfigured them, that their nearest friends could not know them next day, when they were hanging.

APPENDIX.

1642. In the same county 355 persons, men, women and children, were murdered with clubs and stones, being in protection. Mr. Henly, an English gentleman, dwelling in Roche's country, but a Roman Catholic, had his wife and children barbarously stripped, and most of his tenants inhumanly murdered by adjacent English garrisons, he the said Henly, or his tenants, being never in arms: and such cruelty was used, that they stabbed young infants, and left them so half dead on their mother's dead carcasses. In the said Henly's town, and the adjacent villages, at that time, there were murdered about 900 labourers, women, and children.

1643. Cloglegh, being garrisoned by the Irish, and surrendered upon quarter of life to Sir Charles Vavasor, they were all inhumanly murdered, and the hearts of some of them pulled out, and put into their mouths; and many other massacres were committed the same time there on women and children. At Lislee 24 men in protection were murdered by colonel Mynn's soldiers. At Bellauere the same year Teig O'Mungan, and David Broge, blowing by command into pistols, were shot to death by some of captain Bridge's men, and eight poor labourers more killed by them, being in protection, and then employed in saving some harvest of the English.

1642. At Clogheiulty about 238 men, women, and children were murdered, of which number seventeen children were taken by the legs by soldiers, who knocked out their brains against the walls. This was done by Phorbis's men, and the garrison of Bandon Bridge. At Garranne, near Ross, Connor Kennedy, who had protection for himself and his tenants to save their harvest, were murdered by the garrison of Ross, as they were ditching about their corn.

1641. At Bandon Bridge, the garrison there tied 88 Irishmen of the said town back to back, and threw them off the bridge into the river, where they were all drowned. Patrick Hackett, master of a ship in Waterford, the dutchess of Ormond being desirous to be conveyed by him to Dublin, after leaving her safe with her family and goods there, the lords justices and Duke of Ormond gave him a pass for his safe return, who being driven by a storm into Dongarvan, the said master and his men were hanged by direction of the commander in chief there, notwithstanding he produced his said pass. The English party of this county burned O'Sullivan Beare's house in Bantry, and all the rest of that county, killing man, woman, and child, turning many into their houses, then on fire, to be burned therein: and among others Thomas De Bucke, a cooper, about 80 years old, and his wife, being little less; and all this was done without provocation, the said O'Sullivan being a known reliever of the English in that country. Observe that this county is not charged in the late Abstract with any murders.

County

APPENDIX.

County WATERFORD.

1641. In Decy's country the neighbouring English garrisons of the county of Corke, after burning and pillaging all that country, murdered above three thousand persons, men, women, and children, before any rebellion began in Munster, and led 100 labourers prisoners to Caperquine, where being tied by couples, they were cast into the river, and made sport of, to see them drowned. Observe that this county is not charged with any murders to be committed on Protestants.

NUMB. VII.

Extract of the Acts of the General Congregation of the Roman Catholick Bishops and other Clergy, held at Kilkenny on the 10th, 11th, and 13th Days of May, 1642. From Borl. Hist. of the Irish Rebellion, fol. 122.

[See Review, p. 128.]

Act I. IN which war, if some of the Catholicks be found to proceed, out of some particular and unjust title, covetousness, cruelty, revenge, or hatred, or any such unlawful private intention, We declare them grievously to sin, and therefore worthy to be punished, and refrained with ecclesiastical censures, if advised thereof they do not amend.

—— Act IX. Let a faithful inventory be made in every province, of the murthers, burnings, and other crueltys, which are committed by the Puritan enemies, with a quotation of the place, day, cause, manner, and persons, and other circumstances, subscribed by one of public authority.

Act X.—— In every parish let a faithful and sworn messenger be appointed, whereby such crueltys, and other affairs may be written, and sent to the neighbouring places; and likewise from one province to another: let such things be written for the comfort, instruction, and carefulness of the people.

—— Act XVIII. We ordain and decree, that all, and every such, as from the beginning of this present war, have invaded the possessions of goods, as well moveable, as unmoveable,

APPENDIX.

unmoveable, spiritual or temporal, of any Catholick, whether Irish or English, as also of any Irish Protestant, being not an adversary of this cause, and do detain any such goods, shall be excommunicated; and by this present decree, We do excommunicate them, if, admonished, they do not amend. And with the like censure, We do bind such, as henceforward shall invade, or detain such goods.——

Act XIX. We command all and every the churchmen, as well secular, as regular, not to hear the confessions of the aforesaid excommunicated persons, nor to administer unto them the holy Sacrament, under pain of excommunication *ipso facto*.

Act XX. We will, and declare, all those that murther, dismember, or grievously strike, all thieves, unlawful spoilers, robbers of any goods, extorters, together with all such as favour, receive, or any ways assist them, to be excommunicated; and so to remain until they compleatly amend, and satisfy, no less than if they were namely proclaimed excommunicated; and for satisfaction of such crimes, hitherto committed, to be injoined, We leave to the discretion of the ordinarys, and confessors how to absolve them.

——Act XXVI.——We command all, and every the general, colonels, captains, and other officers of our Catholick army, to whom it appertaineth; that they severally punish all transgressors of our aforesaid command, touching murtherers, maimers, strikers, thieves, robbers; and if they fail therein, We command the parish-priests, curates, and chaplains, respectively, to declare them interdicted, and that they shall be excommunicated, if they cause not due satisfaction to be made to the Commonwealth, and the party offended. And this the parish-priests, or chaplains, shall observe, under pain of sentence of excommunication given *ipso facto*.

——Act XXIX. Moreover, We pray, and require all noblemen, magistrates, and all other martial commanders that with their helps and secular forces, they assist and set forward in execution the aforesaid statutes in their several precincts respectively as often as it shall be needful.——

APPENDIX.

Numb. VIII.

Intelligence from his Majesty's army in Scotland, to be presented to the most Honourable the Lord Lieutenant-General of Ireland; written at Inverlochy in Lochaber, the 7th of February, 1644; by an Irish officer of Alexander Macdonnel's Forces.

From Carte's Collection of Original Letters and Papers, concerning the Affairs of England, and Ireland, found among the Duke of Ormonde's Papers. Vol. I. p. 73.

[See Review, p. 179.]

WHEN the Irish forces arrived in Argyle's bounds in Scotland, our general-major, Alexander Macdonnel, sent such of his majesty's commissions and letters to those to whom they were directed, although for the present none was accepted of; which caused our general-major and those forces to march into Badenoch, where they raised the country with them; and from thence to Castle-Blaire in Athol, where the lord marquess of Montrose came unto, and joined them with some other small forces. From thence they marched to St. Johnston, where the enemy had gathered together 8000 foot, and 800 horse, with nine pieces of cannon, his majesty's army not having so much as one horse: for that day, the marquess of Montrose went on foot himself with his target, and pike; the Lord Kilpunt commanding the bow-men, and our general-major of the Irish forces commanding his three regiments. The armies being drawn up on both sides, they both advanced together; and although the battle continued for some space, we lost not one man on our side, yet still advanced, the enemy being 3 or 4 to one: howsoever, God gave us the day; the enemy retreating with their backs towards us, that men might have walked upon the dead corps to the town, being two long miles from the place where the battle was pitched. The chace continued from 8 o'clock in the morning till 9 at night: All their cannon, arms, ammunition, colours, drums, tents, baggage, in a word, none of themselves nor baggage escaped our hands, but their horse and such of the foot as were taken prisoners within the city. This battle, to God's glory, and our Prince's good, was fought the first day of September.

From thence we marched straight to Aberdeen, only surprising such as withstood us, with little or no skirmishing, till the 13th of the same month at Aberdeen, the Covenanters of the North had gathered themselves together, to the number of 3000 foot

APPENDIX.

and 900 horſe, with three pieces of cannon. We had then about 80 horſe: the battle being fairly pitched, it continued for a long ſpace, and the enemy behaved themſelves far better than they did at Johnſton. Yet we loſt not that day above 4, but the enemy were altogether cut off, unleſs ſome few that hid themſelves in the city. The riches of that town, and the riches they got before, hath made all our ſoldiers cavaliers. This battle being ended, only our manner of going down to battle, and how each commanded, I omit till it be drawn, and ſet down in a more ample manner; now tendering only a brevity of our proceedings; for if I ſhould write the whole truth, all that hath been done by our army would be accounted moſt miraculous; which I proteſt I will but ſhew in the leaſt manner I can, leaving the reſt to the report of the enemy themſelves.

AFTER this battle, we marched towards the Highlands again, ſo far as to Caſtle-Blaire, where I was ſent to Ardamuragh, with a party to relieve the caſtle of Migary and the caſtle of Laughaline; Migary caſtle having a leaguer about it, which was raiſed 2 or 3 days before I could come to them; at which time captain of Clanronald, with all his men joyned with Clencoe men, and others, who an inclination to his majeſty's ſervice.

IN the mean time, while I was intereſſed upon the ſervices, the marqueſs of Montroſe marched back to the Low-lands, almoſt the ſame way that he marched before, till they came to a place called Fivy in the ſhire of Aberdeen, where Argyle, with 16 troops of horſe and 3000 foot marched up, and upon a very plain field Argyle was moſt ſhamefully beaten out of the field; and had it not been for his horſe, they had ſuffered as deeply as the reſt; ſo that there was not on our ſide any hurt done, but on their ſide, they loſt many of their beſt horſe, and moſt of all their commanders hurt, and the earl Mareſchal's brother killed. After the armies ſeparated, the lord marqueſs marched again to Caſtle-Blaire in Athol, where I met again with him and ſuch of the Highlands as had joined with me, the day of Fivy was on October, 28th.

FROM Caſtle-Blaire, we marched to Glanurghyes, called M'Callin, M'Conaghy, which lands we all burned and preyed from thence to Lares, alais Laufers; and burned and preyed all this country from thence to Aghenbracke's, whoſe lands and country were burned and preyed; and ſo throughout all Argyle, we left neither houſe nor hold unburned, nor corn nor cattle that belonged to the whole name of Campbell. Such of his majeſty's friends as lived near them joined with us. We then marched to Loughaber, where Mr. Alane came and joined us, but had but few of his men with him. From thence we marched to Glengarry, where the lord of Glengarry joined with us. At this place we got intelligence that Argyle, Aghenbracke, and the whole name of Campbell, with all their forces, and a great number of Lowland-men with them, were come to Inverlonghy in Loughaber, following us. This cauſed us to make a counter-march the neareſt way over the mountains, till we came within

muſket-

musket-shot of the castle of Inverloughy, it then being night, so that the enemy stood to their arms all night, the sentries skirmishing together. By this place of Inverloughy, the sea comes close, and that night Argyle embarked himself in his barge, and there lay till the next morning, sending his orders of discipline to Aghenbracke and the rest of the officers there commanding the battle; which on both sides being pitched, and their cannon planted, the fight began; the enemy giving fire on us on both sides, both with cannon and muskets to their little avail. For only two regiments of our army, playing with musket-shot, advanced till they recovered Argyle's standard, and the standard-bearer, at which their whole army broke; which were so hotly pursued both with foot and horse, that little or none of the whole army escaped us, the officers being the first that were cut off.

There Aghenbracke was killed, with 16 or 17 of the chief lords of Campbell: their other Low-land commanders (only two lieutenant-colonels) all cut off. Four others of the name of Campbell were taken prisoners, as Bearbrick, the young laird Carrindel, Inverleen captain, son of Eniftefinth, and divers others that got quarter, being men of quality. We lost but two or three that day; this battle was fought the 2d. of February.

Numb. IX.

From Carte's Life of the Duke of Ormond, vol. i. fol. 390.

[See Review, p. 157.]

THE Lords of the pale having received no answer from the lords justices to their proposal for a cessation, sent by colonel Read, on March 9th, 1641-2, they renewed that proposal by the earl of Castlehaven, on the 23d of the same month. About the same time, Sir Lucas Dillon, * Hugh Oge O'Conor, and other gentlemen

---

* Hugh O'Conor, the father of this Hugh Oge, was, according to the custom of the Irish, elected chieftain of the family of O'Conor's Dun, in 1581; he compounded by indenture with the lord deputy Perrot in 1585, and was the first of his family, who submitted to have his country governed by the English laws. He married Mary O'Ruare, the daughter of Brian No Murtha O'Ruare, chieftain of Breffny, who having protected some Spaniards thrown on the Sligo coast, after the defeat of their Armada, was tried, condemned, and Executed, on the verdict of a London-jury, in 1589.

Hugh Oge here mentioned, the son of said Hugh O'Conor and Mary O'Ruare, had the estates of Castlerea settled upon them in his father's life-time, and was married to Jane, the daughter of Sir Lucas Dillon of Logh glyn. He was one of the commissioners for the province of Conaught at the council of Kilkenny in 1643.

of the county of Roscommon, proposed a like cessation to the earl of Clanrickard, and the president of Conaught. In the following month the lords of the pale repeated the same proposition. And lord Clanrickard, at the request of the rebels in general, on May 19th, recommended to the state the agreeing to a general cessation, until his majesty's pleasure was further declared, upon their humble supplications. But the justices entertaining different sentiments, and resolving upon a severe punishment of all, without distinction, absolutely rejected the cessation.

Numb. X.

[From Desiderat. Curios. Hibernic.]

A Remonstrance of the Right Honourable James, Earl of Castlehaven, and Lord Audley, addressed to his Majesty King Charles II.

[See Review, p. 157.]

WHEREAS my escape out of sheriff Woodcock's house in Dublin, where I was near twenty weeks a prisoner, is likely to occasion various discourses and conjectures, I have thought fit, by advice of my friends, to remonstrate the truth of my case.

AFTER having, with the rest of the peerage of England, for the space of near a year, served his majesty there, first, in his great council at York, and then in the parliament; but still under the awe and terror, either of the Scotish army at Newcastle, or the rude rabble at London; at length many of the lords (as well wearied with that extream slavery, as unwilling to be any longer eye-witnesses of the affronts daily multiplied on the king and queen, and other intolerable insolencies tending to the destruction of monarchy, and establishing of popular government) retired themselves to their several houses; and I, with his majesty's leave, approved by the lords of parliament, about the feast of S. Michael the archangel, 1641, came into Ireland; where shortly after appeared the sparks of the ensuing war, that now by fire and sword doth rage throughout this kingdom. Upon the first discovery whereof, I with all possible speed

repaired

1643, and lived to see all his estates seized by the Usurper, Oliver Cromwell. Dominic, the present O'Conor Dun, is descended from him in the fourth generation.

This Hugh Oge had two brothers, Charles, who died A. D. 1634, and Brian Roe, who died A. D. 1651. From Charles is descended, in the third generation, my particular and highly esteemed friend, Charles O'Conor of Belanagare, in the county of Roscommon, Esq; now living.

APPENDIX.

repaired to Dublin, and there not only offered my service, but sued to the state for employment, for the suppressing of that commotion; but it was refused; answer being given me by one of the justices, and others of the council, that the character I bear of papist, made me uncapable of trust, nay even of arms, to defend my own house from robbers. At this time the county of Kildare (where I resided) was quiet, and held so till about mid November. But now the tide of confusion began to overflow those banks also, which occasioned my second journey to the justices and council; where after having made a faithful narration of the state of that county, I became an humble suitor, that a troop of horse might be presently sent down, averring, that a small force would then do that, which the month following might be work for an army. But the effect of this journey, was only their lordships thanks, with an unanimous licence from the whole council, that until they were able to relieve me, I should make fair weather, and preserve myself and mine by the respect they knew the country bare me. But this helped me little; for shortly after, most of the chief of that county declared themselves: so that the rest of the winter, I was enforced to stand on my guard, with watch and ward, both day and night, keeping my brother M. Maruin Touchet, or some other, always at Dublin, from time to time, expecting the commands of the state. The winter now past, and fair weather coming on, about Easter the English army (commanded by the lieutenant-general, now marquis of Ormond) in its march to Leix lodged some four miles from my house, whither that night, by the respect of the lieutenant-general, was sent a safeguard. And in thankfulness, the dutchess of Buckingham, the earl of Antrim, and myself, went the next morning to salute his lordship and his army; where we were so received, as stood well with the honour of that great lord and noble commander. After some days, his lordship having now relieved the places in distress, and finished his design, in his return, and in sight of my house, though three miles from it, was the encounter betwixt the English army and the Irish, commonly called the battle of Kilrush; whither, because I *in cuerpo*, with my three or four men, without gun or powder, did not come, and being to pass through thousands of the Irish, I am said, by the malicious, to have discountenanced the king's army. The evening after victory, his lordship's march being near my house, he was pleased, with some of his chief commanders, to refresh themselves there; and in the night, his lordship wanting a guide to conduct him and his army some four miles to their quarters, I would trust none with that charge but myself. Notwithstanding this my respect, it must be given out, that so great an entertainment was never intended for the lieutenant-general and his followers, but rather for the lord viscount Mountgarret, and the rest of the rebels. To this point, divers witnesses were examined against me, though, God knows, I expected not either of their coming thither.

By these misinterpretations of my actions, I thought I must no longer sleep, doubting that my quiet living in the country drew envy on my person, so that I resolved to put myself into the fashion, that is, to leave my house to be burnt, my stock of all sorts

(being

(being of great value) to be a prey to whofoever would take them; and to look at nothing, but to fave myfelf and people, with fome choice goods. To this purpofe, I prefently refolved to move the ftate at Dublin, that I might have licence to go for England, it being the cuftom of this kingdom not to depart without leave; but as I was difpatching the meffenger, a letter unexpected fell into my hands, delivered me by one of my fervants; but the bearer never came to my prefence. I opened it, never afking or confidering from whom it might come, I found it fubfcribed by the vifcounts Gormanftown and Nettervill, and the lord of Slane: it was to this effect; that in obedience to his majefty's proclamation, they, and other united lords and gentlemen, had laid down arms; to intimate which to the ftate, they had fent one lieutenant colonel Read, from whom they had not heard; and that neverthelefs, daily their own and their tenants houfes were burnt, their goods taken, and people killed. They defired that I would mediate with the ftate for a ceffation of arms; and that a place might be appointed, where they and their confederates might meet to draw up their grievances, and fo have free accefs, by way of petition, to prefent them to his majefty. With this letter, I prefently fent another from myfelf to the ftate, wherein I feemed to wifh fome good return might be made, but it happened otherwife; for anfwer to their lordfhips, they would make none at all, alledging they were rebels and traitors, and after many frivolous exceptions taken to my letter, as one, that I did not alfo call them rebels and traitors, they admonifhed me to have nothing to do with them, and inftead of licenfing me to go for England, they commanded I fhould not depart the kingdom without leave. All this while, from the firft opening the ways from Dublin to my houfe, I was frequently at the Englifh garrifons, and had always with me, either troops or troopers of the Englifh army.

AND now finding my unhappinefs, that how candid or fincere foever my actions or meaning was, I muft ftill be miftaken; I packed up all I could conveniently carry, and refolved prefently to go to Dublin, where I would make my abode, till I had leave to pafs for England. But fome few days before my intended departure, news was brought me, that by chance fome of my friends at Dublin had difcovered, that I ftood indicted of high treafon; for it was done with great fecrecy.

AMAZED at this fad and unexpected news, the next morning by five of the clock, I pofted for Dublin, giving order, that all my beft furniture and linen fhould be prefently fent after, which accordingly was done. My ftock of all forts (as the marquis of Ormond and Sir Arthur Loftus well know) I beftowed for the ufe of the Englifh army, and defired nothing in recompence, but only that my people, with the remainder of my goods, might be brought fafe to Dublin, where I was now gone to purge myfelf.

BUT

APPENDIX.

But I continued there for many days, without any notice taken of me; though I presently acquainted the lords justices, and many of the council, of my arrival, and the cause; so that it was then thought, and may yet be believed, that they hoped by that indictment, rather to have frighted me, as they had done thousands of others, into rebellion, as they term it, than that they had any good evidence against me.

But I, not willing to lie long under that title of infamy, went myself to the council, took notice of my charge, and desired, that with all convenient speed, I might be brought to my purgation. Hitherto it is evident, I thought not of my escape. The council, after some debate, confined me to master Woodcock's house, one of the sheriffs of Dublin. From whence, after a day or two, I sent a petition to the state, and it was to this effect, laying down by many particulars the improbability of my associating myself in this war, as that I was a peer of England, that the main of my estate lay there, and the little interest or power I had in this kingdom; that my accusers were of base condition, and would have been taken off for a small sum of money, and that two of them, namely, Ennis and his son, ran away from the English colours with their arms, and afterwards served against them at the battle of Kilrush; and the third, William Collis, had been sadler to some of the Irish army, whereby it is most evident, that beside what other reward those men might be promised, they were made sure of their lives; that the jury who found this indictment, on the evidence of these men, were persons of the same nature and condition, as particularly one Francis Dade, who associated himself with the Irish, changed his religion, and went to Mass. This man having forfeited his life, according to their rule, they make a leading jury-man, and I believe a witness, he not daring to deny what they would have him do or say. In fine, that there was not one gentleman, or scarce a landed-man amongst them. For these reasons, and for that it had been frequently granted to others in the like case, I desired to be bailed. Answer was returned to this modest petition, that the witnesses were no rebels, but espies; so that what I had said, was no impeachment to their testimonies, and in general they thought not fit to grant the petition. Well, though I thought that as well this answer, as the whole proceedings, somewhat harsh, yet I did not much weigh it; for shortly after was to follow Trinity term. At which time I assured myself, that by my innocency I should be set free both from prison and blame.

Oh! but here I was much deceived. For this term must be otherwise employed. For though, through hanging, racking, and barbarous treating of such as submitted on the king's proclamation, thousands had declared themselves for the country, who were in all post haste going to Dublin, to put themselves under the protection of the state; yet there were as many more that stood at a gaze, as most unwilling to run the common course, and yet loth to be handled after this rude manner. Against these, must bills of indictment presently be drawn, and grand-jury-men picked for the purpose.

pose. And to strike the business dead in the eye, fearing these men were not wicked enough, the judges of the king's chief place, on the bench delivered, as part of their charge, that they must not be scrupulous; for that common fame was now evidence enough to find a bill of indictment.

NOTWITHSTANDING this great and holy employment of these reverend fathers of the law, they must yet do something more to shew their grandeur; that was, I by a Habeas Corpus must be brought into the court before them, where after I had been sufficiently looked at by their lordships and the people, I was remanded back to the place whence I came, without any thing said unto me. This term finished, and the jury-men having well acted their parts, some of the judges are dispatched for England, to shew there, that the pen in Ireland had been as active as the sword, and that now, for the destruction of at least all the prisoners, there wanted little, but that old saying, Hang-man, do your office.

IT is no great wonder that now, how innocent soever I was, my head should begin to ake. Yet a session of parliament being shortly to follow, I conceived good hope of fair play there: but when I saw the composure of this great tribunal: that the upper-house consisted of no more than five or six temporal lords, and some bishops; the house of commons (anciently the representative body of the kingdom) for the major part of clerks and clerks-men, few having any land, and those illegally chosen, as by musketteers, and a rabble of such like freeholders: I began to think that such a kind of parliament might err, and feared nothing more than a trial there. And surely I had reason when nothing would serve their turns, but a cessation of Poyning's act, during that session; by which they were freed from transmitting their bills into England, and so might make laws, as in their discretions they thought fit; and I have too great cause to believe, they would have made one for attainting me, and the rest of the prisoners.

ALL this while, no means are untried to make matter against me; for, as before, witnesses were rewarded, by giving them their lives, being forfeited: so now to others, rough language must be used. One John Bird being examined before Sir Robert Meredith, concerning me, and not answering as was expected, the said Sir Robert demanded his religion, the honest man replied, a protestant: Ah! quoth he, by thy answers thou shouldest have a little pope in thy belly.

AND now, having by many such indirect ways, furnished themselves with plenty of evidence, they begin to affront me, by disarming my men, by pulling one master Henry Slingsby out of my chamber; coming by accident with a gentlewoman to visit me, saying, he was a Romish popish jesuit, it being well known, he was no such man; and so carried him to prison.

AND

APPENDIX.

AND laftly, the fheriff's houfe is now thought too weak for fo great a traitor. Hereupon a writ is iffued to the fheriff, to bring me with a ftrong guard to the Inns, where the judges were, being near half a mile: from whence I muft be fent to the caftle, a loathfome prifon of itfelf; but the inhumanity of the gaoler, by name Manwaring, after Hell, makes it the fecond place for mifery and affliction. Well, I thought it now high time, as the judges had fummoned my body, I fhould recollect my wits. And as I ftood confidering my cafe, a paffage in the earl of Strafford's trial occurred to my memory. He ftood much upon his juftification, and demanded the benefit of the law, but mafter St. John replied, that to hares, deer, and other innocent creatures, law was afforded; but to wolves, foxes, and other fuch like vermin, any means might be fought for their deftruction. Now, I finding myfelf hitherto dealt with as one of thefe, although I waved the malice of the wolf, I made fome little ufe of the fox's craft, and for that prefent feigned myfelf fick, and on information thereof given, my attendance on the judges was fpared till the morrow.

HAVING thus gained time, I well pondered all which hath been before related, together with, If I were a traitor, to whom it was? The king, himfelf, I found purfued both with men and fword, by an army of his own people; whofoever followed or adhered unto him, declared rebels and traitors; the queen, his royal confort, flying from place to place, like an exiled or banifhed woman; and, by Mr. Martin's, and divers the like fpeeches in the houfe of commons in England, that his facred majefty was not fit to bear the office of a king, and that he might be depofed; and much more to this effect, as may be feen in divers printed papers: which language in that place going unpunifhed, I could not conceive that the authors of fuch infolencies, or the fwaying malignant part of the ftate here, who from time to time took their directions from them, could adjudge any thing againft his majefty treafon. O, but I remember, that in a book of the king's, relating truly all the paffages, from the firft of this parliament to the twelfth of Auguft, he complains of two great officers, lately fet up in England, who ufurped the regal power, the one is a general for the land, the other admiral of the fea: but to thefe I never owed allegiance, and fo confequently could be no traitor to them. I then began to confider the condition of this kingdom, as that the ftate did chiefly confift of men of mean birth and quality; that moft of them fteered by the influence and power of thofe who were in arms againft the king; that they had by cruel maffacring, hanging, and torturing, been the flaughter of thoufands of innocent men, women, and children, better fubjects than themfelves; that they, by all their actions fhew, looked at nothing but the extirpating of this nation, the deftruction of monarchy, and by the utter fuppreffing of the ancient catholick religion, to fettle and eftablifh puritanifm. To thefe I could be no traitor. Near about the time of this my exigency, I was much cheared by a vifit I received from Sir Arthur Loftus, fon to Sir Adam Loftus, a leading inftrument in all wicked defigns againft his majefty, telling me

APPENDIX.

(as joyful news) that the parliament had lately given the king a total overthrow; and that he was now reduced to so low a condition, that by the next, we should certainly hear the king had submitted to the parliament, and till that were done, things would never do well. Here I took my resolution, with God's help, not tamely to die butchered, and so to have my innocency smothered; but to preserve my life, I hoped more to the honour of God, and service of king Charles, and that by escape. Now forasmuch, as the most immediate way into England was blocked up, I resolved upon a trial, to gain a passage by Wexford into France, and from thence into England; conceiving, I should have been forthwith able to have put myself into a sum of money, to have borne my charges, by the sale of such plate, goods, and stock, as I had in the country; but I was not many hours out of Dublin, before I was pursued by some troops of horse, Sir Arthur Loftus leading them, who that night came to my house in the county of Kildare, and missing me, killed some of my servants, hurt divers, and, after having rifled the house, they set it, and all about it, on fire: and besides all my servants prisoners, they carried away more than the worth of five thousand pounds in plate, and other goods.

Here my wings being clipt, all that I had to carry me abroad, or keep me at home, being thus taken from me, together with the distractions in England, so that I could make little or no account of my estate there; in this streight, I thought fit to apply myself to the great assembly of the kingdom of Ireland, who having given me full satisfaction for their assembling, and that their taking arms was but natural, as to defend themselves and theirs from those aforesaid barbarous cruelties; and that they desired (as may appear by many of their instruments in writing) nothing but the free exercise of their ancient religion, their just liberties, and the preservation of this crown unto his majesty, I having some interest both in honour and estate in the country, associated myself with them; and they, after some time that I was amongst them (more out of charity than merit in me) offered me the generalship of their horse, of the province of Leinster, which I thankfully accepted: and now in my colours bear this device, *Sagittæ tuæ acutæ in corda inimicorum regis.* For the executing whereof, I desire God no longer to prosper my actions, than my heart, hand, sword, and prayers, shall be readily and chearfully employed therein.

Having, with much trouble to the reader, endeavoured to vindicate myself in this remonstrance, I conceive it both proper and charitable, in this place, to labour to acquit him, who, I understand, hath unjustly suffered for my sake, I mean sheriff Allen. The protestant sheriff Woodcock, to whose custody only I was committed, went unpunished for my escape, as really he knew nothing thereof. But sheriff Allen being a catholick, who had no charge of me, nor acquaintance with me, other than that I often saw him, when he came to treat with his brother sheriff about the city affairs, he, poor innocent man, for so I take God to witness he was as to my escape, or as to any word

let

let fall to that effect to my knowledge, or that I can guess, was, with great inhumanity, dragged to prison, most of his goods seized upon and taken away, and a great number of soldiers cessed upon his house. Whereby, and being made uncapable to receive his rents or debts, or to follow any other way he had to gain a living by, his wife and children, from that day forth, were exposed to the charity of their friends, and he condemned to imprisonment for a whole year in misery. How justifiable or conscionable, this proceeding was, I will not argue, much less aggravate, having discharged my conscience thereupon; the matter itself, both to God and the world, crying loud for justice.

Numb. XI.

[From Walsh's History of the Irish Remonstrance.]

To the King's most excellent Majesty.

The humble Remonstrance, Acknowledgement, Protestation, and Petition of the Roman Catholick Clergy of Ireland.

[See Review, p. 291.]

YOUR majesties faithful subjects, the Roman Catholick clergy of your majesties kingdom of Ireland, do most humbly represent this their present state, and deplorable condition.

THAT being intrusted by the indispensable commission of the King of Kings with the cure of souls, and the care of their flocks, in order to the administration of sacraments, and teaching the people that perfect obedience, which for conscience sake, they are bound to pay to your majesties commands, they are loaden with calumnies, and persecuted with severity.

THAT being obliged by the allegiance they owe, and ought to swear, unto your majesty, to reveal all conspiracies and practices against your person, and royal authority, that come to their knowledge, they are themselves clamoured against as conspirators, plotting the destruction of the English among them, without any ground that may give the least colour to so foul a crime, to pass for probable in the judgement of an indifferent person.

THAT their crimes are made as numerous, and as divers, as are the inventions of their adversaries: And because they cannot with freedom appear to justifie their innocence, all the fictions and allegations against them are received as undoubted verities; and

K k k which

which is yet more mischievous, the laity, upon whose consciences the character of priesthood gives them an influence, suffer under the supposition of all the crimes thus falsly imputed to them: it being their adversaries principal design, that the Irish, whose estates they enjoy, should be reputed persons unfit, and no way worthy of any title to your majesties mercy.

THAT no wood comes amiss to make arrows for their destruction; for, as if the Roman Catholick clergy, whom they esteem most criminal, were, or ought to be, a society so perfect, as no evill, no indiscreet person should be found amongst them, they are all of them generally cryed down for any crime, whether true or feigned, which is imputed to one of them; and as if no words could be spoken, no letter written, but with the common consent of all of them, the whole clergy must suffer for that which is laid to the charge of any particular person amongst them.

WE know what odium all the Catholick clergy lyes under, by reason of the calumnies with which our tenets in religion, and our dependence upon the popes authority are aspersed: and we humbly beg your majesties pardon, to vindicate both by the ensuing protestation, which we make in the sight of Heaven, and in the presence of your majesty, sincerely and truly, without equivocation, or mental reservation.

WE do acknowledge and confess your majesty to be our true and lawful king, supreme lord, and rightful sovereign of this realm of Ireland, and of all other your majesties dominions. And therefore we acknowledge and confess ourselves to be obliged, under pain of sin, to obey your majesty in all civil and temporal affairs, as much as any other of your majesties subjects, and as the laws and rules of government in this kingdom do require at our hands. And that, notwithstanding any power or pretension of the pope or see of Rome, or any sentence or declaration of what kind or quality soever, given, or to be given, by the pope, his predecessors, or successors, or by any authority spiritual or temporal proceeding or derived from him, or his see, against your majesty, or royal authority, We will still acknowledge and perform, to the uttermost of our abilities, our faithful loyalty, and true allegiance to your majesty. And we openly disclaim and renounce all foreign power, be it either papal or princely, spiritual or temporal, in as much as it may seem able, or shall pretend to free, discharge, or absolve us from this obligation; or shall any way give us leave or licence to raise tumults, bear armes, or offer any violence to your majesties person, royal authority, or to the state or government. Being all of us ready, not only to discover, and make known to your majesty, and to your ministers, all the treasons made against your majesty, or them, which shall come to our hearing, but also to lose our lives in the defence of your majesties person, and royal authority, and to resist with our best endeavours all conspiracies and attempts against your majesty, be they framed, or sent under what pretence, or patronized by what foreign power or authority soever. And further we profess, that all absolute

solute princes, and supreme governours, of what religion soever they be, are God's lieutenants on earth, and that obedience is due to them, according to the laws of each common wealth respectively, in all civil and temporal affairs. And therefore we do here protest against all doctrine and authority to the contrary.

AND we do hold it impious, and against the word of God, to maintain, that any private subject may kill or murther the annointed of God, his prince, though of a different belief and religion from his. And we abhorr and detest the practice thereof as damnable and wicked.

THESE being the tenets of our religion, in point of loyalty and submission to your majesties commands, and our dependence of the See of Rome no way intrenching upon that perfect obedience, which by our birth, and by all laws divine and human, we are bound to pay to your majesty, our natural and lawful soveraign: We humbly beg, prostrate at your majesties feet, that you would be pleased to protect us from the severe persecution we suffer meerly for our profession in religion: leaving those that are, or hereafter shall be guilty of other crimes (and there have been such in all times, as well by their pens, as by their actions) to the punishment prescribed by the law.

Fr. Oliver Darcy, bishop of Dromore.

Fr. George Dillon, of S. Francis Ord. Guardian of the Irish Franciscans at Paris.
Fr. Philip Roch, of S. Francis Ord. Reader General of divinity.
Fr. Anthony Gearnon, of S. Francis Ord. one of her majesties the queen mothers chaplains.
Fr. John Everard, of S. Francis Ord. Conf. and Preacher.
Fr. Anthony Nash, of S. Francis Ord. Conf. and Preacher.
Fr. William Linch, of S. Francis Order, Conf.
Fr. Nicholas Sall, of S. Francis Ord. Conf. and Preacher.
James Cusack, Doctor of Divinity.
Cornelius Fogorty, Protonot. Apost. and Doctor of the civil and canon law.
Fr. Henry Gibon, of S. Aug. Ord. Conf. and Preacher.
Daniel Dougan, Divine.
Fr. Redmond Moore, of S. Dom. Ord. Conf. and Preacher.

Bartholomew Bellew.
Dennis Fitz Ranna.
Bartholomew Flemming.
Fr. Peter Walsh, of S. Fran. Ord. Reader of Divinity, and Procuratour of the Rom. Cath. clergy, both Sec. and Reg. of Irel.
Fr. Redmond Caron, of S. Fran. Order, Reader Jubilate of Divinity.
Fr. Simon Wafre, of the same Ord. Reader of Divinity.
Fr. James Caverly, of S. Francis Order, Conf. and Preacher.
Fr. John Fitz Gerald, of S. Francis Order, Conf. and Preacher.
Fr. Theobald Burk, of S. Francis Order, Conf. and Preacher.
Fr. Matthew Duff, of S. Francis Order, Conf. and Preacher.
Fr. Peter Goghegan, of S. Francis Order, Conf. and Preacher.

APPENDIX.

Numb. XII.

[From Walsh's History of the Irish Remonstrance.]

To the Kings most excellent Majesty.

The faithful Protestation, and humble Remonstrance of the Roman Catholick Nobility and Gentry of Ireland.

[See Review, p. 293.]

YOUR Majesties faithful subjects, the Roman Catholick nobility and gentry of your majesties kingdom of Ireland, out of a deep sense of those prodigious afflictions, under which the monarchy of Great Britain, has before your majesties happy restauration, groaned these twenty years: and out of our sad thoughts, which daily bring more and more sighs from our breasts, and tears from our eyes, for not only the still and yet continued miseries, and sufferings of the Catholick natives of this our unfortunate country, even amidst, and ever since, the so much famed joyes and triumphs of your sacred majesties most auspicious inauguration; but also for the causes thereof, (whereinto we have made the most narrow search we could) of these our own unparallel'd calamities: and upon reflection upon that allegiance we owe, and ought by all divine and human laws, and which we are, and have been alwayes ready, to swear and perform to your majesty, our only soveraign lord on earth; and on the scandal (notwithstanding) which some persons (who are unwilling to understand aright our religion) cast upon it, as if it were not consistent with all dutiful obedience and faith to the supreme temporal magistrate; and upon consideration likewise, of a further tye of conscience on us, for endeavouring, as much as in us lyes, to clear your majesties royal breast from all fears and jealousies whatsoever, if any, peradventure, your majesty entertain of us, through the suggestion of such as hate our communion or nation; and to wipe off that scandal, and allay the odium under which our church hath layn this last century of years, among other christian people in these nations, of a different way from ours in the worship of God; we humbly crave your majesties pardon, to vindicate both ourselves, and our holy belief, in that particular of our allegiance, by the ensuing protestation. Which (in imitation of the good example given by our clergy, and pursuant to the general doctrine and practice of the catholick church) we make in the sight of Heaven, and in the presence fence of your majesty, sincerely and truly, without equivocation, or mental reservation.

We do acknowledge and confess your majesty to be our true and lawful king, supreme lord, and rightful soveraign of this realm of Ireland, and of all other your majesties dominions. And therefore we acknowledge and confess ourselves to be obliged, under pain of sin, to obey your majesty in all civil and temporal affairs, as much as any other of your majesties subjects, and as the laws and rules of government in this kingdom do require at our hands. And that notwithstanding any power or pretension of the Pope, or See of Rome, or any sentence or declaration, of what kind or quality soever, given, or to be given, by the Pope, his predecessors, or successors, or by any authority, spiritual or temporal, proceeding or derived from him, or his See, against your majesty or royal authority, we will still acknowledge and perform, to the uttermost of our abilities, our faithful loyalty, and true allegiance to your majesty. And we openly disclaim and renounce all foreign power, be it either papal or princely, spiritual or temporal, in as much as it may seem able, or shall pretend to free, discharge, or absolve us from this obligation, or shall any way give us leave or licence to raise tumults, bear armes, or offer any violence to your majesties person, royal authority, or to the state or government; being all of us ready, not only to discover, and make known to your majesty, and to your ministers, all the treasons made against your majesty or them, which shall come to our hearing, but also to lose our lives in the defence of your majesties person, and royal authority; and to resist with our best endeavours, all conspiracies and attempts against your majesty, be they framed or sent under what pretence, or patronized by what foreing power or authority soever. And further we profess, that all absolute princes, and supreme governours, of what religion soever they be, are God's lieutenants on earth; and that obedience is due to them, according to the laws of each commonwealth respectively, in all civil and temporal affairs; and therefore we do here protest against all doctrine and authority to the contrary. And we do hold it impious, and against the word of God, to maintain, that any private subject may kill or murther the annointed of God, his prince, though of a different belief and religion from his. And we abhorr and detest the practice thereof as damnable and wicked.

These being the tenets of our religion in point of loyalty and submission to your majesties authority, and our observance and veneration of, or communion with, the See of Rome, in matters purely spiritual, no way entrenching on that perfect obedience, which, by our birth, by the laws of God and man, we are bound to pay to your majesty, our natural and lawful soveraign.

Prostrate at your majesties feet, we most humbly beg, that all your majesties Roman Catholick subjects of Ireland, who shall by subscription or consent, concurr to this
publick

publick protestation of loyalty, be protected from persecution, for the profession or exercise of their religion, and all former laws, upon that account, against them repealed.

Luke, earl of Fingall.
Moutrogh, earl of Inchequin.
Donoghe, earl of Clancarthy.
Oliver, earl of Tyrconell.
Theobald, earl of Carlingford.
Edmond, viscount Montgarett.
Thomas, viscount Dillon.
Arthur, viscount Jueagh.
William, viscount Clane.
Charles, viscount Muskry.
William, viscount Taaffe.
Oliver, baron of Lowth.
William, baron of Castle-Conell.
Colonel Charles Dillon.
Matthew Plunkett, esquire.
Lieutenant-colonel Ignatius Nugent.
Edward Plunkett esquire.
Nicholas Plunkett knight.
Matthew Plunkett of Dunsany.
James Dillon knight.
Colonel Christopher Brian.
Robert Talbot baronet.
Vullick Burk baronet.
Edward Fiz Harris baronet.
Valentine Brown baronet.
Luke Bath baronet.
Henry Slingsby knight.
John Bellew knight.
Colonel William Burk.
Colonel John Fitz Patrick.
Colonel Brian Mac-Mahon.
Colonel Miles Relly.
Colonel Gilbert Talbott.
Colonel Milo Power.
Lieutenant-colonel Pierce Lacy.
Lieutenant-colonel Vullick Burk.
Lieutenant-colonel Thomas Scurlog.

Esquires and Gentlemen.

Jeoffry Brown of Galway.
John Walsh of Ballyuoher.
Patrick Brian.
James Fitz Gerald of Lackagh.
John Talbot of Malahyde.
Thomas Luttrell of Luttrells-town.
John Holywood of Artayne.
Henry O Neill, son to Sir Phelim O Neill.
Dudley Bagnell of Dunlickny.
Henry Dracott of Mornanton.
Edward Buttler of Monihore.
Nicholas Darcy of Platin.
Patrick Sarsfield of Lucan.
John Mac-na-Mara of Creattlagh.
James Talbott of Bela-connell.
Robert Balf of Corstown.
James Talbot of Templeoge.
Patrick Archer.
Luke Dowdall of Athlumny.
Philip Hore of Killsalaghan.
James Barnewall of Bremore.
James Allen of Saint Wolstans.
Thomas Cantuell of Balymakeddy.
John Cantuell of Cantuells-court.
Edmond Dillon of Stream's-town.
John Flemming of Stahalmock.
Peter Sherlog of Gracedieu.
Christopher Archbold of Tymolin.
Patrick Moore of Duan's-town.
Nicholas Haly of Towrine.
Pierce Butler of Callan.
Pierce Butler of Killuealegher.
John Sedgraw of Cabragh.
Richard Wadding of Killbarry.
Thomas Brown of Clan-Donel-Roe.

Oliver

APPENDIX.

Oliver Caffell of Dundalke.
Patrick Clenton of Irish-town.
Captain Christopher Turner.
John Baggott.
William Grace.
John Arthur of Hogestown.
Marcas Laffan of Greats town.
Chriftopher Aylmer of Balrath.
James Plunkett of Gibiton.
Thomas St. John of Mortles-town.
William Barioge of Rincorran.
Richard Strange of Rockwell-caftle.
James Butler of Ballenckill.

Anthony Colclough.
Thomas Sarsfield of Sarsfieldftown.
Pierce Nangle of Monanimy.
James Wolverftown of Stillorgan.
Michael Brett.
Patrick Boyton of Bally-turny-mac-oris.
James White of Chambolly.
Major Lawrence Dempfy.
Captain Richard Dempfy.
Edward Nugent of Calvin.
Patrick Porter of Kingfton.
Major Marcus Furlong.

Numb. XIII.

[From Lefley's Anfwer to the King. Append.]

Extract of Dr. Gorge, Secretary to General Schomberg in Ireland, his Letter, dated April (or May) 1690, to Collonel James Hamilton, in London, to be communicated to the Lady Vifcountefs Ranelagh, the Lord Maffereen, and others.

[See Review, p. 356.]

YOU know how often and how early we preffed the neceffity of reftoring a Civil Government in this province, and how often and openly we declared that the ruine of the countrey muft be the prejudice, and endanger the ruine, of the army; and that there could be found no hands fo cheap and eafie to be got, or any that would be more hearty and faithfull than the Proteftants of this countrey, who having their particular interefts feconded by natural and religious motives, muft be more zealous in carrying on this war, than any foreign or mercenary foldiers, as is evident by what has been done by the Londonderry and Enefkillen foldiers, who are, and were, made up of the meaneft and loweft people of this and the neighbouring provinces. You cannot forget who offered, and that at their own charge, on our firft landing here, to block up Charlemont, and to raife regiments to fecure the Northern garifons, that the eftablifhed army, might have the more leifure to attend the motions of the publick enemy; and I prefume you cannot but as well remember, who ridiculed, fcorned, and contemned all motions of that kind, and who affirmed, and that openly, that the Proteftants of this province, ought rather to be treated as enemies than friends, and that the beft of them had either bafely complied with K. J. and his party, or cowardly left and deferted their

country

countrey; that the goods and stocks of the Proteſtant inhabitants, once ſeized by the enemy, were forfeited, and ought not to be reſtored, but given as encouragement to the ſoldiers; that all Papiſts ought to be plundered, and none protected; that the reſtoration of civil government was a diminution of the power of the general and the army, and that all the Proteſtants, inhabitants of this province, were falſe to the preſent government, and ought not to be truſted with places of truſt or power; that as their perſons were not to be truſted, ſo their oaths and complaints were neither to be believed nor redreſſed; that ſo an eaſier and a ſafer approach might be made to invade the little left them by the Iriſh.

THAT all endeavours of the ſettlement of a publick revenue were deſigns to oppreſs the army; that free quartering was the leaſt retaliation that Proteſtants could give for being reſtored to their former eſtates; that religion is but canting, and debauchery the neceſſary character of ſoldiers. If to theſe you add the preſſing of horſes at pleaſure, quartering at pleaſure, robbing and plundering at pleaſure, denying the people bread or ſeed of their own corn, though the general by his publick proclamation requires both; and ſome openly and publickly contemning and ſcorning the ſaid proclamation; whereby multitudes of families are already reduced to want of bread, and left only to beg, or ſteal, or ſtarve. Theſe being the practices, and theſe the Principles, and both as well known to you as to me; can it be wondered that the oppreſſed Proteſtants here ſhould report us worſe than the Iriſh? Or can it be wondered that God ſhould purſue us with his dreadfull judgments who have ſo provoked him with our daring ſins? Or can we rationally expect God ſhould fight for us, while we thus fight againſt him? We may as well expect Grapes from Thornes, and Figs from Thiſtles, as ſucceſs to a Proteſtant cauſe from ſuch hands. Can we expect Sodom to deſtroy Babylon, or Debauchery to deſtroy Popery? Our enemy fights with the principle of a miſtaken conſcience againſt us, we againſt the conviction of our own principles againſt them. What I have learned of the enemies principles and practices ſince I left you, I ſhall here inform you, and reduce what I have to ſay to theſe two general heads.

I. THE frequent diſcourſe of their king.

II. HIS publick declarations and proclamations for the well government of his army.

I. As to his private diſcourſe.

1. HE expreſſeth great zeal, and paſſionate affection to his Engliſh ſubjects; in ſo much that both French and Iriſh often ſay of him, as he did of K. David, That he loves his enemies, and hates his friends.

2. HE

APPENDIX.

2. He is heard often to desire his officers, That in their engagement with the English, they should be treated as mistaken subjects, and not as obstinate rebels.

3. He is heard often to declare, That since he rightly understood christianity, he ever asserted christian liberty, as well in his past prosperity, as his present adversity.

4. That all perswasions in matters of religion, Who have most charity and least of severity, are most agreeable to christianity.

5. He is often heard to complain, That he ever observed, an aptitude and propensity in persons of power to persecute such as differ from them.

6. That this natural aptitude to persecute, ought to be restrained by wholesome and effectual laws.

7. That this persecuting spirit influencing the greater number of all perswasions, especially persons in power, is the only cause of his majesty's present sufferings.

8. He is passionately kind to all deserters, and chearfully receives and soon prefers them.

9. He pretending his sufferings to be thus on the account of conscience, seems not to doubt, but God will find some unexpected means, for his restauration, in 1690, as he did in 1660.

10. He is heard frequently to declare against the Dragooning persecution of France, and the barbarous and inhumane murders committed on the protestants of this kingdom in the year 1641, as passionately, and perhaps as sincerely as the Scribes and Pharisees did against their forefathers for persecuting the prophets. To these I think fit to add the particulars of his majesty's publick declarations, which are ordered to be read once every two months in the head of every troop and company in his whole army, and to be fixed up in all the boroughs and market-towns in this kingdom.

1. His majesty is pleased earnestly to recommend the performance of publick and private duties to God, to all under his command, and particularly recommends to the Roman Catholicks of his army frequent confessions, and strict observation of Sundays and Holy-days.

2. He publickly declares what subsistance he allows to every horse, dragoon, and every private soldier in his army, and what is reserved in the pay-master's hands for the accoutrements and the hospital.

3. He avoids and forbids as unneceffary, the charge of all agents, and commands the majors of every regiment to do that work, and to fave the charge.

4. He ftrictly requires the private foldier out of the faid fubfiftence duly and truly to pay his quarters.

5. In cafe they fhall want their fufiftance, they are then required every week to give their refpective landlords a note under their hands, which fhall be received by the Receiver General, as fo much money out of any branch of his majefty's revenue.

6. His majefty forbids all ftraggling of private foldiers from their garrifons without their officers pafs; and requires all officers, either military or civil, to apprehend fuch foldiers having no pafs, and to fend them to their colours, to receive punifhment according to their demerits.

7. His majefty by the fame proclamation, forbids all plundering on any pretence whatfoever, under pain of death without mercy.

8. He requires both officers and soldiers under the pain of his high difpleafure to demean and behave themfelves civilly and refpectfully in their refpective quarters; and to affift and not obftruct the civil magiftrates in the execution of their refpective trufts, efpecially the officers concerned in and about his majefty's revenue.

9. He forbids all officers and foldiers to quarter themfelves on any of his majefty's fubjects, without having a billet or ticket under the hand of the conftable or other civil officer of the place.

10. He ftrictly forbids preffing any countrey-man's horfe on any pretence whatfoever, without having his majefty, his captain general, his lord lieutenant, or deputy-lieutenant's licenfe for his fo doing; and then allows them to prefs the faid horfe but one day's journey, and to fee that the horfe be returned as well as when received; and particularly forbids the preffing any horfe belonging to any plough.

11. His majefty in the fame proclamation, enjoyns fevere penalties on all foreftallers or obftructers of provifion going to either camp or market.

Lastly, The refpective penalties enjoined in the faid proclamation, are feverely and impartially executed on the refpective offenders. My family tells me, that the week before they left Dublin, there were two private foldiers executed before a Proteftant baker's door, for ftealing two loaves not worth a fhilling. And a fortnight before, a lieutenant and enfign were publickly executed at a place, where on pretence of

the

the king's service, they pressed a horse going with provisions to Dublin market; two others were condemned and expected daily to be executed for the like offence: These severe examples confirming the penalties of these publick declarations, contribute so much to the quiet of the country, that were it not for the country rapatees and tories, theirs, 'tis thought, would be much quieter than ours. Some of our foreigners are very uneasie to us; had not the prudence of a discreet major prevented it, last Sunday was seven night had been a bloody day between some of the Danish foot and colonel Langston's regiment of horse. The truth is, too many of the English, as well as Danes and French, are highly oppressive to the poor country; whereas our enemy have reduced themselves to that order, that they exercise violence on none, but the proprieties of such as they know to be absent, or, as they phrase it, in rebellion against them, whose stock, goods, and estates are seized, and set by the civil government, and the proceed applied for and towards the charge of the war. And for their better direction in their seizures, it's reported and believed, that they have copies of the particulars of the Protestants losses, given in to the committee of the late house of Commons at Westminster.

N u m b. XIV.

A Protestation of Allegiance, by thirteen Missioners, to Queen Elizabeth, January 31st, 1602. Taken from Hen. Moore's History of the English Jesuits.

WHEREAS it hath pleased our dread sovereign lady, to take some notice of the faith and loyalty of us, her natural-born subjects, secular priests, (as it appeareth in her late proclamation) and, of her princely clemency, to give a sufficient earnest of some merciful favour towards us (being all subject, by the laws of the realm, unto death, by our return into the country, after our taking the order of priesthood, since the first year of her majesty's reign) and only to demand of us a true profession of our allegiance, thereby to be assured of our fidelity to her majesty's person, and crown, estate and dignity: We, whose names are underwritten, in most humble wise prostrate at her majesty's feet, do acknowledge ourselves infinitely bound unto her majesty therefore; and are most willing to give such assurance and satisfaction in this point, as any Catholic priests can, or ought to give unto their sovereign.

First, Therefore, we acknowledge and confess the queen's majesty to have as full authority, power, and sovereignty over us, and over all the subjects of the realm, as any her highness's predecessors ever had. And farther, we protest, that we are most willing and ready to obey her in all cases and respects, as far forth as ever christian

priests

priests within this realm, or in any other christian country, were bound by the law of God, and christian religion, to obey their temporal prince; as to pay tribute and all other regal duties unto her highness; and to obey her laws, and magistrates, in all civil causes; to pray to God for her prosperous and peaceful reign in this life, according to his blessed will; and that she may hereafter attain everlasting bliss in the life to come. And this our acknowledgement we think to be so grounded upon the word of God, that no authority, no cause, or pretence can, or ought, upon any occasion, to be a sufficient warrant, more unto Us, than to any Protestant, to disobey her majesty in any civil, or temporal matter.

SECONDLY: Whereas for these many years past, diverse conspiracys against her majesty's person and estate, and sundry forcible attempts of * invading and conquering her dominions, have been made, under we know not what pretences and indentments of restoring the Catholic religion by the sword (a course most strange in the world, undertaken peculiarly and solely against her majesty and her kingdoms, and unknown among other princes departed from the religion and obedience of the See Apostolic no less than she) by reason of which violent enterprizes, her majesty, otherwise of singular clemency towards her subjects, hath been greatly moved to ordain and execute severer laws against Catholics (which, by reason of their union with the See Apostolic, in faith and religion, were easily supposed to favour these conspiracys, and invasions) than, perhaps, had ever been enacted, or thought upon, if such hostilities and wars had never been undertaken: We to assure her majesty of our faithful loyalty also in this particular cause, do sincerely protest, and, by this our public act, make known to all the christian world, that in these cases of conspiracys, and practising her majesty's death; of invasions, or whatsoever forcible attempts, which may hereafter be made by any foreign prelate, prince, or potentate whatsoever, either jointly, or severally, for the disturbance, or subversion, of her majesty's person, estate, realm, or dominions, under colour, shew, or pretence, or indentment, of restoring the Catholic religion, in England, or Ireland; We will defend her majesty's person, estate, realms, and dominions, from all such forcible and violent assaults and injuries. And moreover, we will not only ourselves detect, and reveal any conspiracys, or plots, which we shall understand to be undertaken by any prelate, prince, or potentate, against her majesty's person or dominions, for any cause whatsoever (as is before expressed) and likewise, to the best of our power, resist them; but also will earnestly persuade, as much as in us lieth, all Catholics to do the same.

THIRDLY: If upon any excommunications denounced against her majesty, upon any such conspiracys, invasions, or forcible attempts, to be made, as are before expressed, the pope should also excommunicate every one born within her majesty's dominions, that would not forsake the foresaid defence of her majesty and her realms, and take part with such conspirators, or invaders: in these, and all other such like cases,

* The Spanish Armada in 1588.

cafes, we do think ourfelves, and all the lay-catholics born within her majefty's dominions, bound in confcience not to obey this, or any fuch like cenfure; but will defend our prince, and country, accounting it our duty fo to do, and, notwithftanding any authority, or any excommunication whatfoever, either denounced, or to be denounced, (as is before faid) to yield unto her majefty all obedience in temporal caufes.

AND becaufe nothing is more certain, than that, whilft we endeavour to affure her majefty of our dutiful affection and allegiance, by this our chriftian and fincere proteftation, there will not want fuch as will condemn and mifconftrue our lawful act; yea, and by many finifter fuggeftions and calumnies, difcredit our doings with the chriftian world; but chiefly with the pope's holynefs; to the greateft prejudice, and harm, of our good names and perfons, that may be; unlefs maturely we prevent their endeavours therein: we moft humbly befeech her majefty, that, in this our recognizing, and yielding Cæfar's due unto her, we may alfo, by her gracious leave, be permitted, for avoiding obloquies and calumnies, to make known, by like public act, that, by yielding her right unto her, we depart from no bond of that chriftian duty, which we owe unto our fupreme fpiritual paftor: and, therefore, we acknowledge and confefs the bifhops of Rome to be the fucceffors of St. Peter, in that See; and to have as ample, and no more authority, or jurifdiction over us, and other chriftians, than had that apoftle, by the gift and commiffion of Chrift, our Saviour; and that we will obey him fo far forth, as we are bound by the laws of God to do; which, we doubt not but will ftand well with the performance of our duty to our temporal prince, in fuch fort as we have before profeffed. For as we are moft ready to fpend our blood in the defence of her majefty, and our country, fo we will rather lofe our lives, than infringe the lawful authority of Chrift's catholic church.

Robert Drury,	Anthony Champney,	Robert Charnock,
John Jackfon,	William Bifhop,	John Bofwille,
Francis Barnaby,	John Colleton,	Antony Hepburn,
Ofwald Needham,	John Mufh,	Roger Cadwaller.
Richd. Button,		

N. B. Dr. William Bifhop, who was principally concerned in drawing up this proteftation, was afterwards appointed by the See of Rome, bifhop of Calcedon. Dod's Eccl. Hift. V. 2d.

INDEX.

INDEX.

A

ACT of the 2d of Elizabeth fraudulently obtained, p. 30.
Acts of Settlement, p. 301.—Their severity, ib.—By whom procured and modelled, p. 312.
Acts of cruelty and perfidy of the chief governors of Ireland towards the Irish, during the reign of queen Elizabeth, Appen. N°. I.
Agents from the Irish parliament in 1641, returned with the the royal assent for redress of grievances, p. 131. —Disappointed by the sudden adjournment of the parliament, p. 132.—Pray that notice, at least, may be given to the people by proclamation, of their success, ib.—Refused by the lords justices, ib.

B

Bishops (Catholic) assemble in a synod at Waterford; consider the peace concluded with the marquis of Ormond in 1646, p. 210.—Condemn it as contrary to their association-oath; and to the instructions given by the confederates to their commissioners; excommunicate those who adhere to it; and why, p. 210, 211.
Bagnall (Colonel) his speech to the general assembly in support of the peace of 1646, p. 217.—His execution by order of the Cromwellians, p. 218, note.
Bedel (Bishop of Kilmore) draws up a remonstrance of grievances for the Irish in 1641, p. 110.
Burnet (Bishop) his account of the respect, which the Irish insurgents paid to bishop Bedel, in his life-time, and at his death, p. 130.

C

Chichester (Sir Arthur) his government, a puritan, p. 40.
Commons (Irish house of) press the lords justices, in conjunction with the lords, to suffer them to continue together, to concert means to suppress the insurgents in the North; but are refused, p. 133.
Castlehaven (Earl of) offers his service to suppress the northern insurgents, but is imprisoned

INDEX.

imprisoned for his officiousness, p. 157.
—His reasons for joining the confederates, p. 161. See Appen. Nº. X. p. 426.
Cromwell (Oliver) arrives in Ireland, p. 244.— His cruelty at Drogheda, p. 245.—At Wexford, p. 246.
Cromwell (Henry) his humane disposition; befriends the Irish, p. 280.
Cruelty of the English army in Munster, p. 24.

D

Dublin besieged by the Nuncio Renuccini and Owen O'Neale, p. 218.—The Roman clergy of that city declare it to be the duty of those of their communion, to oppose the Nuncio in behalf of the king, p. 220.
Dublin, and all the out-garrisons delivered up by Ormond to the English parliament, p. 228.
Drogheda taken by Cromwell; his inhumanity, and breach of faith on that occasion, p. 245-6.
Depositions concerning the cruelties of the Irish, false, contradictory, and absurd, p. 118.
Desmond (Earl of) his rebellion, forfeiture, and death, p. 14, 15, &c.

E

Extirpation of the Irish Roman Catholics intended and devised by the lords justices, previous to the rebellion of 1641; was the cause of it, p. 137, & passim.
Examples of the cruelty and perfidy of the chief governors of Ireland towards the natives, during the reigns of queen Elizabeth and king James the 1st, p. 40. and Appen. Nº. I.

Expulsion of great numbers of Roman Catholic members from the Irish house of commons, on false pretences, in 1641, p. 168.
Elections and returns to parliament unduely made, p. 68.
Elizabeth (Queen) her insidious order with regard to Tyrone, p. 12.--Merciful, p. 20.
Enlargement of time for hearing the claims of innocent Irish hindered by Ormond, p. 312.
Excommunication denounced by the Presbytery of Bangor, against such of their people as assisted the king's forces after the peace of 1648, p. 264.

F

Fanaticism of the established clergy of Ireland, p. 76.
Faith (Public) frequently broken by the chief governors of Ireland, in the reigns of Elizabeth and James; as also in that of Charles I. Review passim.
Forged commission of Sir Phelim O'Neal to begin the insurrection, confessed by himself, p. 278-9.
Forces (Irish Catholic) in queen Elizabeth's army, during Tyrone's war, p. 28.
Faith, not kept by Protestant governors of Ireland with Popish subjects, Append. Nº. I.
Famine (dreadful) in Ireland, p. 26.

G

General union of the confederate Catholics; their first address to the king, p. 158.
Garrison-soldiers; their cruelty to the Irish, p. 10.
Gray (Lord Leonard) his cruelty at Smirwick, p. 5.

Glamorgan

INDEX

Glamorgan (Earl of) commissioned to conclude a private peace with the confederates, p. 190.—That peace discovered; publickly disavowed by his majesty, but privately approved, ib.

Glamorgan imprisoned in the castle of Dublin; his commission real, p. 194.

H

Histories (Protestant) of the Irish rebellion in 1641, how little to be relied on, p. 120. —Acknowledged to be false, ib.

Hume's account of that rebellion censured, p. 123-8.

Heylin's opinion of the absurdity of the Irish act of the 2d of Elizabeth, p. 38.

I

James-town: proceedings of the Irish Bishops there, against Ormond, p. 256. —Condemned by the generality of the Roman Catholics of Ireland, p. 261.

Inquiry into defective titles, p. 82.—The mischiefs produced by it; and the iniquitous means of carrying it through, p. 84.—Greviously complained of; the king promised to put a stop to it; that promise broken by lord Wentworth's persuasion, p. 70-1.

Jones routs Ormond at Rathmines, p. 245. —His cruelty and perfidy, ib.

Irish: their sufferings under the Cromwellians, p. 305.—The greater, and better part of them assisted queen Elizabeth in her wars in Ireland, p. 28.

K

King (Archbishop) attests the sacred name of God to the truth of what he sets forth in his state of the Protestants of Ireland under king James, p. 327.—Convicted of many falsities asserted in that book, in his life-time, by Mr. Lesley; and never acquitted, either by himself, or his friends, ib.

Kinsale (battle of) the earl of Clanrickard knighted in the field, after the defeat of the Irish, p. 23.—Bloody pursuit of the routed Irish, ib.—An odd old prophecy on that occasion, ib.

L

Loraine (Duke of) applied to by the confederates for his assistance, p. 266.—That application justified, p. 269.

Lesley (Rev. Mr.) a conscientious non-juring clergyman, and therefore worthy of credit in what he relates, p. 326.—Challenges Dr. King to produce vouchers of the truth of his assertions in his state of the Protestants, &c. p. 347.—Offers to produce vouchers of their falsehood, if required; not required, p. 326, & passim.

Londonderry: De Rosen's barbarity when besieging it, p. 342.—King James countermanded it, as soon as he had notice of it, p. 344.

M

Massacre of the protected Irish at Mulloghmaston, in queen Elizabeth's reign, p. 6. —— Of the unoffending Irish in Island Magee, by the Scotch and English puritans, the first committed of either side in the insurrection of 1641, p. 112.

Mountjoy (Lord Deputy) subdues Tyrone, accepts his submission, and brings him with him to England, p. 30, 31.—Recommends

commends lenity towards the Irish, and toleration of their religion, p. 18.—Disputes with White, a jesuit, at Waterford concerning matters of religion, p. 36 — assures, that king James is a Protestant, p. 35.—Accepts their excuse for not having sooner proclaimed him at Waterford, p. 34.

N

Number of cruelties committed by the Irish aggravated by Protestant writers, p. 121.—That number greatly lessened even by the commissioners of the rebellious English parliament residing in Ireland in 1652, p. 122.

Nominees: meriting Irish nominated by the king to be restored to their estates, but not restored, p. 313.

Neale (Owen O') submits to the peace of 1648, but dies soon after, p. 248.

Nobility and gentry of the pale banished from Dublin, p. 136.

Nuncio (Renuccini) charged with high crimes by the confederates; is obliged to leave the kingdom; reproved by the Pope at his return to Rome, p. 239-40.

O

Ormond's implicit obedience to the justices wicked commands, p. 142.—His duplicity, with respect to their character, ib.—His backwardness to conclude the cessation of arms with the confederates, notwithstanding the king's repeated commands, p. 165.—Befriends the Irish, p. 321 —His reluctance to conclude the peace of 1646, p. 184.—His unwillingness to have it proclaimed after it was concluded, p. 203.—His private treaty at the same time with the covenanted Scots in Ulster, to join with them against the confederates, p. 187.—His surrender of the regalia and king's garrisons to the independents in the British parliament, p. 228.—Contrary to the king's order, p. 233.

Orrery (Earl of) imposes on the king, p. 301.

Ormond's rewards after the restoration, p. 320.—He is consulted in every thing relating to the settlement of Ireland, p. 311, note.—And particularly befriends the Cromwellian adventurers and soldiers, p. 313.

P

Phelim (Sir) O'Neale: his imprisonment and trial; cruelties committed by his followers against his order, troubled his conscience very much, p. 278, 280.—His heroic behaviour at his death, ib.

Papists, treated as enemies to God and the prince, p. 4.—Their offer of maintaining 5000 horse, and 500 foot, for the King's service, only to have some toleration of their religion, p. 58-9.—That offer rejected, p. 59.

Protestation of twelve bishops pronounced in Christ-church to dissuade the government from accepting that offer, ib.

Primate Usher's ecclesiastical court as corrupt as the rest, p. 55.—The peace of 1646 concluded, p. 208.——The peace of 1648, p. 242.

Q

Queen Elizabeth: the miserable state of Irish

INDEX.

Irish recusants during her reign, Appen. N°. I.
Qualifications of nocency, and innocency, in the court of claims, rigorous, p. 309.
Qualities of the commissioners of that court, p. 284.
Questioning the recusants for christenings and marriages suspended for a while; and why, p. 88.
Quo-warrantos taken out against the corporations considered, p. 331.

R

Rapparees: who, p. 337.
Renuccini (Pope's Nuncio) arrives in Ireland, p. 195.—Is received with honour by the confederates, ib.—Excommunicates those who adhere to the peace of 1646, p. 210.—Imprisons the promoters of it, p. 216—Is ordered by the body of the confederates to leave the kingdom, p. 239.
Religion (established) more injured in Scotland by king William, than in Ireland by king James, p. 347.—Rather encouraged, in Ireland, by the latter, p. 349.—Hurt by the neglect and immorality of its own clergy, ib.
Remonstrance of grievances delivered to his majesty's commissioners at Trim, p. 163.—Of loyalty, by the Roman Catholic clergy; by Walsh. Append. N°. XII. p. 436.

S

Synod of the established Irish clergy in 1634, p. 76.—Dictated to, and controuled, by lord deputy Wentworth, afterwards earl of Strafford, p. 77.
Simony of the ecclesiastical courts in Ireland, p. 59.
Spaniards invade Ireland, p. 21.
Scots presbyterian ministers flock to Ireland, p. 46.—Receive ordination from the Irish bishops in the form prescribed by themselves, in order to entitle them to church-livings, ib.—Applauded by primate Usher, p. 47.
Strafford (Earl of) lord lieutenant of Ireland, p. 66.—Packs a house of commons, p. 68-9.—Bullies them, p. 171.—The council, p. 67.—And the convocation, 76.—The state of the established clergy in his time, p. 65.
Synod of the Roman Catholic clergy in 1642; their decrees, p. 129.
Swords: breach of public faith to the gentlemen assembled there, p. 140.

T

Tyrone and Tyrconnel (Earls of) attainted for a fictitious plot, p. 43.—Six intire counties in Ulster seized, on that pretence, p. 51.
Timolin (castle) cruelty of Ormond's soldiers to the garrison, after it had surrendered, upon quarter promised, p. 163.
Tyrconnel (Earl of) when very young, inveigled on board a ship, and carried prisoner to Dublin; escapes after seven years imprisonment, p. 12.
Tyrone (Earl of) escapes from Dublin, upon private information that he was to be made a prisoner, notwithstanding his safe

safe conduct, p. 11.—Sues for pardon, and obtains it, 30.

Terms (barbarous) of receiving the Irish to pardon, p. 28-9.

Talbot (Sir Robert) offers to engage against the insurgents, but refused, p. 134.

V U

Verulam (Sir Francis Bacon, Lord of) his advice that lenity should be shewn to the Irish, and some toleration of their religion allowed them, p. 19.—His reasons for that advice, ib.

Usher (Primate) puritanically affected, p. 78.—His shuffling conduct in the convocation 1634, p. 79.

Versatility, and trimming behaviour of the Irish clergy, p. 546.

W

Warner (Doctor) rejects the manuscript depositions, in the possession of the university of Dublin, concerning the cruelties committed on protestants in 1641; his reasons, p. 119—His own pretended authentic copy of the depositions proved to be unauthentic, by an anecdote of the Duke of Ormond, related by himself, ib.—Owns that every protestant history of the Irish rebellion is false, p. 121.

Winter Grant sent by the queen and prince of Wales, to urge Ormond to renew the peace with the confederates; is refused, p. 126.

William Parsons (Sir) lord-justice, promotes the troubles in 1641, p. 34.—Is accused of high crimes and misdemeanors, p. 169.—Imprisoned, ib.

www.ingramcontent.com/pod-product-compliance
Lightning Source LLC
Chambersburg PA
CBHW051848300426
44117CB00006B/313